About Pearson

Pearson is the world's learning company, with presence across 70 countries worldwide. Our unique insights and world-class expertise comes from a long history of working closely with renowned teachers, authors and thought leaders, as a result of which, we have emerged as the preferred choice for millions of teachers and learners across the world.

We believe learning opens up opportunities, creates fulfilling careers and hence better lives. We hence collaborate with the best of minds to deliver you class-leading products, spread across the Higher Education and Test Preparation spectrum.

Superior learning experience and improved outcomes are at the heart of everything we do. This product is the result of one such effort.

Your feedback plays a critical role in the evolution of our products and you can contact us – reachus@pearson.com. We look forward to it.

Machine Learning

Machine Learning

Second Edition

Saikat Dutt

Visiting Faculty, Indian Institute of Management Calcutta
Former Senior Director, Cognizant Technology Solutions

Subramanian Chandramouli

Associate Director, Cognizant Technology Solutions

Amit Kumar Das

Principal Director, LTIMindtree
Former Faculty Member, Institute of Engineering & Management
Kolkata

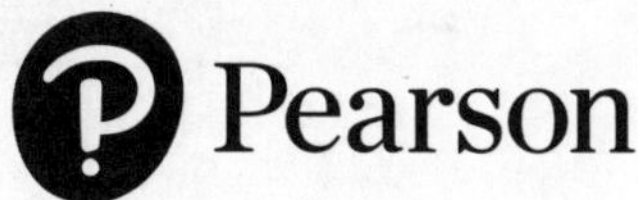

Pearson

Senior Manager—Product: Neha Goomer
Senior Editor—Production: C. Purushothaman

ISBN 978-81-198-9673-8

First Impression, 2025
Fifth Impression, 2026
Sixth Impression

Published by Pearson India Education Services Pvt. Ltd, CIN: U72200TN2005PTC057128.

Head Office: 1st Floor, Berger Tower, Plot No. C-001A/2, Sector 16B, Noida - 201 301, Uttar Pradesh, India.

Registered Office : 6th Floor, Tower A, Unit A and B International Tech Park, Capita Land Chennai, 200 Feet Radial Road, Zamin Pallavaram, Old Pallavaram Chennai – 600117, Tamil Nadu, India
Website: in.pearson.com; Email: companysecretary.india@pearson.com

Compositor: DigiWorld Creative
Printer : Rajkamal Electric Press, Kundli, Haryana-131 028.

This book is dedicated to the people without whom the dream could not have come true – my parents, Tarun Kumar Dutt and Srilekha Dutt; constant inspiration and support from my wife, Adity and unconditional love of my sons Deepro and Devarko.

Saikat Dutt

My sincerest thanks and appreciation go to several people...
My parents Subramanian and Lalitha
My wife Ramya
My son Shri Krishna
My daughter Shri Siva Ranjani
And my colleagues and friends

S. Chandramouli

My humble gratitude goes to -
My parents Juthika Das and Ranajit Kumar Das
My wife Arpana and two lovely daughters Ashmita and Ankita
My academic collaborator, mentor and brother — Saptarsi Goswami and Mrityunjoy Panday

Amit Kumar Das

Contents

6   Bayesian Concept Learning   160

7   Supervised Learning: Classification   187

8   Supervised Learning: Regression   230

9   Unsupervised Learning   266

10   Reinforcement Learning   299

11   Basics of Neural Network   *332*

12   Other Types of Learning   *365*

13 End-to-end ML implementations   384

14 Generative AI & Large Language Models   401

Foreword

I am extremely happy to learn that the book: Machine Learning authored by Mr. Saikat Dutt, Mr. Subramanian Chandramouli, and Dr. Amit Kumar Das is coming up with its second edition. The success of the first edition speaks of the relevance and quality of the book. The new edition includes several enhancements to the topics so that it will be more useful to the two communities: senior undergraduate students of Engineering and early career professionals. I am thrilled to see the notable updates in this edition, such as, inclusion of the latest topics such as Reinforcement Learning, Generative AI, and Large Language Models. Reinforcement Learning is a field that is garnering increased attention due to its applications in diverse domains such as gaming, robotics, and finance. The growing popularity of Generative AI and LLMs has a great impact on today's AI domain. Thus, dedicating an entire chapter to exploring the intricacies of these, has been an invaluable addition. I am also impressed with the incorporation of three end-to-end case studies, which offer a hands-on approach to solving prevalent machine-learning challenges.

One of the distinguishing factors of this book is the presence of ample pictorial representations thus providing visual aids for conceptual elucidation. The real-life examples and use cases, sourced from industry deployments, offer practical illustrations of theoretical concepts in action. Over 1000 meticulously crafted questions, aligned with the latest curriculum of engineering institutes, facilitate both learning and assessment. The coverage of relevant software is extremely helpful for understanding the application of Machine Learning.

The authors have struck a delicate balance between simplicity and depth. For casual readers, the book is impressive due to its simple approach. On the other hand, practitioners will find great value in its meticulous attention to detail and comprehensive coverage of advanced topics. I wish all the success of this edition too and I am confident about that.

Prof. Bimal K. Roy, Padma Shree Awardee
Former Director, Indian Statistical Institute
Former Chairman, National Statistical Commission

Preface

The first edition of this book was published five years back based on requests from Computer Science and IT engineering students. The concept of machine learning was relatively new and at that time there was no popular text book in the market on this topic for end-to-end learning. This book was written specifically for college students, techies, and junior managers so that they understand the machine learning concepts easily. After five years of publication of the first edition, we are quite delighted that the book could serve the purpose for which it was written. It has been able to satisfy the quest of learning of this topic and in the process gained a significant mindshare in the cohort of under-graduate students. The fact that it is the official textbook for several colleges / universities is a testament to the fact that it has succeeded to serve the purpose.

With time there has been some requests on additional topics which have come from the readers. Also, certain new and trending topics have evolved in the area of machine learning. To address these additional needs, new topics have been introduced and the book coverage has got expanded in the process. For example, Reinforcement Learning is an important topic which was not covered in so much details earlier. In the second edition, an elaborate chapter has been introduced on this topic. Also, there was no end-to-end case study provided earlier. In this edition three end-to-end case studies solving popular machine learning problems have been added. Last but not the least, the growing popularity of Generative AI and LLMs have inspired us to include a chapter on GenAI and LLMs. Though a detailed background of deep learning is needed to appreciate the foundational architecture of LLMs, we have kept the things at a little higher level so that readers without any background in deep learning can easily understand and adapt to the concepts of GenAI and LLMs.

With the additional content, we are very hopeful that the second edition of this book will take the knowledge of machine learning to a different level. Readers of this book will gain a thorough understanding of machine learning concepts. Not only students, but the software professionals will find a variety of techniques with sufficient discussions that caters to the needs of the professional environments. Technical managers will get an insight into how to weave machine learning into the overall software engineering process. Students, developers, and technical managers with a basic background in computer science will find the material in this book easily readable.

Pedagogical Features:
Pedagogy is the art and science of how something is taught and how students learn it. How the teaching occurs, the approach to teaching and learning, the way the content is delivered and what the students learn as a result of the process are all included in pedagogy. The following are the pedagogical features of this book:

Start-of-chapter aids:

- Objective: What the reader will gain from the chapter is described at the beginning in the Objective section

In-between chapter aids:

- Examples: Real-life and Industry examples to help the readers relate the topic to the practical applications
- Visualization: A large number of pictures, diagrams, and images are used to facilitate visualization
- 'Did you know?' and 'Points to Ponder' sections highlight important and interesting examples related to the topic discussed in the chapter

End-of-chapter aids:

- Summary: The major concepts discussed in the chapter are reviewed
- Practice Questions: At the end of each chapter, questions are given to facilitate the students to prepare well and the teachers to check the understanding level of the students

List of Reviewers:

Publisher would like to acknowledge following industry and academic leaders for their valuable comments:

It covers the subjects in great detail, is easy to read, and is designed for an Indian readership.

– Alexy Bhowmick, **Assam Don Bosco University, Guwahati**

The language is easy to understand, and the book seems very comprehensive.

– Arindam Ray, **University of South Florida, USA**

In navigating the complex and rapidly evolving domain of machine learning, this manuscript stands out as a comprehensive guide that thoughtfully bridges the gap between foundational principles and cutting-edge advancements. It adeptly balances technical depth with clarity, making advanced concepts accessible to both beginners and seasoned practitioners. Its structured presentation, complemented by quality illustrations and diagrams, facilitates a holistic understanding of machine learning's complexities.

– Diptiman Banerji, **Indian Institute of Management Raipur**

This text book covered the syllabus for Machine Learning and language is easy to understand. The given examples, solved problems are really helpful to understand the concept very easily. The topics list and titles of the topics are more relevant and easy to understand.

– P. V. Siva Kumar, **VNR Vignana Jyothi Institute of Engineering and Technology, Hyderabad**

Generative AI- I find first in this Indian book for the first time which is very much necessary for Machine Learning courses for recent days.

– Saikat Basu, **Maulana Abul Kalam Azad University of Technology, West Bengal**

Great compilation of the topics for anyone in the industry who would like to learn from scratch. Writers have in-depth knowledge of the topics discussed here with very appropriate examples. They have meticulously developed the concept and then provided the theoretical details with programming examples.

– Sarmila Roy, **CTO, AIVOT AI**

This book is exceptionally strong in its educational approach. The seamless flow of language, comprehensive content, abundant figures, examples, and sample questions all contribute to making it easier for both teachers to instruct and students to grasp. The authors have succeeded in simplifying a complex topic, making it accessible even to beginners in the field.

– Sobhan Sen Sarma, **General Manager, Ericsson India Global Services Pvt Ltd**

About the Authors

Saikat Dutt, PMP, PMI-ACP, CSM is also the author of three other books - 'PMI Agile Certified Practitioner-Excel with Ease', 'Software Engineering' and 'Software Project Management' published by Pearson. These books are accepted as textbooks in reputed educational institutes, like IIMC, NITs, Srinidhi Institute of Science & Technology, Anurag University, and many more.  Saikat has vast experience working on AI/ML projects especially focusing on application of those in managing software projects. He is a regular speaker on machine learning topics and involved in reviewing machine learning and AI related papers.

Saikat is a 'Project Management Professional (PMP)' and 'PMI Agile Certified Professional' certified by Project Management Institute (PMI), USA, and a 'Certified Scrum Master (CSM)'. He has over twenty-six years of IT industry experience and expertise in managing large-scale multi-location and mission-critical projects. Saikat has worked with big multinationals in the software industry like Cognizant Technology Solutions, Ushacomm, and CSG International.

Saikat has a keen interest in academics. Since 2014, he has been closely associated with reputed institutions like the Indian Institute of Management Calcutta (IIMC) and the Institute of Engineering and Management (IEM) as a visiting faculty. He is also actively working with IIMC to develop the case studies which are taught in post-graduate courses.

S. Chandramouli, Ph.D., PfMP, PMP, PMI-ACP, is a distinguished alumnus of the Indian Institute of Management Kozhikode (IIM-K) and holds a Doctorate in management from Bharathiar University. He has also earned a Global Business Leader certification from Harvard Business School. He is an expert in technology management, delivery management, competitiveness, IT, organizational culture, and leadership, and has published numerous articles on these topics. He has a Green Belt certification in six-sigma methodology and a master practitioner certification in Neuro Linguistic Programming (NLP). He has received awards for his papers on Portfolio Management at various international forums, such as the "Best practices of Agile program management – SCRUM TEA Model" at the Program and Portfolio Management Conference and the "Strategy Based Service Model – DISCO PMO" at the International IT Service Management Conference. He has 30 publications in National and International Journals and conferences.

Chandramouli has a proven track record of delivering large-scale, mission-critical projects on time and within budget to the customer's satisfaction, which includes Blockchain technologies, AI, Bigdata analytics and machine learning projects. He was an active contributor to PMI's Organization Project Management Maturity Model (OPM3) and Project Management Competency Development Framework (PMCDF) initiatives. He has been a sought-after speaker at various technology and management conferences and has inspired more than 15,000 software professionals worldwide with his insights on Blockchain, AI, machine learning, Bigdata analytics, delivery management, competitiveness, and leadership.

Amit Kumar Das has been working in the IT industry and in academic research / teaching in the area of Data Science for the past 25 years. He is currently working as Principal Director at LTIMindtree. Amit has done Ph.D. at University of Calcutta in the area of Machine Learning and M.Tech. from Birla Institute of Technology & Science, Pilani. Before that, he did graduation in Electrical Engineering from Bengal Engineering College, Shibpur (currently known as IIEST).

Amit has many research papers in the area of data analytics and machine learning published in international journals and conferences. He has also written multiple textbooks on published by Pearson, primarily for the under-graduate students. He also has been a regular speaker in the area of data analytics and machine learning. He is a Senior Member of IEEE.

In the past he has worked at Cognizant Technology Solutions for more than a decade and at Tata Consultancy Services. He started his career in Tata Consultancy Services. He has also worked as faculty member in the Department of Computer Science and Engineering, Institute of Engineering & Management. He has also provided consulting in the area of Data Science with companies like Rebaca Technolgies, Dirac Business Solutions Pvt. Ltd and IT program management support to Department of Higher Education, Government of West Bengal.

Model Syllabus for Machine Learning

Credits: 5

Contacts per week: 3 lectures + 1 tutorial

MODULE I

Introduction to Machine Learning: Human learning and it's types; Machine learning and it's types; well-posed learning problem; applications of machine learning; issues in machine learning

Preparing to model: Basic data types; exploring numerical data; exploring categorical data; exploring relationship between variables; data issues and remediation; data pre-processing

Modelling and Evaluation: Selecting a model; training model – holdout, k-fold cross-validation, bootstrap sampling; model representation and interpretability – under-fitting, over-fitting, bias-variance tradeoff; model performance evaluation – classification, regression, clustering; performance improvement

Feature engineering: Feature construction; feature extraction; feature selection

[12 Lectures]

MODULE II

Brief review of probability: Basic concept of probability, random variables; discrete distributions – binomial, Poisson, Bernoulli, etc.; continuous distribution – uniform, normal, Laplace; central theorem; Monte Carlo approximation

Bayesian concept learning: Bayes theorem – prior and posterior probability, likelihood; concept learning; Bayesian Belief Network

[6 Lectures]

MODULE III

Supervised learning – Classification: Basics of supervised learning – classification; k-Nearestneighbour; decision tree; random forest; support vector machine

Supervised learning – Regression: Simple linear regression; other regression techniques

Unsupervised learning: Basics of unsupervised learning; clustering techniques; association rules

[10 Lectures]

MODULE IV

Basics of Neural Network: Understanding biological neuron and artificial neuron; types of activation functions; early implementations – McCulloch Pitt's, Rosenblatt's Perceptron, ADALINE; architectures of neural network; learning process in ANN; backpropagation

Other types of learning: Representation learning; active learning; instance-based learning; association rule learning; ensemble learning; regularization

Machine Learning Live Case Studies

[8 Lectures]

MODULE V

Reinforcement Learning: Definition, Elements Of RL, Basic Principles, Different RL Algorithms - Dynamic Programming (DP), Monte Carlo Methods, Temporal Difference Learning (TD), Sample Python Implementation Of Q-Learning, Applications Of RL

Generative AI: Brief Context Of NLP, Foundational Architectures of Generative Model, Large Language Models (LLMs), ChatGPT, Applications Of Generative AI, Prompt Engineering, Integrating LLMs into Python using LangChain, Pair programming powered by Prompt Engineering, Best Practices in Prompt Engineering

[12 Lectures]

Lesson Plan

Module #	Chapter #	Chapter Name	Detailed content	Lectures allotted
1	1	Introduction to Machine Learning	Human learning and it's types	Lecture 1
			Machine learning and it's types	
			Well-posed learning problem	
			Applications of machine learning	Lecture 2
			Issues in machine learning	
	2	Preparing to model	Basic data types	Lecture 3
			Exploring numerical data	
			Exploring categorical data	Lecture 4
			Exploring relationship between variables	
			Data issues and remediation	Lecture 5
			Data pre-processing	Lecture 6
	3	Modelling and Evaluation	Selecting a model	Lecture 7 and 8
			Training model - Holdout, k-fold cross-validation, bootstrap sampling	
			Model representation and interpretability - under-fitting, over-fitting, bias-variance tradeoff	

(Continued in next page)

(Continued)

Module #	Chapter #	Chapter Name	Detailed content	Lectures allotted
1	3	Modelling and Evaluation	Model performance evaluation - Classification, regression, clustering	Lecture 9 and 10
			Performance improvement	
	4	Basics of Feature Engineering	Feature construction	Lecture 11
			Feature extraction	
			Feature selection	Lecture 12
2	5	Brief Overview of Probability	Basic concept of probability, Random variables	Lecture 13
			Discrete distributions - Binomial, Poisson, Bernoulli, etc.	Lecture 14
			Continuous distribution - Uniform, Normal, Laplace	Lecture 15
			Central theorem	Lecture 16
			Monte Carlo approximation	
	6	Bayesian concept learning	Bayes theorem - Prior and posterior probability, likelihood	Lecture 17
			Concept learning	Lecture 18
			Bayesian Belief Network	
3	7	Supervised Learning: Classification	Basics of supervised learning - classification	Lecture 19
			k-Nearest Neighbour	Lecture 20
			Decision tree	Lecture 21
			Random Forest	Lecture 22
			Support vector machine	Lecture 23
	8	Supervised Learning: Regression	Simple linear regression	Lecture 24
			Other regression techniques	Lecture 25
	9	Unsupervised learning	Basics of unsupervised learning	Lecture 26 and 27
			Clustering techniques	
			Association rules	Lecture 28

(Continued in next page)

(*Continued*)

Module #	Chapter #	Chapter Name	Detailed content	Lectures allotted
4	10	Reinforcement Learning	Definition, Elements Of RL	Lecture 29
			Basic Principles, Dynamic Programming (DP)	Lecture 30
			Monte Carlo Methods, Temporal Difference Learning (TD)	Lecture 31
			Applications Of RL	Lecture 32
			Sample Python Implementation Of Q-Learning	Lecture 33 and 34
5	11	Basics of Neural Network	Understanding biological neuron and artificial neuron	Lecture 35
			Types of activation functions	
			Early implementations - McCulloch Pitt's, Rosenblatt's Perceptron, ADALINE	Lecture 36
			Architectures of neural network	Lecture 37
			Learning process in ANN	Lecture 38
			Backpropagation	Lecture 39
	12	Other types of learning	Representation Learning, Evolutionary Algorithms	Lecture 40
	14	Generative AI	Brief Context Of NLP	Lecture 41
			Foundational Architectures of Generative Model	Lecture 42
			Large Language Models (LLMs)	Lecture 43
			ChatGPT, Applications Of Generative AI	Lecture 44
			Prompt Engineering, Integrating LLMs into Python	Lecture 45
			Pair programming powered by Prompt Engineering, Best Practices in Prompt Engineering	Lecture 46
	Appendix C	Machine Learning Live Case Studies		Lecture 47 and 48

Digital Component

Pearson and Edureka bring you a unique opportunity to become expert technocrats by combining Pearson's widely circulated educational resources with Edureka's state-of-the-art online learning platform to create an unparalleled learning experience.

Learners can now use Pearson's exceptional educational materials along with Edureka's supplementary video tutorials to augment the learning journey. This collaboration has various benefits, such as:

- Visual learning combined with traditional textbooks allows for a more immersive and comprehensive learning experience, allowing learners to acquire complete proficiency in the domain.
- Learners can evaluate their knowledge using numerous auto-evaluated micro-quizzes offered on the Edureka platform.
- Learners can now put their acquired knowledge into practice by solving the assignments given to them on Edureka platform, which will help them develop a portfolio of completed projects.
- Comprehensive interview preparation materials to help learners prepare for the interviews.

Every topic in the book which has a corresponding video tutorial is tagged with icon. Below is the list of such topics:

Please see inside front cover for access details and join us now to be a part of this transformative journey to upskill yourself with our meticulously designed learning materials and propel your career to the next level.

Chapter 1

Introduction to Machine Learning

OBJECTIVE OF THE CHAPTER:

The objective of this chapter is to venture into the arena of machine learning. New comers struggle a lot to understand the philosophy of machine learning. Also, they do not know where to start from and which problem could be and should be solved using machine learning tools and techniques. This chapter intends to give the new comers a starting point to the journey in machine learning. It starts from a historical journey in this field and takes it forward to give a glimpse of the modern day applications.

1.1 INTRODUCTION

It has been more than 20 years since a computer program defeated the reigning world champion in a game which is considered to need a lot of intelligence to play. The computer program was IBM's Deep Blue and it defeated world chess champion, Gary Kasparov. That was the time, probably, when the most number of people gave serious attention to a fast-evolving field in computer science or more specifically artificial intelligence – i.e. machine learning (ML).

As of today, machine learning is a mature technology area finding its application in almost every sphere of life. It can recommend toys to toddlers much in the same way as it can suggest a technology book to a geek or a rich title in literature to a writer. It predicts the future market to help amateur traders compete with seasoned stock traders. It helps an oncologist find whether a tumour is malignant or benign. It helps

1

in optimizing energy consumption thus helping the cause of Green Earth. Google has become one of the front-runners focusing a lot of its research on machine learning and artificial intelligence – Google self-driving car and Google Brain being two most ambitious projects of Google in its journey of innovation in the field of machine learning. In a nutshell, machine learning has become a way of life, no matter whichever sphere of life we closely look at. But where did it all start from?

The foundation of machine learning started in the 18th and 19th centuries. The first related work dates back to 1763. In that year, Thomas Bayes's work 'An Essay towards solving a Problem in the Doctrine of Chances' was published two years after his death. This is the work underlying Bayes Theorem, a fundamental work on which a number of algorithms of machine learning is based upon. In 1812, the Bayes theorem was actually formalized by the French mathematician Pierre-Simon Laplace. The method of least squares, which is the foundational concept to solve regression problems, was formalized in 1805. In 1913, Andrey Markov came up with the concept of Markov chains.

However, the real start of focused work in the field of machine learning is considered to be Alan Turing's seminal work in 1950. In his paper 'Computing Machinery and Intelligence' (*Mind*, New Series, Vol. 59, No. 236, Oct., 1950, pp. 433–460), Turing posed the question 'Can machines think?' or in other words, 'Do machines have intelligence?'. He was the first to propose that machines can 'learn' and become artificially intelligent. In 1952, Arthur Samuel of IBM laboratory started working on machine learning programs, and first developed programs that could play Checkers. In 1957, Frank Rosenblatt designed the first neural network program simulating the human brain. From then on, for the next 50 years, the journey of machine learning has been fascinating. A number of machine learning algorithms were formulated by different researchers, e.g. the nearest neighbour algorithm in 1969, recurrent neural network in 1982, support vector machines and random forest algorithms in 1995. The latest feather in the cap of machine learning development has been Google's AlphaGo program, which has beaten professional human Go player using machine learning techniques.

Points to Ponder

- While Deep Blue was searching some 200 million positions per second, Kasparov was searching not more than 5–10 positions probably, per second. Yet he played almost at the same level. This clearly shows that humans have some trick up their sleeve that computers could not master yet.
- **Go** is a board game which can be played by two players. It was invented in China almost 2500 years ago and is considered to be the oldest board game. Though it has relatively simple rules, Go is a very complex game (more complex than chess) because of its larger board size and more number of possible moves.

The evolution of machine learning from 1950 is depicted in Figure 1.1.

The rapid development in the area of machine learning has triggered a question in everyone's mind – can machines learn better than human? To find its answer, the first step would be to understand what learning is from a human perspective. Then, more light can be shed on what machine learning is. In the end, we need to know whether machine learning has already surpassed or has the potential to surpass human learning in every facet of life.

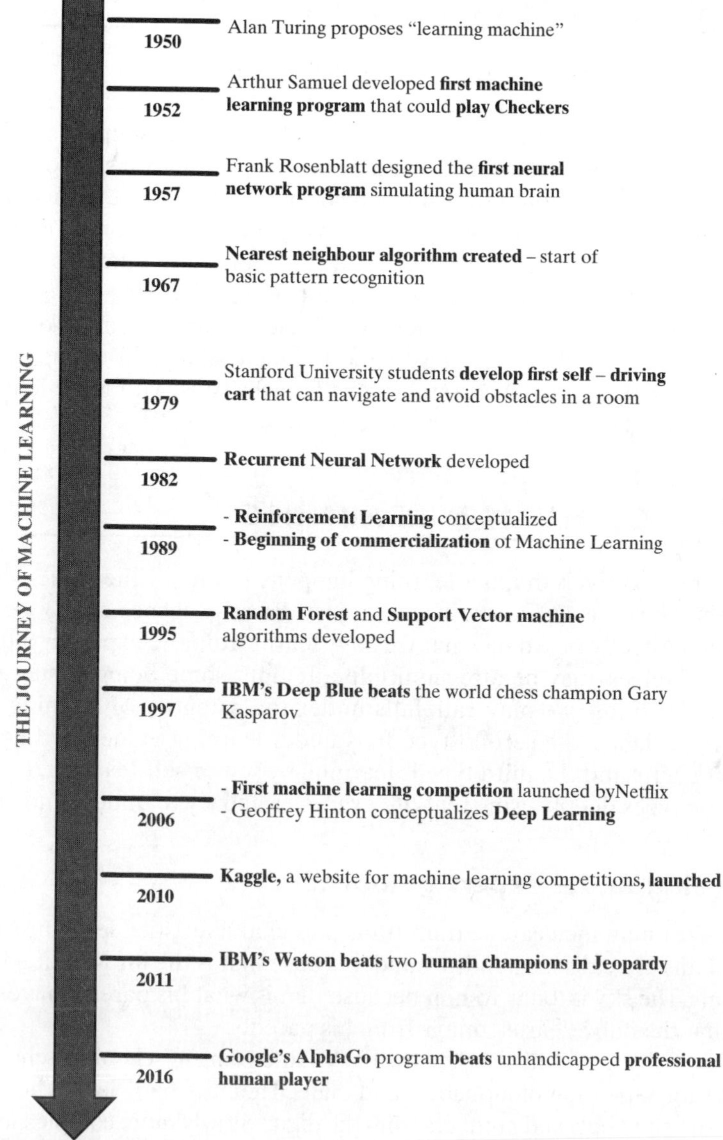

FIG. 1.1

Evolution of machine learning

The idea of generating content through AI was gaining prominence since 1990s and several Deep Learning architectures were being used for that purpose. But a major breakthrough on the generative methods came in the year 2017, with Google Brain's release of the paper "Attention is all you need". The Transformer architecture introduced in that paper had paved the way for rapid development in the areas of Large Language Model and Generative AI. Popular generative models such as GPT, PaLM, LLaMA are built with this architecture. We will cover these advanced topics latter in this book.

1.2   WHAT IS HUMAN LEARNING?

In cognitive science, learning is typically referred to as the process of gaining information through observation. And why do we need to learn? In our daily life, we need to carry out multiple activities. It may be a task as simple as walking down the street or doing the homework. Or it may be some complex task like deciding the angle in which a rocket should be launched so that it can have a particular trajectory. To do a task in a proper way, we need to have prior information on one or more things related to the task. Also, as we keep learning more or in other words acquiring more information, the efficiency in doing the tasks keep improving. For example, with more knowledge, the ability to do homework with less number of mistakes increases. In the same way, information from past rocket launches helps in taking the right precautions and makes more successful rocket launch. Thus, with more learning, tasks can be performed more efficiently.

1.3   TYPES OF HUMAN LEARNING

Thinking intuitively, human learning happens in one of the three ways – (1) either somebody who is an expert in the subject directly teaches us, (2) we build our own notion indirectly based on what we have learnt from the expert in the past, or (3) we do it ourselves, may be after multiple attempts, some being unsuccessful. The first type of learning, we may call, falls under the category of learning directly under expert guidance, the second type falls under learning guided by knowledge gained from experts and the third type is learning by self or self-learning. Let's look at each of these types deeply using real-life examples and try to understand what they mean.

1.3.1   Learning under expert guidance

An infant may inculcate certain traits and characteristics, learning straight from its guardians. He calls his hand, a 'hand', because that is the information he gets from his parents. The sky is 'blue' to him because that is what his parents have taught him. We say that the baby 'learns' things from his parents.

The next phase of life is when the baby starts going to school. In school, he starts with basic familiarization of alphabets and digits. Then the baby learns how to form words from the alphabets and numbers from the digits. Slowly more complex learning happens in the form of sentences, paragraphs, complex mathematics, science, etc. The baby is able to learn all these things from his teacher who already has knowledge on these areas.

Then starts higher studies where the person learns about more complex, application-oriented skills. Engineering students get skilled in one of the disciplines like civil, computer science, electrical, mechanical, etc. medical students learn about anatomy, physiology, pharmacology, etc. There are some experts, in general the teachers, in the respective field who have in-depth subject matter knowledge, who help the students in learning these skills.

Then the person starts working as a professional in some field. Though he might have gone through enough theoretical learning in the respective field, he still needs to learn more about the hands-on application of the knowledge that he has acquired. The professional mentors, by virtue of the knowledge that they have gained through years of hands-on experience, help all new comers in the field to learn on-job.

In all phases of life of a human being, there is an element of guided learning. This learning is imparted by someone, purely because of the fact that he/she has already gathered the knowledge by virtue of his/her experience in that field. So guided learning is the process of gaining information from a person having sufficient knowledge due to the past experience.

1.3.2   Learning guided by knowledge gained from experts

An essential part of learning also happens with the knowledge which has been imparted by teacher or mentor at some point of time in some other form/context. For example, a baby can group together all objects of same colour even if his parents have not specifically taught him to do so. He is able to do so because at some point of time or other his parents have told him which colour is blue, which is red, which is green, etc. A grown-up kid can select one odd word from a set of words because it is a verb and other words being all nouns. He could do this because of his ability to label the words as verbs or nouns, taught by his English teacher long back. In a professional role, a person is able to make out to which customers he should market a campaign from the knowledge about preference that was given by his boss long back.

In all these situations, there is no direct learning. It is some past information shared on some different context, which is used as a learning to make decisions.

1.3.3   Learning by self

In many situations, humans are left to learn on their own. A classic example is a baby learning to walk through obstacles. He bumps on to obstacles and falls down multiple times till he learns that whenever there is an obstacle, he needs to cross over it. He faces the same challenge while learning to ride a cycle as a kid or drive a car as an adult. Not all things are taught by others. A lot of things need to be learnt only from mistakes made in the past. We tend to form a check list on things that we should do, and things that we should not do, based on our experiences.

1.4   WHAT IS MACHINE LEARNING?

Before answering the question 'What is machine learning?' more fundamental questions that peep into one's mind are

- Do machines really learn?
- If so, how do they learn?
- Which problem can we consider as a well-posed learning problem? What are the important features that are required to well-define a learning problem?

At the onset, it is important to formalize the definition of machine learning. This will itself address the first question, i.e. if machines really learn. There are multiple ways to define machine learning. But the one which is perhaps most relevant, concise and accepted universally is the one stated by Tom M. Mitchell, Professor of Machine Learning Department, School of Computer Science, Carnegie Mellon University. Tom M. Mitchell has defined machine learning as

'A computer program is said to learn from experience E with respect to some class of tasks T and performance measure P, if its performance at tasks in T, as measured by P, improves with experience E.'

What this essentially means is that a machine can be considered to learn if it is able to gather experience by doing a certain task and improve its performance in doing the similar tasks in the future. When we talk about past experience, it means past data related to the task. This data is an input to the machine from some source.

In the context of the learning to play checkers, E represents the experience of playing the game, T represents the task of playing checkers and P is the performance measure indicated by the percentage of games won by the player. The same mapping can be applied for any other machine learning problem, for example, image classification problem. In context of image classification, E represents the past data with images having labels or assigned classes (for example whether the image is of a class cat or a class dog or a class elephant etc.), T is the task of assigning class to new, unlabelled images and P is the performance measure indicated by the percentage of images correctly classified.

The first step in any project is defining your problem. Even if the most powerful algorithm is used, the results will be meaningless if the wrong problem is solved.

1.4.1   How do machines learn?

The basic machine learning process can be divided into three parts.

1. **Data Input:** Past data or information is utilized as a basis for future decision-making
2. **Abstraction:** The input data is represented in a broader way through the underlying algorithm
3. **Generalization:** The abstracted representation is generalized to form a framework for making decisions

Figure 1.2 is a schematic representation of the machine learning process.

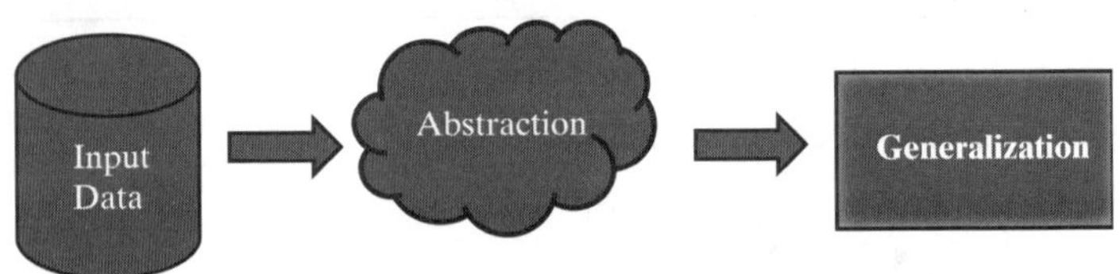

FIG. 1.2
Process of machine learning

Let's put the things in perspective of the human learning process and try to understand the machine learning process more clearly. Reason is, in some sense, machine learning process tries to emulate the process in which humans learn to a large extent.

Let's consider the situation of typical process of learning from classroom and books and preparing for the examination. It is a tendency of many students to try and memorize (we often call it 'learn by heart') as many things as possible. This may work well when the scope of learning is not so vast. Also, the kinds of questions which are asked in the examination are pretty much simple and straightforward. The questions can be answered by simply writing the same things which have been memorized. However, as the scope gets broader and the questions asked in the examination gets more complex, the strategy of memorizing doesn't work well. The number of topics may get too vast for a student to memorize. Also, the capability of memorizing varies from student to student. Together with that, since the questions get more complex, a direct reproduction of the things memorized may not help. The situation continues to get worse as the student graduates to higher classes.

So, what we see in the case of human learning is that just by great memorizing and perfect recall, i.e. just based on knowledge input, students can do well in the examinations only till a certain stage. Beyond that, a better learning strategy needs to be adopted:

1. to be able to deal with the vastness of the subject matter and the related issues in memorizing it

2. to be able to answer questions where a direct answer has not been learnt

A good option is to figure out the key points or ideas amongst a vast pool of knowledge. This helps in creating an outline of topics and a conceptual mapping of those outlined topics with the entire knowledge pool. For example, a broad pool of knowledge may consist of all living animals and their characteristics such as whether they live in land or water, whether they lay eggs, whether they have scales or fur or none, etc. It is a difficult task for any student to memorize the characteristics of all living animals – no matter how much photographic memory he/she may possess. It is better to draw a notion about the basic groups that all living animals belong to and the characteristics which define each of the basic groups. The basic groups of animals are invertebrates and vertebrates. Vertebrates are further grouped as mammals, reptiles, amphibians, fishes, and birds. Here, we have mapped animal groups and their salient characteristics.

1. Invertebrate: Do not have backbones and skeletons
2. Vertebrate
    (a) Fishes: Always live in water and lay eggs
    (b) Amphibians: Semi-aquatic i.e. may live in water or land; smooth skin; lay eggs
    (c) Reptiles: Semi-aquatic like amphibians; scaly skin; lay eggs; cold-blooded
    (d) Birds: Can fly; lay eggs; warm-blooded
    (e) Mammals: Have hair or fur; have milk to feed their young; warm-blooded

This makes it easier to memorize as the scope now reduces to know the animal groups that the animals belong to. Rest of the answers about the characteristics of the animals may be derived from the concept of mapping animal groups and their characteristics.

Moving to the machine learning paradigm, the vast pool of knowledge is available from the data input. However, rather than using it in entirety, a concept map, much in line with the animal group to characteristic mapping explained above, is drawn from the input data. This is nothing but knowledge abstraction as performed by the machine. In the end, the abstracted mapping from the input data can be applied to make critical conclusions. For example, if the group of an animal is given, understanding of the characteristics can be automatically made. Reversely, if the characteristic of an unknown animal is given, a definite conclusion can be made about the animal group it belongs to. This is generalization in context of machine learning.

1.4.1.1   Data Input

Data serves as the primary resource for powering any Machine Learning system. With the growing interconnectivity of physical systems, an immense volume of data is continuously generated. Manual analysis of such vast datasets has become impractical, necessitating the utilization of machine learning models to uncover hidden insights. These models offer a structured approach to dissecting and comprehending data. By examining input data, termed Training Data, and their characteristics, known as Features, machine learning models endeavor to discern underlying patterns. Once identified, these patterns enable consistent interpretation of new data, unveiling latent information within. Depending on the extent of information provided about the input data's nature, datasets are categorized as either labeled or unlabeled.

To illustrate, consider Table 1.1, which records historical data regarding credit card applications, including their final Approval Status—whether "Approved" or "Rejected." When we task a machine learning model with comprehending the relationship between attributes such as Age, Marital Status, and Monthly Income to determine Approval Status autonomously for new applications, we are furnishing the model with labeled historical data and expecting it to predict labels for new data. This endeavor constitutes a Supervised learning task.

Conversely, if we alter Table 1.1 by removing the final labeled column "Approval Status" and anticipate the machine learning model to segment customers into different income ranges based solely on the provided data, we are supplying the model with an unlabeled dataset. This type of task is referred to as an Unsupervised learning task.

Table 1.1

Historical information about credit card applications

Application	Age	Marital Status (M/U)	Monthly Income	Existing Loan? (Y/N)	Approval Status
A1123	39	M	1,00,000	N	Approved
B3421	25	M	1,50,000	Y	Approved
B3392	56	U	25,000	N	Rejected
C8734	49	M	75,000	N	Rejected
….					

We will discuss the role of data in machine learning as well as different machine learning models in detail in the subsequent chapters.

1.4.1.2   *Abstraction*

During the machine learning process, knowledge is fed in the form of input data. However, the data cannot be used in the original shape and form. As we saw in the example above, abstraction helps in deriving a conceptual map based on the input data. This map, or a **model** as it is known in the machine learning paradigm, is summarized knowledge representation of the raw data. The model may be in any one of the following forms

- Computational blocks like if/else rules
- Mathematical equations
- Specific data structures like trees or graphs
- Logical groupings of similar observations

The choice of the model used to solve a specific learning problem is a human task. The decision related to the choice of model is taken based on multiple aspects, some of which are listed below:

- The type of problem to be solved: Whether the problem is related to forecast or prediction, analysis of trend, understanding the different segments or groups of objects, etc.
- Nature of the input data: How exhaustive the input data is, whether the data has no values for many fields, the data types, etc.
- Domain of the problem: If the problem is in a business critical domain with a high rate of data input and need for immediate inference, e.g. fraud detection problem in banking domain.

Once the model is chosen, the next task is to fit the model based on the input data. Let's understand this with an example. In a case where the model is represented by a mathematical equation, say '$y = c_1 + c_2 x$' (the model is known as simple linear regression which we will study in a later chapter), based on the input data, we have to find out the values of c_1 and c_2. Otherwise, the equation (or the model) is of no use. So, fitting the model, in this case, means finding the values of the unknown coefficients or constants of the equation or the model. This process of fitting the model based on the input data is known as training. Also, the input data based on which the model is being finalized is known as training data.

1.4.1.3   *Generalization*

The first part of machine learning process is abstraction i.e. abstract the knowledge which comes as input data in the form of a model. However, this abstraction process, or more popularly training the model, is just one part of machine learning. The other key part is to tune up the abstracted knowledge to a form which can be used to take future decisions. This is achieved as a part of generalization. This part is quite difficult to achieve. This is because the model is trained based on a finite set of data, which may possess a limited set of characteristics. But when we want to apply the model to take decision on a set of unknown data, usually termed as test data, we may encounter two problems:

1. The trained model is aligned with the training data too much, hence may not portray the actual trend.
2. The test data possess certain characteristics apparently unknown to the training data.

Hence, a precise approach of decision-making will not work. An approximate or heuristic approach, much like gut-feeling-based decision-making in human beings, has to be adopted. This approach has the risk of not making a correct decision – quite obviously because certain assumptions that are made may not be true in reality. But just like machines, same mistakes can be made by humans too when a decision is made based on intuition or gut-feeling – in a situation where exact reason-based decision-making is not possible.

1.4.2   Well-posed learning problem

For defining a new problem, which can be solved using machine learning, a simple framework, highlighted below, can be used. This framework also helps in deciding whether the problem is a right candidate to be solved using machine learning. The framework involves answering three questions:

1. What is the problem?
2. Why does the problem need to be solved?
3. How to solve the problem?

Step 1: What is the Problem?

A number of information should be collected to know what is the problem.

Informal description of the problem, e.g. I need a program that will prompt the next word as and when I type a word.

Formalism

Use Tom Mitchell's machine learning formalism stated above to define the T, P, and E for the problem.
For example:

- Task (T): Prompt the next word when I type a word.
- Experience (E): A corpus of commonly used English words and phrases.
- Performance (P): The number of correct words prompted considered as a percentage (which in machine learning paradigm is known as learning accuracy).

Assumptions - Create a list of assumptions about the problem.

Similar problems

What other problems have you seen or can you think of that are similar to the problem that you are trying to solve?

Step 2: Why does the problem need to be solved?

Motivation

What is the motivation for solving the problem? What requirement will it fulfil?

For example, does this problem solve any long-standing business issue like finding out potentially fraudulent transactions? Or the purpose is more trivial like trying to suggest some movies for upcoming weekend.

Solution benefits

Consider the benefits of solving the problem. What capabilities does it enable?

It is important to clearly understand the benefits of solving the problem. These benefits can be articulated to sell the project.

Solution use

How will the solution to the problem be used and the life time of the solution is expected to have?

Step 3: How would I solve the problem?

Try to explore how to solve the problem manually.

Detail out step-by-step data collection, data preparation, and program design to solve the problem. Collect all these details and update the previous sections of the problem definition, especially the assumptions.

Summary

- **Step 1: What is the problem?** Describe the problem informally and formally and list assumptions and similar problems.
- **Step 2: Why does the problem need to be solved?** List the motivation for solving the problem, the benefits that the solution will provide and how the solution will be used.
- **Step 3: How would I solve the problem?** Describe how the problem would be solved manually to flush domain knowledge.

Did you know?

Sony created a series of robotic pets called Aibo. It was built in 1998. Although most models sold were dog-like, other inspirations included lion-cubs. It could express emotions and could also recognize its owner. In 2006, Aibo was added to the Carnegie Mellon University's 'Robot Hall of Fame'. A new generation of Aibo was launched in Japan in January 2018.

1.5   TYPES OF MACHINE LEARNING

As highlighted in Figure 1.3, Machine learning can be classified into three broad categories:

1. **Supervised learning** – Also called predictive learning. A machine predicts the class of unknown objects based on prior class-related information of similar objects.

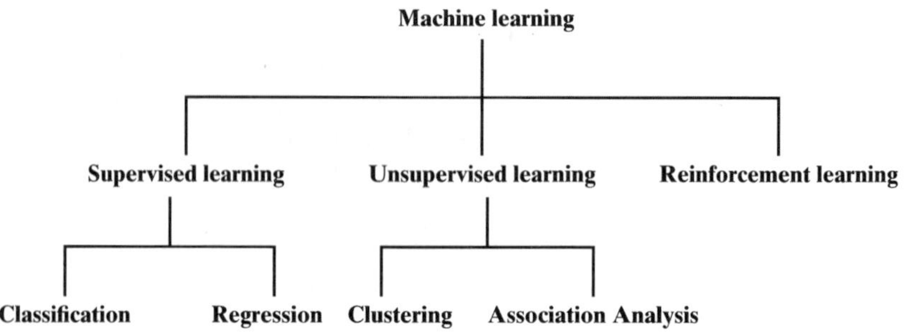

FIG. 1.3
Types of machine learning

Did you know?

Many video games are based on artificial intelligence technique called Expert System. This technique can imitate areas of human behaviour, with a goal to mimic the human ability of senses, perception, and reasoning.

---

2. **Unsupervised learning** – Also called descriptive learning. A machine finds patterns in unknown objects by grouping similar objects together.
3. **Reinforcement learning** – A machine learns to act on its own to achieve the given goals.

1.5.1   Supervised learning

The major motivation of supervised learning is to learn from past information. So what kind of past information does the machine need for supervised learning? It is the information about the task which the machine has to execute. In context of the definition of machine learning, this past information is the experience. Let's try to understand it with an example.

Say a machine is getting images of different objects as input and the task is to segregate the images by either shape or colour of the object. If it is by shape, the images which are of round-shaped objects need to be separated from images of triangular-shaped objects, etc. If the segregation needs to happen based on colour, images of blue objects need to be separated from images of green objects. But how can the machine know what is round shape, or triangular shape? Same way, how can the machine distinguish image of an object based on whether it is blue or green in colour? A machine is very much like a little child whose parents or adults need to guide him with the basic information on shape and colour before he can start doing the task. A machine needs the basic information to be provided to it. This basic input, or the experience in the paradigm of machine learning, is given in the form of **training data**. Training data is the past information on a specific task. In context of the image segregation problem, training data will have past data on different aspects or features on a number of images, along with a tag on whether the image is round or triangular, or blue or green in colour. The tag is called '**label**' and we say that the training data is labelled in case of supervised learning.

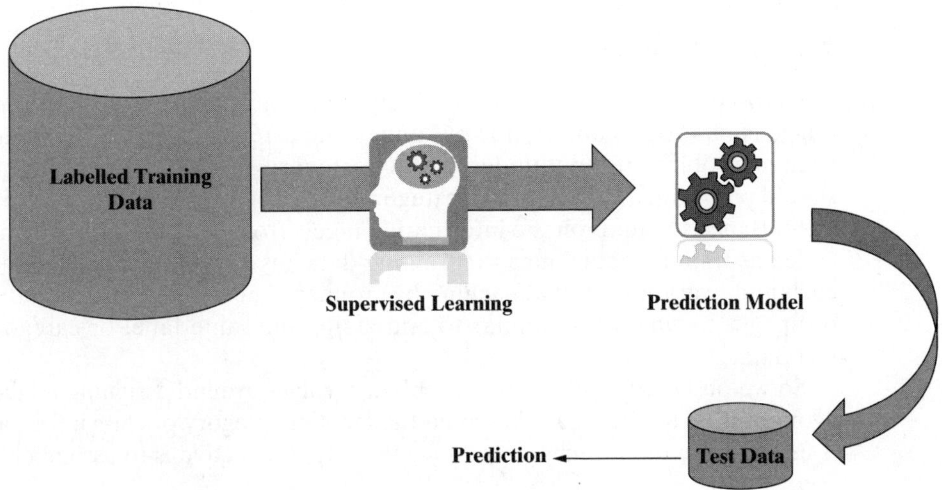

FIG. 1.4
Supervised learning

Figure 1.4 is a simple depiction of the supervised learning process. Labelled training data containing past information comes as an input. Based on the training data, the machine builds a predictive model that can be used on test data to assign a label for each record in the test data.

Some examples of supervised learning are

- Predicting the results of a game
- Predicting whether a tumour is malignant or benign
- Predicting the price of domains like real estate, stocks, etc.
- Classifying texts such as classifying a set of emails as spam or non-spam

Now, let's consider two of the above examples, say 'predicting whether a tumour is malignant or benign' and 'predicting price of domains such as real estate'. Are these two problems same in nature? The answer is 'no'. Though both of them are prediction problems, in one case we are trying to predict which category or class an unknown data belongs to whereas in the other case we are trying to predict an absolute value and not a class. When we are trying to predict a categorical or nominal variable, the problem is known as a **classification** problem. Whereas when we are trying to predict a real-valued variable, the problem falls under the category of **regression**.

Note:

Supervised machine learning is as good as the data used to train it. If the training data is of poor quality, the prediction will also be far from being precise.

Let's try to understand these two areas of supervised learning, i.e. classification and regression in more details.

1.5.1.1   Classification

Let's discuss how to segregate the images of objects based on the shape. If the image is of a round object, it is put under one category, while if the image is of a triangular object, it is put under another category. In which category the machine should put an image of unknown category, also called a **test data** in machine learning parlance, depends on the information it gets from the past data, which we have called as training data. Since the training data has a label or category defined for each and every image, the machine has to map a new image or test data to a set of images to which it is similar to and assign the same label or category to the test data.

So we observe that the whole problem revolves around assigning a label or category or class to a test data based on the label or category or class information that is imparted by the training data. Since the target objective is to assign a class label,

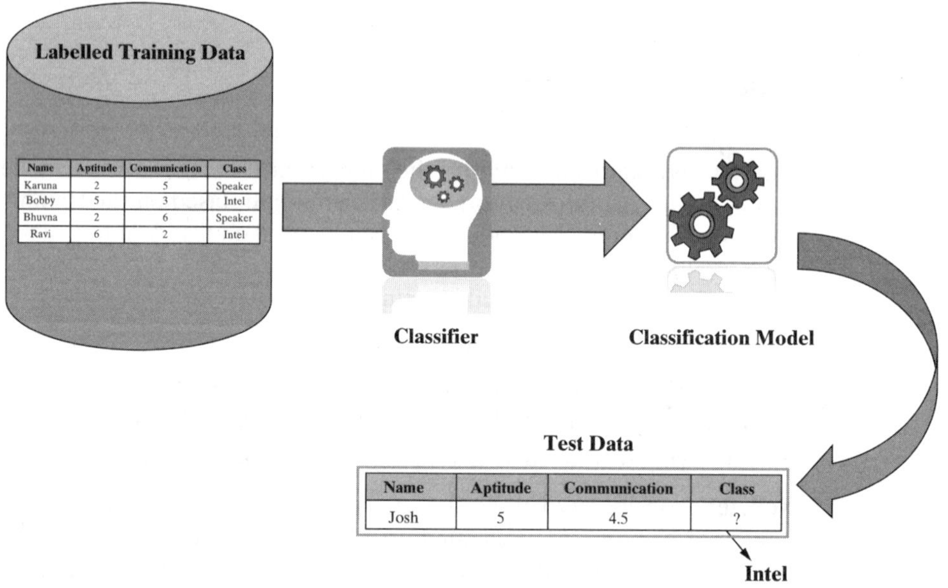

FIG. 1.5
Classification

this type of problem as classification problem. Figure 1.5 depicts the typical process of classification.

There are number of popular machine learning algorithms which help in solving classification problems. To name a few, Naïve Bayes, Decision tree, and k-Nearest Neighbour algorithms are adopted by many machine learning practitioners.

A critical classification problem in context of banking domain is identifying potential fraudulent transactions. Since there are millions of transactions which have to be scrutinized and assured whether it might be a fraud transaction, it is not possible for any human being to carry out this task. Machine learning is effectively leveraged to do this task and this is a classic case of classification. Based on the past transaction data, specifically the ones labelled as fraudulent, all new incoming transactions are marked or labelled as normal or suspicious. The suspicious transactions are subsequently segregated for a closer review.

In summary, classification is a type of supervised learning where a target feature, which is of type categorical, is predicted for test data based on the information imparted by training data. The target categorical feature is known as **class**.

Some typical classification problems include:

- Image classification
- Prediction of disease
- Win–loss prediction of games
- Prediction of natural calamity like earthquake, flood, etc.
- Recognition of handwriting

Did you know?

- Machine learning saves life – ML can spot 52% of breast cancer cells, a year before patients are diagnosed.
- US Postal Service uses machine learning for handwriting recognition.
- Facebook's news feed uses machine learning to personalize each member's feed.

1.5.1.2. Regression

In linear regression, the objective is to predict numerical features like real estate or stock price, temperature, marks in an examination, sales revenue, etc. The underlying predictor variable and the target variable are continuous in nature. In case of linear regression, a straight line relationship is 'fitted' between the predictor variables and the target variables, using the statistical concept of least squares method. As in the case of least squares method, the sum of square of error between actual and predicted values of the target variable is tried to be minimized. In case of simple linear regression, there is only one predictor variable whereas in case of multiple linear regression, multiple predictor variables can be included in the model.

Let's take the example of yearly budgeting exercise of the sales managers. They have to give sales prediction for the next year based on sales figure of previous years vis-à-vis investment being put in. Obviously, the data related to past as well as the data to be predicted are continuous in nature. In a basic approach, a simple linear regression model can be applied with investment as predictor variable and sales revenue as the target variable.

Figure 1.6 shows a typical simple regression model, where regression line is fitted based on values of target variable with respect to different values of predictor variable. A typical linear regression model can be represented in the form –

$$y = \alpha + \beta x$$

where 'x' is the predictor variable and 'y' is the target variable.

The input data come from a famous multivariate data set named Iris introduced by the British statistician and biologist Ronald Fisher. The data set consists of 50 samples from each of three species of Iris – *Iris setosa, Iris virginica,* and *Iris versicolor.* Four features were measured for each sample – sepal length, sepal width, petal length, and petal width. These features can uniquely discriminate the different species of the flower.

The Iris data set is typically used as a training data for solving the classification problem of predicting the flower species based on feature values. However, we can also

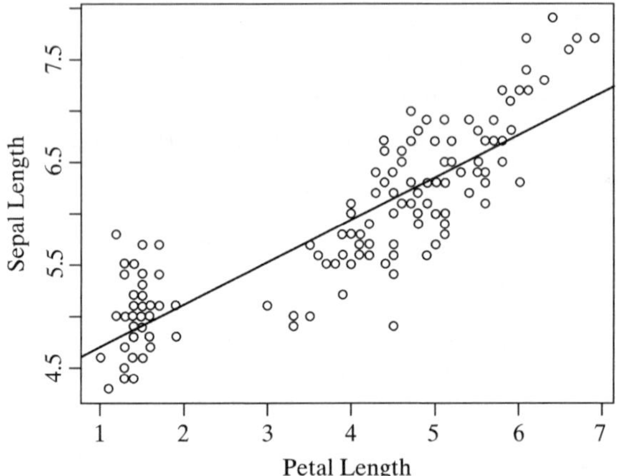

FIG. 1.6

Regression

demonstrate regression using this data set, by predicting the value of one feature using another feature as predictor. In Figure 1.6, petal length is a predictor variable which, when fitted in the simple linear regression model, helps in predicting the value of the target variable sepal length.

Typical applications of regression can be seen in

- Demand forecasting in retails
- Sales prediction for managers
- Price prediction in real estate
- Weather forecast
- Skill demand forecast in job market
- More about regression is discussed in Chapter 8.

1.5.2   Unsupervised learning

Unlike supervised learning, in unsupervised learning, there is no labelled training data to learn from and no prediction to be made. In unsupervised learning, the objective is to take a dataset as input and try to find natural groupings or **patterns** within the data elements or records. Therefore, unsupervised learning is often termed as **descriptive model** and the process of unsupervised learning is referred as **pattern discovery** or **knowledge discovery**. One critical application of unsupervised learning is customer segmentation.

Clustering is the main type of unsupervised learning. It intends to group or organize similar objects together. For that reason, objects belonging to the same cluster

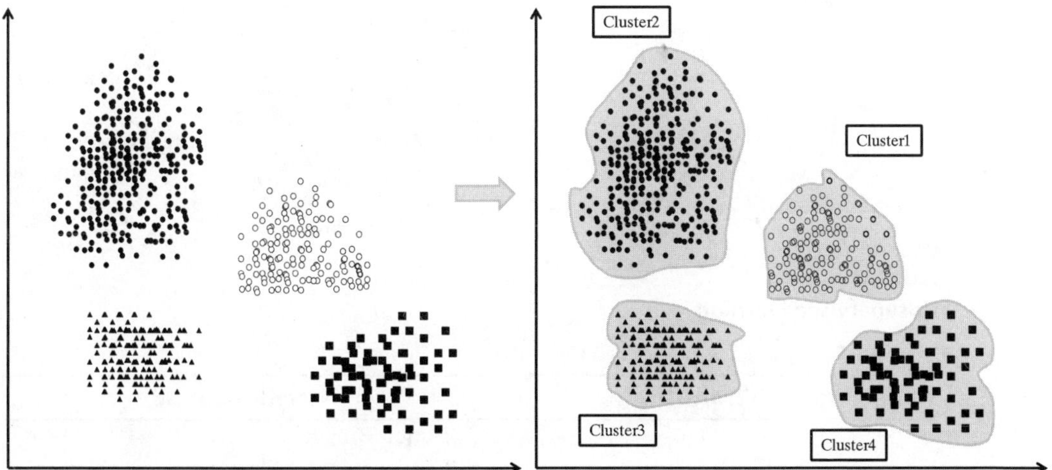

FIG. 1.7
Distance-based clustering

are quite similar to each other while objects belonging to different clusters are quite dissimilar. Hence, the objective of clustering is to discover the intrinsic grouping of unlabelled data and form clusters, as depicted in Figure 1.7. Different measures of similarity can be applied for clustering. One of the most commonly adopted similarity measure is distance. Two data items are considered as a part of the same cluster if the distance between them is less. In the same way, if the distance between the data items is high, the items do not generally belong to the same cluster. This is also known as distance-based clustering. Figure 1.8 depicts the process of clustering at a high level.

Other than clustering of data and getting a summarized view from it, one more variant of unsupervised learning is **association analysis**. As a part of association analysis, the association between data elements is identified. Let's try to understand the approach of association analysis in context of one of the most common examples, i.e. market basket analysis as shown in Figure 1.9. From past transaction data in a grocery store, it may be observed that most of the customers who have bought item A, have also bought item B and item C or at least one of them. This means that there is a strong association of the event 'purchase of item A' with the event 'purchase of

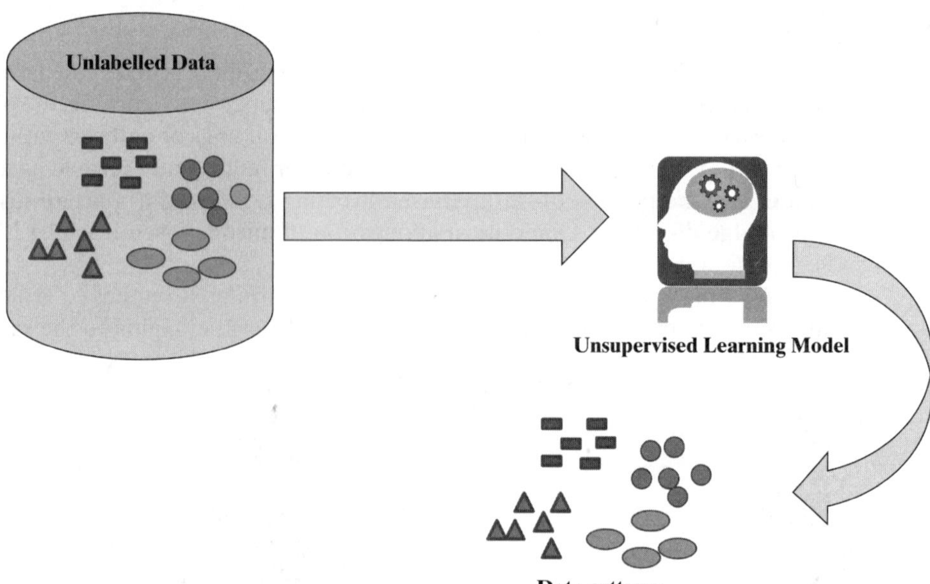

FIG. 1.8
Unsupervised learning

TransID	Items Bought
1	{Butter, Bread}
2	{Ginger, Bread, Milk, Garlic}
3	{Milk, Chicken, Garlic, Ginger}
4	{Bread, Ginger, Chicken, Garlic}
5	{Ginger, Garlic, Cookies, Ice cream}
…	…

Market Basket transactions
Frequent itemsets ➜ (Ginger, Garlic)
Possible association: Ginger ➜ Garlic

FIG. 1.9
Market basket analysis

item B', or 'purchase of item C'. Identifying these sorts of associations is the goal of association analysis. This helps in boosting up sales pipeline, hence a critical input for the sales group. Critical applications of association analysis include market basket analysis and recommender systems. More details about Unsupervised Learning - Clustering and Association Rule can be found in Chapter 9.

1.5.3   Reinforcement learning

We have seen babies learn to walk without any prior knowledge of how to do it. Often we wonder how they really do it. They do it in a relatively simple way.

First they notice somebody else walking around, for example parents or anyone living around. They understand that legs have to be used, one at a time, to take a step. While walking, sometimes they fall down hitting an obstacle, whereas other times they are able to walk smoothly avoiding bumpy obstacles. When they are able to walk overcoming the obstacle, their parents are elated and appreciate the baby with loud claps / or may be a chocolates. When they fall down while circumventing an obstacle, obviously their parents do not give claps or chocolates. Slowly a time comes when the babies learn from mistakes and are able to walk with much ease.

In the same way, machines often learn to do tasks autonomously. Let's try to understand in context of the example of the child learning to walk. The action tried to be achieved is walking, the child is the agent and the place with hurdles on which the

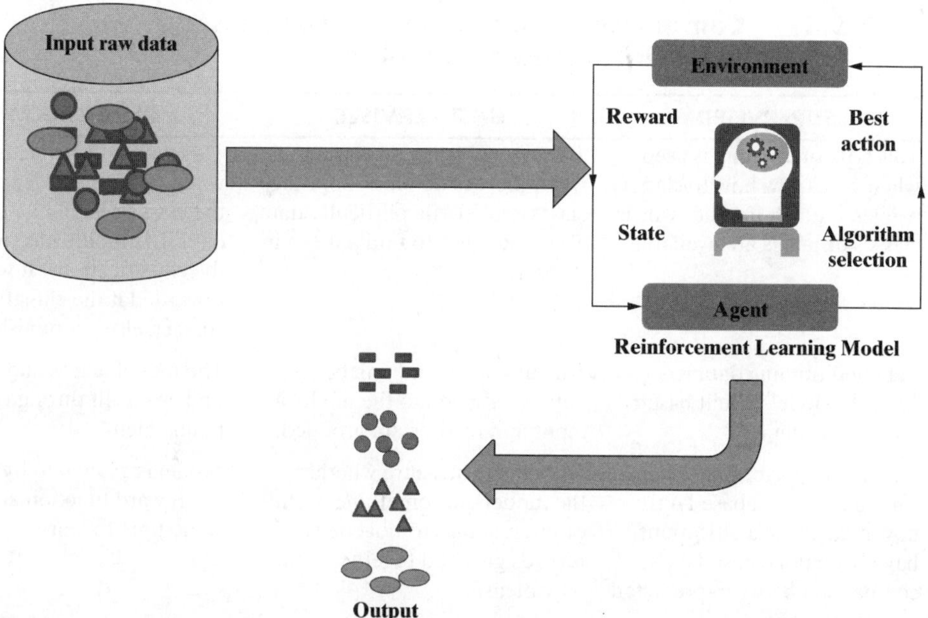

FIG. 1.10
Reinforcement learning

child is trying to walk resembles the environment. It tries to improve its performance of doing the task. When a sub-task is accomplished successfully, a reward is given. When a sub-task is not executed correctly, obviously no reward is given. This continues till the machine is able to complete execution of the whole task. This process of learning is known as reinforcement learning(RL). Figure 1.10 captures the high-level process of reinforcement learning.

One contemporary example of reinforcement learning is self-driving cars. The critical information which it needs to take care of are speed and speed limit in different road segments, traffic conditions, road conditions, weather conditions, etc. The tasks that have to be taken care of are start/stop, accelerate/decelerate, turn to left / right, etc.

Reinforcement Learning is discussed in detail in Chapter 10.

Points to Ponder

- Reinforcement learning is getting more and more attention from both industry and academia. Annual publications count in the area of reinforcement learning in Google Scholar support this view.
- While Deep Blue used brute force to defeat the human chess champion, AlphaGo used RL to defeat the best human Go player.
- RL is an effective tool for personalized online marketing. It considers the demographic details and browsing history of the user real-time to show most relevant advertisements.

■

 ## 1.5.4   Comparison – supervised, unsupervised, and reinforcement learning

SUPERVISED	UNSUPERVISED	REINFORCEMENT
This type of learning is used when you know how to classify a given data, or in other words classes or labels are available.	This type of learning is used when there is no idea about the class or label of a particular data. The model has to find pattern in the data.	This type of learning is used when there is no idea about the class or label of a particular data. The model has to do the classification – it will get rewarded if the classification is correct, else get punished.
Labelled training data is needed. Model is built based on training data.	Any unknown and unlabelled data set is given to the model as input and records are grouped.	The model learns and updates itself through reward/ punishment.
The model performance can be evaluated based on how many misclassifications have been done based on a comparison between predicted and actual values.	Difficult to measure whether the model did something useful or interesting. Homogeneity of records grouped together is the only measure.	Model is evaluated by means of the reward function after it had some time to learn.
There are two types of supervised learning problems – classification and regression.	There are two types of unsupervised learning problems – clustering and association.	No such types.
Simplest one to understand.	More difficult to understand and implement than supervised learning.	Most complex to understand and apply.
Standard algorithms include • Naïve Bayes • k-nearest neighbour (kNN) • Decision tree • Linear regression • Logistic regression • Support Vector Machine SVM), etc.	Standard algorithms are • k-means • Principal Component Analysis (PCA) • Self-organizing map (SOM) • Apriori algorithm • DBSCAN etc.	Standard algorithms are • Q-learning • Sarsa

SUPERVISED	UNSUPERVISED	REINFORCEMENT
Practical applications include • Handwriting recognition • Stock market prediction • Disease prediction • Fraud detection, etc.	Practical applications include • Market basket analysis • Recommender systems • Customer segmentation, etc.	Practical applications include • Self-driving cars • Intelligent robots • AlphaGo Zero (the latest version of DeepMind's AI system playing Go)

1.6 PROBLEMS NOT TO BE SOLVED USING MACHINE LEARNING

Machine learning should not be applied to tasks in which humans are very effective or frequent human intervention is needed. For example, air traffic control is a very complex task needing intense human involvement. At the same time, for very simple tasks which can be implemented using traditional programming paradigms, there is no sense of using machine learning. For example, simple rule-driven or formula-based applications like price calculator engine, dispute tracking application, etc. do not need machine learning techniques.

Machine learning should be used only when the business process has some lapses. If the task is already optimized, incorporating machine learning will not serve to justify the return on investment.

For situations where training data is not sufficient, machine learning cannot be used effectively. This is because, with small training data sets, the impact of bad data is exponentially worse. For the quality of prediction or recommendation to be good, the training data should be sizeable.

1.7 APPLICATIONS OF MACHINE LEARNING

Wherever there is a substantial amount of past data, machine learning can be used to generate actionable insight from the data. Though machine learning is adopted in multiple forms in every business domain, we have covered below three major domains just to give some idea about what type of actions can be done using machine learning.

1.7.1 Banking and finance

In the banking industry, fraudulent transactions, especially the ones related to credit cards, are extremely prevalent. Since the volumes as well as velocity of the transactions are extremely high, high performance machine learning solutions are implemented by almost all leading banks across the globe. The models work on a real-time basis, i.e. the fraudulent transactions are spotted and prevented right at the time of occurrence. This helps in avoiding a lot of operational hassles in settling the disputes that customers will otherwise raise against those fraudulent transactions.

Customers of a bank are often offered lucrative proposals by other competitor banks. Proposals like higher bank interest, lower processing charge of loans, zero balance savings accounts, no overdraft penalty, etc. are offered to customers, with the intent that the customer switches over to the competitor bank. Also, sometimes customers get demotivated by the poor quality of services of the banks and shift to competitor banks. Machine learning helps in preventing or at least reducing the customer churn. Both descriptive and predictive learning can be applied for reducing customer churn. Using descriptive learning, the specific pockets of problem, i.e. a specific bank or a specific zone or a specific type of offering like car loan, may be spotted where maximum churn is happening. Quite obviously, these are troubled areas where further investigation needs to be done to find and fix the root cause. Using predictive learning, the set of vulnerable customers who may leave the bank very soon, can be identified. Proper action can be taken to make sure that the customers stay back.

1.7.2   Insurance

Insurance industry is extremely data intensive. For that reason, machine learning is extensively used in the insurance industry. Two major areas in the insurance industry where machine learning is used are risk prediction during new customer onboarding and claims management. During customer onboarding, based on the past information the risk profile of a new customer needs to be predicted. Based on the quantum of risk predicted, the quote is generated for the prospective customer. When a customer claim comes for settlement, past information related to historic claims along with the adjustor notes are considered to predict whether there is any possibility of the claim to be fraudulent. Other than the past information related to the specific customer, information related to similar customers, i.e. customer belonging to the same geographical location, age group, ethnic group, etc., are also considered to formulate the model.

1.7.3   Healthcare

Wearable device data form a rich source for applying machine learning and predict the health conditions of the person real time. In case there is some health issue which is predicted by the learning model, immediately the person is alerted to take preventive action. In case of some extreme problem, doctors or healthcare providers in the vicinity of the person can be alerted. Suppose an elderly person goes for a morning walk in a park close to his house. Suddenly, while walking, his blood pressure shoots up beyond a certain limit, which is tracked by the wearable. The wearable data is sent to a remote server and a machine learning algorithm is constantly analyzing the streaming data. It also has the history of the elderly person and persons of similar age group. The model predicts some fatality unless immediate action is taken. Alert can be sent to the person to immediately stop walking and take rest. Also, doctors and healthcare providers can be alerted to be on standby.

Machine learning along with computer vision also plays a crucial role in disease diagnosis from medical imaging.

1.8   STATE-OF-THE-ART LANGUAGES/TOOLS IN MACHINE LEARNING

The algorithms related to different machine learning tasks are known to all and can be implemented using any language/platform. It can be implemented using a Java platform or C / C++ language or in .NET. However, there are certain languages and tools which have been developed with a focus for implementing machine learning. Few of them, which are most widely used, are covered below.

1.8.1   Python

Python is one of the most popular, open source programming language widely adopted by machine learning community. It was designed by Guido van Rossum and was first released in 1991. The reference implementation of Python, i.e. CPython, is managed by Python Software Foundation, which is a non-profit organization.

Python has very strong libraries for advanced mathematical functionalities (NumPy), algorithms and mathematical tools (SciPy) and numerical plotting (matplotlib). Built on these libraries, there is a machine learning library named **scikit-learn**, which has various classification, regression, and clustering algorithms embedded in it.

1.8.2   R

R is a language for statistical computing and data analysis. It is an open source language, extremely popular in the academic community – especially among statisticians and data miners. R is considered as a variant of S, a GNU project which was developed at Bell Laboratories. Currently, it is supported by the R Foundation for statistical computing.

R is a very simple programming language with a huge set of libraries available for different stages of machine learning. Some of the libraries standing out in terms of popularity are plyr/dplyr (for data transformation), caret ('Classification and Regression Training' for classification), RJava (to facilitate integration with Java), tm (for text mining), ggplot2 (for data visualization). Other than the libraries, certain packages like Shiny and R Markdown have been developed around R to develop interactive web applications, documents and dashboards on R without much effort.

1.8.3   Matlab

MATLAB (matrix laboratory) is a licenced commercial software with a robust support for a wide range of numerical computing. MATLAB has a huge user base across industry and academia. MATLAB is developed by MathWorks, a company founded in 1984. Being proprietary software, MATLAB is developed much more professionally, tested rigorously, and has comprehensive documentation.

MATLAB also provides extensive support of statistical functions and has a huge number of machine learning algorithms in-built. It also has the ability to scale up for large datasets by parallel processing on clusters and cloud.

1.8.4   SAS

SAS (earlier known as 'Statistical Analysis System') is another licenced commercial software which provides strong support for machine learning functionalities. Developed in C by SAS Institute, SAS had its first release in the year 1976.

SAS is a software suite comprising different components. The basic data management functionalities are embedded in the Base SAS component whereas the other components like SAS/INSIGHT, Enterprise Miner, SAS/STAT, etc. help in specialized functions related to data mining and statistical analysis.

1.8.5   Other languages/tools

There are a host of other languages and tools that also support machine learning functionalities. Owned by IBM, **SPSS** (originally named as Statistical Package for the Social Sciences) is a popular package supporting specialized data mining and statistical analysis. Originally popular for statistical analysis in social science (as the name reflects), SPSS is now popular in other fields as well.

Released in 2012, **Julia** is an open source, liberal licence programming language for numerical analysis and computational science. It has baked in all good things of MATLAB, Python, R, and other programming languages used for machine learning for which it is gaining steady attention from machine learning development community. Another big point in favour of Julia is its ability to implement high-performance machine learning algorithms.

1.9   ISSUES IN MACHINE LEARNING

Machine learning is a field which is relatively new and still evolving. Also, the level of research and kind of use of machine learning tools and technologies varies drastically from country to country. The laws and regulations, cultural background, emotional maturity of people differ drastically in different countries. All these factors make the use of machine learning and the issues originating out of machine learning usage are quite different.

The biggest fear and issue arising out of machine learning is related to privacy and the breach of it. The primary focus of learning is on analyzing data, both past and current, and coming up with insight from the data. This insight may be related to people and the facts revealed might be private enough to be kept confidential. Also, different people have a different preference when it comes to sharing of information. While some people may be open to sharing some level of information publicly, some other people may not want to share it even to all friends and keep it restricted just to family members. Classic examples are a birth date (not the day, but the date as a whole), photographs of a dinner date with family, educational background, etc. Some people share them with all in the social platforms like Facebook while others do not, or if they do, they may restrict it to friends only. When machine learning algorithms are implemented using those information, inadvertently people may get upset. For example, if there is a learning algorithm to do preference-based customer segmentation and the output of the analysis is used for sending targeted marketing campaigns, it will hurt the emotion of people and actually do more harm than good. In certain countries, such events may result in legal actions to be taken by the people affected.

Even if there is no breach of privacy, there may be situations where actions were taken based on machine learning may create an adverse reaction. Let's take the example of knowledge discovery exercise done before starting an election campaign. If a specific area reveals an ethnic majority or skewness of a certain demographic factor, and the campaign pitch carries a message keeping that in mind, it might actually upset the voters and cause an adverse result.

So a very critical consideration before applying machine learning is that proper human judgement should be exercised before using any outcome from machine learning. Only then the decision taken will be beneficial and also not result in any adverse impact.

1.10 SUMMARY

- Machine learning imbibes the philosophy of human learning, i.e. learning from expert guidance and from experience.
- The basic machine learning process can be divided into three parts.
  - ❖ Data Input: Past data or information is utilized as a basis for future decision-making.
  - ❖ Abstraction: The input data is represented in a summarized way
  - ❖ Generalization: The abstracted representation is generalized to form a framework for making decisions.
- Before starting to solve any problem using machine learning, it should be decided whether the problem is a right problem to be solved using machine learning.
- Machine learning can be classified into three broad categories:
  - ❖ Supervised learning: Also called predictive learning. The objective of this learning is to predict class/value of unknown objects based on prior information of similar objects. Examples: predicting whether a tumour is malignant or benign, price prediction in domains such as real estate, stocks, etc.
  - ❖ Unsupervised learning: Also called descriptive learning, helps in finding groups or patterns in unknown objects by grouping similar objects together. Examples: customer segmentation, recommender systems, etc.
  - ❖ Reinforcement learning: A machine learns to act on its own to achieve the given goals. Examples: self-driving cars, intelligent robots, etc.
- Machine learning has been adopted by various industry domains such as Banking and Financial Services, Insurance, Healthcare, Life Sciences, etc. to solve problems.
- Some of the most adopted platforms to implement machine learning include Python, R, MATLAB, SAS, SPPSS, etc.

- To avoid ethical issues, the critical consideration is required before applying machine learning and using any outcome from machine learning.

SAMPLE QUESTIONS

MULTIPLE-CHOICE QUESTIONS (1 MARK EACH):

1. Machine learning is ___ field.
   (a) Inter-disciplinary
   (b) Single
   (c) Multi-disciplinary
   (d) All of the above

2. A computer program is said to learn from __________E with respect to some class of tasks T and performance measure P, if its performance at tasks in T, as measured by P, improves with E.
   (a) Training
   (b) Experience
   (c) Database
   (d) Algorithm

3. __________ has been used to train vehicles to steer correctly and autonomously on road.
   (a) Machine learning
   (b) Data mining
   (c) Neural networks
   (d) Robotics

4. Any hypothesis find an approximation of the target function over a sufficiently large set of training examples will also approximate the target function well over other unobserved examples. This is called _____.
   (a) Hypothesis
   (b) Inductive hypothesis
   (c) Learning
   (d) Concept learning

5. Factors which affect performance of a learner system does not include
   (a) Representation scheme used
   (b) Training scenario
   (c) Type of feedback
   (d) Good data structures

6. Different learning methods does not include
   (a) Memorization
   (b) Analogy
   (c) Deduction
   (d) Introduction

7. A model of language consists of the categories which does not include
   (a) Language units
   (b) Role structure of units
   (c) System constraints
   (d) Structural units

8. How many types are available in machine learning?
   (a) 1
   (b) 2
   (c) 3
   (d) 4

9. The k-means algorithm is a
   (a) Supervised learning algorithm
   (b) Unsupervised learning algorithm
   (c) Semi-supervised learning algorithm
   (d) Weakly supervised learning algorithm

10. The Q-learning algorithm is a
   (a) Supervised learning algorithm
   (b) Unsupervised learning algorithm
   (c) Semi-supervised learning algorithm
   (d) Reinforcement learning algorithm

11. This type of learning to be used when there is no idea about the class or label of a particular data
   (a) Supervised learning algorithm
   (b) Unsupervised learning algorithm
   (c) Semi-supervised learning algorithm
   (d) Reinforcement learning algorithm

12. The model learns and updates itself through reward/punishment in case of
   (a) Supervised learning algorithm
   (b) Unsupervised learning algorithm
   (c) Semi-supervised learning algorithm
   (d) Reinforcement learning algorithm

SHORT-ANSWER TYPE QUESTIONS (5 MARKS EACH):

1. What is human learning? Give any two examples.

2. What are the types of human learning? Are there equivalent forms of machine learning?

3. What is machine learning? What are key tasks of machine learning?

4. Explain the concept of penalty and reward in reinforcement learning.

5. What are concepts of learning as search?

6. What are different objectives of machine learning? How are these related with human learning?

7. Define machine learning and explain the different elements with a real example.

8. Explain the process of abstraction with an example.

9. What is generalization? What role does it play in the process of machine learning?

10. What is classification? Explain the key differences between classification and regression.

11. What is regression? Give example of some practical problems solved using regression.

12. Explain the process of clustering in details.

13. Write short notes on any two of the following:
   (a) Application of machine learning algorithms
   (b) Supervised learning
   (c) Unsupervised learning
   (d) Reinforcement learning

LONG-ANSWER TYPE QUESTIONS (10 MARKS QUESTIONS):

1. What is machine learning? Explain any two business applications of machine learning. What are the possible ethical issues of machine learning applications?

2. Explain how human learning happens:
   (a) Under direct guidance of experts
   (b) Under indirect guidance of experts
   (c) Self-learning

3. Explain the different forms of machine learning with a few examples.

4. Compare the different types of machine learning.

5. What do you mean by a well-posed learning problem? Explain important features that are required to well-define a learning problem.

6. Can all problems be solved using machine learning? Explain your response in detail.

7. What are different tools and technologies available for solving problems in machine learning? Give details about any two of them.

8. What are the different types of supervised learning? Explain them with a sample application in each area.

9. What are the different types of unsupervised learning? Explain them difference with a sample application in each area.

10. Explain, in details, the process of machine learning.
    (a) Write short notes on any two:
        (i) MATLAB
        (ii) Application of machine learning in Healthcare
        (iii) Market basket analysis
        (iv) Simple linear regression
    (b) Write the difference between (any two):
        (i) Abstraction and generalization
        (ii) Supervised and unsupervised learning
        (iii) Classification and regression

Chapter 2

Preparing to Model

OBJECTIVE OF THE CHAPTER:

This chapter gives a detailed view of how to understand the incoming data and create basic understanding about the nature and quality of the data. This information, in turn, helps to select and then how to apply the model. So, the knowledge imparted in this chapter helps a beginner take the first step towards effective modelling and solving a machine learning problem.

2.1 INTRODUCTION

In the last chapter, we got introduced to machine learning. In the beginning, we got a glimpse of the journey of machine learning as an evolving technology. It all started as a proposition from the renowned computer scientist Alan Turing – machines can 'learn' and become artificially intelligent. Gradually, through the next few decades path-breaking innovations came in from Arthur Samuel, Frank Rosenblatt, John Hopfield, Christopher Watkins, Geoffrey Hinton and many other computer scientists. They shaped up concepts of Neural Networks, Recurrent Neural Network, Reinforcement Learning, Deep Learning, etc. which took machine learning to new heights. In parallel, interesting applications of machine learning kept on happening, with organizations like IBM and Google taking a lead. What started with IBM's Deep Blue beating the world chess champion Gary Kasparov, continued with IBM's Watson beating two human champions in a Jeopardy competition.

Google also started with a series of innovations applying machine learning. The Google Brain, Sibyl, Waymo, AlphaGo programs – are all extremely advanced applications of machine learning which have taken the technology a few notches up. Now we can see an all-pervasive presence of machine learning technology in all walks of life.

We have also seen the types of human learning and how that, in some ways, can be related to the types of machine learning – supervised, unsupervised, and reinforcement. Supervised learning, as we saw, implies learning from past data, also called training data, which has got known values or classes. Machines can 'learn' or get 'trained' from the past data and assign classes or values to unknown data, termed as test data. This helps in solving problems related to prediction. This is much like human learning through expert guidance as happens for infants from parents or students through teachers. So, supervised learning in case of machines can be perceived as guided learning from human inputs. Unsupervised machine learning doesn't have labelled data to learn from. It tries to find patterns in unlabelled data. This is much like human beings trying to group together objects of similar shape. This learning is not guided by labelled inputs but uses the knowledge gained from the labels themselves. Last but not the least is reinforcement learning in which machine tries to learn by itself through penalty/reward mechanism – again pretty much in the same way as human self-learning happens.

Lastly, we saw some of the applications of machine learning in different domains such as banking and finance, insurance, and healthcare. Fraud detection is a critical business case which is implemented in almost all banks across the world and uses machine learning predominantly. Risk prediction for new customers is a similar critical case in the insurance industry which finds the application of machine learning. In the healthcare sector, disease prediction makes wide use of machine learning, especially in the developed countries.

While development in machine learning technology has been extensive and its implementation has become widespread, to start as a practitioner, we need to gain some basic understanding. We need to understand how to apply the array of tools and technologies available in the machine learning to solve a problem. In fact, that is going to be very specific to the kind of problem that we are trying to solve. If it is a prediction problem, the kind of activities that will be involved is going to be completely different vis-à-vis if it is a problem where we are trying to unfold a pattern in a data without any past knowledge about the data. So how a machine learning project looks like or what are the salient activities that form the core of a machine learning project will depend on whether it is in the area of supervised or unsupervised or reinforcement learning area. However, irrespective of the variation, some foundational knowledge needs to be built before we start with the core machine learning concepts and key algorithms. In this section, we will have a quick look at a few typical machine learning activities and focus on some of the foundational concepts that all practitioners need to gain as pre-requisites before starting their journey in the area of machine learning.

Points to Ponder

No man is perfect. The same is applicable for machines. To increase the level of accuracy of a machine, human participation should be added to the machine learning process. In short, incorporating human intervention is the recipe for the success of machine learning.

2.2   MACHINE LEARNING ACTIVITIES

The first step in machine learning activity starts with data. In case of supervised learning, it is the labelled training data set followed by test data which is not labelled. In case of unsupervised learning, there is no question of labelled data but the task is to find patterns in the input data. A thorough review and exploration of the data is needed to understand the type of the data, the quality of the data and relationship between the different data elements. Based on that, multiple pre-processing activities may need to be done on the input data before we can go ahead with core machine learning activities. Following are the typical **preparation** activities done once the input data comes into the machine learning system:

- Understand the type of data in the given input data set.
- Explore the data to understand the nature and quality.
- Explore the relationships amongst the data elements, e.g. inter-feature relationship.
- Find potential issues in data.
- Do the necessary remediation, e.g. impute missing data values, etc., if needed.
- Apply pre-processing steps, as necessary.
- Once the data is prepared for modelling, then the learning tasks start off. As a part of it, do the following activities:
    - ❖ The input data is first divided into parts – the training data and the test data (called holdout). This step is applicable for supervised learning only.
    - ❖ Consider different models or learning algorithms for selection.
    - ❖ Train the model based on the training data for supervised learning problem and apply to unknown data. Directly apply the chosen unsupervised model on the input data for unsupervised learning problem.

After the model is selected, trained (for supervised learning), and applied on input data, the performance of the model is evaluated. Based on options available, specific actions can be taken to improve the performance of the model, if possible.

Figure 2.1 depicts the four-step process of machine learning.

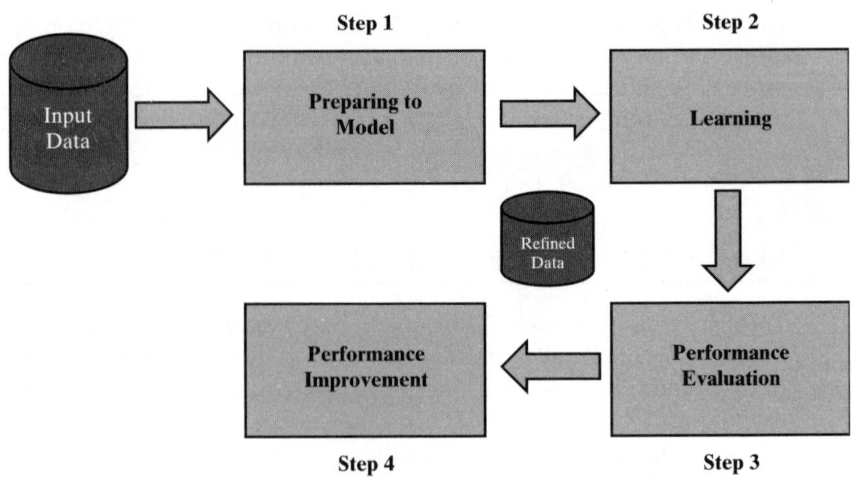

FIG. 2.1
Detailed process of machine learning

Table 2.1 contains a summary of steps and activities involved:

Table 2.1
Activities in Machine Learning

Step #	Step Name	Activities Involved

Step 1	Preparing to Model	• Understand the type of data in the given input data set
		• Explore the data to understand data quality
		• Explore the relationships amongst the data elements, e.g. inter-feature relationship
		• Find potential issues in data
		• Remediate data, if needed
		• Apply following pre-processing steps, as necessary:
		  ✓ Dimensionality reduction
		  ✓ Feature subset selection

Step 2	Learning	• Data partitioning/holdout • Model selection • Cross-validation
Step 3	Performance evaluation	• Examine the model performance, e.g. confusion matrix in case of classification • Visualize performance trade-offs using ROC curves
Step 4	Performance improvement	• Tuning the model • Ensembling • Bagging • Boosting

In this chapter, we will cover the first part, i.e. preparing to model. The remaining parts, i.e. learning, performance evaluation, and performance improvement will be covered in Chapter 3.

2.3   BASIC TYPES OF DATA IN MACHINE LEARNING

Before starting with types of data, let's first understand what a data set is and what are the elements of a data set. A data set is a collection of related information or records. The information may be on some entity or some subject area. For example (Table. 2.2), we may have a data set on students in which each record consists of information about a specific student. Again, we can have a data set on student performance which has records providing performance, i.e. marks on the individual subjects.

Each row of a data set is called a record. Each data set also has multiple attributes, each of which gives information on a specific characteristic. For example,

Table 2.2
Examples of data set

Student data set:

Roll Number	Name	Gender	Age
129/011	Mihir Karmarkar	M	14
129/012	Geeta Iyer	F	15
129/013	Chanda Bose	F	14
129/014	Sreenu Subramanian	M	14
129/015	Pallav Gupta	M	16
129/016	Gajanan Sharma	M	15

Student performance data set:

Roll Number	Maths	Science	Percentage
129/011	89	45	89.33%
129/012	89	47	90.67%
129/013	68	29	64.67%
129/014	83	38	80.67%
129/015	57	23	53.33%
129/016	78	35	75.33%

in the data set on students, there are four attributes namely Roll Number, Name, Gender, and Age, each of which understandably is a specific characteristic about the student entity. Attributes can also be termed as feature, variable, dimension or field. Both the data sets, Student and Student Performance, are having four features or dimensions; hence they are told to have four-dimensional data space. A row or record represents a point in the four-dimensional data space as each row has specific values for each of the four attributes or features. Value of an attribute, quite understandably, may vary from record to record. For example, if we refer to the first two records in the Student data set, the value of attributes Name, Gender, and Age are different (Table 2.3).

Table 2.3

Data set records and attributes

Roll Number	Name	Gender	Age
129/011	Mihir Karmarkar	M	14
129/012	Geeta Iyer	F	15

Now that a context of data sets is given, let's try to understand the different types of data that we generally come across in machine learning problems. Data can broadly be divided into following two types:

1. Qualitative data
2. Quantitative data

Qualitative data provides information about the quality of an object or information which cannot be measured. For example, if we consider the quality of performance of students in terms of 'Good', 'Average', and 'Poor', it falls under the category of qualitative data. Also, name or roll number of students are information that cannot be measured using some scale of measurement. So they would fall under qualitative data. Qualitative data is also called **categorical data**. Qualitative data can be further subdivided into two types as follows:

1. Nominal data
2. Ordinal data

Nominal data is one which has no numeric value, but a named value. It is used for assigning named values to attributes. Nominal values cannot be quantified. Examples of nominal data are

1. Blood group: A, B, O, AB, etc.
2. Nationality: Indian, American, British, etc.
3. Gender: Male, Female, Other

Note:

A special case of nominal data is when only two labels are possible, e.g. pass/fail as a result of an examination. This sub-type of nominal data is called 'dichotomous'.

It is obvious, mathematical operations such as addition, subtraction, multiplication, etc. cannot be performed on nominal data. For that reason, statistical functions such as mean, variance, etc. can also not be applied on nominal data. However, a basic count is possible. So mode, i.e. most frequently occurring value, can be identified for nominal data.

Ordinal data, in addition to possessing the properties of nominal data, can also be naturally ordered. This means ordinal data also assigns named values to attributes but unlike nominal data, they can be arranged in a sequence of increasing or decreasing value so that we can say whether a value is better than or greater than another value. Examples of ordinal data are

1. Customer satisfaction: 'Very Happy', 'Happy', 'Unhappy', etc.
2. Grades: A, B, C, etc.
3. Hardness of Metal: 'Very Hard', 'Hard', 'Soft', etc.

Like nominal data, basic counting is possible for ordinal data. Hence, the mode can be identified. Since ordering is possible in case of ordinal data, median, and quartiles can be identified in addition. Mean can still not be calculated.

Quantitative data relates to information about the quantity of an object – hence it can be measured. For example, if we consider the attribute 'marks', it can be measured using a scale of measurement. Quantitative data is also termed as numeric data. There are two types of quantitative data:

1. Interval data
2. Ratio data

Interval data is numeric data for which not only the order is known, but the exact difference between values is also known. An ideal example of interval data is Celsius temperature. The difference between each value remains the same in Celsius temperature. For example, the difference between 12°C and 18°C degrees is measurable and is 6°C as in the case of difference between 15.5°C and 21.5°C. Other examples include date, time, etc.

For interval data, mathematical operations such as addition and subtraction are possible. For that reason, for interval data, the central tendency can be measured by mean, median, or mode. Standard deviation can also be calculated.

However, interval data do not have something called a 'true zero' value. For example, there is nothing called '0 temperature' or 'no temperature'. Hence, only addition and subtraction applies for interval data. The ratio cannot be applied. This means, we can say a temperature of 40°C is equal to the temperature of 20°C + temperature of 20°C. However, we cannot say the temperature of 40°C means it is twice as hot as in temperature of 20°C.

Ratio data represents numeric data for which exact value can be measured. Absolute zero is available for ratio data. Also, these variables can be added, subtracted, multiplied, or divided. The central tendency can be measured by mean, median, or mode and methods of dispersion such as standard deviation. Examples of ratio data include height, weight, age, salary, etc.

Figure 2.2 gives a summarized view of different types of data that we may find in a typical machine learning problem.

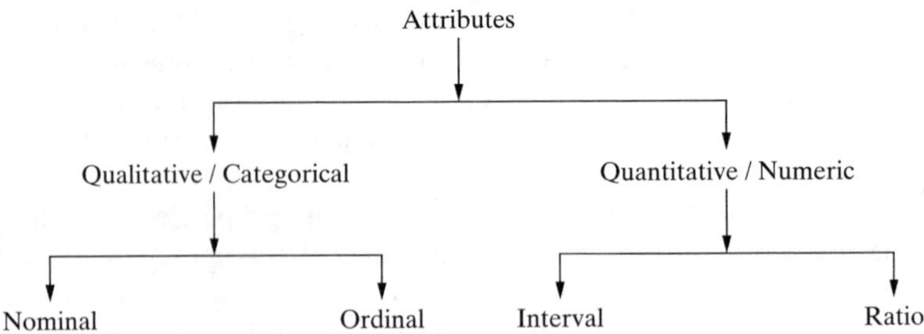

FIG. 2.2
Types of data

Apart from the approach detailed above, attributes can also be categorized into types based on a number of values that can be assigned. The attributes can be either discrete or continuous based on this factor.

Discrete attributes can assume a finite or countably infinite number of values. Nominal attributes such as roll number, street number, pin code, etc. can have a finite number of values whereas numeric attributes such as count, rank of students, etc. can have countably infinite values. A special type of discrete attribute which can assume two values only is called binary attribute. Examples of binary attribute include male/female, positive/negative, yes/no, etc.

Continuous attributes can assume any possible value which is a real number. Examples of continuous attribute include length, height, weight, price, etc.

Note:

In general, nominal and ordinal attributes are discrete. On the other hand, interval and ratio attributes are continuous, barring a few exceptions, e.g. 'count' attribute.

2.4   EXPLORING STRUCTURE OF DATA

By now, we understand that in machine learning, we come across two basic data types – numeric and categorical. With this context in mind, we can delve deeper into understanding a data set. We need to understand that in a data set, which of the attributes are numeric and which are categorical in nature. This is because, the approach of exploring numeric data is different than the approach of exploring categorical data. In case of a standard data set, we may have the data dictionary available for reference. Data dictionary is a metadata repository, i.e. the repository of all information related to the structure of each data element contained in the data set. The data dictionary gives detailed information on each of the attributes – the description as well as the data type and other relevant details. In case the data dictionary is not available, we need to use standard library function of the machine learning tool that we are using and get the details. For the time being, let us move ahead with a standard data set from UCI machine learning repository.

Did you know?

University of California, Irvine (UCI) Machine Learning Repository (http://archive.ics.uci.edu/ml/index.php) is a collection of 400+ data sets which serve as benchmarks for researchers and practitioners in the machine learning community.

The data set that we take as a reference is the Auto MPG data set available in the UCI repository. Table 2.4 is a snapshot of the first few rows of the data set.

Table 2.4
Auto MPG data set

mpg	cylinder	displace-ment	horse-power	weight	accel-eration	model year	origin	car name
18	8	307	130	3504	12	70	1	Chevrolet chevelle malibu
15	8	350	165	3693	11.5	70	1	Buick skylark 320
18	8	318	150	3436	11	70	1	Plymouth satellite
16	8	304	150	3433	12	70	1	Amc rebel sst
17	8	302	140	3449	10.5	70	1	Ford torino
15	8	429	198	4341	10	70	1	Ford galaxie 500
14	8	454	220	4354	9	70	1	Chevrolet impala
14	8	440	215	4312	8.5	70	1	Plymouth fury iii
14	8	455	225	4425	10	70	1	Pontiac catalina
15	8	390	190	3850	8.5	70	1	Amc acbassador dpl
15	8	383	170	3563	10	70	1	Dodge challenger se
14	8	340	160	3609	8	70	1	Plymouth ' cuda 340
15	8	400	150	3761	9.5	70	1	Chevrolet monte carlo
14	8	455	225	3086	10	70	1	Buick estate wagon (sw)
24	4	113	95	2372	15	70	3	Toyota corona mark ii
22	6	198	95	2933	15.5	70	1	Plymouth duster
18	6	199	97	2774	15.5	70	1	Amc hornet

As is quite evident from the data, the attributes such as 'mpg', 'cylinders', 'displacement', 'horsepower', 'weight', 'acceleration', 'model year', and 'origin' are all numeric. Out of these attributes, 'cylinders', 'model year', and 'origin' are discrete in nature as the only finite number of values can be assumed by these attributes. The remaining of the numeric attributes, i.e. 'mpg', 'displacement', 'horsepower', 'weight', and 'acceleration' can assume any real value.

Note:

Since the attributes 'cylinders' or 'origin' have a small number of possible values, one may prefer to treat it as a categorical or qualitative attribute and explore in that way. Anyways, we will treat these attributes as numeric or quantitative as we are trying to show data exploration and related nuances in this section.

Hence, these attributes are continuous in nature. The only remaining attribute 'car name' is of type categorical, or more specifically nominal. This data set is regarding prediction of fuel consumption in miles per gallon, i.e. the numeric attribute 'mpg' is the target attribute.

With this understanding of the data set attributes, we can start exploring the numeric and categorical attributes separately.

 2.4.1   Exploring numerical data

There are two most effective mathematical plots to explore numerical data – box plot and histogram. We will explore all these plots one by one, starting with the most critical one, which is the box plot.

2.4.1.1   *Understanding central tendency*

To understand the nature of numeric variables, we can apply the measures of central tendency of data, i.e. mean and median. In statistics, measures of central tendency help us understand the central point of a set of data. Mean, by definition, is a sum of all data values divided by the count of data elements. For example, mean of a set of observations – 21, 89, 34, 67, and 96 is calculated as below.

$$\text{Mean} = \frac{21+89+34+67+96}{5} = 61.4.$$

If the above set of numbers represents marks of 5 students in a class, the mean marks, or the falling in the middle of the range is 61.4.

Median, on contrary, is the value of the element appearing in the middle of an ordered list of data elements. If we consider the above 5 data elements, the ordered list would be – 21, 34, 67, 89, and 96. Since there are 5 data elements, the 3rd element in the ordered list is considered as the median. Hence, the median value of this set of data is 67.

There might be a natural curiosity to understand why two measures of central tendency are reviewed. The reason is mean and median are impacted differently by data values appearing at the beginning or at the end of the range. Mean being calculated from the cumulative sum of data values, is impacted if too many data elements are having values closer to the far end of the range, i.e. close to the maximum or minimum values. It is especially sensitive to outliers, i.e. the values which are unusually high or low, compared to the other values. Mean is likely to get shifted drastically even due to the presence of a small number of outliers. If we observe that for certain attributes the deviation between values of mean and median are quite high, we should investigate those attributes further and try to find out the root cause along with the need for remediation.

So, in the context of the Auto MPG data set, let's try to find out for each of the numeric attributes the values of mean and median. We can also find out if the deviation between these values is large. In Table 2.5, the comparison between mean and median for all the attributes has been shown. We can see that for the attributes such as 'mpg', 'weight', 'acceleration', and 'model.year' the deviation between mean and median is not significant which means the chance of these attributes having too many outlier values is less. However, the deviation is significant for the attributes 'cylinders', 'displacement' and 'origin'. So, we need to further drill down and look at some more statistics for these attributes. Also, there is some problem in the values of the attribute 'horsepower' because of which the mean and median calculation is not possible.

Table 2.5
Mean vs. Median for Auto MPG

	mpg	cylinders	displacement	horsepower	weight	acceleration	model year	origin
Median	23	4	148.5	?	2804	15.5	76	1
Mean	23.51	5.455	193.4	?	2970	15.57	76.01	1.573
Deviation	2.17	26.67%	23.22%	?	5.59%	0.45%	0.01%	36.43%
	Low	High	High	–	Low	Low	Low	High

With a bit of investigation, we can find out that the problem is occurring because of the 6 data elements, as shown in Table 2.6, do not have value for the attribute 'horsepower'.

Table 2.6
Missing values of attribute 'horsepower' in Auto MPG

mpg	cylinders	displacement	horsepower	weight	acceleration	model year	origin	car name
25	4	98	?	2046	19	71	1	Ford pinto
21	6	200	?	2875	17	74	1	Ford maverick
40.9	4	85	?	1835	17.3	80	2	Renault lecar deluxe
23.6	4	140	?	2905	14.3	80	1	Ford mustang cobra
34.5	4	100	?	2320	15.8	81	2	Renault 18i
23	4	151	?	3035	20.5	82	1	Amc concord di

For that reason, the attribute 'horsepower' is not treated as a numeric. That's why the operations applicable on numeric variables, like mean or median, are failing. So we have to first remediate the missing values of the attribute 'horsepower' before being able to do any kind of exploration. However, we will cover the approach of remediation of missing values a little later.

2.4.1.2   *Understanding data spread*

Now that we have explored the central tendency of the different numeric attributes, we have a clear idea of which attributes have a large deviation between mean and median. Let's look closely at those attributes. To drill down more, we need to look at the entire range of values of the attributes, though not at the level of data elements as that may be too vast to review manually. So we will take a granular view of the data spread in the form of

1. Dispersion of data
2. Position of the different data values

2.4.1.2.1 Measuring data dispersion

Consider the data values of two attributes

1. Attribute 1 values : 44, 46, 48, 45, and 47
2. Attribute 2 values : 34, 46, 59, 39, and 52

Both the set of values have a mean and median of 46. However, the first set of values that is of attribute 1 is more concentrated or clustered around the mean/median value whereas the second set of values of attribute 2 is quite spread out or dispersed. To measure the extent of dispersion of a data, or to find out how much the different values of a data are spread out, the variance of the data is measured. The variance of a data is measured using the formula given below:

$$\text{Variance}\,(x) = \frac{\sum_{i=1}^{n} x_i^2}{n} - \left(\frac{\sum_{i=1}^{n} x_i}{n} \right)^2$$

, where x is the variable or attribute whose variance

is to be measured and n is the number of observations or values of variable x.

Standard deviation of a data is measured as follows:

$$\text{Standard deviation}\,(x) = \sqrt{\text{Variance}\,(x)}$$

Larger value of variance or standard deviation indicates more dispersion in the data and vice versa. In the above example, let's calculate the variance of attribute 1 and that of attribute 2. For attribute 1,

$$\text{Variance} = \frac{\sum_{i=1}^{n} x_i^2}{n} - \left(\frac{\sum_{i=1}^{n} x_i}{n} \right)^2$$

$$= \frac{44^2 + 46^2 + 48^2 + 45^2 + 47^2}{5} - \left(\frac{44 + 46 + 48 + 45 + 47}{5} \right)^2$$

$$= \frac{1936 + 2116 + 2304 + 2025 + 2209}{5} - \left(\frac{230}{5}\right)^2 = \frac{10590}{5} - (46)^2 = 2$$

For attribute 2,

$$\text{Variance} \; = \frac{\sum_{i=1}^{n} x_i^2}{n} - \left(\frac{\sum_{i=1}^{n} x_i}{n}\right)^2$$

$$= \frac{34^2 + 46^2 + 59^2 + 39^2 + 52^2}{5} - \left(\frac{34 + 46 + 59 + 39 + 52}{5}\right)^2$$

$$= \frac{1156 + 2116 + 3481 + 1521 + 2704}{5} - \left(\frac{230}{5}\right)^2 = \frac{10978}{5} - (46)^2 = 79.6$$

So it is quite clear from the measure that attribute 1 values are quite concentrated around the mean while attribute 2 values are extremely spread out. Since this data was small, a visual inspection and understanding were possible and that matches with the measured value.

2.4.1.2.2 Measuring data value position

When the data values of an attribute are arranged in an increasing order, we have seen earlier that median gives the central data value, which divides the entire data set into two halves. Similarly, if the first half of the data is divided into two halves so that each half consists of one-quarter of the data set, then that median of the first half is known as first quartile or Q_1. In the same way, if the second half of the data is divided into two halves, then that median of the second half is known as third quartile or Q_3. The overall median is also known as second quartile or Q_2. So, any data set has five values - minimum, first quartile (Q1), median (Q2), third quartile (Q3), and maximum.

Let's review these values for the attributes 'cylinders', 'displacement', and 'origin'. Table 2.7 captures a summary of the range of statistics for the attributes. If we take the example of the attribute 'displacement', we can see that the difference between minimum value and Q1 is 36.2 and the difference between Q1 and median is 44.3. On the contrary, the difference between median and Q3 is 113.5 and Q3 and the maximum value is 193. In other words, the larger values are more spread out than the smaller ones. This helps in understanding why the value of mean is much higher than that of the median for the attribute 'displacement'. Similarly, in case of attribute 'cylinders', we can observe that the difference between minimum value and median is 1 whereas the difference between median and the maximum value is 4. For the attribute 'origin', the difference between minimum value and median is 0 whereas the difference between median and the maximum value is 2.

Table 2.7

Attribute value drill-down for Auto MPG

	cylinders	displacement	origin
Minimum	3	68	1
Q1	4	104.2	1
Median	4	148.5	1
Q3	8	262	2
Maximum	8	455	3

Note:

Quantiles refer to specific points in a data set which divide the data set into equal parts or equally sized quantities. There are specific variants of quantile, the one dividing data set into four parts being termed as quartile. Another such popular variant is percentile, which divides the data set into 100 parts.

However, we still cannot ascertain whether there is any outlier present in the data. For that, we can better adopt some means to visualize the data. Box plot is an excellent visualization medium for numeric data.

2.4.2   Plotting and exploring numerical data

2.4.2.1   Box plots

Now that we have a fairly clear understanding of the data set attributes in terms of spread and central tendency, let's try to make an attempt to visualize the whole thing as a box-plot. A box plot is an extremely effective mechanism to get a one-shot view and understand the nature of the data. But before we get to review the box plot for different attributes of Auto MPG data set, let's first try to understand a box-plot in general and the interpretation of different aspects in a box plot. As we can see in Figure 2.3, the box plot (also called box and whisker plot) gives a standard visualization of the five-number summary statistics of a data, namely minimum, first quartile (Q1), median (Q2), third quartile (Q3), and maximum. Below is a detailed interpretation of a box plot.

- The central rectangle or the box spans from first to third quartile (i.e. Q1 to Q3), thus giving the inter-quartile range (IQR). Thus IQR can be used as a measure of how spread out the values are.
- Median is given by the line or band within the box.
- The lower whisker extends up to 1.5 times of the inter-quartile range (or IQR) from the bottom of the box, i.e. the first quartile or Q1. However, the actual length of the lower whisker depends on the lowest data value that falls within (Q1 − 1.5 times of IQR). Let's try to understand this with an example. Say for a specific set of data, Q1 = 73, median = 76 and Q3 = 79. Hence, IQR will be 6 (i.e. Q3 − Q1).

So, lower whisker can extend maximum till (Q1 − 1.5 × IQR) = 73 − 1.5 × 6 = 64. However, say there are lower range data values such as 70, 63, and 60. So, the lower whisker will come at 70 as this is the lowest data value larger than 64.

- The upper whisker extends up to 1.5 as times of the inter-quartile range (or IQR) from the top of the box, i.e. the third quartile or Q3. Similar to lower whisker, the actual length of the upper whisker will also depend on the highest data value that falls within (Q3 + 1.5 times of IQR). Let's try to understand this with an example. For the same set of data mentioned in the above point, upper whisker can extend maximum till (Q3 + 1.5 × IQR) = 79 + 1.5 × 6 = 88. If there is higher range of data values like 82, 84, and 89. So, the upper whisker will come at 84 as this is the highest data value lower than 88.

- The data values coming beyond the lower or upper whiskers are the ones which are of unusually low or high values respectively. These are the outliers, which may deserve special consideration.

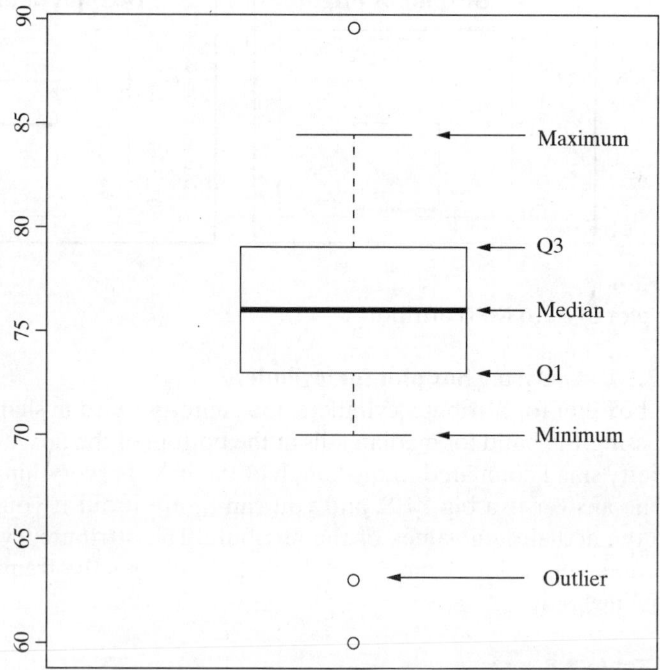

FIG. 2.3
Box plot

Note:

There are different variants of box plots. The one covered above is the Tukey box plot. Famous mathematician John W. Tukey introduced this type of box plot in 1969.

Let's visualize the box plot for the three attributes - 'cylinders', 'displacement', and 'origin'. We will also review the box plot of another attribute in which the deviation between mean and median is very little and see what the basic difference in the respective box plots is. Figure 2.4 presents the respective box plots.

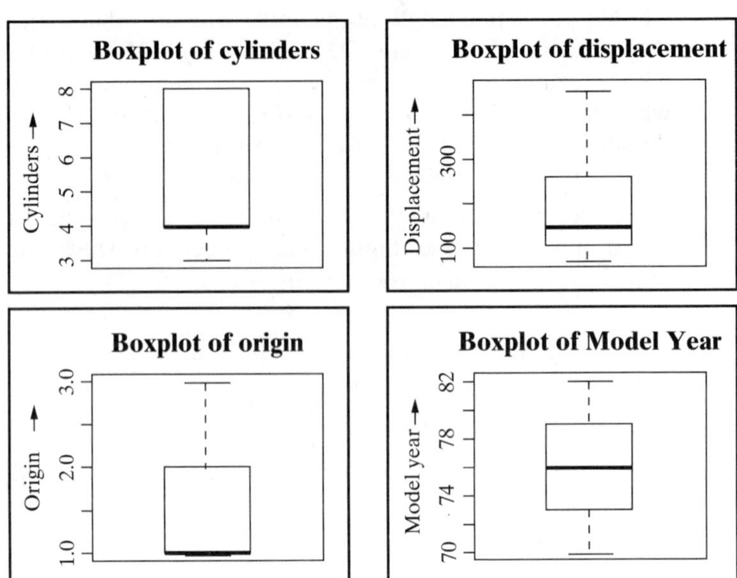

FIG. 2.4
Box plot of Auto MPG attributes

2.4.2.1.1 Analysing box plot for 'cylinders'

The box plot for attribute 'cylinders' looks pretty weird in shape. The upper whisker is missing, the band for median falls at the bottom of the box, even the lower whisker is pretty small compared to the length of the box! Is everything right?

The answer is a big YES, and you can figure it out if you delve a little deeper into the actual data values of the attribute. The attribute 'cylinders' is discrete in nature having values from 3 to 8. Table 2.8 captures the frequency and cumulative frequency of it.

Table 2.8
Frequency of "Cylinders" Attribute

Cylinders	Frequency	Cumulative Frequency
3	4	4
4	204	208 (= 4 + 204)
5	3	211 (= 208 + 3)
6	84	295 (= 211 + 84)
7	0	295 (= 295 + 0)
8	103	398 (= 295 + 103)

As can be observed in the table, the frequency is extremely high for data value 4. Two other data values where the frequency is quite high are 6 and 8. So now if we try to find the quartiles, since the total frequency is 398, the first quartile (Q1), median (Q2), and third quartile (Q3) will be at a cumulative frequency 99.5 (i.e. average of 99th and 100th observation), 199 and 298.5 (i.e. average of 298th and 299th observation), respectively. This way Q1 = 4, median = 4 and Q3 = 8. Since there is no data value beyond 8, there is no upper whisker. Also, since both Q1 and median are 4, the band for median falls on the bottom of the box. Same way, though the lower whisker could have extended till -2 (Q1 – 1.5 × IQR = 4 – 1.5 × 4 = –2), in reality, there is no data value lower than 3. Hence, the lower whisker is also short. In any case, a value of cylinders less than 1 is not possible.

2.4.2.1.2 Analysing box plot for 'origin'

Like the box plot for attribute 'cylinders', the box plot for attribute 'origin' also looks pretty weird in shape. Here the lower whisker is missing and the band for median falls at the bottom of the box! Let's verify if everything right?

Just like the attribute 'cylinders', attribute 'origin' is discrete in nature having values from 1 to 3. Table 2.9 captures the frequency and cumulative frequency (i.e. a summation of frequencies of all previous intervals) of it.

Table 2.9
Frequency of "Origin" Attribute

origin	Frequency	Cumulative Frequency
1	249	249
2	70	319 (= 249 + 70)
3	79	398 (= 319 + 79)

As can be observed in the table, the frequency is extremely high for data value 1. Since the total frequency is 398, the first quartile (Q1), median (Q2), and third quartile (Q3) will be at a cumulative frequency 99.5 (i.e. average of 99th and 100th observation), 199 and 298.5 (i.e. average of 298th and 299th observation), respectively. This way Q1 = 1, median = 1, and Q3 = 2. Since Q1 and median are same in value, the band for median falls on the bottom of the box. There is no data value lower than Q1. Hence, the lower whisker is missing.

2.4.2.1.3 Analysing box plot for 'displacement'

The box plot for the attribute 'displacement' looks better than the previous box plots. However, still, there are few small abnormalities, the cause of which needs to be reviewed. Firstly, the lower whisker is much smaller than an upper whisker. Also, the band for median is closer to the bottom of the box.

Let's take a closer look at the summary data of the attribute 'displacement'. The value of first quartile, Q1 = 104.2, median = 148.5, and third quartile, Q3 = 262. Since (median – Q1) = 44.3 is greater than (Q3 – median) = 113.5, the band for the median is closer to the bottom of the box (which represents Q1). The value of IQR, in this case, is 157.8. So the lower whisker can be 1.5 times 157.8 less than Q1. But minimum data value for the attribute 'displacement' is 68. So, the lower whisker at 15% [(Q1 – minimum)/1.5 × IQR = (104.2 – 68) / (1.5 × 157.8) = 15%] of the permissible length. On the other hand, the maximum data value is 455. So the upper whisker is 81% [(maximum – Q3)/1.5 × IQR = (455 – 262) / (1.5 × 157.8) = 81%] of the permissible length. This is why the upper whisker is much longer than the lower whisker.

2.4.2.1.4 Analysing box plot for 'model Year'

The box plot for the attribute 'model. year' looks perfect. Let's validate is it really what expected to be.

For the attribute 'model.year':

> First quartile, Q1 = 73
>
> Median, Q2 = 76
>
> Third quartile, Q3 = 79

So, the difference between median and Q1 is exactly equal to Q3 and median (both are 3). That is why the band for the median is exactly equidistant from the bottom and top of the box.

$$I\,QR = Q3 - Q1 = 79 - 73 = 6$$

Difference between Q1 and minimum data value (i.e. 70) is also same as maximum data value (i.e. 82) and Q3 (both are 3). So both lower and upper whiskers are expected to be of the same size which is 33% [3 / (1.5 × 6)] of the permissible length.

2.4.2.2 Histogram

Histogram is another plot which helps in effective visualization of numeric attributes. It helps in understanding the distribution of a numeric data into series of intervals, also termed as 'bins'. The important difference between histogram and box plot is

- The focus of histogram is to plot ranges of data values (acting as 'bins'), the number of data elements in each range will depend on the data distribution. Based on that, the size of each bar corresponding to the different ranges will vary.
- The focus of box plot is to divide the data elements in a data set into four equal portions, such that each portion contains an equal number of data elements.

Histograms might be of different shapes depending on the nature of the data, e.g. skewness. Figure 2.5 provides a depiction of different shapes of the histogram that are generally created. These patterns give us a quick understanding of the data and thus act as a great data exploration tool.

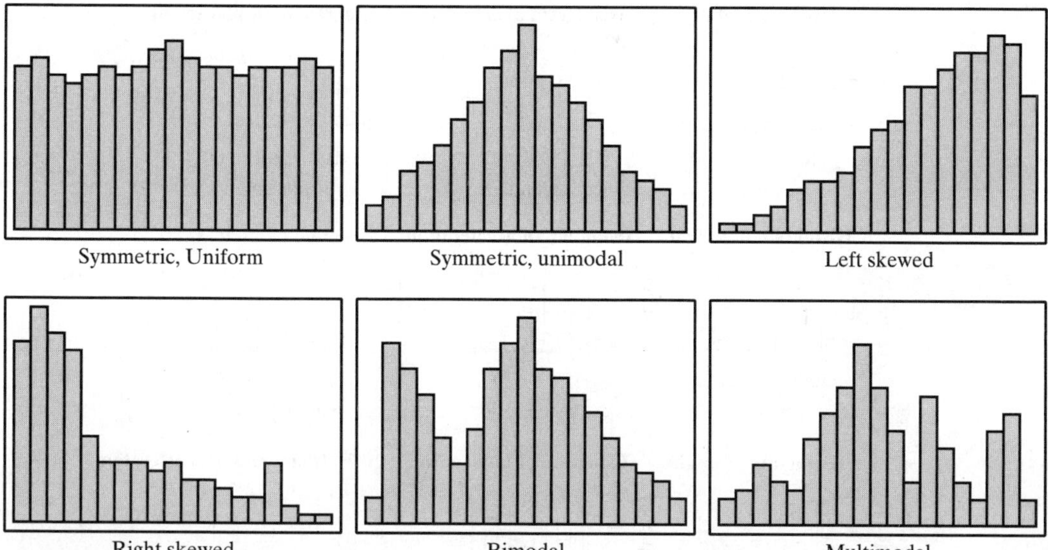

FIG. 2.5
General Histogram shapes

Let's now examine the histograms for the different attributes of Auto MPG data set presented in Figure 2.6. The histograms for 'mpg' and 'weight' are right-skewed. The histogram for 'acceleration' is symmetric and unimodal, whereas the one for 'model.year' is symmetric and uniform. For the remaining attributes, histograms are multimodal in nature.

Now let's dig deep into one of the histograms, say the one for the attribute 'acceleration'. The histogram is composed of a number of bars, one bar appearing for each of the 'bins'. The height of the bar reflects the total count of data elements whose value falls within the specific bin value, or the frequency. Talking in context of the histogram for acceleration, each 'bin' represents an acceleration value interval of 2 units. So the second bin, e.g., reflects acceleration value of 10 to 12 units. The corresponding bar chart height reflects the count of all data elements whose value lies between 10 and 12 units. Also, it is evident from the histogram that it spans over the acceleration value of 8 to 26 units. The frequency of data elements corresponding to the bins first keep on increasing, till it reaches the bin of range 14 to 16 units. At this range, the bar is tallest in size. So we can conclude that a maximum number of data elements fall within this range. After this range, the bar size starts decreasing till the end of the whole range at the acceleration value of 26 units.

Please note that when the histogram is uniform, as in the case of attribute 'model. year', it gives a hint that all values are equally likely to occur.

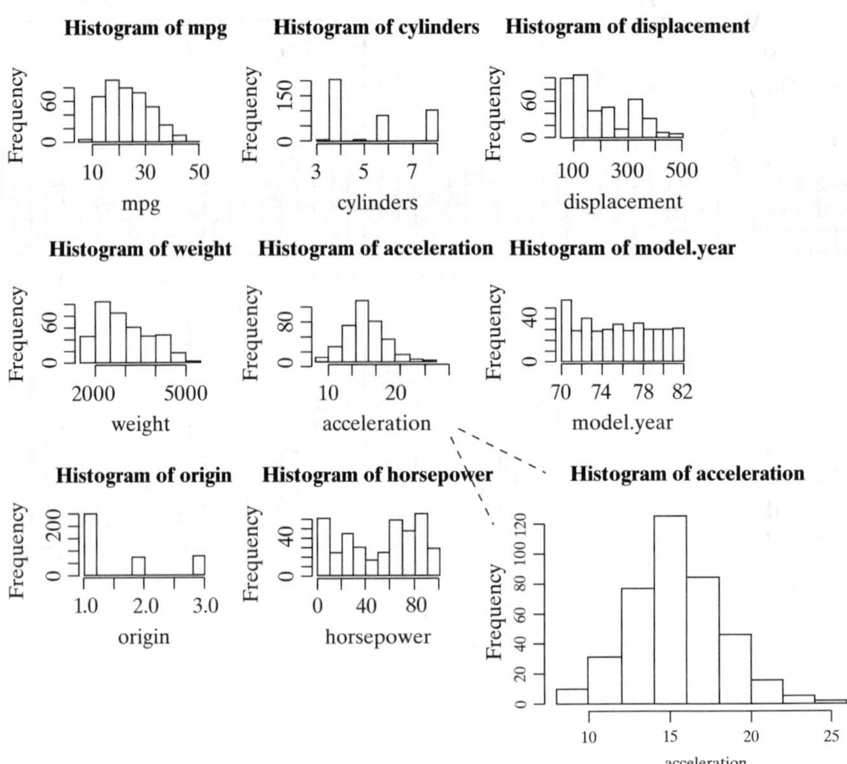

FIG. 2.6
Histogram Auto MPG attributes

2.4.3   Exploring categorical data

We have seen there are multiple ways to explore numeric data. However, there are not many options for exploring categorical data. In the Auto MPG data set, attribute 'car.name' is categorical in nature. Also, as we discussed earlier, we may consider 'cylinders' as a categorical variable instead of a numeric variable.

The first summary which we may be interested in noting is how many unique names are there for the attribute 'car name' or how many unique values are there for 'cylinders' attribute. We can get this as follows:

For attribute 'car name'

[1] Chevrolet chevelle malibu	[2] Buick skylark 320
[3] Plymouth satellite	[4] Amc rebel sst
[5] Ford torino	[6] Ford galaxie 500
[7] Chevrolet impala	[8] Plymouth fury iii
[9] Pontiac catalina	[10] Amc ambassador dpl

For attribute 'cylinders'

8 4 6 3 5

We may also look for a little more details and want to get a table consisting the categories of the attribute and count of the data elements falling into that category. Tables 2.10 and 2.11 contain these details.

For attribute 'car name'

Table 2.10
Count of Categories for 'car name' Attribute

Attribute Value	amc ambassador brougham	amc ambassador dpl	amc ambassador sst	amc concord	amc concord d/l	amc concord dl 6	amc gremlin	...
Count	1	1	1	1	2	2	4	...

For attribute "cylinders"

Table 2.11
Count of Categories for 'Cylinders' Attribute

Attribute Value	3	4	5	6	8
Count	4	204	3	84	103

In the same way, we may also be interested to know the proportion (or percentage) of count of data elements belonging to a category. Say, e.g., for the attributes 'cylinders', the proportion of data elements belonging to the category 4 is 204 ÷ 398 = 0.513, i.e. 51.3%. Tables 2.12 and 2.13 contain the summarization of the categorical attributes by proportion of data elements.

For attribute 'car name'

Table 2.12
Proportion of Categories for "car name" Attribute

Attribute Value	Amc ambassador brougham	Amc ambassador dpl	Amc ambassador sst	Amc concord	Amc concord d/l	Amc concord dl 6	Amc gremlin	...
Count	0.003	0.003	0.003	0.003	0.005	0.005	0.01	...

For attribute 'cylinders'

Table 2.13
Proportion of Categories for "Cylinders" Attribute

Attribute Value	3	4	5	6	8
Count	0.01	0.513	0.008	0.211	0.259

Last but not the least, as we have read in the earlier section on types of data, statistical measure "mode" is applicable on categorical attributes. As we know, like mean and median, mode is also a statistical measure for central tendency of a data. Mode of a data is the data value which appears most often. In context of categorical attribute, it is the category which has highest number of data values. Since mean and median cannot be applied for categorical variables, mode is the sole measure of central tendency.

Let's try to find out the mode for the attributes 'car name' and 'cylinders'. For cylinders, since the number of categories is less and we have the entire table listed above, we can see that the mode is 4, as that is the data value for which frequency is highest. More than 50% of data elements belong to the category 4. However, it is not so evident for the attribute 'car name' from the information given above. When we probe and try to find the mode, it is found to be category 'ford pinto' for which frequency is of highest value 6.

An attribute may have one or more modes. Frequency distribution of an attribute having single mode is called 'unimodal', two modes are called 'bimodal' and multiple modes are called 'multimodal'.

2.4.4   Exploring relationship between variables

Till now we have been exploring single attributes in isolation. One more important angle of data exploration is to explore relationship between attributes. There are multiple plots to enable us explore the relationship between variables. The basic and most commonly used plot is scatter plot.

2.4.4.1   Scatter plot

A scatter plot helps in visualizing bivariate relationships, i.e. relationship between two variables. It is a two-dimensional plot in which points or dots are drawn on coordinates provided by values of the attributes. For example, in a data set there are two attributes – attr_1 and attr_2. We want to understand the relationship between two attributes, i.e. with a change in value of one attribute, say attr_1, how does the value of the other attribute, say attr_2, changes. We can draw a scatter plot, with attr_1 mapped to x-axis and attr_2 mapped in y-axis. So, every point in the plot will have value of attr_1 in the x-coordinate and value of attr_2 in the y-coordinate. As in a two-dimensional plot, attr_1 is said to be the independent variable and attr_2 as the dependent variable.

Let's take a real example in this context. In the data set Auto MPG, there is expected to be some relation between the attributes 'displacement' and 'mpg'. Let's try to verify our intuition using the scatter plot of 'displacement' and 'mpg'. Let's map 'displacement' as the x-coordinate and 'mpg' as the y-coordinate. The scatter plot comes as in Figure 2.7.

As is evident in the scatter plot, there is a definite relation between the two variables. The value of 'mpg' seems to steadily decrease with the increase in the value of 'displacement'. It may come in our mind that what is the extent of relationship? Well, it can be reviewed by calculating the correlation between the variables. Refer to chapter 5 if you want to find more about correlation and how to calculate it. One more interesting fact to notice is that there are certain data values which stand-out of the others. For example, there is one data element which has a mpg of 37 for a displacement of 250. This record is completely different from other data elements having similar displacement value but mpg value in the range of 15 to 25. This gives an indication that of presence of outlier data values.

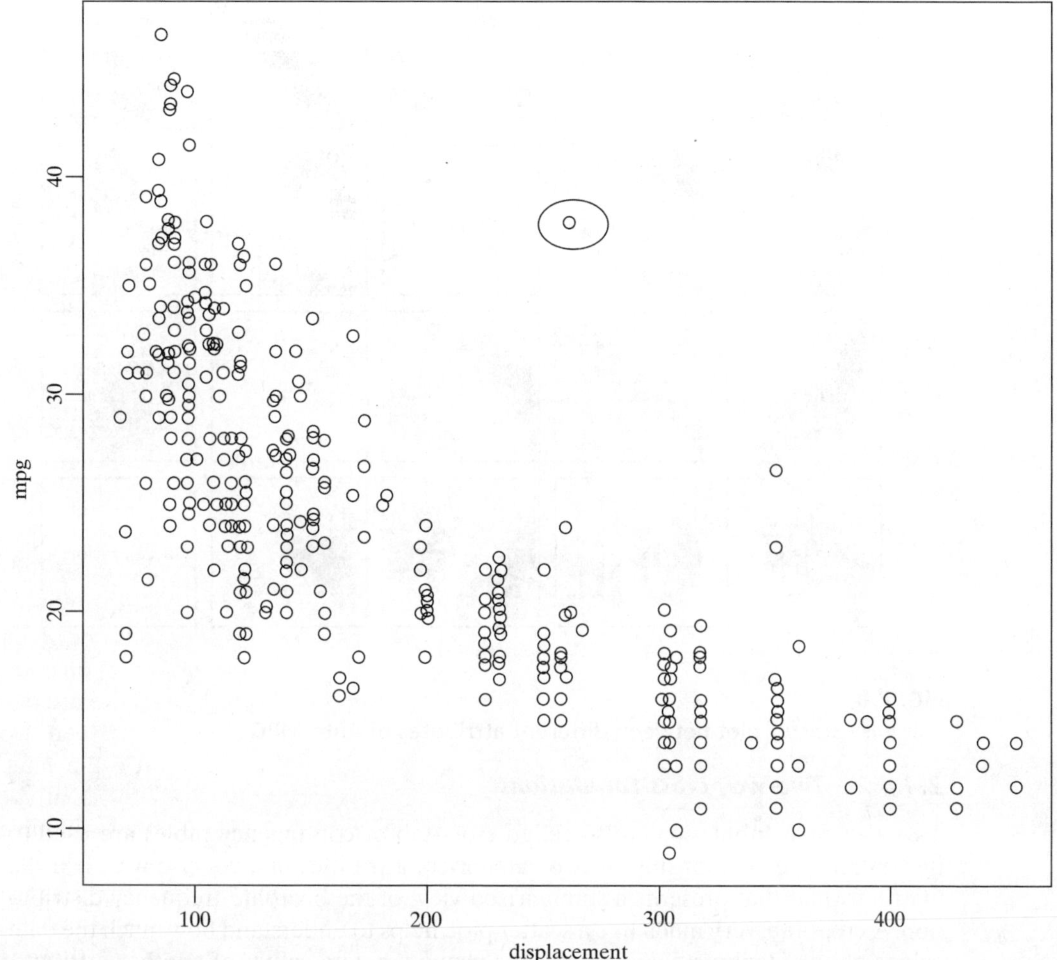

FIG. 2.7
Scatter plot of 'displacement' and 'mpg'

In Figure 2.8, the pair wise relationship among the features – 'mpg', 'displacement', 'horsepower', 'weight', and 'acceleration' have been captured. As you can see, in most of the cases, there is a significant relationship between the attribute pairs. However, in some cases, e.g. between attributes 'weight' and 'acceleration', the relationship doesn't seem to be very strong.

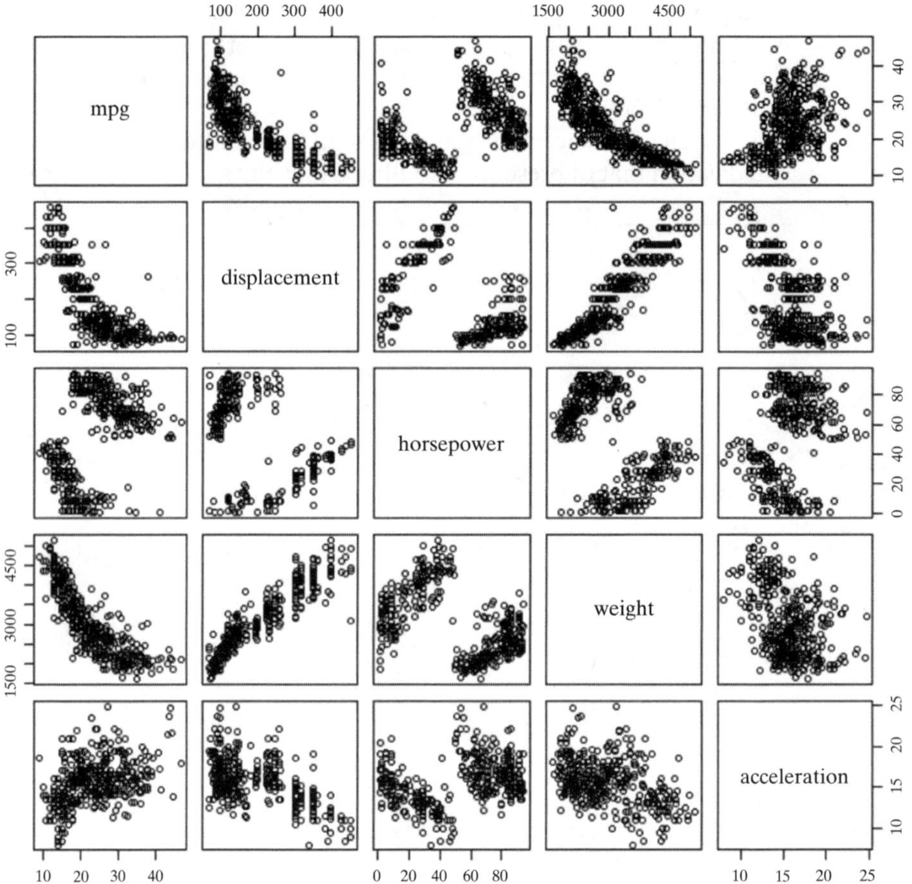

FIG. 2.8
Pair wise scatter plot between different attributes of Auto MPG

2.4.4.2   *Two-way cross-tabulations*

Two-way cross-tabulations (also called cross-tab or contingency table) are used to understand the relationship of two categorical attributes in a concise way. It has a matrix format that presents a summarized view of the bivariate frequency distribution. A cross-tab, very much like a scatter plot, helps to understand how much the data values of one attribute changes with the change in data values of another attribute. Let's try to see with examples, in context of the Auto MPG data set.

Let's assume the attributes 'cylinders', 'model.year', and 'origin' as categorical and try to examine the variation of one with respect to the other. As we understand, attribute 'cylinders' reflects the number of cylinders in a car and assumes values 3, 4, 5, 6, and 8. Attribute 'model.year' captures the model year of each of the car and 'origin' gives the region of the car, the values for origin 1, 2, and 3 corresponding to North America, Europe, and Asia. Below are the cross-tabs. Let's try to understand what information they actually provide.

The first cross-tab, i.e. the one showing relationship between attributes 'model year' and 'origin' help us understand the number of vehicles per year in each of the regions North America, Europe, and Asia. Looking at it in another way, we can get the count of vehicles per region over the different years. All these are in the context of the sample data given in the Auto MPG data set.

Moving to the second cross-tab, it gives the number of 3, 4, 5, 6, or 8 cylinder cars in every region present in the sample data set. The last cross-tab presents the number of 3, 4, 5, 6, or 8 cylinder cars every year.

We may also want to create cross-tabs with a more summarized view like have a cross-tab giving a number of cars having 4 or less cylinders and more than 4 cylinders in each region or by the years. This can be done by rolling up data values by the attribute 'cylinder'. Tables 2.14–2.16 present cross-tabs for different attribute combinations.

'Model year' vs. 'origin'

Table 2.14
Cross-tab for 'Model year' vs. 'Origin'

Origin \ Model Year	70	71	72	73	74	75	76	77	78	79	80	81	82
1	22	20	18	29	15	20	22	18	22	23	7	13	20
2	5	4	5	7	6	6	8	4	6	4	9	4	2
3	2	4	5	4	6	4	4	6	8	2	13	12	9

'Cylinders' vs. 'Origin'

Table 2.15
Cross-tab for 'Cylinders' vs. 'Origin'

Cylinders \ Origin	1	2	3
3	0	0	4
4	72	63	69
5	0	3	0
6	74	4	6
8	103	0	0

'Cylinders' vs. 'Model year'

Table 2.16
Cross-tab for 'Cylinders' vs. 'Model year'

Cylinders \ Model Year	70	71	72	73	74	75	76	77	78	79	80	81	82
3	0	0	1	1	0	0	0	1	0	0	1	0	0
4	7	13	14	11	15	12	15	14	17	12	25	21	28
5	0	0	0	0	0	0	0	0	1	1	1	0	0
6	4	8	0	8	7	12	10	5	12	6	2	7	3
8	18	7	13	20	5	6	9	8	6	10	0	1	0

2.5   DATA QUALITY AND REMEDIATION

2.5.1   Data quality

Success of machine learning depends largely on the quality of data. A data which has the right quality helps to achieve better prediction accuracy, in case of supervised learning. However, it is not realistic to expect that the data will be flawless. We have already come across at least two types of problems:

1. Certain data elements without a value or data with a missing value.
2. Data elements having value surprisingly different from the other elements, which we term as outliers.

There are multiple factors which lead to these data quality issues. Following are some of them:

- **Incorrect sample set selection:** The data may not reflect normal or regular quality due to incorrect selection of sample set. For example, if we are selecting a sample set of sales transactions from a festive period and trying to use that data to predict sales in future. In this case, the prediction will be far apart from the actual scenario, just because the sample set has been selected in a wrong time. Similarly, if we are trying to predict poll results using a training data which doesn't comprise of a right mix of voters from different segments such as age, sex, ethnic diversities, etc., the prediction is bound to be a failure. It may also happen due to incorrect sample size. For example, a sample of small size may not be able to capture all aspects or information needed for right learning of the model.

- **Errors in data collection:** resulting in outliers and missing values

  ❖ In many cases, a person or group of persons are responsible for the collection of data to be used in a learning activity. In this manual process, there is the possibility of wrongly recording data either in terms of value (say 20.67 is wrongly recorded as 206.7 or 2.067) or in terms of a unit of measurement (say cm. is wrongly recorded as m. or mm.). This may result in data elements which have abnormally high or low value from other elements. Such records are termed as *outliers*.

  ❖ It may also happen that the data is not recorded at all. In case of a survey conducted to collect data, it is all the more possible as survey responders may choose not to respond to a certain question. So the data value for that data element in that responder's record is *missing*.

2.5.2   Data remediation

The issues in data quality, as mentioned above, need to be remediated, if the right amount of efficiency has to be achieved in the learning activity. Out of the two major areas mentioned above, the first one can be remedied by proper sampling technique. This is a completely different area – covered as a specialized subject area in statistics. We will not cover that in this book. However, human errors are bound to happen, no matter whatever checks and balances we put in. Hence, proper remedial steps need to be taken for the second area mentioned above. We will discuss how to handle outliers and missing values.

2.5.2.1   Handling outliers

Outliers are data elements with an abnormally high value which may impact prediction accuracy, especially in regression models. Once the outliers are identified and the decision has been taken to amend those values, you may consider one of the following approaches. However, if the outliers are natural, i.e. the value of the data element is surprisingly high or low because of a valid reason, then we should not amend it.

- **Remove outliers:** If the number of records which are outliers is not many, a simple approach may be to remove them.
- **Imputation:** One other way is to impute the value with mean or median or mode. The value of the most similar data element may also be used for imputation.
- **Capping:** For values that lie outside the $1.5|\times|$ IQR limits, we can cap them by replacing those observations below the lower limit with the value of 5th percentile and those that lie above the upper limit, with the value of 95th percentile.

If there is a significant number of outliers, they should be treated separately in the statistical model. In that case, the groups should be treated as two different groups, the model should be built for both groups and then the output can be combined.

2.5.2.2   Handling missing values

In a data set, one or more data elements may have missing values in multiple records. As discussed above, it can be caused by omission on part of the surveyor or a person who is collecting sample data or by the responder, primarily due to his/her unwillingness to respond or lack of understanding needed to provide a response. It may happen that a specific question (based on which the value of a data element originates) is not applicable to a person or object with respect to which data is collected. There are multiple strategies to handle missing value of data elements. Some of those strategies have been discussed below.

2.5.2.2.1   Eliminate records having a missing value of data elements

In case the proportion of data elements having missing values is within a tolerable limit, a simple but effective approach is to remove the records having such data elements. This is possible if the quantum of data left after removing the data elements having missing values is sizeable.

In the case of Auto MPG data set, only in 6 out of 398 records, the value of attribute 'horsepower' is missing. If we get rid of those 6 records, we will still have 392 records, which is definitely a substantial number. So, we can very well eliminate the records and keep working with the remaining data set.

However, this will not be possible if the proportion of records having data elements with missing value is really high as that will reduce the power of model because of reduction in the training data size.

2.5.2.2.2 Imputing missing values

Imputation is a method to assign a value to the data elements having missing values. Mean/mode/median is most frequently assigned value. For quantitative attributes, all missing values are imputed with the mean, median, or mode of the remaining values under the same attribute. For qualitative attributes, all missing values are imputed by the mode of all remaining values of the same attribute. However, another strategy may be identify the similar types of observations whose values are known and use the mean/median/mode of those known values.

For example, in context of the attribute 'horsepower' of the Auto MPG data set, since the attribute is quantitative, we take a mean or median of the remaining data element values and assign that to all data elements having a missing value. So, we may assign the mean, which is 104.47 and assign it to all the six data elements. The other approach is that we can take a similarity based mean or median. If we refer to the six observations with missing values for attribute 'horsepower' as depicted in Table 2.17, 'cylinders' is the attribute which is logically most connected to 'horsepower' because with the increase in number of cylinders of a car, the horsepower of the car is expected to increase. So, for five observations, we can use the mean of data elements of the 'horsepower' attribute having cylinders = 4; i.e. 78.28 and for one observation which has cylinders = 6, we can use a similar mean of data elements with cylinders = 6, i.e. 101.5, to impute value to the missing data elements.

Table 2.17
Missing Values for 'Horsepower' Attribute

mpg	cylin-ders	dis-place-ment	horse-power	weight	accel-eration	model year	origin	car name
25	4	98	?	2046	19	71	1	Ford pinto
21	6	200	?	2875	17	74	1	Ford maverick
40.9	4	85	?	1835	17.3	80	2	Renault lecar deluxe
23.6	4	140	?	2905	14.3	80	1	Ford mustang cobra
34.5	4	100	?	2320	15.8	81	2	Renault 18i
23	4	151	?	3035	20.5	82	1	Amc concord dl

2.5.2.2.3 Estimate missing values

If there are data points similar to the ones with missing attribute values, then the attribute values from those similar data points can be planted in place of the missing value. For finding similar data points or observations, distance function can be used.

For example, let's assume that the weight of a Russian student having age 12 years and height 5 ft. is missing. Then the weight of any other Russian student having age close to 12 years and height close to 5 ft. can be assigned.

2.6   DATA PRE-PROCESSING

2.6.1   Dimensionality reduction

Till the end of the 1990s, very few domains were explored which included data sets with a high number of attributes or features. In general, the data sets used in machine learning used to be in few 10s. However, in the last two decades, there has been a rapid advent of computational biology like genome projects. These projects have produced extremely high-dimensional data sets with 20,000 or more features being very common. Also, there has been a wide-spread adoption of social networking leading to a need for text classification for customer behaviour analysis.

High-dimensional data sets need a high amount of computational space and time. At the same time, not all features are useful – they degrade the performance of machine learning algorithms. Most of the machine learning algorithms perform better if the dimensionality of data set, i.e. the number of features in the data set, is reduced. Dimensionality reduction helps in reducing irrelevance and redundancy in features. Also, it is easier to understand a model if the number of features involved in the learning activity is less.

Dimensionality reduction refers to the techniques of reducing the dimensionality of a data set by creating new attributes by combining the original attributes. The most common approach for dimensionality reduction is known as Principal Component Analysis (PCA). PCA is a statistical technique to convert a set of correlated variables into a set of transformed, uncorrelated variables called principal components. The principal components are a linear combination of the original variables. They are orthogonal to each other. Since principal components are uncorrelated, they capture the maximum amount of variability in the data. However, the only challenge is that the original attributes are lost due to the transformation.

Another commonly used technique which is used for dimensionality reduction is Singular Value Decomposition (SVD).

More about these concepts have been discussed in Chapter 4.

2.6.2   Feature subset selection

Feature subset selection or simply called feature selection, both for supervised as well as unsupervised learning, try to find out the optimal subset of the entire feature set which significantly reduces computational cost without any major impact on the learning accuracy. It may seem that a feature subset may lead to loss of useful information as certain features are going to be excluded from the final set of features used for learning. However, for elimination only features which are not relevant or redundant are selected.

A feature is considered as irrelevant if it plays an insignificant role (or contributes almost no information) in classifying or grouping together a set of data instances. All irrelevant features are eliminated while selecting the final feature subset. A feature is potentially redundant when the information contributed by the feature is more or less same as one or more other features. Among a group of potentially redundant features, a small number of features can be selected as a part of the final feature subset without causing any negative impact to learn model accuracy.

There are different ways to select a feature subset. In Chapter 4, we will be discussing feature selection in details.

2.7   SUMMARY

- A data set is a collection of related information or records.
- Data can be broadly divided into following two types
    - ❖ Qualitative data
    - ❖ Quantitative data
- Qualitative data provides information about the quality of an object or information which cannot be measured. Qualitative data can be further subdivided into two types as follows:
    - ❖ Nominal data: has named value
    - ❖ Ordinal data: has named value which can be naturally ordered
- Quantitative data relates to information about the quantity of an object – hence it can be measured. There are two types of quantitative data:
    - ❖ Interval data: numeric data for which the exact difference between values is known. However, such data do not have something called a 'true zero' value.
    - ❖ Ratio data: numeric data for which exact value can be measured and absolute zero is available.
- Measures of central tendency help to understand the central point of a set of data. Standard measures of central tendency of data are mean, median, and mode.
- Detailed view of the data spread is available in the form of
    - ❖ Dispersion of data:extent of dispersion of a data is measured by variance
    - ❖ Related to the position of the different data values there are five values:minimum, first quartile (Q1), median (Q2), third quartile (Q3), and maximum
- Exploration of numerical data can be best done using box plots and histograms.
- Options for exploration of categorical data are very limited.
- For exploring relations between variables, scatter-plots and two-way cross-tabulations can be effectively used.
- Success of machine learning depends largely on the quality of data. Two common types of data issue are:
    - ❖ Data with a missing value
    - ❖ Data values which are surprisingly different termed as outliers
- High-dimensional data sets need a high amount of computational space and time. Most of the preparing machine learning algorithms perform better if the dimensionality of data set is reduced.
- Some popular dimensionality reduction techniques are PCA, SVD, and feature selection.

SAMPLE QUESTIONS

MULTIPLE-CHOICE QUESTIONS (1 MARK QUESTIONS):

1. Temperature is a
  (a) Interval data
  (b) Ratio data
  (c) Discrete data
  (d) None of the above

2. Principal component is a technique for
  (a) Feature selection
  (b) Dimensionality reduction
  (c) Exploration
  (d) None of the above

3. For bi-variate data exploration, _____ is an effective tool.
  (a) Box plot
  (b) Two-way cross-tab
  (c) Histogram
  (d) None of the above

4. For box plot, the upper and lower whisker length depends on
  (a) Median
  (b) Mean
  (c) IQR
  (d) All of the above

5. Feature selection tries to eliminate features which are
  (a) Rich
  (b) Redundant
  (c) Irrelevant
  (d) Relevant

6. When the number of features increase
  (a) Computation time increases
  (b) Model becomes complex
  (c) Learning accuracy decreases
  (d) All of the above

7. For categorical data, ____ cannot be used as a measure of central tendency.
  (a) Median
  (b) Mean
  (c) Quartile
  (d) None of the above

8. For understanding relationship between two variables, ____ can be used.
  (a) Box plot
  (b) Scatter plot
  (c) Histogram
  (d) None of the above

9. Two common types of data issue are
  (a) Outlier
  (b) Missing value
  (c) Boundary value
  (d) None of the above

10. Exploration of numerical data can be best done using
  (a) Boxplots
  (b) Histograms
  (c) Scatter plot
  (d) None of the above

11. Data can broadly divided into following two types
  (a) Qualitative
  (b) Speculative
  (c) Quantitative
  (d) None of the above

12. Ordinal data can be naturally ____.
  (a) Measured
  (b) Ordered
  (c) Divided
  (d) None of the above

SHORT-ANSWER TYPE QUESTIONS (5 MARKS QUESTIONS):

1. What are the main activities involved when you are preparing to start with modelling in machine learning?

2. What are the basic data types in machine learning? Give an example of each one of them.

3. Differentiate:
   (a) Categorical vs. Numeric attribute
   (b) Dimensionality reduction vs. Feature selection

4. Write short notes on any <u>two</u>:
   (a) Histogram
   (b) Scatter plot
   (c) PCA

5. Why do we need to explore data? Is there a difference in the way of exploring qualitative data vis-a-vis quantitative data?

6. What are different shapes of histogram? What are 'bins'?

7. How can we take care of outliers in data?

8. What are the different measures of central tendency? Why do mean, in certain data sets, differ widely from median?

9. Explain how bivariate relationships can be explored using scatter plot. Can outliers be detected using scatter plot?

10. Explain how cross-tabs can be used to understand relationship between two variables.

LONG-ANSWER TYPE QUESTIONS (10 MARKS QUESTIONS):

1. What are the main activities involved in machine learning? What is meant by data pre-processing?

2. Explain qualitative and quantitative data in details. Differentiate between the two.

3. Prepare a simple data set along with some sample records in it. Have at least one attribute of the different data types used in machine learning.

4. What are the different causes of data issues in machine learning? What are the fallouts?

5. Explain, with proper example, different ways of exploring categorical data.

6. When there are variables with certain values missing, will that impact the learning activity? If so, how can that be addressed?

7. Explain, in details, the different strategies of addressing missing data values.

8. What are the different techniques for data pre-processing? Explain, in brief, dimensionality reduction and feature selection.

9.   (a) What is IQR? How is it measured?
     (b) Explain, in details, the different components of a box plot? When will the lower whisker be longer than the upper whisker? How can outliers be detected using box plot?

10. (a) Write short notes on any <u>two</u>:
         (i)   Interval data
         (ii) Inter-quartile range
         (iii) Cross-tab
     (b) Write the difference between (any <u>two</u>):
         (i)   Nominal and ordinal data
         (ii) Box plot and histogram
         (iii) Mean and median

Chapter 3
Modeling and Evaluation

OBJECTIVE OF THE CHAPTER:

The previous chapter gives a comprehensive understanding of the basic data types in the context of machine learning. It also enables a beginner in the field of machine learning to acquire an understanding of the nature and quality of the data by effective exploration of the data set. In this chapter, the objective is to introduce the basic concepts of learning. In this regard, the information shared concerns the aspects of model selection and application. It also imparts knowledge regarding how to judge the effectiveness of the model in doing a specific learning task, supervised or unsupervised, and how to boost the model performance using different tuning parameters.

3.1 INTRODUCTION

The learning process of machines may seem quite magical to somebody new to machine learning. The thought that a machine can think and take intelligent action may be mesmerizing – much like a science fiction or a fantasy story. However, delving a bit deeper helps them realize that it is not as magical as it may seem to be. In fact, it tries to emulate human learning by applying mathematical and statistical formulations. In that sense, both human and machine learning strive to build formulations or mapping based on a limited number of observations. As introduced in Chapter 1, the basic learning process, irrespective of the fact that the learner is a human or a machine, can be divided into three parts:

"

1. Data Input

2. Abstraction

3. Generalization

Though in Chapter 1 we have understood these aspects in detail, let's quickly refresh our memory with an example. It's a fictitious situation. The detective department of New City Police has got a tip that in a campaign gathering for the upcoming election, a criminal is going to launch an attack on the main candidate. However, it is not known who the person is and quite obviously the person might use some disguise. The only thing that is for sure is the person is a history sheeter or a criminal having a long record of serious crime. From the criminal database, a list of such criminals along with their photographs has been collected. Also, the photos taken by security cameras positioned at different places near the gathering are available to the detective department. They have to match the photos from the criminal database with the faces in the gathering to spot the potential attacker. So the main problem here is to spot the face of the criminal based on the match with the photos in the criminal database.

This can be done using human learning where a person from the detective department can scan through each shortlisted photo and try to match that photo with the faces in the gathering. A person having a strong memory can take a glance at the photos of all criminals in one shot and then try to find a face in the gathering that closely resembles one of the criminal photos that she has viewed. Easy, isn't it? But that is not possible in reality. The number of criminals in the database and hence the count of photos runs in hundreds, if not thousands. So taking a look at all the photos and memorizing them is not possible. Also, an exact match is out of the question as the criminal, in most probability, will come in disguise. The strategy to be taken here is to match the photos in smaller counts and also based on certain salient physical features like the shape of the jaw, the slope of the forehead, the size of the eyes, the structure of the ear, etc. So, the photos from the criminal database form the input data. Based on it, key features can be abstracted. Since human matching for every photo may soon lead to visual as well as mental fatigue, a generalization of abstracted feature-based data is a good way to detect potential criminal faces in the gathering. For example, from the abstracted feature-based data, it is observed that most of the criminals have a shorter distance between the inner corners of the eyes, a smaller angle between the nose and the corners of the mouth, a higher curvature to the upper lip, etc. Hence, a face in the gathering may be classified as 'potentially criminal' based on whether they match these generalized observations. Thus, using the input data, feature-based abstraction could be built and by applying generalization of the abstracted data, human learning could classify the faces as potentially criminal ultimately leading to the spotting of the criminal.

The same thing can be done using machine learning too. Unlike human detection, a machine has no subjective baggage, no emotion, no bias due to past experience, and above all no mental fatigue. The machine can also use the same input data, i.e. criminal database photos, apply computational techniques to abstract feature-based concept maps from the input data and generalize the same in the form of a classification algorithm to decide whether a face in the gathering is potentially criminal or not.

When we talk about the learning process, abstraction is a significant step as it represents raw input data in a summarized and structured format, such that a meaningful insight is obtained from the data. This structured representation of raw input data to the meaningful pattern is called a **model**. The model might have different forms. It might be a mathematical equation, it might be a graph or tree structure, it might be a computational block, etc. The decision regarding which model is to be selected for a specific data set is taken by the learning task, based on the problem to be solved and the type of data. For example, when the problem is related to prediction and the target field is numeric and continuous, the regression model is assigned. The process of assigning a model, and fitting a specific model to a data set is called model **training**. Once the model is trained, the raw input data is summarized into an abstract form.

However, with abstraction, the learner can only summarize the knowledge. This knowledge might be still very broad-based – consisting of a huge number of feature-based data and inter-relations. To generate actionable insight from such broad-based knowledge is very difficult. This is where generalization comes into play. Generalization searches through the huge set of abstracted knowledge to come up with a small and manageable set of key findings. It is not possible to do an exhaustive search by reviewing each of the abstracted findings one by one. A heuristic search is employed, an approach that is also used for human learning (often termed as 'gut-feel'). It is quite obvious that the heuristics sometimes result in erroneous results. If the outcome is systematically incorrect, the learning is said to have a **bias**.

Points to Ponder:

- A machine learning algorithm creates its cognitive capability by building a mathematical formulation or function, known as the target function, based on the features in the input data set.
- Just like a child learning things for the first time needs her parent's guidance to decide whether she is right or wrong, in machine learning someone has to provide some non-learnable parameters, also called hyper-parameters. Without these human inputs, machine learning algorithms cannot be successful.

3.2   SELECTING A MODEL

Now that you are familiar with the basic learning process and have understood model abstraction and generalization in that context, let's try to formalize it in the context of a motivating example. Continuing the thread of the potential attack during the election campaign, the New City Police Department has succeeded in foiling the bid to attack the electoral candidate. However, this was a wake-up call for them and they want to take proactive action to eliminate all criminal activities in the region. They want to find the pattern of criminal activities in the recent past, i.e. they want to see whether the number of criminal incidents per month has any relation with an average income of the local population, weapon sales, the inflow of immigrants, and other such factors. Therefore, an association between potential causes of disturbance and criminal incidents have to be determined. In other words, the goal or target is to develop a model to infer how criminal incidents change based on the potential influencing factors mentioned above.

In the machine learning paradigm, the potential causes of disturbance, e.g. average income of the local population, weapon sales, the inflow of immigrants, etc. are input variables. They are also called predictors, attributes, features, independent variables, or simply variables. The number of criminal incidents is an output variable (also called response or dependent variable). Input variables can be denoted by X, while individual input variables are represented as X_1, X_2, X_3, ..., X_n and output variables by symbol Y. The relationship between X and Y is represented in the general form: $Y = f(X) + e$, where 'f' is the **target function** and 'e' is a random error term.

Note:

Just like a target function concerning a machine learning model, some other functions that are frequently tracked are

- A **cost function** (also called **error function**) helps to measure the extent to which the model is going wrong in estimating the relationship between X and Y. In that sense, the cost function can tell how badly the model is performing. For example, R-squared (to be discussed later in this chapter) is a cost function of a regression model.

- **Loss function** is almost synonymous with cost function – the only difference is loss function is usually a function defined on a data point, while cost function is for the entire training data set.

- Machine learning is an optimization problem. We try to define a model and tune the parameters to find the most suitable solution to a problem. However, we need to have a way to evaluate the quality or optimality of a solution. This is done using an **objective function**. Objective means goal.

- Objective function takes in data and model (along with parameters) as input and returns a value. The target is to find values of the model parameter to maximize or minimize the return value. When the objective is to minimize the value, it becomes synonymous with to cost function. Examples: maximize the reward function in reinforcement learning, maximize the posterior probability in Naive Bayes, and minimize squared error in regression.

But the problem that we just talked about is one specific type of problem in machine learning. We have seen in Chapter 1 that there are three broad categories of machine learning approaches used for resolving different types of problems. Quickly recapitulating, they are

1. Supervised

    (a) Classification
    (b) Regression

    2. Unsupervised

        (a) Clustering

        (b) Association analysis

    3. Reinforcement

For each of the cases, the model that has to be created/trained is different. Multiple factors play a role when we try to select the model for solving a machine-learning problem. The most important factors are (i) the kind of problem we want to solve using machine learning and (ii) the nature of the underlying data. The problem may be related to the prediction of a class value like whether a tumour is malignant or benign, whether the next day will be snowy or rainy, etc. It may be related to prediction – but of some numerical value like what the price of a house should be in the next quarter, what the expected growth of a certain IT stock in the next 7 days, etc. Certain problems are related to the grouping of data like finding customer segments that are using a certain product, movie genres that have had more box office success in the last one year, etc. So, it is very difficult to give generic guidance related to which machine-learning has to be selected. In other words, there is no one model that works best for every machine learning problem. This is what the '**No Free Lunch**' theorem also states.

Any learning model tries to simulate some real-world aspect. However, it is simplified to a large extent removing all intricate details. These simplifications are based on certain assumptions – which are quite dependent on the situation. Based on the exact situation, i.e. the problem in hand and the data characteristics, assumptions may or may not hold. So the same model may yield remarkable results in a certain situation while it may completely fail in a different situation. That's why, while doing the data exploration, which we covered in the previous chapter, we need to understand the data characteristics, combine this understanding with the problem we are trying to solve and then decide which model to be select for solving the problem.

Let's try to understand the philosophy of model selection in a structured way. Machine learning algorithms are broadly of two types: models for supervised learning, which primarily focus on solving predictive problems and models for unsupervised learning, which solve descriptive problems.

3.2.1   Predictive models

Models for supervised learning or predictive models, as is understandable from the name itself, try to predict certain values using the values in an input data set. The learning model attempts to establish a relation between the target feature, i.e. the feature being predicted, and the predictor features. The predictive models have a clear focus on what they want to learn and how they want to learn.

Predictive models, in turn, may need to predict the value of a category or class to which a data instance belongs. Below are some examples:

    (i) Predicting a win/loss in a cricket match

   (ii) Predicting whether a transaction is fraud

  (iii) Predicting whether a customer may move to another product

The models that are used for the prediction of target features of categorical value are known as classification models. The target feature is known as a class and the categories into which classes are divided are called levels. Some of the popular classification models include k-Nearest Neighbor (kNN), Naïve Bayes, and Decision Tree.

Predictive models may also be used to predict numerical values of the target feature based on the predictor features. Below are some examples:

(i) Prediction of revenue growth in the succeeding year

(ii) Prediction of rainfall amount in the coming monsoon

(iii) Prediction of potential flu patients and demand for flu shots next winter

The models that are used for the prediction of the numerical value of the target feature of a data instance are known as regression models. Linear Regression and Logistic Regression models are popular regression models.

Points to Ponder:

- Categorical values can be converted to numerical values and vice versa. For example, for stock price growth prediction, any growth percentage lying between certain ranges may be represented by a categorical value, e.g. 0%–5% as 'low', 5%–10% as 'moderate', 10%–20% as 'high' and > 20% as 'booming'. Similarly, a categorical value can be converted to a numerical value, e.g. in the tumor malignancy detection problem, replace 'benign' as 0 and 'malignant' as 1. This way, the models can be used interchangeably, though they may not work always.

- There are multiple factors to be considered while selecting a model. For example, while selecting the prediction model, the training data size is an important factor to be considered. If the training data set is small, low variance models like Naïve Bayes are supposed to perform better because model overfitting needs to be avoided in this situation. Similarly, when the training data is large, low-bias models like logistic regression should be preferred because they can represent complex relationships more effectively.

Few models like Support Vector Machines and Neural Networks can be used for both classifications as well as for regression.

3.2.2   Descriptive models

Models for unsupervised learning or descriptive models are used to describe a data set or gain insight from a data set. There is no target feature or single feature of interest in the case of unsupervised learning. Based on the value of all features, interesting patterns or insights are derived about the data set.

Descriptive models that group together similar data instances, i.e. data instances having a similar value of the different features are called clustering models. Examples of clustering include

(i) Customer grouping or segmentation based on factors such as, social, demographic, ethnic, etc.

(ii) Grouping of music based on different aspects like genre, language, time period, etc.

(iii) Grouping of commodities in an inventory

The most popular model for clustering is k-Means.

Descriptive models related to pattern discovery are used for market basket analysis of transactional data. In market basket analysis, based on the purchase pattern available in the transactional data, the possibility of purchasing one product based on the purchase of another product is determined. For example, transactional data may reveal a pattern that generally a customer who purchases milk also purchases biscuits at the same time. This can be useful for targeted promotions or in-store setup. Promotions related to biscuits can be sent to customers of milk products or vice versa. Also, in the store products related to milk can be placed close to biscuits.

3.3   TRAINING A MODEL (FOR SUPERVISED LEARNING)

3.3.1   Holdout method

In the case of supervised learning, a model is trained using the labeled input data. However, how can we understand the performance of the model? The test data may not be available immediately. Also, the label value of the test data is not known. That is the reason why a part of the input data is held back (that is how the name holdout originates) for evaluation of the model. This subset of the input data is used as the test data for evaluating the performance of a trained model. In general 70%–80% of the input data (which is obviously labelled) is used for model training. The remaining 20%–30% is used as test data for validation of the performance of the model. However, a different proportion of dividing the input data into training and test data is also acceptable. To make sure that the data in both buckets are similar, the division is done randomly. Random numbers are used to assign data items to the partitions. This method of partitioning the input data into two parts – training and test data (depicted in Figure 3.1), which is by holding back a part of the input data for validating the trained model is known as the holdout method.

Once the model is trained using the training data, the labels of the test data are predicted using the model's target function. Then the predicted value is compared with the actual value of the label. This is possible because the test data is a part of the

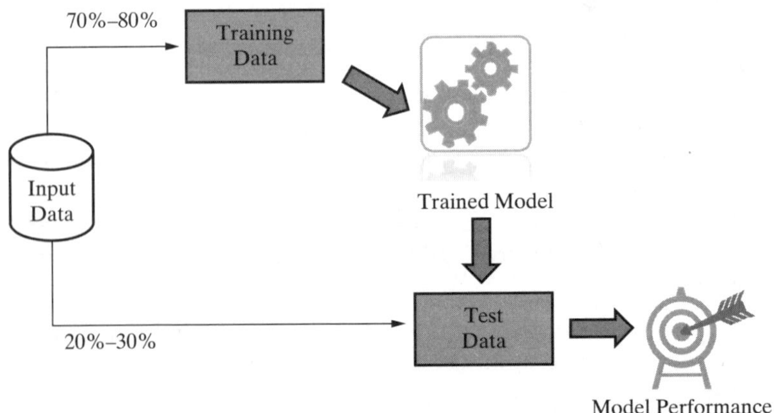

FIG. 3.1
Holdout method

input data with known labels. The performance of the model is in general measured by the accuracy of the prediction of the label value.

In certain cases, the input data is partitioned into three portions –training and test data, and a third validation data. The validation data is used in place of test data, for measuring the model performance. It is used in iterations and to refine the model in each iteration. The test data is used only for once, after the model is refined and finalized, to measure and report the final performance of the model as a reference for future learning efforts. Refer to Figure 3.2 for details.

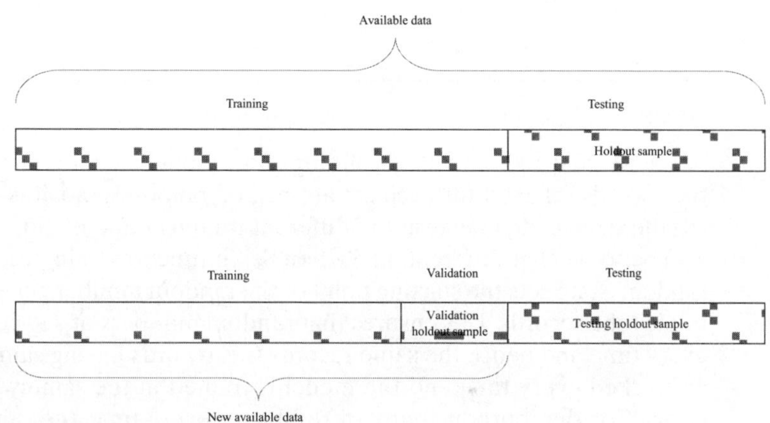

FIG. 3.2
Train-Test-Validation split

An obvious problem in this method is that the division of data of different classes into the training and test data may not be proportionate. This situation is worse if the overall percentage of data related to certain classes is much less compared to other classes. This may happen even though random sampling is employed for test data selection. This problem can be addressed to some extent by applying stratified random sampling in place of sampling. In the case of stratified random sampling, the whole data is broken into several homogenous groups or strata, and a random sample is selected from each such stratum. This ensures that the generated random partitions have equal proportions of each class.

Holdout

The first step before starting to model, in case of supervised learning, is to load the input data, hold out a portion of the input data as test data and have the remaining portion as training data for building the model. Below is the standard way to do it. Scikit-learn provides a function to split input data set into training and test data sets.

```
>>> import pandas as pd

>>> data = pd.read_csv("btissue.csv")
>>> from sklearn.model_selection import train_test_split
```

```
>>> data.shape
(106, 10)

>>> data_train, data_test = train_test_split(data, test_size =
0.3, random_state = 123)    # The parameter test_size sets the ratio
of test data to the input data to 0.3 or 30% and random_state sets
the seed for random number generator

>>> len(data_train)
74
>>> len(data_test)
32
```

Note:

When we do data holdout, i.e. splitting of the input data into training and test data sets, the records selected for each set are picked randomly. So, it is obvious that executing the same code may result in different training data set. So the model trained will also be somewhat different. In Python Scikit function train_test_split, the parameter random_state sets the starting point of the random number generator used internally to pick the records. This ensures that random numbers of a specific sequence is used every time and hence the same records (i.e. records having same sequence number) are picked every time and the model is trained in the same way. This is extremely critical for the reproducibility of results i.e. every time, the same machine learning program generates the same set of results.

 ### 3.3.2   *K*-fold Cross-validation method

The holdout method employing a stratified random sampling approach still heads into issues in certain specific situations. Especially, the smaller data sets may have the challenge of dividing the data of some of the classes proportionally amongst training and test data sets. A special variant of the holdout method called repeated holdout, is sometimes employed to ensure the randomness of the composed data sets. In repeated holdouts, several random holdouts are used to measure the model performance. In the end, the average of all performances is taken. As multiple holdouts have been drawn, the training and test data (and also validation data, in case it is drawn) are more likely to contain representative data from all classes and resemble the original input data closely. This process of repeated holdout is the basis of the k-fold cross-validation technique. In k-fold cross-validation, the data set is divided into k-completely distinct or non-overlapping random partitions called folds. Figure 3.2 depicts an overall approach for k-fold cross-validation.

The value of 'k' in k-fold cross-validation can be set to any number. However, there are two extremely popular approaches:

(i) 10-fold cross-validation (10-fold CV)
(ii) Leave-one-out cross-validation (LOOCV)

10-fold cross-validation is by far the most popular approach. In this approach, for each of the 10 folds, each comprising approximately 10% of the data, one of the folds is used as the test data for validating the performance of the model which was trained based on the remaining 9 folds (or 90% of the data). This is repeated 10 times, once for each of the 10 folds being used as the test data and the remaining folds as the training data.

The average performance across all folds is being reported. Figure 3.3 depicts the detailed approach to selecting the 'k' folds in k-fold cross-validation. As can be observed in the figure, each of the circles resembles a record in the input data set whereas the different colors indicate the different classes that the records belong to.

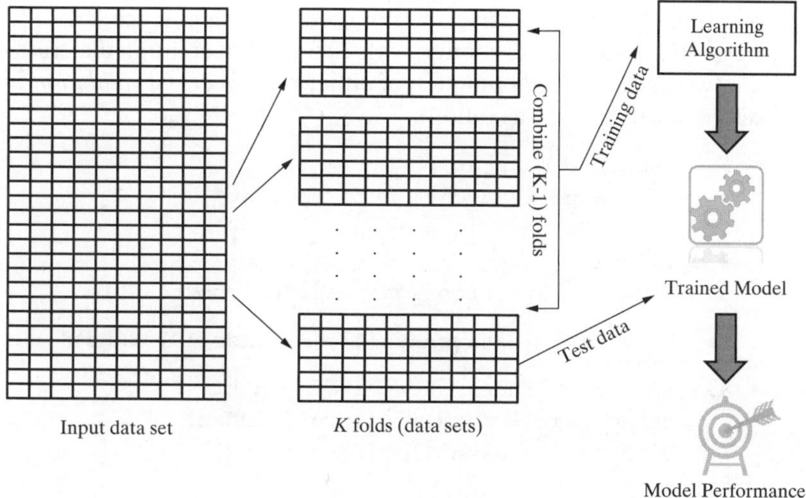

FIG. 3.3
Overall approach for *K*-fold cross-validation

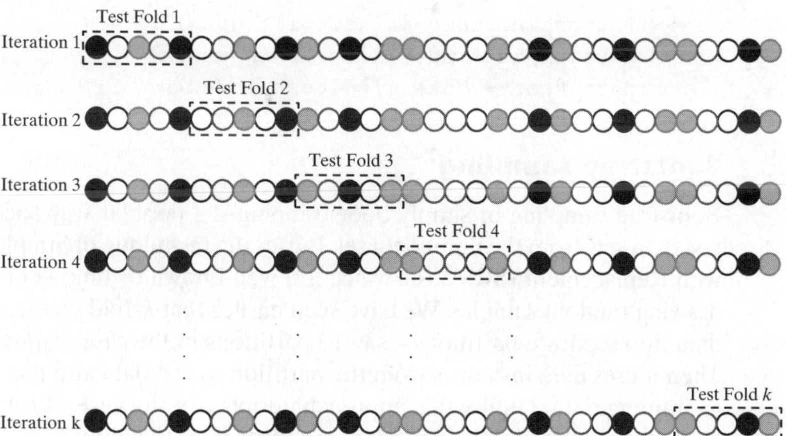

FIG. 3.4
Detailed approach for fold selection

The entire data set is broken into 'k' folds – out of which one fold is selected in each iteration as the test data set. The fold selected as the test data set in each of the 'k' iterations is different. Also, note that though in Figure 3.3 the circles resemble the records in the input data set, the contiguous circles represented as folds do not mean that they are subsequent records in the data set. This is more of a virtual representation and not a physical representation. As already mentioned, the records in a fold are drawn by using a random sampling technique.

Leave-one-out cross-validation (LOOCV) is an extreme case of k-fold cross validation using one record or data instance at a time as test data. This is done to maximize the count of data used to train the model. The number of iterations for which it has to be run is equal to the total number of data in the input data set. Hence, it is computationally very expensive and not used much in practice.

Let's do k-fold cross-validation with 10 folds. For creating the cross-validation, there are two options. *KFold* function of either *sklearn.cross_validation* or *sklearn.model_selection* can be used as follows:

```python
>>> import pandas as pd
>>> data = pd.read_csv("auto-mpg.csv")


# Option 1
>>> from sklearn.cross_validation import KFold

>>> kf = KFold(data.shape[0], n_folds=10, random_state=123)

>>> for train_index, test_index in kf:
    data_train = data.iloc[train_index]
    data_test = data.iloc[test_index]


# Option 2
>>> from sklearn.model_selection import KFold

>>> kf = KFold(n_splits=10)
>>> for train, test in kf.split(data):
    data_train = data.iloc[train_index]
    data_test = data.iloc[test_index]
```

3.3.3 Bootstrap sampling

Bootstrap sampling or simply bootstrapping is a popular way to identify training and test data sets from the input data set. It uses the technique of Simple Random Sampling with Replacement (SRSWR), which is a well-known technique in sampling theory for drawing random samples. We have seen earlier that k-fold cross-validation divides the data into separate partitions – say 10 partitions in the case of 10-fold cross-validation. Then it uses data instances from the partition as test data and the remaining partitions as training data. Unlike this approach adopted in the case of k-fold cross-validation, bootstrapping randomly picks data instances from the input data set, with the possibility of the same data instance being picked multiple times. This essentially means that from the input data set having 'n' data instances, bootstrapping can create one or more training data sets having '*n*' data instances, some of the data instances being repeated multiple times. Figure 3.4 briefly presents the approach followed in bootstrap sampling.

This technique is particularly useful in the case of input data sets of small size, i.e. having a very small number of data instances.

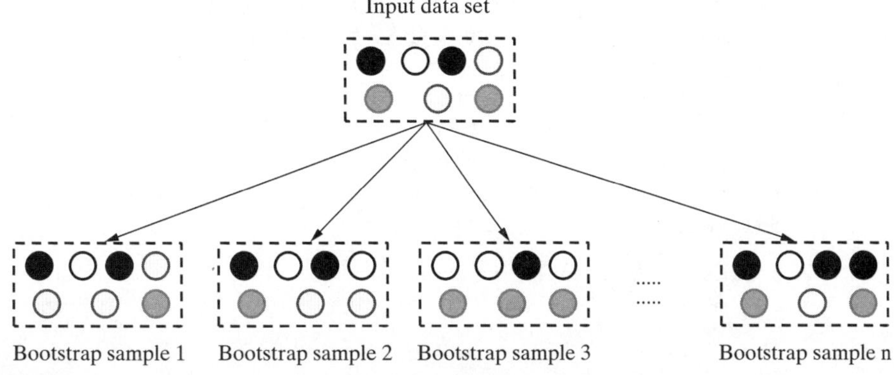

FIG. 3.5
Bootstrap sampling

CROSS-VALIDATION	**BOOTSTRAPPING**
It is a special variant of the holdout method, called repeated holdout. Hence uses a stratified random sampling approach (without replacement). The data set is divided into '*k*' random partitions, with each partition containing approximately $\frac{n}{k}$ number of unique data elements, where '*n*' is the total number of data elements and '*k*' is the total number of folds.	It uses the technique of Simple Random Sampling with Replacement (SRSWR). So the same data instance may be picked up multiple times in a sample.
The number of possible training/test data samples that can be drawn using this technique is finite.	In this technique, since elements can be repeated in the sample, a possible number of training/test data samples is unlimited.

bootstrap resampling is used to generate samples of any given size from the training data. It uses the concept of simple random sampling with repetition. To generate bootstrap sample in Python, *resample* function of sklearn.utils library can be used. Below is a sample code

```
>>> import pandas as pd
>>> from sklearn.utils import resample

>>> data = pd.read_csv("btissue.csv")
>>> X = data.iloc[:,0:9]
>>> X
>>> resample(X, n_samples=200, random_state=0) # Generates a sample
of size 200 (as mentioned in parameter n_samples) with repetition ...
```

Once the model preparatory steps, like data holdout, etc. are over, the actual training happens. The *sklearn* framework in Python provides most of the models which are generally used in machine learning. Below is a sample code.

```
>>> from sklearn.tree import DecisionTreeClassifier
>>> predictors = data.iloc[:,0:7] # Segregating the predictors
>>> target = data.iloc[:,7]   # Segregating the target/class
>>> predictors_train, predictors_test, target_train, target_test =
train_test_split(predictors, target, test_size = 0.3, random_state
= 123)   # Holdout of data
>>> dtree_entropy = DecisionTreeClassifier(criterion = "entropy",
random_state = 100, max_depth=3, min_samples_leaf=5)   #Model is
initialized

# Finally the model is trained
>>> model = dtree_entropy.fit(predictors_train, target_train)
```

3.3.4   Lazy vs. Eager learner

Eager learning follows the general principles of machine learning – it tries to construct a generalized, input-independent target function during the model training phase. It follows the typical steps of machine learning, i.e. abstraction and generalization, and comes up with a trained model at the end of the learning phase. Hence, when the test data comes in for classification, the eager learner is ready with the model and doesn't need to refer back to the training data. Eager learners take more time in the learning phase than lazy learners. Some of the algorithms that adopt the eager learning approach include Decision Trees, Support Vector Machine, Neural Networks, etc.

Lazy learning, on the other hand, completely skips the abstraction and generalization processes, as explained in the context of a typical machine learning process. In that that respect, strictly speaking, a lazy learner doesn't 'learn' anything. It uses the training data in exact and uses the knowledge to classify the unlabelled test data. Since lazy learning uses training data as-is, it is also known as rote learning (i.e. memorization technique based on repetition). Due to its heavy dependency on the given training data instance, it is also known as instance learning. They are also called non-parametric learning. Lazy learners take very little time in training because not much training happens. However, it takes quite some time in classification as for each tuple of test data, a comparison-based assignment of label happens. One of the most popular algorithms for lazy learning is *k*-nearest neighbor.

Note:

Parametric learning models have a finite number of parameters. In the case of non-parametric models, quite contradicting to its name, the number of parameters is potentially infinite.

Models such as Linear Regression and Support Vector Machine, since the coefficients form the learning parameters, are fixed in size. Hence, these models are clubbed as parametric.

On the other hand, in the case of models such as k-Nearest Neighbor (kNN) and decision tree, the number of parameters grows with the size of the training data. Hence, they are considered as non-parametric learning models.

3.4 MODEL REPRESENTATION AND INTERPRETABILITY

We have already seen that the goal of supervised machine learning is to learn or derive a target function that can best determine the target variable from the set of input variables. A key consideration in learning the target function from the training data is the extent of generalization. This is because the input data is just a limited, specific view and the new, unknown data in the test data set may be differing quite a bit from the training data.

The fitness of a target function approximated by a learning algorithm determines how correctly it can classify a set of data it has never seen.

3.4.1 Underfitting

If the target function is kept too simple, it may not be able to capture the essential nuances and represent the underlying data well. A typical case of underfitting may occur when trying to represent non-linear data with a linear model as demonstrated by both cases of underfitting shown in Figure 3.5. Many times underfitting happens due to the unavailability of sufficient training data. Underfitting results in both poor performance with training data as well as poor generalization to test data. Underfitting can be avoided by

1. using more training data
2. reducing features by effective feature selection

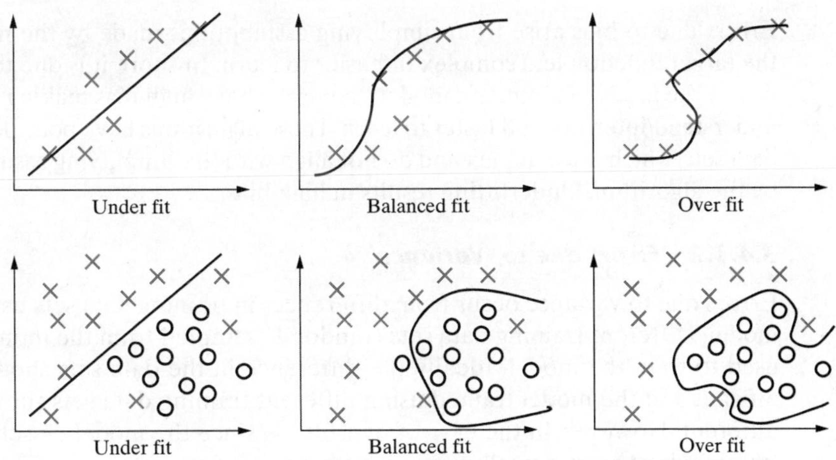

FIG. 3.6
Underfitting and Overfitting of Models

3.4.2   Overfitting

Overfitting refers to a situation where the model has been designed in such a way that it emulates the training data too closely. In such a case, any specific deviation in the training data, like noise or outliers, gets embedded in the model. It adversely impacts the performance of the model on the test data. Overfitting, in many cases, occurs as a result of trying to fit an excessively complex model to closely match the training data. This is represented with a sample data set in Figure 3.5. The target function, in these cases, tries to make sure all training data points are correctly partitioned by the decision boundary. However, more often than not, this exact nature is not replicated in the unknown test data set. Hence, the target function results in tha wrong classification in the test data set. Overfitting results in good performance with a training data set, but poor generalization and hence poor performance with test a data set. Overfitting can be avoided by

1. using re-sampling techniques like k-fold cross-validation
2. hold back of a validation data set
3. remove the nodes that have little or no predictive power for the given machine-learning problem.

Both underfitting and overfitting result in poor classification quality which is reflected by low classification accuracy.

3.4.3   Bias – variance trade-off

In supervised learning, the class value assigned by the learning model built based on the training data may differ from the actual class value. This error in learning can be of two types – errors due to 'bias' and errors due to 'variance'. Let's try to understand each of them in detail.

3.4.3.1   Errors due to 'Bias'

Errors due to bias arise from simplifying assumptions made by the model to make the target function less complex or easier to learn. In short, it is due to the underfitting of the model. Parametric models generally have high bias making them easier to understand/interpret and faster to learn. These algorithms have poor performance on data sets, which are complex and do not align with the simplifying assumptions made by the algorithm. Underfitting results in high bias.

3.4.3.2   Errors due to 'Variance'

Errors due to variance occur from differences in training data sets used to train the model. Different training data sets (randomly sampled from the input data set) are used to train the model. Ideally the difference in the data sets should not be significant and the model trained using different training data sets should not be too different. However, in the case of overfitting, since the model closely matches the training data, even a small difference in training data gets magnified in the model.

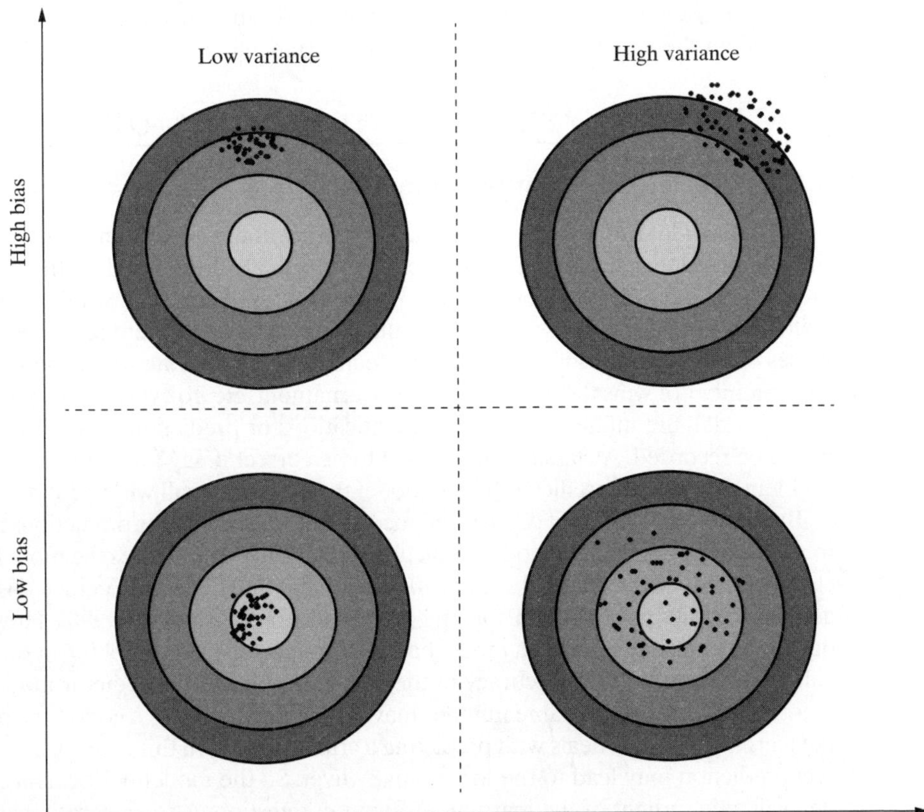

FIG. 3.7
Bias-variance trade-off

So, the problems in training a model can happen because either (a) the model is too simple and hence fails to interpret the data grossly or (b) the model is extremely complex and magnifies even small differences in the training data.

As is quite understandable:

- Increasing the bias will decrease the variance, and
- Increasing the variance will decrease the bias

On one hand, parametric algorithms are generally seen to demonstrate high bias but low variance. On the other hand, non-parametric algorithms demonstrate low bias and high variance.

As can be observed in Figure 3.6, the best solution is to have a model with low bias as well as low variance. However, that may not be possible in reality. Hence, the goal of supervised machine learning is to achieve a balance between bias and variance. The learning algorithm chosen and the user parameters that can be configured help in striking a trade-off between bias and variance. For example, in a popular supervised algorithm k-Nearest Neighbors or kNN, the user-configurable parameter 'k' can be used to do a trade-off between bias and variance. ON one hand, when the value of

'k' is decreased, the model becomes simpler to fit and bias increases. On the other hand, when the value of 'k' is increased, the variance increases.

3.5   EVALUATING PERFORMANCE OF A MODEL

 ### 3.5.1   Supervised learning - classification

In supervised learning, one major task is classification. The responsibility of the classification model is to assign a class label to the target feature based on the value of the predictor features. For example, in the problem of predicting the win/loss in a cricket match, the classifier will assign a class value win/loss to the target feature based on the values of other features like whether the team won the toss, number of spinners in the team, number of wins the team had in the tournament, etc. To evaluate the performance of the model, the number of correct classifications or predictions made by the model has to be recorded. A classification is said to be correct if, say for example in the given problem, it has been predicted by the model that the team will win and it has won.

Based on the number of correct and incorrect classifications or predictions made by a model, the accuracy of the model is calculated. If 99 out of 100 times the model has been classified correctly, e.g. if in 99 out of 100 games what the model has predicted is the same as what the outcome has been, then the model accuracy is said to be 99%. However, it is quite relative to say whether a model has performed well just by looking at the accuracy value. For example, 99% accuracy in the case of a sports win predictor model may be reasonably good but the same number may not be acceptable as a good threshold when the learning problem deals with predicting a critical illness. In this case, even a 1% incorrect prediction may lead to the loss of many lives. So the model performance needs to be evaluated in light of the learning problem in question. Also, in certain cases, erring on the side of caution may be preferred at the cost of overall accuracy. For that reason, we need to look more closely at the model accuracy and also at the same time look at other measures of performance of a model like sensitivity, specificity, precision, etc. So, let's start with looking at model accuracy more closely. And let's try to understand it with an example. There are four possibilities with regard to the cricket match win/loss prediction:

1. the model predicted a win and the team won
2. the model predicted a win and the team lost
3. the model predicted loss and the team won
4. the model predicted loss and the team lost

In this problem, the obvious class of interest is 'win'.

The first case, i.e. the model predicted to win and the team won is a case where the model has correctly classified data instances as the class of interest. These cases are referred to as True Positive (TP) cases.

The second case, i.e. the model predicted to win and the team lost is a case where the model incorrectly classified data instances as the class of interest. These cases are referred to as False Positive (FP) cases.

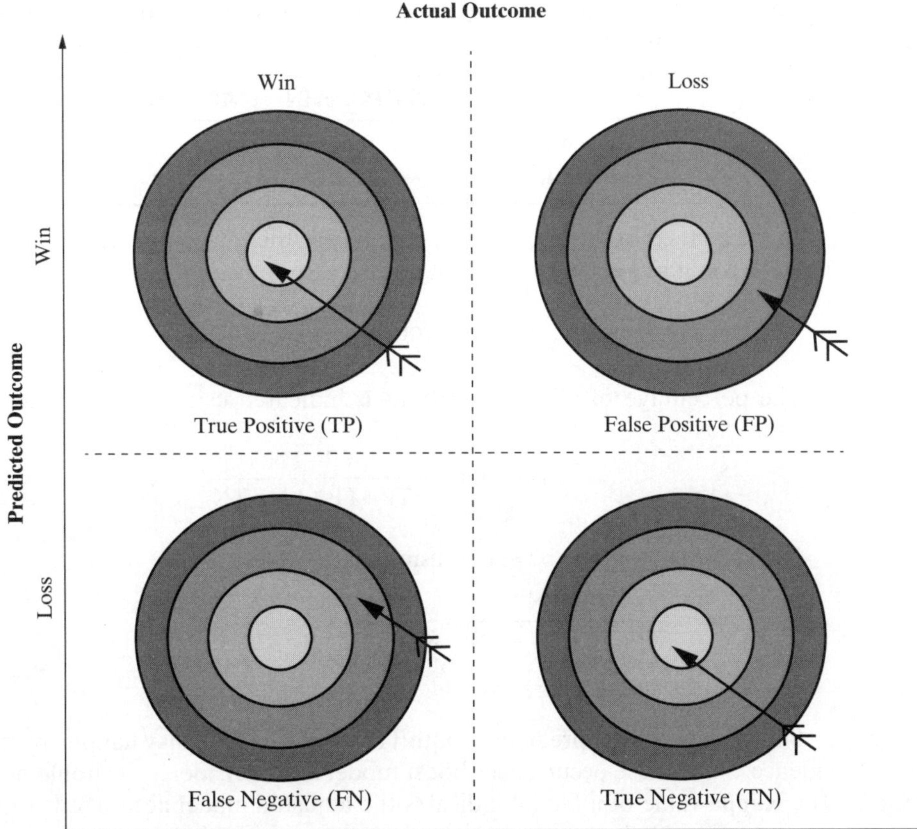

FIG. 3.8
Details of model classification

The third case, i.e. the model predicted loss and the team won is a case where the model has incorrectly classified as not the class of interest. These cases are referred to as False Negative (FN) cases.

The fourth case, i.e. the model predicted loss and the team lost is a case where the model has correctly classified as not the class of interest. These cases are referred to as True Negative (TN) cases. All these four cases are depicted in Figure 3.7.

For any classification model, **model accuracy** is given by a total number of correct classifications (either as the class of interest, i.e. True Positive, or as not the class of interest, i.e. True Negative) divided by a total number of classifications done.

$$\text{Model accuracy} = \frac{TP + TN}{TP + FP + FN + TN}$$

A matrix containing correct and incorrect predictions in the form of TPs, FPs, FNs and TNs is known as a **confusion matrix**. The win/loss prediction of a cricket match has two classes of interest – win and loss. For that reason it will generate a 2 × 2 confusion matrix. For a classification problem involving three classes, the confusion matrix would be 3 × 3, etc.

Let's assume the confusion matrix of the win/loss prediction of the cricket match problem to be as below:

	ACTUAL WIN	ACTUAL LOSS
Predicted Win	85	4
Predicted Loss	2	9

In the context of the above confusion matrix, the total count of TPs = 85, count of FPs = 4, count of FNs, = 2 and count of TNs = 9.

$$\therefore \ \text{Model accuracy} \ = \frac{94}{100} = 94\%$$

The percentage of misclassifications is indicated using the **error rate** which is measured as

$$\text{Error rate} \ = \frac{FP + FN}{TP + FP + FN + TN}$$

In the context of the above confusion matrix,

$$\text{Error rate} \ = \frac{FP + FN}{TP + FP + FN + TN} = \frac{4 + 2}{85 + 4 + 2 + 9} = \frac{6}{100} = 6\%$$

$$= 19 \text{Model accuracy}$$

Sometimes, correct prediction, both TPs as well as TNs, may happen by mere coincidence. Since these occurrences boost model accuracy, ideally it should not happen. The **Kappa** value of a model indicates the adjusted model accuracy. It is calculated using the formula below:

$$\text{Kappa value (k)} = \frac{P(a) - P(p_r)}{1 - P(p_r)}$$

P(a) = Proportion of observed agreement between actual and predicted in the overall data set

$$= \frac{TP + TN}{TP + FP + FN + TN}$$

P(p$_r$) = Proportion of expected agreement between actual and predicted data both in the case of a class of interest as well as the other classes

$$= \frac{TP + FP}{TP + FP + FN + TN} \times \frac{TP + FN}{TP + FP + FN + TN} + \frac{FN + TN}{TP + FP + FN + TN}$$

$$\times \frac{FP + TN}{TP + FP + FN + TN}$$

In the context of the above confusion matrix, the total count of TPs = 85, count of FPs = 4 count of FNs = 2, and count of TNs = 9.

$$\therefore P(a) = \frac{TP+TN}{TP+FP+FN+TN} = \frac{85+9}{85+4+2+9} = \frac{94}{100} = 0.94$$

$$P\left(p_r\right) = \frac{85+4}{85+4+2+9} \times \frac{85+2}{85+4+2+9} + \frac{2+9}{85+4+2+9} \times \frac{4+9}{85+4+2+9}$$

$$= \frac{89}{100} \times \frac{87}{100} + \frac{11}{100} \times \frac{13}{100} = 0.89 \times 0.87 + 0.11 \times 0.13 = 0.7886$$

$$\therefore k = \frac{0.94-0.7886}{1-0.7886} = 0.7162$$

Note:

The kappa value can be 1 at the maximum, which represents perfect agreement between the model's prediction and actual values.

As discussed earlier, in certain learning problems it is critical to have an extremely low number of FN cases, if needed, at the cost of a conservative classification model. Though it is a clear case of misclassification and will impact model accuracy adversely, it is still required as missing each class of interest may have serious consequences. This happens more in problems from medical domains like disease prediction problems. For example, if a tumor is malignant but wrongly classified as benign by the classifier, then the repercussion of such misclassification is fatal. It does not matter if a higher number of tumors that are benign are wrongly classified as malignant. In these problems there are some measures of model performance that are more important than accuracy. Two such critical measurements are the sensitivity and specificity of the model.

The **sensitivity** of a model measures the proportion of TP examples or positive cases that were correctly classified. It is measured as

$$\text{Sensitivity} = \frac{TP}{TP+FN}$$

In the context of the above confusion matrix for the cricket match win prediction problem,

$$\text{Sensitivity} = \frac{TP}{TP+FN} = \frac{85}{85+2} = \frac{85}{87} = 97.7\%$$

So, again taking the example of the malignancy prediction of tumors, the class of interest is 'malignant'. The sensitivity measure gives the proportion of tumors which are actually malignant and have been predicted as malignant. It is quite obvious that for such problems the most critical measure of the performance of a good model is sensitivity. A high value of sensitivity is more desirable than a high value of accuracy.

Specificity is also another good measure to indicate a good balance of a model being excessively conservative or excessively aggressive. The specificity of a model measures the proportion of negative examples which have been correctly classified. In the context, of malignancy prediction of tumors, specificity gives the proportion of benign tumors which have been correctly classified. In the context of the above confusion matrix for the cricket match win prediction problem,

$$\text{Specificity} = \frac{\text{TN}}{\text{TN}+\text{FP}} = \frac{9}{9+4} = \frac{9}{13} = 69.2\%$$

A higher value of specificity will indicate a better model performance. However, it is quite understandable that a conservative approach to reduce False Negatives might push up the number of FPs. The reason for this is that the model, to reduce FNs, is going to classify more tumors as malignant. So the chance that benign tumors will be classified as malignant or FPs will increase.

There are two other performance measures of a supervised learning model which are similar to sensitivity and specificity. These are **precision** and **recall**. While precision gives the proportion of positive predictions that are truly positive, recall gives the proportion of TP cases overall actually positive cases.

$$\text{Precision} = \frac{\text{TP}}{\text{TP}+\text{FP}}$$

Precision indicates the reliability of a model in predicting a class of interest. When the model is related to win / loss prediction of cricket, precision indicates how often it predicts the win correctly. In the context of the above confusion matrix for the cricket match win prediction problem,

$$\text{Precision} = \frac{\text{TP}}{\text{TP}+\text{FP}} = \frac{85}{85+4} = \frac{85}{89} = 95.5\%$$

It is quite understandable that a model with higher precision is perceived to be more reliable.

Recall indicates the proportion of correct prediction of positives to the total number of positives. In the case of win/loss prediction of cricket, recall resembles what proportion of the total wins were predicted correctly.

$$\text{Recall} = \frac{\text{TP}}{\text{TP}+\text{FN}}$$

In the context of the above confusion matrix for the cricket match win prediction problem,

$$\text{Recall} = \frac{\text{TP}}{\text{TP}+\text{FN}} = \frac{85}{85+2} = \frac{85}{87} = 97.7\%$$

3.5.1.1   F-measure

F-measure is another measure of model performance that combines precision and recall. It takes the harmonic mean of precision and recall as calculated as

$$F\text{-measure} = \frac{2\times \text{precision} \times \text{recall}}{\text{precision} + \text{recall}}$$

In the context of the above confusion matrix for the cricket match win prediction problem,

$$F\text{-measure} = \frac{2 \times 0.955 \times 0.977}{0.955 + 0.977} = \frac{1.866}{1.932} = 96.6\%$$

As a combination of multiple measures into one, the *F*-score gives the right measure using which performance of different models can be compared. However, one assumption the calculation is based on is that precision and recall have equal weight, which may not always be true in reality. In certain problems, the disease prediction problems, e.g., precision may be given far more weightage. In that case, different weights may be assigned to precision and recall. However, there may be a serious dilemma regarding what value to be adopted for each and what is the basis for the specific value adopted.

3.5.1.1.1 Receiver operating characteristic (ROC) curves

As we have seen till now, though accuracy is the most popular measure, there are quite several other measures to evaluate the performance of a supervised learning model. However, visualization is an easier and more effective way to understand the model performance. It also helps in comparing the efficiency of the two models.

The Receiver Operating Characteristic (ROC) curve helps in visualizing the performance of a classification model. It shows the efficiency of a model in the detection of true positives while avoiding the occurrence of false positives. To refresh our memory, true positives are those cases where the model has correctly classified data instances as the class of interest. For example, the model has correctly classified the tumors as malignant, in case of a tumor malignancy prediction problem. On the other hand, FPs are those cases where the model incorrectly classified data instances as the class of interest. Using the same example, in this case, the model has incorrectly classified the tumors as malignant, i.e. tumors that are actually benign have been classified as malignant.

$$\text{True Positive Rate TPR} = \frac{TP}{TP + FN}$$

$$\text{False Positive Rate FPR} = \frac{FP}{FP + TN}$$

In the ROC curve, the FP rate is plotted (on the horizontal axis) against the true positive rate (on the vertical axis) at different classification thresholds. If we assume a lower value of the classification threshold, the model classifies more items as positive. Hence, the values of both False Positives and True Positives increase. The area under curve (AUC) value, as shown in Figure 3.8a, is the area of the two-dimensional space under the curve extending from $(0, 0)$ to $(1, 1)$, where each point on the curve gives a set of true and false positive values at a specific classification threshold. This curve gives an indication of the predictive quality of a model. AUC value ranges from 0 to 1, with an AUC of less than 0.5 indicating that the classifier has no predictive ability.

Figure 3.8b shows the curves of two classifiers – classifier 1 and classifier 2. Quite obviously, the AUC of Classifier 1 is more than the AUC of Classifier 2. So, we can draw the inference that Classifier 1 is better than Classifier 2.

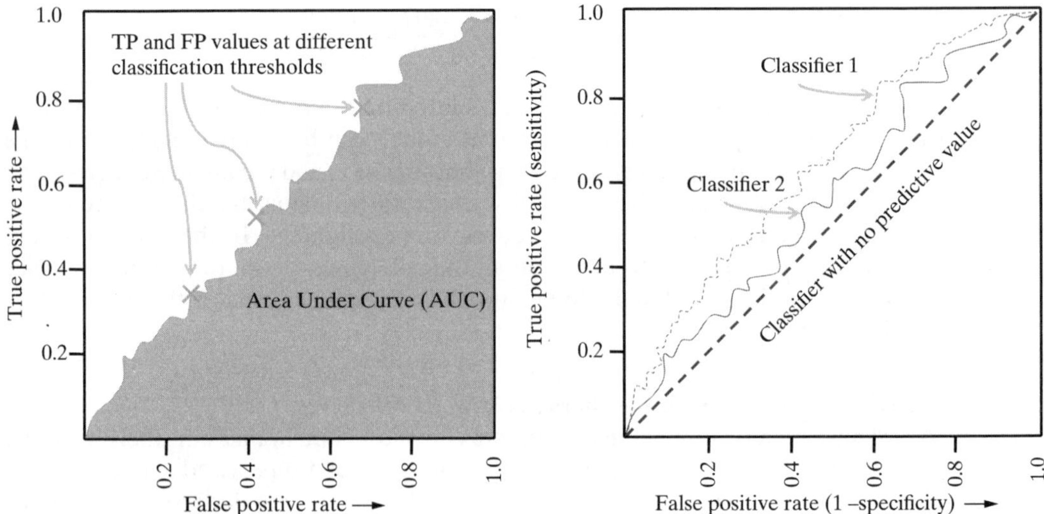

FIG. 3.9
ROC curve

A quick indicative interpretation of the predictive values from 0.5 to 1.0 is given below:

- 0.5 – 0.6 ➔ Almost no predictive ability
- 0.6 – 0.7 ➔ Weak predictive ability
- 0.7 – 0.8 ➔ Fair predictive ability
- 0.8 – 0.9 ➔ Good predictive ability
- 0.9 – 1.0 ➔ Excellent predictive ability

As we have already seen in the primary measure of performance of a classification model is its accuracy. Accuracy of a model is calculated based on correct classifications made by the model compared to total number of classifications. In Python, *sklearn. metrics* provides *accuracy_score* functionality to evaluate the accuracy of a classification model. Below is the code for evaluating the accuracy of a classifier model.

```
>>> from sklearn.metrics import accuracy_score
>>> prediction = model.predict(predictors_test)
>>> accuracy_score(target_test, prediction, normalize = True)
```

The *confusion_matrix* functionality of *sklearn.metrics* helps in generation the confusion matrix, discussed in detail in Chapter 3. Below is the code for finding the confusion matrix of a classifier model. Also, in Figure B.6, is a quick analysis of the output confusion matrix as obtained from the Python code.

```
>>> from sklearn.metrics import confusion_matrix
>>> confusion_matrix(target_test, prediction)
```

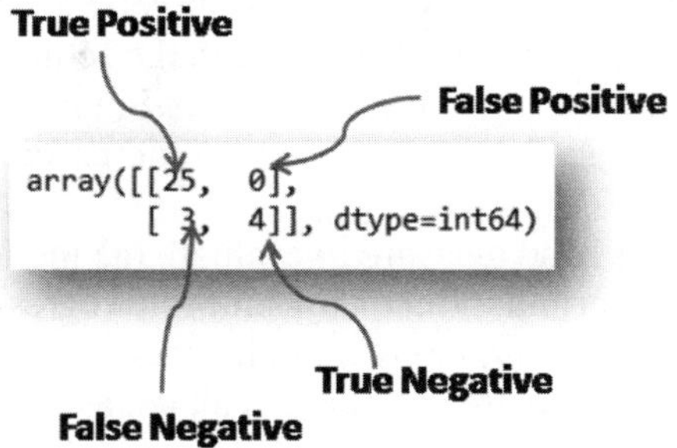

FIG. 3.13
Performance evaluation of a classification model

3.5.2   Supervised learning – regression

A well-fitted regression model churns out predicted values close to actual values. Hence, a regression model which ensures that the difference between predicted and actual values is low can be considered as a good model. Figure 3.9 represents a very simple problem of real estate value prediction solved using a linear regression model. If 'area' is the predictor variable (say x) and 'value' is the target variable (say y), the linear regression model can be represented in the form:

$$y = \alpha + \beta x$$

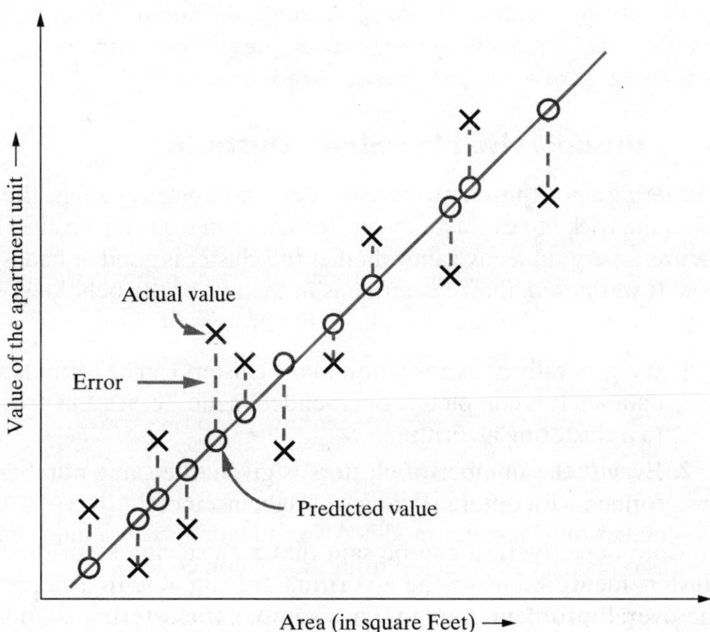

FIG. 3.10
Error – Predicted vs. actual value

For a certain value of x, say $\hat{x}$, the value of y is predicted as $\hat{y}$ whereas the actual value of y is Y (say). The distance between the actual value and the fitted or predicted value, i.e. $\hat{y}$ is known as **residual**. The regression model can be considered to be fitted well if the difference between the actual and predicted value, i.e. the residual value is less.

R-squared is a good measure to evaluate the model fitness. It is also known as the coefficient of determination, or for multiple regression, the coefficient of multiple determination. The R-squared value lies between 0 to 1 (0%–100%) with a larger value representing a better fit. It is calculated as:

$$R^2 = \frac{SST - SSE}{SST}$$

The sum of Squares Total (SST) = squared differences of each observation from the overall mean $= \sum_{i=1}^{n}(y_i - \bar{y})^2$ where $\bar{y}$ is the mean.

The Tum of Squared Errors (SSE) (of prediction) = sum of the squared residuals $= \sum_{i=1}^{n}(Y_i - \hat{y})^2$ where $\hat{y}_i$ is the predicted value of y_i and Y_i is the actual value of y_i.

We have seen in R-squared is an effective measure of performance of a regression model. In Python, *sklearn.metrics* provides *mean_squared_error* and *r2_score* functionality to evaluate the accuracy of a regression model. Below is a sample code.

```
>>> prediction = model.predict(predictors_test)
>>> mean_squared_error(target_test, prediction)
>>> r2_score(target_test, prediction)
```

3.5.3   Unsupervised learning - clustering

Clustering algorithms try to reveal natural groupings amongst the data sets. However, it is quite tricky to evaluate the performance of a clustering algorithm. Clustering, by nature, is very subjective and whether the cluster is good or bad is open to interpretation. It was noted, that 'clustering is in the eye of the beholder'. This stems from the two inherent challenges which lie in the process of clustering:

1. It is generally not known how many clusters can be formulated from a particular data set. It is completely open-ended in most cases and provided as a user input to a clustering algorithm.
2. Even if the number of clusters is given, the same number of clusters can be formed with different groups of data instances.

More objectively, it can be said that a clustering algorithm is successful if the clusters identified using the algorithm are-can able to achieve the right results in the overall problem domain. For example, if clustering is applied for identifying customer segments for a marketing campaign of a new product launch, the clustering can be considered successful only if the marketing campaign ends with success, i.e. it can create the right brand recognition resulting in steady revenue from new product sales. However, there are a couple of popular approaches which are adopted for cluster quality evaluation.

(a) *Internal evaluation*

In this approach, the cluster is assessed based on the underlying data that was clustered. The internal evaluation methods generally measure cluster quality based on the homogeneity of data belonging to the same cluster and heterogeneity of data belonging to different clusters. The homogeneity/heterogeneity is decided by some similarity measure. For example, the **silhouette coefficient**, which is one of the most popular internal evaluation methods, uses distance (Euclidean or Manhattan distances most commonly used) between data elements as a similarity measure. The value of silhouette width ranges between –1 and +1, with a high value indicating high intra-cluster homogeneity and intercluster heterogeneity.

For a data set clustered into 'k' clusters, silhouette width is calculated as:

$$\text{Silhouette width} = \frac{b(i) - an(i)}{\max\{an(i), b(i)\}}$$

$a(i)$ is the average distance between the i th data instance and all other data instances belonging to the same cluster and $b(i)$ is the lowest average distance between the i-the data instance and data instances of all other clusters.

Let's try to understand this in the context of the example depicted in Figure 3.10. There are four clusters namely clusters 1, 2, 3, and 4. Let's consider an arbitrary data element 'i' in cluster 1, resembled by the asterisk. $a(i)$ is the average of the distances $a_{i1}, a_{i2}, \ldots, a_{in_1}$ of the different data elements from the i th data element in cluster 1, assuming there are n_1 data elements in cluster 1. Mathematically,

$$a(i) = \frac{a_{i1} + a_{i2} + \ldots + a_{in_1}}{n_1}$$

In the same way, let's calculate the distance of an arbitrary data element 'i' in cluster 1 with the different data elements from another cluster, say cluster 4m, and take an average of all those distances. Hence,

$$b_{14}(\text{average}) = \frac{b_{14}(1) + b_{14}(2) + \ldots + b_{14}(n_4)}{(n_4)}$$

where n_4 is the total number of elements in cluster 4. In the same way, we can calculate the values of b_{12} (average) and b_{13} (average). $b(i)$ is the minimum of all these values. Hence, we can say that,

$$b(i) = \text{minimum } [b_{12}(\text{average}), b_{13}(\text{average}), b_{14}(\text{average})]$$

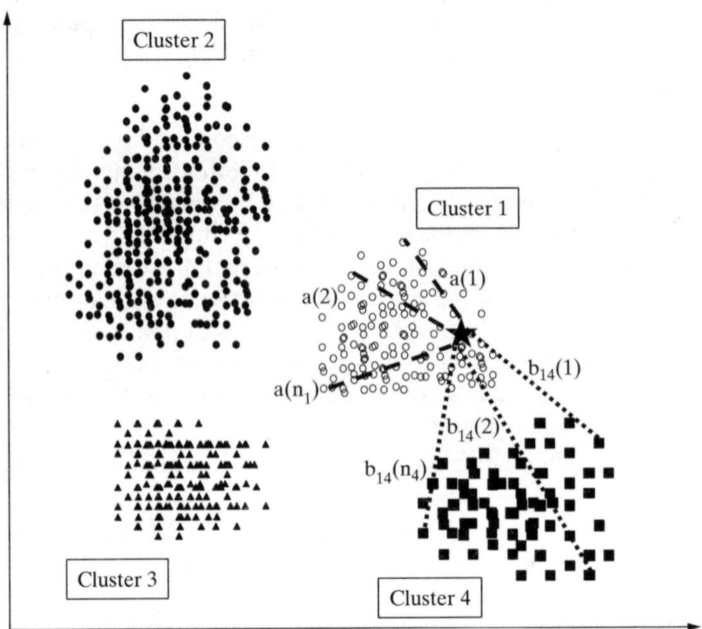

FIG. 3.11
Silhouette width calculation

(b) *External evaluation*

In this approach, the class label is known for the data set subjected to clustering. However, quite obviously, the known class labels are not a part of the data used in clustering. The clustering algorithm is assessed based on how close the results are compared to those known class labels. For example, **purity** is one of the most popular measures of cluster algorithms – evaluates the extent to which clusters contain a single class.

For a data set having 'n' data instances and 'c' known class labels that generate 'k' clusters, purity is measured as:

$$\text{Purity} = \frac{1}{n}\sum_{k} \max(k \cap c)$$

As we have seen in Chapter 3, there are two popular measures of cluster quality – purity and silhouette width. Purity can be calculated only when class label is known for the data set subjected to clustering. On the other hand, silhouette width can be calculated for any data set.

Purity
We will use a Lower Back Pain Symptoms data set released by Kaggle (https://www.kaggle.com/sammy123/lower-back-pain-symptoms-dataset). The data set consists of 310 observations, 13 attributes (12 numeric predictors, 1 binary class attribute).

```
>>> import pandas as pd
>>> import numpy as np
```

```
>>> from sklearn.cluster import KMeans
>>> from sklearn.metrics.cluster import v_measure_score

>>> data = pd.read_csv("spine.csv")
>>> data_woc = data.iloc[:,0:12]    # Stripping out the class vari-
able from the data set ...
>>> data_class = data.iloc[:,12]      # Segregating the target /
class variable ...

>>> f1 = data_woc['pelvic_incidence'].values
>>> f2 = data_woc['pelvic_radius'].values
>>> f3 = data_woc['thoracic_slope'].values
>>> X = np.array(list(zip(f1, f2, f3)))
>>> kmeans = KMeans(n_clusters = 2, random_state = 123)
>>> model = kmeans.fit(X)
>>> cluster_labels = kmeans.predict(X)

>>> v_measure_score(cluster_labels, data_class)
```

Output

```
0.12267025741680369
```

Silhouette Width

For calculating Silhouette Width, *silhouette_score* function of sklearn. metrics library can be used for calculating Silhouette width. Below is the code for calculating Silhouette Width. A full implementation can be found in a later section A.5.3.

```
>>> from sklearn.metrics import silhouette_score

>>> sil = silhouette_score(X, cluster_labels, metric =
'euclidean',sample_size = len(data)) # "X" is a feature matrix
for the feature subset selected for clustering and "data" is the
data set
```

3.6   IMPROVING PERFORMANCE OF A MODEL

Now we have almost reached the end of the journey of building learning models. We have got some idea about what modeling is, how to approach about it to solve a learning problem and how to measure the success of our model. Now comes a million-dollar question. Can we improve the performance of our model? If so, then what are the levers for improving the performance? Even before that comes the question of model selection – which model should be selected for which machine learning task? We have already discussed earlier that the model selection is done on several aspects:

1. Type of learning the task in hand, i.e. supervised or unsupervised

2. Type of the data, i.e. categorical or numeric

3. Sometimes on the problem domain

4. Above all, experience in working with different models to solve problems of diverse domains

So, assuming that the model selection is done, what are the different avenues to improve the performance of models?

One effective way to improve model performance is by tuning model parameters. **Model parameter tuning** is the process of adjusting the model fitting options. For example, in the popular classification model k-Nearest Neighbour (kNN), using different values of 'k' or the number of nearest neighbors to be considered, the model can be tuned. In the same way, several hidden layers can be adjusted to tune the performance in the neural networks model. Most machine learning models have at least one parameter which can be tuned.

As an alternate approach to increasing the performance of one model, several models may be combined. The models in such combination are complimentary to each other, i.e. one model may learn one type of data set well while struggling with another type of data set. Another model may perform well with the data set that the first one struggled with. This approach of combining different models with diverse strengths is known as an **ensemble** (depicted in Figure 3.11). Ensemble helps in averaging out biases of the different underlying models and also reducing the variance. Ensemble methods combine weaker learners to create stronger ones. A performance boost can be expected even if models are built as usual and then ensembled. Following are the typical steps in the ensemble process:

- Build a number of models based on the training data
- For diversifying the models generated, the training data subset can be varied using the <u>allocation function</u>. Sampling techniques like bootstrapping may be used to generate unique training data sets.
- Alternatively, the same training data may be used but the models combined are quite varying, e.g, SVM, neural network, kNN, etc.
- The outputs from the different models are combined using a <u>combination function</u>. A very simple strategy of combining, say in the case of a prediction task using an ensemble, can be majority voting of the different models combined. For example, 3 out of 5 classes predict 'win' and 2 predict 'loss' – then the outcome of the ensemble using a majority vote would be a 'win'.

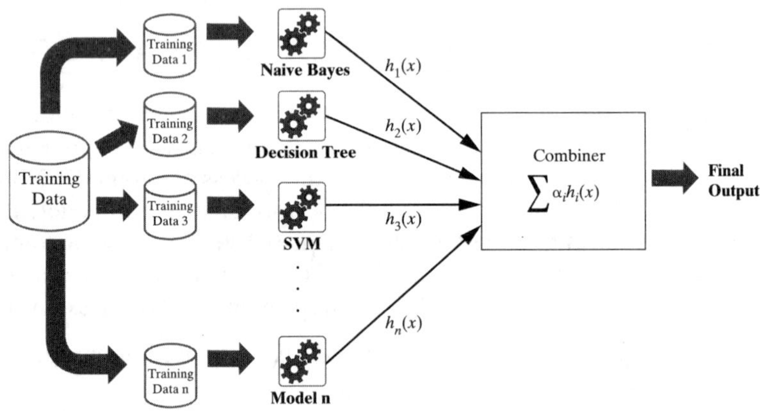

FIG. 3.12
Ensemble

One of the earliest and most popular ensemble models is **bootstrap aggregating** or **bagging**. Bagging uses the bootstrap sampling method (refer to section 3.3.3) to generate multiple training data sets. These training data sets are used to generate (or train) a set of models using the same learning algorithm. Then the outcomes of the models are combined by majority voting (classification) or by average (regression). Bagging is a very simple ensemble technique that can perform well for unstable learners like a decision tree, in which a slight change in data can impact the outcome of a model significantly.

Just like bagging, **boosting** is another key ensemble-based technique. In this type of ensemble, weaker learning models are trained on resampled data, and the outcomes are combined using a weighted voting approach based on the performance of different models. **Adaptive boosting** or **AdaBoost** is a special variant of boosting algorithm. It is based on the idea of generating weak learners and slowly learning

Random forest is another ensemble-based technique. It is an ensemble of decision trees – hence the name random forest to indicate a forest of decision trees. It has been discussed in more detail in chapter 7.

In this chapter, you have been introduced to the crux of machine learning, i.e. modeling. A thorough understanding of the technical aspects elaborated in this chapter is extremely crucial for the success of any machine learning project. For example, the first dilemma comes about which model to select. Again, in the case of supervised learning, how can we deal with the unavailability of sufficient training data? In the same way, once the model is trained in the case of supervised learning or the grouping is done in the case of clustering, how we can understand whether the model training (for supervised) or grouping done (for unsupervised) is good or bad? All these and more have been addressed as a part of this chapter.

3.7   SUMMARY

- Structured representation of raw input data to the meaningful pattern is called a model.
- The process of fitting a specific model to a data set is called model training.
- Models for supervised learning or predictive models try to predict certain values using the input data set.
- Models for unsupervised learning or descriptive models are used to describe a data set or gain insight from a data set.
- The method of partitioning the input data into two parts – training and test data, which is holding back a part of the input data for validating the trained model is known as the holdout method.
- In the k-fold cross-validation technique, the data set is divided into k- completely separate random partitions called folds. It is repeated holdout into 'k' folds. The value of 'k' in k-fold cross-validation can be set to any number. Two extremely popular approaches are:
  ❖ 10-fold cross-validation (10-fold CV)

  ❖ Leave-one-out cross-validation (LOOCV)

- Bootstrap sampling or simply bootstrapping is a popular way to identify training and test data sets from the input data set. It uses the technique of Simple Random Sampling with Replacement (SRSWR). Bootstrapping randomly picks data instances from the input data set, with the possibility of the same data instance being picked multiple times.

- The target function of a model is the function defining the relationship between the input (also called predictor or independent) variables and the output (also called response or dependent or target) variable. It is represented in the general form: $Y = f(X) + e$, where Y is the output variable, X represents the input variables and 'e' is a random error term.

- The fitness of a target function approximated by a learning algorithm determines how correctly it can predict the value or class for a set of data it has never seen.

- If the target function is kept too simple, it may not be able to capture the essential nuances and represent the underlying data well. This is known as underfitting.

- Overfitting refers to a situation where the model has been designed in such a way that it emulates the training data too closely. In such a case, any specific nuance in the training data, like noise or outliers, gets embedded in the model. It adversely impacts the performance of the model on the test data.

- In supervised learning, the value predicted by the learning model built based on the training data may differ from the actual class value. This error in learning can be of two types – errors due to 'bias' and errors due to 'variance'. Errors due to bias arise from simplifying assumptions made by the model whereas errors due to variance occur from over-aligning the model with the training data sets.

- For any classification model, model accuracy is the primary indicator of the goodness of the model. It is given by a total number of correct classifications (either as the class of interest, or as not the class of interest) divided by a total number of classifications done. There are other indicators like error rate, sensitivity, specificity, precision, and recall.

- For unsupervised learning (clustering), silhouette coefficient (or width) is one of the most popular internal evaluation methods. A high value of silhouette width indicates high intra-cluster homogeneity and inter-cluster heterogeneity. In case, a class label is known for the data set, purity is another popular measure that evaluates the extent to which clusters contain a single class.

- Model parameter tuning is the process of adjusting the model fitting options. For example, in the popular classification model k-Nearest Neighbour (kNN), using different values of 'k' or the number of nearest neighbors to be considered, the model can be tuned.

- The approach of combining different models with diverse strengths is known as an ensemble. Ensemble methods combine weaker learners to create stronger ones.

- One of the earliest and most popular ensemble models is bootstrap aggregating or bagging. Bagging uses bootstrapping to generate multiple training data sets. These training data sets are used to generate a set of models using the same learning algorithm.

- Just like bagging, boosting is another key ensemble-based technique. In boosting, weaker learning models are trained on resampled data, and the outcomes are combined using a weighted voting approach based on the performance of different models.

- Adaptive boosting or AdaBoost is a special variant of the boosting algorithm.

SAMPLE QUESTIONS

MULTIPLE-CHOICE QUESTIONS (1 MARK QUESTIONS):

1.   Structured representation of raw input data to meaningful ___ is called a model.
     (a) pattern   (b) data
     (c) object   (d) none of the above

2.   For supervised learning we have ____ model.
     (a) interactive   (b) predictive
     (c) descriptive   (d) prescriptive

3.   For unsupervised learning we have ____ model.
     (a) interactive   (b) predictive
     (c) descriptive   (d) prescriptive

4.   Which of the following measures is not used for a classification model?
     (a) Accuracy   (b) Recall
     (c) Purity   (d) Error rate

5.   Which of the following is a performance measure for regression?
     (a) Accuracy   (c) RMSE
     (b) Recall   (d) Error rate

6.   Which of the following is the measure of cluster quality?
     (a) Purity   (b) Distance
     (c) Accuracy   (d) all of the above

7.   Out of 200 emails, a classification model correctly predicted 150 spam emails and 30 ham emails. What is the accuracy of the model?
     (a) 10%   (b) 90%
     (c) 80%   (d) none of the above

8.   Out of 200 emails, a classification model correctly predicted 150 spam emails and 30 ham emails. What is the error rate of the model?
     (a) 10%   (b) 90%
     (c) 80%   (d) none of the above

9.   There is no one model that works best for every machine learning problem. This is stated as
     (a) Fit gap model theorem   (b) One model theorem
     (c) Free lunch theorem   (d) No free lunch theorem

10. LOOCV in machine learning stands for
    (a) Love one-out cross-validation
    (b) Leave-one-out cross-validation
    (c) Leave-object oriented cross-validation
    (d) Leave-one-out class-validation

SHORT-ANSWER TYPE QUESTIONS (5 MARKS QUESTIONS):

1. What is a model in the context of machine learning? How can you train a model?

2. Explain the "No Free Lunch" theorem in the context of machine learning.

3. Explain, in detail, the process of K-fold cross-validation.

4. Explain the bootstrap sampling. Why is it needed?

5. Why do we need to calculate the Kappa value for a classification model? Show, with a sample set of data, how to calculate the Kappa value of a classification model.

6. Explain the process of an ensemble of models. What role does it play in machine learning?

7. What is the main purpose of a descriptive model? State some real-world problems solved using descriptive models.

8. Explain the process of evaluating a linear regression model.

9. Differentiate (any <u>two</u>):
   - Predictive vs. descriptive models
   - Model underfitting vs. overfitting
   - Cross-validation vs. bootstrapping

10. Write short notes on any <u>two</u>:
    (a) LOOCV
    (b) F-measure
    (c) Silhouette width
    (d) ROC curve

LONG-ANSWER TYPE QUESTIONS (10 MARKS QUESTIONS):

1. What is a target function? Express target function in the context of a real-life example. How is the fitness of a target function measured?

2. What are predictive models? What are descriptive models? Give examples of both types of models. Explain the difference between these types of models.

3. Explain, in detail, the process of evaluating the performance of a classification model. Explain the different parameters of measurement.

4. (a) What is underfitting in the context of machine learning models? What is the major cause of underfitting?
   (b) What is overfitting? When does it happen?
   (c) Explain bias-variance trade-off in context of model fitting.

5. Can the performance of a learning model be improved? If yes, explain how.

6. How would you evaluate the success of an unsupervised learning model? What are the most popular measures of performance for an unsupervised learning model?

7. Is there a way to use a classification model for numerical data or a regression model on a categorical data? Explain your answer.

8. Describe the process of predictive modeling for numerical values. How is it different from predictive modeling for categorical values?

9. While predicting the malignancy of the tumor of a set of patients using a classification model, the following are the data recorded:
(a) Correct predictions – 15 malignant, 75 benign
(b) Incorrect predictions – 3 malignant, 7 benign
Calculate the error rate, Kappa value, sensitivity, precision, and *F*-measure of the model.

10. (a) Write short notes on any <u>two</u>:
    (i) Holdout method
    (ii) 10-fold cross-validation
    (iii) Parameter tuning
(b) Write the difference between (any <u>two</u>):
    (i) Purity vs. Silhouette width
    (ii) Bagging vs. Boosting
    (iii) Lazy vs. Eager learner

Chapter 4

Basics of Feature Engineering

OBJECTIVE OF THE CHAPTER:

In the last three chapters, you have been introduced to the basic concepts of machine learning. Also, the process to start modelling a problem has also been discussed in details. With this context in mind, in this chapter, we will introduce you to another very important aspect of machine learning, that is feature engineering. Though not a core part of the machine learning processes, feature engineering is a critical allied task that we need to perform to make learning more effective. It has three key components - feature construction, feature selection, and feature transformation, each of which will be covered in details in this chapter.

4.1   INTRODUCTION

In the last three chapters, we had a jumpstart to the machine learning process. We first started with what human learning is and how the different types of machine learning emulate the aspects of human learning. We had a detailed view of the different types of problem that can be solved using machine learning techniques. Before applying machine learning to solve the problems, there are certain preparatory steps. These preparatory steps have been covered in details. After that, we have done a step-by-step navigation of the different activities of modelling a problem using machine learning. Modelling alone doesn't help us to realize the effectiveness of machine learning as a problem- solving tool. So we also learnt how to measure the effectiveness of machine learning models in solving problems. In case a specific model is not effective, we can use different levers to boost the effectiveness. Those levers of boosting the model performance were also covered.

Now that we are ready (well almost ready!) to start solving problems using machine learning, we need to touch upon another key aspect which plays a critical role in solving any machine learning problem - feature engineering. Though feature engineering is a part of the preparatory activities which have already been covered in Chapter 2, the criticality and vastness of the area call for treating it separately. This area deals with features of the data set, which form an important input of any machine learning problem - be supervised or unsupervised learning. Feature engineering is a critical preparatory process in machine learning. It is responsible for taking raw input data and converting that to well-aligned features which are ready to be used by the machine learning models.

But before we start discussing feature engineering, let's try to understand more clearly what feature is.

Did you know?

Unstructured data is raw, unorganized data which doesn't follow a specific format or hierarchy. Typical examples of unstructured data include text data from social networks, e.g. Twitter, Facebook, etc. or data from server logs, etc.

 ## 4.1.1   What is a feature?

A feature is an attribute of a data set that is used in a machine learning process. There is a view amongst certain machine learning practitioners that only those attributes which are meaningful to a machine learning problem are to be called as features, but this view has to be taken with a pinch of salt. In fact, selection of the subset of features which are meaningful for machine learning is a sub-area of feature engineering which draws a lot of research interest. The features in a data set are also called its dimensions. So a data set having '*n*' features is called an n-dimensional data set.

Let's take the example of a famous machine learning data set, Iris, introduced by the British statistician and biologist Ronald Fisher, partly shown in Figure 4.1. It has five attributes or features namely Sepal.Length, Sepal.Width, Petal.Length, Petal. Width and Species. Out of these, the feature 'Species' represent the class variable and the remaining features are the predictor variables. It is a five-dimensional data set.

Sepal.Length	Sepal.Width	Petal.Length	Petal.Width	Species
6.7	3.3	5.7	2.5	Virginica
4.9	3	1.4	0.2	Setosa
5.5	2.6	4.4	1.2	Versicolor
6.8	3.2	5.9	2.3	Virginica
5.5	2.5	4	1.3	Versicolor
5.1	3.5	1.4	0.2	Setosa
6.1	3	4.6	1.4	versicolor

FIG. 4.1
Data set features

4.1.2   What is feature engineering?

Feature engineering refers to the process of translating a data set into features such that these features are able to represent the data set more effectively and result in a better learning performance.

As we know already, feature engineering is an important pre-processing step for machine learning. It has two major elements:

1. feature transformation
2. feature subset selection

Feature transformation transforms the data - structured or unstructured, into a new set of features which can represent the underlying problem which machine learning is trying to solve. There are two variants of feature transformation:

1. feature construction
2. feature extraction

Both are sometimes known as <u>feature discovery</u>.

Feature construction   process discovers missing information about the relationships between features and augments the feature space by creating additional features. Hence, if there are 'n' features or dimensions in a data set, after feature construction 'm' more features or dimensions may get added. So at the end, the data set will become '$n + m$' dimensional.

Feature extraction   is the process of extracting or creating a new set of features from the original set of features using some functional mapping.

Unlike feature transformation, in case of **feature subset selection** (or simply **feature selection**) no new feature is generated. The objective of feature selection is to derive a subset of features from the full feature set which is most meaningful in the context of a specific machine learning problem. So, essentially the job of feature selection is to derive a subset F_j $(F_1, F_2, ..., F_m)$ of F_i $(F_1, F_2, ..., F_n)$, where $m < n$, such that F_j is most meaningful and gets the best result for a machine learning problem. We will discuss these concepts in detail in the next section.

Points to Ponder:

Data scientists and machine learning practitioners spend significant amount of time in different feature engineering activities. Selecting the right features has a critical role to play in the success of a machine learning model.

It is quite evident that feature construction expands the feature space, while feature extraction and feature selection reduces the feature space.

4.2   FEATURE TRANSFORMATION

Engineering a good feature space is a crucial prerequisite for the success of any machine learning model. However, often it is not clear which feature is more important. For that reason, all available attributes of the data set are used as features and the problem of identifying the important features is left to the learning model. This is definitely not a feasible approach, particularly for certain domains e.g. medical image classification, text categorization, etc. In case a model has to be trained to classify a document as spam or non-spam, we can represent a document as a bag of words. Then the feature space will contain all unique words occurring across all documents. This will easily be a feature space of a few hundred thousand features. If we start including bigrams or trigrams along with words, the count of features will run in millions. To deal with this problem, feature transformation comes into play. Feature transformation is used as an effective tool for dimensionality reduction and hence for boosting learning model performance. Broadly, there are two distinct goals of feature transformation:

- Achieving best reconstruction of the original features in the data set
- Achieving highest efficiency in the learning task

Did you know?

In the field of natural language processing, 'n-gram' is a contiguous set of n items for example words in a text block or document. Using numerical prefixes, n-gram of size 1 is called unigram (i.e. a single word), size 2 is called bigram (i.e. a two-word phrase), size 3 is called trigram (i.e. a three-word phrase) etc.

4.2.1   Feature construction

Feature construction involves transforming a given set of input features to generate a new set of more powerful features. To understand more clearly, let's take the example of a real estate data set having details of all apartments sold in a specific region.

The data set has three features - apartment length, apartment breadth, and price of the apartment. If it is used as an input to a regression problem, such data can be training data for the regression model. So given the training data, the model should be able to predict the price of an apartment whose price is not known or which has just come up for sale. However, instead of using length and breadth of the apartment as a predictor, it is much convenient and makes more sense to use the area of the apartment, which is not an existing feature of the data set. So such a feature, namely apartment area, can be added to the data set. In other words, we transform the three-dimensional data set to a four-dimensional data set, with the newly 'discovered' feature apartment area being added to the original data set. This is depicted in Figure 4.2.

apartment_length	apartment_breadth	apartment_price
80	59	23,60,000
54	45	12,15,000
78	56	21,84,000
63	63	19,84,000
83	74	30,71,000
92	86	39,56,000

apartment_length	apartment_breadth	apartment_area	apartment_price
80	59	4,720	23,60,000
54	45	2,430	12,15,000
78	56	4,368	21,84,000
63	63	3,969	19,84,000
83	74	6,142	30,71,000
92	86	7,912	39,56,000

FIG. 4.2

Feature construction (example 1)

Note: Though for the sake of simplicity the features apartment length and apartment breadth have been retained in Figure 4.2, in reality, it makes more sense to exclude these features when building the model.

There are certain situations where feature construction is an essential activity before we can start with the machine learning task. These situations are

- when features have categorical value and machine learning needs numeric value inputs
- when features having numeric (continuous) values and need to be converted to ordinal values
- when text-specific feature construction needs to be done

4.2.1.1   Encoding categorical (nominal) variables

Let's take the example of another data set on athletes, as presented in Figure 4.3a. Say the data set has features age, city of origin, parents athlete (i.e. indicate whether any one of the parents was an athlete) and Chance of Win. The feature chance of a win is a class variable while the others are predictor variables. We know that any machine learning algorithm, whether it's a classification algorithm (like kNN) or a regression algorithm, requires numerical figures to learn from. So there are three features - City of origin, Parents athlete, and Chance of win, which are categorical in nature and cannot be used by any machine learning task.

In this case, feature construction can be used to create new dummy features which are usable by machine learning algorithms. Since the feature 'City of origin' has three unique values namely City A, City B, and City C, three dummy features namely origin_ city_A, origin_city_B, and origin_city_C is created. In the same way, dummy features parents_athlete_Y and parents_athlete_N are created for feature 'Parents athlete' and win_chance_Y and win_chance_N are created for feature 'Chance of win'. The dummy features have value 0 or 1 based on the categorical value for the original feature in that row. For example, the second row had a categorical value 'City B' for the feature 'City of origin. So, the newly created features in place of 'City of origin', i.e. origin_city_A, origin_city_B and origin_city_C will have values 0, 1 and 0, respectively. In the same way, parents_athlete_Y and parents_athlete_N will have values 0 and 1, respectively in row 2 as the original feature 'Parents athlete' had a categorical value 'No' in row 2. The entire set of transformation for athletes' data set is shown in Figure 4.3b.

Age (Years)	City of origin	Parents athlete	Chance of win
18	City A	Yes	Y
20	City B	No	Y
23	City B	Yes	Y
19	City A	No	N
18	City C	Yes	N
22	City B	Yes	Y

Age (Years)	origin_city_A	origin.city_B	origin_city_C	parents_athlete_Y	parents_athlete_N	win_chance_Y	win_chance_N
18	1	0	0	1	0	1	0
20	0	1	0	0	1	1	0
23	0	1	0	1	0	1	0
19	1	0	0	0	1	0	1
18	0	0	1	1	0	0	1
22	0	1	0	1	0	1	0

Age (Years)	origin_city_A	origin_city_B	origin_city_C	parents_athlete_Y	win_chance_Y
18	1	0	0	1	1
20	0	1	0	0	1
23	0	1	0	1	1
19	1	0	0	0	0
18	0	0	1	1	0
22	0	1	0	1	1

FIG. 4.3

Feature construction (encoding nominal variables)

However, examining closely, we see that the features 'Parents athlete' and 'Chance of win' in the original data set can have two values only. So creating two features from them is a kind of duplication, since the value of one feature can be decided from the value of the other. To avoid this duplication, we can just leave one feature and eliminate the other, as shown in Figure 4.3c.

4.2.1.2   Encoding categorical (ordinal) variables

Let's take an example of a student data set. Let's assume that there are three variable - science marks, maths marks and grade as shown in Figure 4.4a. As we can see, the grade is an ordinal variable with values A, B, C, and D. To transform this variable to a numeric variable, we can create a feature num_grade mapping a numeric value against each ordinal value. In the context of the current example, grades A, B, C, and D in Figure 4.4a is mapped to values 1, 2, 3, and 4 in the transformed variable shown in Figure 4.4b.

marks_science	marks_maths	Grade
78	75	B
56	62	C
87	90	A
91	95	A
45	42	D
62	57	B

(a)

marks_science	marks_maths	num_grade
78	75	2
56	62	3
87	90	1
91	95	1
45	42	4
62	57	2

(b)

FIG. 4.4
Feature construction (example 1)

4.2.1.3   Transforming numeric (continuous) features to categorical features

Sometimes there is a need of transforming a continuous numerical variable into a categorical variable. For example, we may want to treat the real estate price prediction problem, which is a regression problem, as a real estate price category prediction, which is a classification problem. In that case, we can 'bin' the numerical data into multiple categories based on the data range. In the context of the real estate price prediction example, the original data set has a numerical feature apartment_price as shown in Figure 4.5a. It can be transformed to a categorical variable price-grade either as shown in Figure 4.5b or as shown in Figure 4.5c.

4.2.1.4   Text-specific feature construction

In the current world, text is arguably the most predominant medium of communication. Whether we think about social networks like Facebook or micro-blogging channels like Twitter or emails or short messaging services such as Whatsapp, text plays a major role in the flow of information. Hence, text mining is an important area of research - not only for technology practitioners but also for industry practitioners. However, making sense of text data, due to the inherent unstructured nature of the data, is not

apartment_ area	apartment_ price
4,720	23,60,000
2,430	12,15,000
4,368	21,84,000
3,969	19,84,500
6,142	30,71,000
7,912	39,56,000

(a)

apartment_ area	apartment_ grade
4,720	Medium
2,430	Low
4,368	Medium
3,969	Low
6,142	High
7,912	High

(b)

apartment_ area	apartment_ grade
4,720	2
2,430	1
4,368	2
3,969	1
6,142	3
7,912	3

(c)

FIG. 4.5
Feature construction (numeric to categorical)

so straightforward. In the first place, the text data chunks that we can think about do not have readily available features, like structured data sets, on which machine learning tasks can be executed. All machine learning models need numerical data as input. So the text data in the data sets need to be transformed into numerical features.

Text data, or corpus which is the more popular keyword, is converted to a numerical representation following a process is known as vectorization. In this process, word occurrences in all documents belonging to the corpus are consolidated in the form of bag-of-words. There are three major steps that are followed:

1. tokenize
2. count
3. normalize

In order to tokenize a corpus, the blank spaces and punctuations are used as delimiters to separate out the words, or tokens. Then the number of occurrences of each token is counted, for each document. Lastly, tokens are weighted with reducing importance when they occur in the majority of the documents. A matrix is then formed with each token representing a column and a specific document of the corpus representing each row. Each cell contains the count of occurrence of the token in a specific document. This matrix is known as a document-term matrix (also known as a term-document matrix). Figure 4.6 represents a typical document-term matrix which forms an input to a machine learning model.

This	House	Build	Feeling	Well	Theatre	Movie	Good	Lonely	...
2	1	1	0	0	1	1	1	0	
0	0	0	1	1	0	0	0	0	
1	0	0	2	1	1	0	0	1	
0	0	0	0	1	0	1	1	0	
.	.	.	.	.	.	.	.	.	
.	.	.	.	.	.	.	.	.	
.	.	.	.	.	.	.	.	.	

FIG. 4.6
Feature construction (text-specific)

For doing feature construction, we can use *pandas* library of Python. Following is a small code for implementing feature construction.

```
>>> import pandas as pd

>>> room_length = [18, 20, 10, 12, 18, 11]
>>> room_breadth = [20, 20, 10, 11, 19, 10]
>>> room_type = ['Big', 'Big', 'Normal', 'Normal', 'Big', 'Normal']
>>> data = pd.DataFrame({'Length': room_length, 'Breadth': room_breadth, 'Type': room_type})
>>> data

    Breadth   Length      Type
0        20       18       Big
1        20       20       Big
2        10       10    Normal
3        11       12    Normal
4        19       18       Big
5        10       11    Normal

>>> data['Area'] = data['Length']*data['Breadth']
>>> data

    Breadth   Length      Type    Area
0        20       18       Big     360
1        20       20       Big     400
2        10       10    Normal     100
3        11       12    Normal     132
4        19       18       Big     342
5        10       11    Normal     110
```

B.4.1.1 Dummy coding categorical (nominal) variables:

get_dummies function of **pandas** library can be used to dummy code categorical variables. Following is a sample code for the same.

```
>>> import pandas as pd

>>> age = [18, 20, 23, 19, 18, 22]
>>> city = ['City A', 'City B', 'City B', 'City A', 'City C', 'City B']
>>> data = pd.DataFrame({'age': age, 'city': city})
>>> data

    age    city
0   18   City A
1   20   City B
2   23   City B
3   19   City A
4   18   City C
5   22   City B

>>> dummy_features = pd.get_dummies(data['city'])
>>> data_age = pd.DataFrame(data = data, columns = ['age'])
>>> data_mod = pd.concat([data_age.reset_index(drop=True), dummy_features], axis=1)
>>> data_mod

    age  City A  City B  City C
0   18      1       0       0
1   20      0       1       0
2   23      0       1       0
3   19      1       0       0
4   18      0       0       1
5   22      0       1       0
```

B.4.1.2 Encoding categorical (ordinal) variables:

LabelEncoder function of **sklearn. preprocessing** library can be used to encode categorical variables. Following is a sample code for the same.

```
>>> import pandas as pd
>>> from sklearn import preprocessing

>>> marks_science = [78,56,87,91,45,62]
>>> marks_maths = [75,62,90,95,42,57]
>>> grade = ['B','C','A','A','D','B']
>>> data = pd.DataFrame({'Science marks': marks_science, 'Maths marks': marks_maths, 'Total grade': grade})
>>> data
```

```
   Maths marks  Science marks Total grade
0            75             78           B
1            62             56           C
2            90             87           A
3            95             91           A
4            42             45           D
5            57             62           B
```

```
# Option 1
>>> le = preprocessing.LabelEncoder()
>>> le.fit(data['Total grade'])
>>> data['Total grade'] = le.transform(data['Total grade'])
>>> data
```

```
   Maths marks  Science marks  Total grade
0            75             78            1
1            62             56            2
2            90             87            0
3            95             91            0
4            42             45            3
5            57             62            1
```

```
# Option 2
>>>  target  =  data['Total  grade'].replace(['A','B','C'
,'D'],[0,1,2,3])
>>> predictors = data.iloc[:, 0:2]
>>> data_mod = pd.concat([predictors.reset_index(drop=True), tar-
get], axis=1)
```

B.4.1.3 *Transforming numeric (continuous) features to categorical features:*

```
>>> import pandas as pd

>>> apartment_area = [4720, 2430, 4368, 3969, 6142, 7912]
>>> apartment_price = [2360000,1215000,2184000,1984500,3071000,3
956000]
>>> data = pd.DataFrame({'Area': apartment_area,  'Price':
apartment_price})
>>> data
```

```
   Area     Price
0  4720  2360000
1  2430  1215000
2  4368  2184000
3  3969  1984500
4  6142  3071000
5  7912  3956000
```

```
>>> data ['Price'] = np.where(data['Price'] > 3000000, 'High',
np.where(data['Price'] < 2000000, 'Low', 'Medium'))
>>> data
```

```
     Area    Price
0    4720   Medium
1    2430      Low
2    4368   Medium
3    3969      Low
4    6142     High
5    7912     High
```

4.2.2   Feature extraction

In feature extraction, new features are created from a combination of original features. Some of the commonly used operators for combining the original features include

1. For Boolean features: Conjunctions, Disjunctions, Negation, etc.
2. For nominal features: Cartesian product, M of N, etc.
3. For numerical features: Min, Max, Addition, Subtraction, Multiplication, Division, Average, Equivalence, Inequality, etc.

Let's take an example and try to understand. Say, we have a data set with a feature set F_i $(F_1, F_2, ..., F_n)$. After feature extraction using a mapping function f $(F_1, F_2, ..., F_n)$ say, we will have a set of features $\acute{F_i}(\acute{F_1}, \acute{F_2}, ..., \acute{F_m})$ such that $\acute{F_i} = f(F_i)$ and $m < n$. For example, $F_1 = k_1 F_1 + k_2 F_2$. This is depicted in Figure 4.7.

Feat$_A$	Feat$_B$	Feat$_C$	Feat$_D$		Feat$_1$	Feat$_2$
34	34.5	23	233		41.25	185.80
44	45.56	11	3.44		54.20	53.12
78	22.59	21	4.5	$\rightarrow$	43.73	35.79
22	65.22	11	322.3		65.30	264.10
22	33.8	355	45.2		37.02	238.42
11	122.32	63	23.2		113.39	167.74

$$\text{Feat}_1 = 0.3 \times \text{Feat}_A + 0.9 \times \text{Feat}_A$$
$$\text{Feat}_2 = \text{Feat}_A + 0.5\,\text{Feat}_B + 0.6 \times \text{Feat}_C$$

FIG. 4.7
Feature extraction

Let's discuss the most popular feature extraction algorithms used in machine learning:

4.2.2.1 Principal Component Analysis

Every data set, as we have seen, has multiple attributes or dimensions - many of which might have similarity with each other. For example, the height and weight of a person, in general, are quite related. If the height is more, generally weight is more and vice versa. So if a data set has height and weight as two of the attributes, obviously they are expected to be having quite a bit of similarity. In general, any machine learning algorithm performs better as the number of related attributes or features reduced. In other words, a key to the success of machine learning lies in the fact that the features are less in number as well as the similarity between each other is very less. This is the main guiding philosophy of principal component analysis (PCA) technique of feature extraction.

In PCA, a new set of features are extracted from the original features which are quite dissimilar in nature. So an n-dimensional feature space gets transformed to an m-dimensional feature space, where the dimensions are orthogonal to each other, i.e. completely independent of each other. To understand the concept of orthogonality, we have to step back and do a bit of dip dive into vector space concept in linear algebra.

We all know that a vector is a quantity having both magnitude and direction and hence can determine the position of a point relative to another point in the Euclidean space (i.e. a two or three or 'n' dimensional space). A vector space is a set of vectors. Vector spaces have a property that they can be represented as a linear combination of a smaller set of vectors, called basis vectors. So, any vector 'v' in a vector space can be represented as

$$v = \sum_{i=1}^{n} a_i u_i$$

where, ai represents 'n' scalars and u_i represents the basis vectors. Basis vectors are orthogonal to each other. Orthogonality of vectors in n-dimensional vector space can be thought of an extension of the vectors being perpendicular in a two-dimensional vector space. Two orthogonal vectors are completely unrelated or independent of each other. So the transformation of a set of vectors to the corresponding set of basis vectors such that each vector in the original set can be expressed as a linear combination of basis vectors helps in decomposing the vectors to a number of independent components.

Now, let's extend this notion to the feature space of a data set. The feature vector can be transformed to a vector space of the basis vectors which are termed as principal components. These principal components, just like the basis vectors, are orthogonal to each other. So a set of feature vectors which may have similarity with each other is transformed to a set of principal components which are completely unrelated. However, the principal components capture the variability of the original feature space. Also, the number of principal component derived, much like the basis vectors, is much smaller than the original set of features.

The objective of PCA is to make the transformation in such a way that

1. The new features are distinct, i.e. the covariance between the new features, i. e. the principal components is 0.
2. The principal components are generated in order of the variability in the data that it captures. Hence, the first principal component should capture the maximum variability, the second principal component should capture the next highest variability etc.
3. The sum of variance of the new features or the principal components should be equal to the sum of variance of the original features.

PCA works based on a process called eigenvalue decomposition of a covariance matrix of a data set. Below are the steps to be followed:

1. First, calculate the covariance matrix of a data set.
2. Then, calculate the eigenvalues of the covariance matrix.
3. The eigenvector having highest eigenvalue represents the direction in which there is the highest variance. So this will help in identifying the first principal component.
4. The eigenvector having the next highest eigenvalue represents the direction in which data has the highest remaining variance and also orthogonal to the first direction. So this helps in identifying the second principal component.
5. Like this, identify the top 'k' eigenvectors having top 'k' eigenvalues so as to get the 'k' principal components.

For doing principal component analysis or in other words – to get the principal components of a set of features in a data set, we can use *PCA* function of ***sklearn. decomposition*** library. However, features should be standardized (i.e. transform to unit scale with mean = 0 and variance = 1), for which *StandardScaler* function of ***sklearn.preprocessing*** library can be used. Following is the code using the iris data set. PCA should be applied on the predictors. The target / class variable can be used to visualize the principal components (Figure 4.8).

```
>>> import pandas as pd
>>> import matplotlib.pyplot as plt
>>> from sklearn import datasets
>>> from sklearn.decomposition import PCA
>>> from sklearn.preprocessing import StandardScaler

>>> iris = datasets.load_iris()
>>> predictors = iris.data[:, 0:4]
>>> target = iris.target

>>> predictors = StandardScaler().fit_transform(predictors) #
Standardizing the features
>>> pca = PCA(n_components=2)
```

```
>>> princomp = pca.fit_transform(predictors)
>>> princomp_ds = pd.DataFrame(data = princomp, columns = ['PC 1',
'PC 2'])
>>> princomp_ds

        PC 1        PC 2
0    -2.264542   0.505704
1    -2.086426  -0.655405
2    -2.367950  -0.318477
3    -2.304197  -0.575368
4    -2.388777   0.674767
5    -2.070537   1.518549
6    -2.445711   0.074563
  .         .           .

  .         .           .

  .         .           .

>>> target_ds = pd.DataFrame(data = target, columns = ['class'])

>>> data_mod = pd.concat([princomp_ds.reset_index(drop=True), tar-
get_ds], axis=1)

>>> fig = plt.figure(figsize = (8,8))
>>> pca_plot = fig.add_subplot(1,1,1)
>>> pca_plot.set_xlabel('PC1')
>>> pca_plot.set_ylabel('PC2')
>>> pca_plot.set_title('PCA (2 component)', fontsize = 20)

>>> classes = [0, 1, 2]
>>> colors = ['y', 'r', 'b']
>>> for target, color in zip(classes,colors):
    indices = data_mod['class'] == target
    pca_plot.scatter(data_mod.loc[indices, 'PC 1']
                , data_mod.loc[indices, 'PC 2']
                , c = color
                , s = 50)
>>> legends = ['Setosa', 'Versicolor', 'Virginica']
>>> pca_plot.legend(legends)
```

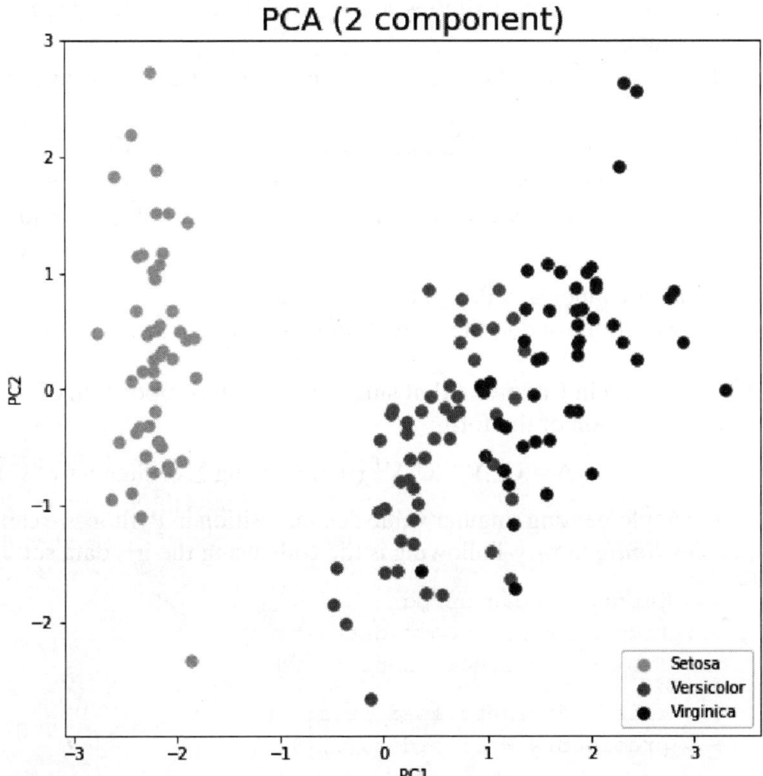

FIG. 4.8
Principal components of iris data set

4.2.2.2 Singular value decomposition

Singular value decomposition (SVD) is a matrix factorization technique commonly used in linear algebra. SVD of a matrix A ($m \times n$) is a factorization of the form:

$$A = U\sum V$$

where, U and V are orthonormal matrices, U is an $m \times m$ unitary matrix, V is an n $\times$ n unitary matrix and Σ is an $m \times n$ rectangular diagonal matrix. The diagonal entries of Σ are known as singular values of matrix A. The columns of U and V are called the left-singular and right-singular vectors of matrix A, respectively.

SVD is generally used in PCA, once the mean of each variable has been removed. Since it is not always advisable to remove the mean of a data attribute, especially when the data set is sparse (as in case of text data), SVD is a good choice for dimensionality reduction in those situations.

SVD of a data matrix is expected to have the properties highlighted below:

1. Patterns in the attributes are captured by the right-singular vectors, i.e. the columns of V.

2. Patterns among the instances are captured by the left-singular, i.e. the columns of U.

3. Larger a singular value, larger is the part of the matrix A that it accounts for and its associated vectors.

4. New data matrix with 'k' attributes is obtained using the equation

$$D' = D \times [v_1, v_2, \ldots, v_k]$$

Thus, the dimensionality gets reduced to k

SVD is often used in the context of text data.

We have seen in Chapter 4 that singular value decomposition of a matrix A (m X n) is a factorization of the form:

$$A = U\Sigma V = UsV^T \text{ (representing } \Sigma \text{ or Sigma by "s")}$$

For implementing singular value decomposition in Python, we can use *svd* function of ***scipy.linalg*** library. Following is the code using the iris data set.

```
>>> import pandas as pd
>>> from sklearn import datasets
>>> from scipy.linalg import svd

>>> iris = datasets.load_iris()
>>> predictors = iris.data[:, 0:4]

>>> U, s, VT = svd(predictors)
>>> print(U)
[[ -6.16171172e-02     1.29969428e-01     -5.58364155e-05  ...,
-9.34637342e-02
    -9.60224157e-02  -8.09922905e-02]
 [ -5.80722977e-02     1.11371452e-01      6.84386629e-02  ...,
3.66755322e-02
    -3.24463474e-02   1.27273399e-02]
 [ -5.67633852e-02     1.18294769e-01      2.31062793e-03  ...,
3.08252776e-02
     1.95234663e-01   1.35567696e-01]
  ...,
 [ -9.40702260e-02     -4.98348018e-02     -4.14958083e-02  ...,
9.81822841e-01
    -2.17978813e-02  -8.85972146e-03]
 [ -9.48993908e-02     -5.62107520e-02     -2.12386574e-01  ...,
-2.14264126e-02
     9.42038920e-01  -2.96933496e-02]
 [ -8.84882764e-02     -5.16210172e-02     -9.51442925e-02  ...,
-8.52768485e-03
    -3.02139863e-02   9.73577349e-01]]
```

```
>>> print(s)

[ 95.95066751    17.72295328    3.46929666    1.87891236]

>>> print(VT)

[[-0.75116805  -0.37978837  -0.51315094  -0.16787934]
 [ 0.28583096   0.54488976  -0.70889874  -0.34475845]
 [ 0.49942378  -0.67502499  -0.05471983  -0.54029889]
 [ 0.32345496  -0.32124324  -0.48077482   0.74902286]]
```

4.2.2.3 *Linear Discriminant Analysis*

Linear discriminant analysis (LDA) is another commonly used feature extraction technique like PCA or SVD. The objective of LDA is similar to the sense that it intends to transform a data set into a lower dimensional feature space. However, unlike PCA, the focus of LDA is not to capture the data set variability. Instead, LDA focuses on class separability, i.e. separating the features based on class separability so as to avoid over-fitting of the machine learning model.

Unlike PCA that calculates eigenvalues of the covariance matrix of the data set, LDA calculates eigenvalues and eigenvectors within a class and inter-class scatter matrices. Below are the steps to be followed:

1. Calculate the mean vectors for the individual classes.
2. Calculate intra-class and inter-class scatter matrices.
3. Calculate eigenvalues and eigenvectors for S_W^{-1} and S_B, where S_W is the intra-class scatter matrix and S_B is the inter-class scatter matrix

$$S_W = \sum_{i=1}^{c} S_i;$$

$$S_i = \sum_{x \in D_i}^{n} (x - m_i)(x - m_i)^T$$

   where, m_i is the mean vector of the i-th class

$$S_B = \sum_{i=1}^{c} N_i (m_i - m)(m_i - m)^T$$

   where, mi is the sample mean for each class, m is the overall mean of the data set, Ni is the sample size of each class
4. Identify the top 'k' eigenvectors having top 'k' eigenvalues

For implementing singular value decomposition in Python, we can use *LinearDiscriminantAnalysis* function of ***sklearn.discriminant_analysis*** library. Following is the code using the UCI data set *btissue*.

```
>>> import pandas as pd
>>> import numpy as np
>>> from sklearn import datasets
>>> from sklearn.discriminant_analysis import
```

```
LinearDiscriminantAnalysis
>>> from sklearn.utils import column_or_1d

>>> data = pd.read_csv("btissue.csv")
>>> X = data.iloc[:,0:9]
>>> y = column_or_1d(data['class'], warn=True) #To generate 1d
array, column_or_1d has been used ...

>>> clf = LinearDiscriminantAnalysis()
>>> lda_fit = clf.fit(X, y)
>>> print(lda_fit)

LinearDiscriminantAnalysis(n_components=None, priors=None,
shrinkage=None,solver='svd', store_covariance=False, tol=0.0001)

>>> pred = clf.predict([[1588.000000, 0.085908, -0.086323,
516.943603, 12895.342130, 25.933331, 141.722204, 416.175649,
1452.331924]])

>>> print(pred)

['con']
```

4.3   FEATURE SUBSET SELECTION

Feature selection is arguably the most critical pre-processing activity in any machine learning project. It intends to select a subset of system attributes or features which makes a most meaningful contribution in a machine learning activity. Let's quickly discuss a practical example to understand the philosophy behind feature selection. Say we are trying to predict the weight of students based on past information about similar students, which is captured in a 'student weight' data set. The student weight data set has features such as Roll Number, Age, Height, and Weight. We can well understand that roll number can have no bearing, whatsoever, in predicting student weight. So we can eliminate the feature roll number and build a feature subset to be considered in this machine learning problem. The subset of features is expected to give better results than the full set. The same has been **depicted** in Figure 4.9.

Roll Number	Age	Height	Weight		Age	Height	Weight
12	12	1.1	23	→	12	1.1	23
14	11	1.05	21.6		11	1.05	21.6
19	13	1.2	24.7		13	1.2	24.7
32	11	1.07	21.3		11	1.07	21.3
38	14	1.24	25.2		14	1.24	25.2
45	12	1.12	23.4		12	1.12	23.4

FIG. 4.9
Feature selection

But before we go forward with more detailed discussion on feature selection, let's try to understand the issues which have made feature selection such a relevant problem to be solved.

4.3.1 Issues in high-dimensional data

With the rapid innovations in the digital space, the volume of data generated has increased to an unbelievable extent. At the same time, breakthroughs in the storage technology area have made storage of large quantity of data quite cheap. This has further motivated the storage and mining of very large and high-dimensionality data sets.

Points to Ponder:

'High-dimensional' refers to the high number of variables or attributes or features present in certain data sets, more so in the domains like DNA analysis, geographic information systems (GIS), social networking, etc. The high-dimensional spaces often have hundreds or thousands of dimensions or attributes, e.g. DNA microarray data can have up to 450,000 variables (gene probes).

Alongside, two new application domains have seen drastic development. One is that of biomedical research, which includes gene selection from microarray data. The other one is text categorization which deals with huge volumes of text data from social networking sites, emails, etc. The first domain, i.e. biomedical research generates data sets having a number of features in the range of a few tens of thousands. The text data generated from different sources also have extremely high dimensions. In a large document corpus having few thousand documents embedded, the number of unique word tokens which represent the feature of the text data set, can also be in the range of a few tens of thousands. To get insight from such high-dimensional data may be a big challenge for any machine learning algorithm. On one hand, very high quantity of computational resources and high amount of time will be required. On the other hand the performance of the model - both for supervised and unsupervised machine learning task, also degrades sharply due to unnecessary noise in the data. Also, a model built on an extremely high number of features may be very difficult to understand. For this reason, it is necessary to take a subset of the features instead of the full set.

The objective of feature selection is three-fold:

- Having faster and more cost-effective (i.e. less need for computational resources) learning model
- Improving the efficiency of the learning model
- Having a better understanding of the underlying model that generated the data

4.3.2   Key drivers of feature selection — feature relevance and redundancy

4.3.2.1   Feature relevance

In supervised learning, the input data set which is the training data set, has a class label attached. A model is inducted based on the training data set - so that the inducted model can assign class labels to new, unlabelled data. Each of the predictor variables, is expected to contribute information to decide the value of the class label. In case a variable is not contributing any information, it is said to be irrelevant. In case the information contribution for prediction is very little, the variable is said to be weakly relevant. Remaining variables, which make a significant contribution to the prediction task are said to be strongly relevant variables.

In unsupervised learning, there is no training data set or labelled data. Grouping of similar data instances are done and similarity of data instances are evaluated based on the value of different variables. Certain variables do not contribute any useful information for deciding the similarity of dissimilarity of data instances. Hence, those variables make no significant information contribution in the grouping process. These variables are marked as irrelevant variables in the context of the unsupervised machine learning task.

To get a perspective, we can think of the simple example of the student data set that we discussed at the beginning of this section. Roll number of a student doesn't contribute any significant information in predicting what the Weight of a student would be. Similarly, if we are trying to group together students with similar academic capabilities, Roll number can really not contribute any information whatsoever. So, in context of the supervised task of predicting student Weight or the unsupervised task of grouping students with similar academic merit, the variable Roll number is quite irrelevant.

Any feature which is irrelevant in the context of a machine learning task is a candidate for rejection when we are selecting a subset of features. We can consider whether the weakly relevant features are to be rejected or not on a case-to-case basis.

4.3.2.2   Feature redundancy

A feature may contribute information which is similar to the information contributed by one or more other features. For example, in the weight prediction problem referred earlier in the section, both the features Age and Height contribute similar information. This is because with an increase in Age, Weight is expected to increase. Similarly, with the increase of Height also Weight is expected to increase. Also, Age and Height increase with each other. So, in context of the Weight prediction problem, Age and Height contribute similar information. In other words, irrespective of whether the feature height is present as a part of the feature subset, the learning model will give almost same results. In the same way, without age being part of the predictor variables, the outcome of the learning model will be more or less same. In this kind of a situation when one feature is similar to another feature, the feature is said to be potentially redundant in the context of the learning problem.

All features having potential redundancy are candidates for rejection in the final feature subset. Only a small number of representative features out of a set of potentially redundant features are considered for being a part of the final feature subset.

So, in a nutshell, the main objective of feature selection is to remove all features which are irrelevant and take a representative subset of the features which are potentially redundant. This leads to a meaningful feature subset in context of a specific learning task.

Now, the question is how to find out which of the features are irrelevant or which features have potential redundancy. For that multiple measures are being used, some of which have been covered in the next sub-section.

4.3.3   Measures of feature relevance and redundancy

4.3.3.1   Measures of feature relevance

As mentioned earlier, feature relevance is to be gauged by the amount of information contributed by a feature. For supervised learning, mutual information is considered as a good measure of information contribution of a feature to decide the value of the class label. That's why it is a good indicator of the relevance of a feature with respect to the class variable. Higher the value of mutual information of a feature, more relevant is that feature. Mutual information can be calculated as follows:

$$MI(C,f) = H(C) + H(f) - H(C,f)$$

where, marginal entropy of the class, $H(C) = -\sum_{i=1}^{k} p(C_i) \log_2 p(C_i)$

marginal entropy of the feature 'x', $H(f) = -\sum_{c} p(f = x) \log_2 p(f = x)$

and K = number of classes, C = class variable, f = feature set that take discrete values.

In case of unsupervised learning, there is no class variable. Hence, feature-to-class mutual information cannot be used to measure the information contribution of the features. In case of unsupervised learning, the entropy of the set of features without one feature at a time is calculated for all the features. Then, the features are ranked in a descending order of information gain from a feature and top 'β' percentage (value of 'β' is a design parameter of the algorithm) of features are selected as relevant features. The entropy of a feature f is calculated using Shannon's formula below:

$$H(f) = -\sum_{x} p(f = x) \log_2 p(f = x)$$

$\sum_{x}$ is used only for features that take discrete values. For continuous features, it should be replaced by discretization performed first to estimate probabilities $p(f = x)$.

4.3.3.2   Measures of Feature redundancy

Feature redundancy, as we have already discussed, is based on similar information contribution by multiple features. There are multiple measures of similarity of information contribution, salient ones being

1. Correlation-based measures
2. Distance-based measures, and
3. Other coefficient-based measure

1. Correlation-based similarity measure

Correlation is a measure of linear dependency between two random variables. Pearson's product moment correlation coefficient is one of the most popular and accepted measures of correlation between two random variables. For two random feature variables F_1 and F_2, Pearson correlation coefficient is defined as:

$$\alpha = \frac{cov(F_1, F_2)}{\sqrt{var(F_1) \cdot var(F_2)}}$$

$$cov(F_1, F_2) = \sum \left(F_{1_i} - \overline{F_1}\right) \cdot \left(F_{2_i} - \overline{F_2}\right)$$

$$var(F_1) = \sum \left(F_{1_i} - \overline{F_1}\right)^2, \text{ where } \overline{F_1} = \frac{1}{n} \cdot \sum F_{1_i}$$

$$var(F_2) = \sum \left(F_{2_i} - \overline{F_2}\right)^2, \text{ where } \overline{F_2} = \frac{1}{n} \cdot \sum F_{2_i}$$

Correlation values range between +1 and −1. A correlation of 1 (+ / −) indicates perfect correlation, i.e. the two features having a perfect linear relationship. In case the correlation is 0, then the features seem to have no linear relationship. Generally, for all feature selection problems, a threshold value is adopted to decide whether two features have adequate similarity or not.

2. Distance-based similarity measure

The most common distance measure is the **Euclidean distance**, which, between two features F_1 and F_2 are calculated as:

$$d(F_1, F_2) = \sqrt{\sum_{i=1}^{n} \left(F_{1_i} - F_{2_i}\right)^2}$$

where F_1 and F_2 are features of an n-dimensional data set. Refer to the Figure 4.9. The data set has two features, aptitude (F_1) and communication (F_2) under consideration. The Euclidean distance between the features has been calculated using the formula provided above.

Aptitude (F_1)	Communication (F_2)	($F_1 - F_2$)	($F_1 - F_2$)^2
2	6	−4	16
3	5.5	−2.5	6.25
6	4	2	4
7	2.5	4.5	20.25
8	3	5	25
6	5.5	0.5	0.25
6	7	−1	1
7	6	1	1
8	6	2	4
9	7	2	4
			81.75

FIG. 4.10
Distance calculation between features

A more generalized form of the Euclidean distance is the **Minkowski distance**, measured as

$$d(F_1, F_2) = \sqrt{\sum_{i=1}^{n}\left(F_{1_i} - F_{2_i}\right)^r}$$

Minkowski distance takes the form of Euclidean distance (also called **L_2 norm**) when $r = 2$.

At $r = 1$, it takes the form of **Manhattan distance** (also called **L_1 norm**), as shown below:

$$d(F_1, F_2) = \sum_{i=1}^{n}\left|F_{1_i} - F_{2_i}\right|$$

A specific example of Manhattan distance, used more frequently to calculate the distance between binary vectors is the **Hamming distance**. For example, the Hamming distance between two vectors 01101011 and 11001001 is 3, as illustrated in Figure 4.10a.

3. Other similarity measures

Jaccard index/coefficient is used as a measure of similarity between two features. The **Jaccard distance**, a measure of dissimilarity between two features, is complementary of Jaccard index.

For two features having binary values, Jaccard index is measured as

$$J = \frac{n_{11}}{n_{01} + n_{10} + n_{11}}$$

where, n_{11} = number of cases where both the features have value 1
n_{01} = number of cases where the feature 1 has value 0 and feature 2 has value 1
n_{10} = number of cases where the feature 1 has value 1 and feature 2 has value 0

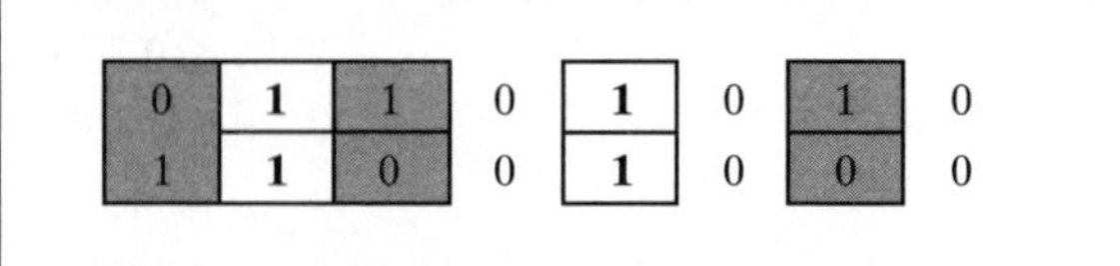

(a) Hamming distance measurement

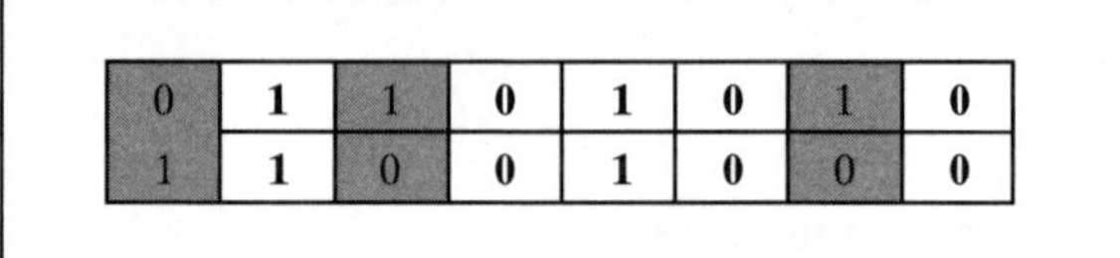

(b) Jaccard coefficient measurement

(c) SMC measurement

FIG. 4.11

Distance measures between features

Jaccard distance, $d_J = 1 - J$

Let's consider two features F_1 and F_2 having values $(0, 1, 1, 0, 1, 0, 1, 0)$ and $(1, 1, 0, 0, 1, 0, 0, 0)$. Figure 4.10b shows the identification of the values of n_{11}, n_{01} and n_{10}. As shown, the cases where both the values are 0 have been left out without border — as an indication of the fact that they will be excluded in the calculation of Jaccard coefficient.

Jaccard coefficient of F_1 and $F_2, J = \dfrac{n_{11}}{n_{01} + n_{10} + n_{11}} = \dfrac{2}{1+2+2} = \dfrac{2}{5}$ or 0.4.

Jaccard distance between F_1 and $F_2, d_J = 1 - J = \dfrac{1}{2}$ or 0.6

Simple matching·coefficient (SMC) is almost same as Jaccard coeficient except the fact that it includes a number of cases where both the features have a value of 0.

$$SMC = \dfrac{n_{11} + n_{00}}{n_{00} + n_{01} + n_{10} + n_{11}}$$

where, n_{11} = number of cases where both the features have value 1

n_{01} = number of cases where the feature 1 has value 0 and feature 2 has value 1

n_{10} = number of cases where the feature 1 has value 1 and feature 2 has value 0

n_{00} = number of cases where both the features have value 0

Quite understandably, the total count of rows, $n = n_{00} + n_{01} + n_{10} + n_{11}$. As shown in Figure 4.10c, all values have been included in the calculation of SMC.

$$\therefore \text{SMC of } F_1 \text{ and } F_2 = \frac{n_{11} + n_{00}}{n_{00} + n_{01} + n_{10} + n_{11}} = \frac{2+3}{3+1+2+2} = \frac{1}{2} \text{ or } 0.5.$$

One more measure of similarity using similarity coefficient calculation is **Cosine Similarity**. Let's take the example of a typical text classification problem. The text corpus needs to be first transformed into features with a word token being a feature and the number of times the word occurs in a document comes as a value in each row. There are thousands of features in such a text data set. However, the data set is sparse in nature as only a few words do appear in a document, and hence in a row of the data set. So each row has very few non-zero values. However, the non-zero values can be anything integer value as the same word may occur any number of times. Also, considering the sparsity of the data set, the 0-0 matches (which obviously is going to be pretty high) need to be ignored. Cosine similarity which is one of the most popular measures in text classification is calculated as:

$$cos(x, y) = \frac{x \cdot y}{\|x\| \cdot \|y\|}$$

where, x.y = vector dot product of x and $y = \sum_{i=1}^{n} x_i y_i$

$$\|x\| = \sqrt{\sum_{i=1}^{n} x_i^2} \text{ and } \|y\| = \sqrt{\sum_{i=1}^{n} y_i^2}$$

Let's calculate the cosine similarity of x and y, where $x = (2, 4, 0, 0, 2, 1, 3, 0, 0)$ and $y = (2, 1, 0, 0, 3, 2, 1, 0, 1)$.

In this case, $x.y = 2*2 + 4*1 + 0*0 + 0*0 + 2*3 + 1*2 + 3*1 + 0*0 + 0*1 = 19$

$$\|x\| = \sqrt{2^2 + 4^2 + 0^2 + 0^2 + 2^2 + 1^2 + 3^2 + 0^2 + 0^2} = \sqrt{34} = 5.83$$

$$\|y\| = \sqrt{2^2 + 1^2 + 0^2 + 0^2 + 3^2 + 2^2 + 1^2 + 0^2 + 1^2} = \sqrt{20} = 4.47$$

$$\therefore cos(x, y) = \frac{19}{5.83 * 4.47} = 0.729$$

Cosine similarity actually measures the angle (refer to Fig. 4.12) between x and y vectors. Hence, if cosine similarity has a value 1, the angle between x and y is 0° which means x and y are same except for the magnitude. If cosine similarity is 0, the angle between x and y is 90°. Hence, they do not share any similarity (in case of text data, no term/word is common). In the above example, the angle comes to be 43.2°.

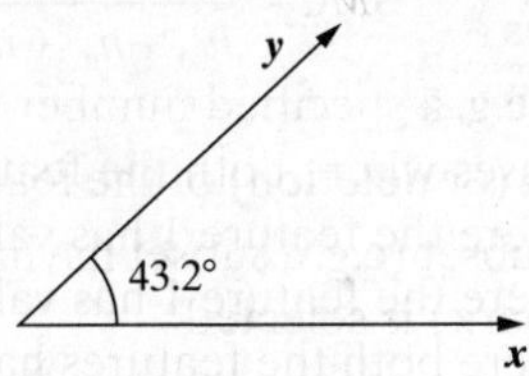

FIG. 4.12
Cosine similarity

4.3.4   Overall feature selection process

Feature selection is the process of selecting a subset of features in a data set. As depicted in Figure 4.13, a typical feature selection process consists of four steps:

1. generation of possible subsets
2. subset evaluation
3. stop searching based on some stopping criterion
4. 4validation of the result

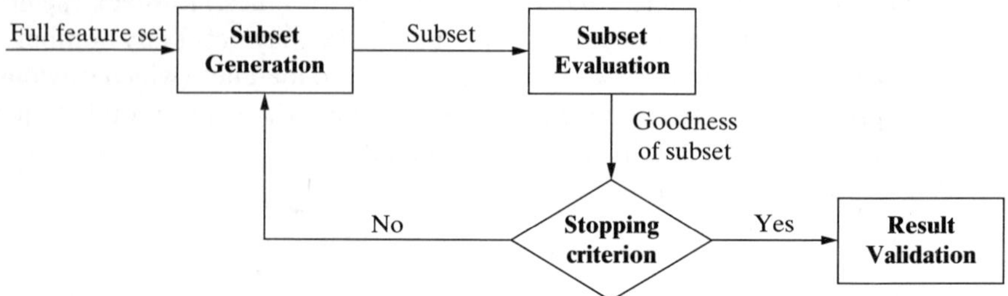

FIG. 4.13
Feature selection process

Subset generation, which is the first step of any feature selection algorithm, is a search procedure which ideally should produce all possible candidate subsets. However, for an n-dimensional data set, 2^n subsets can be generated. So, as the value of 'n' becomes high, finding an optimal subset from all the 2^n candidate subsets becomes intractable. For that reason, different approximate search strat-egies are employed to find candidate subsets for evaluation. On one hand, the search may start with an empty set and keep adding features. This search strategy is termed as a sequential forward selection. On the other hand, a search may start with a full set and successively remove features. This strategy is termed as sequen-tial backward elimination. In certain cases, search start with both ends and add and remove features simultaneously. This strategy is termed as a bi-directional selection.

Each candidate subset is then evaluated and compared with the previous best performing subset based on certain **evaluation criterion**. If the new subset performs better, it replaces the previous one.

This cycle of subset generation and evaluation continues till a pre-defined **stopping criterion** is fulfilled. Some commonly used stopping criteria are

1. the search completes
2. some given bound (e.g. a specified number of iterations) is reached
3. subsequent addition (or deletion) of the feature is not producing a better subset
4. a sufficiently good subset (e.g. a subset having better classification accuracy than the existing benchmark) is selected

Then the selected best subset is **validated** either against prior benchmarks or by experiments using real-life or synthetic but authentic data sets. In case of supervised learning, the accuracy of the learning model may be the performance parameter considered for validation. The accuracy of the model using the subset derived is compared against the model accuracy of the subset derived using some other benchmark algorithm. In case of unsupervised, the cluster quality may be the parameter for validation.

 ### 4.3.5   Feature selection approaches

There are four types of approach for feature selection:

1. Filter approach
2. Wrapper approach
3. Hybrid approach
4. Embedded approach

In the **filter approach** (as depicted in Fig. 4.14), the feature subset is selected based on statistical measures done to assess the merits of the features from the data perspective. No learning algorithm is employed to evaluate the goodness of the feature selected. Some of the common statistical tests conducted on features as a part of filter approach are - Pearson's correlation, information gain, Fisher score, analysis of variance (ANOVA), Chi-Square, etc.

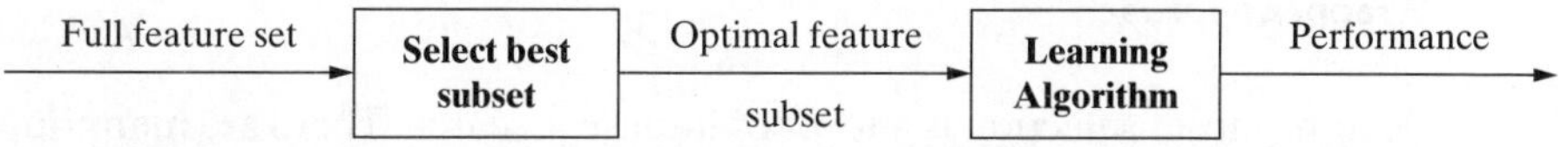

FIG. 4.14
Filter approach

In the **wrapper approach** (as depicted in Fig. 4.15), identification of best feature subset is done using the induction algorithm as a black box. The feature selection algorithm searches for a good feature subset using the induction algorithm itself as a part of the evaluation function. Since for every candidate subset, the learning model is trained and the result is evaluated by running the learning algorithm, wrapper approach is computationally very expensive. However, the performance is generally superior compared to filter approach.

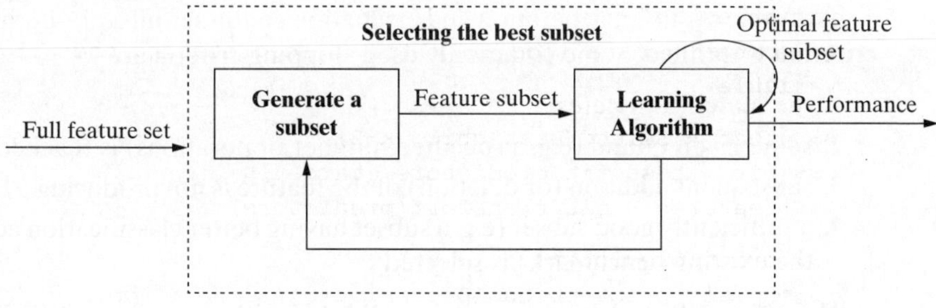

FIG. 4.15
Wrapper approach

Hybrid approach takes the advantage of both filter and wrapper approaches. A typical hybrid algorithm makes use of both the statistical tests as used in filter approach to decide the best subsets for a given cardinality and a learning algorithm to select the final best subset among the best subsets across different cardinalities.

Embedded approach (as depicted in Fig. 4.16) is quite similar to wrapper approach as it also uses and inductive algorithm to evaluate the generated feature subsets. However, the difference is it performs feature selection and classification simultaneously.

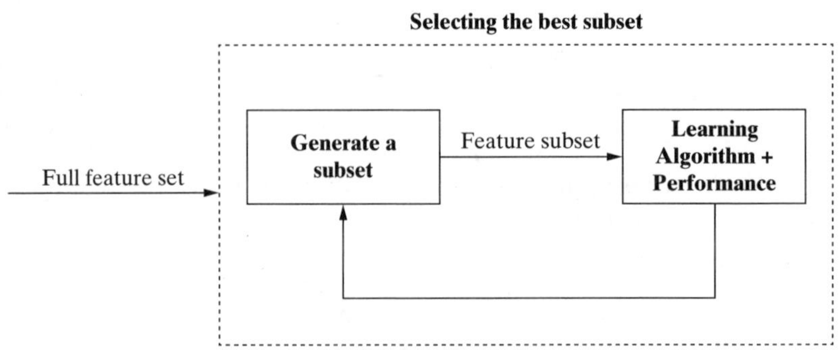

FIG. 4.16
Wrapper approach

Feature subset selection is a topic of intense research. There are many approaches to select a subset of features which can improve model performance. It is not possible to cover all such approaches as a part of this text. However, *sklearn.feature_selection* module can be used for applying basic feature selection. There are multiple options of feature selection offered by the module, one of which is presented below:

```
>>> import pandas as pd
>>> import numpy as np
>>> from sklearn.feature_selection import SelectKBest
>>> from sklearn.feature_selection import chi2

>>> data = pd.read_csv("apndcts.csv")
>>> predictors = data.iloc[:,0:7] # Seggretating the predictor
variables ...
>>> target = data.iloc[:,7]       # Seggretating the target / class
variable ...

>>> test = SelectKBest(chi2, k=2)
>>> fit = test.fit(predictors, target)
>>> features = fit.transform(predictors)

>>> print(predictors.columns)
>>> np.set_printoptions(precision=3)
>>> print(fit.scores_)
```

Output:
```
Index(['At1', ' At2', ' At3', ' At4', ' At5', ' At6', ' At7'],
dtype='object')
```

Scores for each feature:
```
[ 1.771  1.627  2.391  1.084  1.673  1.647  2.236]
```

4.4   SUMMARY

- A feature is an attribute of a data set that is used in a machine learning process.

- Feature engineering is an important pre-processing step for machine learning, having two major elements:

  1. feature transformation
  2. feature subset selection

- Feature transformation transforms data into a new set of features which can represent the underlying machine learning problem

- There are two variants of feature transformation:

  1. feature construction
  2. feature extraction

- Feature construction process discovers missing information about the relationships between features and augments the feature space by creating additional features.

- Feature extraction is the process of extracting or creating a new set of features from the original set of features using some functional mapping.

- Some popular feature extraction algorithms used in machine learning:

  1. Principal Component Analysis (PCA)
  2. Singular Value Decomposition (SVD)
  3. Linear Discriminant Analysis (LDA)

- Feature subset selection is intended to derive a subset of features from the full feature set. No new feature is generated.

- The objective of feature selection is three-fold:

  1. Having faster and more cost-effective (i.e. less need for computational resources) learning model
  2. Improving the efficiency of the learning model
  3. Having a better understanding of the underlying model that generated the data

Feature selection intends to remove all features which are irrelevant and take a representative subset of the features which are potentially redundant. This leads to a meaningful feature subset in context of a specific learning task.

- Feature relevance is indicated by the information gain from a feature measured in terms of relative entropy.

- Feature redundancy is based on similar information contributed by multiple features measured by feature-to-feature:

  1. Correlation
  2. Distance (Minkowski distances, e.g. Manhattan, Euclidean, etc. used as most popular measures)
  3. Other coefficient-based (Jaccard, SMC, Cosine similarity, etc.)

- Main approaches for feature selection are

  1. Filter
  2. Wrapper
  3. Hybrid
  4. Embedded

SAMPLE QUESTIONS

MULTIPLE-CHOICE QUESTIONS

1. Engineering a good feature space is a crucial ___ for the success of any machine learning model.
   (a) Pre-requisite
   (b) Process
   (c) Objective
   (d) None of the above

2. n-gram of size 1 is called
   (a) Bigram
   (b) Unigram
   (c) Trigram
   (d) None of the above

3. Feature ___ involves transforming a given set of input features to generate a new set of more powerful features.
   (a) Selection
   (b) Engineering
   (c) Transformation
   (d) Re-engineering

4. Conversion of a text corpus to a numerical representation is done using process.
   (a) Tokenization
   (b) Normalization
   (c) Vectorization
   (d) None of the above

5. approach uses induction algorithm for subset validation.
   (a) Filter
   (b) Hybrid
   (c) Wrapper
   (d) Embedded

6. In feature extraction, some of the commonly used are used for combining the origi-nal features.
   (a) Operators   (b) Delimiters
   (c) Words   (d) All of the above

7. Hamming distance between binary vectors 1001 and 0101 is
   (a) 1   (b) 2
   (c) 3   (d) 4

8. PCA is a technique for
   (a) Feature extraction   (b) Feature construction
   (c) Feature selection   (d) None of the above

9. The new features created in PCA are known as
   (a) Principal components   (b) Eigenvectors
   (c) Secondary components   (d) None of the above

10. In LDA, intra-class and inter-class matrices are calculated.
   (a) Scatter   (b) Adjacency
   (c) Similarity   (d) None of the above

11. Cosine similarity is most popularly used in
   (a) Text classification   (b) Image classification
   (c) Feature selection   (d) None of the above

12. This approach is quite similar to wrapper approach as it also uses and inductive algo-rithm to evaluate the generated feature subsets.
   (a) Embedded approach   (b) Filter approach
   (c) Pro Wrapper approach   (d) Hybrid approach

13. _______ In approach, identification of best feature subset is done using the induction algorithm as a black box.
   (a) Embedded   (b) Filter
   (c) Wrapper   (d) Hybrid

SHORT-ANSWER TYPE QUESTIONS (5 MARKS EACH)

1. What is a feature? Explain with an example.

2. What are the different situations which necessitate feature construction?

3. Explain the process of encoding nominal variables.

4. Explain the process of transforming numeric features to categorical features.

5. Explain the wrapper approach of feature selection. What are the merits and de-merits of this approach?

6. When can a feature be termed as irrelevant? How can it be measured?

7. When can a feature be termed as redundant? What are the measures to determine the potentially redundant features?

8. What are the different distance measures that can be used to determine similarity of features?

9. Compare Euclidean distance with Manhattan distance?

10. Differentiate feature transformation with feature selection

11. Write short notes on any <u>two</u>:
(a) SVD
(b) Hybrid method of feature selection
(c) Silhouette width
(d) ROC curve

LONG-ANSWER TYPE QUESTIONS (10 MARKS QUESTIONS)

1. What is feature engineering? Explain, in details, the different aspects of feature engineering?

2. What is feature selection? Why is it needed? What are the different approaches of feature selection?

3. Explain the filter and wrapper approaches of feature selection. What are the merits and demerits of these approaches?

4. (a) Explain the overall process of feature selection
(b) Explain, with an example, the main underlying concept of feature extraction. What are the most popular algorithms for feature extraction?

5. Explain the process of feature engineering in context of a text categorization problem.

6. Why is cosine similarity a suitable measure in context of text categorization? Two rows in a document-term matrix have values - $(2, 3, 2, 0, 2, 3, 3, 0, 1)$ and $(2, 1, 0, 0, 3, 2, 1, 3, 1)$. Find the cosine similarity.

7. (a) How can we calculate Hamming distance? Find the Hamming distance between 10001011 and 11001111.
(b) Compare the Jaccard index and similarity matching coefficient of two features having values $(1, 1, 0, 0, 1, 0, 1, 1)$ and $(1, 0, 0, 1, 1, 0, 0, 1)$.

8. What do you understand by a high-dimensional data set? Give a few practical examples? What is the challenge while applying machine learning technique on a high-dimensional data set? How can that be addressed?

9. (a) Write short notes on any <u>two</u>:
    (i) PCA
    (ii) Vectorization
    (iii) Embedded method
(b) Write the difference between (<u>any two</u>):
    (i) Sequential forward selection vs. sequential backward elimination
    (ii) Filter vs. wrapper method of feature selection
    (iii) Jaccard coefficient vs. SMC

Chapter 5
Brief Overview of Probability

OBJECTIVE OF THE CHAPTER

The principles of machine learning are largely dependent on effectively handling the uncertainty in data and predicting the outcome based on data in hand. All the learning processes we will be discussing in later chapters of this book expects the readers to understand the foundational rules of probability, the concept of random and continuous variables, distribution, and sampling principles and few basic principles such as central limit theorem, hypothesis testing, and Monte Carlo approximations. As these rules, theorems, and principles form the basis of learning principles, we will be discussing those in this chapter with examples and illustrations.

5.1 INTRODUCTION

As we discussed in previous chapters, machine learning provides us a set of methods that can automatically detect patterns in data, and then can be used to predict future data, or to perform other kinds of decision making under uncertainty. The best way to perform such activities on top of huge data set known as **big data** is to use the tools of probability theory because probability theory can be applied to any situation involving uncertainty. In machine learning there may be uncertainties in different forms like arriving at the best prediction of future given the past data, arriving at the best model based on certain data, arriving at the confidence level while predicting the future outcome based on past data, etc. The probabilistic approach used in machine learning is closely related to the field of statistics, but the emphasis is in a different

"

direction as we see in this chapter. In this chapter we will discuss the tools, equations, and models of probability that are useful for machine learning domain.

5.2   IMPORTANCE OF STATISTICAL TOOLS IN MACHINE LEARNING

In machine learning, we train the system by using a limited data set called 'training data' and based on the confidence level of the training data we expect the machine learning algorithm to depict the behaviour of the larger set of actual data. If we have observation on a subset of events, called 'sample', then there will be some uncertainty in attributing the sample results to the whole set or population. So, the question was how a limited knowledge of a sample set can be used to predict the behaviour of a real set with some confidence. It was realized by mathematicians that even if some knowledge is based on a sample, if we know the amount of uncertainty related to it, then it can be used in an optimum way without causing loss of knowledge. Refer Figure 5.1

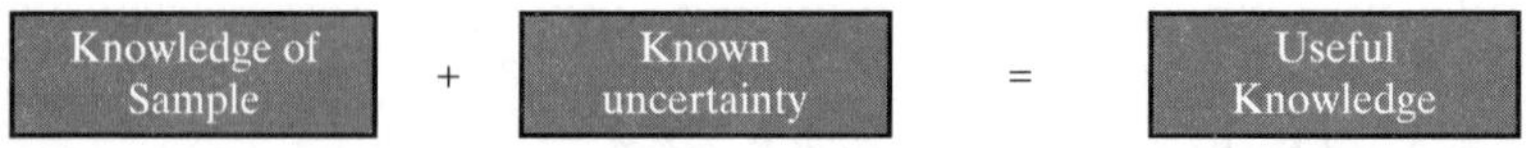

FIG. 5.1
Knowledge and uncertainty

Probability theory provides a mathematical foundation for quantifying this uncertainty of the knowledge. As the knowledge about the training data comes in the form of **interdependent** feature sets, the conditional probability theories (especially the Bayes theorem), discussed later in this chapter form the basis for deriving required confidence level of the training data.

Different distribution principles discussed in this chapter create the view of how the data set that we will be dealing with in machine learning can behave, in terms of their feature distributions. It is important to understand the mathematical function behind each of these distributions so that we can understand how the data is spread out from its average value – denoted by the mean and the variance. While choosing the samples from these distribution sets we should be able to calculate to what extent the sample is representing the actual behaviour of the full data set. These along with the test of hypothesis principles build the basis for finding out the uncertainty in the training data set to represent the actual data set which is the fundamental principle of machine learning.

5.3   CONCEPT OF PROBABILITY – FREQUENTIST AND BAYESIAN INTERPRETATION

The concept of probability is not new. In our day to day life, we use the concept of probability in many places. For example, when we talk about probabilities of getting the heads and the tails when a coin is flipped are equal, we actually intend to say that if a coin is flipped many times, the coin will land heads a same number of times as it lands tails. This is the **frequentist** interpretation of probability. This interpretation represents the long run frequencies of events. Another important interpretation of probability tries to quantify the uncertainty of some event and thus focuses on information rather than repeated trials. This is called the **Bayesian** interpretation of probability. Taking the same example of coin flipping is interpreted as – the coin is equally likely to land heads or tails when we flip the coin next.

The reason the Bayesian interpretation can be used to model the uncertainty of events is that it does not expect the long run frequencies of the events to happen. For example, if we have to compute the probability of Brazil winning 2018 football world cup final, that event can happen only once and can't be repeated over and over again to calculate its probability. But still, we should be able to quantify the uncertainty about the event and which is only possible if we interpret probability the Bayesian way. To give some more machine learning oriented examples, we are starting a new software implementation project for a large customer and want to compute the probability of this project getting into customer escalation based on data from similar projects in the past, or we want to compute the probability of a tumor to be malignant or not based on the probability distribution of such cases among the patients of similar profile. In all these cases it is not possible to do a repeated trial of the event and the Bayesian concept is valid for computing the uncertainty. So, in this book, we will focus on the Bayesian interpretation to develop our machine learning models. The basic formulae of probability remain the same anyway irrespective of whatever interpretation we adopt.

5.3.1   A brief review of probability theory

We will briefly touch upon the basic probability theory in this section just as a refresher so that we can move to the building blocks of machine learning way of use of probability. As discussed in previous chapters, the basic concept of machine learning is that we want to have a limited set of 'Training' data that we use as a representative of a large set of Actual data and through probability distribution we try to find out how an event which is matching with the training data can represent the outcome with some confidence.

5.3.1.1   Foundation rules

We will review the basic rules of probability in this section.

Let us introduce few notations that will be used throughout this book.

$p(A)$ denotes the probability that the event A is true. For example, A might be the logical statement 'Brazil is going to win the next football world cup final'. The expression $0 \leq p(A) \leq 1$ denotes that the probability of this event happening lies between 0 and 1, where $p(A) = 0$ means the event will definitely not happen, and $p(A) = 1$ means the event will definitely happen. The notation $p(\bar{A})$ denotes the probability of the event not A; this is defined as $p(\bar{A}) = 1 - p(A)$. It is also common practice to write $A = 1$ to mean the event A is true, and $A = 0$ to mean the event A is false. So, this is a binary event where the event is either true or false but can't be something indefinite.

The probability of selecting an event A, from a sample size of X is defined as $p(A) = \dfrac{n}{X}$, where n is the number of times the instance of event A is present in the sample of size X.

5.3.1.2 *Probability of a union of two events*

We are often interested to find out the probability of one or multiple events occurring. For example, we may win a bet if either England or Brazil enters the semi-finals of football World Cup. The Union of the two events A and B written as A, is the event that occurs if either or both of the events occur. The probability of union of these two events is as in equation 5.1.

$$p(A \cup B) = p(A) + p(B) - p(A \cap B) \tag{5.1}$$

For two mutually exclusive events, this equation takes a special form as in equation 5.2.

$$p(A) + p(B), \text{if } A \text{ and } B \text{ are mutually exclusive, meaning p (A intersection B)} = 0 \tag{5.2}$$

5.3.1.3 *Joint probabilities*

The probability of the joint event A and B is defined as the **product rule**:

$$p(A, B) = p(A \cap B) = p(A \mid B) \cdot p(B) \tag{5.3}$$

where p(A|B) is defined as the conditional probability of event A happening if event B happens. Based on this **joint distribution** on two events $p(A, B)$,we can define the **marginal distribution** as follows:

$$p(A) = \sum_b p(A, B) = \sum_b p(A \mid B = b) p(B = b) \tag{5.4}$$

summing up the all probable states of B gives the total probability formulae, which is also called **sum rule or the rule of total probability**.

Same way, $p(B)$ can be defined as

$$p(B) = \sum_a p(A, B) = \sum_a p(B \mid A = a) p(A = a) \tag{5.5}$$

This formula can be extended for the countably infinite number of events in the set and **chain rule** of probability can be derived if the product rule is applied multiple times as

$$p(X_{1:N}) = p(X_1) p(X_2 \mid X_1) p(X_3 \mid X_2, X_1)$$

$$p(X_4 \mid X_1, X_2, X_3) \dots p(X_N \mid X_{1:N} - 1) \tag{5.6}$$

5.3.1.4 Conditional probability

We define the **conditional probability** of event A, given that event B is true, as follows:

$$p(A\,|\,B) = p(A, B)\,/\,p(B), \text{ if } p(B) > 0 \tag{5.7}$$

where, $p(A, B)$ is the joint probability of A and B and can also be denoted as $p(A \cap B)$

Similarly,

$$p(B\,|\,A) = p(B, A)\,/\,p(A), \text{ if } p(A) > 0 \tag{5.8}$$

Illustration. In a toy-making shop, the automated machine produces few defective pieces. It is observed that in a lot of 1,000 toy parts, 25 are defective. If two random samples are selected for testing without replacement (meaning that the first sample is not put back to the lot and thus the second sample is selected from the lot size of 999) from the lot, calculate the probability that both the samples are defective.

Solution: Let A denote the probability of first part being defective and B denote the second part being defective. Here, we have to employ the conditional probability of the second part being found defective when the first part is already found defective.

By law of probability, $\quad p(A) = \dfrac{25}{1000} = 0.025$

As we are selecting the second sample without replacing the first sample into the lot and the first one is already found defective, there are now 24 defective pieces out of 999 pieces left in the lot.

Thus
$$p(B\,|\,A) = \frac{24}{999} = 0.024$$

As
$$p(A, B) = p(A \cap B) = p(B\,|\,A)p(A)$$
$$= 0.025 \times 0.024$$
$$= 0.006006$$

which is the probability of both the parts being found defective.

5.3.1.5 Bayes rule

The **Bayes rule**, also known as **Bayes Theorem,** can be derived by combining the definition of conditional probability with the product and sum rules, as below:

$$p(A\,|\,B) = \frac{p(B\,|\,A)p(A)}{p(B)} \tag{5.9}$$

$$p(A = a\,|\,B = b) = \frac{p(A = a, B = b)}{p(B = b)}$$

$$= \frac{p(A = a)p(B = b\,|\,A = a)}{\sum_a p(A = a)p(B = b\,|\,A = a)} \tag{5.10}$$

Illustration: Flagging an email as spam based on the sender name of the email

Let's take an example to identify the probability of an email to be really spam based on the name of the sender. We often receive email from mail id containing junk characters or words such as bulk, mass etc. which turn out to be a spam mail. So, we want our machine learning agent to flag the spam emails for us so that we can easily delete them.

Let's also assume that we have knowledge about the reliability of the assumption that emails with sender names 'mass' and 'bulk' are spam email is 80% meaning that if some email has sender name with 'mass' or 'bulk' then the email will be spam with probability 0.8. The probability of false alarm is 10% meaning that the agent will show the positive result as spam even if the email is not a spam with a probability 0.1. Also, we have a prior knowledge that only 0.4% of the total emails received are spam.

Solution:

Let x be the event of the flag being set as spam because the sender name has the words 'mass' or 'bulk' and y be the event of some mail really being spam.

So, $p(x = 1|y = 1) = 0.8$, which is the probability of the flag being positive if the email is spam.

Many times this probability is wrongly interpreted as the probability of an email being spam if the flag is positive. But that is not true, because we will then ignore the prior knowledge that only 0.4% of the emails are actually spam and also there can be a false alarm in 10% of the cases.

So, $p(y = 1) = 0.004$ and $p(y = 0) = 1 - p(y = 1) = 0.996$

$$p(x = 1 \mid y = 0) = 0.1$$

Combining these terms using the Bayes rule, we can compute the correct answer as follows:

$$p(y = 1 \mid x = 1) = \frac{p(x = 1 \mid y = 1)p(y = 1)}{p(x = 1 \mid y = 1)p(y = 1) + p(x = 1 \mid y = 0)p(y = 0)}$$

$$= \frac{0.8 \times 0.004}{0.8 \times 0.004 + 0.1 \times 0.996}$$

$$= 0.031$$

This means that if we combine our prior knowledge with the actual test results then there is only about a 3% chance of emails actually being spam if the sender name contains the terms 'bulk' or 'mass'. This is significantly lower than the earlier assumption of 80% chance and thus calls for additional checks before someone starts deleting such emails based on only this flag.

Details of the practice application of Bayes theorem in machine learning is discussed in Chapter 6.

5.4   RANDOM VARIABLES

Let's take an example of tossing a coin once. We can associate random variables X and Y as

$X(\text{H}) = 1$, $X(\text{T}) = 0$, which means this variable is associated with the outcome of the coin facing head.

$Y(H) = 0$, $Y(T) = 1$, which means this variable is associated with the outcome of the coin facing tails.

Here in the sample space S which is the outcome related to tossing the coin once, random variables represent the single-valued real function $[X(\zeta)]$ that assigns a real number, called its value to each sample point of S. A random variable is not a variable but is a function. The sample space S is called the domain of random variable X and the collection of all the numbers, i.e. values of $X(\zeta)$, is termed the range of the random variable.

We can define the event $(X = x)$ where x is a fixed real number as

$$(X = x) = \{\zeta : X(\zeta) = x\}$$

Accordingly, we can define the following events for fixed numbers x, x_1, and x_2:

$$(X \leq x) = \{\zeta : X(\zeta) \leq x\}$$
$$(X > x) = \{\zeta : X(\zeta) > x\}$$
$$(x_1 < X \leq x_2) = \{\zeta : x_1 < X(\zeta) \leq x_2\}$$

The probabilities of these events are denoted by

$$P(X = x) = P\{\zeta : X(\zeta) = x\}$$
$$P(X \leq x) = P\{\zeta : X(\zeta) \leq x\}$$
$$P(X > x) = P\{\zeta : X(\zeta) > x\}$$
$$P(x_1 < X \leq x_2) = P\{\zeta : x_1 < X(\zeta) \leq x_2\}$$

We will use the term cdf in this book to denote the **distribution function** or **cumulative distribution function,** which takes the form of random variable X as

$$F_x(x) = P(X \leq x) -\infty < x < \infty$$

Some of the important properties of $F_x(x)$ are

$$0 \leq F_x(x) \leq 1$$
$$F_x(x_1) \leq F_x(x_2) \quad \text{if } x_1 < x_2$$
$$\lim_{n \to \infty} F_x(x) = F_x(\infty) = 1$$
$$\lim_{n \to \infty} F_x(x) = F_x(-\infty) = 0$$

5.4.1   Discrete random variables

Let us extend the concept of binary events by defining a **discrete random variable** X. Let X be a random variable with cdf $F_x(x)$ and it changes values only in jumps (a countable number of them) and remains constant between the jumps then it is called a discrete random variable. So, the definition of a discrete random variable is that its range or the set X contains a finite or countably infinite number of points.

Let us consider that the jumps of $F_x(x)$ of the discrete random variable X is occurring at points $x_1, x_2, x_3....$, where this sequence represents a finite or countably infinite set and $x_i < x_j$ if $i < j$. See Figure 5.2.

Then $F_x(x_i) - F_x(x_{i-1}) = P(X \leq x_i) - P(X \leq x_{i-1}) = P(X = x_i)$ (5.11)

We can denote this through notation as

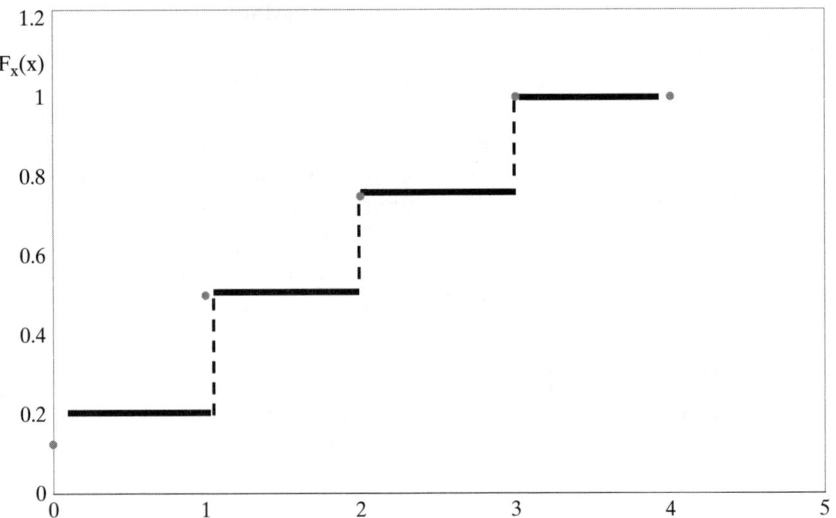

FIG. 5.2
A discrete random variable X with cdf $F_x(x) = p(X \leq x)$ for x = 0, 1, 2, 3, 4, and $F_x(x)$
has jumps at x = 0, 1, 2, 3, 4

$$p(x) = p(X = x) \qquad (5.12)$$

The probability of the event that $X = x$ is denoted as $p(X = x)$, or just $p(x)$ for short. p is called a **probability mass function (pmf)**.

This satisfies the properties $0 \leq p(x) \leq 1$ and $\sum_{x \in X} p(x) = 1$.

The cumulative distribution function (cdf) $F_x(x)$ of a discrete random variable X can be denoted as

$$F_x(x) = P(X \leq x) = \sum_{x \in X} p(x) \qquad (5.13)$$

Refer to Figure 5.3, the pmf is defined on a finite **state space** $X = \{1, 2, 3, 4\}$ that shows a uniform distribution with $p(x) = \dfrac{1}{2}$ This distribution means that X is always equal to the value $\dfrac{1}{2}$, in other words, it is a constant.

Example. Suppose X is a discrete random variable with $R_{X \in} \{0,1,2,...\}$ .we can prove $EX = \sum_{k=0}^{\infty} P(X > k)$.

From the equation above,

$$P(X > 0) = P_X(1) + P_X(2) + P_X(3) + P_X(4) + \cdots,$$
$$P(X > 1) = P_X(2) + P_X(3) + P_X(4) + \cdots,$$
$$P(X > 2) = P_X(3) + P_X(4) + P_X(5) + \cdots.$$

Thus,

$$\sum_{k=0}^{\infty} P(X > k) = P(X > 0) + P(X > 1) + P(X > 2) + \ldots$$
$$= P_X(1) + 2P_X(2) + 3P_X(3) + 4P_X(4) + \ldots$$
$$= EX$$

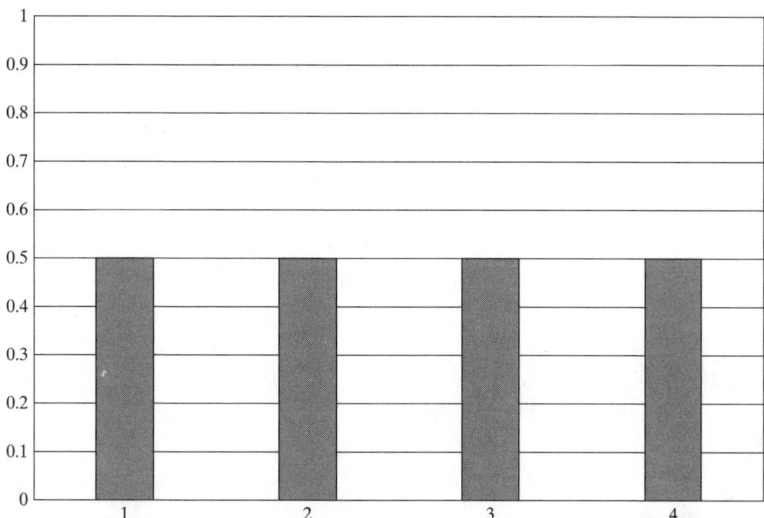

FIG. 5.3

A uniform distribution within the set {1, 2, 3, 4} where $p(x = k) = \dfrac{1}{2}$

DISCUSSION POINTS

Discuss few examples of discrete random variables in practical life. How do you think the behaviour is different from the continuous random variables?

5.4.2   Continuous random variables

We have discussed the probabilities of uncertain discrete quantities. But most of the real-life events are continuous in nature. For example, if we have to measure the actual time taken to finish an activity then there can be an infinite number of possible ways to complete the activity and thus the measurement is continuous and not discrete as it is not similar to the discrete event of rolling a dice or flipping a coin. Here, the function $F_x(x)$ describing the event is continuous and also has a derivative $\dfrac{dF_x(x)}{dx}$ that exists and is piecewise continuous. The **probability density function (pdf)** of the continuous random variable x is defined as

$$f_x(x) = \frac{dF_x(x)}{dx}$$

We will now see how to extend probability to reason about uncertain continuous quantities. The probability that x lies in any interval $a \leq x \leq b$ can be computed as follows.

We can define the events $A = (x \leq a)$, $B = (x \leq b)$, and $W = (a < x \leq b)$. We have that $B = A \cup W$, and since A and W are mutually exclusive, according to the sum rules:

$$p(B) = p(A) + p(W) \tag{5.14}$$

and hence,

$$p(W) = p(B) - p(A) \tag{5.15}$$

Define the function $F(q) = p(X \le q)$. The **cumulative distribution function (cdf)** of random variable X can be obtained by

$$F_x(x) = p(X \le x) = \int_{-\infty}^{x} f(x)dx$$

which is a monotonically increasing function. Using this notation, we have

$$p(a < X \le b) = F(b) - F(a) \tag{5.16}$$

using the pdf of x, we can compute the probability of the continuous variable being in a finite interval as follows:

$$p(a < X \le b) = \int_{b}^{a} f(x)dx \tag{5.17}$$

As the size of the interval gets smaller, it is possible to write

$$P(x \le X \le x + dx) \approx p(x)dx \tag{5.18}$$

5.4.2.1   Mean and variance

The mean in statistical terms represents the weighted average (often called as an expected value) of the all the possible values of random variable X and each value is weighted by its probability. It is denoted by μ_x or $E(X)$ and defined as

$$\mu_x = E(X) = \sum_{k} x_k P_x(x_k) \text{ when } X \text{ is discrete} \tag{5.19}$$

$$\mu_x = E(X) = \int_{-\infty}^{\infty} x f_x(x)dx \text{ when } X \text{ is continuous} \tag{5.20}$$

mean is one of the important parameters for a probability distribution.

Variance of a random variable X measures the spread or dispersion of X. If $E(X)$ is the mean of the random variable X, then the variance is given by

$$\sigma_x^2 = Var(X) = E\left\{[X - E(X)]^2\right\} \tag{5.21}$$

so, $$\sigma_x^2 = \sum_{k}(x_k - \mu_x)^2 P_x(x_k) \text{ when } X \text{ is discrete} \tag{5.22}$$

$$\sigma_x^2 = \int_{-\infty}^{\infty}(x - \mu_x)^2 f_x(x)dx \text{ when } X \text{ is continuous} \tag{5.23}$$

Points to ponder:

The difference between Probability Density Function (pdf) and the Probability Mass Function (pmf) is that the former is associated with the continuous random variable and the latter is associated with the discrete random variable. While pmf represents the probability that a discrete random variable is exactly equal to some value, the pdf does not represent a probability by itself. The integration of pdf over a continuous interval yields the probability.

5.5   SOME COMMON DISCRETE DISTRIBUTIONS

In this section, we will discuss some commonly used parametric distributions defined on discrete state spaces, both finite and countably infinite.

5.5.1   Bernoulli distributions

When we have a situation where the outcome of a trial is withered 'success' or 'failure', then the behaviour of the random variable X can be represented by Bernoulli distribution. Such trials or experiments are termed as Bernoulli trials.

So we can derive that, a random variable X is called Bernoulli random variable with parameter p when its pmf takes the form of

$$P_x(k) = P(X = k) = p^k (1-p)^{1-k}$$

$$k = 0,1 \qquad\qquad (5.24)$$

Where $0 \le p \le 1$. So, using the cdf $F_x(x)$ of Bernoulli random variable is expressed as

$$F_x(x) = \begin{cases} 0 & x < 0 \\ 1-p & 0 \le x < 1 \\ 1 & X \ge 1 \end{cases} \qquad\qquad (5.25)$$

The mean and variance of Bernoulli random variable X are

$$\mu = E(X) = p$$

$$\sigma^2 = Var(X) = p(1-p)$$

here, the probability of success is p and probability of failure is $1 - p$. This is obviously just a special case of a Binomial distribution with $n = 1$ as we will discuss below.

5.5.2   Binomial distribution

If n independent Bernoulli trials are performed and X represents the number of success in those n trials, then X is called a binomial random variable. That's the reason a Bernoulli random variable is a special case of binomial random variable with parameters $(1, p)$.

The pmf of X with parameters (n, p) is given by

$$P_x(k) = P(X = k) = \binom{n}{k} p^k (1-p)^{n-k} \quad k = 0,1...n \qquad\qquad (5.26)$$

Where, $0 \le p \le 1$ and

$\binom{n}{k} = \dfrac{n!}{k!(n-k)!}$ is also called the binomial coefficient which is the number of ways to choose k items from n.

For example, if we toss a coin n times. Let $X \in \{0, ..., n\}$ be the number of heads. If the probability of heads is p, then we say X has a **binomial** distribution, written as $X \sim Bin(n, p)$.

The corresponding cdf of x is

$$F_x = \sum_{k=0}^{n} \binom{n}{k} p^k (1-p)^{n-k} \quad n \le x \le n+1 \qquad\qquad (5.27)$$

This distribution has the following mean and variance:

$$\mu = E(X) = np \tag{5.28}$$

$$\sigma^2 = Var(X) = np(1-p) \tag{5.29}$$

Figure 5.4 shows the binomial distribution of $n = 6$ and $p = 0.6$

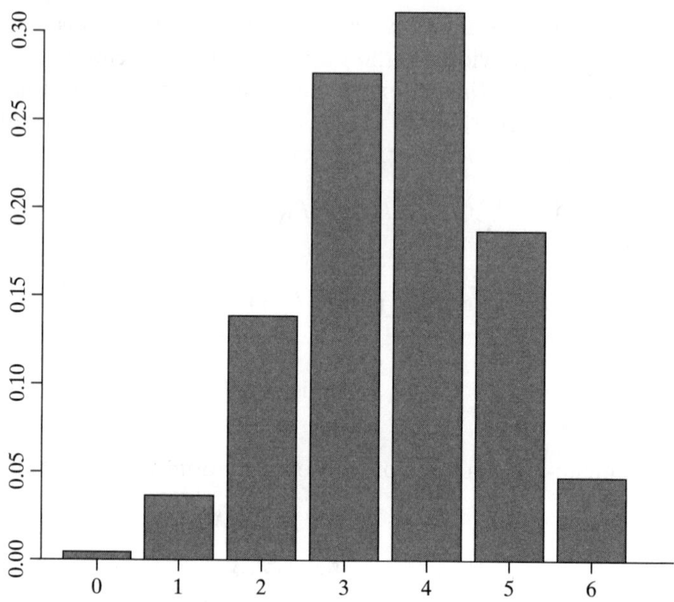

FIG. 5.4
A binomial distribution of n = 6 and p = 0.6

5.5.3   The multinomial and multinoulli distributions

The binomial distribution can be used to model the outcomes of coin tosses, or for experiments where the outcome can be either success or failure. But to model the outcomes of tossing a K-sided die, or for experiments where the outcome can be multiple, we can use the **multinomial** distribution. This is defined as: let $\mathbf{x} = (x_1, ..., x_K)$ be a random vector, where x_j is the number of times side j of the die occurs. Then $\mathbf{x}$ has the following pmf:

$$\left(p_1 + p_2 + ... + p_k \right)^n = \Sigma \binom{n}{x_1 x_2 ... x_k} p_1^{x_1} p_2^{x_2} \cdots p_k^{x_k} \tag{5.30}$$

where, $x_1 + x_2 + ... x_K = n$ and
the multinomial coefficient is defined as

$$\binom{n}{x_1 x_2 ... x_k} = \frac{n!}{x_1! x_2! ... x_k!} \tag{5.31}$$

and the summation is over the set of all non-negative integers $x_1, x_2, ... x_k$ whose sum is n.

Now consider a special case of $n = 1$, which is like rolling a K-sided dice once, so $\mathbf{x}$ will be a vector of 0s and 1s (a bit vector), in which only one bit can be turned on. This means, if the dice shows up face k, then the k'th bit will be on. We can consider

x as being a scalar categorical random variable with K states or values, and $\mathbf{x}$ is its **dummy encoding** with $\mathbf{x} = [\Pi(x = 1), \ldots, \Pi(x = K)]$.

For example, if $K = 3$, this states that 1, 2, and 3 can be encoded as $(1, 0, 0)$, $(0, 1, 0)$, and $(0, 0, 1)$. This is also called a **one-hot encoding**, as we interpret that only one of the K 'wires' is 'hot' or on. This very common special case is known as a **categorical** or **discrete** distribution and because of the analogy with the Binomial/ Bernoulli distinction, Gustavo Lacerda suggested that this is called the **multinoulli distribution.**

5.5.4   Poisson distribution

Poisson random variable has a wide range of application as it may be used as an approximation for binomial with parameter (n,p) when n is large and p is small and thus np is of moderate size. An example application area is, if a fax machine has a faulty transmission line, then the probability of receiving an erroneous digit within a certain page transmitted can be calculated using a Poisson random variable.

So, a random variable X is called a Poisson random variable with parameter (>0) when the pmf looks like

$$p_x(k) = P(X = k) = e^{-\lambda}\frac{\lambda^k}{k!} \text{ where } k = 0,1,\ldots \tag{5.32}$$

the cdf is given as:

$$F_x(x) = e^{-\lambda}\sum_{k=0}^{n}\frac{\lambda^k}{k!}, n \leq x \leq n+1 \tag{5.33}$$

Figure 5.5 shows the Poisson distribution with $= 2$

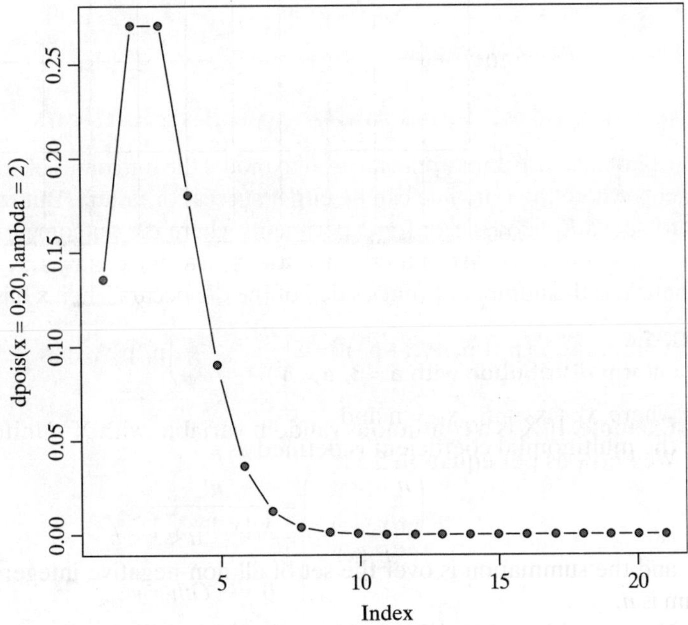

FIG. 5.5

A Poisson distribution with = 2

5.6   SOME COMMON CONTINUOUS DISTRIBUTIONS

In this section we present some commonly used univariate (one-dimensional) continuous probability distributions.

5.6.1   Uniform distribution

The pdf of a uniform random variable is given by:

$$F_x(x) = \begin{cases} \dfrac{1}{b-a} & a < x < b \\ 0 & \textit{Otherwise} \end{cases} \tag{5.34}$$

And the cdf of X is:

$$F_x(x) = \begin{cases} 0 & X \le a \\ \dfrac{x-a}{b-a} & a < x < b \\ 1 & x \ge b \end{cases} \tag{5.35}$$

See Figure 5.6 that represents a uniform distribution with a = 3, b = 8 with increment 0.5.

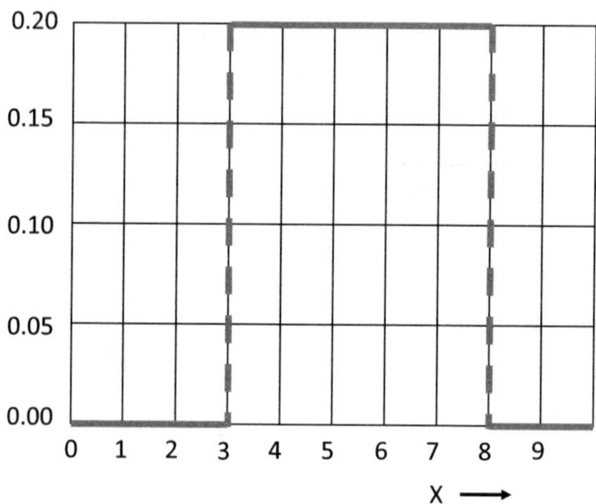

FIG. 5.6

A uniform distribution with a = 3, b = 8

Example. If X is a continuous random variable with X~Uniform(a,b). Find E(X). We know as per equation 5.33

$$F_x(x) = \begin{cases} \dfrac{1}{b-a} & a < x < b \\ 0 & \textit{Otherwise} \end{cases}$$

$$E(X) = \int_{-\infty}^{\infty} x F_x(x)\,dx$$

$$= \int_a^b x\left(\frac{1}{b-a}\right)dx$$

So,

$$= \frac{1}{b-a}\left[\frac{1}{2}x^2\right]_a^b = \frac{a+b}{2}$$

This is also corroborated by the fact that because X is uniformly distributed over the interval $[a, b]$ we can expect the mean to be at the middle point, $E(X) = \dfrac{a+b}{2}$

The mean and variance of a uniform random variable X are

$$\mu = E(X) = \frac{a+b}{2} \tag{5.36}$$

$$\sigma^2 = \mathrm{Var}(X) = \frac{(b-a)^2}{12} \tag{5.37}$$

This is a useful distribution when we don't have any prior knowledge of the actual pdf and all continuous values in the same range seems to be equally likely.

5.6.2   Gaussian (normal) distribution

The most widely used distribution in statistics and machine learning is the Gaussian or normal distribution. Its pdf is given by

$$f_x(x) = \frac{1}{\sqrt{2\pi}\sigma}\,e^{-(x-\mu)^2/(2\sigma^2)} \tag{5.38}$$

and the corresponding cdf looks like

$$F_x(x) = \frac{1}{\sqrt{2\pi}\sigma}\int_{-\infty}^{x} e^{-(\zeta-\mu)^2/(2\sigma^2)}\,d\zeta = \frac{1}{\sqrt{2\pi}}\int_{-\infty}^{(x-\mu)/\sigma} e^{-\zeta^2/2}\,d\zeta \tag{5.39}$$

For easier reference a function $\Phi(z)$ is defined as

$$\Phi(z) = \frac{1}{\sqrt{2\pi}}\int_{-\infty}^{z} e^{-\zeta^2/2}\,d\zeta \tag{5.40}$$

Which will help us evaluate the value of $F_x(x)$ which can be written as

$$F_x(x) = \Phi\left(\frac{x-\mu}{\sigma}\right) \tag{5.41}$$

It can be derived that

$$\Phi(-z) = 1 - \Phi(z)$$

Figure 5.7 shows the normal distribution graph with mean = 4, s.d. = 12.

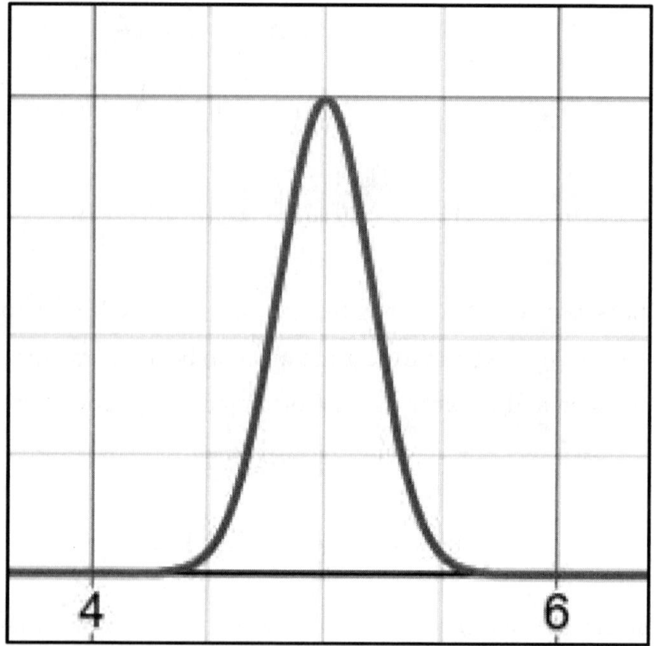

FIG. 5.7
A normal distribution graph

For a normal random variable, mean and variance are

$$\mu_x = E(X) = \mu \tag{5.42}$$

$$\sigma_x^2 = Var(X) = \sigma^2 \tag{5.43}$$

the notation $N(\mu; \sigma^2)$ is used to denote that $p(X = x) = N(x|\mu; \sigma^2)$.

A standard normal random variable is defined as the one whose mean is 0 and variance is 1 which means $Z = N(0;1)$. The plot for this is sometimes called the bell curve, (see Fig 5.8)

The Gaussian or Normal distribution is the most widely used distribution in the study of random phenomena in nature statistics due to few reasons:

1. It has two parameters that are easy to interpret, and which capture some of the most basic properties of a distribution, namely its mean and variance.

2. The central limit theorem (Section 5.8) provides the result that sums of independent random variables have an approximately Gaussian distribution, which makes it a good choice for modelling residual errors or 'noise'.

3. The Gaussian distribution makes the least number of assumptions, subject to the constraint of having a specified mean and variance and thus is a good default choice in many cases.

4. Its simple mathematical form is easy to implement, but often highly effective.

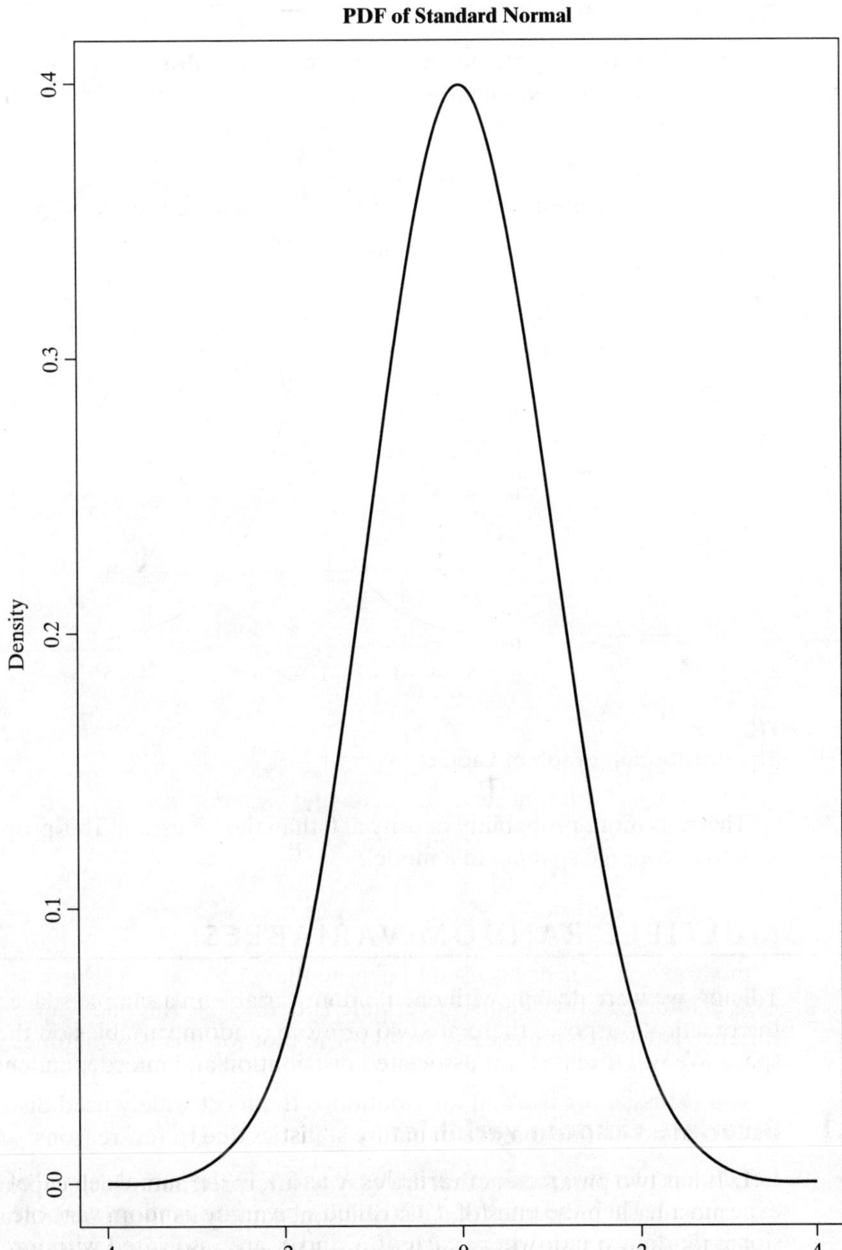

FIG. 5.8
A standard normal distribution graph

5.6.3   The laplace distribution

Another distribution with heavy tails is the **Laplace distribution,** which is also known as the **double-sided exponential** distribution. This has the following pdf:

$$\text{Lap}(x\,|\,\mu,b) = \frac{1}{2b}\, e^{-\frac{|x-m|}{b}} \tag{5.44}$$

Here μ is a location parameter and $b > 0$ is a scale parameter.

Figure 5.9 represents the distribution of Laplace $\left(0, \dfrac{1}{\sqrt{2}}\right)$.

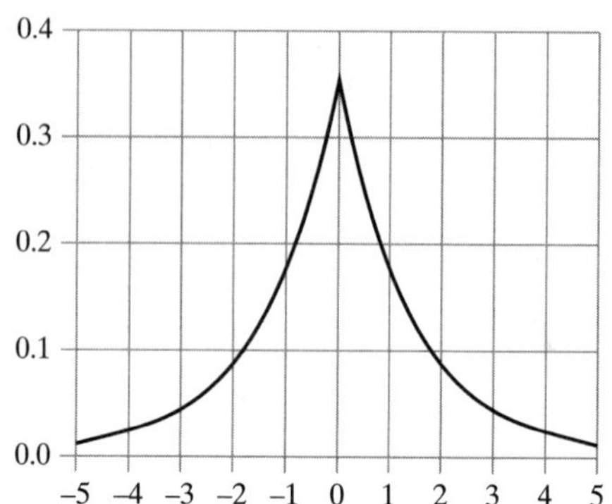

FIG. 5.9
The distribution graph of Laplace $\left(0, \dfrac{1}{\sqrt{2}}\right)$

This puts more probability density at 0 than the Gaussian. This property is a useful way to encourage sparsity in a model.

5.7   MULTIPLE RANDOM VARIABLES

Till now we were dealing with one random variable in a sample space, but in most of the practical purposes there are two or more random variables on the same sample space. We will discuss their associated distribution and interdependence.

5.7.1   Bivariate random variables

Let us consider two random variables X and Y in the sample space of S of a random experiment. Then the pair (X, Y) is called s bivariate random variable or two-dimensional random vector where each of X and Y are associated with a real number for every element of S. The range space of bivariate random variable (X, Y) is denoted by R_{xy} and (X, Y) can be considered as a function that to each point in S assigns a point (x, y) in the plane.

$$R_{xy} = \{(x, y); \zeta \in S \text{ and } X(\zeta) = x, Y(\zeta) = y\} \tag{5.45}$$

(X, Y) is called a discrete bivariate random variable if the random variables X and Y both by themselves are discrete. Similarly, (X, Y) is called a continuous bivariate random variable if the random variables X and Y both are continuous and is called a mixed bivariate random variable if one of X and Y is discrete and the other is continuous.

5.7.2   Joint distribution functions

The joint cumulative distribution function (or joint cdf) of X and Y is defined as:

$$F_{XY}(x, y) = P(X \leq x, Y \leq y) \tag{5.46}$$

For the event $(X \leq x, Y \leq y)$, we can define
$A = \{\zeta \in S; X(\zeta) \leq x\}$ and $B = \{\zeta \in S; Y(\zeta) \leq y\}$
And $P(A) = F_X(x)$ and $P(B) = F_Y(y)$
Then, $F_{XY}(x, y) = P(A \cap B)$.
For certain values of x and y, if A and B are independent events of S, then

$$F_{XY}(x, y) = P(A \cap B) = P(A)P(B) = F_X(x)F_Y(y) \tag{5.47}$$

Few important properties of joint cdf of two random variables which are similar to that of the cdf of single random variable are

1. $0 \leq F_{XY}(x, y) \leq 1$
If $x_1 \leq x_2$ and $y_1 \leq y_2$, then
$F_{XY}(x_1, y_1) \leq F_{XY}(x_2, y_1) \leq F_{XY}(x_2, y_2)$
2. $F_{XY}(x_1, y_1) \leq F_{XY}(x_1, y_2) \leq F_{XY}(x_2, y_2)$
3. $\lim\limits_{\substack{x \to \infty \\ y \to \infty}} F_{XY}(x, y) = F_{XY}(\infty, \infty) = 1$

4. $\lim\limits_{x \to -\infty} F_{XY}(x, y) = F_{XY}(-\infty, y) = 0$

5. $\lim\limits_{y \to -\infty} F_{XY}(x, y) = F_{XY}(x, -\infty) = 0$

6. $P(x_1 < X \leq x_2, Y \leq y) = F_{XY}(x_2, y) - F_{XY}(x_1, y)$
$P(X < x, y_1 < Y \leq y_2) = F_{XY}(x, y_2) - F_{XY}(x, y_1)$

5.7.3   Joint probability mass functions

For the discrete bivariate random variable (X, Y) if it takes the values (x_i, y_j) for certain allowable integers I and j, then the joint probability mass function (joint pmf) of (X, Y) is given by

$$p_{XY}(x_i, y_j) = P(X = x_i, Y = y_j) \tag{5.48}$$

Few important properties of $p_{XY}(x_i, y_j)$ are

1. $0 \leq p_{XY}(x_i, y_j) \leq 1$

2. $\sum\limits_{xi} \sum\limits_{yj} p_{XY}(x_i, y_j) = 1$

3. $P[(X, Y) \in A] = \sum(x_i, y_j) \in R_A \sum p_{XY}(x_i, y_j)$, where the summation is done over the points (x_i, y_j) in the range space R_A.

The joint cdf of a discrete bivariate random variable (X, Y) is given by

$$F_{XY}(x, y) = \sum_{x_j \leq xy} \sum_{j \leq y} P_{XY}(x_i, y_j) \tag{5.49}$$

5.7.4   Joint probability density functions

In case (X, Y) is a continuous bivariate random variable with cdf $F_{XY}(x, y)$ and then the function,

$$f_{XY}(x, y) = \frac{\partial^2 F_{XY}(x, y)}{\partial x \partial y} \tag{5.50}$$

is called the joint probability density function (joint pdf) of (X, Y). Thus, integrating, we get

$$F_{XY}(x, y) = \int_{-\infty}^{x} \int_{-\infty}^{y} {}^{x} f_{xy}(\zeta, \varepsilon) d\varepsilon d\zeta \tag{5.51}$$

Few important properties of $f_{xy}(x, y)$ are

1. $f_{xy}(x, y) \geq 0$

2. $\int_{-\infty}^{\infty} \int_{-\infty}^{\infty} x(x, y) dx dy = 1$

3. $P[(X, Y) \in A] = \int_{R_A} f_{xy}(x, y) dx dy$

5.7.5   Conditional distributions

While working with a discrete bivariate random variable, it is important to deduce the conditional probability function as X and Y are related in the finite space. Based on the joint pmf of (X, Y) the conditional pmf of Y when $X = x_i$ is defined as

$$P_{Y|X}(y_j \mid x_i) = \frac{P_{XY}(x_i, y_j)}{P_X(x_i)} \quad \text{when } P_X(x_i) > 0 \text{ and} \tag{5.52}$$

$$P_{X|Y}(x_j \mid y_i) = \frac{P_{XY}(x_i, y_j)}{P_Y(y_j)} \quad \text{when } P_Y(y_j) > 0 \text{when} \tag{5.53}$$

Note few important properties of $P_{Y|X}(y_j|x_i)$:

1. $0 \leq P_{Y|X}(y_j \mid x_i) \leq 1$

2. $\sum_{yj} P_{Y|X}(y_j \mid x_i) = 1$

In the same way, when (X, Y) is a continuous bivariate random variable and has joint pdf $f_{XY}(x, y)$, then the conditional cdf of Y in case $X = x$ is defined as

$$f_{Y|X}(y \mid x) = \frac{f_{xy}(x, y)}{f_X(x)} \quad \text{when } f_X(x) > 0 \text{ and} \tag{5.54}$$

$$f_{X|Y}(x \mid y) = \frac{f_{xy}(x, y)}{f_Y(y)} \quad \text{when } f_Y(x) > 0 \tag{5.55}$$

Note few important properties of $f_{Y|X}(y|x)$:

1. $f_{Y|X}(y|x) \geq 0$

2. $\int_{-\infty}^{\infty} f_{Y|X}(y\,|\,x)dy = 1$

5.7.6   Covariance and correlation

The **covariance** between two random variables X and Y measure the degree to which X and Y are (linearly) related, which means how X varies with Y and vice versa.

$$\mathrm{Cov}(X, Y) = E(XY) - E(X)E(Y) \tag{5.56}$$

So, if the variance is the measure of how a random variable varies with itself, then the covariance is the measure of how two random variables vary with each other.

Covariance can be between 0 and infinity. Sometimes, it is more convenient to work with a normalized measure, because covariance alone may not have enough information about the relationship among the random variables. For example, let's define 3 different random variables based on flipping of a coin:

$$X(n) = \begin{cases} 2 \; \textit{if } n \textit{ is head} \\ 1 \; \textit{if } n \textit{ is tail} \end{cases}$$

$$Y(n) = \begin{cases} 20 \; \textit{if } n \textit{ is head} \\ 10 \; \textit{if } n \textit{ is tail} \end{cases}$$

$$Z(n) = \begin{cases} 200 \; \textit{if } n \textit{ is head} \\ 100 \; \textit{if } n \textit{ is tail} \end{cases}$$

Just by looking into these random variables we can understand that they are essentially the same just a constant multiplied at their output. But the covariance of them will be very different when calculating with the equation 5.55:

$$\mathrm{Cov}(X,Y) = 2.5, \mathrm{Cov}(X,Z) = 25, \mathrm{Cov}(Y,Z) = 250$$

To solve this problem, it is necessary to add a normalizing term that provides this intelligence: $\sqrt{\mathrm{Var}(X) \cdot \mathrm{Var}(Y)}$

$$\text{So, Corr } (X, Y) = \frac{\mathrm{Cov}(X,Y)}{\sqrt{\mathrm{Var}(X) \cdot \mathrm{Var}(Y)}} \tag{5.57}$$

If Cov $(X,Y) = 0$, then we can say X and Y are uncorrelated. Then from equation 5.55, X and Y are uncorrelated if

$$E(X, Y) = E(X)\,E(Y)$$

If X and Y are independent then it can be shown that they are uncorrelated, but note that the converse is not true in general.

So, we should remember

- The outcomes of a Random Variable weighted by their probability is Expectation, $E(X)$.
- The difference between Expectation of a squared Random Variable and the Expectation of that Random Variable squared is Variance: $E(X^2) - E(X)^2$.
- Covariance, $E(XY) - E(X)E(Y)$ is the same as Variance, but here two Random Variables are compared, rather than a single Random Variable against itself.

- Correlation, Corr $(X, Y) = \dfrac{\text{Cov}(X, Y)}{\sqrt{\text{Var}(X) \cdot \text{Var}(Y)}}$ is the Covariance normalized.

Few important properties of correlation are

1. $-1 \le \text{corr}\,[X, Y] \le 1$. Hence, in a correlation matrix, each entry on the diagonal is 1, and the other entries are between -1 and 1.

2. $\text{corr}\,[X, Y] = 1$ if and only if $Y = aX + b$ for some parameters a and b, i.e., if there is a *linear* relationship between X and Y.

3. From property 2 it may seem that the correlation coefficient is related to the slope of the regression line, i.e., the coefficient a in the expression $Y = aX + b$. However, the regression coefficient is in fact given by $a = \text{cov}[X, Y]\,/\text{var}\,[X]$. A better way to interpret the correlation coefficient is as a degree of linearity.

5.8   CENTRAL LIMIT THEOREM

This is one of the most important theorems in probability theory. It states that if $X_1,\ldots X_n$ is a sequence of independent identically distributed random variables and each having mean μ and variance σ^2 and $\overline{X}_n = \dfrac{1}{n}\sum_{n=1}^{n} X_i = \dfrac{1}{n}\left(X_{1+\ldots} X_n\right)$

$$Z_n = \frac{X_1 + \ldots + X_n - n\mu}{\sigma\sqrt{n}} = \frac{\overline{X}_n - \mu}{\sigma\sqrt{n}} \tag{5.58}$$

As $n \to \infty$ (meaning for a very large but finite set) then Z_n tends to the standard normal.

$$\lim_{n \to \infty} Z_n\, N(0;1) \tag{5.59}$$

Or

$$\lim_{n \to \infty} F_{z_n}(z) = \lim_{n \to \infty} P\left(Z_n \le z\right) = \Phi(z) \tag{5.60}$$

where, $\Phi(z)$ is the cdf of a standard normal random variable.

So, according to the central limit theorem, irrespective of the distribution of the individual X_i's the distribution of the sum $S_n = X_1 + \ldots X_n$ is approximately normal for large n. This is the very important result as whenever we need to deal with a random variable which is the sum of a large number of random variables than using central limit theorem we can assume that this sum is normally distributed.

5.9   SAMPLING DISTRIBUTIONS

As we discussed earlier in this chapter, an important application of statistics in machine learning is how to draw a conclusion about a set or population based on the probability model of random samples of the set. For example, based on the malignancy sample test results of some random tumour cases we want to estimate the proportion of all tumours which are malignant and thus advise the doctors on the requirement or non-requirement of biopsy on each tumour case. As we can understand, different random samples may give different estimates, if we can get some knowledge about the variability of all possible estimates derived from the random samples, then we should be able to arrive at reasonable conclusions. Some of the terminologies used in this section are defined below:

Population is a finite set of objects being investigated.

Random sample refers to a sample of objects drawn from a population in a way that every member of the population has the same chance of being chosen.

Sampling distribution refers to the probability distribution of a random variable defined in a space of random samples.

5.9.1   Sampling with replacement

While choosing the samples from the population if each object chosen is returned to the population before the next object is chosen, then it is called the sampling with replacement. In this case, repetitions are allowed. That means, if the sample size n is chosen from the population size of N, then the number of such samples is

$$N \times N \times \ldots \ldots \times N = N^n \text{ , because each object can be repeated.}$$

Also, the probability of each sample being chosen is the same and is $.\dfrac{1}{N^n}$

For example, let's choose a random sample of 2 patients from a population of 3 patients $\{A, B, C\}$ and replacement is allowed. There can be 9 such ordered pairs, like:

$$(A, A), (A, B), (A, C), (B, A), (B, B), (B, C), (C, A), (C, B), (C, C)$$

That means the number of random samples of 2 from the population of 3 is

$$N^n = 3^2 = 9$$

and each of the random sample has probability $\dfrac{1}{N^n} = \dfrac{1}{9}$ of being chosen.

5.9.2   Sampling without replacement

In case, we don't return the object being chosen to the population before choosing the next object, then the random sample of size n is defined as the unordered subset of n objects from the population and called sampling without replacement. The number of such samples that can be drawn from the population size of N is

$$\binom{N}{n} = \frac{N!}{n!(N-n)!}$$

In our previous example, the unordered sample of 2 that can be created from the population of 3 patients when replacement is not allowed is

$(A, B), (A, C), (B, C)$

$$\binom{3}{2} = \frac{3!}{2!(3-2)!} = 3$$

Also, each of these 3 samples of size 2 has the probability of getting chosen as $\dfrac{1}{3}$

5.9.3   Mean and variance of sample

Let us consider X as a random variable with mean μ and standard deviation from a population N. A random sample of size n, drawn without replacement will generate n values $x_1, x_2.....,x_n$ for X. When samples are drawn with replacement, these values are independent of each other and can be considered as values of n independent random variables $X_1, X_2,...., X_n$, each having mean μ and variance σ^2. The sample mean is a random variable $\bar{X}$ as

$$\overline{X} = \frac{X_1 + X_2 + ... + X_n}{n} \tag{5.61}$$

As $\overline{X}$ is a random variable, it also has a mean $\mu_{\bar{X}}$ and variance $\sigma_{\bar{X}}^2$ and it is related to population parameters as:

$$\mu_{\bar{x}} = \mu \text{ and } \sigma_{\bar{x}}^2 = \frac{\sigma^2}{n} \tag{5.62}$$

for a large number of n, if X is approximately normally distributed, then $\overline{X}$ will also be normally distributed.

When the samples are drawn without replacement, then the sample values $x_1, x_2.....,x_n$ for random variable X are not independent. The sample mean $\overline{X}$ has the mean $\mu_{\bar{X}}$ and variance σ_X^2 given by:

$$\mu_{\bar{x}} = \mu \text{ and } \sigma_{\bar{X}}^2 = \frac{\sigma^2}{n}\left(\frac{N-n}{N-1}\right) \tag{5.63}$$

where, N is the size of the population and n < N. Also if X is normally distributed then also has a normal distribution.

Now, based on the central limit theorem, if the sample size of a random variable based on a finite population is large then the sample mean is approximately normally distributed irrespective of the distribution of the population. For most of the practical applications of sampling, when the sample size is large enough (as a rule of thumb ≥ 30) the sample mean is approximately normally distributed. Also, when a random sample is drawn from a large population, it can be assumed that the values $x_1, x_2.....,x_n$ are independent. This assumption of independence is one of the key to application of probability theory in statistical inference. We use the terms like 'population is much larger than the sample size' or 'population is large compared to its sample size', etc. to denote that the population is large enough to make the samples independent of each other. In practice, if $\sqrt{\frac{N-n}{N-1}} \cong 1$, then independence may be assumed.

5.10   HYPOTHESIS TESTING

While dealing with random variables a common situation is when we have to make certain decisions or choices based on the observations or data which are random in nature. The solutions for dealing with these situations is called decision theory or hypothesis testing and it is a widely used process in real life situations. As we discussed earlier, the key component of machine learning is to use a sample-based training data which can be used to represent the larger set of actual data and it is important to estimate how confidently an outcome can be related to the behaviour of the training data so that the decisions on the actual data can be made. So, hypothesis testing is an integral part of machine learning.

In terms of statistics, a hypothesis is an assumption about the probability law of the random variables. Take, e.g. a random sample $(X_1,\ldots\ldots X_n)$ of a random variable whose pdf on parameter κ is given by $f(x, \kappa) = f(x_1, x_2\ldots., x_n; \kappa)$. We want to test the assumption $\kappa = \kappa_0$ against the assumption $\kappa = \kappa_1$. In this case, the assumption $\kappa = \kappa_0$ is called null hypothesis and is denoted by H_0. Assumption $\kappa = \kappa_1$ is called alternate hypothesis and is denoted by H_1.

$$H_0: \kappa = \kappa_0$$

$$H_1: \kappa = \kappa_1$$

A simple hypothesis is the one where all the parameters are specified with an exact value, like H_0 or H_1 in this case. But if the parameters don't have an exact value, like $H_1:\kappa \neq \kappa_1$ then H_1 is composite.

Concept of hypothesis testing is the decision process used for validating a hypothesis. We can interpret a decision process by dividing an observation space, say R into two regions – R_0 and R_1. If $x = (x_1,\ldots..x_n)$ are the set of observation, then if $x \in R_0$ the decision is in favor of H_0 and if $x \in R_1$ then the decision is in favor of H_1. The region R_0 is called acceptance region as the null hypothesis is accepted and R_1 is the rejection region. There are 4 possible decisions based on the two regions in observation space:

1. H_0 is true; accept H_0➡ this is a correct decision

2. H_0 is true; reject H_0 (which means accept H_1) ➡ this is an incorrect decision

3. H_1 is true; accept H_1➡ this is a correct decision

4. H_1 is true; reject H_1 (which means accept H_0) ➡ this is an incorrect decision

So, we can see there is the possibility of 2 correct and 2 incorrect decisions and the corresponding actions. The erroneous decisions can be termed as:

Type I error: reject H_0 (or accept H_1) when H_0 is true. The example of this situation is in a malignancy test of a tumour, a benign tumour is accepted as malignant tumour and corresponding treatment is started. This is also called Alpha error where good is interpreted as bad.

Type II error: reject H_1 (or accept H_0) when H_1 is true. The example of this situation is in a malignancy test of a tumour, a malignant tumour is accepted as a benign tumour and no treatment for malignancy is started. This is also called Beta error where bad is interpreted as good and can have a more devastating impact.

The probabilities of Type I and Type II errors are

$$P_I = P(D_1 \mid H_0) = P(x \in R_1; H_0)$$
$$P_{II} = P(D_0 \mid H_1) = P(x \in R_0; H_1)$$

where, D_i $(I = 0, 1)$ denotes the event that the decision is for accepting H_i. P_I is also denoted by α and known as level of significance whereas P_{II} is denoted by β and is known as the power of the test. Here, α and β are not independent of each other as they represent the probabilities of the event from same decision problem.

So, normally a decrease in one type of error leads to an increase in another type of when the sample size is fixed. Though it is desirable to reduce both types of errors it is only possible by increasing the sample size. In all practical applications of hypothesis testing, each of the four possible outcomes and courses of actions are associated with relative importance or certain cost and thus the final goal can be to reduce the overall cost.

So, the probabilities of correct decisions are

$$P(D_0 \mid H_0) = P(x \in R_0; H_0)$$
$$P(D_1 \mid H_1) = P(x \in R_1; H_1)$$

5.11 MONTE CARLO APPROXIMATION

Though we discussed the distribution functions of the random variables, in practical situations it is difficult to compute them using the change of variables formula. Monte Carlo approximation provides a simple but powerful alternative to this. Let's first generate S samples from the distribution, as $x1, \ldots, x_S$. For these samples, we can approximate the distribution of $f(X)$ by using the empirical distribution of $\{f(x_s)\}_{s=1}^{S}$.

In principle, Monte Carlo methods can be used to solve any problem which has a probabilistic interpretation. We know that by the law of large numbers, integrals described by the expected value of some random variable can be approximated by taking the empirical mean (or the sample mean) of independent samples of the random variable. A widely used sampler is Markov chain Monte Carlo (MCMC) sampler for parametrizing the probability distribution of a random variable. The main idea is to design a judicious Markov chain model with a prescribed stationary probability distribution. Monte Carlo techniques are now widely used in statistics and machine learning as well. Using the Monte Carlo technique, we can approximate the expected value of any function of a random variable by simply drawing samples from the population of the random variable, and then computing the arithmetic mean of the function applied to the samples, as follows:

$$E[f(X)] = \int f(x)p(x)dx \approx \frac{1}{S}\sum_{S=1}^{S} f(x_s) \text{ where } x_s \sim p(X). \qquad (5.64)$$

This is also called Monte Carlo integration, and is easier to evaluate than the numerical integration which attempts to evaluate the function at a fixed grid of points. Monte Carlo evaluates the function only in places where there is a non-negligible probability.

For different functions $f()$, the approximation of some important quantities can be obtained

- $\bar{x} = \dfrac{1}{S}\sum_{s=1}^{s} x_s \rightarrow E[X]$

- $\dfrac{1}{S}\sum_{s=1}^{S}(x_S - \bar{x})^2 \rightarrow \text{var}[X]$

- $\dfrac{1}{S}\#\{x_s \leq c\} \rightarrow P(X \leq c)$

- $\text{median}\{x_1, \ldots, x_s\} \rightarrow \text{median}(X)$

5.12 SUMMARY

1. Frequentist interpretation of probability represents the long run frequencies of events whereas the Bayesian interpretation of probability tries to quantify the uncertainty of some event and thus focuses on information rather than repeated trials.

2. According to the Bayes rule, $p(A|B) = p(B|A)\, p(A)/\, p(B)$.

3. A discrete random variable is expressed with the probability mass function (pmf) $p(x) = p(X = x)$.

4. A continuous random variable is expressed with the probability density function (pdf) $p(x) = p(X = x)$.

5. The cumulative distribution function (cdf) of random variable X can be obtained by $F_x(x) = p(X \le x) = \int_{-\infty}^{x} f_x(x)dx$

6. The equation to find out the mean for random variable X is:

$$\mu_x = E(X) = \sum_k x_k p_x(x_k) \text{ when } X \text{ is discrete}$$

$$\mu_x = E(X) = \int_{-\infty}^{\infty} x f_x(x)dx \text{ when } X \text{ is continuous.}$$

7. The equation to find out the variance for random variable X is

$$\sigma_x^2 = \text{Var}(X) = E\left\{[X - E(X)]^2\right\} \text{ so,}$$

$$\sigma_x^2 = \sum_k (x_k - \mu_x)^2 p_x(x_k) \text{ when } X \text{ is discrete}$$

$$\sigma_x^2 = \int_{-\infty}^{\infty} (x - \mu_x)^2 f_x(x)dx \text{ when } X \text{ is continuous.}$$

8. When we have a situation where the outcome of a trial is withered 'success' or 'failure', then the behaviour of the random variable X can be represented by Bernoulli distribution.

9. If n independent Bernoulli trials are performed and X represents the number of success in those n trials, then X is called a binomial random variable.

10. To model the outcomes of tossing a K-sided die, or for experiments where the outcome can be multiple, we can use the multinomial distribution.

11. The Poisson random variable has a wide range of application as it may be used as an approximation for binomial with parameter (n, p) when n is large and p is small and thus np is of moderate size.

12. Uniform distribution, Gaussian (normal) distribution, Laplace distribution are examples for few important continuous random distributions.

13. If there are two random variables X and Y in the sample space of S of a random experiment, then the pair (X, Y) is called as bivariate random variable.

14. The covariance between two random variables X and Y measures the degree to which X and Y are (linearly) related.

15. According to the central limit theorem, irrespective of the distribution of the individual X_i's the distribution of the sum $S_n - X_1 + \dots X_n$ is approximately normal for large n.

16. In hypothesis testing:

Type I error: reject H_0 (or accept H_1) when H_0 is true.

Type II error: reject H_1 (or accept H_0) when H_1 is true.

17. Using the Monte Carlo technique, we can approximate the expected value of any function of a random variable by simply drawing samples from the population of the random variable, and then computing the arithmetic mean of the function applied to the samples.

SAMPLE QUESTIONS

MULTIPLE-CHOICE QUESTIONS (1 MARK EACH)

1. The probabilistic approach used in machine learning is closely related to:
(a) Statistics
(b) Physics
(c) Mathematics
(d) Psychology

2. This type of interpretation of probability tries to quantify the uncertainty of some event and thus focuses on information rather than repeated trials.
(a) Frequency interpretation of probability
(b) Gaussian interpretation of probability
(c) Machine learning interpretation of probability
(d) Bayesian interpretation of probability

3. The reason the Bayesian interpretation can be used to model the uncertainty of events is that it does not expect the long run frequencies of the events to happen.
(a) True
(b) False

4. $p(A,B) = p() = p(A|B)\, p(B)$ is referred as:
(a) Conditional probability
(b) Unconditional probability
(c) Bayes rule
(d) Product rule

5. Based on this **joint distribution** on two events $p(A,B)$, we can define the **this distribution** as follows:

6. $p(A) = p(A,B) = p(A|B = b)\, p(B = b)$
(a) Conditional distribution
(b) Marginal distribution
(c) Bayes distribution
(d) Normal distribution

7. We can define this probability as $p(A|B) = p(A,B)/p(B)$ if $p(B) > 0$
(a) Conditional probability
(b) Marginal probability
(c) Bayes probability
(d) Normal probability

8. In statistical terms, this represents the weighted average score.
(a) Variance
(c) Median
(b) Mean
(d) More

9. The **covariance** between two random variables X and Y measures the degree to which X and Y are (linearly) related, which means how X varies with Y and vice versa. What is the formula for Cov (X,Y)?
(a) $\text{Cov}(X,Y) = E(XY) - E(X)E(Y)$
(b) $\text{Cov}(X,Y) = E(XY) + E(X)E(Y)$
(c) $\text{Cov}(X,Y) = E(XY)/E(X)E(Y)$
(d) $\text{Cov}(X,Y) = E(X)E(Y)/E(XY)$

10. The binomial distribution can be used to model the outcomes of coin tosses.
(a) True
(b) False

11. Two events A and B are called mutually exclusive if they can happen together.
(a) True
(b) False

SHORT-ANSWER TYPE QUESTIONS (5 MARKS EACH)

1. Define the Bayesian interpretation of probability.

2. Define probability of a union of two events with equation.

3. What is joint probability? What is its formula?

4. What is chain rule of probability?

5. What is conditional probability means? What is the formula of it?

6. What are continuous random variables?

7. What are Bernoulli distributions? What is the formula of it?

8. What is binomial distribution? What is the formula?

9. What is Poisson distribution? What is the formula?

10. Define covariance.

11. Define correlation

12. Define sampling with replacement. Give example.

13. What is sampling without replacement? Give example.

14. What is hypothesis? Give example.

LONG-ANSWER TYPE QUESTIONS (10 MARKS QUESTIONS)

1. Let X be a discrete random variable with the following PMF

$$P_X(x) = \begin{cases} 0.1 \ for \ x = 0.2 \\ 0.2 \ for \ x = 0.4 \\ 0.2 \ for \ x = 0.5 \\ 0.3 \ for \ x = 0.8 \\ 0.2 \ for \ x = 1 \\ 0 \ otherwise \end{cases}$$

(a) Find the range R_X of the random variable X.
(b) Find P($X \leq 0.5$)
(c) Find P($0.25 < X < 0.75$)
(d) Find P($X = 0.2 | X < 0.6$)

2. Two equal and fair dice are rolled and we observed two numbers X and Y.
   (a) Find R_X, R_Y and the PMFs of X and Y.
   (b) Find $P(X = 2, Y = 6)$.
   (c) Find $P(X > 3 | Y = 2)$.
   (d) If $Z = X + Y$. Find the range and PMF of Z.
   (e) Find $P(X = 4 | Z = 8)$.

3. In an exam, there were 20 multiple-choice questions. Each question had 44 possible options. A student knew the answer to 10 questions, but the other 10 questions were unknown to him and he chose answers randomly. If the score of the student X is equal to the total number of correct answers, then find out the PMF of X. What is P($X > 15$)?

4. The number of students arriving at a college between a time interval is a Poisson random variable. On an average 10 students arrive per hour. Let X be the number of students arriving from 10 am to 11:30 am. What is P($10 < X \leq 15$)?

5. If we have two independent random variables X and Y such that $X \sim$ Poisson(α) and $Y \sim$ Poisson(β). Define a new random variable as $Z = X + Y$. Find out the PMF of Z.

6. There is a discrete random variable X with the pmf.

$$P_x(x) = \begin{cases} \dfrac{1}{4} & \text{when } x = -2 \\[2mm] \dfrac{1}{8} & \text{when } x = -1 \dfrac{1}{4} \text{ when } x = 20 \text{ otherwise} \text{wen } x = 0 \\[2mm] \dfrac{11}{84} & \text{when } x = 1 \end{cases}$$

If we define a new random variable $Y = (X + 1)^2$ then
(a) Find the range of Y.
(b) Find the pmf of Y.

7. If X is a continuous random variable with PDF

(a) $f_X(x) = \begin{cases} cx2 & |x| \leq 1 \\ 0 & Otherwise \end{cases}$ Find the constant cc.

(b) Find EX and Var(X).

(c) Find $P\left(X \geq \dfrac{1}{2} \right)$.

8. If X is a continuous random variable with pdf
$$f_x(x) = \begin{cases} 4x^3 & 0 < x \leq 1 \\ 0 & otherwise \end{cases}$$

Find $P\left(X \leq \dfrac{2}{3} \mid X \rangle \dfrac{1}{3} \right)$

9. If $X \sim$ Uniform $\left(\dfrac{-\pi}{2}, \pi \right)$ and $Y = \sin(X)$, then find $f_Y(y)$.

10. If X is a random variable with CDF

$$F_X(x) = \begin{cases} 1 & X \geq 1 \\ \dfrac{1}{2} + \dfrac{x}{2} & \text{where } 0 \leq X < 1 \\ 0 & \text{where } x < 0 \end{cases}$$

(a) What kind of random variable is X: discrete, continuous, or mixed?
(b) Find the PDF of X, $f_X(x)$.
(c) Find $E(e^X)$.
(d) Find $P(X = 0|X \leq 0.5)$.

11. There are two random variables X and Y with joint PMF given in Table below
(a) Find $P(X \leq 2, Y \leq 4)$.
(b) Find the marginal PMFs of X and Y.
(c) Find $P(Y = 2|X = 1)$.
(d) Are X and Y independent?

(L)	$Y = 2$	$Y = 4$	$Y = 5$
$X = 1$	1/12	1/24	1/24
$X = 2$	1/6	1/12	1/8
$X = 3$	¼	1/8	1/12

12. There is a box containing 40 white shirts and 60 black shirts. If we choose 10 shirts (without replacement) at random, then find the joint PMF of X and Y where X is the number of white shirts and Y is the number of black shirts.

13. If X and Y are two jointly continuous random variables with joint PDF

$$f_{XY}(x, y) = \begin{cases} 6xy & \text{where } 0 \leq x \leq 1, 0 \leq y \leq \sqrt{x} \\ 0 & \text{otherwise} \end{cases}$$

(a) Find $f_X(x)$ and $f_Y(y)$.
(b) Are X and Y independent to each other?
(c) Find the conditional PDF of X given $Y = y$, $f_{X|Y}(x|y)$.
(d) Find $E[X|Y = y]$, for $0 \leq y \leq 1$.
(e) Find $\text{Var}(X|Y = y)$, for $0 \leq y \leq 1$.

14. There are 100 men on a ship. If X_i is the weight of the ith man on the ship and Xi's are independent and identically distributed and also $EX_i = \mu = 170$ and $\sigma_{Xi} = \sigma = 30$. Find the probability that the total weight of the men on the ship exceeds 18,000.

15. Let $X_1, X_2, \ldots\ldots, X_{25}$ are the independent and identically distributed. And have the following PMF

$$P_X(k) = \begin{cases} 0.6 & k = 1 \\ 0.4 & k = -1 \\ 0 & \text{otherwise} \end{cases}$$

If $Y = X_1 + X_2 + \ldots + X_n$, estimate $P(4 \leq Y \leq 6)$ using central limit theorem.

Chapter 6

Bayesian Concept Learning

OBJECTIVE OF THE CHAPTER:

Principles of probability for classification are an important area of machine learning algorithms. In our practical life, our decisions are affected by our prior knowledge or belief about an event. Thus, an event that is otherwise very unlikely to occur may be considered by us seriously to occur in certain situations if we know that in the past, the event had certainly occurred when other events were observed. The same concept is applied in machine learning using Bayes' theorem and the related algorithms discussed in this chapter. The concepts of probabilities discussed in the previous chapters are used extensively in this chapter.

6.1 INTRODUCTION

In the last chapter, we discussed the rules of probability and possible uses of probability, distribution functions, and hypothesis testing principles in the machine learning domain. In this chapter, we will discuss the details of the Bayesian theorem and how it provides the basis for machine learning concepts. The technique was derived from the work of the 18th century mathematician Thomas Bayes. He developed the foundational mathematical principles, known as Bayesian methods, which describe the probability of events, and more importantly, how probabilities should be revised when there is additional information available.

6.2   WHY BAYESIAN METHODS ARE IMPORTANT?

Bayesian learning algorithms, like the naive Bayes classifier, are highly practical approaches to certain types of learning problems as they can calculate explicit probabilities for hypotheses. In many cases, they are equally competitive or even outperform the other learning algorithms, including decision tree and neural network algorithms.

Bayesian classifiers use a simple idea that the training data are utilized to calculate an observed probability of each class based on feature values. When the same classifier is used later for unclassified data, it uses the observed probabilities to predict the most likely class for the new features. The application of the observations from the training data can also be thought of as applying our prior knowledge or prior belief to the probability of an outcome, so that it has higher probability of meeting the actual or real-life outcome. This simple concept is used in Bayes' rule and applied for training a machine in machine learning terms. Some of the real-life uses of Bayesian classifiers are as follows:

- Text-based classification such as spam or junk mail filtering, author identification, or topic categorization
- Medical diagnosis such as given the presence of a set of observed symptoms during a disease, identifying the probability of new patients having the disease
- Network security such as detecting illegal intrusion or anomaly in computer networks

One of the strengths of Bayesian classifiers is that they utilize all available parameters to subtly change the predictions, while many other algorithms tend to ignore the features that have weak effects. Bayesian classifiers assume that even if few individual parameters have small effect on the outcome, the collective effect of those parameters could be quite large. For such learning tasks, the naive Bayes classifier is most effective.

Some of the features of Bayesian learning methods that have made them popular are as follows:

- Prior knowledge of the candidate hypothesis is combined with the observed data for arriving at the final probability of a hypothesis. So, two important components are the prior probability of each candidate hypothesis and the probability distribution over the observed data set for each possible hypothesis.
- The Bayesian approach to learning is more flexible than the other approaches because each observed training pattern can influence the outcome of the hypothesis by increasing or decreasing the estimated probability about the hypothesis, whereas most of the other algorithms tend to eliminate a hypothesis if that is inconsistent with the single training pattern.
- Bayesian methods can perform better than the other methods while validating the hypotheses that make probabilistic predictions. For example, when starting a new software project, on the basis of the demographics of the project, we can predict the probability of encountering challenges during execution of the project.

- Through the easy approach of Bayesian methods, it is possible to classify new instances by combining the predictions of multiple hypotheses, weighted by their respective probabilities.

- In some cases, when Bayesian methods cannot compute the outcome deterministically, they can be used to create a standard for the optimal decision against which the performance of other methods can be measured.

As we discussed above, the success of the Bayesian method largely depends on the availability of initial knowledge about the probabilities of the hypothesis set. So, if these probabilities are not known to us in advance, we have to use some background knowledge, previous data or assumptions about the data set, and the related probability distribution functions to apply this method. Moreover, it normally involves high computational cost to arrive at the optimal Bayes hypothesis.

6.3   BAYES' THEOREM

Before we discuss Bayes' theorem and its application in concept learning, we should be clear about what is ***concept learning***. Let us take an example of how a child starts to learn meaning of new words, e.g. 'ball'. The child is provided with positive examples of 'objects' which are 'ball'. At first, the child may be confused with many different colours, shapes and sizes of the balls and may also get confused with some objects which look similar to ball, like a balloon or a globe. The child's parent continuously feeds her positive examples like 'that is a ball', 'this is a green ball', 'bring me that small ball', etc. Seldom there are negative examples used for such concept teaching, like 'this is a non-ball', but the parent may clear the confusion of the child when it points to a balloon and says it is a ball by saying 'that is not a ball'. But it is observed that the learning is most influenced through positive examples rather than through negative examples, and the expectation is that the child will be able to identify the object 'ball' from a wide variety of objects and different types of balls kept together once the concept of a ball is clear to her. We can extend this example to explain how we can expect machines to learn through the feeding of positive examples, which forms the basis for concept learning.

To relate the above-mentioned learning concept with the mathematical model of Bayes, we can correlate the learning process of 'meaning of a word' as equivalent to learning, a concept using binary classification. Let us define a concept set C and a corresponding function $f(k)$. We also define $f(k) = 1$, when k is within the set C and $f(k) = 0$ otherwise. Our aim is to learn the indicator function f that defines which elements are within the set C. So, by using the function f, we will be able to classify the element either inside or outside our concept set. In Bayes' theorem, we will learn how to use standard probability calculation to determine the uncertainty about the function f, and we can validate the classification by feeding positive examples.

There are few notations that will be introduced before going into the details of Bayes' theorem. In Chapter 5, we already discussed Bayes' probability rule as given below:

$$P(A \mid B) = \frac{P(B \mid A)P(A)}{P(B)}$$

where A and B are conditionally related events and $p(A|B)$ denotes the probability of event A occurring when event B has already occurred.

Let us assume that we have a training data set D where we have noted some observed data. Our task is to determine the best hypothesis in space H by using the knowledge of D.

6.3.1   Prior

The prior knowledge or belief about the probabilities of various hypotheses in H is called Prior in context of Bayes' theorem. For example, if we have to determine whether a particular type of tumour is malignant for a patient, the prior knowledge of such tumours becoming malignant can be used to validate our current hypothesis and is a prior probability or simply called Prior.

Let us introduce few notations to explain the concepts. We will assume that $P(h)$ is the initial probability of a hypothesis 'h' that the patient has a malignant tumour based only on the malignancy test, without considering the prior knowledge of the correctness of the test process or the so-called training data. Similarly, $P(T)$ is the prior probability that the training data will be observed or, in this case, the probability of positive malignancy test results. We will denote $P(T|h)$ as the probability of observing data T in a space where 'h' holds true, which means the probability of the test results showing a positive value when the tumour is actually malignant.

6.3.2   Posterior

The probability that a particular hypothesis holds for a data set based on the Prior is called the posterior probability or simply Posterior. In the above example, the probability of the hypothesis that the patient has a malignant tumour considering the Prior of correctness of the malignancy test is a posterior probability. In our notation, we will say that we are interested in finding out $P(h|T)$, which means whether the hypothesis holds true given the observed training data T. This is called the posterior probability or simply Posterior in machine learning language. So, the prior probability $P(h)$, which represents the probability of the hypothesis independent of the training data (Prior), now gets refined with the introduction of influence of the training data as $P(h|T)$.

According to Bayes' theorem

$$P(h \mid T) = \frac{P(T \mid h)P(h)}{P(T)}$$

combines the prior and posterior probabilities together.

From the above equation, we can deduce that $P(h|T)$ increases as $P(h)$ and $P(T|h)$ increases and also as $P(T)$ decreases. The simple explanation is that when there is more probability that T can occur independently of h then it is less probable that h can get support from T in its occurrence.

It is a common question in machine learning problems to find out the maximum probable hypothesis h from a set of hypotheses H ($h \in H$) given the observed training data T. This maximally probable hypothesis is called the ***maximum a posteriori (MAP)*** hypothesis. By using Bayes' theorem, we can identify the MAP hypothesis from the posterior probability of each candidate hypothesis:

$$h_{\mathrm{MAP}} = \mathrm{argmax}_{h \in H} P(h \mid T)$$

$$= \mathrm{argmax}_{h \in H} \frac{P(T \mid h)P(h)}{P(T)}$$

and as $P(T)$ is a constant independent of h, in this case, we can write

$$= \mathrm{argmax}_{h \in H} P(T \mid h)P(h) \tag{6.1}$$

6.3.3   Likelihood

In certain machine learning problems, we can further simplify equation 6.1 if every hypothesis in H has equal probable priori as $P(h_i) = P(h_j)$, and then, we can determine $P(h \mid T)$ from the probability $P(T \mid h)$ only. Thus, $P(T \mid h)$ is called the likelihood of data T given h, and any hypothesis that maximizes $P(T \mid h)$ is called the maximum likelihood (ML) hypothesis, h_{ML}. See figure 6.1 and 6.2 for the conceptual and mathematical representation of Bayes theorem and the relationship of Prior, Posterior and Likelihood.

$$h_{\mathrm{ML}} = \mathrm{argmax}_{h \in H} P(T \mid h) \tag{6.2}$$

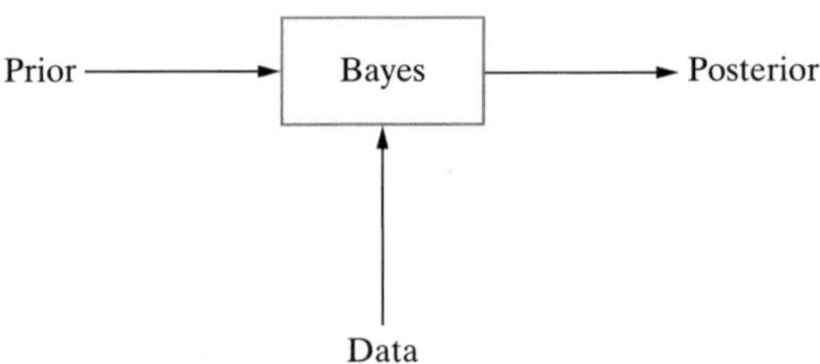

FIG. 6.1
Bayes' theorem

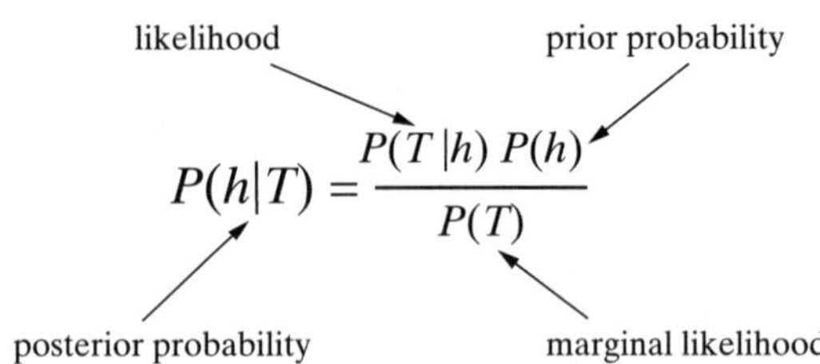

FIG. 6.2
Concept of prior, posterior, and likelihood

Points to ponder:

Arriving at the refined probability of an event in the light of probability of a related event is a powerful concept and relates very closely with our day-to-day handling of events and using our knowledge to influence the decisions.

∎

Example. Let us take the example of malignancy identification in a particular patient's tumour as an application for Bayes rule. We will calculate how the prior knowledge of the percentage of cancer cases in a sample population and probability of the test result being correct influence the probability outcome of the correct diagnosis. We have two alternative hypotheses: (1) a particular tumour is of malignant type and (2) a particular tumour is non-malignant type. The priori available are—1. only 0.5% of the population has this kind of tumour which is malignant, 2. the laboratory report has some amount of incorrectness as it could detect the malignancy was present only with 98% accuracy whereas could show the malignancy was not present correctly only in 97% of cases. This means the test predicted malignancy was present which actually was a false alarm in 2% of the cases, and also missed detecting the real malignant tumour in 3% of the cases.

Solution: Let us denote Malignant Tumour = MT, Positive Lab Test = PT, Negative Lab Test = NT

h_1 = the particular tumour is of malignant type = MT in our example

h_2 = the particular tumour is not malignant type = !MT in our example

$$P(\text{MT}) = 0.005 \qquad P(!\text{MT}) = 0.995$$
$$P(\text{PT}\,|\,\text{MT}) = 0.98 \qquad P(\text{PT}\,|\,!\text{MT}) = 0.02$$
$$P(\text{NT}\,|\,!\text{MT}) = 0.97 \qquad P(\text{NT}\,|\,\text{MT}) = 0.03$$

So, for the new patient, if the laboratory test report shows positive result, let us see if we should declare this as the malignancy case or not:

$$P(h_1\,|\,\text{PT}) = \frac{P(\text{PT}\,|\,h_1)\cdot P(h_1)}{P(\text{PT})}$$
$$= P(\text{PT}\,|\,\text{MT})P(\text{MT})$$
$$= 0.98 \times 0.005$$
$$= 0.0049$$
$$= 0.49\%$$

$$P(h_2\,|\,\text{PT}) = \frac{P(\text{PT}\,|\,h_2)\cdot P(h_2)}{P(\text{PT})}$$
$$= P(\text{PT}\,|\,!\text{MT})P(!\text{MT})$$
$$= 0.02 \times 0.995$$
$$= 0.0199$$
$$= 1.99\%$$

As $P(h_2|\text{PT})$ is higher than $P(h_1|\text{PT})$, it is clear that the hypothesis h_2 has more probability of being true. So, $h_{\text{MAP}} = h_2 = !\text{MT}$.

This indicates that even if the posterior probability of malignancy is significantly higher than that of non-malignancy, the probability of this patient not having malignancy is still higher on the basis of the prior knowledge. Also, it should be noted that through Bayes' theorem, we identified the probability of one hypothesis being higher than the other hypothesis, and we did not completely accept or reject the hypothesis by this theorem. Furthermore, there is very high dependency on the availability of the prior data for successful application of Bayes' theorem.

6.4   BAYES' THEOREM AND CONCEPT LEARNING

One simplistic view of concept learning can be that if we feed the machine with the training data, then it can calculate the posterior probability of the hypotheses and outputs the most probable hypothesis. This is also called brute-force Bayesian learning algorithm, and it is also observed that consistency in providing the right probable hypothesis by this algorithm is very comparable to the other algorithms.

6.4.1   Brute-force Bayesian algorithm

We will now discuss how to use the MAP hypothesis output to design a simple learning algorithm called brute-force map learning algorithm. Let us assume that the learner considers a finite hypothesis space H in which the learner will try to learn some target concept $c{:}X \rightarrow \{0,1\}$ where X is the instance space corresponding to H. The sequence of training examples is $\{(x_1, t_1), (x_2, t_2),\ldots, (x_m, t_m)\}$, where x_i is the instance of X and t_i is the target concept of x_i defined as $t_i = c(x_i)$. Without impacting the efficiency of the algorithm, we can assume that the sequence of instances of x $\{x_1,\ldots,x_m\}$ is held fixed, and then, the sequence of target values becomes $T = \{t_1,\ldots,t_m\}$.

For calculating the highest posterior probability, we can use Bayes' theorem as discussed earlier in this chapter:

Calculate the posterior probability of each hypothesis h in H:

$$P(h\,|\,T) = \frac{P(T\,|\,h)P(h)}{P(T)}$$

Identify the h_{MAP} with the highest posterior probability

$$h_{\mathrm{MAP}} = \mathrm{argmax}_{h \in H}P(h\,|\,T)$$

Please note that calculating the posterior probability for each hypothesis requires a very high volume of computation, and for a large volume of hypothesis space, this may be difficult to achieve.

Let us try to connect the concept learning problem with the problem of identifying the h_{MAP}. On the basis of the probability distribution of $P(h)$ and $P(T|h)$, we can derive the prior knowledge of the learning task. There are few important assumptions to be made as follows:

1. The training data or target sequence T is noise free, which means that it is a direct function of X only (i.e. $t_i = c(x_i)$)

2. The concept c lies within the hypothesis space H

3. Each hypothesis is equally probable and independent of each other

On the basis of assumption 3, we can say that each hypothesis h within the space H has equal prior probability, and also because of assumption 2, we can say that these prior probabilities sum up to 1. So, we can write

$$P(h) = \frac{1}{|H|} \text{ for all } h \text{ within } H \tag{6.3}$$

$P(T|h)$ is the probability of observing the target values t_i in the fixed set of instances $\{x_i,..., x_m\}$ in the space where h holds true and describes the concept c correctly. Using assumption 1 mentioned above, we can say that if T is consistent with h, then the probability of data T given the hypothesis h is 1 and is 0 otherwise:

$$P(T\,|\,h) = \begin{cases} 1 & \text{if } t_i = h\left(x_i\right) \text{ for all } t_i \text{ within } T \\ 0 & \text{otherwise} \end{cases}$$

$$\tag{6.4}$$

Using Bayes' theorem to identify the posterior probability

$$P(h\,|\,T) = \frac{P(T\,|\,h)P(h)}{P(T)} \tag{6.5}$$

For the cases when h is inconsistent with the training data T, using 6.5 we get

$$P(h\,|\,T) = \frac{0 \times P(h)}{P(T)} = 0, \text{ when } h \text{ is inconsistent with } T,$$

and when h is consistent with T

$$P(h\,|\,T) = \frac{1 \times \dfrac{1}{|H|}}{P(T)} = \frac{1}{|H|\,P(T)} \tag{6.6}$$

Now, if we define a subset of the hypothesis H which is consistent with T as H_D, then by using the total probability equation, we get

$$P(T) = \sum_{h_i \in H_D} P\left(T\,|\,h_i\right) P\left(h_i\right)$$

$$= \sum_{h_i \in H_D} 1 \cdot \frac{1}{|H|} + \sum_{h_i \notin H_D} 0 \cdot \frac{1}{|H|}$$

$$= \sum_{h_i \in H_D} 1 \cdot \frac{1}{|H|}$$

$$= \frac{|H_D|}{|H|}$$

This makes 6.5 as

$$P(h\,|\,T) = \cfrac{1}{|H|\cdot\cfrac{|H_D|}{|H|}}$$

$$= \frac{1}{|H_D|}$$

So, with our set of assumptions about $P(h)$ and $P(T|h)$, we get the posterior probability $P(h|T)$ as

$$P(h\,|\,T) = \begin{cases} \dfrac{1}{|H_D|} & \text{if } h \text{ is consistent with } T \\ 0 & \text{otherwise} \end{cases} \qquad (6.5)$$

where H_D is the number of hypotheses from the space H which are consistent with target data set T. The interpretation of this evaluation is that initially, each hypothesis has equal probability and, as we introduce the training data, the posterior probability of inconsistent hypotheses becomes zero and the total probability that sums up to 1 is distributed equally among the consistent hypotheses in the set. So, under this condition, each consistent hypothesis is a MAP hypothesis with posterior probability $= \dfrac{1}{|H_D|}$.

6.4.2   Concept of consistent learners

From the above discussion, we understand the behaviour of the general class of learner whom we call as consistent learners. So, the group of learners who commit zero error over the training data and output the hypothesis are called *consistent learners*. If the training data is noise free and deterministic (i.e. $P(D|h) = 1$ if D and h are consistent and 0 otherwise) and if there is uniform prior probability distribution over H (so, $P(h_m) = P(h_n)$ for all m, n), then every consistent learner outputs the MAP hypothesis. An important application of this conclusion is that Bayes' theorem can characterize the behaviour of learning algorithms even when the algorithm does not explicitly manipulate the probability. As it can help to identify the optimal distributions of $P(h)$ and $P(T|h)$ under which the algorithm outputs the MAP hypothesis, the knowledge can be used to characterize the assumptions under which the algorithms behave optimally.

Though we discussed in this section a special case of Bayesian output which corresponds to the noise-free training data and deterministic predictions of hypotheses where $P(T|h)$ takes on value of either 1 or 0, the theorem can be used with the same effectiveness for noisy training data and additional assumptions about the probability distribution governing the noise.

6.4.3   Bayes optimal classifier

In this section, we will discuss the use of the MAP hypothesis to answer the question what is the most probable classification of the new instance given the training data. To illustrate the concept, let us assume three hypotheses h_1, h_2, and h_3 in the hypothesis space H. Let the posterior probability of these hypotheses be 0.4, 0.3, and 0.3, respectively. There is a new instance x, which is classified as true by h_1, but false by h_2 and h_3.

Then the most probable classification of the new instance (x) can be obtained by combining the predictions of all hypotheses weighed by their corresponding posterior probabilities. By denoting the possible classification of the new instance as c_i from the set C, the probability $P(c_i|T)$ that the correct classification for the new instance is c_i is

$$P\left(c_i \mid T\right) = \sum_{h_i \in H} P\left(c_i \mid h_i\right) P\left(h_i \mid T\right)$$

The optimal classification is for which $P(c_i|T)$ is maximum is

$$\text{Bayes optimal classifier} = \underset{c_i \in C}{\operatorname{argmax}} \sum_{h_i \in H} P\left(c_i \mid h_i\right) P\left(h_i \mid T\right)$$

Points to ponder:

The approach in the Bayes optimal classifier is to calculate the most probable classification of each new instance on the basis of the combined predictions of all alternative hypotheses, weighted by their posterior probabilities.

■

So, extending the above example,
The set of possible outcomes for the new instance x is within the set $C = \{\text{True, False}\}$ and

$$P\left(h_1 \mid T\right) = 0.4, P\left(\text{False} \mid h_1\right) = 0, P\left(\text{True} \mid h_1\right) = 1$$
$$P\left(h_2 \mid T\right) = 0.3, P\left(\text{False} \mid h_2\right) = 1, P\left(\text{True} \mid h_2\right) = 0$$
$$P\left(h_3 \mid T\right) = 0.3, P\left(\text{False} \mid h_3\right) = 1, P\left(\text{True} \mid h_3\right) = 0$$

Then,

$$\sum_{h_i \in H} P\left(\text{True} \mid h_i\right) P\left(h_i \mid T\right) = 0.4$$

$$\sum_{h_i \in H} P\left(\text{False} \mid h_i\right) P\left(h_i \mid T\right) = 0.6$$

and

$$\underset{c_i \in \{\text{True, False}\}}{\operatorname{argmax}} \sum_{h_i \in H} P\left(c_i \mid h_i\right) P\left(h_i \mid T\right) = \text{False}$$

This method maximizes the probability that the new instance is classified correctly when the available training data, hypothesis space and the prior probabilities of the hypotheses are known. This is thus also called Bayes optimal classifier.

6.4.4   Naïve Bayes classifier

Naïve Bayes is a simple technique for building classifiers: models that assign class labels to problem instances. The basic idea of Bayes rule is that the outcome of a hypothesis can be predicted on the basis of some evidence (E) that can be observed.

From Bayes rule, we observed that

1. A prior probability of hypothesis h or $P(h)$: This is the probability of an event or hypothesis before the evidence is observed.

2. A posterior probability of h or $P(h|D)$: This is the probability of an event after the evidence is observed within the population D.

$$\text{Posterior probability} = \frac{\textbf{(Prior probability} \times \textbf{Conditional Probability)}}{\textbf{Evidence}}$$

Posterior Probability is of the format 'What is the probability that a particular object belongs to class i given its observed feature values?'

For example, a person has height and weight of 182 cm and 68 kg, respectively. What is the probability that this person belongs to the class 'basketball player'? This can be predicted using the Naïve Bayes classifier. This is known as probabilistic classifications.

In machine learning, a probabilistic classifier is a classifier that can be foreseen, given a perception or information (input), a likelihood calculation over a set of classes, instead of just yielding (outputting) the most likely class that the perception (observation) should belong to. Parameter estimation for Naïve Bayes models uses the method of ML.

Bayes' theorem is used when new information can be used to revise previously determined probabilities. Depending on the particular nature of the probability model, Naïve Bayes classifiers can be trained very professionally in a supervised learning setting.

Let us see the basis of deriving the principles of Naïve Bayes classifiers. We take a learning task where each instance x has some attributes and the target function ($f(x)$) can take any value from the finite set of classification values C. We also have a set of training examples for target function, and the set of attributes $\{a_1, a_2, ..., a_n\}$ for the new instance are known to us. Our task is to predict the classification of the new instance.

According to the approach in Bayes' theorem, the classification of the new instance is performed by assigning the most probable target classification C_{MAP} on the basis of the attribute values of the new instance $\{a_1, a_2, ..., a_n\}$. So,

$$C_{\text{MAP}} = \underset{c_i \in C}{\overset{\text{argmax}}{\sum_{h_i \in H}}} P(c_i \mid a_1, a_2, ..., a_n)$$

which can be rewritten using Bayes' theorem as

$$C_{\text{MAP}} = \underset{c_i \in C}{\overset{\text{argmax}}{\sum_{h_i \in H}}} \frac{P(a_1, a_2, ..., a_n \mid c_i) P(c_i)}{P(a_1, ... a_n)}$$

As combined probability of the attributes defining the new instance fully is always 1

$$C_{\text{MAP}} = \underset{c_i \in C}{\overset{\text{argmax}}{\sum_{h_i \in H}}} P(a_1, a_2, ..., a_n \mid c_i) P(c_i) \tag{6.8}$$

So, to get the most probable classifier, we have to evaluate the two terms $P(a_1, a_2, ..., a_n|c_i)$ and $P(c_i)$. In a practical scenario, it is possible to calculate $P(c_i)$ by calculating the frequency of each target value c_i in the training data set. But the $P(a_1, a_2, ..., a_n|c_i)$ cannot be estimated easily and needs a very high effort of calculation. The reason is that the number of these terms is equal to the product of number of possible instances and the number of possible target values, and thus, each instance in the instance space needs to be visited many times to arrive at the estimate of the occurrence. Thus, the Naïve Bayes classifier makes a simple assumption that the attribute values are conditionally independent of each other for the target value. So, applying this simplification, we can now say that for a target value of an instance, the probability of observing the combination $a_1, a_2, ..., a_n$ is the product of probabilities of individual attributes $P(a_i|c_j)$.

$$P\left(a_1, a_2, ..., a_n \mid c_j\right) = \prod_i P\left(a_i \mid c_j\right)$$

Then, from equation 6.7, we get the approach for the Naïve Bayes classifier as

$$C_{NB} = \underset{c_i \in C}{\overset{\text{argmax}}{\sum_{h_i \in H}}} P\left(c_i\right) \prod_i P\left(a_i \mid c_j\right) \tag{6.9}$$

Here, we will be able to compute $P(a_i|c_j)$ as we have to calculate this only for the number of distinct attributes values (a_i) times the number of distinct target values (c_j), which is much smaller set than the product of both the sets. The most important reason for the popularity of the Naïve Bayes classifier approach is that it is not required to search the whole hypothesis space for this algorithm, but rather we can arrive at the target classifier by simply counting the frequencies of various data combinations within the training example.

To summarize, a Naïve Bayes classifier is a primary probabilistic classifier based on a view of applying Bayes' theorem (from Bayesian inference with strong naive) independence assumptions. The prior probabilities in Bayes' theorem that are changed with the help of newly available information are classified as posterior probabilities.

A key benefit of the naive Bayes classifier is that it requires only a little bit of training information (data) to gauge the parameters (mean and differences of the variables) essential for the classification (arrangement). In the Naïve Bayes classifier, independent variables are always assumed, and only the changes (variances) of the factors/variables for each class should be determined and not the whole covariance matrix. Because of the rather naïve assumption that all features of the dataset are equally important and independent, this is called Naïve Bayes classifier.

Naïve Bayes classifiers are direct linear classifiers that are known for being the straightforward, yet extremely proficient result. The modified version of Naïve Bayes classifier originates from the assumption that information collection (data set) is commonly autonomous (mutually independent). In most of the practical scenarios, the 'independence' assumption is regularly violated. However, Naïve Bayes classifiers still tend to perform exceptionally well.

Some of the key strengths and weaknesses of Naïve Bayes classifiers are described in Table 6.1.

Table 6.1
Strengths and Weaknesses of Bayes Classifiers

Strengths	Weakness
Simple and fast in calculation but yet effective in result	The basis assumption of equal importance and independence often does not hold true
In situations where there are noisy and missing data, it performs well	If the target dataset contains large numbers of numeric features, then the reliability of the outcome becomes limited
Works equally well when smaller number of data is present for training as well as very large number of training data is available	Though the predicted classes have a high reliability, estimated probabilities have relatively lower reliability
Easy and straightforward way to obtain the estimated probability of a prediction	

Example. Let us assume that we want to predict the outcome of a football world cup match on the basis of the past performance data of the playing teams. We have training data available (refer Fig. 6.3) for actual match outcome, while four parameters are considered – Weather Condition (Rainy, Overcast, or Sunny), how many matches won were by this team out of the last three matches (one match, two matches, or three matches), Humidity Condition (High or Normal), and whether they won the toss (True or False). Using Naïve Bayesian, you need to classify the conditions when this team wins and then predict the probability of this team winning a particular match when Weather Conditions = Rainy, they won two of the last three matches, Humidity = Normal and they won the toss in the particular match.

Weather Condition	Wins in last 3 matches	Humidity	Win toss	Won match?
Rainy	3 wins	High	FALSE	No
Rainy	3 wins	High	TRUE	No
OverCast	3 wins	High	FALSE	Yes
Sunny	2 wins	High	FALSE	Yes
Sunny	1 win	Normal	FALSE	Yes
Sunny	1 win	Normal	TRUE	No
OverCast	1 win	Normal	TRUE	Yes
Rainy	2 wins	High	FALSE	No
Rainy	1 win	Normal	FALSE	Yes
Sunny	2 wins	Normal	FALSE	Yes
Rainy	2 wins	Normal	TRUE	Yes
OverCast	2 wins	High	TRUE	Yes
OverCast	3 wins	Normal	FALSE	Yes
Sunny	2 wins	High	TRUE	No

FIG. 6.3
Training data for the Naïve Bayesian method

6.4.4.1   *Naïve Bayes classifier steps*

Step 1: First construct a frequency table. A frequency table is drawn for each attribute against the target outcome. For example, in Figure 6.3, the various attributes are (1) Weather Condition, (2) How many matches won by this team in last three matches, (3) Humidity Condition, and (4) whether they won the toss and the target outcome is will they win the match or not?

Step 2: Identify the cumulative probability for 'Won match = Yes' and the probability for 'Won match = No' on the basis of all the attributes. Otherwise, simply multiply probabilities of all favourable conditions to derive 'YES' condition. Multiply probabilities of all non-favourable conditions to derive 'No' condition.

Step 3: Calculate probability through normalization by applying the below formula

$$P(\text{Yes}) = \frac{P(\text{Yes})}{P(\text{Yes}) + P(\text{No})}$$

$$P(\text{No}) = \frac{P(\text{No})}{P(\text{Yes}) + P(\text{No})}$$

$P(\text{Yes})$ will give the overall probability of favourable condition in the given scenario.

$P(\text{No})$ will give the overall probability of non-favourable condition in the given scenario.

Solving the above problem with Naive Bayes

Step 1: Construct a frequency table. The posterior probability can be easily derived by constructing a frequency table for each attribute against the target. For example, frequency of Weather Condition variable with values 'Sunny' when the target value Won match is 'Yes', is, 3/(3+4+2) = 3/9.

Figure 6.4 shows the frequency table thus constructed.

Step 2:

To predict whether the team will win for given weather conditions (a_1) = Rainy, Wins in last three matches (a_2) = 2 wins, Humidity (a_3) = Normal and Win toss (a_4) = True, we need to choose 'Yes' from the above table for the given conditions.

From Bayes' theorem, we get

$$P\left(\text{Win match} \mid a_1 \cap a_2 \cap a_3 \cap a_4\right) = \frac{P\left(a_1 \cap a_2 \cap a_3 \cap a_4 \mid \text{Win match}\right) P(\text{Win match})}{P\left(a_1 \cap a_2 \cap a_3 \cap a_4\right)}$$

This equation becomes much easier to resolve if we recall that Naïve Bayes classifier assumes independence among events. This is specifically true for

Weather condition	Won Match	
	Yes	No
Sunny	3	2
OverCast	4	0
Rainy	2	3
Total	9	5

Humidity	Won Match	
	Yes	No
High	3	4
Normal	6	1
Total	9	5

Wins in last 3 matches	Won Match	
	Yes	No
3 wins	2	2
1 win	4	2
2 wins	3	1
Total	9	5

Win toss	Won Match	
	Yes	No
FALSE	6	2
TRUE	3	3
Total	9	5

FIG. 6.4
Construct frequency table

class-conditional independence, which means that the events are independent so long as they are conditioned on the same class value. Also, we know that if the events are independent, then the probability rule says, $P(A \cap B) = P(A) P(B)$, which helps in simplifying the above equation significantly as

$$P\left(\text{Win match} \mid a_1 \cap a_2 \cap a_3 \cap a_4\right)$$

$$= \frac{P\left(a_1 \mid \text{Win match}\right) P\left(a_2 \mid \text{Win match}\right) P\left(a_3 \mid \text{Win match}\right) P\left(a_4 \mid \text{Win match}\right) P\left(\text{Win match}\right)}{P\left(a_1\right) P\left(a_2\right) P\left(a_3\right) P\left(a_4\right)}$$

$$= 2/9*4/9*6/9*9/14$$

$$= 0.014109347$$

This should be compared with

$$P\left(!\text{Win match} \mid a_1 \cap a_2 \cap a_3 \cap a_4\right)$$

$$= \frac{P\left(a_1 \mid !\text{Win match}\right) P\left(a_2 \mid !\text{Win match}\right) P\left(a_3 \mid !\text{in match}\right) P\left(a_4 \mid !\text{Win match}\right) P\left(!\text{Win match}\right)}{P\left(a_1\right) P\left(a_2\right) P\left(a_3\right) P\left(a_4\right)}$$

$$= 3/5*2/5*1/5*5/14$$

$$= 0.010285714$$

Step 3: by normalizing the above two probabilities, we can ensure that the sum of these two probabilities is 1.

$$P(\text{Win match}) = \frac{P(\text{Win match})}{P(\text{Win match}) + P(!\text{Win match})}$$

$$= \frac{0.014109347}{0.014109347 + 0.010285714}$$

$$= 0.578368999$$

$$P(!\text{Win match}) = \frac{P(!\text{Win match})}{P(\text{Win match}) + P(!\text{Win match})}$$

$$= \frac{0.010285714}{0.014109347 + 0.010285714}$$

$$= 0.421631001$$

Conclusion: This shows that there is 58% probability that the team will win if the above conditions become true for that particular day. Thus, Naïve Bayes classifier provides a simple yet powerful way to consider the influence of multiple attributes on the target outcome and refine the uncertainty of the event on the basis of the prior knowledge because it is able to simplify the calculation through independence assumption.

For Naive Bayes classifier implementation, *GaussianNB* library of **sklearn.naive_bayes** has been used. The full code for the implementation is given below.

```
>>> import pandas as pd
>>> from sklearn.model_selection import train_test_split
>>> from sklearn.metrics import accuracy_score
>>> from sklearn.naive_bayes import GaussianNB

>>> data = pd.read_csv("apndcts.csv")

>>> predictors = data.iloc[:,0:7] # Segregating the predictor
variables ...
>>> target = data.iloc[:,7]        # Segregating the target / class
variable ...

>>> predictors_train, predictors_test, target_train, target_test =
train_test_split(predictors, target, test_size = 0.3, random_state
= 123)

>>> gnb = GaussianNB()

# First train model / classifier with the input dataset (training
data part of it)
>>> model = gnb.fit(predictors_train, target_train)

# Make prediction using the trained model
>>> prediction = model.predict(predictors_test)

# Time to check the prediction accuracy ...
>>> accuracy_score(target_test, prediction, normalize = True)
```

Output Accuracy:
0.90625

6.4.5   Applications of Naïve Bayes classifier

Text classification: Naïve Bayes classifier is among the most successful known algorithms for learning to classify text documents. It classifies the document where the probability of classifying the text is more. It uses the above algorithm to check the permutation and combination of the probability of classifying a document under a particular 'Title'. It has various applications in document categorization, language detection, and sentiment detection, which are very useful for traditional retailers, e-retailors, and other businesses on judging the sentiments of their clients on the basis of keywords in feedback forms, social media comments, etc.

Spam filtering: Spam filtering is the best known use of Naïve Bayesian text classification. Presently, almost all the email providers have this as a built-in functionality, which makes use of a Naïve Bayes classifier to identify spam email on the basis of certain conditions and also the probability of classifying an email as 'Spam'. Naïve Bayesian spam sifting has turned into a mainstream mechanism to recognize illegitimate a spam email from an honest-to-goodness email (sometimes called 'ham'). Users can also install separate email filtering programmes. Server-side email filters such as DSPAM, Spam Assassin, Spam Bayes, and ASSP make use of Bayesian spam filtering techniques, and the functionality is sometimes embedded within the mail server software itself.

Hybrid Recommender System: It uses Naïve Bayes classifier and collaborative filtering. Recommender systems (used by e-retailors like eBay, Alibaba, Target, Flipkart, etc.) apply machine learning and data mining techniques for filtering unseen information and can predict whether a user would like a given resource. For example, when we log in to these retailer websites, on the basis of the usage of texts used by the login and the historical data of purchase, it automatically recommends the product for the particular login persona. One of the algorithms is combining a Naïve Bayes classification approach with collaborative filtering, and experimental results show that this algorithm provides better performance regarding accuracy and coverage than other algorithms.

Online Sentiment Analysis: The online applications use supervised machine learning (Naïve Bayes) and useful computing. In the case of sentiment analysis, let us assume there are three sentiments such as nice, nasty, or neutral, and Naïve Bayes classifier is used to distinguish between them. Simple emotion modelling combines a statistically based classifier with a dynamical model. The Naïve Bayes classifier employs 'single words' and 'word pairs' like features and determines the sentiments of the users. It allocates user utterances into nice, nasty, and neutral classes, labelled as +1, −1, and 0, respectively. This binary output drives a simple first-order dynamical system, whose emotional state represents the simulated emotional state of the experiment's personification.

6.4.6   Handling Continuous Numeric Features in Naïve Bayes Classifier

In the above example, we saw that the Naïve Bayes classifier model uses a frequency table of the training data for its calculation. Thus, each attribute data should be categorical in nature so that the combination of class and feature values can be created. But this is not possible in the case of continuous numeric data as it does not have the categories of data.

The workaround that is applied in these cases is discretizing the continuous data on the basis of some data range. This is also called binning as the individual categories are termed as bins. For example, let us assume we want to market a certain credit card to all the customers who are visiting a particular bank. We have to classify the persons who are visiting a bank as either interested candidate for taking a new card or non-interested candidate for a new card, and on the basis of this classification, the representative will approach the customer for sale. In this case, the customers visit the bank continuously during banking hours and have different values for the attributes we want to evaluate before classifying them into the interested/non-interested categories.

If we plot the number of customers visiting the bank during the 8 hours of banking time, the distribution graph will be a continuous graph. But if we introduce a logic to categorize the customers according to their time of entering the bank, then we will be able to put the customers in 'bins' or buckets for our analysis. We can then try to assess what time range is best suited for targeting the customers who will have interest in the new credit card. The bins created by categorizing the customers by their time of entry looks like Figure 6.5.

This creates eight natural bins for us (or we may change the number of bins by changing our categorizing criteria), which can now be used for Bayes analysis.

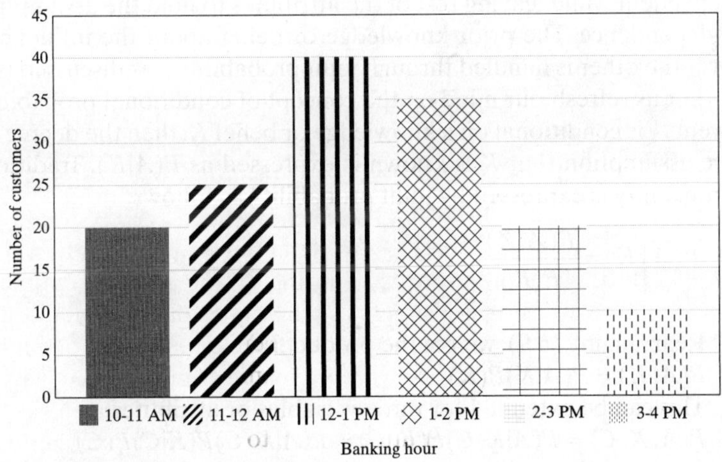

FIG. 6.5
The distribution of bins based on the time of entry of customers in the bank

6.5   BAYESIAN BELIEF NETWORK

We must have noted that a significant assumption in the Naïve Bayes classifier was that the attribute values $a_1, a_2, ..., a_n$ are conditionally independent for a target value. The Naïve Bayes classifier generates optimal output when this condition is met. Though this assumption significantly reduces the complexity of computation, in many practical scenarios, this requirement of conditional independence becomes

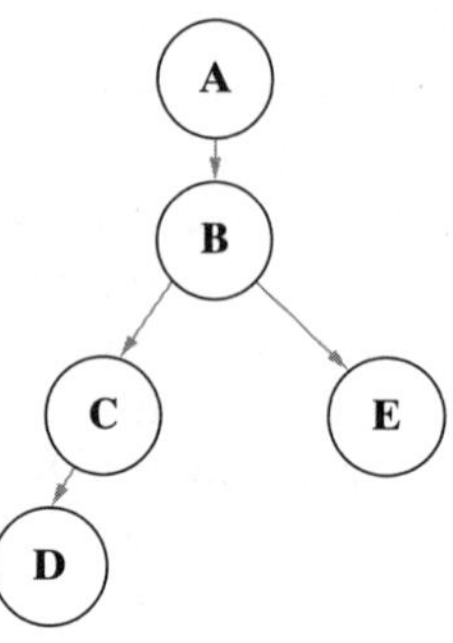

FIG. 6.6
Chain rule

a difficult constraint for the application of this algorithm. So, in this section, we will discuss the approach of Bayesian Belief network, which assumes that within the set of attributes, the probability distribution can have conditional probability relationship as well as conditional independence assumptions. This is different from the Naïve Bayes assumption of conditional independence of all the attributes as the belief network provides the flexibility of declaring a subset of the attributes as conditionally dependent while leaving rest of the attributes to hold the assumptions of conditional independence. The prior knowledge or belief about the influence of one attribute over the other is handled through joint probabilities as discussed later in this section.

Let us refresh our mind on the concept of conditional probability. If an uncertain event A is conditional on a knowledge or belief K, then the degree of belief in A with the assumption that K is known is expressed as $P(A|K)$. Traditionally, conditional probability is expressed by joint probability as follows:

$$P(A \mid K) = \frac{P(A, K)}{P(K)}$$

(6.10)

Rearranging (6.9), we get the product rule
$P(A, K) = P(A|K)P(K)$
This can be extended for three variables or attributes as
$P(A, K, C) = P(A|K, C)P(K, C) = P(A|K, C)P(K|C)P(C)$
For a set of n attributes, the generalized form of the product rule becomes
$P(A_1, A_2, ..., A_n) = P(A_1|A_2, ..., A_n)P(A_2|A_3, ..., A_n)P(A_{n-1}|A_n)P(A_n)$ (6.10)
This generalized version of the product rule is called the Chain Rule.

Let us understand the chain rule by using the diagram in Figure 6.6. From the joint probability formula 6.10, we can write

$$P(A, B, C, D, E) = P(A|B, C, D, E)P(B|C, D, E)P(C|D, E)P(D|E)P(E)$$

But from Figure 6.6, it is evident that E is not related to C and D, which means that the probabilities of variables C and D are not influenced by E and vice versa. Similarly, A is directly influenced only by B. By applying this knowledge of independence, we can simplify the above equation as

$$P(A, B, C, D, E) = P(A|B)P(B|C, D)P(C|D)P(D)P(E)$$

Let us discuss this concept of independence and conditional independence in detail in the next section.

6.5.1   Independence and conditional independence

We represent the conditional probability of A with knowledge of K as $P(A|K)$. The variables A and K are said to be independent if $P(A|K) = P(A)$, which means that there is no influence of K on the uncertainty of A. Similarly, the joint probability can be written as $P(A,K) = P(A)P(K)$.

Extending this concept, the variables A and K are said to be conditionally independent given C if $P(A|C) = P(A|K, C)$.

This concept of conditional independence can also be extended to a set of attributes. We can say that the set of variables $A_1, A_2,..., A_n$ is conditionally independent of the set of variables $B_1, B_2,..., B_m$ given the set of variables $C_1, C_2,..., C_l$ if

$$P(A_1, A_2, ... , A_n|B_1, B_2, ... ,B_m, C_1, C_2, ... , C_l) = P(A_1, A_2, ... , A_n|C_1, C_2, ... , C_l)$$

If we compare this definition with our assumption in the Naïve Bayes classifier, we see that the Naïve Bayes classifier assumes that the instance attribute A_1 is conditionally independent of the instance attribute A_2, given the target value V, which can be written using the general product rule and application of conditional independence formula as

$$P(A_1, A_2|V) = P(A_1|A_2, V)P(A_2, V) = P(A_1, V)P(A_2, V)$$

A Bayesian Belief network describes the joint probability distribution of a set of attributes in their joint space. In Figure 6.7, a Bayesian Belief network is presented. The diagram consists of nodes and arcs. The nodes represent the discrete or continuous variables for which we are interested to calculate the conditional probabilities. The arc represents the causal relationship of the variables.

The two important information points we get from this network graph are used for the determining the joint probability of the variables. First, the arcs assert that the node variables are conditionally independent of its non-descendants in the network given its immediate predecessors in the network. If two variables A and B are connected through a directed path, then B is called the descendent of A. Second, the conditional probability table for each variable provides the probability distribution of that variable given the values of its immediate predecessors. We can use Bayesian probability to calculate different behaviours of the variables in Figure 6.7.

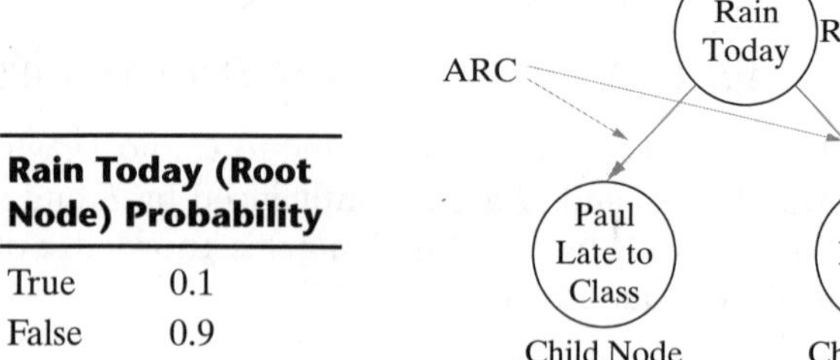

Rain Today (Root Node) Probability

True	0.1
False	0.9

Node Conditional probability	**Rain Today**	
	True	**False**
Paul Late to Class	True 0.6	0.5
	False 0.4	0.5

Node Conditional probability	**Rain Today**	
	True	**False**
Tim Late to Class	True 0.8	0.1
	False 0.2	0.9

FIG. 6.7
Bayesian belief network

1. The unconditional probability that Tim is late to class –

    P(Tim is late to class)

    $= P$(Tim late|Rain Today)P(Rain Today)

      $+ P$(Tim late|No Rain Today)$*P$(No Rain Today)

    $= (0.8 \times 0.1) \times (0.1 \times 0.9)$

    $= 0.17$

    From this unconditional probability, the most important use of the Bayesian Belief network is to find out the revised probability on the basis of the prior knowledge. If we assume that there was rain today, then the probability table can quickly provide us the information about the probability of Paul being late to class or the probability of Tim being late to class from the probability distribution table itself. But if we do not know whether there was rain today or not, but we only know that Tim is late to class today, then we can arrive at the following probabilities –

2. The revised probability that there was rain today –

$$P(\text{Rain Today} \,|\, \text{Tim late to class}) = \frac{P(\text{Tim late} \,|\, \text{Rain today})P(\text{Rain today})}{P(\text{Tim late})}$$

$$= \frac{(0.8 \times 0.1)}{0.17}$$

$$= 0.47$$

$$= P(\text{Rain Today}) \text{ as Tim late to class is already known}$$

3. The revised probability that Paul will be late to class today –

P(Paul late to class today)

$= P$(Paul late|Rain today)P(Rain today)

$+ P$(Paul late|No rain today)P(No rain today)

$= (0.6 \times 0.47) + (0.5 \times (190.47)\,)$

$= 0.55$

Here, we used the concept of hard evidence and soft evidence. Hard evidence (instantiation) of a node is evidence that the state of the variable is definitely as a particular value. In our above example, we had hard evidence that 'Tim is late to class'. If a particular node is instantiated, then it will block propagation of evidence further down to its child nodes. Soft evidence for a node is the evidence that provides the prior probability values for the node. The node 'Paul is late to class' is soft evidenced with the prior knowledge that 'Tim is late to class'.

Note

There can be two main scenarios faced in the Bayesian Belief network learning problem. First, the network structure might be available in advance or can be inferred from the training data. Second, all the network variables either are directly observable in each training example or some of the variables may be unobservable. Learning the conditional probability tables is a straightforward problem when the network structure is given in advance and the variables are fully observable in the training examples. But in the case the network structure is available and only *some* of the variable values are observable in the training data, then the learning problem is more difficult. This is topic of much research, and some of the advanced topics for identifying the node values include algorithms such as Gradient Ascent Training and the EM algorithm.

The Bayesian Belief network can represent much more complex scenarios with dependence and independence concepts. There are three types of connections possible in a Bayesian Belief network.

Diverging Connection: In this type of connection, the evidence can be transmitted between two child nodes of the same parent provided that the parent is not instantiated. In Figure 6.7, we already saw the behaviour of diverging connection.

Serial Connection: In this type of connection, any evidence entered at the beginning of the connection can be transmitted through the directed path provided that no intermediate node on the path is instantiated (see Fig. 6.8 for illustration).

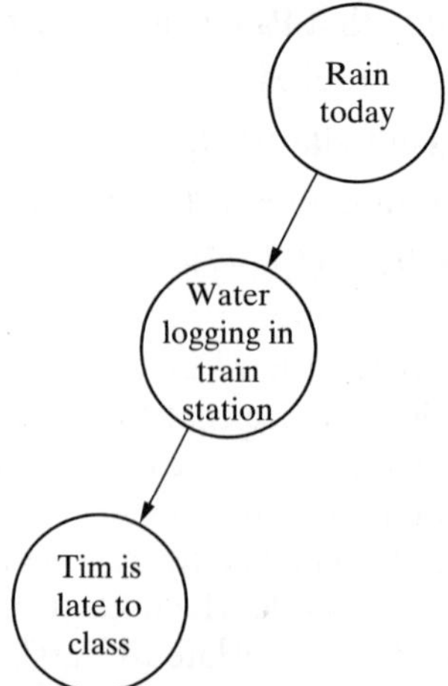

FIG. 6.8
Serial connection

Converging Connection: In this type of connection, the evidence can only be transmitted between two parents when the child (converging) node has received some evidence and that evidence can be soft or hard (see Fig. 6.9 for illustration).

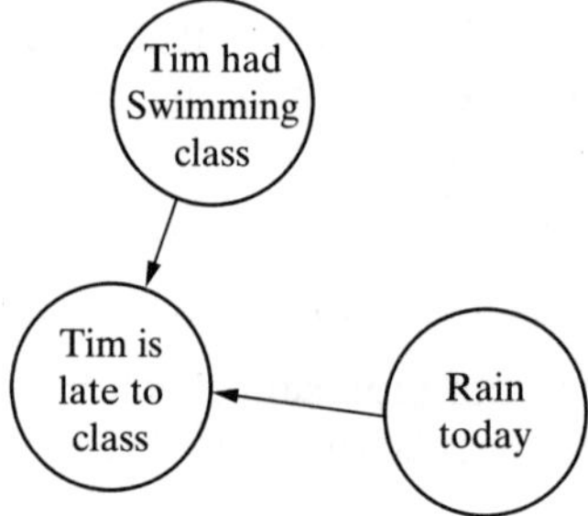

FIG. 6.9
Convergent connection

As discussed above, by using the Bayesian network, we would like to infer the value of a target variable on the basis of the observed values of some other variables. Please note that it will not be possible to infer a single value in the case of random variables we are dealing with, but our intention is to infer the probability distribution of the target variable given the observed values of other variables. In general, the Bayesian network can be used to compute the probability distribution of any subset of node variables given the values or distribution of the remaining variables.

6.5.2 Use of the Bayesian Belief network in machine learning

We have seen that the Bayesian network creates a complete model for the variables and their relationships and thus can be used to answer probabilistic queries about them. A common use of the network is to find out the updated knowledge about the state of a subset of variables, while the state of the other subset (known as the evidence variables) is observed. This concept, often known as probabilistic inference process of computing the posterior distribution of variables, given some evidences, provides a universal sufficient statistic for applications related to detections. Thus if one wants to choose the values for a subset of variables in order to minimize some expected loss functions or decision errors, then this method is quiet effective. In other words, the Bayesian network is a mechanism for automatically applying Bayes' theorem to complex problems. Bayesian networks are used for modelling beliefs in domains like computational biology and bioinformatics such as protein structure and gene regulatory networks, medicines, forensics, document classification, information retrieval, image processing, decision support systems, sports betting and gaming, property market analysis and various other fields.

6.6 SUMMARY

- Bayesian methods introduced a basis for probabilistic learning methods that consider the knowledge about the **prior** probabilities of alternative hypotheses and the probability of **likelihood** or observing various training data given the hypothesis. It then assigns a **posterior** probability to each candidate hypothesis on the basis of the assumed priors and the observed data.

- The **MAP** hypothesis is the most probable hypothesis given the data. As no other hypothesis is more likely, this is also the optimal hypothesis.

- The Bayes optimal classifier calculates the most probable classification of each new instance by combining the predictions of all alternative hypotheses, weighted by their posterior probabilities.

- **Naïve Bayes classifier** makes the naïve assumption that the attribute values are conditionally independent given the classification of the instance. This simplifying assumption considerably reduces the calculation overhead without losing the effectiveness of the outcome. With this assumption in effect, the Naïve Bayes classifier outputs the MAP classification.

- The Naïve Bayes classifier has been found to be useful in many practical applications and is considered as one of the powerful learning methods. Even when the assumption of conditional independence is not met, the Naïve Bayes classifier is quite effective in providing a standard for the other learning methods.

- **Bayesian Belief network** provides the mechanism to handle more practical scenario of considering the conditional independence of a subset of variables while considering the joint probability distribution of the remaining variables given the observation.

SAMPLE QUESTIONS

MULTIPLE-CHOICE QUESTIONS (1 MARK EACH)

1. Three companies X, Y, and Z supply 40%, 45%, and 15% of the uniforms to a school. Past experience shows that 2%, 3%, and 4% of the uniforms supplied by these companies are defective. If a uniform was found to be defective, what is the probability that the uniform was supplied by Company X?
   (a) $^{34}/_{69}$
   (b) $^{25}/_{55}$
   (c) $^{16}/_{55}$
   (d) $^{16}/_{12}$

2. A box of apples contains 10 apples, of which 6 are defective. If 3 of the apples are removed from the box in succession without replacement, what is the probability that all the 3 apples are defective?
   (a) (6*5*4)/ (10*10*10)
   (b) (6*5*4)/ (10*9*8)
   (c) (3*3*3)/ (10*10*10)
   (d) (3*2*1)/ (10*9*8)

3. Two boxes containing chocolates are placed on a table. The boxes are labelled B_1 and B_2. Box B_1 contains 6 dark chocolates and 5 white chocolates. Box B_2 contains 3 dark chocolates and 8 orange chocolates. The boxes are arranged so that the probability of selecting box B_1 is $^1/_3$ and the probability of selecting box B_2 is $^2/_3$. Sneha is blindfolded and asked to select a chocolate. She will win Rs. 10,000 if she selects a dark chocolate. What is the probability that Sneha will win Rs. 10,000 (that is, she will select a dark chocolate)?
   (a) $^7/_{33}$
   (b) $^6/_{33}$
   (c) $^{11}/_{33}$
   (d) $^{10}/_{33}$

4. Two boxes containing chocolates are placed on a table. The boxes are labelled B_1 and B_2. Box B_1 contains 6 Cadbury chocolates and 5 Amul chocolates. Box B_2 contains 3 Cadbury chocolates and 8 Nestle chocolates. The boxes are arranged so that the probability of selecting box B_1 is $^1/_3$ and the probability of selecting box B_2 is $^2/_3$. Sneha is blindfolded and asked to select a chocolate. She will win Rs. 10,000 if she selects a Cadbury chocolate. If she win Rs 10,000, what is the probability that she selected a Cadbury chocolate from the first box?
   (a) $^7/_{12}$
   (b) $^6/_{12}$
   (c) $^{11}/_{12}$
   (d) $^{10}/_{33}$

5. In a certain basketball club, there are 4% of male players who are over 6 feet tall and 1% of female players who are over 6 feet tall. The ratio of male to female players in the total player population is male:female = 2:3. A player is selected at random from among all those who are over 6 feet tall. What is the probability that the player is a female?
   (a) 3/11
   (b) 2/5
   (c) 2/11
   (d) 1/11

6. The probability that a particular hypothesis holds for a data set based on the Prior is called
   (a) Independent probabilities
   (b) Posterior probabilities
   (c) Interior probabilities
   (d) Dependent probabilities

7. One main disadvantage of Bayesian classifiers is that they utilize all available parameters to subtly change the predictions.
   (a) True
   (b) False

8. In a bolt factory, machines A1, A2, and A3 manufacture respectively 25%, 35%, and 40% of the total output. Of these 5%, 4%, and 2% are defective bolts. A bolt is drawn at random from the product and is found to be defective. What is the probability that it was manufactured by machine A2?
(a) 0.0952
(b) 0.452
(c) 0.952
(d) 0.125

9. Bayesian methods can perform better than the other methods while validating the hypotheses that make probabilistic predictions.
(a) True
(b) False

10. Naïve Bayes classifier makes the naïve assumption that the attribute values are conditionally dependent given the classification of the instance.
(a) True
(b) False

SHORT-ANSWER TYPE QUESTIONS (5 MARKS EACH)

1. What is prior probability? Give an example.

2. What is posterior probability? Give an example.

3. What is likelihood probability? Give an example.

4. What is Naïve Bayes classifier? Why is it named so?

5. What is optimal Bayes classifier?

6. Write any two features of Bayesian learning methods.

7. Define the concept of consistent learners.

8. Write any two strengths of Bayes classifier.

9. Write any two weaknesses of Bayes classifier.

10. Explain how Naïve Bayes classifier is used for
(a) Text classification
(b) Spam filtering
(c) Market sentiment analysis

LONG-ANSWER TYPE QUESTIONS (10 MARKS EACH)

1. Explain the concept of Prior, Posterior, and Likelihood with an example.

2. How Bayes' theorem supports the concept learning principle?

3. Explain Naïve Bayes classifier with an example of its use in practical life.

4. Is it possible to use Naïve Bayes classifier for continuous numeric data? If so, how?

5. What are Bayesian Belief networks? Where are they used? Can they solve all types of problems?

6. In an airport security checking system, the passengers are checked to find out any intruder. Let I with $i \in \{0, 1\}$ be the random variable which indicates whether somebody is an intruder ($i = 1$) or not ($i = 0$) and A with $a \in \{0, 1\}$ be the variable indicating alarm. An alarm will be raised if an intruder is identified with probability $P(A = 1|I = 1) = 0.98$ and a non-intruder with probability $P(A = 1|I = 0) = 0.001$, which implies the error factor. In the population of passengers, the probability of someone is intruder is $P(I = 1) = 0.00001$. What is the probability that an alarm is raised when a person actually is an intruder?

7.   An antibiotic resistance test (random variable T) has 1% false positives (i.e. 1% of those not resistance to an antibiotic show positive result in the test) and 5% false negatives (i.e. 5% of those actually resistant to an antibiotic test negative). Let us assume that 2% of those tested are resistant to antibiotics. Determine the probability that somebody who tests positive is actually resistant (random variable D).

8.   For preparation of the exam, a student knows that one question is to be solved in the exam which is either of types A, B, or C. The probabilities of A, B, or C appearing in the exam are 30%, 20%, and 50% respectively. During the preparation, the student solved 9 of 10 problems of type A, 2 of 10 problems of type B, and 6 of 10 problems of type C.
   (a) What is the probability that the student will solve the problem of the exam?
   (b) Given that the student solved the problem, what is the probability that it was of type A?

9.   A CCTV is installed in a bank to monitor the incoming customers and take a photograph. Though there are continuous flows of customers, we create bins of timeframe of 5 min each. In each time frame of 5 min, there may be a customer moving into the bank with 5% probability or there is no customer (again, for simplicity, we assume that either there is 1 customer or none, not the case of multiple customers). If there is a customer, it will be detected by the CCTV with a probability of 99%. If there is no customer, the camera will take a false photograph by detecting other thing's movement with a probability of 10%.
   (a) How many customers enter the bank on average per day (10 hours)?
   (b) How many false photographs (there is a photograph taken even though there is no customer) and how many missed photographs (there is no photograph even though there is a customer) are there on average per day?
   (c) If there is a photograph, what is the probability that there is indeed a customer?

10.   Draw the Bayesian Belief network to represent the conditional independence assumptions of the Naïve Bayes classifier for the match winning prediction problem of Section 6.4.4. Construct the conditional probability table associated with the node Won Toss.

Chapter 7

Supervised Learning: Classification

 **7.1   INTRODUCTION**

OBJECTIVE OF THE CHAPTER:

In the last chapter on Bayesian Concept Learning, you were introduced to an important supervised learning algorithm – the Naïve Bayes algorithm. As we have seen, it is a very simple but powerful classifier based on Bayes' theorem of conditional probability. However, other than the Naïve Bayes classifier, there are more algorithms for classification. This chapter will focus on other classification algorithms.

The first algorithm we will delve into in this chapter is k-Nearest Neighbour (kNN), which tries to classify unlabelled data instances based on the similarity with the labelled instances in the training data.

Then, another critical classifier, named as decision tree, will be explained in detail. Decision tree, as the name suggests, is a classifier based on a series of logical decisions, which resembles a tree with branches.

Next, we will explore the random forest classifier, which, in very simplistic terms, can be thought as a collection of many decision trees.

Finally, a very powerful and popular classifier named Support Vector Machine (SVM) will be explored.

So, by the end of this chapter, you will gain enough knowledge to start solving a classification problem by using some standard classifiers.

7.2   EXAMPLE OF SUPERVISED LEARNING

In supervised learning, the labelled training data provide the basis for learning. According to the definition of machine learning, this labelled training data is the experience or prior knowledge or belief. It is called supervised learning because the process of learning from the training data by a machine can be related to a teacher supervising the learning process of a student who is new to the subject. Here, the teacher is the training data.

Training data is the past information with known value of class field or '**label**'. Hence, we say that the '**training data is labelled**' in the case of supervised learning (refer Fig. 7.1). Contrary to this, there is no labelled training data for unsupervised

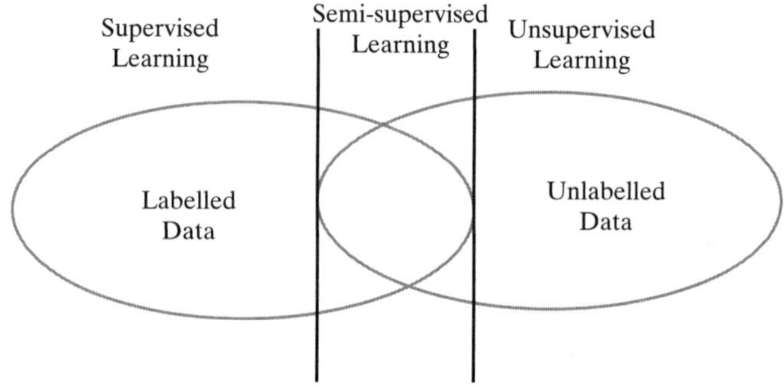

FIG. 7.1
Supervised learning vs. unsupervised learning

learning. Semi-supervised learning, as depicted in Figure 7.1, uses a small amount of labelled data along with unlabelled data for training.

In a hospital, many patients are treated in the general wards. In comparison, the number of beds in the Intensive Care Unit (ICU) is much less. So, it is always a cause of worry for the hospital management that if the health condition of a number of patients in the general ward suddenly aggravates and they would have to be moved to ICU. Without previous planning and preparations, such a spike in demand becomes difficult for the hospital to manage. This problem can be addressed in a much better way if it is possible to predict which of the patients in the normal wards have a possibility of their health condition deteriorating and thus need to be moved to ICU.

This kind of prediction problem comes under the purview of supervised learning or, more specifically, under classification. The hospital already has all past patient records. The records of the patients whose health condition aggravated in the past and had to be moved to ICU can form the training data for this prediction problem. Test results of newly admitted patients are used to classify them as high-risk or low-risk patients.

Some more examples of supervised learning are as follows:

- Prediction of results of a game based on the past analysis of results
- Predicting whether a tumour is malignant or benign on the basis of the analysis of data
- Price prediction in domains such as real estate, stocks, etc.

Did you know?

'IBM Watson Health' developed by IBM software provides evidence-backed cancer care to each patient by understanding millions of data points. 'Watson for Oncology' helps physicians quickly identify vital information in a patient's medical record, surface relevant evidence, and explore various treatment options for patients (Source: https://www.ibm.com/watson/health/oncology-and-genomics/oncology).

 ## 7.3 CLASSIFICATION MODEL

Let us consider two examples, say 'predicting whether a tumour is malignant or benign' and 'price prediction in the domain of real estate'. Are these two problems same in nature?

The answer is 'no'. It is true that both of them are problems related to prediction. However, for tumour prediction, we are trying to predict which category or class, i.e. 'malignant' or 'benign', an unknown input data related to tumour belongs to. In the other case, that is, for price prediction, we are trying to predict an absolute value and not a class.

When we are trying to predict a categorical or nominal variable, the problem is known as a classification problem. A classification problem is one where the output variable is a category such as 'red' or 'blue' or 'malignant tumour' or 'benign tumour', etc.

Whereas when we are trying to predict a numerical variable such as 'price', 'weight', etc. the problem falls under the category of regression.

Note that:

Supervised machine learning is as good as the data used to train it. If the training data is poor in quality, the prediction will also be far from being precise.

We can observe that in classification, the whole problem centres around assigning a label or category or class to a test data on the basis of the label or category or class information that is imparted by the training data. Because the target objective is to assign a class label, we call this type of problem as a classification problem. Figure 7.2 depicts the typical process of classification where a classification model is obtained from the labelled training data by a classifier algorithm. On the basis of the model, a class label (e.g. 'Intel' as in the case of the test data referred in Fig. 7.2) is assigned to the test data.

A critical classification problem in the context of the banking domain is identifying potentially fraudulent transactions. Because there are millions of transactions which

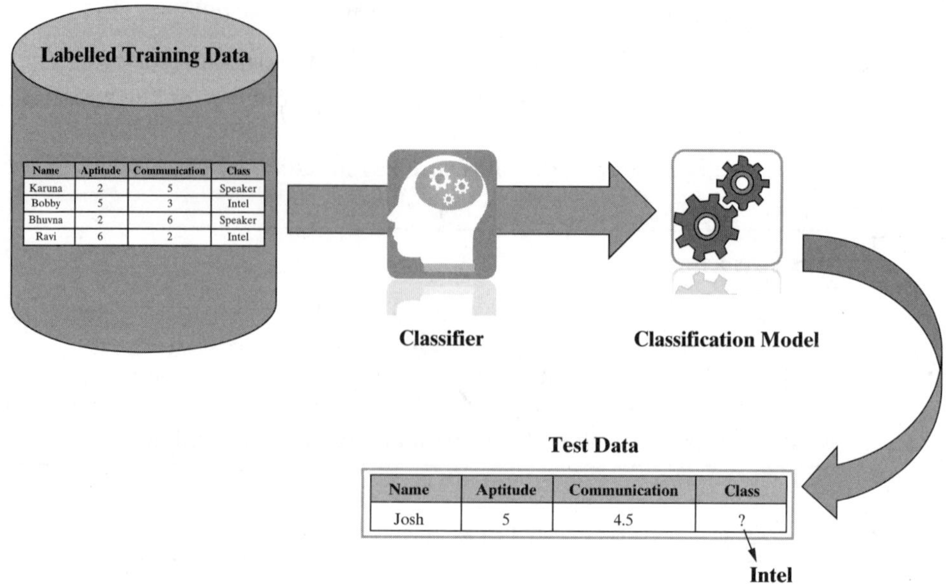

FIG. 7.2
Classification model

have to be scrutinized to identify whether a particular transaction might be a fraud transaction, it is not possible for any human being to carry out this task. Machine learning is leveraged efficiently to do this task, and this is a classic case of classification. On the basis of the past transaction data, especially the ones labelled as fraudulent, all new incoming transactions are marked or labelled as usual or suspicious. The suspicious transactions are subsequently segregated for a closer review.

In summary, classification is a type of supervised learning where a target feature, which is of categorical type, is predicted for test data on the basis of the information imparted by the training data. The target categorical feature is known as **class**.

Some typical classification problems include the following:

- Image classification
- Disease prediction
- Win–loss prediction of games
- Prediction of natural calamity such as earthquake, flood, etc.
- Handwriting recognition:

Did you know?

- Machine learning saves lives – it can spot 52% of breast cancer cells at least a year before patients are diagnosed
- US Postal Service uses machine learning for handwriting recognition
- Facebook's news feed uses machine learning to personalize each member's feed

7.4   CLASSIFICATION LEARNING STEPS

First, there is a problem which is to be solved, and then, the required data (related to the problem, which is already stored in the system) is evaluated and pre-processed based on the algorithm. Algorithm selection is a critical point in supervised learning.

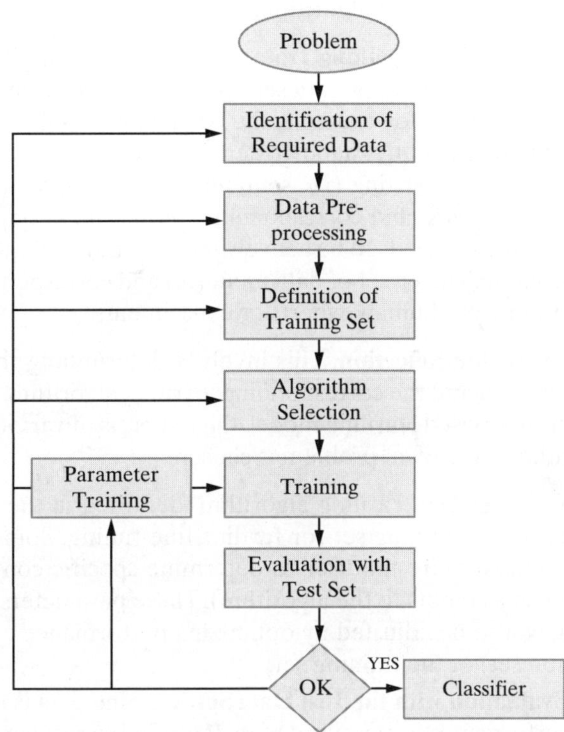

FIG. 7.3
Classification model steps

The result after iterative training rounds is a classifier for the problem in hand (refer Fig. 7.3).

Problem Identification: Identifying the problem is the first step in the supervised learning model. The problem needs to be a well-formed problem, i.e. a problem with well-defined goals and benefit, which has a long-term impact.

Identification of Required Data: On the basis of the problem identified above, the required data set that precisely represents the identified problem needs to be identified/evaluated. For example: If the problem is to predict whether a tumour is malignant or benign, then the corresponding patient data sets related to malignant tumour and benign tumours are to be identified.

Data Pre-processing: This is related to the cleaning/transforming the data set. This step ensures that all the unnecessary/irrelevant data elements are removed. Data pre-processing refers to the transformations applied to the identified data before feeding the same into the algorithm. Because the data is gathered from different sources, it is usually collected in a raw format and is not ready for immediate analysis. This step ensures that the data is ready to be fed into the machine learning algorithm.

Definition of Training Data Set: Before starting the analysis, the user should decide what kind of data set is to be used as a training set. In the case of signature analysis, for example, the training data set might be a single handwritten alphabet, an entire handwritten word (i.e. a group of the alphabets) or an entire line of handwriting (i.e. sentences or a group of words). Thus, a set of 'input meta-objects' and corresponding 'output meta-objects' are also gathered. The training set needs to be actively representative of the real-world use of the given scenario. Thus, a set of data input (X) and corresponding outputs (Y) is gathered either from human experts or experiments.

Algorithm Selection: This involves determining the structure of the learning function and the corresponding learning algorithm. This is the most critical step of supervised learning model. On the basis of various parameters, the best algorithm for a given problem is chosen.

Training: The learning algorithm identified in the previous step is run on the gathered training set for further fine tuning. Some supervised learning algorithms require the user to determine specific control parameters (which are given as inputs to the algorithm). These parameters (inputs given to algorithm) may also be adjusted by optimizing performance on a subset (called as validation set) of the training set.

Evaluation with the Test Data Set: Training data is run on the algorithm, and its performance is measured here. If a suitable result is not obtained, further training of parameters may be required.

7.5   COMMON CLASSIFICATION ALGORITHMS

Let us now delve into some common classification algorithms. Following are the most common classification algorithms, out of which we have already learnt about the Naïve Bayes classifier in Chapter 6. We will cover details of the other algorithms in this chapter.

1. *k*-Nearest Neighbour (*k*NN)
2. Decision tree
3. Random forest
4. Support Vector Machine (SVM)
5. Naïve Bayes classifier (discussed in Chapter 6)

7.5.1   *k*-Nearest Neighbour (*k*NN)

The *k*NN algorithm is a simple but extremely powerful classification algorithm. The name of the algorithm originates from the underlying philosophy of *k*NN – i.e. people having similar background or mindset tend to stay close to each other. In other words, neighbours in a locality have a similar background. In the same way, as a part of the *k*NN algorithm, the unknown and unlabelled data which comes for a prediction problem is judged on the basis of the training data set elements which are similar to the unknown element. So, the class label of the unknown element is assigned on the basis of the class labels of the similar training data set elements (metaphorically can be considered as neighbours of the unknown element). Let us try to understand the algorithm with a simple data set.

7.5.1.1   How kNN works

Let us consider a very simple Student data set as depicted in Figure 7.4. It consists of 15 students studying in a class. Each of the students has been assigned a score on a scale of 10 on two performance parameters – 'Aptitude' and 'Communication'. Also, a class value is assigned to each student based on the following criteria:

1. Students having good communication skills as well as a good level of aptitude have been classified as 'Leader'
2. Students having good communication skills but not so good level of aptitude have been classified as 'Speaker'
3. Students having not so good communication skill but a good level of aptitude have been classified as 'Intel'

Name	Aptitude	Communication	Class
Karuna	2	5	Speaker
Bhuvna	2	6	Speaker
Gaurav	7	6	Leader
Parul	7	2.5	Intel
Dinesh	8	6	Leader
Jani	4	7	Speaker
Bobby	5	3	Intel
Parimal	3	5.5	Speaker
Govind	8	3	Intel
Susant	6	5.5	Leader
Gouri	6	4	Intel
Bharat	6	7	Leader
Ravi	6	2	Intel
Pradeep	9	7	Leader
Josh	5	4.5	Intel

FIG. 7.4
Student data set

As we have already seen in Chapter 3, while building a classification model, a part of the labelled input data is retained as test data. The remaining portion of the input data is used to train the model – hence known as training data. The motivation to retain a part of the data as test data is to evaluate the performance of the model. As we have seen, the performance of the classification model is measured by the number of correct classifications made by the model when applied to an unknown data set. However, it is not possible during model testing to know the actual label value of an unknown data. Therefore, the test data, which is a part of the labelled input data, is used for this purpose. If the class value predicted for most of the test data elements matches with the actual class value that they have, then we say that the classification model possesses a good accuracy. In context of the Student data set, to keep the things simple, we assume one data element of the input data set as the test data. As depicted in Figure 7.5, the record of the student named Josh is assumed to be the test data. Now that we have the training data and test data identified, we can start with the modelling.

As we have already discussed, in the *k*NN algorithm, the class label of the test data elements is decided by the class label of the training data elements which are neighbouring, i.e. similar in nature. But there are two challenges:

1. What is the basis of this similarity or when can we say that two data elements are similar?

2. How many similar elements should be considered for deciding the class label of each test data element?

To answer the first question, though there are many measures of similarity, the most common approach adopted by *k*NN to measure similarity between two data elements is Euclidean distance. Considering a very simple data set having two features (say f_1 and f_2), Euclidean distance between two data elements d_1 and d_2 can be measured by

	Name	Aptitude	Communication	Class
	Karuna	2	5	Speaker
	Bhuvna	2	6	Speaker
	Gaurav	7	6	Leader
	Parul	7	2.5	Intel
	Dinesh	8	6	Leader
	Jani	4	7	Speaker
Training Data	Bobby	5	3	Intel
	Parimal	3	5.5	Speaker
	Govind	8	3	Intel
	Susant	6	5.5	Leader
	Gouri	6	4	Intel
	Bharat	6	7	Leader
	Ravi	6	2	Intel
	Pradeep	9	7	Leader
Test Data →	Josh	5	4.5	Intel

FIG. 7.5
Segregated student data set

$$\text{Euclidean distance } = \sqrt{\left(f_{11}-f_{12}\right)^2 + \left(f_{21}-f_{22}\right)^2}$$

where f_{11} = value of feature f_1 for data element d_1

f_{12} = value of feature f_1 for data element d_2

f_{21} = value of feature f_2 for data element d_1

f_{22} = value of feature f_2 for data element d_2

So, as depicted in Figure 7.6, the training data points of the Student data set considering only the features 'Aptitude' and 'Communication' can be represented as dots in a two-dimensional feature space. As shown in the figure, the training data points having the same class value are coming close to each other. The reason for considering

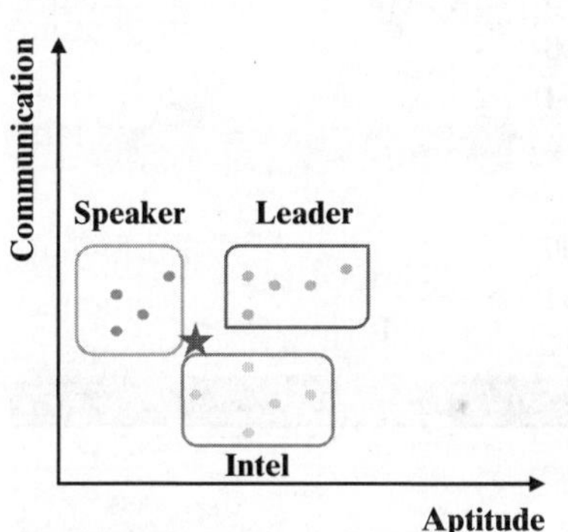

FIG. 7.6

2-D representation of the student data set

Name	Aptitude	Communication	Class
Karuna	2	5	Speaker
Bhuvna	2	6	Speaker
Gaurav	7	6	Leader
Parul	7	2.5	Intel
Dinesh	8	6	Leader
Jani	4	7	Speaker
Bobby	5	3	Intel
Parimal	3	5.5	Speaker
Govind	8	3	Intel
Susant	6	5.5	Leader
Gouri	6	4	Intel
Bharat	6	7	Leader
Ravi	6	2	Intel
Pradeep	9	7	Leader

Name	Aptitude	Communication	Class
★ Josh	5	4.5	???

two-dimensional data space is that we are considering just the two features of the Student data set, i.e. 'Aptitude' and 'Communication', for doing the classification. The feature 'Name' is ignored because, as we can understand, it has no role to play in deciding the class value. The test data point for student Josh is represented as an asterisk in the same space. To find out the closest or nearest neighbours of the test data point, Euclidean distance of the different dots need to be calculated from the asterisk. Then, the class value of the closest neighbours helps in assigning the class value of the test data element.

Now, let us try to find the answer to the second question, i.e. how many similar elements should be considered. The answer lies in the value of 'k' which is a user-defined parameter given as an input to the algorithm. In the kNN algorithm, the value of 'k' indicates the number of neighbours that need to be considered. For example, if the value of k is 3, only three nearest neighbours or three training data elements closest to the test data element are considered. Out of the three data elements, the class which is predominant is considered as the class label to be assigned to the test data. In case the value of k is 1, only the closest training data element is considered. The class label of that data element is directly assigned to the test data element. This is depicted in Figure 7.7.

Let us now try to find out the outcome of the algorithm for the Student data set we have. In other words, we want to see what class value kNN will assign for the test

Name	Aptitude	Communication	Class	Distance	$k = 1$	$k = 2$	$k = 3$
Karuna	2	5	Speaker	3.041			
Bhuvna	2	6	Speaker	3.354			
Parimal	3	5.5	Speaker	2.236			
Jani	4	7	Speaker	2.693			
Bobby	5	3	Intel	1.500			1.500
Ravi	6	2	Intel	2.693			
Gouri	6	4	Intel	1.118	1.118	1.118	1.118
Parul	7	2.5	Intel	2.828			
Govind	8	3	Intel	3.354			
Susant	6	5.5	Leader	1.414			
Bharat	6	7	Leader	2.693			
Gaurav	7	6	Leader	2.500			
Dinesh	8	6	Leader	3.354			
Pradeep	9	7	Leader	4.717			
Josh	5	4.5	???				

FIG. 7.7
Distance calculation between test and training points

data for student Josh. Again, let us refer back to Figure 7.7. As is evident, when the value of k is taken as 1, only one training data point needs to be considered. The training record for student Gouri comes as the closest one to test record of Josh, with a distance value of 1.118. Gouri has class value 'Intel'. So, the test data point is also assigned a class label value 'Intel'. When the value of k is assumed as 3, the closest neighbours of Josh in the training data set are Gouri, Susant, and Bobby with distances being 1.118, 1.414, and 1.5, respectively. Gouri and Bobby have class value 'Intel', while Susant has class value 'Leader'. In this case, the class value of Josh is decided by majority voting. Because the class value of 'Intel' is formed by the majority of the neighbours, the class value of Josh is assigned as 'Intel'. This same process can be extended for any value of k.

But it is often a tricky decision to decide the value of k. The reasons are as follows:

- If the value of k is very large (in the extreme case equal to the total number of records in the training data), the class label of the majority class of the training data set will be assigned to the test data regardless of the class labels of the neighbours nearest to the test data.
- If the value of k is very small (in the extreme case equal to 1), the class value of a noisy data or outlier in the training data set which is the nearest neighbour to the test data will be assigned to the test data.

The best k value is somewhere between these two extremes.

Few strategies, highlighted below, are adopted by machine learning practitioners to arrive at a value for k.

- One common practice is to set k equal to the square root of the number of training records.
- An alternative approach is to test several k values on a variety of test data sets and choose the one that delivers the best performance.
- Another interesting approach is to choose a larger value of k, but apply a weighted voting process in which the vote of close neighbours is considered more influential than the vote of distant neighbours.

7.5.1.2   kNN algorithm

Input: Training data set, test data set (or data points), value of 'k' (i.e. number of nearest neighbours to be considered)

Steps:

Do for all test data points

Calculate the distance (usually Euclidean distance) of the test data point from the different training data points.

Find the closest 'k' training data points, i.e. training data points whose distances are least from the test data point.

If $k = 1$

Then assign class label of the training data point to the test data point

Else

Whichever class label is predominantly present in the training data points, assign that class label to the test data point

End do

k-Nearest Neighbour (kNN) classifier is implemented through *KNeighborsClassifier* library of ***sklearn. neighbors***. The full code for the implementation is given below.

```
>>> import pandas as pd
>>> from sklearn.model_selection import train_test_split
>>> from sklearn.metrics import accuracy_score
```

```
>>> from sklearn.neighbors import KNeighborsClassifier

>>> data = pd.read_csv("apndcts.csv")

>>> predictors = data.iloc[:,0:7] # Seggretating the predictor
variables ...
>>> target = data.iloc[:,7]      # Seggretating the target / class
variable ...

>>> predictors_train, predictors_test, target_train, target_test =
train_test_split(predictors, target, test_size = 0.3, random_state
= 123)

>>> nn = KNeighborsClassifier(n_neighbors = 3)  # Instantiate the
model with 3 neighbors ...

# First train model / classifier with the input dataset (training
data part of it)
>>> model = nn.fit(predictors_train, target_train)

# Time to check the prediction accuracy ...
>>> nn.score(predictors_test, target_test)
```

Output Accuracy:
0.875

7.5.1.3   *Why the kNN algorithm is called a lazy learner?*

We have already discussed in Chapter 3 that eager learners follow the general steps of machine learning, i.e. perform an abstraction of the information obtained from the input data and then follow it through by a generalization step. However, as we have seen in the case of the kNN algorithm, these steps are completely skipped. It stores the training data and directly applies the philosophy of nearest neighbourhood finding to arrive at the classification. So, for *k*NN, there is no learning happening in the real sense. Therefore, *k*NN falls under the category of lazy learner.

7.5.1.4   *Strengths of the kNN algorithm*

- Extremely simple algorithm – easy to understand
- Very effective in certain situations, e.g. for recommender system design
- Very fast or almost no time required for the training phase

7.5.1.5   *Weaknesses of the kNN algorithm*

- Does not learn anything in the real sense. Classification is done completely on the basis of the training data. So, it has a heavy reliance on the training data. If the training data does not represent the problem domain comprehensively, the algorithm fails to make an effective classification.

- Because there is no model trained in real sense and the classification is done completely on the basis of the training data, the classification process is very slow.
- Also, a large amount of computational space is required to load the training data for classification.

7.5.1.6   *Application of the kNN algorithm*

One of the most popular areas in machine learning where the *k*NN algorithm is widely adopted is recommender systems. As we know, recommender systems recommend users different items which are similar to a particular item that the user seems to like. The liking pattern may be revealed from past purchases or browsing history and the similar items are identified using the *k*NN algorithm.

Another area where there is widespread adoption of *k*NN is searching documents/contents similar to a given document/content. This is a core area under information retrieval and is known as concept search.

7.5.2   Decision tree

Decision tree learning is one of the most widely adopted algorithms for classification. As the name indicates, it builds a model in the form of a tree structure. Its grouping exactness is focused with different strategies, and it is exceptionally productive.

A decision tree is used for multi-dimensional analysis with multiple classes. It is characterized by fast execution time and ease in the interpretation of the rules. The goal of decision tree learning is to create a model (based on the past data called past vector) that predicts the value of the output variable based on the input variables in the feature vector.

Each node (or decision node) of a decision tree corresponds to one of the feature vector. From every node, there are edges to children, wherein there is an edge for each of the possible values (or range of values) of the feature associated with the node. The tree terminates at different leaf nodes (or terminal nodes) where each leaf node represents a possible value for the output variable. The output variable is determined by following a path that starts at the root and is guided by the values of the input variables.

A decision tree is usually represented in the format depicted in Figure 7.8.

Each internal node (represented by boxes) tests an attribute (represented as 'A'/'B' within the boxes). Each branch corresponds to an attribute value (T/F) in the above case. Each leaf node assigns a classification. The first node is called as 'Root' Node. Branches from the root node are called as 'Leaf' Nodes where 'A' is the Root Node (first node). 'B' is the Branch Node. 'T' & 'F' are Leaf Nodes.

Thus, a decision tree consists of three types of nodes:

- Root Node
- Branch Node
- Leaf Node

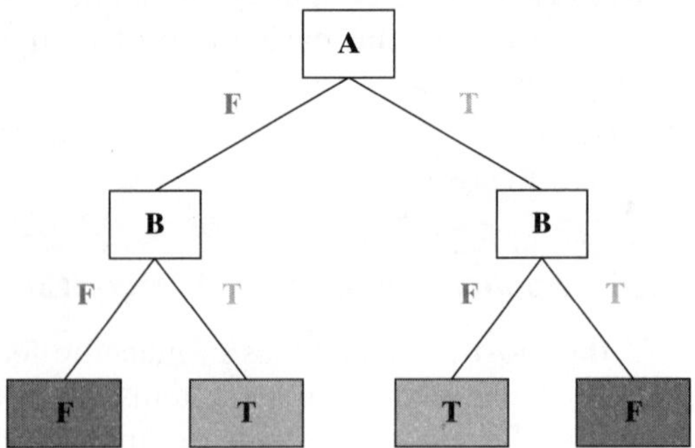

FIG. 7.8
Decision tree structure

Figure 7.9 shows an example decision tree for a car driving – the decision to be taken is whether to 'Keep Going' or to 'Stop', which depends on various situations as depicted in the figure. If the signal is RED in colour, then the car should be stopped. If there is not enough gas (petrol) in the car, the car should be stopped at the next available gas station.

7.5.2.1 Building a decision tree

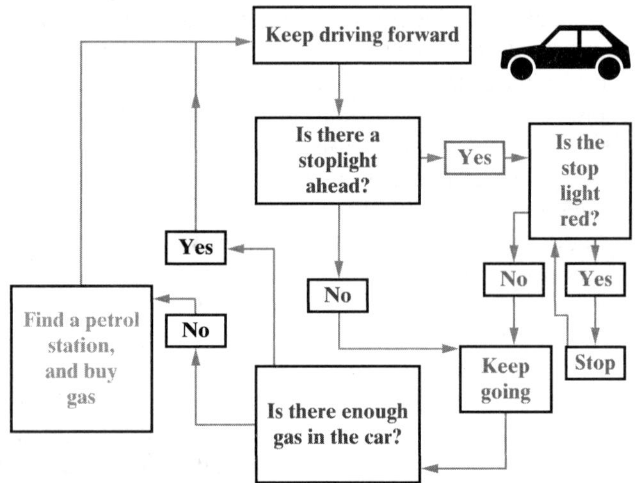

FIG. 7.9
Decision tree example

Decision trees are built corresponding to the training data following an approach called recursive partitioning. The approach splits the data into multiple subsets on the basis of the feature values. It starts from the root node, which is nothing but the entire data set. It first selects the feature which predicts the target class in the strongest way. The decision tree splits the data set into multiple partitions, with data in each partition having a distinct value for the feature based on which the partitioning has happened. This is the first set of branches. Likewise, the algorithm continues splitting the nodes on the basis of the feature which helps in the best partition. This continues till a stopping criterion is reached. The usual stopping criteria are –

1. All or most of the examples at a particular node have the same class
2. All features have been used up in the partitioning
3. The tree has grown to a pre-defined threshold limit

Let us try to understand this in the context of an example. Global Technology Solutions (GTS), a leading provider of IT solutions, is coming to College of Engineering and Management (CEM) for hiring B.Tech. students. Last year during campus recruitment, they had shortlisted 18 students for the final interview. Being a company of international repute, they follow a stringent interview process to select only the best of the students. The information related to the interview evaluation results of shortlisted students (hiding the names) on the basis of different evaluation parameters is available for reference in Figure 7.10. Chandra, a student of CEM, wants to find out if he may be offered a job in GTS. His CGPA is quite high. His self-evaluation on the other parameters is as follows:

Communication – Bad; Aptitude – High; Programming skills – Bad

Training data for GTS recruitment

CGPA	Communication	Aptitude	Programming Skill	Job offered?
High	Good	High	Good	Yes
Medium	Good	High	Good	Yes
Low	Bad	Low	Good	No
Low	Good	Low	Bad	No
High	Good	High	Bad	Yes
High	Good	High	Good	Yes
Medium	Bad	Low	Bad	No
Medium	Bad	Low	Good	No
High	Bad	High	Good	Yes
Medium	Good	High	Good	Yes
Low	Bad	High	Bad	No
Low	Bad	High	Bad	No
Medium	Good	High	Bad	Yes
Low	Good	Low	Good	No
High	Bad	Low	Bad	No
Medium	Bad	High	Good	No
High	Bad	Low	Bad	No
Medium	Good	High	Bad	Yes

FIG. 7.10

Let us try to solve this problem, i.e. predicting whether Chandra will get a job offer, by using the decision tree model. First, we need to draw the decision tree corresponding to the training data given in Figure 7.10. According to the table, job offer condition (i.e. the outcome) is FALSE for all the cases where **Aptitude = Low**, irrespective of other conditions. So, the feature Aptitude can be taken up as the first node of the decision tree.

For **Aptitude = High**, job offer condition is TRUE for all the cases where **Communication = Good**. For cases where **Communication = Bad**, job offer condition is TRUE for all the cases where **CGPA = High**.

Figure 7.11 depicts the complete decision tree diagram for the table given in Figure 7.10.

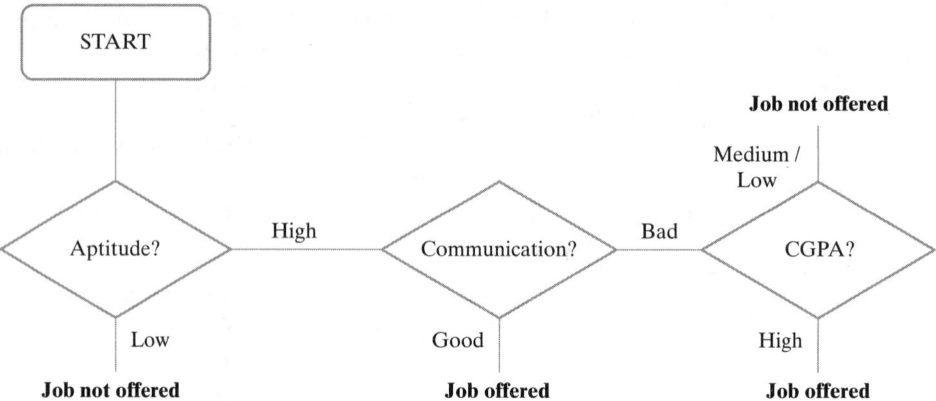

FIG. 7.11
Decision tree based on the training data

7.5.2.2   Searching a decision tree

By using the above decision tree depicted in Figure 7.11, we need to predict whether Chandra might get a job offer for the given parameter values: CGPA = **High**, Communication = **Bad**, Aptitude = **High**, Programming skills = **Bad**. There are multiple ways to search through the trained decision tree for a solution to the given prediction problem.

Exhaustive search
1. Place the item in the first group (class). Recursively examine solutions with the item in the first group (class).
2. Place the item in the second group (class). Recursively examine solutions with the item in the second group (class).
3. Repeat the above steps until the solution is reached.

Exhaustive search travels through the decision tree exhaustively, but it will take much time when the decision tree is big with multiple leaves and multiple attribute values.

Branch and bound search

Branch and bound uses an existing best solution to sidestep searching of the entire decision tree in full. When the algorithm starts, the best solution is well defined to have the worst possible value; thus, any solution it finds out is an improvement. This makes the algorithm initially run down to the left-most branch of the tree, even though that is unlikely to produce a realistic result. In the partitioning problem, that solution corresponds to putting every item in one group, and it is an unacceptable solution. A programme can speed up the process by using a fast heuristic to find an initial solution. This can be used as an input for branch and bound. If the heuristic is right, the savings can be substantial.

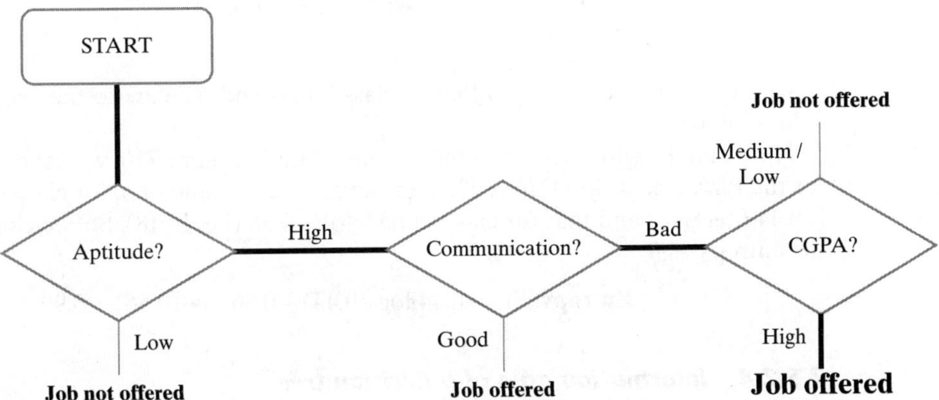

FIG. 7.12
Decision tree based on the training data (depicting a sample path)

Figure 7.12 depicts a sample path (thick line) for the conditions CGPA = **High**, Communication = Bad, Aptitude = High and Programming skills = Bad. According to the above decision tree, the prediction can be made as Chandra **will get the job offer**.

There are many implementations of decision tree, the most prominent ones being C5.0, CART (Classification and Regression Tree), CHAID (Chi-square Automatic Interaction Detector) and ID3 (Iterative Dichotomiser 3) algorithms. The biggest challenge of a decision tree algorithm is to find out which feature to split upon. The main driver for identifying the feature is that the data should be split in such a way that the partitions created by the split should contain examples belonging to a single class. If that happens, the partitions are considered to be **pure**. Entropy is a measure of impurity of an attribute or feature adopted by many algorithms such as ID3 and C5.0. The information gain is calculated on the basis of the decrease in entropy (S) after a data set is split according to a particular attribute (A). Constructing a decision tree is all about finding an attribute that returns the highest information gain (i.e. the most homogeneous branches).

Note:

Like information gain, there are other measures like Gini index or chi-square for individual nodes to decide the feature on the basis of which the split has to be applied. The CART algorithm uses Gini index, while the CHAID algorithm uses chi-square for deciding the feature for applying split.

7.5.2.3   *Entropy of a decision tree*

Let us say S is the sample set of training examples. Then, Entropy (S) measuring the impurity of S is defined as

$$\textbf{Entropy}(S) = \sum_{i=1}^{c} - p_i \log_2 p_i$$

where c is the number of different class labels and p refers to the proportion of values falling into the i-th class label.

For example, with respect to the training data in Figure 7.10, we have two values for the target class 'Job Offered?' – Yes and No. The value of p_i for class value 'Yes' is 0.44 (i.e. 8/18) and that for class value 'No' is 0.56 (i.e. 10/18). So, we can calculate the entropy as

$$\textbf{Entropy}(S) = -0.44 \log_2(0.44) - 0.56 \log_2(0.56) = 0.99.$$

7.5.2.4   *Information gain of a decision tree*

The information gain is created on the basis of the decrease in entropy (S) after a data set is split according to a particular attribute (A). Constructing a decision tree is all about finding an attribute that returns the highest information gain (i.e. the most homogeneous branches). If the information gain is 0, it means that there is no reduction in entropy due to split of the data set according to that particular feature. On the other hand, the maximum amount of information gain which may happen is the entropy of the data set before the split.

Information gain for a particular feature A is calculated by the difference in entropy before a split (or S_{bs}) with the entropy after the split (S_{as}).

$$\textbf{Information Gain } (S, A) = \textbf{Entropy } (S_{bs}) - \textbf{Entropy } (S_{as})$$

For calculating the entropy after split, entropy for all partitions needs to be considered. Then, the weighted summation of the entropy for each partition can be taken as the total entropy after split. For performing weighted summation, the proportion of examples falling into each partition is used as weight.

$$\textbf{Entropy}\left(S_{as}\right) = \sum_{i=1}^{n} w_i \text{ Entropy }\left(p_i\right)$$

Let us examine the value of information gain for the training data set shown in Figure 7.10. We will find the value of entropy at the beginning before any split happens and then again after the split happens. We will compare the values for all the cases –

(a) Original data set:

	Yes	No	Total
Count	8	10	18
pi	0.44	0.56	
-pi*log(pi)	0.52	0.47	0.99

Total Entropy = 0.99

(b) Splitted data set (based on the feature 'CGPA'):

CGPA = High

	Yes	No	Total
Count	4	2	6
pi	0.67	0.33	
-pi*log(pi)	0.39	0.53	0.92

CGPA = Medium

	Yes	No	Total
Count	4	3	7
pi	0.57	0.43	
-pi*log(pi)	0.46	0.52	0.99

CGPA = Low

	Yes	No	Total
Count	0	5	5
pi	0.00	1.00	
-pi*log(pi)	0.00	0.00	0.00

Total Entropy = 0.69   **Information Gain = 0.30**

(c) Splitted data set (based on the feature 'Communication'):

Communication = Good

	Yes	No	Total
Count	7	2	9
pi	0.78	0.22	
-pi*log(pi)	0.28	0.48	0.76

Communication = Bad

	Yes	No	Total
Count	1	8	9
pi	0.11	0.89	
-pi*log(pi)	0.35	0.15	0.50

Total Entropy = 0.63   **Information Gain = 0.36**

(d) Splitted data set (based on the feature 'Aptitude'):

Aptitude = High

	Yes	No	Total
Count	8	3	11
pi	0.73	0.27	
-pi*log(pi)	0.33	0.51	0.85

Aptitude = Low

	Yes	No	Total
Count	0	7	7
pi	0.00	1.00	
-pi*log(pi)	0.00	0.00	0.00

Total Entropy = 0.52   **Information Gain = 0.47**

(e) Splitted data set (based on the feature 'Programming Skill'):

Programming Skill = Good

	Yes	No	Total
Count	5	4	9
pi	0.56	0.44	
-pi*log(pi)	0.47	0.52	0.99

Programming Skill = Bad

	Yes	No	Total
Count	3	6	9
pi	0.33	0.67	
-pi*log(pi)	0.53	0.39	092

Total Entropy = 0.95   **Information Gain = 0.04**

FIG. 7.13A
Entropy and information gain calculation (Level 1)

1. when the feature 'CGPA' is used for the split
2. when the feature 'Communication' is used for the split
3. when the feature 'Aptitude' is used for the split
4. when the feature 'Programming Skills' is used for the split

Figure 7.13a gives the entropy values for the first level split for each of the cases mentioned above.

As calculated, entropy of the data set before split (i.e. Entropy (S_{bs})) = 0.99, and entropy of the data set after split (i.e. Entropy (S_{as})) is

- 0.69 when the feature 'CGPA' is used for split
- 0.63 when the feature 'Communication' is used for split
- 0.52 when the feature 'Aptitude' is used for split
- 0.95 when the feature 'Programming skill' is used for split

Therefore, the information gain from the feature 'CGPA' = 0.99 − 0.69 = 0.3, whereas the information gain from the feature 'Communication' = 0.99 − 0.63 = 0.36. Likewise, the information gain for 'Aptitude' and 'Programming skills' is 0.47 and 0.04, respectively.

Hence, it is quite evident that among all the features, 'Aptitude' results in the best information gain when adopted for the split. So, at the first level, a split will be applied according to the value of 'Aptitude' or in other words, 'Aptitude' will be the first node of the decision tree formed. One important point to be noted here is that for **Aptitude = Low**, entropy is 0, which indicates that always the result will be the same irrespective of the values of the other features. Hence, the branch towards Aptitude = Low will not continue any further.

Aptitude = High

CGPA	Communication	Programming Skill	Job offered?
High	Good	Good	Yes
Medium	Good	Good	Yes
High	Good	Bad	Yes
High	Good	Good	Yes
High	Bad	Good	Yes
Medium	Good	Good	Yes
Low	Bad	Bad	No
Low	Bad	Bad	No
Medium	Good	Bad	Yes
Medium	Bad	Good	No
Medium	Good	Bad	Yes

FIG. 7.13B (*Continued*)

(a) Level 2 starting set:

	Yes	No	Total
Count	8	3	11
pi	0.73	0.27	
-pi*log(pi)	0.33	0.51	0.85

Total Entropy = 0.85

(b) Splitted data set (based on the feature 'CGPA'):

CGPA = High

	Yes	No	Total
Count	4	0	4
pi	1.00	0.00	
-pi*log(pi)	0.00	0.00	0.00

Total Entropy = 0.33

CGPA = Medium

	Yes	No	Total
Count	4	1	5
pi	0.80	0.20	
-pi*log(pi)	0.26	0.46	0.72

Information Gain = 0.52

CGPA = Low

	Yes	No	Total
Count	0	2	2
pi	0.00	1.00	
-pi*log(pi)	0.00	0.00	0.00

(c) Splitted data set (based on the feature 'Communication'):

Communication = Good

	Yes	No	Total
Count	7	0	7
pi	1.00	0.00	
-pi*log(pi)	0.00	0.00	0.00

Total Entropy = 0.30

Communication = Bad

	Yes	No	Total
Count	1	3	4
pi	0.25	0.75	
-pi*log(pi)	0.50	0.31	0.81

Information Gain = 0.55

(d) Spitted data set (based on the feature 'Programming Skill'):

Programming Skill = Good

	Yes	No	Total
Count	5	1	6
pi	0.83	0.17	
-pi*log(pi)	0.22	0.43	0.65

Total Entropy = 0.80

Programming Skill = Bad

	Yes	No	Total
Count	3	2	5
pi	0.60	0.40	
-pi*log(pi)	0.44	0.53	0.97

Information Gain = 0.05

FIG. 7.13B
Entropy and information gain calculation (Level 2)

As a part of level 2, we will thus have only one branch to navigate in this case – the one for **Aptitude = High**. Figure 7.13b presents calculations for level 2. As can be seen from the figure, the entropy value is as follows:

- 0.85 before the split
- 0.33 when the feature 'CGPA' is used for split
- 0.30 when the feature 'Communication' is used for split
- 0.80 when the feature 'Programming skill' is used for split

Entropy and information gain calculation (Level 3)

Aptitude = High & Communication = Bad

CGPA	Programming Skill	Job offered?
High	Good	Yes
Low	Bad	No
Low	Bad	No
Medium	Good	No

(a) Level 2 starting set:

	Yes	No	Total
Count	1	3	4
pi	0.25	0.75	
-pi*log(pi)	0.50	0.31	0.81

Total Entropy = 0.81

(b) Splitted data set (based on the feature 'CGPA'):

CGPA = High

	Yes	No	Total
Count	1	0	1
pi	1.00	0.00	
-pi*log(pi)	0.00	0.00	0.00

CGPA = Medium

	Yes	No	Total
Count	0	1	1
pi	0.00	1.00	
-pi*log(pi)	0.00	0.00	0.00

CGPA = Low

	Yes	No	Total
Count	0	2	2
pi	0.00	1.00	
-pi*log(pi)	0.00	0.00	0.00

Total Entropy = 0.00   **Information Gain = 0.81**

(c) Splitted data set (based on the feature 'Programming Skill'):

Programming Skill = Good

	Yes	No	Total
Count	0	2	2
pi	0.00	1.00	
-pi*log(pi)	0.00	0.00	0.00

Programming Skill = Bad

	Yes	No	Total
Count	1	1	2
pi	0.50	0.50	
-pi*log(pi)	0.50	0.50	1.00

Total Entropy = 0.50   **Information Gain = 0.31**

FIG. 7.13C

Hence, the information gain after split with the features CGPA, Communication and Programming Skill is 0.52, 0.55 and 0.05, respectively. Hence, the feature Communication should be used for this split as it results in the highest information gain. So, at the second level, a split will be applied on the basis of the value of 'Communication'. Again, the point to be noted here is that for **Communication = Good**, entropy is 0, which indicates that always the result will be the same irrespective of the values of the other features. Hence, the branch towards Communication = Good will not continue any further.

As a part of level 3, we will thus have only one branch to navigate in this case – the one for **Communication = Bad**. Figure 7.13c presents calculations for level 3. As can be seen from the figure, the entropy value is as follows:

- 0.81 before the split
- 0 when the feature 'CGPA' is used for split
- 0.50 when the feature 'Programming Skill' is used for split

Hence, the information gain after split with the feature CGPA is 0.81, which is the maximum possible information gain (as the entropy before split was 0.81). Hence, as obvious, a split will be applied on the basis of the value of 'CGPA'. Because the maximum information gain is already achieved, the tree will not continue any further.

7.5.2.5 *Algorithm for decision tree*

Input: Training data set, test data set (or data points)

Steps:

    Do for all attributes

        Calculate the entropy E_i of the attribute F_i

        if $E_i < E_{min}$

           then $E_{min} = E_i$ and $F_{min} = F_i$

        end if

    End do

        Split the data set into subsets using the attribute F_{min}

        Draw a decision tree node containing the attribute F_{min} and split the data set into subsets

        Repeat the above steps until the full tree is drawn covering all the attributes of the original table.

Decision Tree classifier can be implemented using *DecisionTreeClassifier* library of *sklearn. tree* has been used. The full code for the implementation is given below.

```
>>> import pandas as pd
>>> from sklearn.model_selection import train_test_split
>>> from sklearn.metrics import accuracy_score
```

```
>>> from sklearn.tree import DecisionTreeClassifier

>>> data = pd.read_csv("apndcts.csv")

>>> predictors = data.iloc[:,0:7] # Seggretating the predictor
variables ...
>>> target = data.iloc[:,7]        # Seggretating the target / class
variable ...

>>> predictors_train, predictors_test, target_train, target_test =
train_test_split(predictors, target, test_size = 0.3, random_state
= 123)

>>> dtree_entropy = DecisionTreeClassifier(criterion = "entropy",
random_state = 100, max_depth=3, min_samples_leaf=5)

# First train model / classifier with the input dataset (training
data part of it)
>>> model = dtree_entropy.fit(predictors_train, target_train)

# Make prediction using the trained model
>>> prediction = dtree_entropy.predict(predictors_test)

# Time to check the prediction accuracy ...
>>> accuracy_score(target_test, prediction, normalize = True)
```

Output Accuracy:
0.84375

7.5.2.6   *Avoiding overfitting in decision tree – pruning*

The decision tree algorithm, unless a stopping criterion is applied, may keep growing indefinitely – splitting for every feature and dividing into smaller partitions till the point that the data is perfectly classified. This, as is quite evident, results in overfitting problem. To prevent a decision tree getting overfitted to the training data, pruning of the decision tree is essential. Pruning a decision tree reduces the size of the tree such that the model is more generalized and can classify unknown and unlabelled data in a better way.

There are two approaches of pruning:

- Pre-pruning: Stop growing the tree before it reaches perfection.
- Post-pruning: Allow the tree to grow entirely and then post-prune some of the branches from it.

In the case of pre-pruning, the tree is stopped from further growing once it reaches a certain number of decision nodes or decisions. Hence, in this strategy, the algorithm avoids overfitting as well as optimizes computational cost. However, it also stands a chance to ignore important information contributed by a feature which was skipped, thereby resulting in miss out of certain patterns in the data.

On the other hand, in the case of post-pruning, the tree is allowed to grow to the full extent. Then, by using certain pruning criterion, e.g. error rates at the nodes, the size of the tree is reduced. This is a more effective approach in terms of classification accuracy as it considers all minute information available from the training data. However, the computational cost is obviously more than that of pre-pruning.

7.5.2.7   Strengths of decision tree

- It produces very simple understandable rules. For smaller trees, not much mathematical and computational knowledge is required to understand this model.
- Works well for most of the problems.
- It can handle both numerical and categorical variables.
- Can work well both with small and large training data sets.
- Decision trees provide a definite clue of which features are more useful for classification.

7.5.2.8   Weaknesses of decision tree

- Decision tree models are often biased towards features having more number of possible values, i.e. levels.
- This model gets overfitted or underfitted quite easily.
- Decision trees are prone to errors in classification problems with many classes and relatively small number of training examples.
- A decision tree can be computationally expensive to train.
- Large trees are complex to understand.

7.5.2.9   Application of decision tree

Decision tree can be applied in a data set in which there is a finite list of attributes and each data instance stores a value for that attribute (e.g. 'High' for the attribute CGPA). When each attribute has a small number of distinct values (e.g. 'High', 'Medium', 'Low'), it is easier/quicker for the decision tree to suggest (or choose) an effective solution. This algorithm can be extended to handle real-value attributes (e.g. a floating point temperature).

The most straightforward case exists when there are only two possible values for an attribute (Boolean classification). Example: Communication has only two values as 'Good' or 'Bad'. It is also easy to extend the decision tree to create a target function with more than two possible output values. Example: CGPA can take one of the values from 'High', 'Medium', and 'Low'. Irrespective of whether it is a binary value/ multiple values, it is discrete in nature. For example, Aptitude can take the value of either 'High' or 'Low'. It is not possible to assign the value of both 'High' and 'Low' to the attribute Aptitude to draw a decision tree.

There should be no infinite loops on taking a decision. As we move from the root node to the next level node, it should move step-by-step towards the decision node. Otherwise, the algorithm may not give the final result for a given data. If a set of code goes in a loop, it would repeat itself forever, unless the system crashes.

A decision tree can be used even for some instances with missing attributes and instances with errors in the classification of examples or in the attribute values describing those examples; such instances are handled well by decision trees, thereby making them a robust learning method.

Points to Ponder

Balancing overfitting and underfitting in decision tree is a very tricky topic, involving more of an art than science. The way to master this art is experience in working with more number of data sets with a lot of diversity.

■

7.5.3   Random forest model

Random forest is an ensemble classifier, i.e. a combining classifier that uses and combines many decision tree classifiers. Ensembling is usually done using the concept of bagging with different feature sets. The reason for using large number of trees in random forest is to train the trees enough such that contribution from each feature comes in a number of models. After the random forest is generated by combining the trees, majority vote is applied to combine the output of the different trees. A simplified random forest model is depicted in Figure 7.14. The result from the ensemble model is usually better than that from the individual decision tree models.

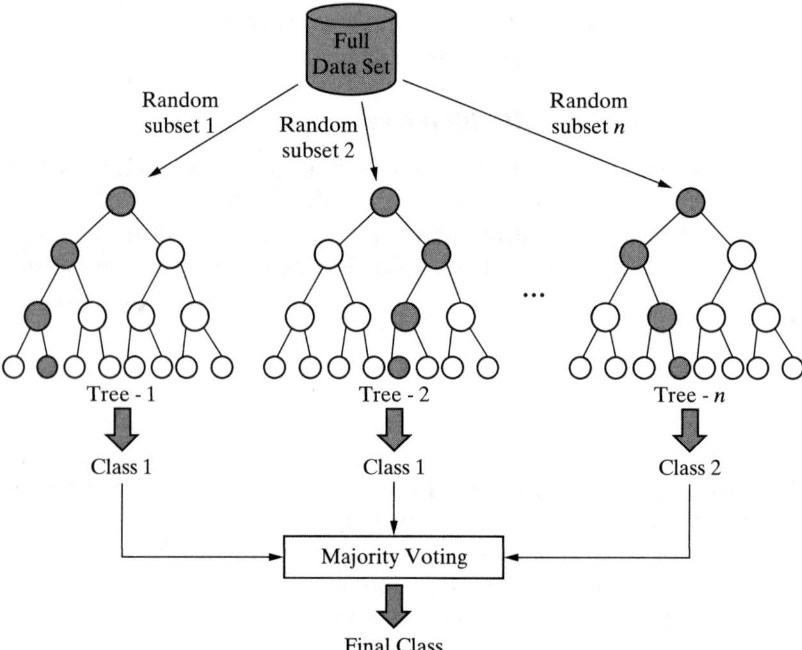

FIG. 7.14
Random forest model

7.5.3.1   *How does random forest work?*

The random forest algorithm works as follows:

1. If there are *N* variables or features in the input data set, select a subset of '*m*' (*m < N*) features at random out of the *N* features. Also, the observations or data instances should be picked randomly.

2. Use the best split principle on these '*m*' features to calculate the number of nodes '*d*'.

3. Keep splitting the nodes to child nodes till the tree is grown to the maximum possible extent.

4. Select a different subset of the training data 'with replacement' to train another decision tree following steps (1) to (3). Repeat this to build and train '*n*' decision trees.

5. Final class assignment is done on the basis of the majority votes from the '*n*' trees.

For implementing Random Forest classifier, RandomForestClassifier library of *sklearn. ensemble* has been used. The full code for the implementation is given below.

In the code below, in addition to reviewing the model accuracy, we will also review the confusion matrix.

```
>>> import pandas as pd
>>> from sklearn.model_selection import train_test_split
>>> from sklearn.metrics import accuracy_score
>>> from sklearn.metrics import confusion_matrix
>>> from sklearn.ensemble import RandomForestClassifier

>>> data = pd.read_csv("apndcts.csv")

>>> predictors = data.iloc[:,0:7] # Segregating the predictor
variables ...
>>> target = data.iloc[:,7]       # Segregating the target / class
variable ...

>>> predictors_train, predictors_test, target_train, target_test =
train_test_split(predictors, target, test_size = 0.3, random_state
= 123)

>>> rf = RandomForestClassifier()

# First train model / classifier with the input dataset (training
data part of it)
>>> model = rf.fit(predictors_train, target_train)

# Make prediction using the trained model
>>> prediction = rf.predict(predictors_test)

# Time to check the prediction accuracy...
>>> accuracy_score(target_test, prediction, normalize = True)
```

```
# And this time let's look at the confusion matrix too...
>>> confusion_matrix(target_test, prediction)
```

Output Accuracy:

Accuracy ⇒ 0.875

Confusion matrix ⇒ array([[25, 0],

[4, 3]], dtype=int64)

Points to Ponder

In the random forest classifier, if the number of trees is assumed to be excessively large, the model may get overfitted. In an extreme case of overfitting, the model may mimic the training data, and training error might be almost 0. However, when the model is run on an unseen sample, it may result in a very high validation error.

■

7.5.3.2   Out-of-bag (OOB) error in random forest

In random forests, we have seen, that each tree is constructed using a different bootstrap sample from the original data. The samples left out of the bootstrap and not used in the construction of the i-th tree can be used to measure the performance of the model. At the end of the run, predictions for each such sample evaluated each time are tallied, and the final prediction for that sample is obtained by taking a vote. The total error rate of predictions for such samples is termed as out-of-bag (OOB) error rate.

The error rate shown in the confusion matrix reflects the OOB error rate. Because of this reason, the error rate displayed is often surprisingly high.

7.5.3.3   Strengths of random forest

- It runs efficiently on large and expansive data sets.
- It has a robust method for estimating missing data and maintains precision when a large proportion of the data is absent.
- It has powerful techniques for balancing errors in a class population of unbalanced data sets.
- It gives estimates (or assessments) about which features are the most important ones in the overall classification.
- It generates an internal unbiased estimate (gauge) of the generalization error as the forest generation progresses.
- Generated forests can be saved for future use on other data.
- Lastly, the random forest algorithm can be used to solve both classification and regression problems.

7.5.3.4 *Weaknesses of random forest*

- This model, because it combines a number of decision tree models, is not as easy to understand as a decision tree model.
- It is computationally much more expensive than a simple model like decision tree.

7.5.3.5 *Application of random forest*

Random forest is a very powerful classifier which combines the versatility of many decision tree models into a single model. Because of the superior results, this ensemble model is gaining wide adoption and popularity amongst the machine learning practitioners to solve a wide range of classification problems.

7.5.4 Support vector machines

SVM is a model, which can do linear classification as well as regression. SVM is based on the concept of a surface, called a hyperplane, which draws a boundary between data instances plotted in the multi-dimensional feature space. The output prediction of an SVM is one of two conceivable classes which are already defined in the training data. In summary, the SVM algorithm builds an N-dimensional hyperplane model that assigns future instances into one of the two possible output classes.

7.5.4.1 *Classification using hyperplanes*

In SVM, a model is built to discriminate the data instances belonging to different classes. Let us assume for the sake of simplicity that the data instances are linearly separable. In this case, when mapped in a two-dimensional space, the data instances belonging to different classes fall in different sides of a straight line drawn in the two-dimensional space as depicted in Figure 7.15a. If the same concept is extended to a multi-dimensional feature space, the straight line dividing data instances belonging to different classes transforms to a hyperplane as depicted in Figure 7.15b.

Thus, an SVM model is a representation of the input instances as points in the feature space, which are mapped so that an apparent gap between them divides the instances of the separate classes. In other words, the goal of the SVM analysis is to find a plane, or rather a hyperplane, which separates the instances on the basis of their classes. New examples (i.e. new instances) are then mapped into that same space and predicted to belong to a class on the basis of which side of the gap the new instance will fall on. In summary, in the overall training process, the SVM algorithm analyses input data and identifies a surface in the multi-dimensional feature space called the hyperplane. There may be many possible hyperplanes, and one of the challenges with the SVM model is to find the optimal hyperplane.

Training data sets which have a substantial grouping periphery will function well with SVM. Generalization error in terms of SVM is the measure of how accurately and precisely this SVM model can predict values for previously unseen data (new data). A hard margin in terms of SVM means that an SVM model is inflexible in classification and tries to work exceptionally fit in the training set, thereby causing overfitting.

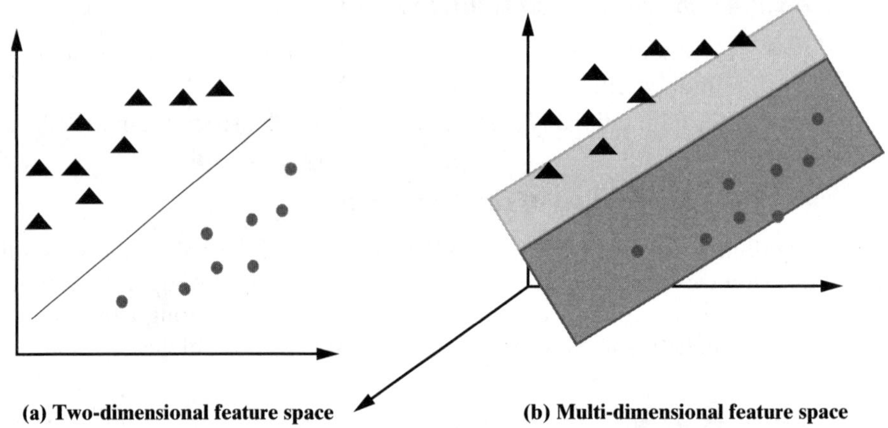

(a) Two-dimensional feature space   (b) Multi-dimensional feature space

FIG. 7.15
Linearly separable data instances

Support Vectors: Support vectors are the data points (representing classes), the critical component in a data set, which are near the identified set of lines (hyperplane). If support vectors are removed, they will alter the position of the dividing hyperplane.

Hyperplane and Margin: For an N-dimensional feature space, hyperplane is a flat subspace of dimension $(N-1)$ that separates and classifies a set of data. For example, if we consider a two-dimensional feature space (which is nothing but a data set having two features and a class variable), a hyperplane will be a one-dimensional subspace or a straight line. In the same way, for a three-dimensional feature space (data set having three features and a class variable), hyperplane is a two-dimensional subspace or a simple plane. However, quite understandably, it is difficult to visualize a feature space greater than three dimensions, much like for a subspace or hyperplane having more than three dimensions.

Mathematically, in a two-dimensional space, hyperplane can be defined by the equation:

$c_0 + c_1 X_1 + c_2 X_2 = 0$, which is nothing but an equation of a straight line.

Extending this concept to an N-dimensional space, hyperplane can be defined by the equation:

$c_0 + c_1 X_1 + c_2 X_2 + \ldots + c_N X_N = 0$ which, in short, can be represented as follows:

$$\vec{c} \cdot \vec{X} + c_0 = 0$$

Spontaneously, the further (or more distance) from the hyperplane the data points lie, the more confident we can be about correct categorization. So, when a new testing data point/data set is added, the side of the hyperplane it lands on will decide the class that we assign to it. The distance between hyperplane and data points is known as **margin**.

7.5.4.2 *Identifying the correct hyperplane in SVM*

As we have already discussed, there may be multiple options for hyperplanes dividing the data instances belonging to the different classes. We need to identify which one will result in the best classification. Let us examine a few scenarios before arriving to that conclusion. For the sake of simplicity of visualization, the hyperplanes have been shown as straight lines in most of the diagrams.

Scenario 1

As depicted in Figure 7.16, in this scenario, we have three hyperplanes: A, B, and C. Now, we need to identify the correct hyperplane which better segregates the two classes represented by the triangles and circles. As we can see, hyperplane 'A' has performed this task quite well.

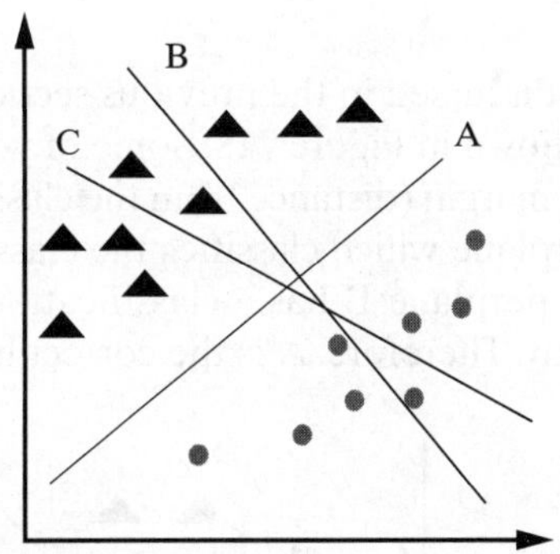

FIG. 7.16
Support vector machine: Scenario 1

Scenario 2

As depicted in Figure 7.17, we have three hyperplanes: A, B, and C. We have to identify the correct hyperplane which classifies the triangles and circles in the best possible way. Here, maximizing the distances between the nearest data points of both the classes and hyperplane will help us decide the correct hyperplane. This distance is called as **margin**.

In Figure 7.17b, you can see that the margin for hyperplane A is high as compared to those for both B and C. Hence, hyperplane A is the correct hyperplane. Another quick reason for selecting the hyperplane with higher margin (distance) is robustness. If we select a hyperplane having a lower margin (distance), then there is a high probability of misclassification.

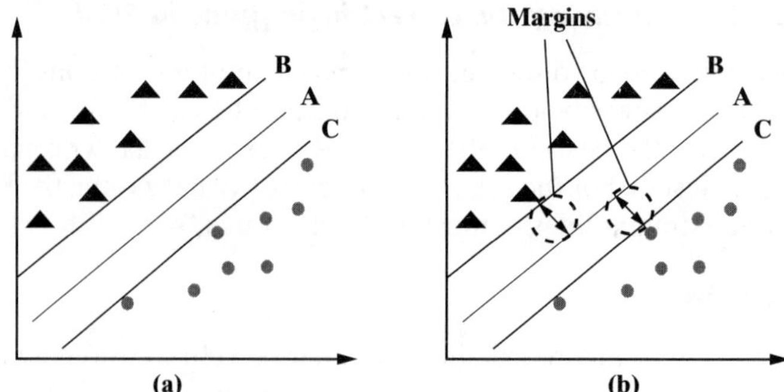

FIG. 7.17
Support vector machine: Scenario 2

Scenario 3

Use the rules as discussed in the previous section to identify the correct hyperplane in the scenario shown in Figure 7.18. Some of you might have selected hyperplane B as it has a higher margin (distance from the class) than A. But, here is the catch; SVM selects the hyperplane which classifies the classes accurately before maximizing the margin. Here, hyperplane B has a classification error, and A has classified all data instances correctly. Therefore, A is the correct hyperplane.

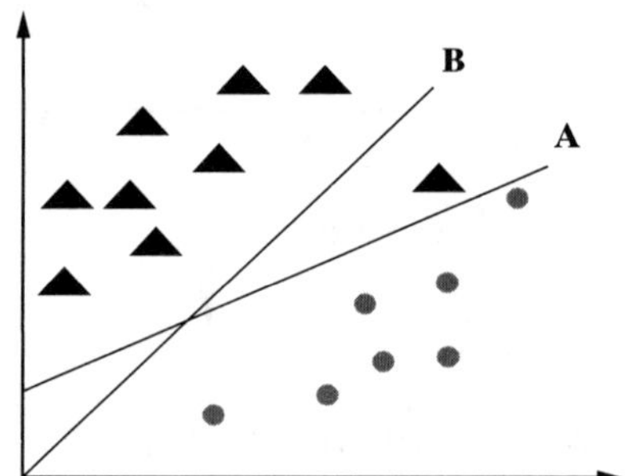

FIG. 7.18
Support vector machine: Scenario 3

Scenario 4

In this scenario, as shown in Figure 7.19a, it is not possible to distinctly segregate the two classes by using a straight line, as one data instance belonging to one of the classes (triangle) lies in the territory of the other class (circle) as an outlier.

One triangle at the other end is like an outlier for the triangle class. SVM has a feature to ignore outliers and find the hyperplane that has the maximum margin (hyperplane A, as shown in Fig. 7.19b). Hence, we can say that SVM is robust to outliers.

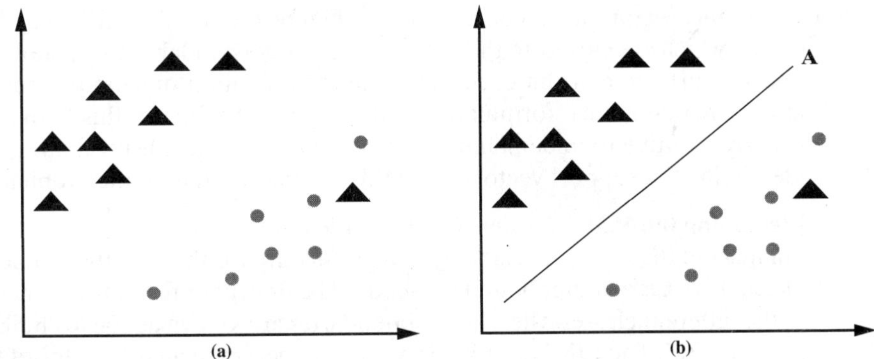

FIG. 7.19
Support vector machine: Scenario 4

So, by summarizing the observations from the different scenarios, we can say that

1. The hyperplane should segregate the data instances belonging to the two classes in the best possible way.
2. It should maximize the distances between the nearest data points of both the classes, i.e. maximize the margin.
3. If there is a need to prioritize between higher margin and lesser misclassification, the hyperplane should try to reduce misclassifications.

Our next focus is to find out a way to identify a hyperplane which maximizes the margin.

7.5.4.3   *Maximum margin hyperplane*

Finding the Maximum Margin Hyperplane (MMH) is nothing but identifying the hyperplane which has the largest separation with the data instances of the two classes. Though any set of three hyperplanes can do the correct classification, why do we need to search for the set of hyperplanes causing the largest separation? The answer is that doing so helps us in achieving more generalization and hence less number of issues in the classification of unknown data.

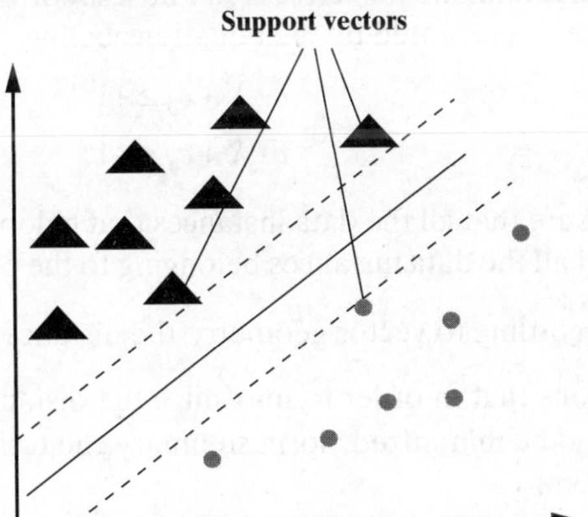

FIG. 7.20
Support vectors

Support vectors, as can be observed in Figure 7.20, are data instances from the two classes which are closest to the MMH. Quite understandably, there should be at least one support vector from each class. The identification of support vectors requires intense mathematical formulation, which is out of scope of this book. However, it is fairly intuitive to understand that modelling a problem using SVM is nothing but identifying the support vectors and MMH corresponding to the problem space.

Identifying the MMH for linearly separable data

Finding out the MMH is relatively straightforward for the data that is linearly separable. In this case, an outer boundary needs to be drawn for the data instances belonging to the different classes. These outer boundaries are known as convex hull, as depicted in Figure 7.21. The MMH can be drawn as the perpendicular bisector of the shortest line (i.e. the connecting line having the shortest length) between the convex hulls.

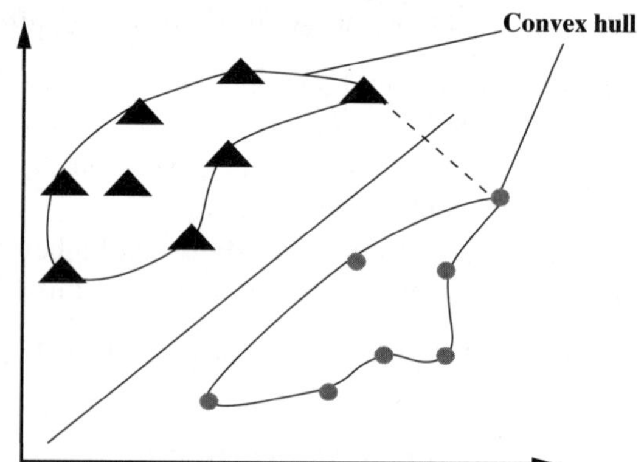

FIG. 7.21
Drawing the MMH for linearly separable data

We have already seen earlier that a hyperplane in the N-dimensional feature space can be represented by the equation: $\vec{c} \cdot \vec{X} + c_0 = 0$

Using this equation, the objective is to find a set of values for the vector such that two hyperplanes, represented by the equations below, can be specified.

$$\vec{c} \cdot \vec{X} + c_0 \geq +1$$

$$\vec{c} \cdot \vec{X} + c_0 \leq -1$$

This is to ensure that all the data instances that belong to one class falls above one hyperplane and all the data instances belonging to the other class falls below another hyperplane. According to vector geometry, the distance of these planes should be $\frac{2}{\vec{c}}$.

It is quite obvious that in order to maximize the distance between hyperplanes, the value of $\vec{c}$ should be minimized. So, in summary, the task of SVM is to solve the optimization problem:

$$\min\left(\frac{1}{2}\vec{c}\right)$$

Identifying the MMH for non-linearly separable data

Now that we have a clear understanding of how to identify the MMH for a linearly separable data set, let us do some study about how non-linearly separable data needs to be handled by SVM. For this, we have to use a slack variable ξ, which provides some soft margin for data instances in one class that fall on the wrong side of the hyperplane. As depicted in Figure 7.22, a data instance belonging to the circle class falls on the side of the hyperplane designated for the data instances belonging to the triangle class. The same issue also happens for a data instance belonging to the triangle class.

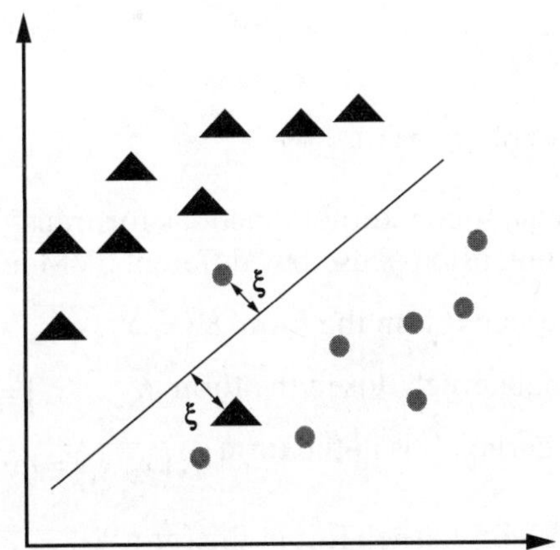

FIG. 7.22
Drawing the MMH for non-linearly separable data

A cost value 'C' is imposed on all such data instances that fall on the wrong side of the hyperplane. The task of SVM is now to minimize the total cost due to such data instances in order to solve the revised optimization problem:

$$\min\left(\frac{1}{2}\vec{c}^{\,2}\right)+C\sum_{i=1}^{N}\xi_i$$

7.5.4.4   Kernel trick

As we have seen in the last section, one way to deal with non-linearly separable data is by using a slack variable and an optimization function to minimize the cost value. However, this is not the only way to use SVM to solve machine learning problems involving non-linearly separable data sets. SVM has a technique called the **kernel trick** to deal with non-linearly separable data. As shown in Figure 7.23, these are functions which can transform lower dimensional input space to a higher dimensional space. In the process, it converts linearly non-separable data to a linearly separable data. These functions are called **kernels**.

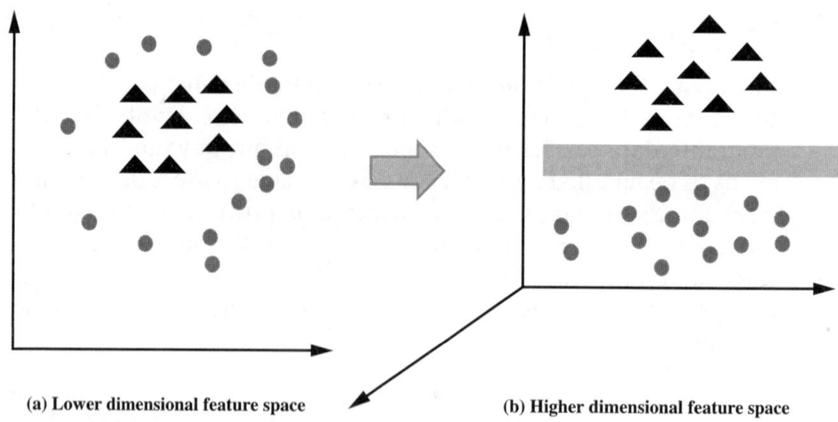

FIG. 7.23
Kernel trick in SVM

Some of the common kernel functions for transforming from a lower dimension 'i' to a higher dimension 'j' used by different SVM implementations are as follows:

- Linear kernel: It is in the form $K\left(\vec{x_i},\vec{x_j}\right)=\vec{x_i}\cdot\vec{x_j}$

- Polynomial kernel: It is in the form $K\left(\vec{x_i},\vec{x_j}\right)=\left(\vec{x_i}\cdot\vec{x_j}+1\right)^{d}$

- Sigmoid kernel: It is in the form $K\left(\vec{x_i},\vec{x_j}\right)=\tanh\left(k\vec{x_i}\cdot\vec{x_j}-\partial\right)$

- Gaussian RBF kernel: It is in the form $K\left(\vec{x_i},\vec{x_j}\right)=e^{\dfrac{-x_i-x_j^2}{2\sigma^2}}$

When data instances of the classes are closer to each other, this method can be used. The effectiveness of SVM depends both on the

- selection of the kernel function
- adoption of values for the kernel parameters

For implementing Random Forest classifier, *svm* library of **sklearn** framework has been used. The full code for the implementation is given below.

```
>>> import pandas as pd
>>> from sklearn.model_selection import train_test_split
>>> from sklearn.metrics import accuracy_score
>>> from sklearn import svm

>>> data = pd.read_csv("apndcts.csv")

>>> predictors = data.iloc[:,0:7] # Seggretating the predictor
variables ...
>>> target = data.iloc[:,7]       # Seggretating the target / class
variable ...

>>> predictors_train, predictors_test, target_train, target_test =
```

```
train_test_split(predictors, target, test_size = 0.3, random_state
= 123)

>>> svm = svm.SVC(kernel='linear')   # SVC with linear kernel

# First train model / classifier with the input dataset (training
data part of it)
>>> model = svm.fit(predictors_train, target_train)

# Make prediction using the trained model
>>> prediction = svm.predict(predictors_test)

# Time to check the prediction accuracy ...
>>> accuracy_score(target_test, prediction, normalize = True)
```

Output Accuracy:
0.78125

Note:

Instead of linear kernel, we can use RBF or polynomial degree kernel as shown in
the code below:
```
>>> rbf_svc = svm.SVC (kernel = 'rbf', gamma = 0.7, C = 1.0)
>>> poly_svc = svm.SVC (kernel = 'poly', degree = 3, C = 1.0)
```

7.5.4.5   Strengths of SVM

- SVM can be used for both classification and regression.
- It is robust, i.e. not much impacted by data with noise or outliers.
- The prediction results using this model are very promising.

7.5.4.6   Weaknesses of SVM

- SVM is applicable only for binary classification, i.e. when there are only two
  classes in the problem domain.
- The SVM model is very complex – almost like a black box when it deals with a
  high-dimensional data set. Hence, it is very difficult and close to impossible to
  understand the model in such cases.
- It is slow for a large dataset, i.e. a data set with either a large number of features
  or a large number of instances.
- It is quite memory-intensive.

7.5.4.7   Application of SVM

SVM is most effective when it is used for binary classification, i.e. for solving a
machine learning problem with two classes. One common problem on which SVM
can be applied is in the field of bioinformatics – more specifically, in detecting cancer
and other genetic disorders. It can also be used in detecting the image of a face by

binary classification of images into face and non-face components. More such applications can be described.

7.6   SUMMARY

1. The objective of classification is to predict the class of unknown objects on the basis of prior class-related information of similar objects. This learning could be used when how to classify a given data is known or, in other words, class values of data instances are available.

2. A critical classification problem in the context of the banking domain is identifying potentially fraudulent transactions. Because there are millions of transactions which have to be scrutinized to identify whether a particular transaction might be a fraud transaction, it is not possible for any human being to carry out this task.

3. Common classification algorithms are kNN, decision tree, random forest, SVM, and Naïve Bayes.

4. The kNN algorithm is among the best and the simplest of machine learning algorithms. A new instance is classified by a majority vote of its neighbours, with the instance being allocated the class that is predominant among its kNN.

5. Decision tree learning is the most broadly utilized classifier. It is characterized by fast execution time and ease in the interpretation of the rules.

6. The decision tree algorithm needs to find out the attribute splitting by which results in highest information gain. For a sample of training examples S, entropy measures the impurity of S.

$$\textbf{Entropy}(S) = \sum_{i=1}^{C} -p_i \log_2 p_i$$

where c is the number of different class labels and p refers to the proportion of values falling into the i-th class label.

7. Information gain is created on the basis of the decrease in entropy (S) after a dataset is split based on a particular attribute (A). Information gain for a particular feature A is calculated by the difference in entropy before a split (S_{bs}) with the entropy after the split (S_{as}).

Information Gain (S, A) = Entropy (S_{bs}) - Entropy (S_{as})

8. Random forest is an ensemble classifier (combining classifier) which uses and combines many decision tree models. The result from an ensemble model is usually better than that from one of the individual models.

9. An SVM is a binary linear classifier. The output prediction of an SVM is one of the two conceivable classes which are already defined in the training data. SVM is also an example of a linear classifier and a maximum margin classifier.

10. SVM has a new technique called the kernel trick. These are functions, which take a lower dimensional input space and transform it to a higher dimensional space and in the process converts a non-linearly separable problem to a linearly separable problem. These functions are called kernels. When all the classes are closer to each other, this method can be used.

MULTIPLE-CHOICE QUESTIONS

1. Predicting whether a tumour is malignant or benign is an example of?
    (a) Unsupervised Learning
    (b) Supervised Regression Problem
    (c) Supervised Classification Problem
    (d) Categorical Attribute

2. Price prediction in the domain of real estate is an example of?
    (a) Unsupervised Learning
    (b) Supervised Regression Problem
    (c) Supervised Classification Problem
    (d) Categorical Attribute

3. Let us consider two examples, say 'predicting whether a tumour is malignant or benign' and 'price prediction in the domain of real estate'. These two problems are same in nature.
    (a) TRUE   (b) FALSE

4. Supervised machine learning is as good as the data used to train it.
    (a) TRUE   (b) FALSE

5. Which is a type of machine learning where a target feature, which is of categorical type, is predicted for the test data on the basis of the information imparted by the training data?
    (a) Unsupervised Learning   (b) Supervised Regression
    (c) Supervised Classification   (d) Categorical Attribute

6. Classification is a type of supervised learning where a target feature, which is of categorical type, is predicted for the test data on the basis of the information imparted by the training data. The target categorical feature is known as?
    (a) Object   (b) Variable
    (c) Method   (d) Class

7. This is the first step in the supervised learning model.
    (a) Problem Identification
    (b) Identification of Required Data
    (c) Data Pre-processing
    (d) Definition of Training Data Set

8. This is the cleaning/transforming the data set in the supervised learning model.
    (a) Problem Identification
    (b) Identification of Required Data
    (c) Data Pre-processing
    (d) Definition of Training Data Set

9. This refers to the transformations applied to the identified data before feeding the same into the algorithm.
    (a) Problem Identification
    (b) Identification of Required Data
    (c) Data Pre-processing
    (d) Definition of Training Data Set

10. This step of supervised learning determines 'the type of training data set'.
(a) Problem Identification
(b) Identification of Required Data
(c) Data Pre-processing
(d) Definition of Training Data Set

11. Entire design of the programme is done over here in supervised learning.
(a) Problem Identification
(b) Training
(c) Data Pre-processing
(d) Definition of Training Data Set

12. Training data run on the algorithm is called as?
(a) Program   (b) Training
(c) Training Information   (d) Learned Function

13. SVM is an example of?
(a) Linear Classifier and Maximum Margin Classifier
(b) Non-linear Classifier and Maximum Margin Classifier
(c) Linear Classifier and Minimum Margin Classifier
(d) Non-linear Classifier and Minimum Margin Classifier

14. ---------- in terms of SVM means that an SVM is inflexible in classification
(a) Hard Margin   (b) Soft Margin
(c) Linear Margin   (d) Non-linear Classifier

15. ---------- are the data points (representing classes), the important component in a data set, which are near the identified set of lines (hyperplane).
(a) Hard Margin   (b) Soft Margin
(c) Linear Margin   (d) Support Vectors

16. ---------- is a line that linearly separates and classifies a set of data.
(a) Hyperplane   (b) Soft Margin
(c) Linear Margin   (d) Support Vectors

17. The distance between hyperplane and data points is called as:
(a) Hyper Plan   (b) Margins
(c) Error   (d) Support Vectors

18. Which of the following is true about SVM?
(a) It is useful only in high-dimensional spaces
(b) It always gives an approximate value
(c) It is accurate
(d) Understanding SVM is difficult

19. Which of the following is true about SVM?
(a) It is useful only in high-dimensional spaces
(b) It requires less memory
(c) SVM does not perform well when we have a large data set
(d) SVM performs well when we have a large data set

20. What is the meaning of hard margin in SVM?
(a) SVM allows very low error in classification
(b) SVM allows high amount of error in classification
(c) Underfitting
(d) SVM is highly flexible

21. What sizes of training data sets are not best suited for SVM?
 (a) Large data sets
 (b) Very small training data sets
 (c) Medium size training data sets
 (d) Training data set size does not matter

22. Support Vectors are near the hyperplane.
 (a) True   (b) False

23. In SVM, these functions take a lower dimensional input space and transform it to a higher dimensional space.
 (a) Kernels   (b) Vector
 (c) Support Vector   (d) Hyperplane

24. Which of the following options is true about the kNN algorithm?
 (a) It can be used only for classification
 (b) It can be used only for regression
 (c) It can be used for both classification and regression
 (d) It is not possible to use for both classification and regression

25. Which of the following will be Euclidean distance between the two data points A(4,3) and B(2,3)?
 (a) 1   (b) 2
 (c) 4   (d) 8

26. Which of the following will be Manhattan distance between the two data points A(8,3) and B(4,3)?
 (a) 1   (b) 2
 (c) 4   (d) 8

27. When you find many noises in data, which of the following options would you consider in kNN?
 (a) Increase the value of k (b) Decrease the value of k
 (c) Noise does not depend on k (d) $K = 0$

28. What would be the relationship between the training time taken by 1-NN, 2-NN, and 3-NN?
 (a) 1-NN > 2-NN > 3-NN   (b) 1-NN < 2-NN < 3-NN
 (c) 1-NN ~ 2-NN ~ 3-NN   (d) None of these

29. Which of the following algorithms is an example of the ensemble learning algorithm?
 (a) Random Forest   (b) Decision Tree
 (c) kNN   (d) SVM

30. Which of the following is not an inductive bias in a decision tree?
 (a) It prefers longer tree over shorter tree
 (b) Trees that place nodes near the root with high information gain are preferred
 (c) Overfitting is a natural phenomenon in a decision tree
 (d) Prefer the shortest hypothesis that fits the data

SHORT-ANSWER TYPE QUESTIONS (5 MARKS EACH)

1. What is supervised learning? Why it is called so?
2. Give an example of supervised learning in a hospital industry.
3. Give any three examples of supervised learning.
4. What is classification and regression in a supervised learning?
5. Give some examples of common classification algorithms.
6. Explain, in brief, the SVM model.
7. What is cost of misclassification in SVM?
8. Define Support Vectors in the SVM model.
9. Define kernel in the SVM model.
10. What are the factors determining the effectiveness of SVM?
11. What are the advantages of the SVM model?
12. What are the disadvantages of the SVM model?
13. Write notes on
    - validation error in the kNN algorithm
    - choosing k value in the kNN algorithm
    - inductive bias in a decision tree
14. What are the advantages of the kNN algorithm?
15. What are the disadvantages of the kNN algorithm?
16. Explain, in brief, the decision tree algorithm.
17. What is node and leaf in decision tree?
18. What is entropy of a decision tree?
19. Define information gain in a decision tree.
20. Write any three strengths of the decision tree method.
21. Write any three weaknesses of the decision tree method.
22. Explain, in brief, the random forest model?

LONG-ANSWER TYPE QUESTIONS (10 MARKS EACH)

1. Distinguish between supervised learning, semi-supervised learning, and unsupervised learning.
2. Explain any five examples of classification problems in detail.
3. Explain classification steps in detail.
4. Discuss the SVM model in detail with different scenarios.
5. What are the advantages and disadvantages associated with SVM?
6. Discuss the kNN model in detail.
7. Discuss the error rate and validation error in the kNN algorithm.

8. Discuss how to calculate the distance between the test data and the training data for kNN.

9. Write the algorithm for kNN.

10. What is decision tree? What are the different types of nodes? Explain in detail

11. Explain various options of searching a decision tree.

12. Discuss the decision tree algorithm in detail.

13. What is inductive bias in a decision tree? How to avoid overfitting?

14. What are the strengths and weaknesses of the decision tree method?

15. Discuss appropriate problems for decision tree learning in detail.

16. Discuss the random forest model in detail. What are the features of random forest?

17. Discuss OOB error and variable importance in random forest.

Chapter 8

Supervised Learning: Regression

8.1   INTRODUCTION

OBJECTIVE OF THE CHAPTER:

In the last two chapters, you have got quite a good conceptual overview of supervised learning algorithm for categorical data prediction. You got a detailed understanding of all the popular models of classification that are used by machine learning practitioners to solve a wide array of prediction problems where the target variable is a categorical variable.

In this chapter, we will build concepts on prediction of numerical variables – which is another key area of supervised learning. This area, known as regression, focuses on solving problems such as predicting value of real estate, demand forecast in retail, weather forecast, etc.

First, you will be introduced to the most popular and simplest algorithm, namely simple linear regression. This model roots from the statistical concept of fitting a straight line and the least squares method. We will explore this algorithm in detail. In this same context, we will also explore the concept of multiple linear regression.

We will then briefly touch upon the other important algorithms in regression, namely multivariate adaptive regression splines, logistic regression, and maximum likelihood estimation.

By the end of this chapter, you will gain sufficient knowledge in all the aspects of supervised learning and become ready to start solving problems on your own.

8.2   EXAMPLE OF REGRESSION

We have mentioned many times that real estate price prediction is a problem that can be solved by supervised learning or, more specifically, by regression. So, what this problem really is? Let us delve a little deeper into the problem.

New City is the primary hub of the commercial activities in the country. In the last couple of decades, with increasing globalization, commercial activities have intensified in New City. Together with that, a large number of people have come and settled in the city with a dream to achieve professional growth in their lives. As an obvious fall-out, a large number of housing projects have started in every nook and corner of the city. But the demand for apartments has still outgrown the supply. To get benefit from this boom in real estate business, Karen has started a digital market agency for buying and selling real estates (including apartments, independent houses, town houses, etc.). Initially, when the business was small, she used to interact with buyers and sellers personally and help them arrive at a price quote – either for selling a property (for a seller) or for buying a property (for a buyer). Her long experience in real estate business helped her develop an intuition on what the correct price quote of a property could be – given the value of certain standard parameters such as area (sq. m.) of the property, location, floor, number of years since purchase, amenities available, etc. However, with the huge surge in the business, she is facing a big challenge. She is not able to manage personal interactions as well as setting the correct price quote for the properties all alone. She hired an assistant for managing customer interactions. But the assistant, being new in the real estate business, is struggling with price quotations. How can Karen solve this problem?

Fortunately, Karen has a friend, Frank, who is a data scientist with in-depth knowledge in machine learning models. Frank comes up with a solution to Karen's problem. He builds a model which can predict the correct value of a real estate if it has certain standard inputs such as area (sq. m.) of the property, location, floor, number of years since purchase, amenities available, etc. Wow, that sounds to be like Karen herself doing the job! Curious to know what model Frank has used? Yes, you guessed it right. He used a regression model to solve Karen's real estate price prediction problem.

So, we just discussed about one problem which can be solved using regression. In the same way, a bunch of other problems related to prediction of numerical value can be solved using the regression model. In the context of regression, dependent variable (Y) is the one whose value is to be predicted, e.g. the price quote of the real estate in the context of Karen's problem. This variable is presumed to be functionally related to one (say, X) or more independent variables called predictors. In the context of Karen's problem, Frank used area of the property, location, floor, etc. as predictors of the model that he built. In other words, the dependent variable depends on independent variable(s) or predictor(s). Regression is essentially finding a relationship (or) association between the dependent variable (Y) and the independent variable(s) (X), i.e. to find the function 'f' for the association $Y = f(X)$.

8.3   COMMON REGRESSION ALGORITHMS

The most common regression algorithms are

- Simple linear regression
- Multiple linear regression
- Polynomial regression
- Multivariate adaptive regression splines
- Logistic regression
- Maximum likelihood estimation (least squares)

8.3.1   Simple Linear Regression

As the name indicates, simple linear regression is the simplest regression model which involves only one predictor. This model assumes a linear relationship between the dependent variable and the predictor variable as shown in Figure 8.1.

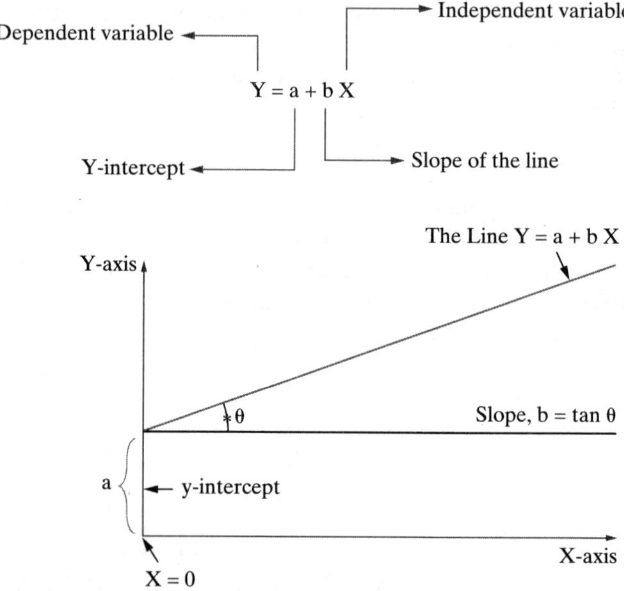

FIG. 8.1
Simple linear regression

In the context of Karen's problem, if we take Price of a Property as the dependent variable and the Area of the Property (in sq. m.) as the predictor variable, we can build a model using simple linear regression.

$$\text{Price}_{\text{Property}} = f(\text{Area}_{\text{Property}})$$

Assuming a linear association, we can reformulate the model as

$$\text{Price}_{\text{Property}} = a + b.\,\text{Area}_{\text{Property}}$$

where 'a' and 'b' are intercept and slope of the straight line, respectively.

Just to recall, straight lines can be defined in a slope–intercept form $Y = (a + bX)$, where a = intercept and b = slope of the straight line. The value of intercept indicates the value of Y when $X = 0$. It is known as 'the intercept or Y intercept' because it specifies where the straight line crosses the vertical or Y-axis (refer to Fig. 8.1).

8.3.1.1   *Slope of the simple linear regression model*

The Slope of a straight line represents how much the line in a graph changes in the vertical direction (Y-axis) over a change in the horizontal direction (X-axis) as shown in Figure 8.2.

Slope = Change in Y/Change in X

Rise is the change in Y-axis ($Y_2 - Y_1$) and Run is the change in X-axis ($X_2 - X_1$). So, slope is represented as given below:

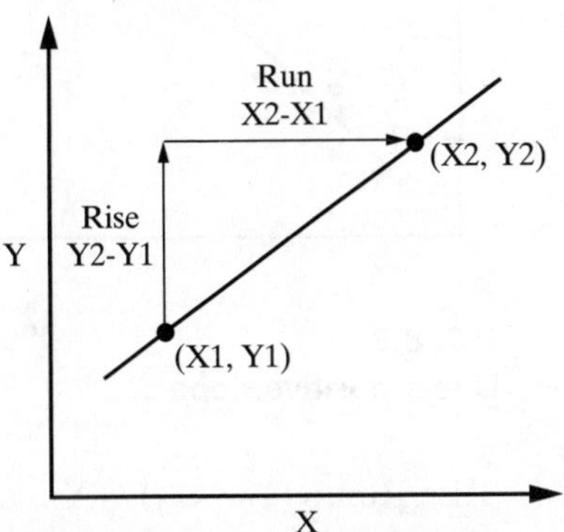

FIG. 8.2
Rise and run representation

$$\text{Slope} = \frac{\text{Rise}}{\text{Run}} = \frac{Y2 - Y1}{X2 - X1}$$

Example of slope

Let us find the slope of the graph where the lower point on the line is represented as $(-3, -2)$ and the higher point on the line is represented as $(2, 2)$.

$(X_1, Y_1) = (-3, -2)$ and $(X_2, Y_2) = (2, 2)$

Rise $= (Y_2 - Y_1) = (2 - (-2)) = 2 + 2 = 4$

Run $= (X_2 - X_1) = (2 - (-3)) = 2 + 3 = 5$

Slope = Rise/Run = 4/5 = 0.8

There can be two types of slopes in a linear regression model: positive slope and negative slope. Different types of regression lines based on the type of slope include

- Linear positive slope
- Curve linear positive slope
- Linear negative slope
- Curve linear negative slope

Linear positive slope

A positive slope always moves upward on a graph from left to right (refer to Fig. 8.3).

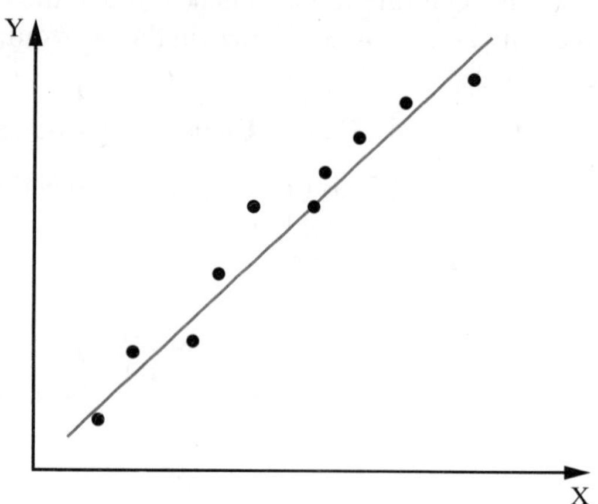

FIG. 8.3
Linear positive slope

$$\text{Slope} = \text{Rise/Run} = (Y_2 - Y_1) / (X_2 - X_1) = \text{Delta } (Y) / \text{Delta}(X)$$

- Scenario 1 for positive slope: Delta (Y) is positive and Delta (X) is positive
- Scenario 2 for positive slope: Delta (Y) is negative and Delta (X) is negative

Curve linear positive slope

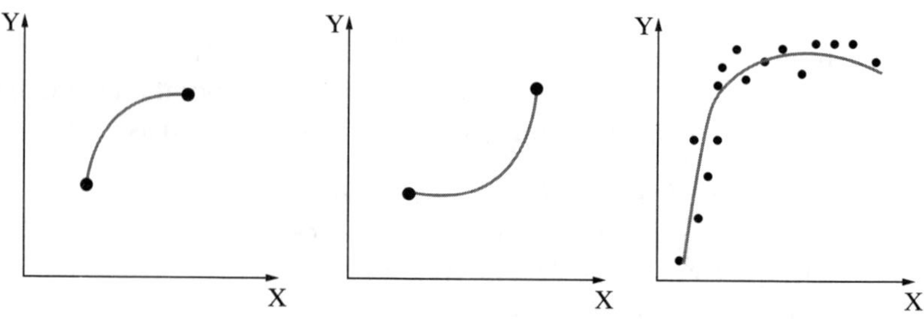

FIG. 8.4
Curve linear positive slope

Curves in these graphs (refer to Fig. 8.4) slope upward from left to right.

$$\text{Slope} = (Y_2 - Y_1) / (X_2 - X_1) = \text{Delta}(Y) / \text{Delta}(X)$$

The Slope for a variable (X) may vary between two graphs, but it will always be positive; hence, the above graphs are called as graphs with curve linear positive slope.

Linear negative slope

A negative slope always moves downward on a graph from left to right. As X value (on X-axis) increases, Y value decreases (refer to Fig. 8.5).

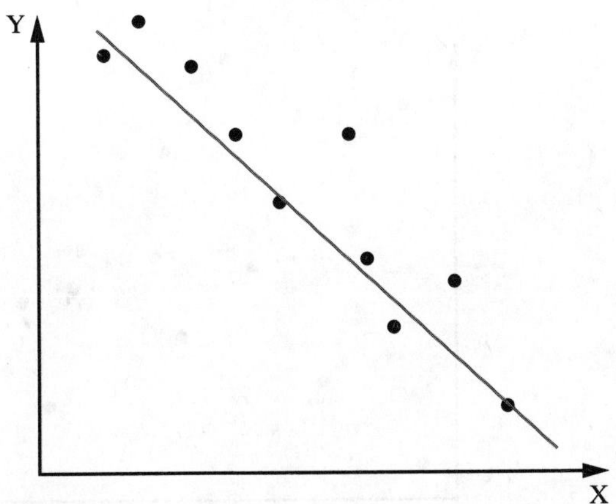

FIG. 8.5
Linear negative slope

$$\text{Slope} = \text{Rise/Run} = (Y_2 - Y_1) / (X_2 - X_1) = \text{Delta}(Y) / \text{Delta}(X)$$

- Scenario 1 for negative slope: Delta (Y) is positive and Delta (X) is negative
- Scenario 2 for negative slope: Delta (Y) is negative and Delta (X) is positive

Curve linear negative slope

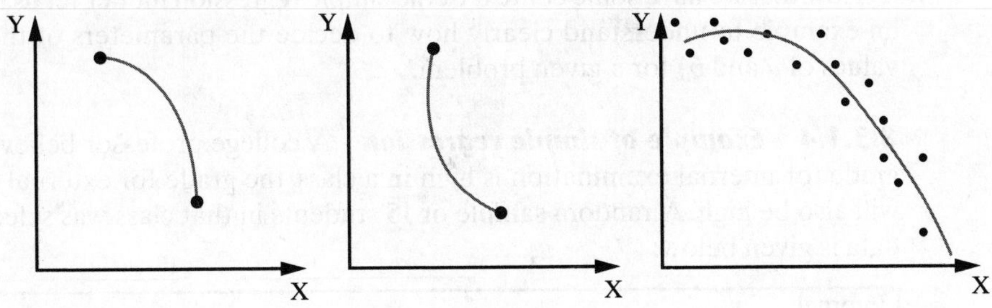

FIG. 8.6
Curve linear negative slope

Curves in these graphs (refer to Fig. 8.6) slope downward from left to right.

$$\text{Slope} = (Y_2 - Y_1) / (X_2 - X_1) = \text{Delta } (Y) / \text{Delta}(X)$$

The Slope for a variable (X) may vary between two graphs, but it will always be negative; hence, the above graphs are called as graphs with curve linear negative slope.

8.3.1.2   No relationship graph   Scatter graph shown in Figure 8.7 indicates 'no relationship' curve as it is very difficult to conclude whether the relationship between X and Y is positive or negative.

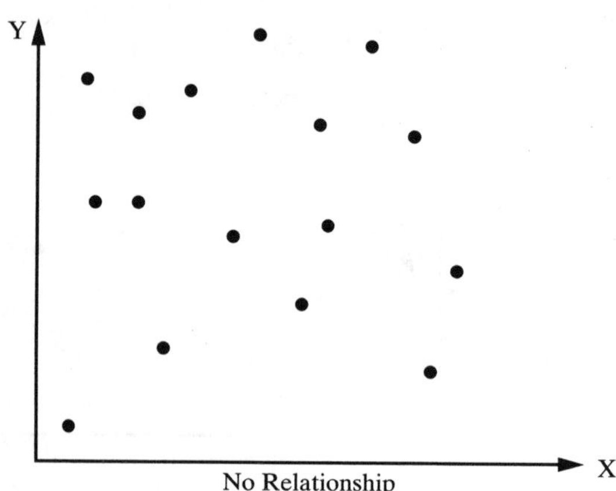

FIG. 8.7
No relationship graph

8.3.1.3   Error in simple regression   The regression equation model in machine learning uses the above slope–intercept format in algorithms. X and Y values are provided to the machine, and it identifies the values of a (intercept) and b (slope) by relating the values of X and Y. However, identifying the exact match of values for a and b is not always possible. There will be some error value (ε) associated with it. This error is called marginal or residual error.

$$Y = (a + bX) + \varepsilon$$

Now that we have some context of the simple regression model, let us try to explore an example to understand clearly how to decide the parameters of the model (i.e. values of a and b) for a given problem.

8.3.1.4   Example of simple regression   A college professor believes that if the grade for internal examination is high in a class, the grade for external examination will also be high. A random sample of 15 students in that class was selected, and the data is given below:

Internal Exam	15	23	18	23	24	22	22	19	19	16	24	11	24	16	23
External Exam	49	63	58	60	58	61	60	63	60	52	62	30	59	49	68

A scatter plot was drawn to explore the relationship between the independent variable (internal marks) mapped to X-axis and dependent variable (external marks) mapped to Y-axis as depicted in Figure 8.8.

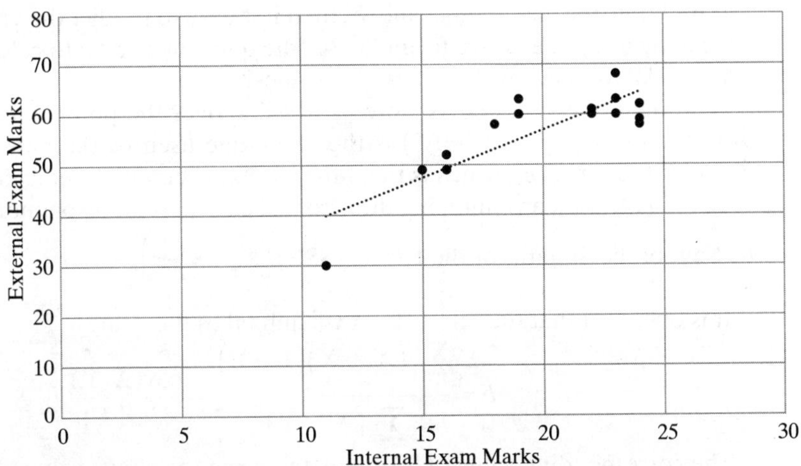

FIG. 8.8

Scatter plot and regression line

As you can observe from the above graph, the line (i.e. the regression line) does not predict the data exactly (refer to Fig. 8.8). Instead, it just cuts through the data. Some predictions are lower than expected, while some others are higher than expected.

Residual is the distance between the predicted point (on the regression line) and the actual point as depicted in Figure 8.9.

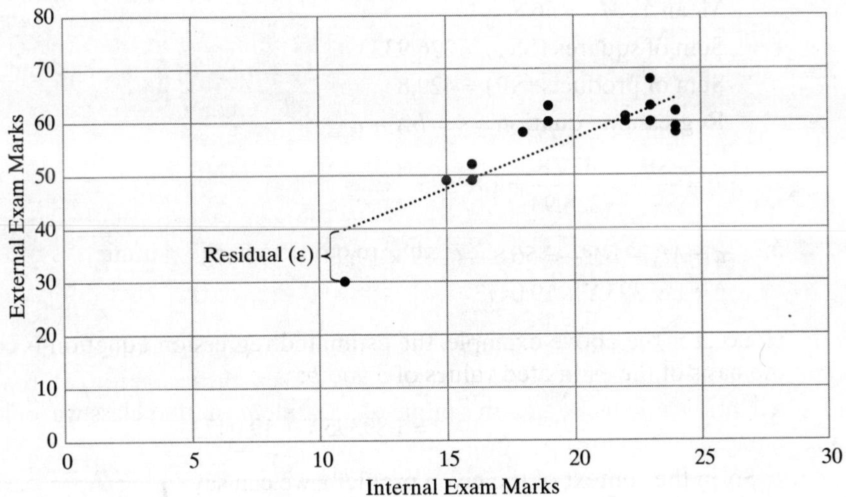

FIG. 8.9

Residual error

As we know, in simple linear regression, the line is drawn using the regression formula.

$$Y = (a + bX) + \varepsilon$$

If we know the values of 'a' and 'b', then it is easy to predict the value of Y for any given X by using the above formula. But the question is how to calculate the values of 'a' and 'b' for a given set of X and Y values?

A straight line is drawn as close as possible over the points on the scatter plot. Ordinary Least Squares (OLS) is the technique used to estimate a line that will minimize the error (ε), which is the difference between the predicted and the actual values of Y. This means summing the errors of each prediction or, more appropriately, the Sum of the Squares of the Errors (SSE) $\left(\text{i.e. } \sum_i \varepsilon_i^2 \right)$.

It is observed that the SSE is least when b takes the value

$$b = \frac{\sum_i \left(X_i - \overline{X}\right)\left(Y_i - \overline{Y}\right)}{\sum_i \left(X_i - \overline{X}\right)^2} = \frac{\text{cov}(X,Y)}{\text{Var}(X)}$$

The corresponding value of 'a' calculated using the above value of 'b' is

$$a = \overline{Y} - b\overline{X}$$

So, let us calculate the value of a and b for the given example. For detailed calculation, refer to Figure 8.10.

Calculation summary

Sum of $X = 299$

Sum of $Y = 852$

Mean $X, M_X = 19.93$

Mean $Y, M_Y = 56.8$

Sum of squares (SS_X) = 226.9333

Sum of products (SP) = 429.8

Regression equation = $\hat{y} = bX + a$

$$b = \frac{\text{SP}}{\text{SS}_X} = \frac{429.8}{226.93} = 1.89395$$

$a = M_Y - bM_X = 56.8 - (1.89 \times 19.93) = 19.0473$

$\hat{y} = 1.89395X + 19.0473$

Hence, for the above example, the estimated regression equation is constructed on the basis of the estimated values of a and b:

$$\hat{y} = 1.89395X + 19.0473$$

So, in the context of the given problem, we can say

Marks in external exam = 19.04 + 1.89 × (Marks in internal exam)

or, $M_{\text{Ext}} = 19.04 + 1.89 \times M_{\text{Int}}$

| | | Step 2 | | Step 3 | Step 5 |
X	Y	X- mean (X)	Y- Mean (Y)	$(Xi - \bar{X})(Yi - \bar{Y})$	$(Xi - \bar{X}^2)$
15	49	4.93	-7.8	38.454	24.3049
23	63	3.07	6.2	19.034	9.4249
18	58	1.93	1.2	2.316	3.7249
23	60	3.07	3.2	9.824	9.4249
24	58	4.07	1.2	4.884	16.5649
22	61	2.07	4.2	8.694	4.2849
22	60	2.07	3.2	6.624	4.2849
19	63	0.93	6.2	5.766	0.8649
19	60	0.93	3.2	2.976	0.8649
16	52	3.93	4.8	18.864	15.4449
24	62	4.07	5.2	21.164	16.5649
11	30	8.93	26.8	239.324	79.7449
24	59	4.07	2.2	8.954	16.5649
16	49	3.93	7.8	30.654	15.4449
23	68	3.07	11.2	34.384	9.4249
19.9	**56.8**		$\Sigma(Xi - \bar{X})(Yi - \bar{Y})$	**429.8**	**226.9335**

Step 1   Step 4   Step 6

Step 7: Divide (step4 / step6)

b = 429.28 / 226.93 = 1.89

Step 8: Calculate a using the value of b

$a = \bar{Y} - b\bar{X}$

a = 56.8 − 1.89 × 19.9

a = 19.05

FIG. 8.10
Detailed calculation of regression parameters

The model built above can be represented graphically as

- an extended version (refer to Fig. 8.11)
- a zoom-in version (refer to Fig. 8.12)

Interpretation of the intercept

As we have already seen, the simple linear regression model built on the data in the example is

$$M_{Ext} = 19.04 + 1.89 \times M_{Int}$$

The value of the intercept from the above equation is 19.05. However, none of the internal mark is 0. So, intercept = 19.05 indicates that 19.05 is the portion of the external examination marks not explained by the internal examination marks.

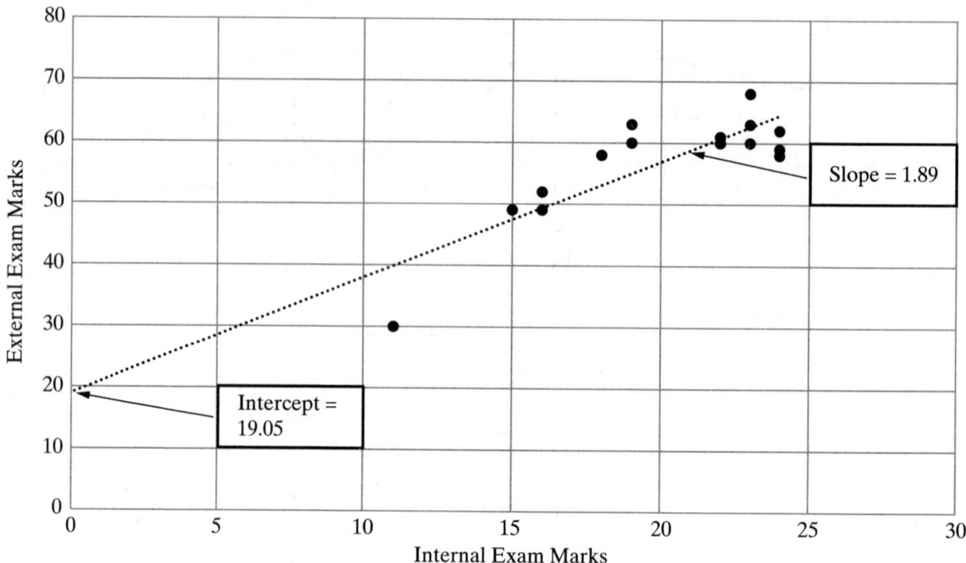

FIG. 8.11
Extended version of the regression graph

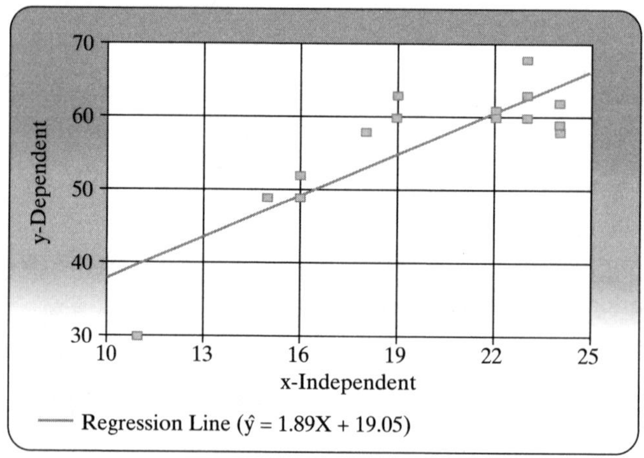

FIG. 8.12
Zoom-in regression line

Slope measures the estimated change in the average value of Y as a result of a one-unit change in X. Here, slope = 1.89 tells us that the average value of the external examination marks increases by 1.89 for each additional 1 mark in the internal examination.

Now that we have a complete understanding of how to build a simple linear regression model for a given problem, it is time to summarize the algorithm.

8.3.1.5   OLS algorithm

- Step 1: Calculate the mean of X and Y
- Step 2: Calculate the errors of X and Y
- Step 3: Get the product
- Step 4: Get the summation of the products
- Step 5: Square the difference of X
- Step 6: Get the sum of the squared difference
- Step 7: Divide output of step 4 by output of step 6 to calculate 'b'
- Step 8: Calculate 'a' using the value of 'b'

8.3.1.6   *Maximum and minimum point of curves*   Maximum (shown in Fig. 8.13) and minimum points (shown in Fig. 8.14) on a graph are found at points where the slope of the curve is zero. It becomes zero either from positive or negative value. The maximum point is the point on the curve of the graph with the highest y-coordinate and a slope of zero. The minimum point is the point on the curve of the graph with the lowest y-coordinate and a slope of zero.

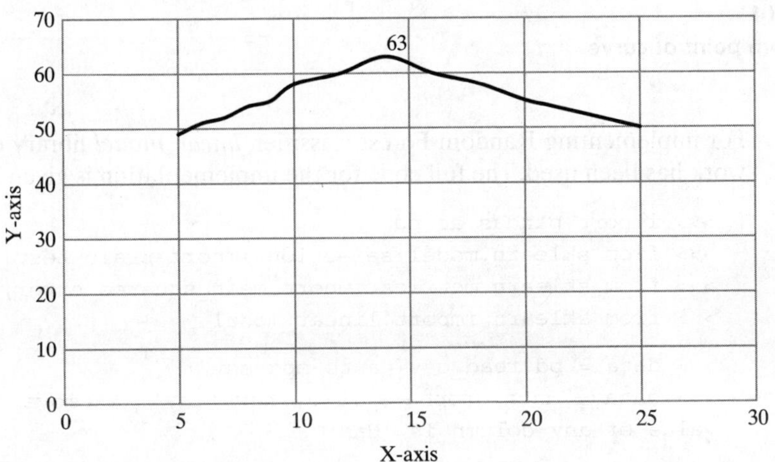

FIG. 8.13
Maximum point of curve

Point 63 is at the maximum point for this curve (refer to Fig. 8.13). Point 63 is at the highest point on this curve. It has a greater y-coordinate value than any other point on the curve and has a slope of zero.

Point 40 (marked with an arrow in Fig. 8.14) is the minimum point for this curve. Point 40 is at the lowest point on this curve. It has a lesser y-coordinate value than any other point on the curve and has a slope of zero.

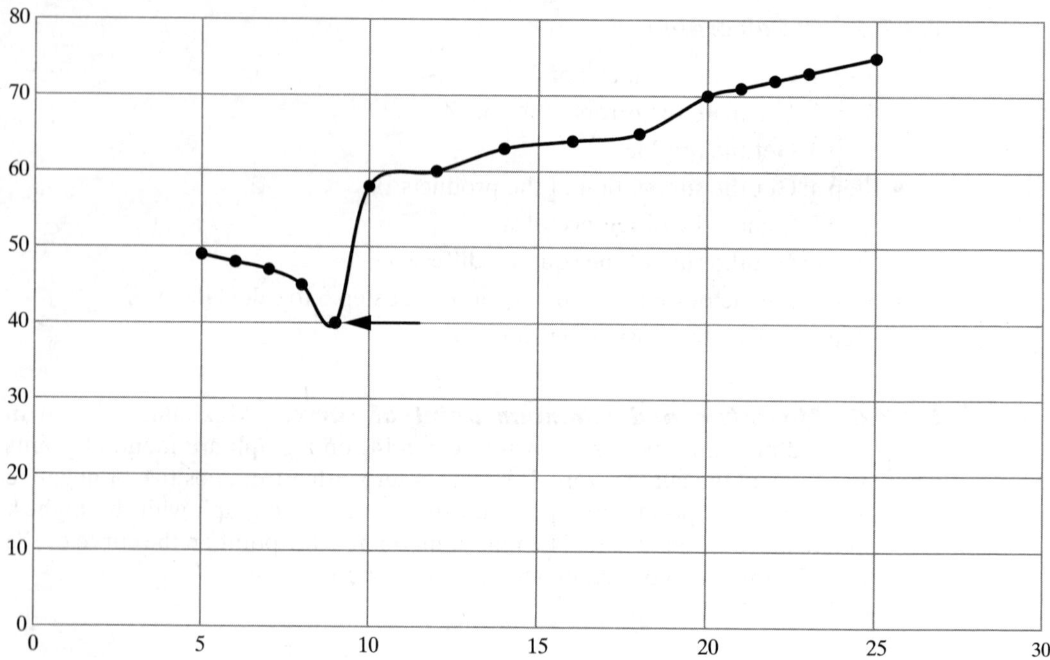

FIG. 8.14
Minimum point of curve

For implementing Random Forest classifier, *linear_model* library of **sklearn** frame-work has been used. The full code for the implementation is given below.

```
>>> import pandas as pd
>>> from sklearn.model_selection import train_test_split
>>> from sklearn.metrics import mean_squared_error, r2_score
>>> from sklearn import linear_model

>>> data = pd.read_csv("auto-mpg.csv")
>>> data = data.dropna(axis=0, how='any') #Remove all rows where
value of any column is 'NaN'

>>> predictors = data.iloc[:,1:7] # Seggretating the predictor
variables ...
>>> target = data.iloc[:,0]       # Seggretating the target / class
variable ...

>>> predictors_train, predictors_test, target_train, target_test =
train_test_split(predictors, target, test_size = 0.3, random_state
= 123)

>>> lm = linear_model.LinearRegression()

# First train model / classifier with the input dataset (training
data part of it)
```

```
>>> model = lm.fit(predictors_train, target_train)

# Make prediction using the trained model
>>> prediction = model.predict(predictors_test)

>>> mean_squared_error(target_test, prediction)

>>> r2_score(target_test, prediction)
```

Output Accuracy:
Mean squared error ⮕ 20.869480380073597
R^2 score ⮕ 0.63425991602097787

8.3.2   Multiple Linear Regression

In a multiple regression model, two or more independent variables, i.e. predictors are involved in the model. If we think in the context of Karen's problem, in the last section, we came up with a simple linear regression by considering Price of a Property as the dependent variable and the Area of the Property (in sq. m.) as the predictor variable. However, location, floor, number of years since purchase, amenities available, etc. are also important predictors which should not be ignored. Thus, if we consider Price of a Property (in \$) as the dependent variable and Area of the Property (in sq. m.), location, floor, number of years since purchase and amenities available as the independent variables, we can form a multiple regression equation as shown below:

$$\text{Price}_{\text{Property}} = f(\text{Area}_{\text{Property}}, \text{location}, \text{floor}, \text{Ageing}, \text{Amenities})$$

The simple linear regression model and the multiple regression model assume that the dependent variable is continuous.

The following expression describes the equation involving the relationship with two predictor variables, namely X_1 and X_2.

$$\hat{Y} = a + b_1 X_1 + b_2 X_2$$

The model describes a plane in the three-dimensional space of $\hat{Y}$, X_1, and X_2. Parameter 'a' is the intercept of this plane. Parameters 'b_1' and 'b_2' are referred to as **partial regression coefficients**. Parameter b_1 represents the change in the mean response corresponding to a unit change in X_1 when X_2 is held constant. Parameter b_2 represents the change in the mean response corresponding to a unit change in X_2 when X_1 is held constant.

Consider the following example of a multiple linear regression model with two predictor variables, namely X_1 and X_2 (refer to Fig. 8.15).

$$\hat{Y} = 22 + 0.3 X_1 + 1.2 X_2$$

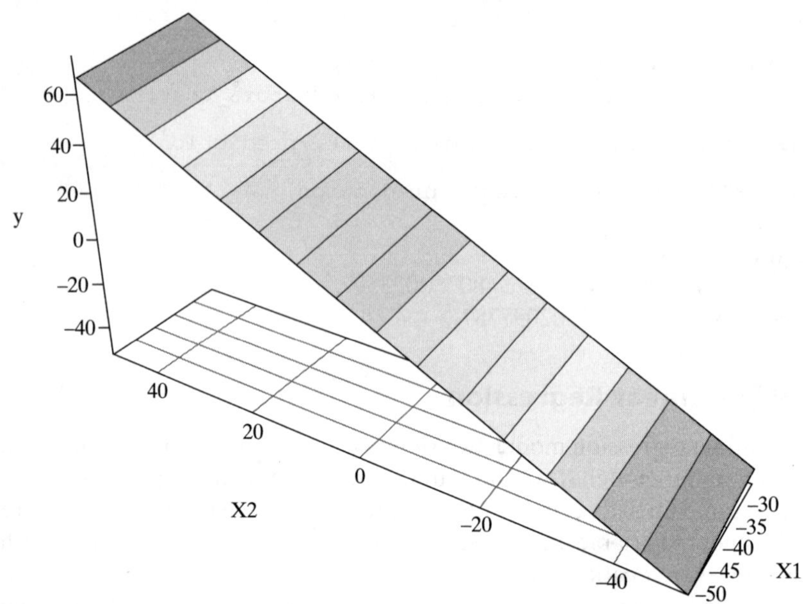

FIG. 8.15
Multiple regression plane

Multiple regression for estimating equation when there are 'n' predictor variables is as follows:

$$\hat{Y} = a + b_1X_1 + b_2X_2 + b_3X_3 + ... + b_nX_n$$

While finding the best fit line, we can fit either a polynomial or curvilinear regression. These are known as polynomial or curvilinear regression, respectively.

8.3.3   Assumptions in Regression Analysis

1. The dependent variable (Y) can be calculated / predicated as a linear function of a specific set of independent variables (X's) plus an error term (ε).

2. The number of observations (n) is greater than the number of parameters (k) to be estimated, i.e. $n > k$.

3. Relationships determined by regression are only relationships of association based on the data set and not necessarily of cause and effect of the defined class.

4. Regression line can be valid only over a limited range of data. If the line is extended (outside the range of extrapolation), it may only lead to wrong predictions.

5. If the business conditions change and the business assumptions underlying the regression model are no longer valid, then the past data set will no longer be able to predict future trends.

6. Variance is the same for all values of X (homoskedasticity).

7. The error term (ε) is normally distributed. This also means that the mean of the error (ε) has an expected value of 0.

8. The values of the error (ε) are independent and are not related to any values of X. This means that there are no relationships between a particular X, Y that are related to another specific value of X, Y.

Given the above assumptions, the OLS estimator is the **Best Linear Unbiased Estimator (BLUE)**, and this is called as **Gauss-Markov Theorem**.

8.3.4   Main Problems in Regression Analysis

In multiple regressions, there are two primary problems: multicollinearity and heteroskedasticity.

8.3.4.1   *Multicollinearity*

Two variables are perfectly collinear if there is an exact linear relationship between them. Multicollinearity is the situation in which the degree of correlation is not only between the dependent variable and the independent variable, but there is also a strong correlation within (among) the independent variables themselves. A multiple regression equation can make good predictions when there is multicollinearity, but it is difficult for us to determine how the dependent variable will change if each independent variable is changed one at a time. When multicollinearity is present, it increases the standard errors of the coefficients. By overinflating the standard errors, multicollinearity tries to make some variables statistically insignificant when they actually should be significant (with lower standard errors). One way to gauge multicollinearity is to calculate the Variance Inflation Factor (VIF), which assesses how much the variance of an estimated regression coefficient increases if the predictors are correlated. If no factors are correlated, the VIFs will be equal to 1.

The assumption of no perfect collinearity states that there is no exact linear relationship among the independent variables. This assumption implies two aspects of the data on the independent variables. First, none of the independent variables, other than the variable associated with the intercept term, can be a constant. Second, variation in the X's is necessary. In general, the more variation in the independent variables, the better will be the OLS estimates in terms of identifying the impacts of the different independent variables on the dependent variable.

8.3.4.2   *Heteroskedasticity*

Heteroskedasticity refers to the changing variance of the error term. If the variance of the error term is not constant across data sets, there will be erroneous predictions. In general, for a regression equation to make accurate predictions, the error term should be independent, identically (normally) distributed (iid).

Mathematically, this assumption is written as

$$\mathrm{var}\left(u_i \mid X\right) = \sigma^2 \text{ and}$$

$$\mathrm{cov}\left(u_i u_j \mid X\right) = 0 \text{ for } i \neq j$$

where 'var' represents the variance, 'cov' represents the covariance, 'u' represents the error terms, and 'X' represents the independent variables.

This assumption is more commonly written as

$$\text{var}\left(u_i\right) = \sigma^2 \text{ and}$$

$$\text{cov}\left(u_i u_j\right) = 0 \text{ for } i \neq j.$$

8.3.5 Improving Accuracy of the Linear Regression Model

Let us understand bias and variance in the regression model before exploring how to improve the same. The concept of bias and variance is similar to accuracy and prediction. Accuracy refers to how close the estimation is near the actual value, whereas prediction refers to continuous estimation of the value.

High bias = low accuracy (not close to real value)

High variance = low prediction (values are scattered)

Low bias = high accuracy (close to real value)

Low variance = high prediction (values are close to each other)

Let us say we have a regression model which is highly accurate and highly predictive; therefore, the overall error of our model will be low, implying a low bias (high accuracy) and low variance (high prediction). This is highly preferable. Similarly, we can say that if the variance increases (low prediction), the spread of our data points increases, which results in less accurate prediction. As the bias increases (low accuracy), the error between our predicted value and the observed values increases. Therefore, balancing out bias and accuracy is essential in a regression model.

In the linear regression model, it is assumed that the number of observations (n) is greater than the number of parameters (k) to be estimated, i.e. $n > k$, and in that case, the least squares estimates tend to have low variance and hence will perform well on test observations.

However, if observations (n) is not much larger than parameters (k), then there can be high variability in the least squares fit, resulting in overfitting and leading to poor predictions.

If $k > n$, then linear regression is not usable. This also indicates infinite variance, and so, the method cannot be used at all.

Accuracy of linear regression can be improved using the following three methods:

1. Shrinkage Approach
2. Subset Selection
3. Dimensionality (Variable) Reduction

8.3.5.1 Shrinkage (Regularization) approach   By limiting (shrinking) the estimated coefficients, we can try to reduce the variance at the cost of a negligible increase in bias. This can in turn lead to substantial improvements in the accuracy of the model.

Few variables used in the multiple regression model are in fact not associated with the overall response and are called as irrelevant variables; this may lead to unnecessary complexity in the regression model.

This approach involves fitting a model involving all predictors. However, the estimated coefficients are shrunken towards zero relative to the least squares estimates. This shrinkage (also known as regularization) has the effect of reducing the overall variance. Some of the coefficients may also be estimated to be exactly zero, thereby indirectly performing variable selection. The two best-known techniques for shrinking the regression coefficients towards zero are

1. ridge regression
2. lasso (Least Absolute Shrinkage Selector Operator)

Ridge regression performs L2 regularization, i.e. it adds penalty equivalent to square of the magnitude of coefficients

Minimization objective of ridge = LS Obj + α × (sum of square of coefficients)

Ridge regression *(include all k predictors in the final model)* is very similar to least squares, except that the coefficients are estimated by minimizing a slightly different quantity. If $k > n$, then the least squares estimates do not even have a unique solution, whereas ridge regression can still perform well by trading off a small increase in bias for a large decrease in variance. Thus, ridge regression works best in situations where the least squares estimates have high variance. One disadvantage with ridge regression is that it will include all k predictors in the final model. This may not be a problem for prediction accuracy, but it can create a challenge in model interpretation in settings in which the number of variables k is quite large. Ridge regression will perform better when the response is a function of many predictors, all with coefficients of roughly equal size.

Lasso regression performs L1 regularization, i.e. it adds penalty equivalent to the absolute value of the magnitude of coefficients.

Minimization objective of ridge = LS Obj + α × (absolute value of the magnitude of coefficients)

The *lasso* overcomes this disadvantage by forcing some of the coefficients to zero value. We can say that the lasso yields sparse models (involving only subset) that are simpler as well as more interpretable. The lasso can be expected to perform better in a setting where a relatively small number of predictors have substantial coefficients, and the remaining predictors have coefficients that are very small or equal to zero.

8.3.5.2 Subset selection   Identify a subset of the predictors that is assumed to be related to the response and then fit a model using OLS on the selected reduced subset of variables. There are two methods in which subset of the regression can be selected:

1. Best subset selection (considers all the possible (2^k))
2. Stepwise subset selection

   (a) Forward stepwise selection (0 to k)
   (b) Backward stepwise selection (k to 0)

In best subset selection, we fit a separate least squares regression for each possible subset of the k predictors. For computational reasons, best subset selection cannot be applied with very large value of predictors (k). The best subset selection procedure considers all the possible (2^k) models containing subsets of the p predictors.

The stepwise subset selection method can be applied to choose the best subset. There are two stepwise subset selection:

1. Forward stepwise selection (0 to k)

2. Backward stepwise selection (k to 0)

Forward stepwise selection is a computationally efficient alternative to best subset selection. Forward stepwise considers a much smaller set of models, that too step by step, compared to best set selection. Forward stepwise selection begins with a model containing no predictors, and then, predictors are added one by one to the model, until all the k predictors are included in the model. In particular, at each step, the variable (X) that gives the highest additional improvement to the fit is added.

Backward stepwise selection begins with the least squares model which contains all k predictors and then iteratively removes the least useful predictor one by one.

8.3.5.3   Dimensionality reduction (Variable reduction)   The earlier methods, namely subset selection and shrinkage, control variance either by using a subset of the original variables or by shrinking their coefficients towards zero. In dimensionality reduction, predictors (X) are transformed, and the model is set up using the transformed variables after dimensionality reduction. The number of variables is reduced using the dimensionality reduction method. Principal component analysis is one of the most important dimensionality (variable) reduction techniques.

8.3.6   Locally Weighted Linear Regression

Linear Regression works very well when the independent and dependent variables are related to each other linearly. But if the dependent variable does not have a simple linear relationship with the independent variables, then Linear Regression does not provide correct predictions. Please see the dataset plotted in figure 8.19. We can clearly see that the dependent variable (Tips) is not linearly related to independent variable (Total_bill).

A non-parametric approach, like the Locally Weighted Linear Regression (LWLR) algorithm can be used to solve this type of prediction problem.

Parametric Learning Algorithms

In these models, a function is derived with a fixed set of parameters from the training data. As these parameters become fixed in number, the model already knows about these parameters and is not dependent on the data. The training data can be erased from the computer memory and the prediction can be done through the model (which is just a function now) with the parameters.

For example, in this equation, $y = m_0 + m_1 x_1 + m_2 x_2$, the parameters m_0, m_1, m_2 are fixed and optimized using the training data and with the help of input variables x_1 and x_2, it can predict the dependent variable y.

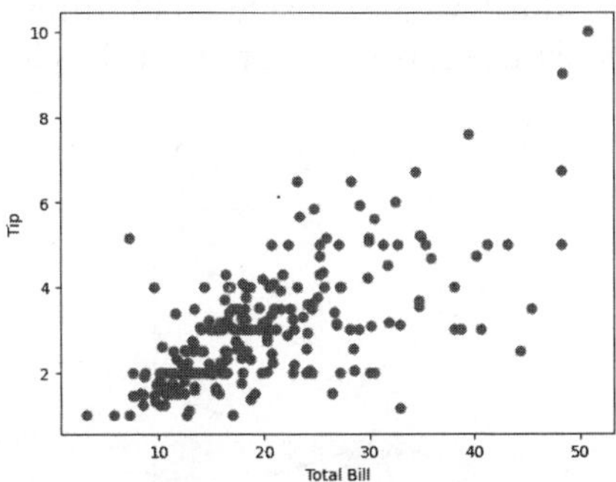

Dataset available in Kaggle/tips.csv. Structure of the data is as below:

	total_bill	tip	sex	smoker	day	time	size
0	16.99	1.01	Female	No	Sun	Dinner	2
1	10.34	1.66	Male	No	Sun	Dinner	3
2	21.01	3.50	Male	No	Sun	Dinner	3
3	23.68	3.31	Male	No	Sun	Dinner	2
4	24.59	3.61	Female	No	Sun	Dinner	4

FIG. 8.16
Non-linearly related dataset

Non-Parametric Learning Algorithms

On the other hand, non-parametric algorithms do not assume any mapping function between the input and output variables. They have the freedom to choose any functional form from the training data. So, the data needs to be always retained in the computer to make the predictions. We can understand that this type of algorithm is not suitable if the dataset is very large.

Let's check how a non-parametric approach can be taken for the dataset mentioned in Figure 8.19. It is evident that we can't fit a straight line for this dataset, as this data is non-linear and we will end up with large errors in our prediction in that case. So, the fitted line should be a curve line which can minimize the error. Locally Weighted Linear Regression algorithm which is a non-parametric model works on the following principle:

- the model is given an input point (x) for which it has to make a prediction
- it then assigns weightages (wi's) to all the input data points (xi's) around this point (x) in such a way that higher weightages (close to 1) are provided to the data points closer to x, whereas lower weightages (Locally Weighted Linear Regression (LWLR) algorithm can be used in those cases. Locally Weighted Linear Regression (LWLR) algorithm can be used in those cases (close to 0) are assigned to the data points farther from x.

- it then fits a straight line to those weighted xi's data. A circular area is marked to identify xi's which will be considered for fitting the line. This results in fitting a line with the data points which are near the circle, as shown in figure 8.20

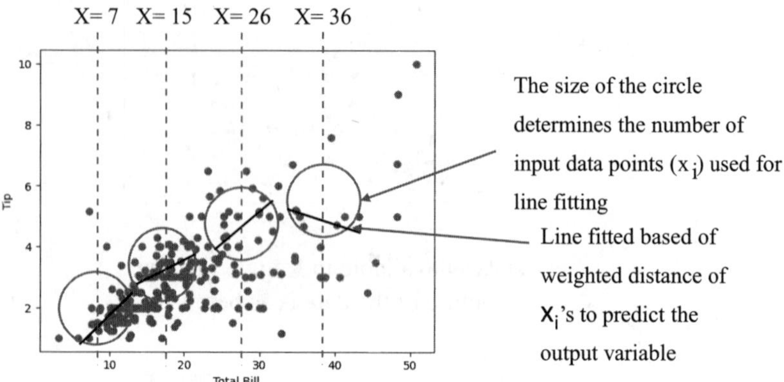

FIG. 8.17
Concept of Locally Weighted Linear Regression

So, we identified two important aspects for building the model – the weightage (wi) and the size of circle (τ – Tau).

The loss function in this case can be written as:

$$\sum_{i=1}^{m} w_i \left(y_i - \theta^T x_i \right)^2$$

Where
$$w_i = e^{-\frac{(x_i - x)^T (x_i - x)}{2}}$$
(8.1),

x is the point where the model needs to do prediction, and x_i is the ith training data

It is evident that in equation (8.1) if

$|x_i - x|$ is small, then w_i is close to 1.

$|x_i - x|$ is large, then w_i is close to 0.

The weight decreases as the distance between the predicting data and training data increases. We will find the weight matrix for each training input x_i. Weight matrix is always a diagonal matrix.

The size of the circle (τ) also controls the weight function and thus it can be introduced as a hyperparameter in equation (1)

$$w_i = e^{-\frac{(x_i - x)^T (x_i - x)}{2\tau^2}}$$

We can make the circle fatter or thinner by changing the value of τ (tau).

By taking partial derivative of the loss function and equating it to zero, we get a closed-form solution of the algorithm which gives the prediction parameter θ directly. This means that we don't have to train the model, but we can get the value of dependent variable directly from the dataset.

$$\theta = (X^T W^X)^{-1} (X^T W^Y)$$
$$Y = \theta^T X$$

Sample python implementation of LWLR is given below

```python
import numpy as np
import pandas as pd
import matplotlib.pyplot as plt

#Kernel smoothing function to create the weight matrix for the
# prediction data (point): w_i = e^(- ((x_i-x).T (x_i-x))/(2τ^2 ))
def kernel_func(point, X, tau):
m,n = np.shape(X)
weights = np.mat(np.eye(m)) #creates the diagonal matrix
for j in range(m):
diff = point - X[j]
temp = diff * diff.T/(-2 * tau ** 2)
weights[j,j] = np.exp(temp)
return weights

# function to calculate the dependent variable theta directly
# from the training data and weights θ = [(X.T WX)] ^ (-1) (X.T WY)

def local_weight(point, X, ymat, tau):
W = kernel_func(point, X, tau)

theta = (X.T * (W*X)).I * (X.T * W * ymat.T)

return theta

# main part to read the input data and call regression function
df = pd.read_csv("tips.csv")
print(df.head())
plt.scatter(df.total_bill, df.tip)
plt.xlabel('Total Bill')
plt.ylabel('Tip')
plt.show()
```

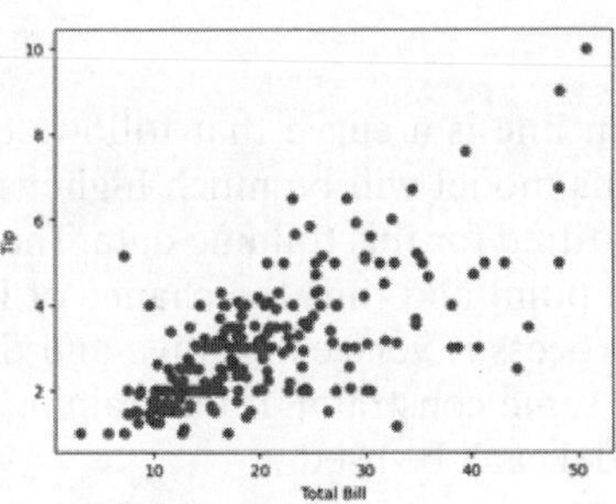

```python
# create matrix for regression function
x_matrix = np.mat(df.total_bill)
y_matrix = np.mat(df.tip)
m = np.shape(x_matrix)[1]
one = np.ones((1,m), dtype=int)
data_point_matrix = np.hstack((one.T, x_matrix.T))
tau = 0.5  # setting the size of tau
y_predict = np.zeros(m)

# locally weighted linear regression creates predicted output
for i in range(m):
theta_ = local_weight(data_point_matrix[i], data_point_matrix, y_
matrix, tau)
y_predict [i] = theta_ * data_point_matrix [i]

# plot the resulting curve based on predicted data
xsort = data_point_matrix.copy()
xsort.sort(axis=0)
plt.scatter(df.total_bill, df.tip, color = 'green')
plt.plot(xsort[:,1], y_predict [data_point_matrix[:,1].argsort
(0)], color = 'red', linewidth = 5)

plt.xlabel('Total_bill')
plt.ylabel('Tip')
plt.show()
```

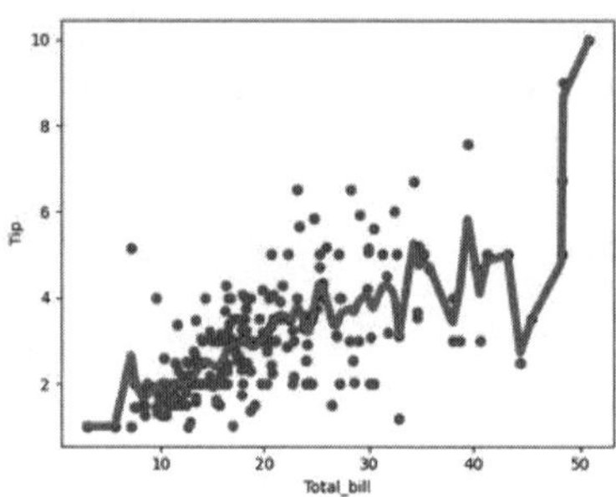

Note that the final fitted prediction line is a curve that follows the density of the data points. So, the accuracy of this model will be much higher than a simple linear regression model, if that is force-fitted for this training data. The local weights are calculated in relation to each data point and thus the chance of large errors is minimized. But, on the flip side, the process is very exhaustive and thus consumes huge computing resources. Due to the same constraint, if the training dataset has a large number of features, then this model can't be used.

Points to Ponder:

- Try to fit a linear regression model for the tips.csv data and see how the prediction line comes out
- Using the accuracy function also check the accuracy of the linear regression model vs that of the locally weighted linear regression model for this dataset

When to use Locally weighted Linear Regression?
- if the number of features is small.
- if feature selection is not required

8.3.7   Polynomial Regression Model

The Polynomial regression model is the extension of the simple linear model by adding extra predictors obtained by raising (squaring) each of the original predictors to a power. For example, if there are three variables, X, X^2, and X^3 are used as predictors. This approach provides a simple way to yield a non-linear fit to data.

$$f(x) = c_0 + c_1 \cdot X^1 + c_2 \cdot X^2 + c_3 \cdot X^3$$

In the above equation, $c_0, c_1, c_2,$ and c_3 are the coefficients.
Example: Let us use the below data set of (X, Y) for degree 3 polynomial.

Internal Exam (X)	15	23	18	23	24	22	22	19	19	16	24	11	24	16	23
External Exam (Y)	49	63	58	60	58	61	60	63	60	52	62	30	59	49	68

As you can observe, the regression line (refer to Fig. 8.18) is slightly curved for polynomial degree 3 with the above 15 data points. The regression line will curve further if we increase the polynomial degree (refer to Fig. 8.19). At the extreme value as shown below, the regression line will be overfitting into all the original values of X.

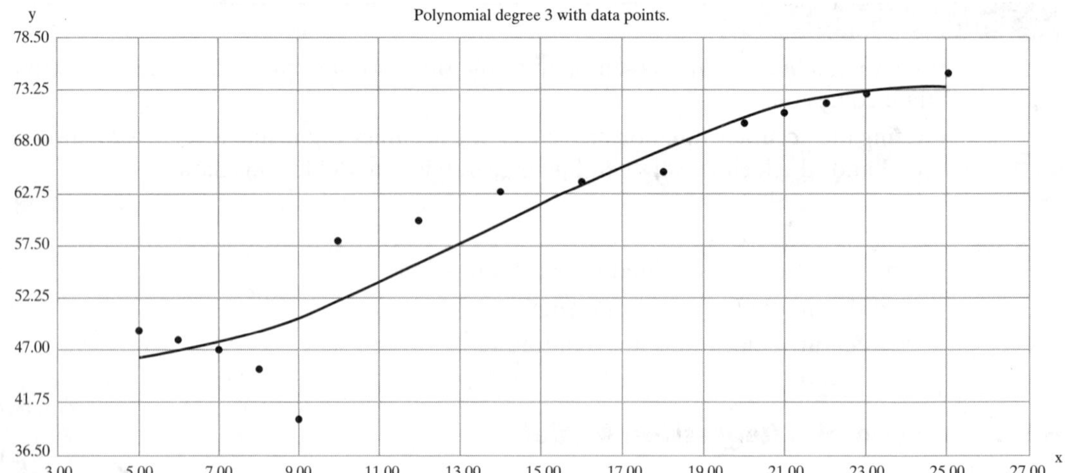

FIG. 8.18

Polynomial regression degree 3

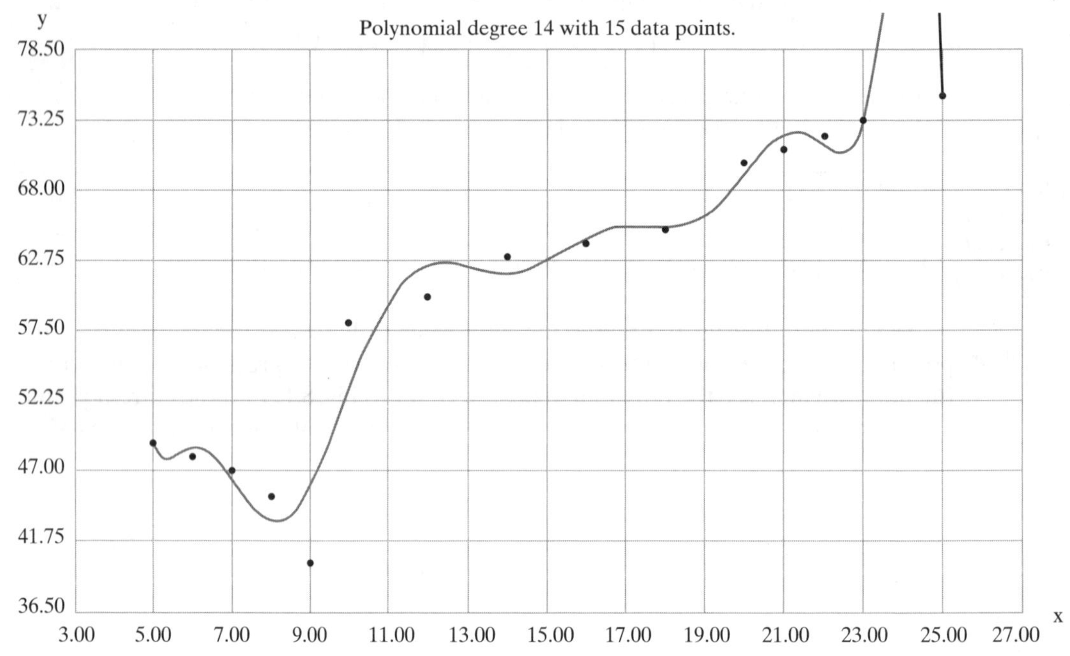

FIG. 8.19

Polynomial regression degree 14

8.3.8   Logistic Regression

Logistic regression is both classification and regression technique depending on the scenario used. Logistic regression (logit regression) is a type of regression analysis used for predicting the outcome of a categorical dependent variable similar to OLS regression. In logistic regression, dependent variable (Y) is binary (0,1) and independent variables (X) are continuous in nature. The probabilities describing the possible outcomes (probability that $Y = 1$) of a single trial are modelled as a logistic function of the predictor variables. In the logistic regression model, there is no R^2 to gauge the fit of the overall model; however, a chi-square test is used to gauge how well the logistic regression model fits the data. The goal of logistic regression is to predict the likelihood that Y is equal to 1 (probability that $Y = 1$ rather than 0) given certain values of X. That is, if X and Y have a strong positive linear relationship, the probability that a person will have a score of $Y = 1$ will increase as values of X increase. So, we are predicting probabilities rather than the scores of the dependent variable.

For example, we might try to predict whether or not a small project will succeed or fail on the basis of the number of years of experience of the project manager handling the project. We presume that those project managers who have been managing projects for many years will be more likely to succeed. This means that as X (the number of years of experience of project manager) increases, the probability that Y will be equal to 1 (success of the new project) will tend to increase. If we take a hypothetical example in which 60 already executed projects were studied and the years of experience of project managers ranges from 0 to 20 years, we could represent this tendency to increase the probability that $Y = 1$ with a graph.

To illustrate this, it is convenient to segregate years of experience into categories (i.e. 0–8, 9–16, 17–24, 25–32, 33–40). If we compute the mean score on Y (averaging the 0s and 1s) for each category of years of experience, we will get something like

X	Y
0–8	0.27
9–16	0.5
17–24	0.6
25–32	0.66
33–40	0.93

When the graph is drawn for the above values of X and Y, it appears like the graph in Figure 8.18. As X increases, the probability that $Y = 1$ increases. In other words, when the project manager has more years of experience, a larger percentage of projects succeed. A perfect relationship represents a perfectly curved S rather than a straight line, as was the case in OLS regression. So, to model this relationship, we need some fancy algebra / mathematics that accounts for the bends in the curve.

An explanation of logistic regression begins with an explanation of the logistic function, which always takes values between zero and one. The logistic formulae are stated in terms of the probability that $Y = 1$, which is referred to as P. The probability that Y is 0 is $1 - P$.

$$\ln\left(\frac{P}{1-P}\right) = a + bX$$

$$\ln(p/1-p) = \beta_0 + \beta_1 X_1 + \beta_2 X_2 + \ldots + \varepsilon$$

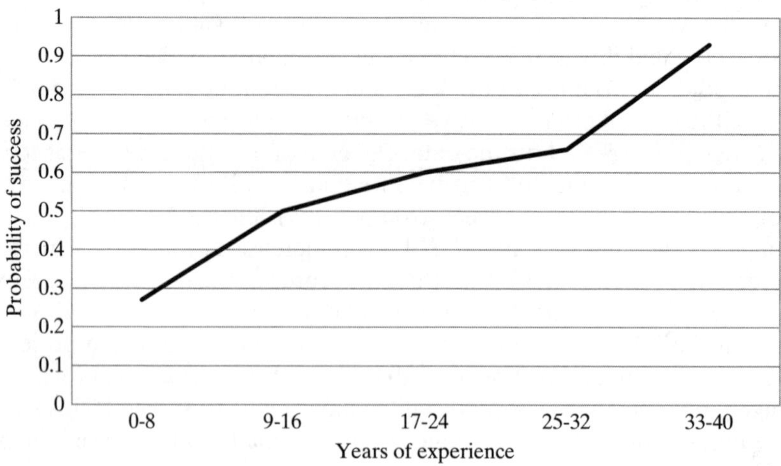

FIG. 8.20
Logistic regression

The 'ln' symbol refers to a natural logarithm and $a + bX$ is the regression line equation. Probability (P) can also be computed from the regression equation. So, if we know the regression equation, we could, theoretically, calculate the expected probability that $Y = 1$ for a given value of X.

$$P = \frac{\exp(a + bX)}{1 + \exp(a + bx)} = \frac{e^{a + bx}}{1 + e^{a + bx}}$$

'exp' is the exponent function, which is sometimes also written as e.

Let us say we have a model that can predict whether a person is male or female on the basis of their height. Given a height of 150 cm, we need to predict whether the person is male or female.

If we assume that the coefficients of $a = -100$ and $b = 0.6$. Using the above equation, we can calculate the probability of male given a height of 150 cm or more formally $P(\text{male}|\text{height} = 150)$.

$$y = e^{\wedge}(a + b \times X) / \left(1 + e^{\wedge}(a + b \times X)\right)$$

$$y = \exp(-100 + 0.6 \times 150) / (1 + \text{EXP}(-100 + 0.6 \times 150)$$

$$y = 0.000046$$

or a probability of near zero that the person is a male.

Assumptions in logistic regression

The following assumptions must hold when building a logistic regression model:

- There exists a linear relationship between logit function and independent variables
- The dependent variable Y must be categorical (1/0) and take binary value, e.g. if pass then $Y = 1$; else $Y = 0$

- The data meets the 'iid' criterion, i.e. the error terms, ε, are independent from one another and identically distributed
- The error term follows a binomial distribution $[n, p]$
  - ✓ n = # of records in the data
  - ✓ p = probability of success (pass, responder)

8.3.9   Multi-Class Logistic Regression

In the previous section, we mentioned that the independent variable (Y) should be categorical in nature and should have two possible values for Logistic Regression algorithm to work, as it uses a binomial probability distribution function. But that can restrict the use of logistic regression in many real-life situations. For example, if a logistic regression program needs to determine the species of a flower, based on petal and sepal dimensions of the samples, where the number of species has more than two possibilities, then the Binary Logistic Regression algorithm will not work. In such cases the Logistic Regression model is modified to support multi-class classification problem.

One way to achieve this is to split the multi-class classification problem into multiple binary classification problems and fit a binary logistic regression model to each sub-problem. One vs Rest (OVR) is an example of such wrapper model.

The alternative is to change the logistic regression model to support the prediction of multiple class labels directly. This requires a change in the loss function used to train the model (like changing from log function to cross-entropy function) and a change in the output from a single probability value to one probability for each class label. The probability distribution that can be used for multi-class probabilities is called multinomial probability distribution. The logistic regression model that is adapted to work with a multinomial probability distribution is called **Multinomial Logistic Regression**.

One vs Rest Classification:
One vs Rest classification breaks down the dataset (D) that contains k classes into k binary classifier models. The idea is to classify a data point either as part of the current class k_i or part of rest of the classes. Each model is used to distinguish the ith class from everything else.

Example: Let us have 3 classes C_1, C_2, C_3. We will build 3 binary models, one for each class:

$$\text{Model 1} - C_1 \text{ or not } C_1$$
$$\text{Model 2} - C_2 \text{ or not } C_2$$
$$\text{Model 3} - C_3 \text{ or not } C_3$$

After these 3 models are run, based on the confidence score about the prediction of each model the final class can be determined. A visual representation of the One vs Rest approach is in Figure 8.21

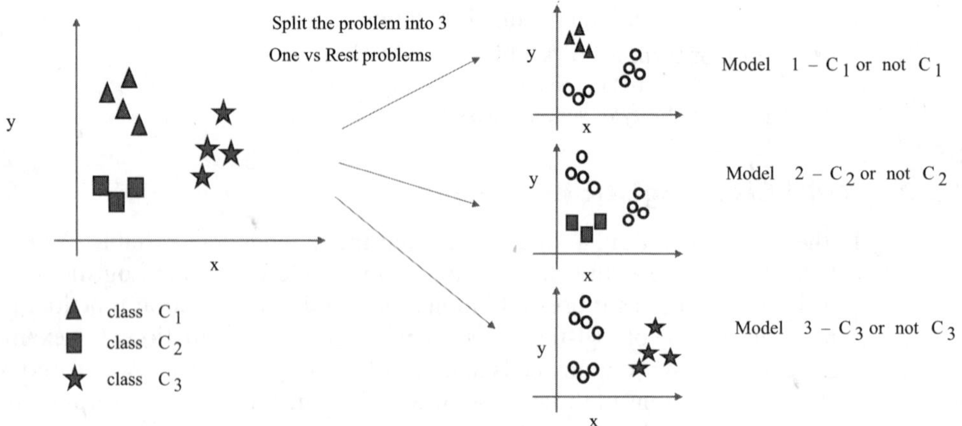

FIG. 8.21
One vs Rest Problem

A more widely used approach is to adapt the standard logistic regression model and interpret the array of probabilities for each sample (as we discussed earlier, for each sample we will get k probability values for k label classes). Full Python code for running the multi-class logistic regression model is provided below:

Dataset used: https://www.kaggle.com/datasets/uciml/iris

The structure of this data is like this –

	Id	SepalLengthCm	SepalWidthCm	PetalLengthCm	PetalWidthCm	Species
0	1	5.1	3.5	1.4	0.2	Iris-setosa
1	2	4.9	3.0	1.4	0.2	Iris-setosa
2	3	4.7	3.2	1.3	0.2	Iris-setosa
3	4	4.6	3.1	1.5	0.2	Iris-setosa
4	5	5.0	3.6	1.4	0.2	Iris-setosa

There are 3 types of species in the dataset –

- Iris-setosa,
- Iris-versicolor and
- Iris-virginica.

Based on the parameters 'SepalLengthCm', 'SepalWidthCm', 'PetalLengthCm', and 'PetalWidthCm', the model needs to predict the type of species for any sample.

```python
from sklearn.linear_model import LogisticRegression
from sklearn.preprocessing import StandardScaler
```

```python
data = pd.read_csv("Iris.csv")
predictors = data.iloc[:,0:5] # Seggretating the predictor variables
target = data.iloc[:,6]       # Seggretating the target / class
variable
predictors_train, predictors_test, target_train, target_test =
train_test_split(predictors, target, test_size = 0.3, random_state
= 123)
# LogisticRegression is affected by scale. So, we have to scale
the data # in the featureset. We can transform the data into unit
scale (mean=0,
# variance = 1) for better performance
scaler = StandardScaler()
scaler.fit (predictors_train)
x_train = scaler.transform(predictors_train)
scaler.fit (predictors_test)
x_test = scaler.transform (predictors_test)
# LogisticRegression class instance is created
LogR = LogisticRegression(
multi_class = 'multinomial',
solver='lbfgs', #Specifies algorithm in the optimization problem
random_state=0)            -------- (Line A)
LogR.fit(predictors_train, target_train)
y_pred = LogR.predict(predictors_test)
y_pred
>>> [Out]: array(['Iris-versicolor', 'Iris-setosa',.... ,
'Iris-setosa', 'Iris-setosa'], dtype=object)        --- (Line B)
LogR.score(predictor_test, target_test) # score gives the R squared
value
>>> [Out] Accuracy: 68.56%
# checking the prediction with 1 sample
y_pred = LogR.predict(predictors_test[4:5])
>>> [Out]: array(['Iris-versicolor'], dtype=object) -------- (Line
C)
LogR.predict_proba(predictor_test[4:5])   # shows the probability
of different class choices
>>> [Out]: array([[0.01056367, 0.94450094, 0.0449354 ]]) ----
(Line D)
```

Few lines in the code need our attention. In Line A, we created an instance of the logistic regression model. We have set the multi_class parameter as 'multinomial' and also have set a solver which can work with multinomial distribution. This instructs the model to use the multinomial distribution to solve this classification problem.

Points to Ponder:

But is it really necessary to explicitly set multi_class parameters? Let's have a close look into the definition of the logistic regression model -

LogisticRegression(C=1.0, class_weight=None, dual=False, fit_intercept=True, intercept_scaling=1, l1_ratio=None, max_iter=100, multi_class='auto', n_jobs=None, penalty='l2', random_state=None, solver='lbfgs', tol=0.0001, verbose=0, warm_start=False)

We can see that the multi_class parameter has a default value of 'auto'. This does the automatic selection of binary and multinomial. If the label data is binary then 'auto' does binary classification, and if the data is multi classification then 'auto' does multi classification.

■

In Line B, we can see that predicted labels are exactly one per sample. But if we check the predict_proba function in Line D, it shows that for each sample three probability values are returned. This is equal to the number of label class. Then how is the final output zeroing in on one particular class label for each sample? The final output of the model picks up the class label corresponding to the highest probability in predict_proba(). In our example, for the sample in row 5 of our dataset the predicted probability was highest for the second label ('Iris-versicolor'), and thus the model tags that label to this sample as in Line C.

8.3.10 Maximum Likelihood Estimation

The coefficients in a logistic regression are estimated using a process called Maximum Likelihood Estimation (MLE). First, let us understand what is likelihood function before moving to MLE. A fair coin outcome flips equally heads and tails of the same number of times. If we toss the coin 10 times, it is expected that we get five times Head and five times Tail.

Let us now discuss about the probability of getting only Head as an outcome; it is $5/10 = 0.5$ in the above case. Whenever this number (P) is greater than 0.5, it is said to be in favour of Head. Whenever P is lesser than 0.5, it is said to be against the outcome of getting Head.

Let us represent 'n' flips of coin as $X_1, X_2, X_3, ..., X_n$. Now X_i can take the value of 1 or 0.

$X_i = 1$ if Head is the outcome

$X_i = 0$ if Tail is the outcome

When we use the Bernoulli distribution represents each flip of the coin:

$$f\left(x_i \mid \theta\right) = \theta^{x_i}(1-\theta)^{1-x_i}$$

Each observation X_i is independent and also identically distributed (iid), and the joint distribution simplifies to a product of distributions.

$$f\left(x_1, ..., x_n \mid \theta\right)_{i=1}^{n} f\left(x_i \mid \theta\right) = \theta^{x_1}(1-\theta)^{1-x_1} ... \theta^{x_n}(1-\theta)^{1-x_n} = \theta^{\#H}(1-\theta)^{n-\#H},$$

where #H is the number of flips that resulted in the expected outcome (heads in this case).

The likelihood equation is

$$L(\theta|x) = \prod_{i=1}^{n} f(x_i | \theta)$$

But the likelihood function is not a probability. The likelihood for some coins may be 0.25 or 0 or 1.

MLE is about predicting the value for the parameters that maximizes the likelihood function.

$$\log L(\theta| x) = \sum_{i=1}^{n} \log f(x_i |\theta)$$

8.4   SUMMARY

- In supervised learning, when we are trying to predict a real-value variable such as 'Price', 'Weight', etc., the problem falls under the category of regression. A regression problem tries to forecast results as a continuous output.
- Dependent Variable (Y) is the value to be predicted. This variable is presumed to be functionally related to the independent variable (X). In other words, dependent variable(s) depends on independent variable(s).
- Independent Variable (X) is called as predictor. The independent variable (X) is used in a regression model to estimate the value of the dependent variable (Y).
- Regression is essentially finding a relationship (or) association between the dependent variable (Y) and the independent variables (X).
- If the regression involves only one independent variable, it is called simple regression. Thus, if we take 'Price of a used car' as the dependent variable and the 'Year of manufacturing of the car' as the independent variable, we can build a simple regression.
- Slope represents how much the line in a graph changes in the vertical direction (Y-axis) over a change in the horizontal direction (X-axis). Slope is also referred as the rate of change in a graph.
- Maximum and minimum points on a graph are found at points where the slope of the curve is zero. It becomes zero either from positive or from negative value.
- If two or more independent variables are involved, it is called multiple regression. Thus, if we take 'Price of a used car' as the dependent variable and year of manufacturing (Year), brand of the car (Brand), and mileage run (Miles run) as the independent variables, we can form a multiple regression equation as given below:

Price of a used car ($\$$) = function (Year, Brand, Miles run)

- Multicollinearity is the situation in which the degree of correlation is not only between the dependent variable and the independent variable, but there also exists a strong correlation within (among) the independent variables itself.

- Heteroskedasticity refers to the changing variance of the error term. If the variance of the error term is not constant across data sets, there will be erroneous predictions. In general, for a regression equation to make accurate predictions, the error term should be independent, normally (identically) distributed (iid). The error terms should not be related to each other.
- Accuracy of linear regression can be improved using the following three methods:

  1. Shrinkage Approach
  2. Subset Selection
  3. Dimensionality Reduction

- Polynomial regression model is the extension of the simple linear model by adding extra predictors, obtained by raising (squaring) each of the original predictors to a power. For example, if there are three variables, X, X^2, and X^3 are used as predictors.
- In logistic regression, the dependent variable (Y) is binary (0,1) and independent variables (X) are continuous in nature. The probabilities describing the possible outcomes (probability that $Y = 1$) of a single trial are modelled as a function of the explanatory (predictor) variables by using a logistic function.

SAMPLE QUESTIONS

MULTIPLE-CHOICE QUESTIONS

1. When we are trying to predict a real-value variable such as '\$', 'Weight', the problem falls under the category of
   (a) Unsupervised learning
   (b) Supervised regression problem
   (c) Supervised classification problem
   (d) Categorical attribute

2. Price prediction of crude oil is an example of
   (a) Unsupervised learning
   (b) Supervised regression problem
   (c) Supervised classification problem
   (d) Categorical attribute

3. Value to be predicted in machine learning is called as
   (a) Slope   (b) Regression
   (c) Independent variable   (d) Dependent variable

4. This is called as predictor.
   (a) Slope   (b) Regression
   (c) Independent variable   (d) Dependent variable

5. This is essentially finding a relationship (or) association between the dependent variable (Y) and the independent variables (X).
   (a) Slope   (b) Regression
   (c) Classification   (d) Categorization

6.   If the regression involves only one independent variable, it is called as
   (a) Multiple regression   (b) One regression
   (c) Simple regression   (d) Independent regression

7.   Which equation represents simple imperfect relationship?
   (a) $Y = (a + bx) + \varepsilon$
   (b) $Y = (a + bx)$
   (c) DY = Change in Y / Change in X
   (d) $Y = a + b1X1 + b2X2$

8.   Which equation represents simple perfect relationship?
   (a) $Y = (a + bx) + \varepsilon$
   (b) $Y = (a + bx)$
   (c) DY = Change in Y / Change in X
   (d) $Y = a + b1X1 + b2X2$

9.   What is the formula for slope in a simple linear equation?
   (a) $Y = (a + bx) + €$
   (b) $Y = (a + bx)$
   (c) DY = Change in Y / Change in X
   (d) $Y = a + b1X1 + b2X2$

10.   This slope always moves upward on a graph from left to right.
   (a) Multilinear slope   (b) No relationship slope
   (c) Negative slope   (d) Positive slope

11.   This slope always moves downwards on a graph from left to right.
   (a) Multilinear slope   (b) No relationship slope
   (c) Negative slope   (d) Positive slope

12.   Maximum and minimum points on a graph are found at points where the slope of the curve is
   (a) Zero   (b) One
   (c) 0.5   (d) Random number

13.   In the OLS algorithm, the first step is
   (a) Calculate the mean of Y and X
   (b) Calculate the errors of X and Y
   (c) Get the product (multiply)
   (d) Sum the products

14.   In the OLS algorithm, the last step is
   (a) Calculate 'a' using the value of 'b'
   (b) Calculate 'b' using the value of 'a'
   (c) Get the product (multiply)
   (d) Sum the products

15.   Which equation below is called as Unexplained Variation?
   (a) SSR (Sum of Squares due to Regression)
   (b) SSE (Sum of Squares due to Error)
   (c) SST (Sum of Squares Total):
   (d) R-square (R2)

16. Which equation below is called as Explained Variation?
(a) SSR (Sum of Squares due to Regression)
(b) SSE (Sum of Squares due to Error)
(c) SST (Sum of Squares Total):
(d) R-square (R2)

17. When new predictors (X) are added to the multiple linear regression model, how does R^2 behave?
(a) Decreasing
(b) Increasing or decreasing
(c) Increasing and decreasing
(d) Increasing or remains constant

18. Predicting stochastic events precisely is not possible.
(a) True
(b) False

SHORT-ANSWER TYPE QUESTIONS (5 MARKS EACH)

1. What is a dependent variable and an independent variable in a linear equation?

2. What is simple linear regression? Give one example.

3. Define slope in a linear regression.

4. Find the slope of the graph where the lower point on the line is represented as $(-3, -2)$ and the higher point on the line is represented as $(2, 2)$.

5. What are the conditions of a positive slope in linear regression?

6. What are the conditions of a negative slope in linear regression?

7. What is multiple linear regression?

8. Define sum of squares due to error in multiple linear regression.

9. Define sum of squares due to regression in multiple linear regression.

10. What is multicollinearity in regression equation?

11. What is heteroskedasticity?

12. Explain ridge regression.

13. Explain lasso regression.

14. What is polynomial regression?

15. Explain basis function.

16. Explain logistic regression.

LONG-ANSWER TYPE QUESTIONS (10 MARKS EACH)

1. Define simple linear regression using a graph explaining slope and intercept.

2. Explain rise, run, and slope in a graph.

3. Explain slope, linear positive slope, and linear negative slope in a graph along with various conditions leading to the slope.

4. Explain curve linear negative slope and curve linear positive slope in a graph.

5. Explain maximum and minimum point of curves through a graph.

6. Explain ordinary least square with formula for a and b.

7. Explain the OLS algorithm with steps.

8. What is standard error of the regression? Draw a graph to represent the same.

9. Explain multiple linear regression with an example.

10. Explain the assumptions in regression analysis and BLUE concept.

11. Explain two main problems in regression analysis.

12. How to improve accuracy of the linear regression model?

13. Explain polynomial regression model in detail with an example.

14. Explain logistic regression in detail.

15. What are the assumptions in logistic regression?

16. Discuss maximum likelihood estimation in detail.

Chapter 9
Unsupervised Learning

OBJECTIVE OF THE CHAPTER:

We have discussed how to train our machines with past data on the basis of which they can learn, gain intelligence, and apply that intelligence on a new set of data. There are, however, situations when we do not have any prior knowledge of the data set we are working with, but we still want to discover interesting relationships among the attributes of the data or group the data in logical segments for easy analysis. The task of the machine is then to identify this knowledge without any prior training and that is the space of unsupervised learning. In this chapter, we will discuss how Clustering algorithms help in grouping data sets into logical segments and the association analysis which enables to identify a pattern or relationship of attributes within the data set. An interesting application of the association analysis is the Market Basket Analysis, which is used widely by retailers and advertisers across the globe.

9.1   INTRODUCTION

Unsupervised learning is a machine learning concept where the unlabelled and unclassified information is analysed to discover hidden knowledge. The algorithms work on the data without any prior training, but they are constructed in such a way that they can identify patterns, groupings, sorting order, and numerous other interesting knowledge from the set of data.

9.2 UNSUPERVISED VS SUPERVISED LEARNING

Till now, we have discussed about supervised learning where the aim was to predict the outcome variable Y on the basis of the feature set $X_1{:}X_2{:}... X_n$, and we discussed methods such as *regression* and *classification* for the same. We will now introduce the concept of unsupervised learning where the objective is to observe only the features $X_1{:}X_2{:}... X_n$; we are not going to predict any outcome variable, but rather our intention is to find out the association between the features or their grouping to understand the nature of the data. This analysis may reveal an interesting correlation between the features or a common behaviour within the subgroup of the data, which provides better understanding of the data.

In terms of statistics, a supervised learning algorithm will try to learn the probability of outcome Y for a particular input X, which is called the posterior probability. Unsupervised learning is closely related to density estimation in statistics. Here, every input and the corresponding targets are concatenated to create a new set of input such as $\{(X_1, Y_1), (X_2, Y_2),..., (X_n, Y_n)\}$, which leads to a better understanding of the correlation of X and Y; this probability notation is called the joint probability.

Let us take an example of how unsupervised learning helps in pushing movie promotions to the correct group of people. In earlier days, movie promotions were blind push of the same data to all demography, such that everyone used to watch the same posters or trailers irrespective of their choice or preference. So, in most of the cases, the person watching the promotion or trailer would end up ignoring it, which leads to waste of effort and money on the promotion. But with the advent of smart devices and apps, there is now a huge database available to understand what type of movie is liked by what segment of the demography. Machine learning helps to find out the pattern or the repeated behaviour of the smaller groups/clusters within this database to provide the intelligence about liking or disliking of certain types of movies by different groups within the demography. So, by using this intelligence, the smart apps can push only the relevant movie promotions or trailers to the selected groups, which will significantly increase the chance of targeting the right interested person for the movie.

We will discuss two methods in this chapter for explaining the principle underlying unsupervised learning – Clustering and Association Analysis. **Clustering** is a broad class of methods used for discovering unknown subgroups in data, which is the most important concept in unsupervised learning. Another technique is **Association Analysis** which identifies a low-dimensional representation of the observations that can explain the variance and identify the association rule for the explanation.

9.3 APPLICATION OF UNSUPERVISED LEARNING

Because of its flexibility that it can work on uncategorized and unlabelled data, there are many domains where unsupervised learning finds its application. Few examples of such applications are as follows:

- Segmentation of target consumer populations by an advertisement consulting agency on the basis of few dimensions such as demography, financial data,

> purchasing habits, etc. so that the advertisers can reach their target consumers efficiently

- Anomaly or fraud detection in the banking sector by identifying the pattern of loan defaulters
- Image processing and image segmentation such as face recognition, expression identification, etc.
- Grouping of important characteristics in genes to identify important influencers in new areas of genetics
- Utilization by data scientists to reduce the dimensionalities in sample data to simplify modelling
- Document clustering and identifying potential labelling options

Today, unsupervised learning is used in many areas involving Artificial Intelligence (AI) and Machine Learning (ML). Chat bots, self-driven cars, and many more recent innovations are results of the combination of unsupervised and supervised learning.

So, in this chapter, we will cover two major aspects of unsupervised learning, namely *Clustering* which helps in segmentation of the set of objects into groups of similar objects and *Association Analysis* which is related to the identification of relationships among objects in a data set.

9.4   CLUSTERING

Clustering refers to a broad set of techniques for finding subgroups, or clusters, in a data set on the basis of the characteristics of the objects within that data set in such a manner that the objects within the group are similar (or related to each other) but are different from (or unrelated to) the objects from the other groups. The effectiveness of clustering depends on how similar or related the objects within a group are or how different or unrelated the objects in different groups are from each other. It is often domain specific to define what is meant by two objects to be similar or dissimilar and thus is an important aspect of the unsupervised machine learning task.

As an example, suppose we want to run some advertisements of a new movie for a countrywide promotional activity. We have data for the age, location, financial condition, and political stability of the people in different parts of the country. We may want to run a different type of campaign for the different parts grouped according to the data we have. Any logical grouping obtained by analysing the characteristics of the people will help us in driving the campaigns in a more targeted way. Clustering analysis can help in this activity by analysing different ways to group the set of people and arriving at different types of clusters.

There are many different fields where cluster analysis is used effectively, such as

- Text data mining: this includes tasks such as text categorization, text clustering, document summarization, concept extraction, sentiment analysis, and entity relation modelling
- Customer segmentation: creating clusters of customers on the basis of parameters such as demographics, financial conditions, buying habits, etc., which can be used by retailers and advertisers to promote their products in the correct segment

- Anomaly checking: checking of anomalous behaviours such as fraudulent bank transaction, unauthorized computer intrusion, suspicious movements on a radar scanner, etc.
- Data mining: simplify the data mining task by grouping a large number of features from an extremely large data set to make the analysis manageable

In this section, we will discuss the methods related to the machine learning task of clustering, which involves finding natural groupings of data. The focus will be on

- how clustering tasks differ from classification tasks and how clustering defines groups
- a classic and easy-to-understand clustering algorithm, namely k-means, which is used for clustering along with the k-medoids algorithm
- application of clustering in real-life scenarios

9.4.1   Clustering as a machine learning task

The primary driver of clustering knowledge is discovery rather than prediction, because we may not even know what we are looking for before starting the clustering analysis. So, clustering is defined as an unsupervised machine learning task that automatically divides the data into **clusters** or groups of similar items. The analysis achieves this without prior knowledge of the types of groups required and thus can provide an insight into the natural groupings within the data set. The primary guideline of clustering task is that the data inside a cluster should be very similar to each other but very different from those outside the cluster. We can assume that the definition of similarity might vary across applications, but the basic idea is always the same, that is, to create the group such that related elements are placed together. Using this principle, whenever a large set of diverse and varied data is presented for analysis, clustering enables to represent the data in a smaller number of groups. It helps to reduce the complexity and provides insight into patterns of relationships to generate meaningful and actionable structures within the data. The effectiveness of clustering is measured by the homogeneity within a group as well as the difference between distinct groups. See Figure 9.1 for reference.

From the above discussion, it may seem that through clustering, we are trying to label the objects with class labels. But clustering is somewhat different from the classification and numeric prediction discussed in supervised learning chapters. In each of these cases, the goal was to create a model that relates features to an outcome or to other features and the model identifies patterns within the data. In contrast, clustering creates new data. Unlabelled objects are given a cluster label which is inferred entirely from the relationship of attributes within the data.

Let us take an example. You were invited to take a session on Machine Learning in a reputed university for induction of their professors on the subject. Before you create the material for the session, you want to know the level of acquaintance of the professors on the subject so that the session is successful. But you do not want to ask the inviting university, but rather do some analysis on your own on the basis of the data available freely. As Machine Learning is the intersection of Statistics and Computer Science, you focused on identifying the professors from these two areas also. So, you searched the list of research publications of these professors from the internet, and by using the machine learning algorithm, you now want to group the papers and thus infer the expertise of the professors into three buckets – Statistics, Computer Science, and Machine Learning.

After plotting the number of publications of these professors in the two core areas, namely Statistics and Computer Science, you obtain a scatter plot as shown in Figure 9.2.

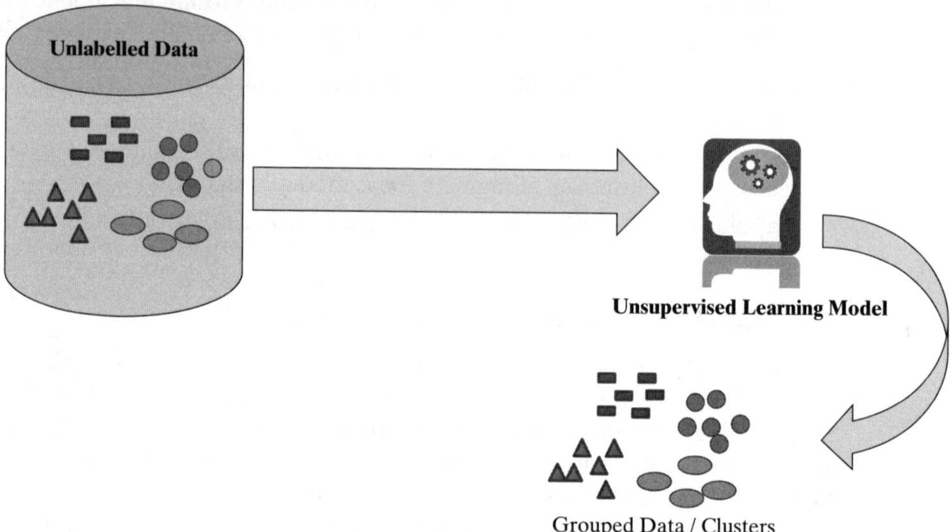

FIG. 9.1
Unsupervised learning – clustering

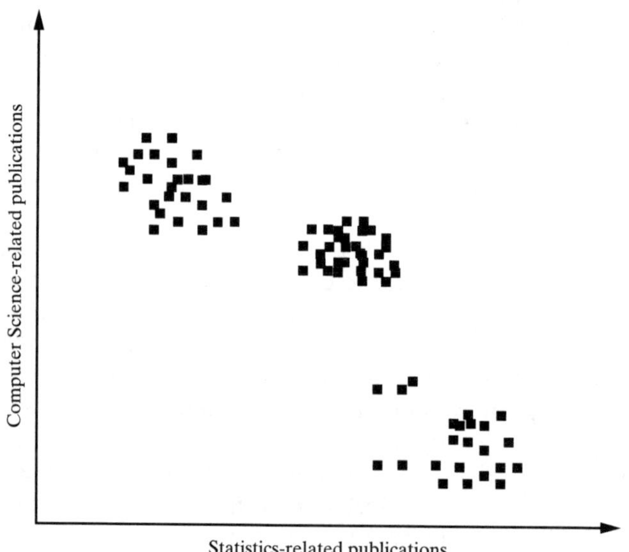

FIG. 9.2
Data set for the conference attendees

Some inferences that can be derived from the pattern analysis of the data is that there seems to be three groups or clusters emerging from the data. The pure statisticians have very less Computer Science-related papers, whereas the pure Computer Science professors have less number of statistics-related papers than Computer Science-related papers. There is a third cluster of professors who have published papers on both these areas and thus can be assumed to be the persons knowledgeable in machine learning concepts, as shown in Figure 9.3.

Thus, in the above problem, we used visual indication of logical grouping of data to identify a pattern or cluster and labelled the data in three different clusters. The main driver for our clustering was the closeness of the points to each other to form a group. The clustering algorithm uses a very similar approach to measure how closely the data points are related and decides whether they can be labelled as a homogeneous group. In the next section, we will discuss few important algorithms for clustering.

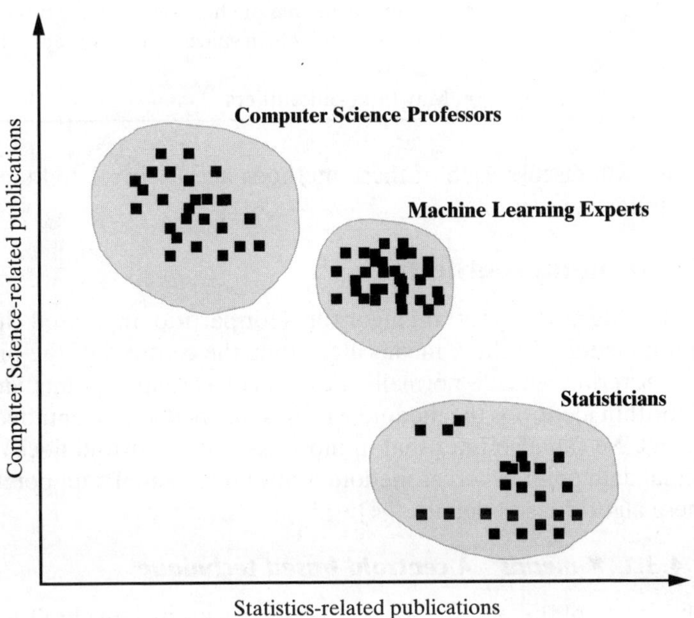

FIG. 9.3
Clusters for the conference attendees

9.4.2   Different types of clustering techniques

The major clustering techniques are

- Partitioning methods,
- Hierarchical methods, and
- Density-based methods.

Their approach towards creating the clusters, way to measure the quality of the clusters, and applicability are different. **Table 9.1** summarizes the main characteristics of each method for each reference.

Table 9.1
Different Clustering Methods

Method	Characteristics
Partitioning methods	• Uses mean or medoid (etc.) to represent cluster centre • Adopts distance-based approach to refine clusters • Finds mutually exclusive clusters of spherical or nearly spherical shape • Effective for data sets of small to medium size
Hierarchical methods	• Creates hierarchical or tree-like structure through decomposition or merger • Uses distance between the nearest or furthest points in neighbouring clusters as a guideline for refinement • Erroneous merges or splits cannot be corrected at subsequent levels
Density-based methods	• Useful for identifying arbitrarily shaped clusters • Guiding principle of cluster creation is the identification of dense regions of objects in space which are separated by low-density regions • May filter out outliers

We will discuss each of these methods and their related techniques in details in the following sections.

9.4.3   Partitioning methods

Two of the most important algorithms for partitioning-based clustering are k-means and k-medoid. In the k-means algorithm, the centroid of the prototype is identified for clustering, which is normally the mean of a group of points. Similarly, the k-medoid algorithm identifies the medoid which is the most representative point for a group of points. We can also infer that in most cases, the centroid does not correspond to an actual data point, whereas medoid is always an actual data point. Let us discuss both these algorithms in detail.

9.4.3.1 K-means - A centroid-based technique

This is one of the oldest and most popularly used algorithm for clustering. The basic principles used by this algorithm also serves as the basis for other more sophisticated and complex algorithms. **Table 9.2** provides the strengths and weaknesses of this algorithm.

The principle of the k-means algorithm is to assign each of the 'n' data points to one of the K clusters where 'K' is a user-defined parameter as the number of clusters desired. The objective is to maximize the homogeneity within the clusters and also to maximize the differences between the clusters. The homogeneity and differences are measured in terms of the distance between the objects or points in the data set.

Algorithm 9.1 shows the simple algorithm of K-means

Step 1: Select K points in the data space and mark them as initial centroids

loop
Step 2: Assign each point in the data space to the nearest centroid to form K clusters

Table 9.2
Strengths and Weaknesses of K-means

Strengths	Weaknesses
• The principle used for identifying the clusters is very simple and involves very less complexity of statistical terms • The algorithm is very flexible and thus can be adjusted for most scenarios and complexities • The performance and efficiency are very high and comparable to those of any sophisticated algorithm in term of dividing the data into useful clusters	• The algorithm involves an element of random chance and thus may not find the optimal set of cluster in some cases • The starting point of guessing the number natural clusters within the data requires some experience of the user, so that the final outcome is efficient

Step 3: Measure the distance of each point in the cluster from the centroid

Step 4: Calculate the Sum of Squared Error (SSE) to measure the quality of the clusters *(described later in this chapter)*

Step 5: Identify the new centroid of each cluster on the basis of distance between points

Step 6: Repeat Steps 2 to 5 to refine until centroids do not change

end loop

Let us understand this algorithm with an example. In Figure 9.4, we have certain set of data points, and we will apply the k-means algorithm to find out the clusters generated from this data set. Let us fix $K = 4$, implying that we want to create four clusters out of this data set. As the first step, we assign four random points from the data set as the centroids, as represented by the * signs, and we assign the data points to the nearest centroid to create four clusters. In the second step, on the basis of the

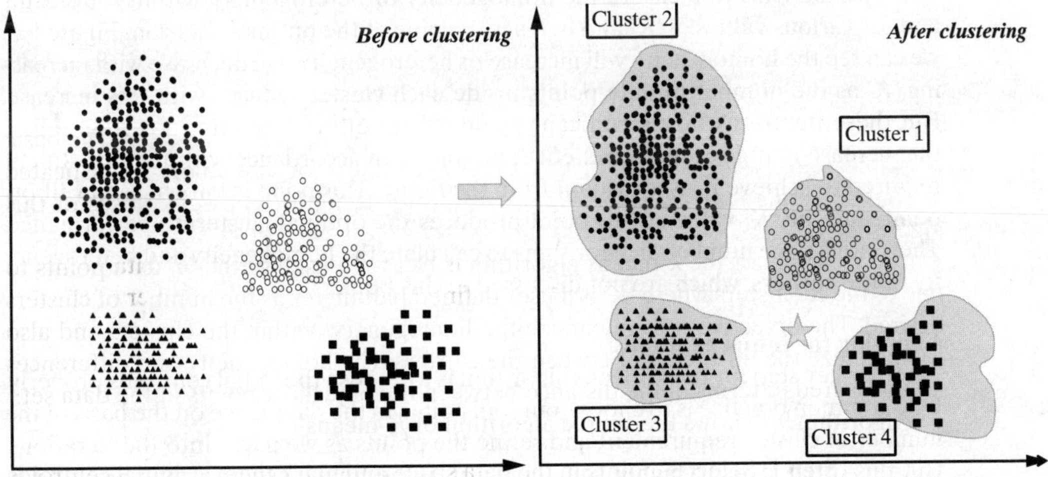

FIG. 9.4

Clustering concept – before and after clustering

distance of the points from the corresponding centroids, the centroids are updated and points are reassigned to the updated centroids. After three iterations, we found that the centroids are not moving as there is no scope for refinement, and thus, the k-means algorithm will terminate. This provides us the most logical four groupings or cluster of the data sets where the homogeneity within the groups is highest and difference between the groups is maximum.

Choosing appropriate number of clusters

One of the most important success factors in arriving at correct clustering is to start with the correct number of cluster assumptions. Different numbers of starting cluster lead to completely different types of data split. It will always help if we have some prior knowledge about the number of clusters and we start our k-means algorithm with that prior knowledge. For example, if we are clustering the data of the students of a university, it is always better to start with the number of departments in that university. Sometimes, the business needs or resource limitations drive the number of required clusters. For example, if a movie maker wants to cluster the movies on the basis of combination of two parameters – budget of the movie: high or low, and casting of the movie: star or non-star, then there are 4 possible combinations, and thus, there can be four clusters to split the data.

For a small data set, sometimes a rule of thumb that is followed is

$$K = \sqrt{\frac{n}{2}}$$

which means that K is set as the square root of $n/2$ for a data set of n examples. But unfortunately, this thumb rule does not work well for large data sets. There are several statistical methods to arrive at the suitable number of clusters.

Elbow method

This method tries to measure the homogeneity or heterogeneity within the cluster and for various values of 'K' and helps in arriving at the optimal 'K'. From Figure 9.5, we can see the homogeneity will increase or heterogeneity will decrease with increasing 'K' as the number of data points inside each cluster reduces with this increase. But these iterations take significant computation effort, and after a certain point, the increase in homogeneity benefit is no longer in accordance with the investment required to achieve it, as is evident from the figure. This point is known as the elbow point, and the 'K' value at this point produces the optimal clustering performance. There are a large number of algorithms to calculate the homogeneity and heterogeneity of the clusters, which are not discussed in this book.

Choosing the initial centroids

Another key step for the k-means algorithm is to choose the initial centroids properly. One common practice is to choose random points in the data space on the basis of the number of cluster requirement and refine the points as we move into the iterations. But this often leads to higher squared error in the final clustering, thus resulting in sub-optimal clustering solution. The assumption for selecting random centroids is that multiple subsequent runs will minimize the SSE and identify the optimal clusters.

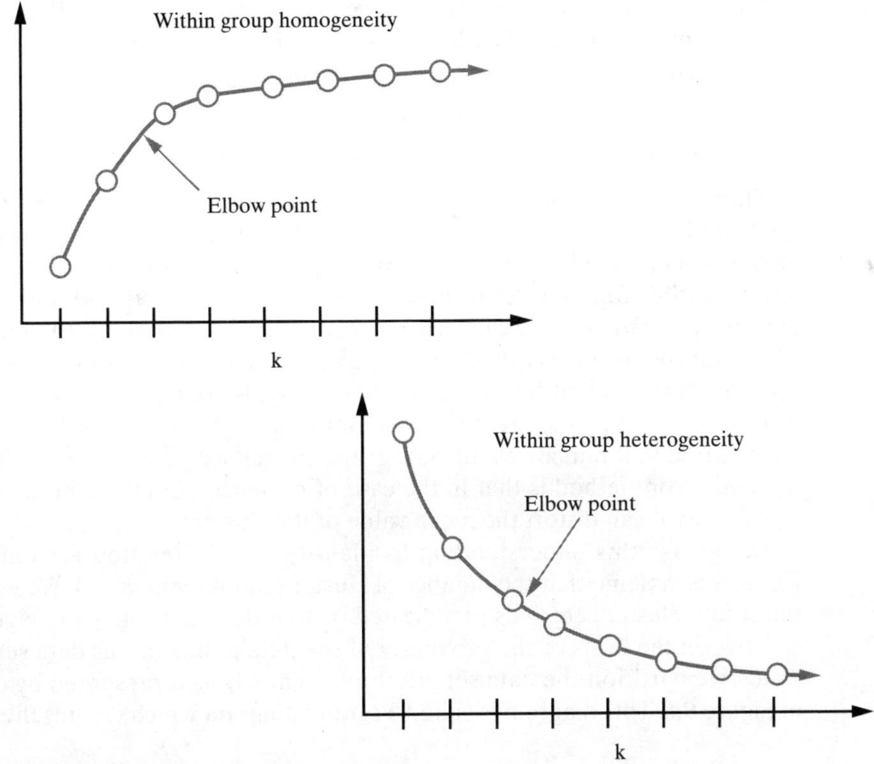

FIG. 9.5
Elbow point to determine the appropriate number of clusters

But this is often not true on the basis of the spread of the data set and the number of clusters sought. So, one effective approach is to employ the hierarchical clustering technique on sample points from the data set and then arrive at sample K clusters. The centroids of these initial K clusters are used as the initial centroids. This approach is practical when the data set has small number of points and K is relatively small compared to the data points. There are procedures such as bisecting k-means and use of post-processing to fix initial clustering issues; these procedures can produce better quality initial centroids and thus better SSE for the final clusters.

Recomputing cluster centroids
We discussed in the k-means algorithm that the iterative step is to recalculate the centroids of the data set after each iteration. The proximities of the data points from each other within a cluster is measured to minimize the distances. The distance of the data point from its nearest centroid can also be calculated to minimize the distances to arrive at the refined centroid. The Euclidean distance between two data points is measured as follows:

$$\text{dist}(x, y) = \sqrt{\sum_{1}^{n} (x_i - y_i)^2} \tag{9.1}$$

Using this function, the distance between the example data and its nearest centroid and the objective is calculated to minimize this distance. The measure of quality of clustering uses the SSE technique. The formula used is as follows:

$$\text{SSE} = \sum_{i=1}^{k} \sum_{x \in C_i} \text{dist}\left(c_i, x\right)^2 \tag{9.2}$$

where dist() calculates the Euclidean distance between the centroid c_i of the cluster C_i and the data points x in the cluster. The summation of such distances over all the 'K' clusters gives the total sum of squared error. As you can understand, the lower the SSE for a clustering solution, the better is the representative position of the centroid. Thus, in our clustering algorithm in Algorithm 9.1, the recomputation of the centroid involves calculating the SSE of each new centroid and arriving at the optimal centroid identification. After the centroids are repositioned, the data points nearest to the centroids are assigned to form the refined clusters. It is observed that the centroid that minimizes the SSE of the cluster is its mean. One limitation of the squared error method is that in the case of presence of outliers in the data set, the squared error can distort the mean value of the clusters.

Let us use this understanding to identify the cluster step for the data set in Figure 9.6. Assume that the number of cluster requirement, $K = 4$. We will randomly select four cluster centroids as indicated by four different colours in Figure 9.7.

Now, on the basis of the proximity of the data points in this data set to the centroids, we partition the data set into four segments as represented by dashed lines in Figure 9.8. This diagram is called **Voronoi diagram** which creates the boundaries

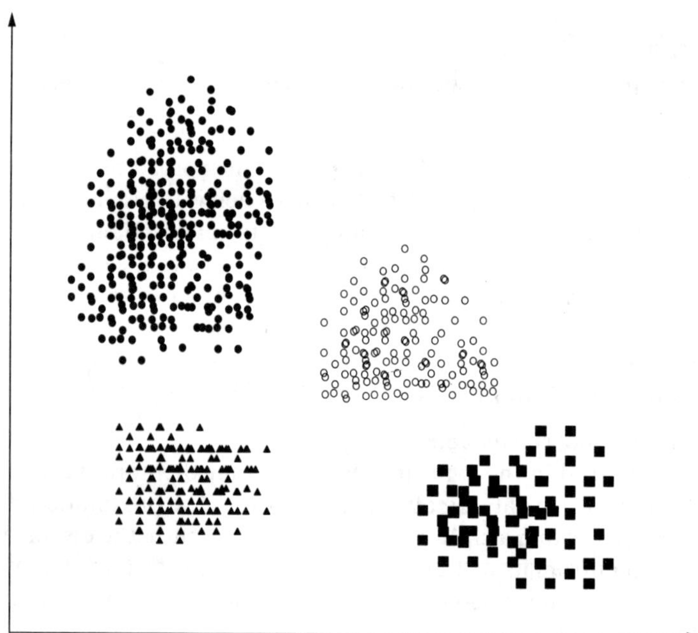

FIG. 9.6
Clustering of data set

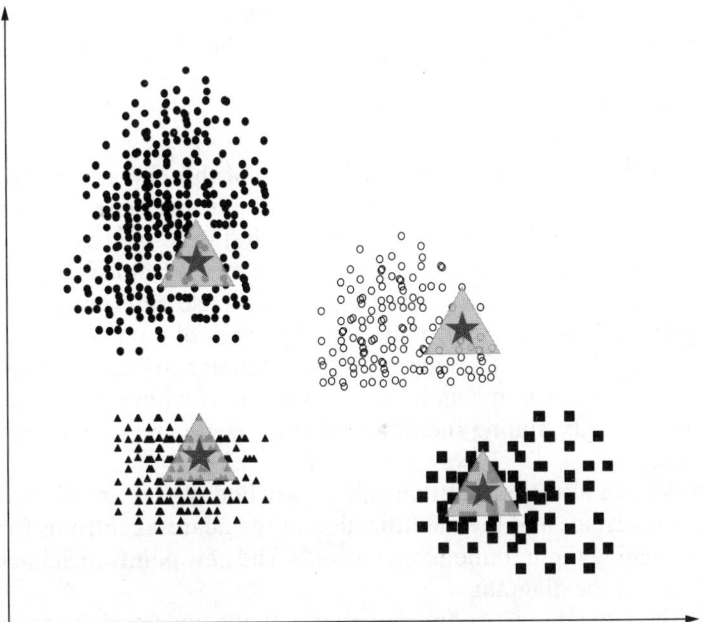

FIG. 9.7
Clustering with initial centroids

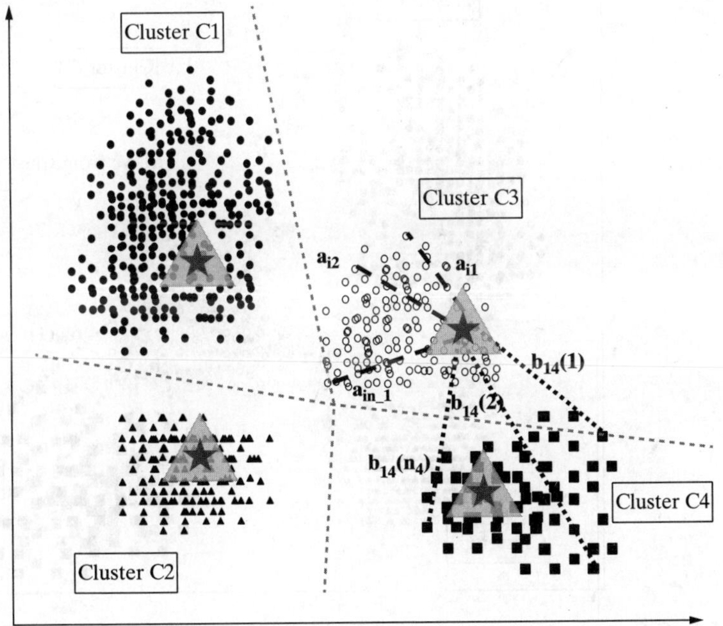

FIG. 9.8
Iteration 1: Four clusters and distance of points from the centroids

of the clusters. We got the initial four clusters, namely C_1, C_2, C_3, and C_4, created by the dashed lines from the vertex of the clusters, which is the point with the maximal distance from the centre of the clusters. It is now easy to understand the areas covered by each cluster and the data points within each cluster through this representation.

The next step is to calculate the SSE of this clustering and update the position of the centroids. We can also proceed by our understanding that the new centroid should be the mean of the data points in the respective clusters. The distances of the data points currently marked as Cluster C_3 from the centroid of cluster C_3 are marked as a_{i1}, a_{i2},..., a_{in} in the figure and those determine the homogeneity within cluster C_3. On the other hand, the distances of data points of cluster C_4 from the centroid of cluster C_3 determine the heterogeneity among these two different clusters. Our aim is to maximize the homogeneity within the clusters and maximize the heterogeneity among the different clusters. So, the revised centroids are as shown in Figure 9.9.

We can also find out that the cluster boundaries are refined on the basis of the new centroids and the identification of the nearest centroids for the data points and reassigning them to the new centroids. The new points reclaimed by each cluster are shown in the diagram.

The k-means algorithm continues with the update of the centroid according to the new cluster and reassignment of the points, until no more data points are changed

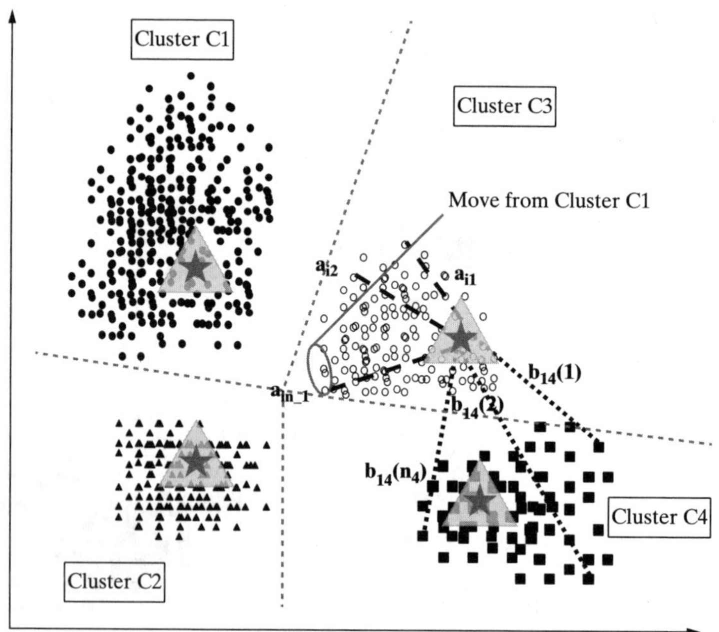

FIG. 9.9

Iteration 2: Centroids recomputed and points redistributed among the clusters according to the nearest centroid

due to the centroid shift. At this point, the algorithm stops. Figure 9.10 shows the final clustering of the data set we used. The complexity of the k-means algorithm is $O\,(nKt)$, where 'n' is the total number of data points or objects in the data set, K is the number of clusters, and 't' is the number of iterations. Normally, 'K' and 't' are kept much smaller than 'n', and thus, the k-means method is relatively scalable and efficient in processing large data sets.

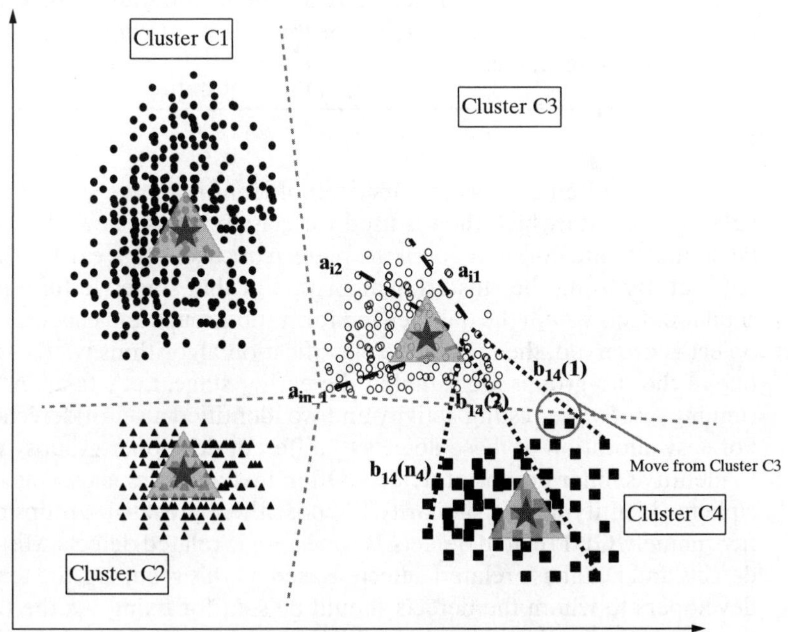

FIG. 9.10

Iteration 3: Final cluster arrangement: Centroids recomputed and points redistributed among the clusters according to the nearest centroid

Points to Ponder:

Because of the distance-based approach from the centroid to all points in the data set, the k-means method may not always converge to the global optimum and often terminates at a local optimum. The result of the clustering largely depends on the initial random selection of cluster centres.

k-means often produce local optimum and not global optimum. Also, the result depends on the initial selection of random cluster centroids. It is a common practice to run the k-means algorithm multiple times with different cluster centres to identify the optimal clusters. The necessity to set the initial 'K' values is also perceived as a disadvantage of the k-means algorithm. There are methods to overcome this problem, such as defining a range for 'K' and then comparing the results of clustering with those different 'K' values to arrive at the best possible cluster. The ways to improve cluster performance is an area of further study, and many different techniques are employed to achieve that. This is out of scope of this book but can be pursued for advanced machine learning studies.

Note:

Clustering is often used as the first step of identifying the subgroups within a unlabeled set of data which then is used for classifying the new observed data. At the beginning we are not clear about the pattern or classes that exist within the unlabeled data set. By using the clustering algorithm at that stage we find out the groups of similar objects within the data set and form sub-groups and classes. Later when a new object is observed, then using the classification algorithms we try to place that into one of the sub-groups identified in the earlier stage. Let's take an example. We are running a software testing activity and we identified a set of defects in the software. For easy allocation of these defects to different developer groups, the team is trying to identify similar groups of defects. Often text analytics is used as the guiding principle for identifying this similarity. Suppose there are 4 sub-groups of defects identified, namely, GUI related defects, Business logic related defects, Missing requirement defects and Database related defects. Based on this grouping, the team identified the developers to whom the defects should be sent for fixing. As the testing continues, there are new defects getting created. We have the categories of defects identified now and thus the team can use classification algorithms to assign the new defect to one of the 4 identified groups or classes which will make it easy to identify the developer who should be fixing it.

For the implementation of $k$means algorithm, *KMeans* function of **sklearn.cluster** library has been used. Also, since silhouette width is a more generic performance measure, it has been used here. *silhouette_score* function of **sklearn. metrics** library has been used for calculating Silhouette width. The full code for the implementation is given below (Figure B.8).

```
>>> import pandas as pd
>>> import numpy as np
```

```
>>> import matplotlib.pyplot as plt
>>> from mpl_toolkits.mplot3d import Axes3D
>>> from sklearn.cluster import KMeans
>>> from sklearn.metrics import silhouette_score

>>> data = pd.read_csv("spinem.csv")

>>> f1 = data['pelvic_incidence'].values
>>> f2 = data['pelvic_radius'].values
>>> f3 = data['thoracic_slope'].values
>>> X = np.array(list(zip(f1, f2, f3)))
>>> kmeans = KMeans(n_clusters = 3, random_state = 123)
>>> model = kmeans.fit(X)
>>> cluster_labels = kmeans.predict(X)
>>> C = kmeans.cluster_centers_
>>> sil = silhouette_score(X, cluster_labels,
metric='euclidean',sample_size = len(data))
>>> print(C)
>>> print(sil)

#For 2-D plot of the data points along with the centroids ...
>>> fig = plt.figure()
>>> plt.scatter(X[:, 0], X[:, 1])
>>> plt.scatter(C[:, 0], C[:, 1], marker='*', s=1000)

#For 3-D plot of the data points along with the centroids ...
>>> fig = plt.figure()
>>> ax = Axes3D(fig)
>>> ax.scatter(X[:, 0], X[:, 1], X[:, 2])
>>> ax.scatter(C[:, 0], C[:, 1],  C[:, 2], marker='*', c='#050505',
s=1000)
```

Output Accuracy:
Centroids:
```
[[  46.42903837   124.47018491    13.26250567]
 [  80.49567418   120.00557969    12.78133516]
 [  62.59438009   103.64870812    13.03697051]]
```

Silhouette width:
```
0.352350820437
```

2-D plot:

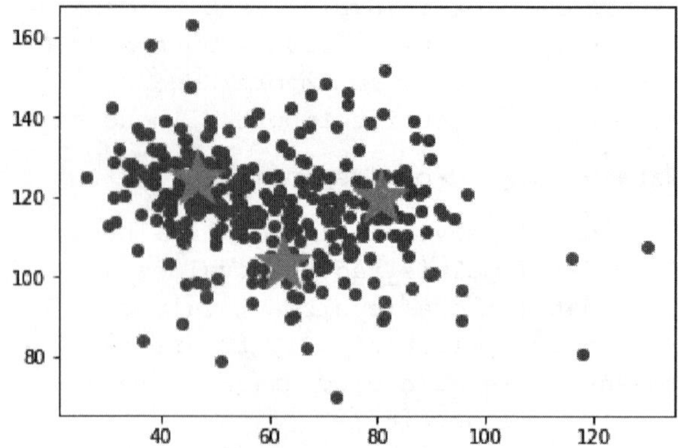

3-D plot:

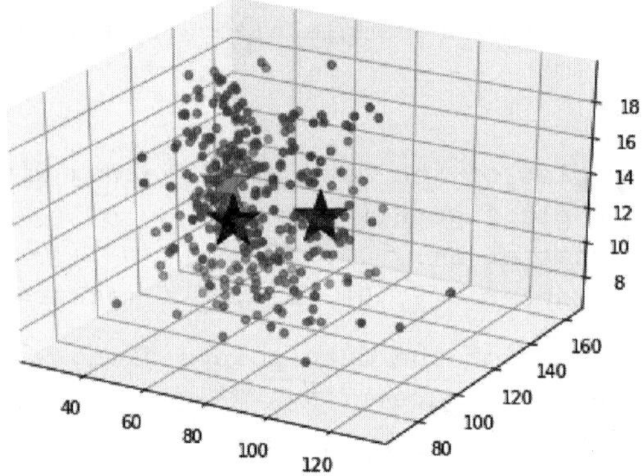

FIG. B.8
2-D and 3-D plots of clustering

9.4.4   *K*-Medoids: a representative object-based technique

As discussed earlier, the *k*-means algorithm is sensitive to outliers in the data set and inadvertently produces skewed clusters when the means of the data points are used as centroids. Let us take an example of eight data points, and for simplicity, we can consider them to be 1-D data with values 1, 2, 3, 6, 9, 10, 11, and 25. Point 25 is the outlier, and it affects the cluster formation negatively when the mean of the points is considered as centroids.

With $K = 2$, the initial clusters we arrived at are $\{1, 2, 3, 6\}$ and $\{9, 10, 11, 25\}$.

$$\text{The mean of the cluster } \{1,2,3,6\} = \frac{12}{4} = 3,$$

$$\text{and the mean of the cluster } \{9,10,12,25\} = \frac{56}{4} = 14.$$

So, the SSE within the clusters is

$$(1-3)^2 + (2-3)^2 + (3-3)^2 + (6-3)^2 + (9-14)^2$$
$$+(10-14)^2 + (12-14)^2 + (25-14)^2 = 179$$

If we compare this with the cluster $\{1, 2, 3, 6, 9\}$ and $\{10, 11, 25\}$,

$$\text{the mean of the cluster } \{1, 2, 3, 6, 9\} = \frac{21}{5} = 4.2,$$

$$\text{and the mean of the cluster } \{10, 12, 25\} = \frac{47}{3} = 15.67 .$$

So, the SSE within the clusters is

$$(1-4.2)^2 + (2-4.2)^2 + (3-4.2)^2 + (6-4.2)^2 + (9-4.2)^2$$
$$+(10-15.67)^2 + (12-15.67)^2 + (25-15.67)^2 = 113.84$$

Because the SSE of the second clustering is lower, k-means tend to put point 9 in the same cluster with $1, 2, 3$, and 6 though the point is logically nearer to points 10 and 11. This skewedness is introduced due to the outlier point 25, which shifts the mean away from the centre of the cluster.

k-medoids provides a solution to this problem. Instead of considering the mean of the data points in the cluster, k-medoids considers k representative data points from the existing points in the data set as the centre of the clusters. It then assigns the data points according to their distance from these centres to form k clusters. Note that the medoids in this case are actual data points or objects from the data set and not an imaginary point as in the case when the mean of the data sets within cluster is used as the centroid in the k-means technique. The SSE is calculated as

$$\text{SSE} = \sum_{i=1}^{k} \sum_{x \in C_i} \text{dist}(o_i, x)^2 \tag{9.3}$$

where o_i is the representative point or object of cluster C_i.

Thus, the k-medoids method groups n objects in k clusters by minimizing the SSE. Because of the use of medoids from the actual representative data points, k-medoids is less influenced by the outliers in the data. One of the practical implementation of the k-medoids principle is the Partitioning Around Medoids (PAM) algorithm. Refer to Algorithm 2 table:

Algorithm 2: PAM

Step 1: Randomly choose k points in the data set as the initial representative points
loop
Step 2: Assign each of the remaining points to the cluster which has the nearest representative point
Step 3: Randomly select a non-representative point o_r in each cluster
Step 4: Swap the representative point o_j with o_r and compute the new SSE after swapping

Step 5: If SSEnew < SSEold, then swap o_j with o_r to form the new set of k representative objects;
Step 6: Refine the k clusters on the basis of the nearest representative point. Logic continues until there is no change
end loop

In this algorithm, we replaced the current representative object with a non-representative object and checked if it improves the quality of clustering. In the iterative process, all possible replacements are attempted until the quality of clusters no longer improves.

If $o_1,\ldots, o_k$ are the current set of representative objects or medoids and there is a non-representative object o_r, then to determine whether o_r is a good replacement of o_j $(1 \leq j \leq k)$, the distance of each object x is calculated from its nearest medoid from the set $\{o_1, o_2,\ldots, o_{j-1}, o_r, o_{j+1},\ldots, o_k\}$ and the SSE is calculated. If the SSE after replacing o_j with o_r decreases, it means that o_r represents the cluster better than o_j, and the data points in the set are reassigned according to the nearest medoids now.

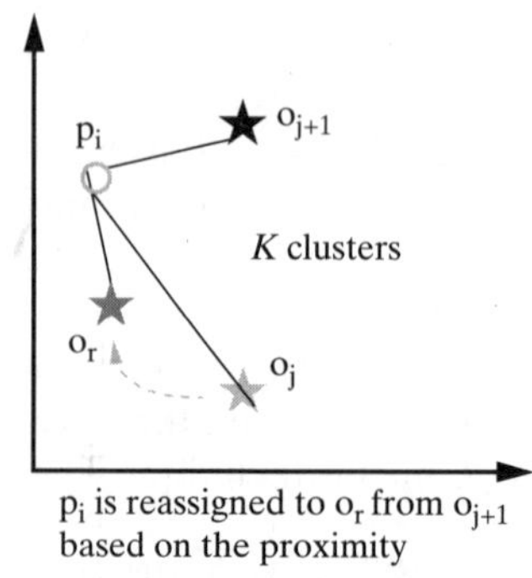

FIG. 9.11

PAM algorithm: Reassignment of points to different clusters

As shown in Figure 9.11, point p_i was belonging to the cluster with medoid o_{j+1} in the first iteration, but after o_j was replaced by o_r, it was found that p_i is nearest to the new random medoid and thus gets assigned to it. In this way, the clusters get refined after each medoid is replaced with a new non-representative medoid. Each time a reassignment is done, the SSE based on the new medoid is calculated. The difference between the SSE before and after the swap indicates whether or not the replacement is improving the quality of the clustering by bringing the most similar points together.

Points to Ponder:

k-medoids methods like PAM works well for small set of data, but they are not scalable for large set of data because of computational overhead. A sample-based technique is used in the case of large data set where the sample should be a good representative of the whole data set.

Though the k-medoids algorithm provides an effective way to eliminate the noise or outliers in the data set, which was the problem in the k-means algorithm, it is expensive in terms of calculations. The complexity of each iteration in the k-medoids algorithm is $O\left(k(n-k)^2\right)$. For large value of 'n' and 'k', this calculation becomes much costlier than that of the k-means algorithm.

9.4.5 Hierarchical clustering

Till now, we have discussed the various methods for partitioning the data into different clusters. But there are situations when the data needs to be partitioned into groups at different levels such as in a hierarchy. The hierarchical clustering methods are used to group the data into hierarchy or tree-like structure. For example, in a machine learning problem of organizing employees of a university in different departments, first the employees are grouped under the different departments in the university, and then within each department, the employees can be grouped according to their roles such as professors, assistant professors, supervisors, lab assistants, etc. This creates a hierarchical structure of the employee data and eases visualization and analysis. Similarly, there may be a data set which has an underlying hierarchy structure that we want to discover and we can use the hierarchical clustering methods to achieve that.

There are two main hierarchical clustering methods: agglomerative clustering and divisive clustering. Agglomerative clustering is a bottom-up technique which starts with individual objects as clusters and then iteratively merges them to form larger clusters. On the other hand, the divisive method starts with one cluster with all given objects and then splits it iteratively to form smaller clusters. See Figure 9.12.

The agglomerative hierarchical clustering method uses the bottom-up strategy. It starts with each object forming its own cluster and then iteratively merges the clusters according to their similarity to form larger clusters. It terminates either when a certain clustering condition imposed by the user is achieved or all the clusters merge into a single cluster.

The divisive hierarchical clustering method uses a top-down strategy. The starting point is the largest cluster with all the objects in it, and then, it is split recursively to form smaller and smaller clusters, thus forming the hierarchy. The end of iterations is achieved when the objects in the final clusters are sufficiently homogeneous to each other or the final clusters contain only one object or the user-defined clustering condition is achieved.

In both these cases, it is important to select the split and merger points carefully, because the subsequent splits or mergers will use the result of the previous ones and there is no option to perform any object swapping between the clusters or rectify the decisions made in previous steps, which may result in poor clustering quality at the end.

A dendrogram is a commonly used tree structure representation of step-by-step creation of hierarchical clustering. It shows how the clusters are **merged** iteratively (in the case of agglomerative clustering) or **split** iteratively (in the case of divisive

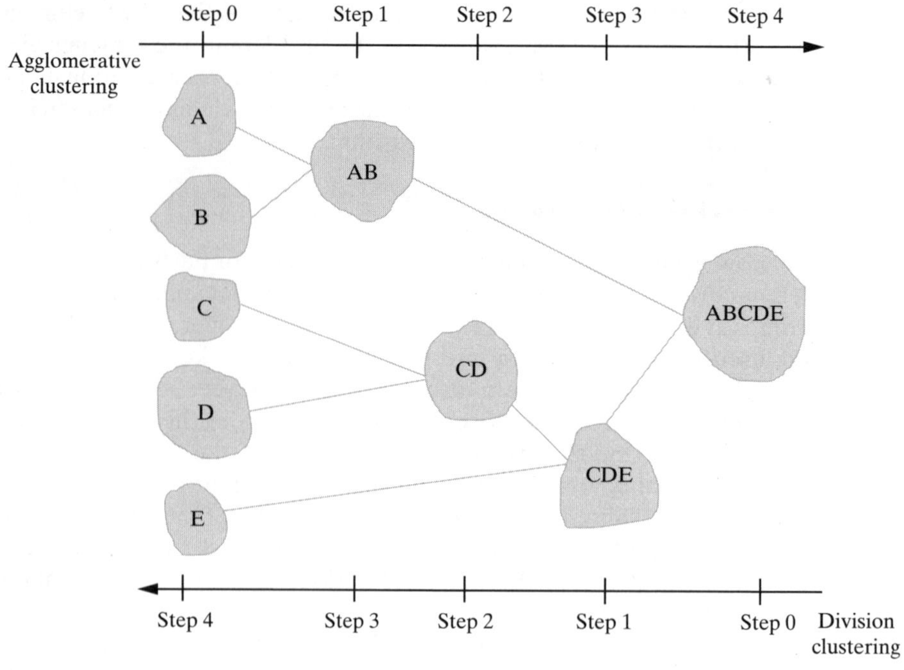

FIG. 9.12

Agglomerative and divisive hierarchical clustering

clustering) to arrive at the optimal clustering solution. Figure 9.13 shows a dendrogram with four levels and how the objects are merged or split at each level to arrive at the hierarchical clustering.

One of the core measures of proximities between clusters is the distance between them. There are four standard methods to measure the distance between clusters:

Let C_i and C_j be the two clusters with n_i and n_j respectively. p_i and p_j represents the points in clusters C_i and C_j respectively. We will denote the mean of cluster C_i as m_i.

Minimum distance
$$D_{\min}\left(C_i, C_j\right) = \min_{p_i \in C_i, p_j \in C_j}\left\{\left\|p_i - p_j\right\|\right\} \tag{9.4}$$

Maximum distance
$$D_{\max}\left(C_i, C_j\right) = \max_{p_i \in C_i, p_j \in C_j}\left\{\left\|p_i - p_j\right\|\right\} \tag{9.5}$$

Mean distance $D_{\text{mean}}\left(C_i, C_j\right) = \left\{\left\|m_i - m_j\right\|\right\}$ $\hspace{2cm}$ (9.6)

Average distance $D_{\text{avg}}\left(C_i, C_j\right) = \dfrac{1}{n_i n_j}\displaystyle\sum_{p_i \in C_i, p_j \in C_j}\left|p_i - p_j\right|$ $\hspace{1cm}$ (9.7)

Refer to Figure 9.14 for understanding the concept of these distances.

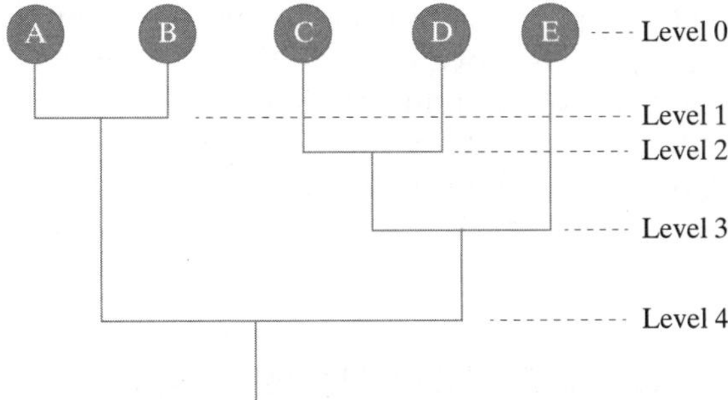

FIG. 9.13
Dendrogram representation of hierarchical clustering

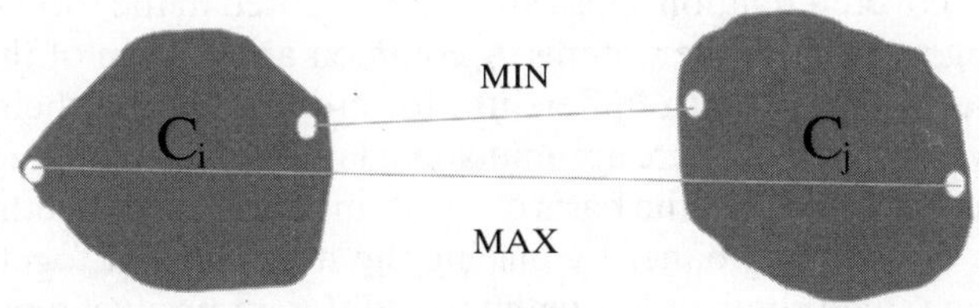

FIG. 9.14
Distance measure in algorithmic methods

Often the distance measure is used to decide when to terminate the clustering algorithm. For example, in an agglomerative clustering, the merging iterations may be stopped once the MIN distance between two neighbouring clusters becomes less than the user-defined threshold. So, when an algorithm uses the minimum distance D_{min} to measure the distance between the clusters, then it is referred to as nearest neighbour clustering algorithm, and if the decision to stop the algorithm is based on a user-defined limit on D_{min}, then it is called single linkage algorithm.

On the other hand, when an algorithm uses the maximum distance D_{max} to measure the distance between the clusters, then it is referred to as furthest neighbour clustering algorithm, and if the decision to stop the algorithm is based on a user-defined limit on D_{max} then it is called complete linkage algorithm.

As minimum and maximum measures provide two extreme options to measure distance between the clusters, they are prone to the outliers and noisy data. Instead, the use of mean and average distance helps in avoiding such problem and provides more consistent results.

9.4.6 Density-based methods - DBSCAN

You might have noticed that when we used the partitioning and hierarchical clustering methods, the resulting clusters are spherical or nearly spherical in nature. In the case of the other shaped clusters such as S-shaped or uneven shaped clusters, the above two types of method do not provide accurate results. The density-based clustering approach provides a solution to identify clusters of arbitrary shapes. The principle is based on identifying the dense area and sparse area within the data set and then run the clustering algorithm. DBSCAN is one of the popular density-based algorithm which creates clusters by using connected regions with high density.

9.5   FINDING PATTERN USING ASSOCIATION RULE

Association rule presents a methodology that is useful for identifying interesting relationships hidden in large data sets. It is also known as **association analysis**, and the discovered relationships can be represented in the form of association rules comprising a set of frequent items. A common application of this analysis is the **Market Basket Analysis** that retailers use for cross-selling of their products. For example, every large grocery store accumulates a large volume of data about the buying pattern of the customers. On the basis of the items purchased together, the retailers can push some cross-selling either by placing the items bought together in adjacent areas or creating some combo offer with those different product types. The below association rule signifies that people who have bought bread and milk have often bought egg also; so, for the retailer, it makes sense that these items are placed together for new opportunities for cross-selling.

$$\{Bread, Milk\} \rightarrow \{Egg\}$$

The application of association analysis is also widespread in other domains such as bioinformatics, medical diagnosis, scientific data analysis, and web data mining. For example, by discovering the interesting relationship between food habit and patients developing breast cancer, a new cancer prevention mechanism can be found which will benefit thousands of people in the world. In this book, we will mainly illustrate the analysis techniques by using the market basket example, but it can be used more widely across domains to identify association among items in transactional data. The huge pool of data generated everyday through tracked transactions such as barcode scanner, online purchase, and inventory tracking systems has enabled for machine learning systems to learn from this wealth of data. We will discuss the methods for finding useful associations in large databases by using simple statistical performance measures while managing the peculiarities of working with such transactional data. One significant challenge in working with the large volume of data is that it may be computationally very expensive to discover patterns from such data. Moreover, there may be cases when some of the associations occurred by chance, which can lead to potentially false knowledge. While discussing the association analysis, we will discuss both these points.

We will use the transaction data in the table below for our examples of association analysis. This simplified version of the market basket data will show how the association rules can be effectively used for the market basket analysis.

9.5.1   Definition of common terms

Let us understand few common terminologies used in association analysis.

9.5.1.1   Itemset

One or more items are grouped together and are surrounded by brackets to indicate that they form a set, or more specifically, an **itemset** that appears in the data with some regularity. For example, in **Table 9.3**, {Bread, Milk, Egg} can be grouped together to form an itemset as those are frequently bought together. To generalize this concept, if $I = \{i_1, i_2, \ldots, i_n\}$ are the items in a market basket data and $T = \{t_1, t_2, \ldots, t_n\}$ are the set of all the transactions, then each transaction t_i contains a subset of items from I. A collection of zero or more items is called an itemset. A null itemset is the one which does not contain any item. In the association analysis, an itemset is called k-itemset if it contains k number of items. Thus, the itemset {Bread, Milk, Egg} is a three-itemset.

Table 9.3
Market Basket Transaction Data

Transaction Number	Purchased Items
1	{Bread, Milk, Egg, Butter, Salt, Apple}
2	{Bread, Milk, Egg, Apple}
3	{Bread, Milk, Butter, Apple}
4	{Milk, Egg, Butter, Apple}
5	{Bread, Egg, Salt}
6	{Bread, Milk, Egg, Apple}

9.5.1.2   Support count

Support count denotes the number of transactions in which a particular itemset is present. This is a very important property of an itemset as it denotes the frequency of occurrence for the itemset. This is expressed as

$$\sigma(X) = \left|\{t_i \mid X \subseteq t_i, t_i \varepsilon T\}\right|$$

where $|\{\}|$ denotes the number of elements in a set

In **Table 9.3**, the itemset {Bread, Milk, Egg} occurs together three times and thus have a support count of 3.

9.5.2   Association rule

The result of the market basket analysis is expressed as a set of **association rules** that specify patterns of relationships among items. A typical rule might be expressed as {Bread, Milk}→{Egg}, which denotes that if Bread and Milk are purchased, then Egg is also likely to be purchased. Thus, association rules are learned from subsets of itemsets. For example, the preceding rule was identified from the set of *{Bread, Milk, Egg}*.

It should be noted that an association rule is an expression of $X \rightarrow Y$ where X and Y are disjoint itemsets, i.e. $X \cap Y = 0$.

Support and confidence are the two concepts that are used for measuring the strength of an association rule. Support denotes how often a rule is applicable to a given data set. Confidence indicates how often the items in Y appear in transactions that contain X in a total transaction of N. Confidence denotes the predictive power or accuracy of the rule. So, the mathematical expressions are

$$\text{Support, } s(X \rightarrow Y) = \frac{\sigma(X \cup Y)}{N} \tag{9.8}$$

$$\text{Confidence, } c(X \rightarrow Y) = \frac{\sigma(X \cup Y)}{\sigma(X)} \tag{9.9}$$

In our data set 9.3, if we consider the association rule {Bread, Milk} $\rightarrow$ {Egg}, then from the above formula

$$\text{Support } s \,(\{\text{ Bread, Milk }\} \rightarrow \{\text{ Egg }\}) = \frac{\text{support count of } \{\text{ Bread, Milk, Egg }\}}{\text{Total transactions, N}}$$

$$= \frac{3}{6}$$

$$= 0.5$$

$$\text{Confidence } c(\{\text{ Bread, Milk }\} \rightarrow \{\text{ Egg }\}) = \frac{\text{support count of } \{\text{ Bread, Milk, Egg }\}}{\text{support count of } \{\text{ Bread, Milk }\}}$$

$$= \frac{3}{4}$$

$$= 0.75$$

It is important to understand the role of support and confidence in the association analysis. A low support may indicate that the rule has occurred by chance. Also, from its application perspective, this rule may not be a very attractive business investment as the items are seldom bought together by the customers. Thus, support can provide the intelligence of identifying the most interesting rules for analysis.

Similarly, confidence provides the measurement for reliability of the inference of a rule. Higher confidence of a rule $X \rightarrow Y$ denotes more likelihood of Y to be present in transactions that contain X as it is the estimate of the conditional Y probability of Y given X.

Also, understand that the confidence of X leading to Y is not the same as the confidence of Y leading to X. In our example, confidence of {Bread, Milk} $\rightarrow$ {Egg} = 0.75 but confidence of {Egg} $\rightarrow$ {Bread, Milk} = $\frac{3}{5}$ = 0.6. Here, the rule {Bread, Milk} $\rightarrow$ {Egg} is the strong rule.

Association rules were developed in the context of Big Data and data science and are not used for prediction. They are used for unsupervised knowledge discovery in large databases, unlike the classification and numeric prediction algorithms. Still we will find that association rule learners are closely related to and share many features of the classification rule learners. As association rule learners are unsupervised, there is no need for the algorithm to be trained; this means that no prior labelling of the data is required. The programme is simply run on a data set in the hope that interesting associations are found.

Obviously, the downside is that there is not an easy way to objectively measure the performance of a rule learner, aside from evaluating them for qualitative usefulness. Also, note that the association rule analysis is used to search for interesting connections among a very large number of variables. Though human beings are capable of such insight quite intuitively, sometimes it requires expert-level knowledge or a great deal of experience to achieve the performance of a rule-learning algorithm. Additionally, some data may be too large or complex for humans to decipher and analyse so easily.

9.5.3   The apriori algorithm for association rule learning

As discussed earlier, the main challenge of discovering an association rule and learning from it is the large volume of transactional data and the related complexity. Because of the variation of features in transactional data, the number of feature sets within a data set usually becomes very large. This leads to the problem of handling a very large number of itemsets, which grows exponentially with the number of features. If there are k items which may or may not be part of an itemset, then there is 2^k ways of creating itemsets with those items. For example, if a seller is dealing with 100 different items, then the learner need to evaluate $2^{100} = 1 \times e^{30}$ itemsets for arriving at the rule, which is computationally impossible. So, it is important to filter out the most important (and thus manageable in size) itemsets and use the resources on those to arrive at the reasonably efficient association rules.

The first step for us is to decide the minimum support and minimum confidence of the association rules. From a set of transaction T, let us assume that we will find out all the rules that have support $\geq$ minS and confidence $\geq$ minC, where minS and minC are the support and confidence thresholds, respectively, for the rules to be considered acceptable. Now, even if we put the minS = 20% and minC = 50%, it is seen that more than 80% of the rules are discarded; this means that a large portion of the computational efforts could have been avoided if the itemsets for consideration were first pruned and the itemsets which cannot generate association rules with reasonable support and confidence were removed. The approach to achieve this goal is discussed below.

Step 1: decouple the support and confidence requirements. According to formula 9.8, the support of the rule $X \rightarrow Y$ is dependent only on the support of its corresponding itemsets. For example, all the below rules have the same support as their itemsets are the same {Bread, Milk, Egg}:

- {Bread, Milk} $\rightarrow$ {Egg}
- {Bread, Egg} $\rightarrow$ {Milk}
- {Egg, Milk} $\rightarrow$ {Bread}

- {Bread} → {Egg, Milk}
- {Milk} → {Bread, Egg}
- {Egg} → {Bread, Milk}

So, the same treatment can be applied to this association rule on the basis of the frequency of the itemset. In this case, if the itemset {Bread, Milk, Egg} is rare in the basket transactions, then all these six rules can be discarded without computing their individual support and confidence values. This identifies some important strategies for arriving at the association rules:

1. **Generate Frequent Itemset:** Once the min$S$ is set for a particular assignment, identify all the itemsets that satisfy min$S$. These itemsets are called frequent itemsets.

2. **Generate Rules:** From the frequent itemsets found in the previous step, discover all the high confidence rules. These are called strong rules.

Please note that the computation requirement for identifying frequent itemsets is more intense than the rule generation. So, different techniques have been evolved to optimize the performance for frequent itemset generation as well as rule discovery as discussed in the next section.

9.5.4   Build the apriori principle rules

One of the most widely used algorithm to reduce the number of itemsets to search for the association rule is known as Apriori. It has proven to be successful in simplifying the association rule learning to a great extent. The principle got its name from the fact that the algorithm utilizes a simple prior belief (i.e. *a priori*) about the properties of frequent itemsets:

If an itemset is frequent, then all of its subsets must also be frequent.

This principle significantly restricts the number of itemsets to be searched for rule generation. For example, if in a market basket analysis, it is found that an item like 'Salt' is not so frequently bought along with the breakfast items, then it is fine to remove all the itemsets containing salt for rule generation as their contribution to the support and confidence of the rule will be insignificant.

The converse also holds true:

If an itemset is frequent, then all the supersets must be frequent too.

These are very powerful principles which help in pruning the exponential search space based on the support measure and is known as support-based pruning. The key property of the support measure used here is that the support for an itemset never exceeds the support for its subsets. This is also known as the anti-monotone property of the support measure.

Let us use the transaction data in **Table 9.3** to illustrate the Apriori principle and its use. From the full itemset of six items {Bread, Milk, Egg, Butter, Salt, Apple}, there are 2^6 ways to create baskets or itemsets (including the null itemset) as shown in Figure 9.15:

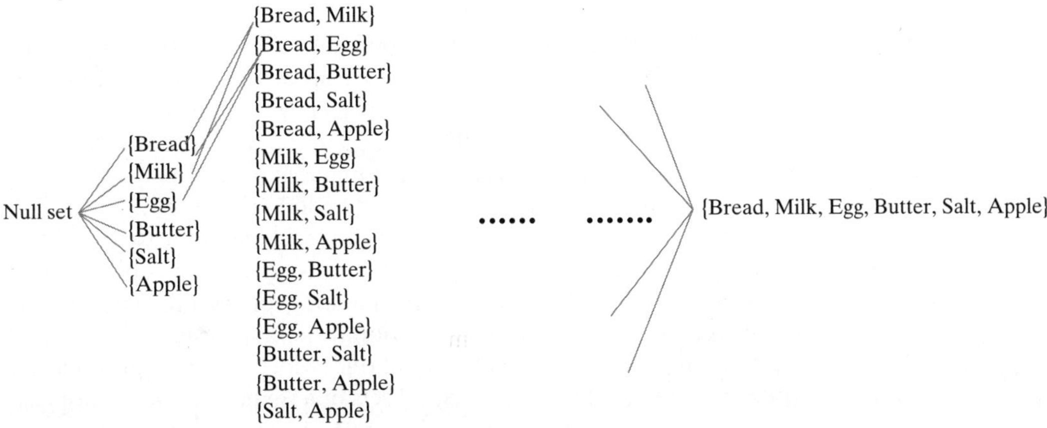

FIG. 9.15
Sixty-four ways to create itemsets from 6 items

Without applying any filtering logic, the brute-force approach would involve cal-culating the support count for each itemset in Figure 9.16. Thus, by comparing each item in the generated itemset with the actual transactions mentioned in **Table 9.3**, we can determine the support count of the itemset. For example, if {Bread, Milk} is present in any transactions in **Table 9.3**, then its support count will be incremented by 1. As we can understand, this is a very computation heavy activity, and as discussed earlier, many of the computations may get wasted at a later point of time because some itemsets will be found to be infrequent in the transactions. To get an idea of the total computations to be done, the number of comparisons to be done is $T \times N \times L$, where T is the number of transactions (6 in our case), N is the number of candidate itemsets (64 in our case), and L is the maximum transaction width (6 in our case).

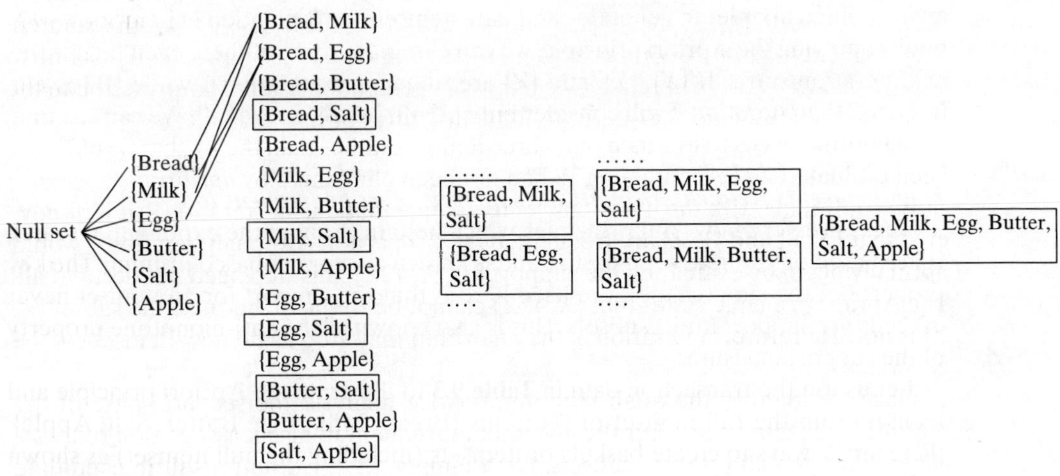

FIG. 9.16
Discarding the itemsets consisting of Salt

Let us apply the Apriori principle on this data set to reduce the number of candidate itemsets (N). We could identify from the transaction **Table 9.3** that Salt is an infrequent item. So, by applying the Apriori principle, we can say that all the itemsets which are superset of Salt will be infrequent and thus can be discarded from comparison to discover the association rule as shown in Figure 9.16.

This approach reduces the computation effort for a good number of itemsets and will make our search process more efficient. Thus, in each such iteration, we can determine the support count of each itemset, and on the basis of the min support value fixed for our analysis, any itemset in the hierarchy that does not meet the min support criteria can be discarded to make the rule generation faster and easier.

To generalize the example in order to build a set of rules with the Apriori principle, we will use the Apriori principle that states that all subsets of a frequent itemset must also be frequent. In other words, if $\{X, Y\}$ is frequent, then both $\{X\}$ and $\{Y\}$ must be frequent. Also by definition, the support metric indicates how frequently an itemset appears in the data. Thus, if we know that $\{X\}$ does not meet a desired support threshold, there is no reason to consider $\{X, Y\}$ or any itemset containing $\{X\}$; it cannot possibly be frequent.

This logic of the Apriori algorithm excludes potential association rules prior to actually evaluating them. The actual process of creating rules involves two phases:

- Identifying all itemsets that meet a minimum support threshold set for the analysis
- Creating rules from these itemsets that meet a minimum confidence threshold which identifies the strong rules

The first phase involves multiple iterations where each successive iteration requires evaluating the support of storing a set of increasingly large itemsets. For instance, iteration 1 evaluates the set of one-item itemsets (one-itemsets), iteration 2 involves evaluating the two-itemsets, etc.. The result of each iteration N is a set of all N-itemsets that meet the minimum support threshold. Normally, all the itemsets from iteration N are combined in order to generate candidate itemsets for evaluation in iteration $N + 1$, but by applying the Apriori principle, we can eliminate some of them even before the next iteration starts. If $\{X\}$, $\{Y\}$, and $\{Z\}$ are frequent in iteration 1 while $\{W\}$ is not frequent, then iteration 2 will consider only $\{X, Y\}$, $\{X, Z\}$, and $\{Y, Z\}$. We can see that the algorithm needs to evaluate only three itemsets rather than the six that would have been evaluated if sets containing W had not been eliminated by *apriori*.

By continuing with the iterations, let us assume that during iteration 2, it is discovered that $\{X, Y\}$ and $\{Y, Z\}$ are frequent, but $\{X, Z\}$ is not. Although iteration 3 would normally begin by evaluating the support for $\{X, Y, Z\}$, this step need not occur at all. The Apriori principle states that $\{X, Y, Z\}$ cannot be frequent, because the subset $\{X, Z\}$ is not. Therefore, in iteration 3, the algorithm may stop as no new itemset can be generated.

Once we identify the qualifying itemsets for analysis, the second phase of the Apriori algorithm begins. For the given set of frequent itemsets, association rules are generated from all possible subsets. For example, $\{X, Y\}$ would result in candidate rules for $\{X\} \rightarrow \{Y\}$ and $\{Y\} \rightarrow \{X\}$. These rules are evaluated against a minimum confidence threshold, and any rule that does not meet the desired confidence level is eliminated, thus finally yielding the set of strong rules.

Though the Apriori principle is widely used in the market basket analysis and other applications of association rule help in the discovery of new relationship among objects, there are certain strengths and weaknesses we need to keep in mind before employing it over the target data set:

Strengths	Weaknesses
• Provides reasonable accuracy while working with very large amounts of transactional data • Discovers rules that are easy to understand • Provides valuable insight into the unexpected knowledge in data sets, which is a key aspect of learning	• Not very accurate in the case the data set is small as the smaller occurrences of itemsets may not be due to chance • Some effort is involved to separate the insight from the common sense • In the case of widespread presence of random patterns, the principle can draw spurious conclusions

9.6   SUMMARY

- Unsupervised learning is a machine learning concept where the unlabelled and unclassified information is analysed to discover hidden knowledge. The algorithm works on the data without any prior training, but they are constructed in such a way that they can identify patterns, groupings, sorting order, and numerous other interesting knowledge from the set of data.

- Clustering refers to a broad set of techniques for finding subgroups, or clusters, in a data set based on the characteristics of the objects within the data set itself in such a manner that the objects within the group are similar (or related to each other) but are different from (or unrelated to) the objects from the other groups.

- The major clustering techniques are classified in three board categories
  - ❖ Partitioning methods,
  - ❖ Hierarchical methods, and
  - ❖ Density-based methods.

- k-means and k-medoids are the most popular partitioning techniques.

- The principle of k-means algorithm is to assign each of the n data points to one of the k clusters, where k is a user-defined parameter as the number of clusters desired. The objective is to maximize the homogeneity within the clusters and to maximize the differences between the clusters. The homogeneity and differences are measured in terms of the distance between the points.

- k-medoids considers representative data points from the existing points in the data set as the centre of the clusters. It then assigns the data points according to their distance from these centres to form the clusters.

- The hierarchical clustering methods are used to group the data into hierarchy or tree-like structure.
- There are two main hierarchical clustering methods: agglomerative clustering and divisive clustering. Agglomerative clustering is a bottom-up technique which starts with individual objects as clusters and then iteratively merges them to form larger clusters. On the other hand, the divisive method starts with one cluster with all given objects and then splits it iteratively to form smaller clusters.
- DBSCAN is one of the density-based clustering approaches that provide a solution to identify clusters of arbitrary shapes. The principle is based on identifying the dense area and sparse area within the data set and then running the clustering algorithm.
- Association rule presents a methodology that is useful for identifying interesting relationships hidden in large data sets. It is also known as association analysis, and the discovered relationships can be represented in the form of association rules comprising a set of frequent items.
- A common application of this analysis is the Market Basket Analysis that retailers use for cross-selling of their products.

SAMPLE QUESTIONS

MULTIPLE-CHOICE QUESTIONS (1 MARK EACH)

1. k-means clustering algorithm is an example of which type of clustering method?
   (a) Hierarchical
   (b) Partitioning
   (c) Density based
   (d) Random

2. Which of the below statement describes the difference between agglomerative and divisive clustering techniques correctly?
   (a) Agglomerative is a bottom-up technique, but divisive is a top-down technique
   (b) Agglomerative is a top-down technique, but divisive is a bottom-up technique
   (c) Agglomerative technique can start with a single cluster
   (d) Divisive technique can end with a single cluster

3. Which of the below is an advantage of k-medoids algorithm over k-means algorithm?
   (a) both are equally error prone
   (b) k-medoids can handle larger data set than k-means
   (c) k-medoids helps in reducing the effect of the outliers in the objects
   (d) k-medoids needs less computation to arrive at the final clustering

4. The principle underlying the Market Basket Analysis is known as
   (a) Association rule
   (b) Bisecting rule
   (c) k-means
   (d) Bayes' theorem

5. A Voronoi diagram is used in which type of clustering?
  (a) Hierarchical
  (b) Partitioning
  (c) Density based
  (d) Intuition based

6. SSE of a clustering measures:
  (a) Initial number of set clusters
  (b) Number of clusters generated
  (c) Cost of clustering
  (d) Quality of clustering

7. One of the disadvantages of k-means algorithm is that the outliers may reduce the quality of the final clustering.
  (a) True
  (b) False

8. Which of the following can be possible termination conditions in K-Means?
  (a) For a fixed number of iterations.
  (b) Assignment of observations to clusters does not change between iterations. Except for cases with a bad local minimum.
  (c) Centroids do not change between successive iterations.
  (d) All of the above

9. Which of the following clustering algorithm is most sensitive to outliers?
  (a) K-means clustering algorithm
  (b) K-medians clustering algorithm
  (c) K-medoids clustering algorithm
  (d) K-modes clustering algorithm

10. In which of the following situations the K-Means clustering fails to give good results?
  (a) Data points with outliers
  (b) Data points with different densities
  (c) Data points with round shapes
  (d) All of the above

SHORT-ANSWER TYPE QUESTIONS (5 MARKS EACH)

1. How unsupervised learning is different from supervised learning? Explain with some examples.

2. Mention few application areas of unsupervised learning.

3. What are the broad three categories of clustering techniques? Explain the characteristics of each briefly.

4. Describe how the quality of clustering is measured in the k-means algorithm?

5. Describe the main difference in the approach of k-means and k-medoids algorithms with a neat diagram.

6. What is a dendrogram? Explain its use.

7. What is SSE? What is its use in the context of the k-means algorithm?

8. Explain the k-means method with a step-by-step algorithm.

9. Describe the concept of single link and complete link in the context of hierarchical clustering.

10. How apriori principle helps in reducing the calculation overhead for a market basket analysis? Provide an example to explain.

LONG-ANSWER TYPE QUESTIONS (10 MARKS EACH)

1. You are given a set of one-dimensional data points: $\{5, 10, 15, 20, 25, 30, 35\}$. Assume that $k = 2$ and first set of random centroid is selected as $\{15, 32\}$ and then it is refined with $\{12, 30\}$.
   (a) Create two clusters with each set of centroid mentioned above following the k-means approach
   (b) Calculate the SSE for each set of centroid

2. Explain how the Market Basket Analysis uses the concepts of association analysis.

3. Explain the Apriori algorithm for association rule learning with an example.

4. How the distance between clusters is measured in hierarchical clustering? Explain the use of this measure in making decision on when to stop the iteration.

5. How to recompute the cluster centroids in the k-means algorithm?

6. Discuss one technique to choose the appropriate number of clusters at the beginning of clustering exercise.

7. Discuss the strengths and weaknesses of the k-means algorithm.

8. Explain the concept of clustering with a neat diagram.

9. During a research work, you found 7 observations as described with the data points below. You want to create 3 clusters from these observations using K-means algorithm. After first iteration, the clusters C1, C2, C3 has following observations:

   C1: $\{(2,2), (4,4), (6,6)\}$

   C2: $\{(0,4), (4,0)\}$

   C3: $\{(5,5), (9,9)\}$

   If you want to run a second iteration then what will be the cluster centroids? What will be the SSE of this clustering?

10. In a software project, the team is trying to identify the similarity of software defects identified during testing. They wanted to create 5 clusters of similar defects based on the text analytics of the defect descriptions. Once the 5 clusters of defects are identified, any new defect created is to be classified as one of the types identified through clustering. Explain this approach through a neat diagram. Assume 20 Defect data points which are clustered among 5 clusters and k-means algorithm was used.

Chapter 10
Reinforcement Learning

OBJECTIVE OF THE CHAPTER:

We discussed Supervised and Unsupervised learning in earlier chapters. The third type of learning is Reinforcement Learning (RL) where an AI agent learns from the consequences of its actions to perform a set of tasks within an environment. The popularity of RL is increasing rapidly within the AI community because of its usefulness in advanced AI applications like autonomous robots, self-driving cars, gaming, self-learning chatbots, and many more. The objective of this chapter is to provide an understanding of how RL works, its implementation, and its applications in modern industries.

10.1   INTRODUCTION

In previous chapters, we have discussed Supervised and Unsupervised learning in detail. In supervised learning, the agent is trained with labeled data. The labels are the correct actions a knowledgeable external supervisor identifies based on the training data that describes the situation. The objective is that the system will generalize or extrapolate the learning from these training data, and create a generalized ruleset so that the system can act correctly in situations outside the training data. However, the robustness of the rule is still dependent on the richness of the training data and the agent can't explore new actions outside the rule set. We can easily understand that in a highly interactive environment (for example a self-driven car), it is not practical to identify examples of all the possible situations and train the agent on how to act in those situations. It is expected that the agent will explore and learn from its own experience. Reinforcement Learning addresses this area. As we have seen earlier, unsupervised learning also does not depend on labeled data, but its goal is very different - identifying the hidden pattern within the data.

 10.2   WHAT IS REINFORCEMENT LEARNING (RL)?

Throughout our lives, the most significant portion of learning happens through interacting with our environment and gaining knowledge about the consequences of our actions in this environment. When we have a clear goal in mind, from these consequences or feedback, we can identify what is a right or a wrong action for a situation. For example, while conversing with someone, we constantly watch how our environment is responding and try to influence it to achieve our goal.

The computational approach to learning from interactions with the environment and analyzing the response to generate maximum reward (positive outcome) is the basis for Reinforcement Learning.

Reinforcement learning is a type of machine learning paradigm where the learner learns to map the actions to a situation and the goal is to maximize a numerical *reward* value. There is no expert to guide the learner on the right action (through labeled data), but it must discover which actions yield maximum reward value through *trial and error*. An interesting factor that impacts the learning path in RL is that the agent's current action may not only impact the immediate reward but may also impact the next action and as a result *all subsequent rewards*. These are very powerful learning concepts and mimic animal learning very closely. So, two key features behind all reinforcement learning algorithms are - **trial-and-error** and **delayed rewards or total cumulative rewards.**

The trial-and-error concept is closely related to the idea of *exploration* and *exploitation*. When the agent takes the known steps that have proven to be successful in yielding high reward values, then it is told to be *exploiting* the knowledge. On the other hand, when the agent tries out unknown paths and by doing that identifies the new ways to achieve higher rewards, it is termed as *exploration*. It is evident that without exploration the agent can't gain experience or have a probability to improve from the current max reward. But to do so, it may go through multiple failure paths. The balancing act between exploitation and exploration actions is one of the intensively studied areas of mathematics.

Points to Ponder:

- As there is no labeled data to train the agent, some may argue that reinforcement learning is a type of unsupervised learning, but there are significant differences. The reinforcement learning agent can benefit from learning the pattern in the data, but the agent's objective is not fulfilled by only that. It aims to maximize the reward signal within the environment.

In the subsequent chapters, we will discuss all these concepts in detail.

10.3   ELEMENTS OF REINFORCEMENT LEARNING

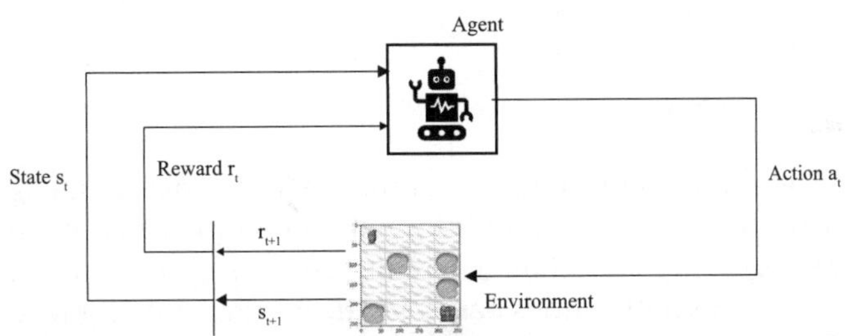

FIG. 10.1
Agent-Environment Interaction

 ## 10.3.1   Agent

An agent in the RL domain is the one who makes decisions on what action to take in an environment and in a particular state. It is the learner in RL. In the real world, it can be compared with the abstract decision-making unit like the CPU of a robot which makes the decision based on all the input from the robot's environment and applies the rules to take the best action for the situation.

10.3.2 Environment

Everything that the agent interacts with is called an environment. The environment can comprise anything that is outside the agent. In RL it can be demonstrated by the problem to be solved. Based on the properties of the environment, it can be classified as –

- *Deterministic vs. Stochastic environments* – an environment is called deterministic if the outcome is known based on the current state and action. For example, in a chess game, it is clear what will be the new state if a piece is moved. So, it is a deterministic environment. But if the outcome is not certain and only a probability of the possible outcomes can be estimated, then the environment is called a stochastic environment. For example, it is not certain what will be the outcome if a dice is rolled.

- *Fully observable vs. Partially observable environment* – when the state of the system is visible to the agent at all times, then it is called a fully observable environment. For example, in chess, the players can see the position of all the pieces on the board and thus it is a fully observable environment. But if the agent can't determine the state of the whole system all the time, then it is a partially observable environment.

For example, in a game of poker, the players can't see the cards in other players' hands.

- *Discrete vs. Continuous environments* – within an environment, if only a finite set of actions is possible for moving from one state to another, then it is called a discrete environment. For example, the number of possible actions is limited in chess. On the other hand, if the set of actions available is infinite, then it is called a continuous environment. For example, there can be infinite possible routes for traveling from one place to another.

10.3.3 State

The state is the representation of the environment that an agent is in a specific time step. It is defined as a set of information that the agent has at a given point in time. The state is very important in a reinforcement learning context as the agent needs to plan its next set of actions based on the current situation, the reward it can get from the environment, and the goal.

10.3.4 Policy

Policy is a strategy that the agent uses to achieve the goal. So, a policy defines the mapping from the perceived states of the environment to actions to be taken when in those states. Policy is a core component of reinforcement learning as it alone can drive the action of the agent. It can be deterministic, meaning that the environment state combination can provide the action information or it can be stochastic, meaning that the combination will return only the probabilities of different actions. In its simplest form, a policy π is a function that takes a state s as input and returns an action a. That is:

$$\pi(s) \to a$$

In this way, a policy is typically used by the agent to decide what action 'a' should be executed when it is in a given state 's'.

If the policy is stochastic instead of deterministic, then instead of returning a unique action 'a', the policy returns a probability distribution over a set of actions.

$$\pi(s) \to p(a)$$

For a policy-based reinforcement learning algorithm, the aim is to learn an optimal policy that achieves a specific goal.

10.3.5 Reward

After each action step, the environment sends a single number to the agent, which is termed a reward. These rewards define the goal of the reinforcement learning program because reinforcement learning algorithms have the goal of maximizing the rewards that can be accumulated by the agent over the long run. The effect of an action can be positive or negative, which is equivalent to reward and punishment in the real world. Through multiple trial-and-error the agent must learn to accumulate as much reward as possible and to do so it may have to alter the policy. Thus, reward becomes the key factor while creating or fine-tuning a policy. For example, if an action by a policy yields a low reward, then the agent may choose to take a different action in a similar situation in the future.

If we take these entities together, then the agent and environment interact at a sequence of discrete time steps, t = 0, 1, 2, 3… At each time step t, the agent receives some information of the environment's state, s_t -> S, where S is the set of possible states, and on that basis selects an action, at -> $A(s_t)$, where $A(s_t)$ is the set of actions available in that state. As a result of the action, it will receive a reward rt and keep on accumulating the rewards for all state-action pairs. After one time step, as a consequence of its action, the agent moves to a new state, s_{t+1}. Refer to Figure 10.1 to see the agent-environment interaction.

10.3.6 Value function

A value function defines long-term gain while reward defines immediate gain. When an agent takes an action in the current state, it can expect a certain reward. The action also affects the subsequent state's actions. The sum of all the rewards that can be accumulated by the agent starting from the current state to all the probable future states is termed as the value of the current state. In the real world, we can bring an analogy of pleasure or pain to reward, which is immediate effect, and long-term happiness or sadness to value function which is the accumulation of continuous pleasure or pain over a timeline. While it is a relatively straightforward task to calculate the immediate reward as it is given back by the environment directly, optimization of the value function is a complex problem to solve. For example, a particular step action may yield low immediate reward, but because its subsequent steps are yielding high rewards, the total accumulated reward over all probable future actions - the value of the step can be actually high, or vice versa. The value must be estimated and re-estimated over the entire lifespan of the agent based on the sequence of actions that the agent makes. While discussing different reinforcement learning algorithms, we will note that a key consideration of those algorithms is how to maximize the value function most efficiently.

10.3.7 Model

A model is a replica of the environment that imitates the behavior of the environment. This helps in deriving inferences about future courses of action based on prior knowledge about how the environment will behave in such a situation. So, an agent can identify the reward of a state and that of all probable future states without actually experiencing those situations. Models are well suited for planning as the future course of action can be decided based on the knowledge gained from the model of the environment. The technique of solving reinforcement learning problems using models is called the *model-based* approach and the main aim of the agent is to explore the environment to learn the model. On the other hand, the techniques that depend on exploration and exploitation of the environment to gather knowledge about it and identify the maximum value or optimal policy is termed a *model-free* approach.

10.3.8 Introduction to the Farama Foundation's 'The Frozen Lake' RL Environment

Let us take a famous gaming problem of *The Frozen Lake*. This game involves crossing a frozen lake by walking over it to reach the goal without falling into one of the holes. Refer to Figure 10.2. The lake is divided into a 4x4 grid world. The game starts with the agent placed at the location [1,1] and the goal is located at the far end of [4,4]. Holes are located at [2,2], [4,2], [4,3] and [1,4] locations. The player makes moves until it reaches the goal or it falls into a hole.

There are 4 different discrete actions possible in the action space – 0. Move Up, 1. Move Down, 2. Move Left, 3. Move Right.

The observation space has 16 discrete numbers. It is defined as the player's current position as (current_row - 1) * no_of_rows + (current_colum – 1). For example, the position of the goal is represented by 3 * 4 + 3 = 15.

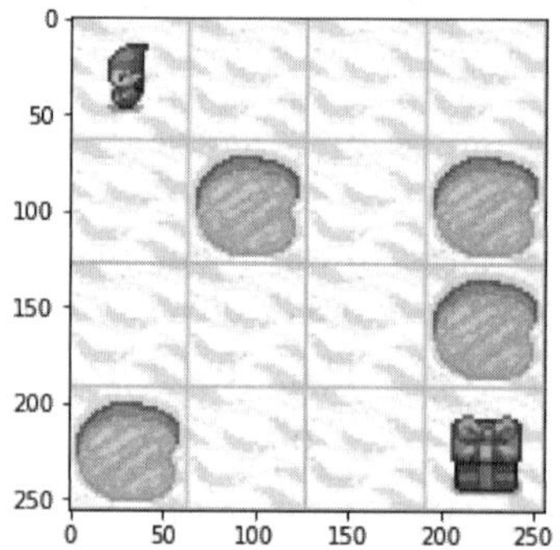

FIG. 10.2

The Frozen Lake Environment

More documentation about this environment can be found at https://gymnasium.farama.org/environments/toy_text/frozen_lake/

In Figure 10.3 different components of the Frozen Lake problem are explained.

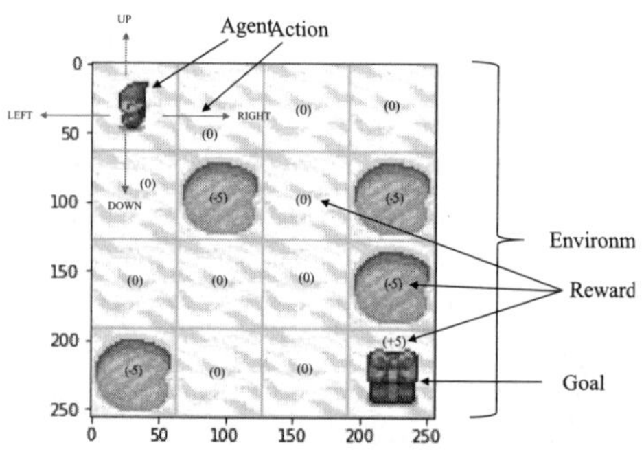

FIG. 10.3

Different elements of RL in The Frozen Lake environment

The **state** of the agent corresponds to its location on the lake grid, in this case, $s_t = (x, y)$ and $s_1 = (1, 1)$.

The **action** space, in this example, consists of four possible behaviors: move up, move down, move left, and move right.

The probability matrix P contains all pairwise combinations of states (s, s') for all actions in A. It's Bernoulli-distributed, and looks like this:

$$P_{down}((1,1),(1,2)) = 1; P_{down}((1,1),(1,3)) = 0;....; P_{right}((3,4),(4,4)) = 1$$

We can define the **reward function** R as (this is different than how Gymnasium defined it) –

- If it's in an empty cell, the agent receives a reward of 0, which means it is not earning an immediate reward so that it can look for accumulating rewards in the future
- If the agent is in a cell with a hole, it then receives a reward of – 5, which acts like a punishment and the expectation is that the agent will avoid this action in the future after learning
- If the agent successfully reaches the goal cell: (4, 4) then it will earn a reward of +5
- The simulation runs for an arbitrary finite number of time steps but terminates early if the agent reaches a hole or the final goal cell.

Let's consider two policies π_1 and π_2. We can indicate a policy as a sequence of actions starting from the state of the agent at (1,1):

- π_1: down -> down -> down: Hole
- π_2: right -> right -> down -> down -> down -> right: Goal achieved

By computing the value function, we get:

- $R(\pi_1)$: 0 + 0 -5 = -5
- $R(\pi_2)$: 0 + 0 + 0 + 0 + 0 + 5 = +5

The evaluation of the policies suggests that the value is maximized with $\pi2$, which the agent chooses as its policy for this task. Refer to Figure 10.4

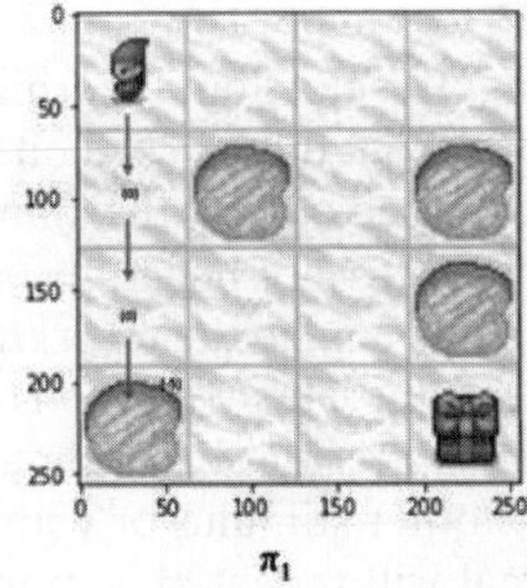

π_1

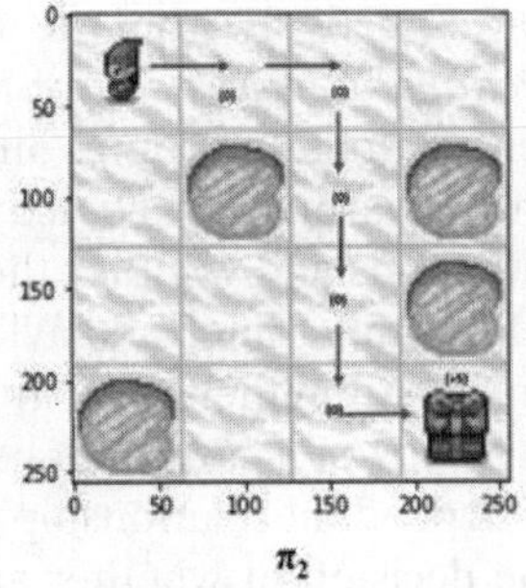

π_2

FIG. 10.4
Action – Policy – Reward concept

There are three distinct approaches to implementing RL algorithms which we can understand based on the discussion about value, policy, and model:

1. Value-based:

   In the value-based approach, the objective of the agent is to find the optimal value function, which can maximize the value at a state under any policy. So, the agent looks for long-term returns at any state(s) under the policy π. The idea is that an optimal value function leads to optimal policy. By minimizing the loss between the predicted and the target value, the approximate true action-value function is arrived at and we get the policy directly from the value function.

2. Policy-based:

   The second approach is to find the optimal policy for the maximum future rewards without using the value function. Here the policy is parameterized and the objective is to maximize the performance of that policy so that the action performed in each step helps to maximize the future reward.

   The policy-based approach uses two types of policies:

   ❖ Deterministic policy: the policy (π) outputs the same action (A) at any state.
   ❖ Stochastic policy: instead of a particular action, the policy outputs the probability distribution of the actions.

3. Model-based:

   A model-based approach is the third type, where a virtual model is created for the environment. The objective of the agent is to explore the environment to learn the model.

10.4 REINFORCEMENT LEARNING PRINCIPLES

Research around learning, especially on how to reinforce learning is not new. More than 100 years back in 1911, Edward Thorndike introduced the concept of the "Law of Effect". In his paper, he described that an animal will repeat an action if the action produces satisfaction and will avoid an action if it causes discomfort. Moreover, the degree of pursuance or deterrence is directly proportional to the level of pleasure or pain respectively from the action. The Law of Effect also combined the concepts of *selectional* and *associative* learning. In selectional learning, the animal tries out different options and routes and selects from them based on the outcome of each. In associative learning, the choice is made based on how the animal associates its options with situations and whether those are positive or negative.

On this similar line, Ian Pavlov formally coined the term *"reinforcement"* in 1927 in the context strengthening of animal learning. He mentioned that reinforcement is the strengthening of a pattern of behavior as a result of an animal receiving a stimulus in a time-dependent relationship with another stimulus or with a response. This means that the decision of whether an animal will repeat an action in the future or not is affected by the reaction they have received shortly after they have taken the action. These concepts built the fundamentals *of trial-and-error* learning.

The idea of implementing the concepts in computer programming came out in 1948 when Alan Turing described in his report the design of a 'pleasure-pain system' that worked along the lines of the Law of Effect.

"When a configuration is reached for which, the action is undetermined, a random choice for the missing data is made and the appropriate entry is made in the description, tentatively, and is applied. When a pain stimulus occurs, all tentative entries are canceled, and when a pleasure stimulus occurs, they are all made permanent." - Turing, 1948

A second line of research that was going on at that time was related to "optimal control" and its solutions using value functions and dynamic programming. The idea was to design a controller that can maximize or minimize the measure of a dynamic system's behavior over time. Richard Bellman proposed an approach in the mid-1950s in which he suggested that a functional equation can be formulated using the dynamic system's state and a value function – "optimal return function" and the equation is known as the *Bellman equation*. Dynamic programming is the category of methods that solve optimal control problems by solving this equation. Bellman also proposed a discrete stochastic version of the optimal control problem, known as *Markov Decision Processes* (*MDPs*). Though dynamic programming and MDPs were not related to any learning problem at that time, these became an essential part of solving RL problems as they provided a way to gradually reach correct answers through successive approximations, which was closely related to any learning problem.

A third, though less distinctive line of research that contributed to the development of modern reinforcement learning was temporal-difference learning. In 1959 Arthur Samuel proposed the implementation of a learning method that included *temporal-difference* ideas. The principle works based on the differences between temporally successive estimates of the same quantity, for example, the probability of achieving a total reward over a continuous time state. Arthur Samuel's famous checkers-playing program proved the efficacy of this learning method.

All these streams of research started coming together in 1989 when Chris Watkins developed the Q-learning model by bringing temporal difference and optimal control streams. We will discuss in this chapter how different modern RL algorithms implemented and fine-tuned these basic principles to achieve remarkable success in the RL domain.

1. Markov Property

In section 10.3 we discussed different elements of RL – like the state, action, reward, and policy. Let's see how to formulate any RL problem mathematically using those elements.

An RL problem is said to have *Markov property* if the future state depends only on the present and not on the past. This is named after the Russian mathematician Andrey Markov. Mathematically this can be represented as -

$$P\left[S_{t+1} \mid S_t\right] = P\left[S_{t+1} \mid S_1, S_2, \ldots, S_t\right]$$

where S_t denotes the current state of the agent and S_{t+1} denotes the next state.

As we can see in the LHS of the equation, the transition from state S_t to S_{t+1} is entirely independent of the past and thus the RHS of the equation which has all the history from states S_1 to S_t gets captured within the current state S_t, if the process has Markov property.

Let's remember the definition of *Transition Probability* in this context. It is the probability that the agent will move from one state to another state. Drawing the similarity to moving from Markov State S_t to S_{t+1} i.e. from the current state to any other successor state, the state transition probability and the transition matrix are given by

$$P_{ss'} = P[S_{t+1} = s' \mid S_t = s] = \begin{bmatrix} p_{11} & p_{12} & \cdots & p_{1n} \\ p_{21} & p_{22} & \cdots & p_{2n} \\ \cdots & \cdots & \cdots & \cdots \\ p_{n1} & p_{n2} & \cdots & p_{nn} \end{bmatrix} \text{"To State"}$$

$$\text{"From State"}$$

Here p_{12} represents the state transition probability of moving from state S_1 to state S_2 and so on. It should be noted that the sum of probabilities along the rows is always 1. This means that if we add up the probabilities of moving from one current state to multiple other future states, then the sum of such probabilities always needs to be 1. So,

$$p_{11} + p_{12} + p_{13} + \ldots + p_{1n} = 1$$

2. Markov Process or Markov Chain

Now that we discussed state transition probability, let's understand how random processes are mathematically represented as Markov Chains or Markov Processes. A random process is a sequence of random states $(S_1, S_2 .. S_n)$ that demonstrate Markov property. Thus, the environment can be represented using the states (S) and state transition probability matrix ($P_{ss'}$). In a discrete environment, it is called a Markov chain and in a continuous environment, it is termed a Markov process. Refer to Figure 10.5. In this example, we have 3 fully observable states A, B, and C. The probability of transitioning from one state to another or staying in the same state is provided above the arrows.

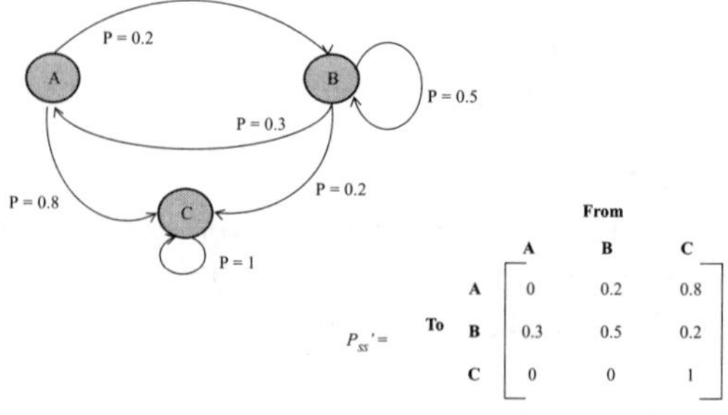

$$P_{ss'} = \begin{array}{c|ccc} & A & B & C \\ \hline A & 0 & 0.2 & 0.8 \\ B & 0.3 & 0.5 & 0.2 \\ C & 0 & 0 & 1 \end{array}$$

FIG. 10.5
Markov chain and process

We can create several random sets of states by sequencing the states like, A – B – C - C, A – B - B – C, and so on. The probability of being in a state S_{t+m} at a time step t + m starting from state St is mathematically represented as,

$p_{t+n} = p_t P_{ss'}^n$, where n is the number of steps between S_t and $S_{t + m}$.

When n -> ∞ (steady state), then the above equation can be generalized as,

$$p = pP_{ss'}$$

We can get an insight into which state of the Markov chain is visited in the long run by solving this equation. This is called the Chapman-Kolmogorov equation.

3. Markov Reward Process

Let's add the concept of reward as a result of moving from one state to another. A reward function evaluates how useful it is to transition from one state to another. This will guide the agent to choose which transition is good and which is not. Before we get into the Markov Reward Process (MRP), we should understand the terms – reward, return, and discount factor well.

Rewards are the numerical values an agent receives based on the action taken while being in a state in the environment. The reward can be positive or negative based on the action taken by the agent.

Return is the cumulative reward that the agent receives from the environment while completing a sequence of state transitions, called episodes. In RL the goal is to maximize the cumulative reward or return, rather than the reward an agent receives from the current state. So,

Return = $G_t = R_{t+1} + R_{t+2} + \ldots + R_T$, where R_{t+1} is the reward received at time step t = 0, to R_T which is the reward received at the final time step T

Points to Ponder:

- Episodic Task – these tasks have a terminal or end state and contain a finite set of states. For example, in the frozen lake environment, the agent starts from the initial state, moves along the path and the game ends either if the agent falls into the pond or reaches the destination. Once the game is restarted, the agent will start from the initial state. So, every episode is independent.
- Continuous Task – the tasks that do not have a terminal state and thus never end are called continuous tasks. For example, learning a language is a continuous task. Calculating the returns of continuous tasks is tricky as they have an infinite set of states.

■

Discount factor (γ) is the value that determines how much importance is given to the current and future rewards. The return equation using the discount factor becomes

$$G_t = R_{t+1} + \gamma R_{t+2} + \gamma^2 R_{t+3} \ldots = \sum_{\infty}^{n=0} \gamma^n R_{t+n+1}$$

$$= R_{t+1} + \gamma \left(R_{t+2} + \gamma^2 R_{t+3} \ldots \right)$$

$$= R_{t+1} + \gamma G_{t+1} \tag{10.1}$$

So, if we define $G_T = 0$, or the return from the terminal step as zero, then this recursive equation works for all $t < T$.

The discount factor has a value between 0 and 1. So, if we choose a value closer to zero, then the future rewards get less significance, as the factor γ^n reduces the future values drastically. On the other hand, if we keep its value closer to 1, then all the future rewards will matter for calculating the return. Balancing the discount factor value is an important task in RL problems. So, there are two important aspects handled by γ –

- It handles the uncertainty of the future, as immediate rewards are valued more than the future rewards

- It helps to avoid infinite returns problem in continuous tasks as γ^n becomes very small as the value of n increases

In our earlier Markov process, we considered only the state transition and its probability. When a reward function is added on the Markov process then it represents a finite Markov Reward Process. The finite MRP can be represented by a tuple of $(S, P_{ss'}, R, \gamma)$,

Where   S = finite set of states

$P_{ss'}$ = state transition probability

R = reward function $R_{ss'} = E\ [R_{t+1} \mid S_t = s, S_{t+1} = s']$, the expectation of the reward that the agent will get for moving from states s to s' in time t to t+1

γ = discount factor $0 \le \gamma \le 1$

in our earlier Figure 10.5 if we add rewards then the diagram will look like Figure 10.6

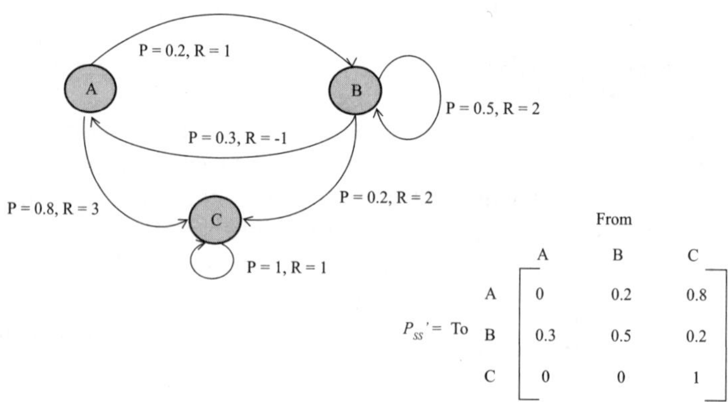

$$P_{ss}' = \text{To} \quad \begin{array}{c|ccc} & A & B & C \\ A & 0 & 0.2 & 0.8 \\ B & 0.3 & 0.5 & 0.2 \\ C & 0 & 0 & 1 \end{array}$$

FIG. 10.6

Markov reward process

From the definition of the *expected value* of a random variable, which is the value of the variable multiplied by its probability, we get the expected value of transitioning from state A, $\mathbb{E}[R^A]$ as $\Sigma r\ p(r)$, the value of reward associated with the state change multiplied by the transition probability of the state change. In our example in Figure

10.6, state A can change to state B or state C with rewards and probabilities $(1, 0.2)$ and $(3, 0.8)$ respectively. So,

$$\mathbb{E}[R^A] = 1 \times 0.2 + 3 \times 0.8 = 2.6.$$

This is the foundation for the value function and Markov Decision Process.

4. Bellman Equation for Value Function

The value function of a state determines how good it is for an agent to be in a particular state. The agent must take some action to find out the value or goodness of a particular state and thus the concept of policy comes into play here. As we discussed previously, a policy defines what actions to be taken in a particular state, s. So, the *state-value function* for policy π can be defined as,

$$v_\pi(s) = \mathbb{E}_\pi \left[G_t \mid S_t = s \right] = \mathbb{E}_\pi \left[\sum_{\infty}^{n=0} \gamma^n R_{t+n+1} \mid S_t = s \right], \text{ for all } s \in S \qquad (10.2)$$

where, $v_\pi(s)$ or value of the state, s under the *policy* is the expected return the agent can get starting from state, s to subsequent states, following a policy till the terminal state. *The value of the terminal state is defined to be zero.*

Similarly, the *state-action-value function* for policy π can be defined as,

$$q_\pi(s,a) = \mathbb{E}_\pi \left[G_t \mid S_t = s, A_t = a \right] = \mathbb{E}_\pi \left[\sum_{n=0}^{\infty} \gamma^n R_{t+n+1} \mid S_t = s, A_t = a \right] \qquad (10.3)$$

where $q_\pi(s,a)$ is the value of taking action a, in state, s under a policy π and is defined as the expected return starting from s, taking action a and following the policy π thereafter.

Based on Figure 10.6, if we take an episode with starting state A and terminal state C and which stays in state B in-between like, A – B – B – C, then the expected return with a discount factor of 0.5 is:

$$G_t = 1 + 2 * 0.5 + 2 * (0.5)^2 = 2.5$$

So, the value of State A is 2.5 for following the policy A – B – B – C.

Bellman's equation helps in finding out the optimal policies and value functions to maximize the return. But the complexity is that the reward is not a deterministic variable, but it is a random variable and thus return Gt also becomes a random variable. So, we can't maximize Gt directly, but we must maximize the expected returns, which we expressed in equations (10.2) and (10.3). From the above example, we can understand that the policy will change with experience and thus the value function will also change for different policies. Bellman equation aims to identify the optimal value function that can maximize the value compared to all other value functions.

Did you know?

- The Bellman equation is named after Dr. Richard Bellman who is called the Father of Dynamic Programming. In his paper "Theory of Dynamic Programming" in 1954, he explained with examples the principles of dynamic programming to solve RL problems. In very simple terms, dynamic programming algorithms try to solve complex problems by breaking those down into simple sub-problems and solving the sub-problems recursively, meaning with functions that call themselves.

Also, recall from our discussion in section 10.3 that a Policy π (a|s) is the probability of selecting an action, a if we are in state, s at time, t.

$$\pi(a|s)= Probability\ (A_t = a,\ S_t = s)$$

The fundamental property that is used for RL and dynamic programming is that they satisfy the recursive property, similar to what we have already established for the return (equation 10.1). So, equations (10.2) and (10.3) satisfy the below relationship between the value of state, s and its successor states, s'

$$v_\pi(s) = \mathbb{E}_\pi\left[G_t \mid S_t = s\right]$$

$$= \mathbb{E}_\pi\left[R_{t+1} + \gamma G_{t+1} \mid S_t = s\right] \tag{10.4}$$

$$= \sum_a \pi(a\mid s)\sum_{s'}\sum_r p(s',r\mid s,a)\left[r+\gamma\mathbb{E}_\pi\left[G_{t+1}\mid S_{t+1} = s'\right]\right]$$

$$= \sum_a \pi(a\mid s)\sum_{s',r}p(s',r\mid s,a)\left[r+\gamma v_\pi(s')\right] \text{ for all } s \in S \tag{10.5}$$

It is important to note that the value function of the current state, s is now related to the value function of the successor state, s', which enables us to iteratively compute the value function. This equation is called *Bellman equation for the state value function* and is one of the most important equations in RL. Similarly, the state-action function can be expressed as the recursive function with its successor state-action pair. In the next sections, we will discuss the approaches to solving this equation to identify the optimal value function.

A finite Markov Decision Process (MDP) is a mathematical model where the agent makes some decision or takes action based on its current state following a policy. It is a tuple of (S, A, Pss', R(s|a), γ) where:

- S is a set of states,
- A is the set of actions the agent can take,
- $P_{ss'}$ is the transition probability matrix,
- R(s|a) is the reward function,
- γ is the discount factor.

MDPs are a classical formalization of sequential decision-making problems where actions not only influence the immediate reward, but also the successor states and through those the future rewards. *The goal of RL is to find an optimal policy that will achieve a high value of cumulative reward over the long run.* Keeping this goal in mind, a policy π is considered better than or equal to policy π' if its return is better than or equal to that of π' for all states. Mathematically,

$$\pi \geq \pi' \text{ if and only if } v_\pi(s) \geq v_{\pi'}(s) \text{ for all } s \in S$$

So, there is always at least one policy that is better than or equal to all other policies, and this policy is called *optimal policy.* Optimal policy(s) are denoted by the following notation:

$$v_*(s) = max_\pi v_\pi(s),\ for\ all\ s \in S \tag{10.6}$$

Optimal policies share the same optimal action-value function, denoted as below:

$$q_*(s,a) = max_\pi q_\pi(s,a),\ for\ all\ s \in S \tag{10.7}$$

Here, for the state-action pair (s, a), this function gives the expected return by taking action, a in state, s, and then following the optimal policy. So, q_* can be written in terms of v_* as:

$$q_*(s,a) = \mathbb{E}\left[R_{t+1} + \gamma v_*\left(S_{t+1}\right) \mid S_t = s, A_t = a\right] \tag{10.8}$$

In equation (10.6), v_* is the optimal value function and thus it should satisfy the consistency condition that we discussed in Bellman's equation for state-value in equation (10.4). But as this is optimal value function, its consistency condition can be written without reference to any specific policy. This is the *Bellman optimality equation for v_**. Thus, we can deduce that the value of a state under an optimal policy must be equal to the expected return for the best action from that state:

$$v_*(s) = max_{a \in A(s)} \, q_{\pi*}(s,a)$$
$$= max_a \, \mathbb{E}_{\pi*}\left[G_t \mid S_t = s, A_t = a\right]$$
$$= max_a \, \mathbb{E}_{\pi*}\left[R_{t+1} + \gamma v_*\left(S_{t+1}\right) \mid S_t = s, A_t = a\right]$$
$$= max_a \, \Sigma_{s',r} \, p(s',r \mid s,a)\left[r + \gamma v_*\left(s'\right)\right] \tag{10.9}$$

Similar to equation (10.9), which is the Bellman Optimality equation for v_*, we can deduce the *Bellman Optimality equation for q_** as,

$$q_*(s) = \mathbb{E}\left[R_{t+1} + \gamma \, max_{a'} \, q_*\left(S_{t+1}, a'\right) \mid S_t = s, A_t = a\right]$$
$$= \Sigma_{s',r} \, p(s',r \mid s,a)\left[r + \gamma \, max_{a'} q_*\left(s' \, a'\right)\right] \tag{10.10}$$

Now that we have understood how the Bellman equation works, we can try to find out the value functions for the Frozen Lake environment with the parameters set in section 10.3.8. We will represent the environment as a grid world and the notations used are as below:

<Cell number>

<immediate reward>

<Value function>

To calculate the value function of a state (cell here), we need the immediate reward of the state, s, and the value function of the next state, s'. We will use the simplified optimality function for state-value:

$$V(s) = max\left[\, R(s) + \gamma V(s')\right]$$

Iteration 1:

Let's assume $\gamma = 0.9$ for our case. We will start with the calculation of the value function from the state immediately before the Goal state as we know that $V_{16} = 0$, as this is a terminal state. One of the episodes is $S_1 - S_5 - S_9 - S_{10} - S_{14} - S_{15} - S_{16}$

$$V_{15} = max \, (R_{15} + 0.9*(V_{16})) = 0 + 0.9*(+5) = 4.5$$

$$V_{14} = \max (R_{14} + 0.9*(V_{15})) = 0 + 0.9*(4.5) = 4.05$$

$$V_{13} = 0 \text{ as this is a terminal state}$$

As V_{13} is a terminal step, an alternative path to the goal should be explored. Let's assume that the path is V_9, V_{10}, V_{14} and we will use the next state-value functions accordingly.

$$V_{10} = \max (R_{10} + 0.9*(V_{14})) = 0 + 0.9*(4.05) = 3.64$$

$$V_9 = \max (R_9 + 0.9*(V_{10})) = 0 + 0.9*(3.64) = 3.29$$

$$V_5 = \max (R_5 + 0.9*(V_9)) = 0 + 0.9*(3.29) = 2.95$$

$$V_1 = \max (R_1 + 0.9*(V_5)) = 0 + 0.9*(2.95) = 2.66$$

In the same way, we can calculate the value function for other cells.

$$V_{11} = \max (R_{11} + 0.9*(V_{10})) = 0 + 0.9*(3.64) = 3.29$$

$$V_7 = \max (R_7 + 0.9*(V_{11})) = 0 + 0.9*(3.29) = 2.95$$

$$V_3 = \max (R_3 + 0.9*(V_7)) = 0 + 0.9*(2.95) = 2.66$$

$$V_2 = \max (R_2 + 0.9*(V_3)) = 0 + 0.9*(2.66) = 2.39$$

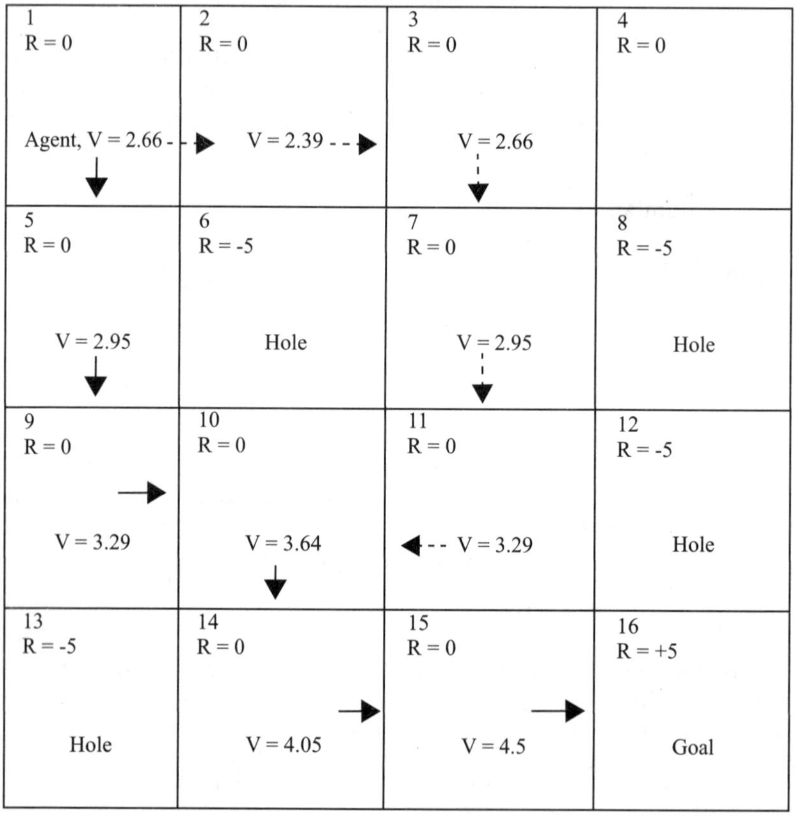

1 $R = 0$ Agent, $V = 2.66$ →	2 $R = 0$ $V = 2.39$ →	3 $R = 0$ $V = 2.66$ ↓	4 $R = 0$
5 $R = 0$ $V = 2.95$ ↓	6 $R = -5$ Hole	7 $R = 0$ $V = 2.95$ ↓	8 $R = -5$ Hole
9 $R = 0$ $V = 3.29$	10 $R = 0$ → $V = 3.64$ ↓	11 $R = 0$ ← $V = 3.29$	12 $R = -5$ Hole
13 $R = -5$ Hole	14 $R = 0$ $V = 4.05$ →	15 $R = 0$ $V = 4.5$ →	16 $R = +5$ Goal

We can see that when the agent is in S_1, it won't move to right to S_2 but will move down to S_5 as $V_5 > V_2$. In this same way, it tries to identify the optimal path or policy to reach the goal.

Iteration 2...n:

Note that the value functions derived in *Iteration 1* may not be the optimal solution for this grid world. The reason is, that many of the cells can be reached from multiple paths and we should identify which of those is most efficient, meaning generates the most return. For example, S_{11} can be reached from S_{10} as well as from S_7 and we should calculate V_{11} for both paths and take the max value for the optimal solution. So, for each terminal episode, the value functions are evaluated, and fine-tuned and finally, the optimal policy (set of actions) is chosen based on the one that provides the maximum cumulative value or return. This is the key concept of the Bellman equation and optimality.

It may seem an easy task to solve the optimality equations to learn the optimal policies. But in reality, the computational cost to generate the optimal policy is prohibitively high, especially when the lengths of the episodes are very large. Memory requirement is also a constraint as building up approximations of value functions, policies and models requires a large amount of memory. So, some sort of approximation strategy is required to balance the acceptable optimality level and the resource availability. Because of the online nature of RL problems, it is often possible to focus on frequently occurring states and learn the best policies for them, rather than putting effort into states that seldom occur. This is the key aspect to be kept in mind while solving MDPs for RL problems. We will discuss a few such algorithms to compute optimal policies in the MDP environment in the next section.

10.5   REINFORCEMENT LEARNING ALGORITHMS

10.5.1   Dynamic Programming (DP)

Dynamic Programming (DP) is a set of algorithms that are used to compute optimal policies in a perfect model of the environment, like MDP. The key idea is to search for the optimal policy by using the value functions where the problem is broken down into multiple sub-problems and the result of a sub-problem is used in similar sub-problems, instead of independently solving those. To be solved through a dynamic programming approach, a problem should have the following properties – a) we should be able to divide the problem into similar sub-problems, and b) if we can find the optimal solution for a sub-problem, then that solution can be used to find the optimal solution for the overall problem. As we have seen in the Bellman equation (10.4), MDPs possess these properties because the value of a state is equal to the immediate value plus the value of the next step. This demonstrates the suitability for applying DP. As the computational overhead of a classical DP method is very high, most of the algorithms attempt to achieve almost the same effect as DP with less computational cost and without assuming the perfect environment, though the fundamental theory of DP is followed.

In Dynamic Programming, the key concept is to first identify the value function that will satisfy the Bellman equation and then using the optimal value function identify the optimal policy. The process is logically divided into 3 steps –

1. **Policy Evaluation/ Prediction:** if we have an MDP with the parameters (S, A, P, R, and γ) and a given policy π, then we aim to identify the value function by evaluating the policy using Bellman's Expectation Equations (10.2) and (10.3)

2. **Policy Improvement:** the value function obtained in the previous step is optimized.

3. **Policy Iteration/ Control:** From the optimal value function v_*, the optimal policies q_* can be easily obtained through Bellman's Optimality Equations (10.9 and 10.10)

10.5.1.1 Policy Evaluation or Prediction

The policy evaluation involves the computation of state value function v_π for an arbitrary policy π. Please recall the Bellman equation 10.5 in previous section as:

$$v_\pi(s) = \sum \pi(a_a\ s)\sum_{s',r} p(s',r\,|\,s,a)\left[r + \gamma v_\pi(s')\right] \text{ for all } s \in S$$

which provides a unique value of v_π when either $\gamma<1$ or all states get terminated eventually. When the environment's properties are completely known, then the above equation becomes a system of $|S|$ simultaneous linear equations of $|S|$ unknowns (v_π $(s), s \in S$). An algorithm called *iterative policy evaluation* is used to compute the value function. Here a sequence of approximate value functions $v_0, v_1, v_2, \ldots$ is considered, each mapping $S^+$to $\mathbb{R}$ (real numbers). Initial approximation v_0 is chosen arbitrarily and in each successive approximation is obtained by Bellman equation as an update rule:

$$v_{k+1}(s) = \mathbb{E}_\pi\left[R_{t+1} + \gamma v_k(S_{t+1})\,|\,S_t = s\right]$$
$$= \sum_a \pi(a\,|\,s)\sum_{s',r} p(s',r\,|\,s,a)\left[r + \gamma v_k(s')\right]$$

Please note that the value of the terminal state should always be considered as 0.

This implies that each successive approximation v_{k+1} is computed from v_k through iterative policy evaluation on each state, s. The old value of of s is replaced by the new value obtained from the old values of successor states of s, and the expected immediate rewards, for all the one-step transitions possible for the policy under consideration. This way, each iteration of iterative policy evaluation updates the value of every state once to produce a new approximate value function v_{k+1}.

10.5.1.2 Policy Improvement

Now that we have evaluated $v_\pi(s)$ which gives how good it is to follow the current policy from s, we should also evaluate whether we should change the policy to deterministically choose an action a $\neq \pi(s)$ to improve the value function. This value can be obtained as:

$$q_\pi(s,a) = \mathbb{E}\left[R_{t+1} + \gamma v_\pi\left(S_{t+1}\right) \mid S_t = s, A_t = a\right]$$

$$= \sum_{s',r} p\left(s',r \mid s,a\right)\left[r + \gamma v_\pi\left(s'\right)\right]$$

If q_π is greater than v_π then it is better to select a in s and then to follow π thereafter than to follow π all the time and also it can be inferred that it is better to select action a every time when s is encountered and the new policy is better one overall. This is called the *policy improvement theorem* and can be expressed as

$q_\pi\left(s, \pi'\left(s\right)\right) \geq v_\pi\left(s\right)$, π *and* π' are any pair of deterministic policies for all $s \in S$

Then the policy π' must be better or as least as good as π and thus obtain great or equal expected return

$$v_{\pi'}\left(s\right) \geq v_\pi\left(s\right)$$

10.5.1.3 *Policy Iteration or Control*

Once we obtain improved policy v_π', we can use the same equation o improve it again and obtain an even better policy v_π''. This way each policy is evaluated and then improved in iterations until it reaches the optimal value function and optimal policy. This is shown diagrammatically in Figure 10.7. As finite MDP consists only a finite number of policies, this process is guaranteed to converge to an optimal policy and optimal value function within a finite number of iterations. This process is called *policy iteration.*

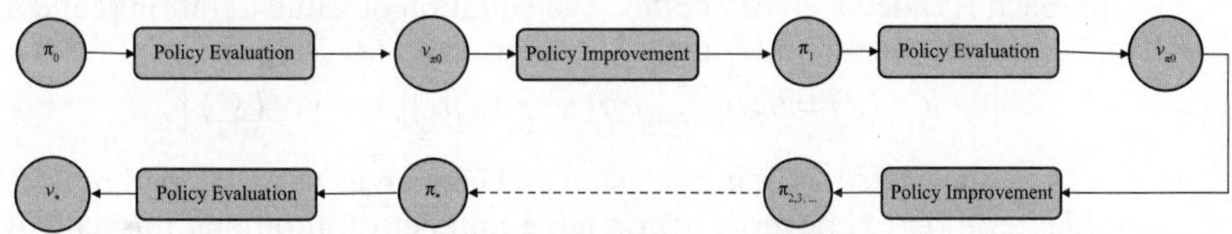

FIG. 10.7
Policy Iteration

The flow of Policy Iteration (iterative policy evaluation) to estimate $\pi \approx \pi_*$ looks like below:

---

1. Initialize $V(s) \in \mathbb{R}$, $\pi(s) \in A(s)$ for all s $\in$ S arbitrarily, except $V(Terminal)=0$

2. Policy evaluation

    Loop:

        diff = 0

        For each $s \in s$, Loop:

            $v = V(s)$

            $V(s) = \sum_{s',r} p\left(s',r \mid s,\pi(s)\right)\left[r + \gamma V\left(s'\right)\right]$

        diff = max $\left(\text{diff}, |v - V(s)|\right)$

> until diff $< \varepsilon$, a very small number to check whether improvements are happening
>
> **3.** Policy Improvement
>
> policy-is-stable = True
> For each $s \in s$, Loop:
>   Old-action = $\pi(s)$
> $$\pi(s) = argmax_a \sum_{s',r} p(s',r \mid s,a)\left[r + \gamma V(s')\right]$$
>   If old-action $\neq \pi(s)$
>   policy-is-stable = False
>   If policy-is-stable then
>   stop, return $V \approx v_*$ and $\pi \approx \pi_*$
>   else
>   move to step 2

10.5.1.4 *Value Iteration*

It is evident from the policy iteration logic that each of its iterations needs to perform policy evaluation. In the real world, this may involve iterative computation with multiple sweeps through the state set, and for large state sets this can be prohibitively expensive. To optimize the computation requirement without losing the convergence guarantee of policy iteration, the policy evaluation step is truncated in an algorithm called *value iteration*. Here, policy iteration is stopped after just one sweep (one update of each state) because the maximum value for a particular state is taken. This approach is called a *greedy policy*. The equation of value iteration that combines the policy improvement and truncated policy evaluation steps is:

$$v_{k+1}(s) = max_a \sum_{s',r} p(s',r \mid s,a)\left[r + \gamma v_k(s')\right] \tag{10.10a}$$

The policy gets better in each step and converges to v_*. Instead of waiting for the value iteration to converge over a large number of iterations, normally we stop the iterations when the improvement of the value function becomes very small over each sweep. Please note that equation (10.10) can be directly obtained from the Bellman Optimality equation (10.9) by turning it into an update function.

The complete flow of Value Iteration for estimating $\pi \approx \pi_*$ looks like below:

> Initialize $V(s)$ for all $s \in S^+$ arbitrarily, except $V(Terminal) = 0$
> loop for each $s \in S$
>
> **1.** diff = 0
> **2.** $v = V(s)$
> **3.** $V(s) = max_a \sum_{s',r} p(s',r \mid s,a)\left[r + \gamma V(s')\right]$
> **4.** diff = max $(\text{diff}, |v - V(s)|)$
> until diff $< \Delta$, where Δ is a very small number to check whether improvements are happening
> Compute the deterministic policy $\pi \approx \pi^*$ such that
> **5.** $\pi(s) = argmax_a \sum_{s',r} p(s',r \mid s,a)\left[r + \gamma V(s')\right]$

10.5.1.5 Generalized Policy Iteration (GPI)

We have seen that in Policy Iteration, two simultaneous and interacting processes occur back-to-back – the policy evaluation makes the value function consistent with the current policy and the policy improvement makes the policy greedy with respect to the current value function. We have also seen that in the Value Iteration, efficiency is gained with these two processes being performed simultaneously within a single iteration. So, as long as both processes continue to update all states, the final goal of convergence to optimal value function and optimal policy is achieved.

Generalized Policy Iteration (GPI) is the term that is used to refer to the idea of letting the policy evaluation and policy-improvement processes interact, independent of the granularity of the two processes. Almost all reinforcement learning methods can be described as GPI. The principal concept of GPI is explained in Figure 10.8

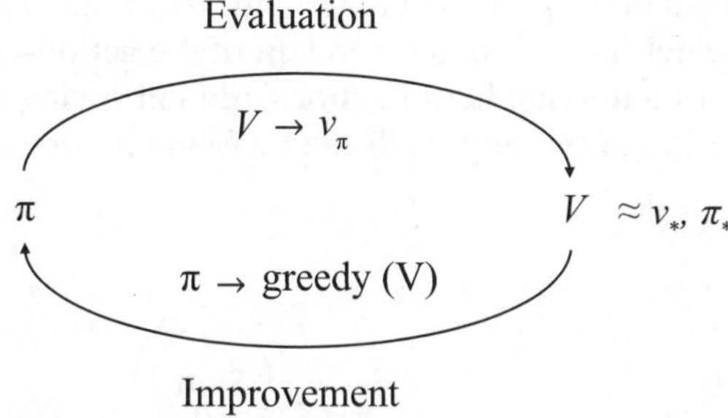

FIG. 10.8
Generalized Policy Iteration (GPI)

The policy is being improved with respect to the value function and the value function is driven toward the value function for the policy. The value function stabilizes once it is consistent with the current policy and the policy stabilizes once it is greedy for the current value function. Thus, the cycle stops once both the processes stabilize, as it reaches the Bellman optimality equation and the policy and the value function are optimal. In GPI, the two processes together achieve the optimality goal though neither of them is attempting to achieve it directly.

10.5.2 Monte Carlo Methods

In the previous section, we discussed solving RL problems for MDPs, where we assumed that we have full knowledge of the environment, like the complete probability distribution of all the possible transitions, the reward function, etc. which was the basis for using dynamic programming. But in the real world we may not have the full knowledge of the environment and a new class of RL called model-free learning comes into the picture there. Monte Carlo Methods are one such class of model-free algorithms. In essence, Monte Carlo methods are learning methods that require only *experience* – sample sequences of states, actions, and rewards from actual or simulated interactions with the environment. The methods work by averaging sample returns. The key assumption is that the experience is divided into episodes and that all episodes terminate at the end irrespective of the actions taken. The value estimates and policies change only after the completion of an episode. The agent takes action and obtains rewards during an episode and we take an average of the rewards when the episode terminates.

$$V(S_t) = V(S_t) + \alpha \left[G_t - V(S_t) \right] \tag{10.11}$$

where G_t is actual return following time t and α is a constant step-size parameter

Epsilon-Greedy Action Selection: in section 10.2 we briefly discussed the exploitation vs exploration approach in RL. Extreme dependence either on exploitation or on exploration is detrimental to any model. So, a balance is struck with the use of a small number ε (epsilon) to instruct the algorithm when to exploit and when to explore. This is called the Epsilon-Greedy Action Selection approach. Please refer to Figure 10.9. The algorithm exploits, i.e., chooses the optimal action that generated the highest reward in the past most of the time. For a small probability (ε) it explores, i.e., randomly selects an action independent of the action-value estimates. This opens up the room for identifying better actions and improving the policy further. The actual implementation of this approach can be found in section 10.6 Python code base.

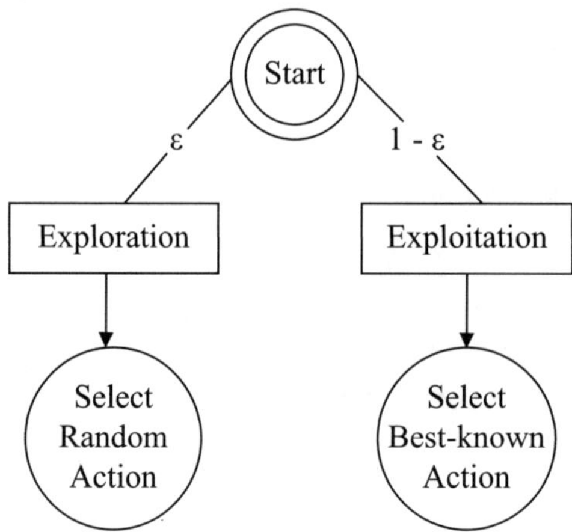

FIG. 10.9
Epsilon-greedy action selection

10.5.3 Temporal Difference Learning (TD)

One of the most effective learning processes in RL is Temporal Difference (TD) learning, which combines the ideas of Monte Carlo methods and DP methods. Similar to Monte Carlo methods, TD methods do not depend on the knowledge of the environment's dynamics or the model and thus learn directly from the experience. Also, similar to DP, TD methods update the estimates based in part on other learned estimates and do not wait for the final outcome. The steps include Prediction and Control which is a standardized approach for RL algorithms. Please note that DP, Monte Carlo, and TD all use some variation of GPI for the control problem, which aims to find out the optimal policy, but these methods are different in their approaches to the prediction problem, which aims to estimate the value function v_π for a given policy π.

10.5.3.1 TD Prediction

Similar to Monte Carlo methods, TD methods use experience to solve prediction problems. But the main difference in approach is that the Monte Carlo methods wait until an episode completes and the return is known, and then use that return to update the estimate for $V(S_t)$ [refer to equation 10.11]; whereas, TD methods need to wait only until the next time step. The update is done immediately after transitioning to S_{t+1} and receiving R_{t+1} at t+1, using the observed reward R_{t+1} and the estimate $V(S_{t+1})$:

$$V(S_t)= V(S_t)+ \alpha\,[R_{t+1} + \gamma V(S_{t+1}) - V(S_t)] \tag{10.12}$$

The flow of the algorithm can be seen as below:

Policy π is given as input which needs to be evaluated

Initialize $V(s)$ for all $s \in S^+$ arbitrarily, except $V(Terminal) = 0$, step size $\alpha \in (0,1]$

{α is a real number between 0 and 1, which denotes the learning rate or step size. If this is set to zero, then the agent learns nothing from the new actions, whereas making it 1 means that the agent will completely ignore prior knowledge and use only the most recent information. The higher the value of α, faster the changes in value function.}

For each episode, Loop:
    Initialize S
    For each step of the episode, loop:

      1. A = action given by π for S

      2. Take action A, observe R, S′

      3. $V(S_t)= V(S_t)+ \alpha\,[R_{t+1}+\gamma V(S_{t+1}) - V(S_t)]$

      4. S = S′

until S is terminal

TD methods use the best parts of both Monte Carlo and DP methods and thus offer advantages over both of them. The advantage over DP methods is that they do not need a model of the environment – its next-state transition probability distribution and the reward. The advantage over Monte Carlo methods is that TD can be implemented in a fully online incremental way. The reason is that Monte Carlo methods need to wait for an episode to end while TD needs to wait only till the next time step. In real-life situations, some of the problems may have very long running episodes which delay the learning significantly making the process slower. If the constant step-size parameter is kept sufficiently small then TD methods converge to v_π very efficiently.

There are two different approaches to implementing TD prediction methods – on-policy and off-policy, as we will discuss in the subsequent chapters. In on-policy methods, the value function ($Q(s, a)$) is learned by following the current policy π (s|a) based on which the actions are chosen. But in off-policy methods, the actions need not follow the current policy, but a different policy can be followed and can even be chosen at random (through exploration). Both these types of methods find an optimal policy in the long run.

10.5.3.2 On-Policy TD Control – SARSA

Here we start by learning the action-value function rather than learning the state-value function. The aim is to estimate q_π (s, a)for the current behavior policy π for all state s and actions a. So, instead of learning just the values of the states by transitioning from state to state, we will learn the values of the state-action pairs transitioning from state-action pair to state-action pair. The TD prediction equation of (10.12) will get updated to:

$$Q(S_t, A_t) = Q(S_t, A_t)+ \alpha\, [R_{t+1} + \gamma Q(S_{t+1}, A_{t+1}) - Q(S_t,A_t)] \qquad (10.13)$$

The update is made after each transition from non-terminal states. If S_{t+1} is terminal then $Q(S_{t+1},A_{t+1})$ is defined as zero. You can see that the above equation uses every element of the group of events, $(S_t, A_t, R_{t+1}, S_{t+1}, A_{t+1})$ [(**S**tate-**A**ction-**R**eward-**S**tate-**A**ction)] which has driven the algorithm's name - SARSA. The flow of the SARSA control algorithm is given below, where the main idea is that we continuously estimate qπ for the behavior policy π and at the same time change π to greediness with respect to q_π to finally arrive at the optimum q*.

Policy π is given as input which needs to be evaluated

Initialize $Q(s, a)$ for all $s \in S^+$, a $\in$ A(s) arbitrarily, except $Q(Terminal) = 0$, step size $\alpha \in (0,1]$, small $\varepsilon > 0$

For each episode, Loop:

  Initialize S

  Choose A from S using policy derived from Q (e.g. ε-greedy)

  For each step of the episode, loop:

    1. Take action A, observe R, S'

    2. Choose A' from S' using policy derived from Q (e.g. ε-greedy)

    3. $Q(S_t, A_t) = Q(S_t, A_t)+ \alpha\, [R_{t+1} + \gamma Q(S_{t+1}, A_{t+1}) - Q(S_t,A_t)]$

    4. S = S', A = A'

  until S is terminal

The algorithm stores a table of state (S)-action (A) estimate pairs for each Q-value. This table is known as a Q-table.

10.5.3.3 Off-Policy TD Control – Q-learning

In 1989 Chris Watkins developed an off-policy TD control algorithm called Q-learning which significantly simplified the algorithm and enabled early convergence proofs. The driving equation is:

$$Q(S_t, A_t) = Q(S_t, A_t) + \alpha\,[R_{t+1} + \gamma\,max_a\,Q(S_{t+1}, A_{t+1}) - Q(S_t, A_t)] \qquad (10.13)$$

As it is evident from the equation, the optimal action-value function q* is obtained directly from the learned action-value function Q, independent of the policy being followed. The policy only plays a role in determining which state-action pairs are visited and updated, but as long as it is ensured that all pairs continue to be updated, the algorithm converges correctly. This is a model-free learning process, which means that the agent explores the environment and learns directly from it, without constructing an internal model or MDP. The Agent only knows about the possible states and actions in an environment at the beginning and then discovers the state transitions and rewards by exploration.

The sample algorithm of Q-learning is shown below. Python implementation of this algorithm can be found in section 10.6.

Initialize parameters: step size $\alpha \in (0,1]$, small $\varepsilon > 0$

Initialize Q(s, a) for all s $\in$ S$^+$, a $\in$ A(s) , arbitrarily, except *Q(Terminal,.)*=0
For each episode, loop
    Initialize S
    For each step of the episode, loop:
    Choose A from S using policy derived from Q, with the ε-greedy approach
    Take action A, observe R, S′
    $Q(S, A) = Q(S, A) + \alpha[R + \gamma\,max_a\,Q(S', a) - Q(S, A)]$
    S = S′
Until S is terminal

10.6   SAMPLE PYTHON IMPLEMENTATION OF Q-LEARNING

```python
# This program implements a sample reinforcement learning algo-
rithm with
# q-learning. The agent learns to reach the end of the frozen lake
through
# trial and error. Note the features like balancing of exploration
and #exploitation, use of value function

import numpy as np
import matplotlib.pyplot as plt
import gymnasium


# defining an agent that learns with q-learning
```

```python
class GenericAgent:
def __init__(
        self,
        learning_rate:float,
        initial_epsilon: float,
        epsilon_decay: float,
        final_epsilon:float,
        discount_factor:float = 0.95
):

        self.q_values = np.zeros((env.observation_space.n, env.
action_space.n))
        self.lr = learning_rate
        self.discount_factor = discount_factor
        self.epsilon = initial_epsilon
        self.epsilon_decay = epsilon_decay
        self.final_epsilon = final_epsilon

# this function returns a random action (exploration) or the best
known #action(exploitation) based on the epsilon value
    def get_action(self, obs:tuple[int, int, bool])->int:
    if np.random.random() < self.epsilon:
    return env.action_space.sample()
    else:
        return int(np.argmax(self.q_values[obs,:]))


# this function calculates the q-value and updates the q-value
table for #reference while calculating the total cumulative reward
of a state-action
        def update(self,
        obs:tuple[int, int, bool],
        action:int,
        reward:float,
        terminated:bool,
        next_obs: tuple[int, int, bool]):

    future_q_value = (not terminated * np.max(self.q_values[next_
obs,:]))

    temporal_difference = (reward + self.discount_factor*future_q_
value - self.q_values[obs, action])
    self.q_values[obs, action] = (self.q_values[obs, action] +
self.lr * temporal_difference)

    def decay_epsilon(self):
    self.epsilon  =  max(self.final_epsilon,  self.epsilon
- epsilon_decay)
```

```python
## actual algorithm starts here
learning_rate = 0.01
n_episodes = 10000                # number of times the learning
sequence will run


start_epsilon = 1.0      # at start it goes for exploration and then
moves toward
                    # explotation through epsilon decay function
epsilon_decay = start_epsilon/(n_episodes/2)

final_epsilon = 0.1

# initiation of openAI.gymnasium's Frozenlake environment
env = gymnasium.make('FrozenLake-v1', render_mode="rgb_array")

agent = GenericAgent(learning_rate, start_epsilon, epsilon_decay,
                    final_epsilon)

episode_reward = []

for episode in range(n_episodes):
    obs, info = env.reset()
    done = False
    total_episode_reward = 0
    terminated = False

while not done:
    action = agent.get_action(obs) #either explores or exploits
    # step function returns next observation space, reward value
of current
    # action and a signal whether the termination action is reached,
like
    # it has fallen into the lake

    next_obs, reward, terminated, truncated, info = env.step(action)

    agent.update(obs, action, reward, terminated, next_obs)
    frame = env.render()

    plt.imshow(frame)
    plt.show()
    done = terminated or truncated
    obs = next_obs
    total_episode_reward = total_episode_reward + reward

    episode_reward.append( total_episode_reward)
    agent.decay_epsilon()

    for i in range(10):
    print ("Mean reward of episode {} is {}".format((i+1)*1000,
np.mean(episode_reward[i*1000:(i+1)*1000])))
```

The mean reward of 1000 episodes will look like below.

```
>> Mean reward of episode 1000 is 0.026
>> Mean reward of episode 2000 is 0.027
>> Mean reward of episode 3000 is 0.044
>> Mean reward of episode 4000 is 0.053
>> Mean reward of episode 5000 is 0.081
>> Mean reward of episode 6000 is 0.093
>> Mean reward of episode 7000 is 0.092
>> Mean reward of episode 8000 is 0.077
>> Mean reward of episode 9000 is 0.091
>> Mean reward of episode 10000 is 0.096
```

Note that the mean reward value started with a low value as the agent was still learning, but steadily increased as it could maximize the value function much better and use the right policy based on the experience it gained over multiple runs. Can you think of few practical applications of the above algorithm? We have seen that the Agent has learnt to avoid the obstacles on its own and reached the final destination discovering the shortest path. Similar agents like, a self-driving car, an autonomous robot, a computer-player in a game can use this algorithm to continuously learn the policies in the environment and fine-tune their actions.

10.7   APPLICATIONS OF RL

The use of machine learning in solving real-life problems is not new. But, with the advancement in the field of reinforcement learning, the agents now have more capability to recommend or take actions, based on the long-term gain/loss from such actions. In many real-life and industry situations, the volume of data produced is very high, making it difficult to analyze it and create training data from it by manually labeling it. Also, some tasks are dangerous and can't be accomplished by humans. Thus, it is difficult for anyone to train the agent in those situations. The capability of reinforcement learning agents to learn on their own in such situations has made it a popular choice of machine learning algorithm.

Robotics and Industrial Automation

Autonomous robots and industrial machines that can create an adaptive control to learn from their actions and refine future behavior are important examples of the use of RL. Robots and autonomous parts are used widely in applications, like, holding and handling parts of different shapes and sizes, assembling end products, inspecting products for defects, tracking and managing inventory, traveling short and long distances, delivering goods, etc.

Case study: Google's Deepmind has used RL powered agent to manage the cooling systems of Google Data Centres. The workflow that the agent follows is:

1. Measure the environmental conditions within the data center every 5 min
2. Analyse different settings and how those will affect future energy consumption

3. Use sets of standard safety criteria as the guiding policy and identify the actions that will have minimal power consumption

4. Sends and implements the actions

The outcome is very impressive – this led to a 40% reduction in energy spend and thus is a huge step towards sustainability.

Case study: manipulating the complex grasping mechanism for robotic arms was a challenging task when it was attempted to be implemented using only static learning models and vision-based controls. Instead, an RL-based model was developed in 2018, called QT-Opt, that continuously updated the grasping strategy based on the most recent observations and optimized it for long-term grasping success. Application of this RL-based model on real robots by Google AI found that the success rate of grasping increased from 78% to 96% which is very significant in this domain.

Natural Language Processing (NLP)

Text summarization, question-answer-based conversation, and machine translation are a few examples where RL is used in NLP. For example, during machine translation, standard supervised learning is used to predict the words, but the system learns when to use the predicted word or when to wait for more input using the RL model. RL in NLP is now widely implemented by customer service departments in many major organizations.

ChatGPT is a very pertinent example of how language models can be fine-tuned using RL. A language model can generate impressive texts in response to human prompts. But understanding whether the generated text is 'good' in the context of the conversation, was a long-standing challenge. In the case of ChatGPT, human feedback is used as the measure for this performance and it is called reinforcement learning from human feedback (RLHF). The important attributes of the sequence of conversation, like, coherence, informativity, and ease of answering are rewarded in this learning model.

Healthcare

The healthcare sector was one of the early adopters of machine learning. Diagnostic report analysis, medical diagnosis, and ailment prediction have been using machine learning models for quite some time now. With the use of RL, the concept of dynamic treatment regimes (DTRs) has evolved. Based on diagnostic reports, clinical assessment of the patient, and the previous outcomes the learning agent can produce output with suggested treatment type, drug dosages, and appointment timings during a patient's treatment. The result is very encouraging and can reduce the time, energy, and effort in creating an end-to-end treatment strategy.

Gaming

Due to an RL agent's ability to learn and fine-tune its actions through continuous learning, gaming is an area where it is used very extensively. The rules of the game form the policy. In the simulated game environment, the agent navigates, attacks, defends, and strategizes, with a final goal of accumulating a target reward or winning the game.

Did you know?

AlphaGo Zero was able to learn the game of Go from scratch by using reinforcement learning. For 40 days it played against itself. During this, a neural network generated two outputs – a continuous value of the board's state |–1, +1| from the perspective of the current player and a policy which is a probability vector over all possible actions. The estimate of this policy for a given state is improved using Monte Carlo tree search (a reinforcement learning algorithm). After 40 days of self-training, Alpha Go Zero was able to outperform the previous version of AlphaGo known as Master which had defeated world number one Ke Jie.

Self-driving cars

Various aspects of self-driving cars, like, learning speed limits of various places, and avoiding collision, are controlled by deep reinforcement learning. As the autonomous car is supposed to work in real environments, it is not possible to train it for all the possible situations that the car (agent) may encounter on the road. So, the agent learns on its own to identify the best actions, based on the predicted future outcomes. AWS Deep Racer is an autonomous car that is designed to test model self-driving cars in physical tracks. The input from the cameras fitted to the car is used by RL to control the throttle and direction.

Other than the above examples, many other sectors are using RL successfully, like, the finance sector for evaluating trading strategy, recommendation systems in media and e-commerce platforms, pushing targeted marketing and advertisement content based on success rate, etc. The industries are yet to explore the full potential of RL and there will be more widespread interest in this field in the future!

10.8 SUMMARY

- Reinforcement learning is a type of machine learning where the learner learns to map the actions to a situation, to maximize a numerical reward value. The computational approach to learning from interactions with the environment and analyzing the response to generate maximum reward is the basis for Reinforcement Learning.

- An agent makes decisions on what action to take in an environment and in a particular state.

- Everything that the agent interacts with is called an environment.

- The state is the representation of the environment that an agent is in a specific time step. It is defined as a set of information that the agent has at a given point in time.

- Policy is a strategy that the agent uses to achieve the goal. So, a policy defines the mapping from the perceived states of the environment to actions to be taken when in those states.

- After each action step, the environment sends a single number to the agent, which is termed a reward. These rewards define the goal of the reinforcement learning program because reinforcement learning algorithms have the goal of maximizing the rewards that can be accumulated by the agent over the long run.

- A value function defines long-term gain The sum of all the rewards that can be accumulated by the agent starting from the current state to all the probable future states is termed as the value of the current state.

- An RL problem is said to have Markov property if the future state depends only on the present and not on the past.

- Rewards vs Returns: Rewards are the numerical values an agent receives based on the action taken while being in a state in the environment. Return is the cumulative reward that the agent receives from the environment while completing a sequence of state transitions, called episodes.

- Discount factor (γ) is the value that determines how much importance is given to the current and future rewards.

- Bellman's equation helps in finding out the optimal policies and value functions to maximize the return.

- A set of algorithms that identify the optimal policy in an environment are
  & Dynamic Programming (DP)
  & Monte Carlo Methods
  & Temporal Difference Learning
    - On-Policy TD Control – SARSA
    - Off-Policy TD Control – Q-learning

- Almost all the industry sectors have started using reinforcement learning extensively, especially for its ability to learn on its own.

SAMPLE QUESTIONS

MULTIPLE-CHOICE QUESTIONS

1. Reinforcement learning methods learned through ____?
   (a) Experience
   (b) Predictions
   (c) Analyzing the data

2. What is an agent in reinforcement learning?
   (a) Agent is the situation in which rewards are being exchanged
   (b) Agent is the simple value in reinforcement learning.
   (c) An agent is an entity that explores the environment.

3. What are actions in reinforcement learning?
   (a) Actions are the moves that the agent takes inside the environment.
   (b) Actions are the functions that the environment takes.
   (c) Actions are the feedback that an agent provides.

4.   Which of the following is the practical example of reinforcement learning?
(a) House pricing prediction   (b) Market basket analysis
(c) Text classification   (d) Driverless cars

5.   What are the Rewards of Reinforcement learning?
(a) An agent's action is evaluated based on feedback returned from the environment.
(b) The environment gives value in return which is known as a reward.
(c) A reward is a result returned by the environment after an agent takes an action.

6.   In which of the following approaches of reinforcement learning, do we find the optimal value function?
(a) Value-based
(b) Policy-based
(c) Model-based.

7.   The agent's main objective is to _____the total number of rewards for good actions.?
(a) Experience
(b) Predictions
(c) Analyzing the data

8.   Which element in reinforcement learning defines the behavior of the agent?
(a) Policy   (b) Reward Signal
(c) Value Function   (d) none of the above

9.   Which of the following elements of reinforcement learning imitates the behavior of the environment?
(a) Policy   (b) Reward Signal
(c) Value Function   (d) none of the above

10.   Gamma (γ) in the Bellman equation is known as?
(a) Value factor
(b) Discount factor
(c) Environment factor

11.   Why do we use MDP in reinforcement learning?
(a) We use MDP to formalize the reinforcement learning problems.
(b) We use MDP to predict reinforcement learning problems.
(c) We use MDP to analyze the reinforcement learning problems.

12.   Which of the following algorithms will find the best course of action, based on the agent's current state, without using a model and off-policy reinforcement learning?
(a) Q-learning
(b) Markov property
(c) State-action-reward-state-action
(d) Deep Q neural network

SHORT-ANSWER TYPE QUESTIONS (5 MARKS EACH)

1. Explain Markov Decision Process.
2. Explain the principle of Q-learning with a flow of the algorithm.
3. Explain various practical applications of RL
4. Why reinforcement learning is the same as supervised or unsupervised learning?

LONG-ANSWER TYPE QUESTIONS (10 MARKS EACH)

1. What is reinforcement learning? Explain with an example.
2. Explain key components of reinforcement learning.
3. Explain value-based, model-based, and policy-based reinforcement learning.
4. What is the Bellman equation? How is it used in RL?

Chapter 11

Basics of Neural Network

OBJECTIVE OF THE CHAPTER:

In the last 9 chapters, you have been introduced to the concepts of machine learning in great details. You started with how to decide whether a problem can be solved with machine learning, and once you have made that decision, you learnt how to start with the modelling of the problem in the machine learning paradigm. In that context, you were introduced to three types of machine learning – supervised, unsupervised, and reinforcement. Then, you explored all different popular algorithms of supervised and unsupervised learning. Now, you have gained quite some background on machine learning basics, and it is time for you to get introduced to the concept of neural network.

Well, you have already seen right at the beginning of the book how the machine learning process maps with the human learning process. Now, it is time to see how the human nervous system has been mimicked in the computer world in the form of an artificial neural network or simply a neural network. This chapter gives a brief view of neural networks and how it helps in different forms of learning.

11.1   INTRODUCTION

In the previous chapters, we were slowly unveiling the mystery of machine learning, i.e. how a machine learns to perform tasks and improves with time from experience, by expert guidance or by itself. Machine learning, as we have seen, mimics the human form of learning. On the other hand, human learning, or for that matter every action of a human being, is controlled by the nervous system. In any human being, the nervous system coordinates the different actions by transmitting signals to and from different parts of the body. The nervous system is constituted of a special type of cell, called **neuron** or **nerve cell**, which has special structures allowing it to receive or send signals to other neurons. Neurons connect with each other to transmit signals to or receive signals from other neurons. This structure essentially forms a network of neurons or a neural network.

By virtue of billions of networked neurons that it possesses, the biological neural network is a massively large and complex parallel computing network. It is because of this massive parallel computing network that the nervous system helps human beings to perform actions or take decisions at a speed and with such ease that the fastest supercomputer of the world will also be envy of. For example, let us think of the superb flying catches taken by the fielders in the cricket world cup. It is a combination of superior calculation based on past cricketing experience, understanding of local on-ground conditions, and anticipation of how hard the ball has been hit that the fielder takes the decision about when to jump, where to jump, and how much to jump. This is a highly complex task, and you may think that not every human being is skilled enough for such a magical action. In that case, let us think of something much simpler. Let us consider about a very simple, daily activity, namely swimming in the pool. Apparently, swimming may look very trivial, but think about the parallel actions and decisions that need to be taken to swim. It needs the right combination of body position, limb movement, breathe in/out, etc. to swim. To add to the challenge is the fact that water is few hundred times denser than air. So, to orient the body movement in that scale difference is a difficult proposition in itself. Coordinating the actions and taking the decisions for such a complex task, which may appear to be trivial, are possible because of the massive parallel complex network, i.e. the neural network.

The fascinating capability of the biological neural network has inspired the inception of artificial neural network (ANN). An ANN is made up of artificial neurons. In its most generic form, an ANN is a machine designed to model the functioning of the nervous system or, more specifically, the neurons. The only difference is that the biological form of neuron is replicated in the electronic or digital form of neuron. Digital neurons or artificial neurons form the smallest processing units of the ANNs. As we move on, let us first do a deep dive into the structure of the biological neuron and then try to see how that has been modelled in the artificial neuron.

 ## 11.2   UNDERSTANDING THE BIOLOGICAL NEURON

The human nervous system has two main parts –

- the central nervous system (CNS) consisting of the brain and spinal cord
- the peripheral nervous system consisting of nerves and ganglia outside the brain and spinal cord.

The CNS integrates all information, in the form of signals, from the different parts of the body. The peripheral nervous system, on the other hand, connects the CNS with the limbs and organs. Neurons are basic structural units of the CNS. A neuron is able to receive, process, and transmit information in the form of chemical and electrical signals. Figure 11.1 presents the structure of a neuron. It has three main parts to carry out its primary functionality of receiving and transmitting information:

1. **Dendrites** – to receive signals from neighbouring neurons.
2. **Soma** – main body of the neuron which accumulates the signals coming from the different dendrites. It 'fires' when a sufficient amount of signal is accumulated.
3. **Axon** – last part of the neuron which receives signal from soma, once the neuron 'fires', and passes it on to the neighbouring neurons through the axon terminals (to the adjacent dendrite of the neighbouring neurons).

There is a very small gap between the axon terminal of one neuron and the adjacent dendrite of the neighbouring neuron. This small gap is known as **synapse**. The signals transmitted through synapse may be excitatory or inhibitory.

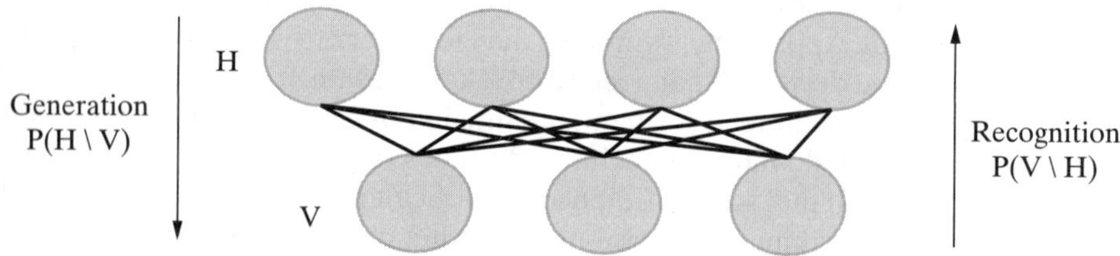

FIG. 11.1
Structure of biological neuron

Points to Ponder:

The adult human brain, which forms the main part of the central nervous system, is approximately 1.3 kg in weight and 1200 cm^3 in volume. It is estimated to contain about 100 billion (i.e. 10^{11}) neurons and 10 times more glial or glue cells. Glial cells act as support cells for the neurons. It is believed that neurons represent about 10% of all cells in the brain. On an average, each neuron is connected to 10^5 other neurons, which means that altogether there are 10^{16} connections.

The axon, a human neuron, is 10–12 μm in diameter. Each synapse spans a gap of about a millionth of an inch wide.

11.3   EXPLORING THE ARTIFICIAL NEURON

The biological neural network has been modelled in the form of ANN with artificial neurons simulating the function of biological neurons. As depicted in Figure 11.2, input signal x_i ($x_1, x_2, ..., x_n$) comes to an artificial neuron. Each neuron has three major components:

(i) A set of 'i' **synapses** having weight w_i. A signal x_i forms the input to the i-th synapse having weight w_i. The value of weight w_i may be positive or negative. A positive weight has an excitatory effect, while a negative weight has an inhibitory effect on the output of the summation junction, y_{sum}.

(ii) A **summation junction** for the input signals is weighted by the respective synaptic weight. Because it is a linear combiner or adder of the weighted input signals, the output of the summation junction, y_{sum}, can be expressed as follows:

$$y_{sum} = \sum_{i=1}^{n} w_i x_i$$

[Note: Typically, a neural network also includes a bias which adjusts the input of the activation function. However, for the sake of simplicity, we are ignoring bias for the time being. In the case of a bias 'b', the value of y_{sum} would have been as follows:

$$y_{sum} = b + \sum_{i=1}^{n} w_i x_i$$

(iii) A **threshold activation function** (or simply **activation function**, also called **squashing function**) results in an output signal only when an input signal exceeding a specific threshold value comes as an input. It is similar in behaviour to the biological neuron which transmits the signal only when the total input signal meets the firing threshold.

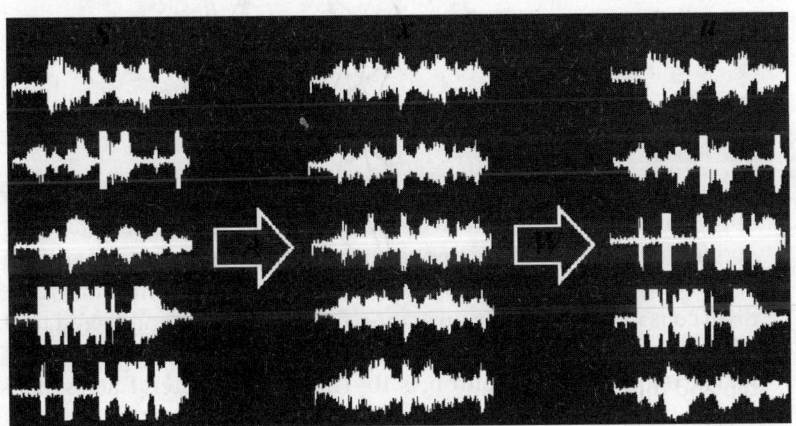

FIG. 11.2
Structure of an artificial neuron

Output of the activation function, y_{out}, can be expressed as follows:

$$y_{out} = f(y_{sum})$$

11.4   TYPES OF ACTIVATION FUNCTIONS

There are different types of activation functions. The most commonly used activation functions are highlighted below.

11.4.1   Identity function

Identity function is used as an activation function for the input layer. It is a linear function having the form

$$y_{out} = f(x) = x, \text{ for all } x$$

As obvious, the output remains the same as the input.

11.4.2 Threshold/step function

Step/threshold function is a commonly used activation function. As depicted in Figure 11.3a, **step function** gives 1 as output if the input is either 0 or positive. If the input is negative, the step function gives 0 as output. Expressing mathematically,

$$y_{out} = f(y_{sum}) = \begin{cases} 1, & x \geq 0 \\ 0, & x < 0 \end{cases}$$

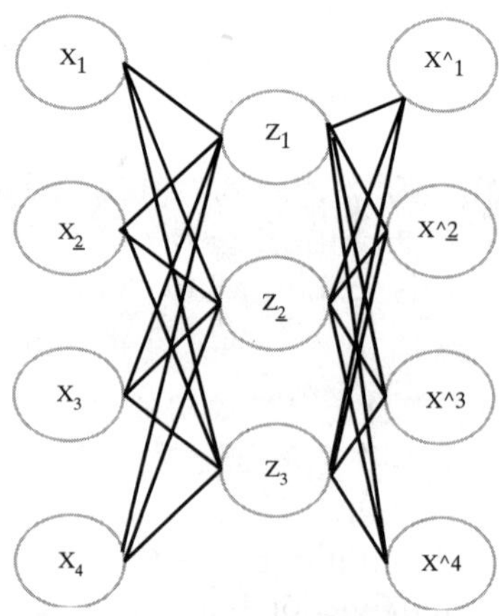

FIG. 11.3
Step and threshold functions

The **threshold function** (depicted in Fig. 11.3b) is almost like the step function, with the only difference being the fact that θ is used as a threshold value instead of 0. Expressing mathematically,

$$y_{out} = f(y_{sum}) = \begin{cases} 1, & x \geq \theta \\ 0, & x < \theta \end{cases}$$

11.4.3 ReLU (Rectified Linear Unit) function

ReLU is the most popularly used activation function in the areas of convolutional neural networks and deep learning. It is of the form

$$f(x) = \begin{cases} x, & x \geq 0 \\ 0, & x < 0 \end{cases}$$

This means that $f(x)$ is zero when x is less than zero and $f(x)$ is equal to x when x is above or equal to zero. Figure 11.4 depicts the curve for a ReLU activation function.

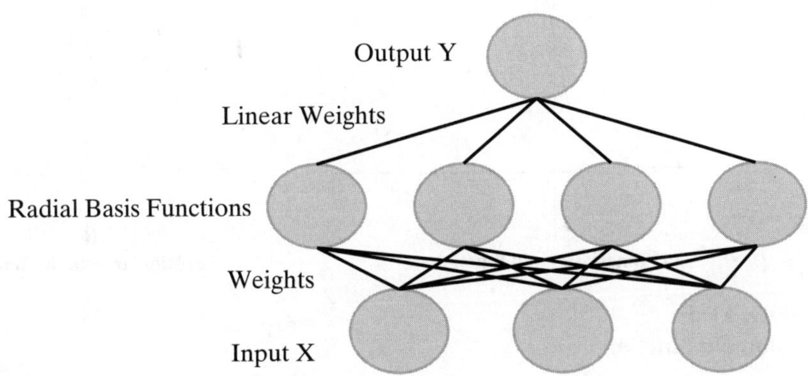

FIG. 11.4
ReLU function

This function is differentiable, except at a single point x = 0. In that sense, the derivative of a ReLU is actually a sub-derivative.

11.4.4 Sigmoid function

Sigmoid function, depicted in Figure 11.5, is by far the most commonly used activation function in neural networks. The need for sigmoid function stems from the fact that many learning algorithms require the activation function to be differentiable and hence continuous. Step function is not suitable in those situations as it is not continuous. There are two types of sigmoid function:

1. Binary sigmoid function
2. Bipolar sigmoid function

11.4.4.1 Binary sigmoid function

A binary sigmoid function, depicted in Figure 11.5a, is of the form

$$y_{out} = f(x) = \frac{1}{1+e^{-kx}}$$

where k = steepness or slope parameter of the sigmoid function. By varying the value of k, sigmoid functions with different slopes can be obtained. It has range of $(0, 1)$.

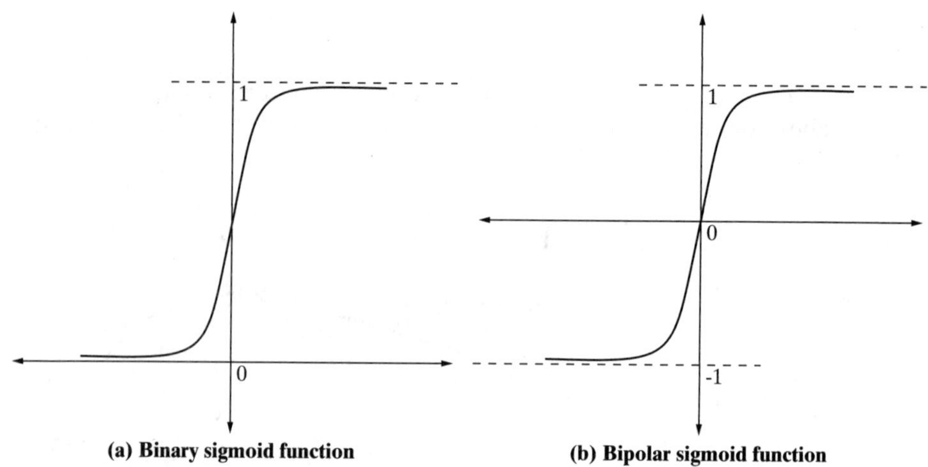

(a) Binary sigmoid function   (b) Bipolar sigmoid function

FIG. 11.5
Sigmoid function

The slope at origin is $k/4$. As the value of k becomes very large, the sigmoid function becomes a threshold function.

11.4.4.2 Bipolar sigmoid function

A bipolar sigmoid function, depicted in Figure 11.5b, is of the form

$$y_{\text{out}} = f(x) = \frac{1 - e^{-kx}}{1 + e^{-kx}}$$

The range of values of sigmoid functions can be varied depending on the application. However, the range of $(-1, +1)$ is most commonly adopted.

11.4.5 Hyperbolic tangent function

Hyperbolic tangent function is another continuous activation function, which is bipolar in nature. It is a widely adopted activation function for a special type of neural network known as backpropagation network (discussed elaborately in Section 11.8). The hyperbolic tangent function is of the form

$$y_{\text{out}} = f(x) = \frac{e^{x} - e^{-x}}{e^{x} + e^{-x}}$$

This function is similar to the bipolar sigmoid function.

Note that all the activation functions defined in Sections 11.4.2 and 11.4.4 have values ranging between 0 and 1. However, in some cases, it is desirable to have values ranging from −1 to +1. In that case, there will be a need to reframe the activation function. For example, in the case of step function, the revised definition would be as follows:

$$y_{\text{out}} = f\left(y_{\text{sum}}\right) = \begin{cases} 1, x > 0 \\ 0, x = 0 \\ -1, x < 0 \end{cases}$$

Did you know?

Works related to neural network dates long back to the 1940s. Warren McCulloch and Walter Pitts in 1943 created a computational network inspired by the biological processes in the brain. This model paved the way for neural networks.

The next notable work in the area of neural network was in the late 1940s by the Canadian psychologist Donald Olding Hebb. He proposed a learning hypothesis based on the neurons and synaptic connection between neurons. This became popular as Hebbian learning.

In 1958, the American psychologist Frank Rosenblatt refined the Hebbian concept and evolved the concept of perceptron. It was almost at the same time, in 1960, that Professor Bernard Widrow of Stanford University came up with an early single-layer ANN named ADALINE (Adaptive Linear Neuron or later Adaptive Linear Element). Marvin Lee Minsky and Seymour Aubrey Papert stated two key issues of perceptron in their research paper in 1969. The first issue stated was the inability of perceptron of processing the XOR (exclusive-OR) circuit. The other issue was lack of processing power of computers to effectively handle the large neural networks.

From here till the middle of the 1970s, there was a slowdown in the research work related to neural networks. There was a renewed interest generated in neural networks and learning with Werbos' backpropagation algorithm in 1975. Slowly, as the computing ability of the computers increased drastically, a lot of research on neural network has been conducted in the later decades. Neural network evolved further as deep neural networks and started to be implemented in solving large-scale learning problems such as image recognition, thereby getting a more popular name as deep learning.

11.5   EARLY IMPLEMENTATIONS OF ANN

11.5.1 McCulloch–Pitts model of neuron

The McCulloch–Pitts neural model (depicted in Fig. 11.6), which was the earliest ANN model, has only two types of inputs – excitatory and inhibitory. The excitatory inputs have weights of positive magnitude and the inhibitory inputs have weights of negative magnitude. The inputs of the McCulloch–Pitts neuron could be either 0 or 1. It has a threshold function as activation function. So, the output signal y_{out} is 1 if the input y_{sum} is greater than or equal to a given threshold value, else 0.

Simple McCulloch–Pitts neurons can be used to design logical operations. For that purpose, the connection weights need to be correctly decided along with the threshold

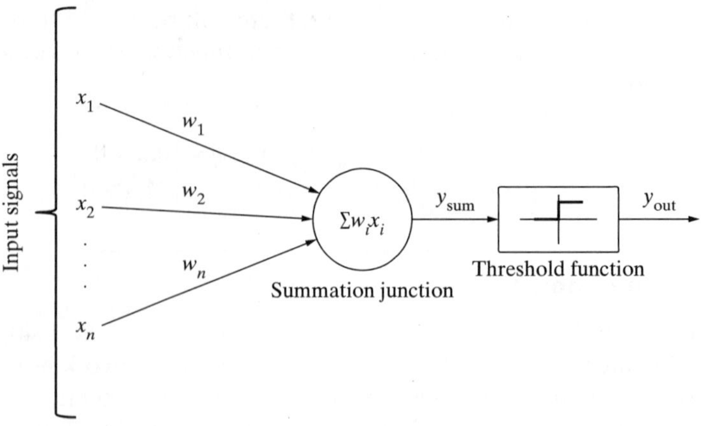

FIG. 11.6
McCulloch–Pitts neuron

function (rather the threshold value of the activation function). Let us take a small example.

John carries an umbrella if it is sunny or if it is raining. There are four given situations. We need to decide when John will carry the umbrella. The situations are as follows:

- Situation 1 – It is not raining nor is it sunny.
- Situation 2 – It is not raining, but it is sunny.
- Situation 3 – It is raining, and it is not sunny.
- Situation 4 – Wow, it is so strange! It is raining as well as it is sunny.

To analyse the situations using the McCulloch–Pitts neural model, we can consider the input signals as follows:

- $x_1 \rightarrow$ Is it raining?
- $x_2 \rightarrow$ Is it sunny?

So, the value of both x_1 and x_2 can be either 0 or 1. We can use the value of both weights x_1 and x_2 as 1 and a threshold value of the activation function as 1. So, the neural model will look as Figure 11.7a.

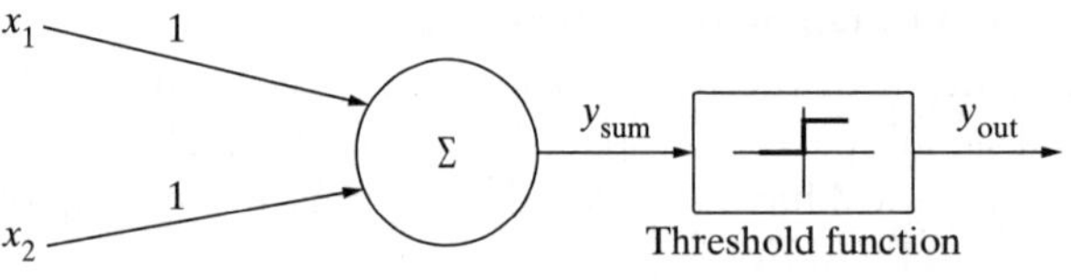

(a) McCulloch–Pitts neural model

FIG. 11.7
McCulloch–Pitts neural model (illustration)

Formally, we can say,

$$y_{sum} = \sum_{i=1}^{2} w_i x_i$$

$$y_{out} = f(y_{sum}) = \begin{cases} 1, & x \geq 1 \\ 0, & x < 1 \end{cases}$$

The truth table built with respect to the problem is depicted in **Figure 11.7b**. From the truth table, we can conclude that in the situations where the value of y_{out} is 1, John needs to carry an umbrella. Hence, he will need to carry an umbrella in situations 2, 3, and 4. Surprised, as it looks like a typical logic problem related to 'OR' function? Do not worry, it is really an implementation of logical OR using the McCulloch–Pitts neural model.

11.5.2 Rosenblatt's perceptron

Rosenblatt's perceptron is built around the McCulloch–Pitts neural model. The perceptron, as depicted in Figure 11.7, receives a set of input x_1, x_2,..., x_n. The linear combiner or the adder node computes the linear combination of the inputs applied to the synapses with synaptic weights being w_1, w_2, ..., w_n. Then, the hard limiter checks whether the resulting sum is positive or negative. If the input of the hard limiter node is positive, the output is +1, and if the input is negative, the output is –1. Mathematically, the hard limiter input is

$$v = \sum_{i=1}^{n} w_i x_i$$

However, perceptron includes an adjustable value or bias as an additional weight w_0. This additional weight w_0 is attached to a dummy input x_0, which is always assigned a value of 1. This consideration modifies the above equation to

$$v = \sum_{i=0}^{n} w_i x_i$$

The output is decided by the expression

$$y_{out} = f(v) = \begin{cases} +1, v > 0 \\ -1, v < 0 \end{cases}$$

The objective of perceptron is to classify a set of inputs into two classes, c_1 and c_2. This can be done using a very simple decision rule – assign the inputs $x_0, x_1, x_2, ...,$ x_n to c_1 if the output of the perceptron, i.e. y_{out}, is +1 and c_2 if y_{out} is –1. So, for an n-dimensional signal space, i.e. a space for 'n' input signals $x_0, x_1, x_2, ..., x_n$, the simplest form of perceptron will have two decision regions, resembling two classes, separated by a hyperplane defined by

$$\sum_{i=0}^{n} w_i x_i = 0$$

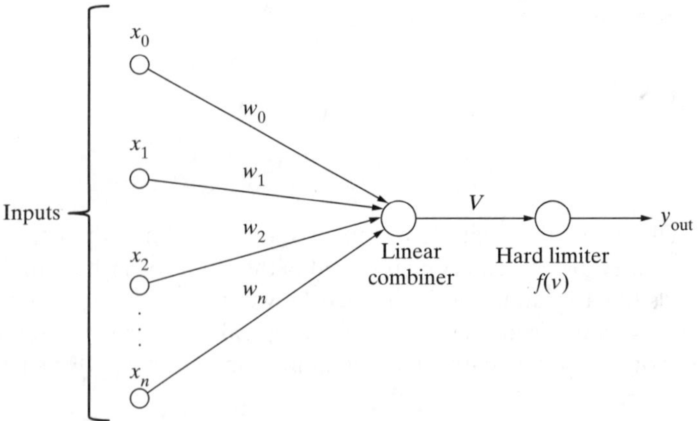

FIG. 11.8
Rosenblatt's perceptron

Therefore, for two input signals denoted by variables x_1 and x_2, the decision boundary is a straight line of the form

$$w_0 x_0 + w_1 x_1 + w_2 x_2 = 0$$
$$\text{or, } w_0 + w_1 x_1 + w_2 x_2 = 0 [\, x_0 = 1]$$

So, for a perceptron having the values of synaptic weights w_0, w_1, and w_2 as -2, $\frac{1}{2}$, and $\frac{1}{4}$, respectively, the linear decision boundary will be of the form

$$-2 + \frac{1}{2}x_1 + \frac{1}{4} x_2 = 0$$
$$\text{or, } 2x_1 + x_2 = 8$$

So, any point (x_1, x_2) which lies above the decision boundary, as depicted by Figure 11.9, will be assigned to class c_1 and the points which lie below the boundary are assigned to class c_2.

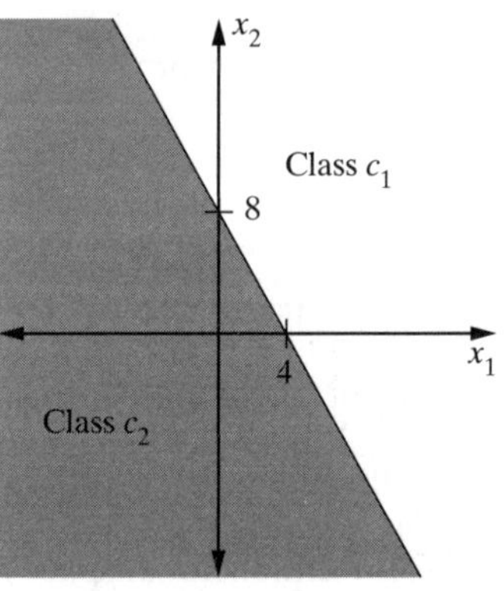

FIG. 11.9
Perceptron decision boundary

Let us examine if this perceptron is able to classify a set of points given below:

$p_1 = (5, 2)$ and $p_2 = (-1, 12)$ belonging to c_1

$p_3 = (3, -5)$ and $p_4 = (-2, -1)$ belonging to c_2

As depicted in Figure 11.10, we can see that on the basis of activation function output, only points p_1 and p_2 generate an output of 1. Hence, they are assigned to class c_1 as expected. On the other hand, p_3 and p_4 points having activation function output as negative generate an output of 0. Hence, they are assigned to class c_2, again as expected.

point	$v = \Sigma w_i x_i$	$y_{out} = f(v)$	Class
p_1	$-2 + (\frac{1}{2})*5 + (\frac{1}{4})*2 = 1$	1	c_1
p_2	$-2 + (\frac{1}{2})*(-1) + (\frac{1}{4})*12 = 0.5$	1	c_1
p_3	$-2 + (\frac{1}{2})*3 + (\frac{1}{4})*(-5) = -1.75$	0	c_2
p_4	$-2 + (\frac{1}{2})*(-2) + (\frac{1}{4})*(-1) = -3.25$	0	c_2

FIG. 11.10

Class assignment through perceptron

The same classification is obtained by mapping the points in the input space, as shown in Figure 11.11.

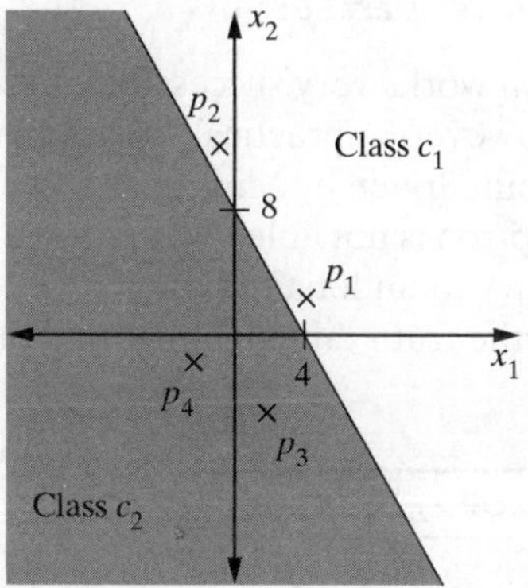

FIG. 11.11

Classification by decision boundary

Thus, we can see that for a data set with linearly separable classes, perceptrons can always be employed to solve classification problems using decision lines (for two-dimensional space), decision planes (for three-dimensional space), or decision hyperplanes (for n-dimensional space).

Appropriate values of the synaptic weights $w_0, w_1, w_2, \ldots, w_n$ can be obtained by training a perceptron. However, one assumption for perceptron to work properly is that the two classes should be linearly separable (as depicted in Figure 11.12a), i.e. the classes should be sufficiently separated from each other. Otherwise, if the classes are

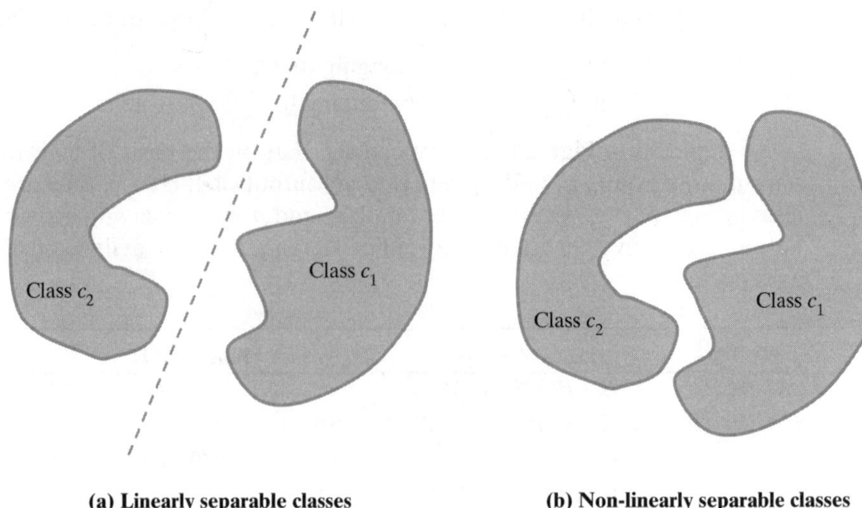

(a) Linearly separable classes   (b) Non-linearly separable classes

FIG. 11.12
Class separability

non-linearly separable (as depicted in Figure 11.12b), then the classification problem cannot be solved by perceptron.

11.5.2.1 Multi-layer perceptron

A basic perceptron works very successfully for data sets which possess linearly separable patterns. However, in practical situation, that is an ideal situation to have. This was exactly the point driven by Minsky and Papert in their work (1969). They showed that a basic perceptron is not able to learn to compute even a simple 2-bit XOR. Why is that so? Let us try to understand.

Figure 11.13 is the truth table highlighting output of a 2-bit XOR function.

x_1	x_2	x_1 **XOR** x_2	**Class**
1	1	0	c_2
1	0	1	c_1
0	1	1	c_1
0	0	0	c_2

FIG. 11.13
Class separability of XOR function output

As we can see in Figure 11.13, the data is not linearly separable. Only a curved decision boundary can separate the classes properly.

To address this issue, the other option is to use two decision lines in place of one. Figure 11.14 shows how a linear decision boundary with two decision lines can clearly partition the data.

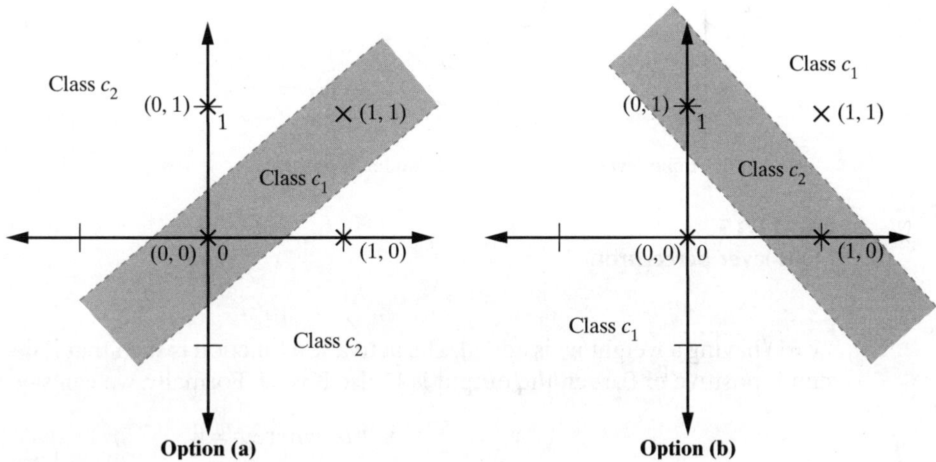

FIG. 11.14
Classification with two decision lines in XOR function output

This is the philosophy used to design the multi-layer perceptron model. The major highlights of this model are as follows:

- The neural network contains one or more intermediate layers between the input and the output nodes, which are hidden from both input and output nodes.
- Each neuron in the network includes a non-linear activation function that is differentiable.
- The neurons in each layer are connected with some or all the neurons in the previous layer.

The diagram in Figure 11.15 resembles a fully connected multi-layer perceptron with multiple hidden layers between the input and output layers. It is called fully connected because any neuron in any layer of the perceptron is connected with all neurons (or input nodes in the case of the first hidden layer) in the previous layer. The signals flow from one layer to another layer from left to right.

11.5.3 ADALINE network model

Adaptive Linear Neural Element (ADALINE) is an early single-layer ANN developed by Professor Bernard Widrow of Stanford University. As depicted in Figure 11.16, it has only output neuron. The output value can be +1 or −1. A bias input x_0 (where

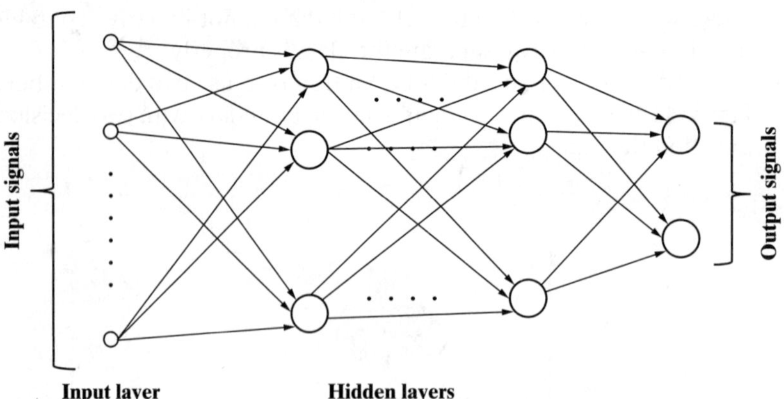

FIG. 11.15
Multi-layer perceptron

$x_0 = 1$) having a weight w_0 is added. The activation function is such that if the weighted sum is positive or 0, then the output is 1, else it is −1. Formally, we can say,

$$y_{sum} = \sum_{i=1}^{n} w_i x_i + b, \text{ where } b = w_0$$

$$y_{out} = f(y_{sum}) = \begin{cases} 1, x \geq 1 \\ -1, x < 1 \end{cases}$$

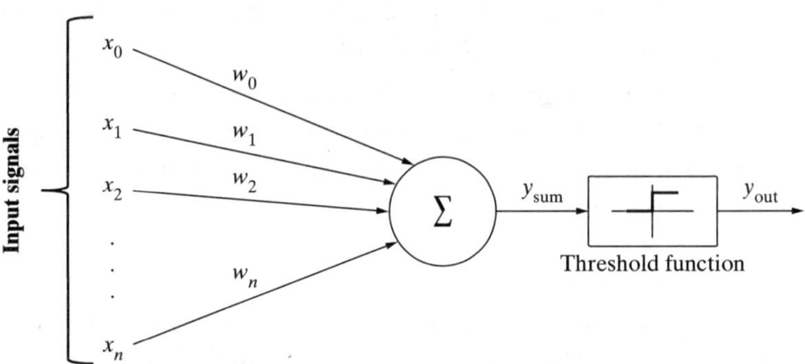

FIG. 11.16
ADALINE network

The supervised learning algorithm adopted by the ADALINE network is known as Least Mean Square (LMS) or Delta rule.

A network combining a number of ADALINEs is termed as MADALINE (many ADALINE). MADALINE networks can be used to solve problems related to non-linear separability.

Note:

Both perceptron and ADALINE are neural network models. Both of them are classifiers for binary classification. They have linear decision boundary and use a threshold activation function.

11.6   ARCHITECTURES OF NEURAL NETWORK

As we have seen till now, ANN is a computational system consisting of a large number of interconnected units called artificial neurons. The connection between artificial neurons can transmit signal from one neuron to another. There are multiple possibilities for connecting the neurons based on which architecture we are going to adopt for a specific solution. Some of the choices are listed below:

- There may be just two layers of neuron in the network – the input and output layer.
- Other than the input and output layers, there may be one or more intermediate 'hidden' layers of neuron.
- The neurons may be connected with one or more of the neurons in the next layer.
- The neurons may be connected with all neurons in the next layer.
- There may be single or multiple output signals. If there are multiple output signals, they might be connected with each other.
- The output from one layer may become input to neurons in the same or preceding layer.

11.6.1   Single-layer feed forward network

Single-layer feed forward is the simplest and most basic architecture of ANNs. It consists of only two layers as depicted in Figure 11.17 – the input layer and the output layer. The input layer consists of a set of 'm' input neurons $X_1, X_2, ..., X_m$ connected to each of the 'n' output neurons $Y_1, Y_2, ..., Y_n$. The connections carry weights w_{11}, $w_{12}, ..., w_{mn}$. The input layer of neurons does not conduct any processing – they pass the input signals to the output neurons. The computations are performed only by the neurons in the output layer. So, though it has two layers of neurons, only one layer is performing the computation. This is the reason why the network is known as single layer in spite of having two layers of neurons. Also, the signals always flow from the input layer to the output layer. Hence, this network is known as feed forward.

The net signal input to the output neurons is given by

$$y_{\text{in\_}k} + x_1 w_{1k} + x_2 w_{2k} + ... + x_m w_{mk} = \sum_{i=1}^{m} x_i w_{ik},$$

for the k-th output neuron. The signal output from each output neuron will depend on the activation function used.

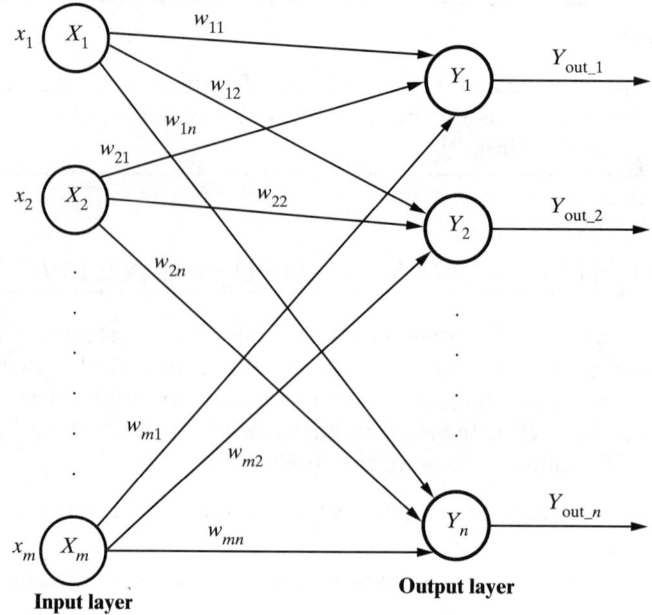

FIG. 11.17
Single-layer feed forward

11.6.2 Multi-layer feed forward ANNs

The multi-layer feed forward network is quite similar to the single-layer feed forward network, except for the fact that there are one or more intermediate layers of neurons between the input and the output layers. Hence, the network is termed as multi-layer. The structure of this network is depicted in Figure 11.18.

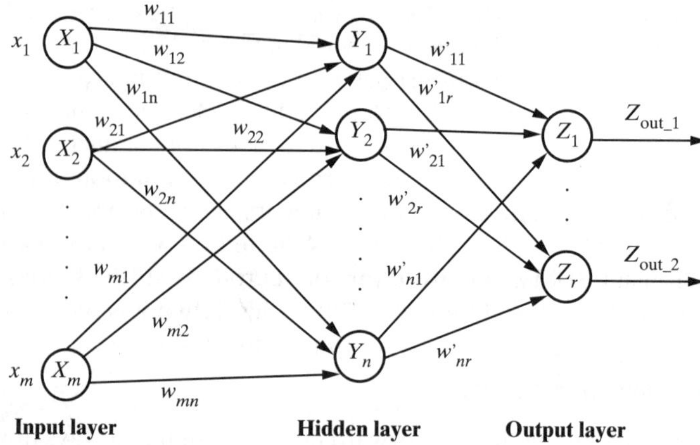

FIG. 11.18
Multi-layer feed forward

Each of the layers may have varying number of neurons. For example, the one shown in Figure 11.18 has 'm' neurons in the input layer and 'r' neurons in the output layer, and there is only one hidden layer with 'n' neurons.

The net signal input to the neuron in the hidden layer is given by

$$y_{\text{in}\_k} = x_1 w_{1k} + x_2 w_{2k} + \ldots + x_m w_{mk} = \sum_{i=1}^{m} x_i w_{ik},$$

for the k-th hidden layer neuron. The net signal input to the neuron in the output layer is given by

$$z_{\text{in}\_k} = y_{\text{out}\_1} w'_{1k} + y_{\text{out}\_2} w'_{2k} + \ldots + y_{\text{out}\_n} w'_{nk} = \sum_{i=1}^{n} y_{\text{out}\_i} w'_{ik},$$

for the k-th output layer neuron.

11.6.3 Competitive network

The competitive network is almost the same in structure as the single-layer feed forward network. The only difference is that the output neurons are connected with each other (either partially or fully). Figure 11.19 depicts a fully connected competitive network.

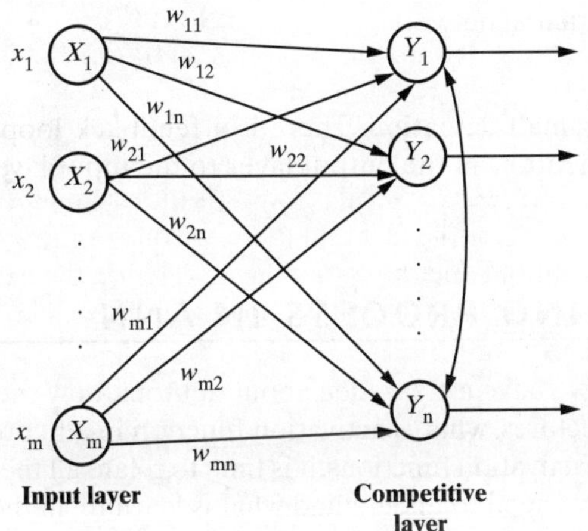

FIG. 11.19

Competitive network

In competitive networks, for a given input, the output neurons compete amongst themselves to represent the input. It represents a form of unsupervised learning algorithm in ANN that is suitable to find clusters in a data set.

11.6.4 Recurrent network

We have seen that in feed forward networks, signals always flow from the input layer towards the output layer (through the hidden layers in the case of multi-layer feed forward networks), i.e. in one direction. In the case of recurrent neural networks,

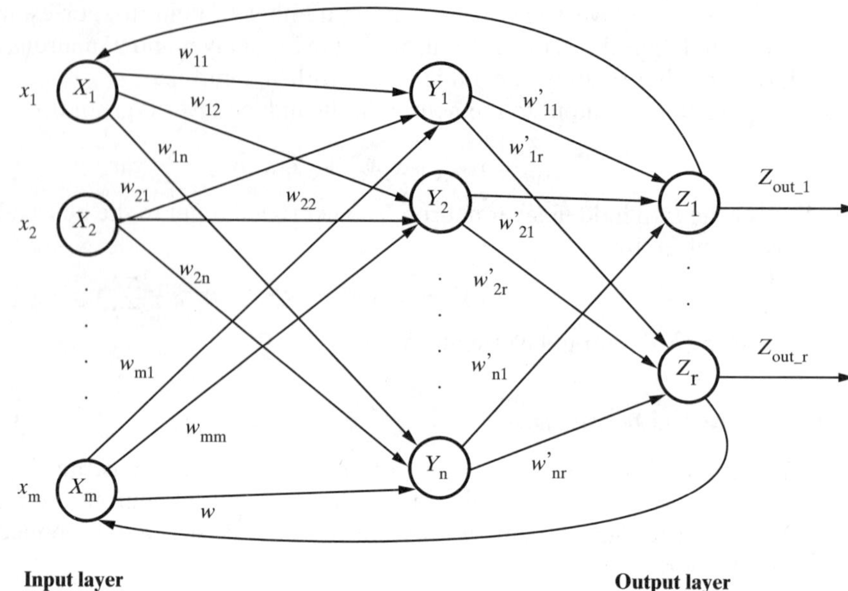

FIG. 11.20
Recurrent neural network

there is a small deviation. There is a feedback loop, as depicted in Figure 11.20, from the neurons in the output layer to the input layer neurons. There may also be self-loops.

11.7   LEARNING PROCESS IN ANN

Now that we have a clear idea about neurons, how they form networks using different architectures, what is activation function in a neuron, and what are the different choices of activation functions, it is time to relate all these to our main focus, i.e. learning. First, we need to understand what is learning in the context of ANNs? There are four major aspects which need to be decided:

(a) The number of layers in the network
(b) The direction of signal flow
(c) The number of nodes in each layer
(d) The value of weights attached with each interconnection between neurons

11.7.1 Number of layers

As we have seen earlier, a neural network may have a single layer or multi-layer. In the case of a single layer, a set of neurons in the input layer receives signal, i.e. a single feature per neuron, from the data set. The value of the feature is transformed by the activation function of the input neuron. The signals processed by the neurons in the input layer are then forwarded to the neurons in the output layer. The neurons in the output layer use their own activation function to generate the final prediction.

More complex networks may be designed with multiple hidden layers between the input layer and the output layer. Most of the multi-layer networks are fully connected.

11.7.2 Direction of signal flow

In certain networks, termed as feed forward networks, signal is always fed in one direction, i.e. from the input layer towards the output layer through the hidden layers, if there is any. However, certain networks, such as the recurrent network, also allow signals to travel from the output layer to the input layer.

This is also an important consideration for choosing the correct learning model.

11.7.3 Number of nodes in layers

In the case of a multi-layer network, the number of nodes in each layer can be varied. However, the number of nodes or neurons in the input layer is equal to the number of features of the input data set. Similarly, the number of output nodes will depend on possible outcomes, e.g. number of classes in the case of supervised learning. So, the number of nodes in each of the hidden layers is to be chosen by the user. A larger number of nodes in the hidden layer help in improving the performance. However, too many nodes may result in overfitting as well as an increased computational expense.

11.7.4 Weight of interconnection between neurons

Deciding the value of weights attached with each interconnection between neurons so that a specific learning problem can be solved correctly is quite a difficult problem by itself. Let us try to understand it in the context of a problem. Let us take a step back and look at the problem in Section 11.6.2.

We have a set of points with known labels as given below. We have to train an ANN model using this data, so that it can classify a new test data, say p_5 (3, –2).

- $p_1 = (5, 2)$ and $p_2 = (-1, 12)$ belonging to c_1
- $p_3 = (3, -5)$ and $p_4 = (-2, -1)$ belonging to c_2

When we were discussing the problem in Section 11.6.2, we assumed the values of the synaptic weights w_0, w_1, and w_2 as –2, ½, and ¼, respectively. But where on earth did we get those values from? Will we get these weight values for every learning problem that we will attempt to solve using ANN? The answer is a big NO.

For solving a learning problem using ANN, we can start with a set of values for the synaptic weights and keep doing changes to those values in multiple iterations. In the case of supervised learning, the objective to be pursued is to reduce the number of misclassifications. Ideally, the iterations for making changes in weight values should be continued till there is no misclassification. However, in practice, such a stopping criterion may not be possible to achieve. Practical stopping criteria may be the rate of misclassification less than a specific threshold value, say 1%, or the maximum number of iterations reaches a threshold, say 25, etc. There may be other practical challenges to deal with, such as the rate of misclassification is not reducing progressively. This may become a bigger problem when the number of interconnections and hence the number of weights keeps increasing. There are ways to deal with those challenges, which we will see in more details in the next section.

So, to summarize, learning process using ANN is a combination of multiple aspects – which include deciding the number of hidden layers, number of nodes in each of the hidden layers, direction of signal flow, and last but not the least, deciding the connection weights.

Multi-layer feed forward network is a commonly adopted architecture. It has been observed that a neural network with even one hidden layer can be used to reasonably approximate any continuous function. The learning method adopted to train a multi-layer feed forward network is termed as backpropagation, which we will study in the next section.

11.8   BACKPROPAGATION

We have already seen that one of the most critical activities of training an ANN is to assign the inter-neuron connection weights. It can be a very intense work, more so for the neural networks having a high number of hidden layers or a high number of nodes in a layer. In 1986, an efficient method of training an ANN was discovered. In this method, errors, i.e. difference in output values of the output layer and the expected values, are propagated back from the output layer to the preceding layers. Hence, the algorithm implementing this method is known as backpropagation, i.e. propagating the errors backward to the preceding layers.

The backpropagation algorithm is applicable for multi-layer feed forward networks. It is a supervised learning algorithm which continues adjusting the weights of the connected neurons with an objective to reduce the deviation of the output signal from the target output. This algorithm consists of multiple iterations, also known as **epochs**. Each epoch consists of two phases –

- A **forward phase** in which the signals flow from the neurons in the input layer to the neurons in the output layer through the hidden layers. The weights of the interconnections and activation functions are used during the flow. In the output layer, the output signals are generated.

- A **backward phase** in which the output signal is compared with the expected value. The computed errors are propagated backwards from the output to the preceding layers. The errors propagated back are used to adjust the interconnection weights between the layers.

The iterations continue till a stopping criterion is reached. Figure 11.21 depicts a reasonably simplified version of the backpropagation algorithm.

One main part of the algorithm is adjusting the interconnection weights. This is done using a technique termed as **gradient descent**. In simple terms, the algorithm calculates the partial derivative of the activation function by each interconnection weight to identify the 'gradient' or extent of change of the weight required to minimize the

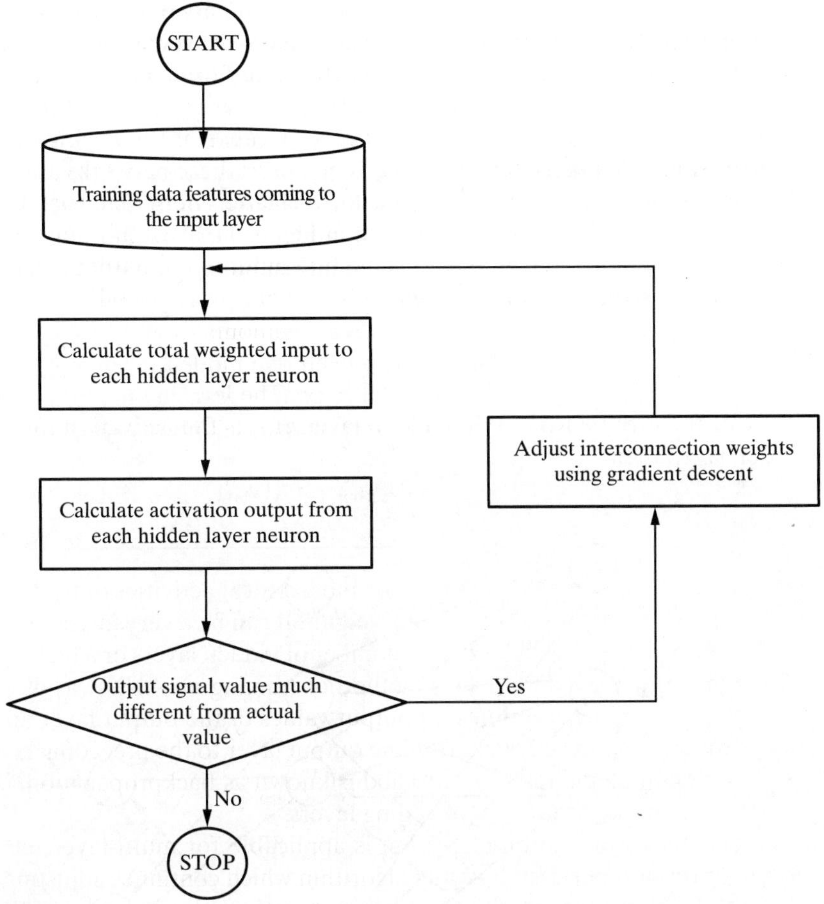

FIG. 11.21
Backpropagation algorithm

cost function. Quite understandably, therefore, the activation function needs to be differentiable. Let us try to understand this in a bit more details.

Points to Ponder:

A real-world simile for the gradient descent algorithm is a blind person trying to come down from a hill top without anyone to assist. The person is not able to see. So, for the person who is not able to see the path of descent, the only option is to check in which direction the land slope feels to be downward. One challenge of this approach arises when the person reaches a point which feels to be the lowest, as all the points surrounding it is higher in slope, but in reality it is not so. Such a point, which is local minima and not global minima, may be deceiving and stalls the algorithm before reaching the real global minima.

We have already seen that multi-layer neural networks have multiple hidden layers. During the learning phase, the interconnection weights are adjusted on the basis of the errors generated by the network, i.e. difference in the output signal of the network vis-à-vis the expected value. These errors generated at the output layer are propagated back to the preceding layers. Because of the backward propagation of errors which happens during the learning phase, these networks are also called backpropagation networks or simply backpropagation nets. One such backpropagation net with one hidden layer is depicted in Figure 11.22. In this network, X_0 is the bias input to the hidden layer and Y_0 is the bias input to the output layer.

The net signal input to the hidden layer neurons is given by

$$y_{in\_k} = x_0 w_{0k} + x_1 w_{1k} + x_2 w_{2k} + \ldots + x_m w_{mk} = w_{0k} + \sum_{i=1}^{m} x_i w_{ik},$$

for the k-th neuron in the hidden layer. If f_y is the activation function of the hidden layer, then

$$y_{out\_k} = f_y(y_{in\_k})$$

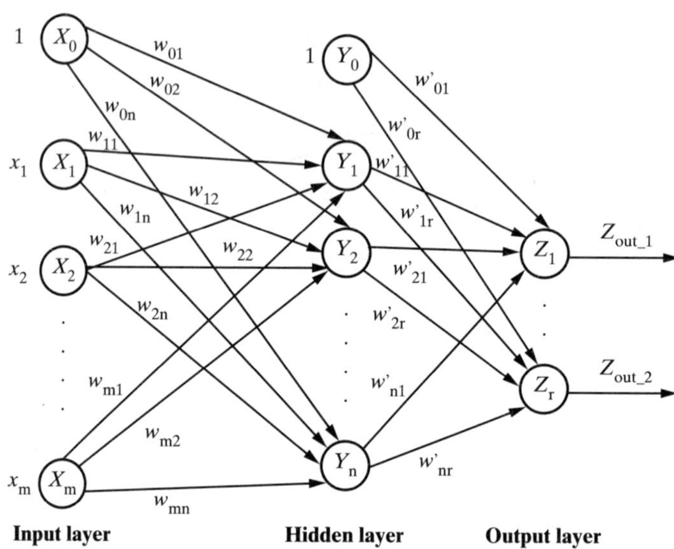

FIG. 11.22

Backpropagation net

The net signal input to the output layer neurons is given by

$$z_{in\_k} = y_0 w'_{0k} + y_{out\_1} w'_{1k} + y_{out\_2} w'_{2k} + \ldots + y_{out\_n} w'_{nk} = w'_{0k} + \sum_{i=1}^{n} y_{out\_i} w'_{ik},$$

for the k-th neuron in the output layer. Note that the input signals to X_0 and Y_0 are assumed as 1. If f_z is the activation function of the hidden layer, then

$$z_{out\_k} = f_z(z_{in\_k})$$

If t_k is the target output of the k-th output neuron, then the cost function defined as the squared error of the output layer is given by

$$E = \frac{1}{2}\sum_{k=1}^{n}\left(t_k - z_{\text{out\_}k}\right)^2$$

$$= \frac{1}{2}\sum_{k=1}^{n}\left(t_k - f_z\left(z_{\text{in\_}k}\right)\right)^2$$

Note:

There are two types of gradient descent algorithms. When a full data set is used in one shot to compute the gradient, it is known as **full batch gradient** descent. In the case of **stochastic gradient descent**, which is also known as **incremental gradient descent**, smaller samples of the data are taken iteratively and used in the gradient computation. Thus, stochastic gradient descent tries to identify the global minima.

So, as a part of the gradient descent algorithm, partial derivative of the cost function E has to be done with respect to each of the interconnection weights $w'_{01}, w'_{02}, ..., w'_{nr}$. Mathematically, it can be represented as follows:

$$\frac{\partial E}{\partial w'_{jk}} = \frac{\partial}{\partial w'_{jk}}\left\{\frac{1}{2}\sum_{k=1}^{n}\left(t_k - f_z\left(z_{\text{in\_}k}\right)\right)^2\right\},$$

for the interconnection weight between the j-th neuron in the hidden layer and the k-th neuron in the output layer. This expression can be deduced to

$$\frac{\partial E}{\partial w'_{jk}} = -\left(t_k - z_{\text{out\_}k}\right)\cdot f'_z\left(z_{\text{in\_}k}\right)\cdot\frac{\partial}{\partial w'_{jk}}\left(\sum_{i=0}^{n} y_{\text{out\_}i}\cdot w_{ik}\right),$$

where $f'_z\left(z_{\text{in\_}k}\right) = \dfrac{\partial}{\partial w'_{jk}}\left(f_z\left(z_{\text{in\_}k}\right)\right)$

$$\text{or,}\ \ \frac{\partial E}{\partial w'_{jk}} = -\left(t_k - z_{\text{out\_}k}\right)\cdot f'_z\left(z_{\text{in\_}k}\right)\cdot y_{\text{out\_}i}$$

If we assume $\delta w_k = -\left(t_k - z_{\text{out\_}k}\right)\cdot f'_z\left(z_{\text{in\_}k}\right)$ as a component of the weight adjustment needed for weight w_{jk} corresponding to the k-th output neuron, then

$$\frac{\partial E}{\partial w'_{jk}} = \delta w'_k \cdot y_{\text{out\_}i}$$

On the basis of this, the weights and bias need to be updated as follows:

For weights: $\Delta w_{jk} = -\alpha \cdot \dfrac{\partial E}{\partial w'_{jk}} = -\alpha \cdot \delta w'_k \cdot y_{\text{out\_}i}$

Hence, $w'_{jk}(\text{new}) = w'_{jk}(\text{old}) + \Delta w'_{jk}$

For bias: $\Delta w_{0k} = -\alpha.\delta w'_k$

Hence, $w'_{0k}(\text{new}) = w'_{0k}(\text{old}) + \Delta w'_{0k}$

Note that 'α' is the learning rate of the neural network.

In the same way, we can perform the calculations for the interconnection weights between the input and hidden layers. The weights and bias for the interconnection between the input and hidden layers need to be updated as follows:

For weights: $\Delta w_{ij} = -\alpha \cdot \dfrac{\partial E}{\partial w_{ij}} = -\alpha \cdot \delta w_j \cdot x_{out\_i}$

Hence, $w_{ij}(\text{ new }) = w_{ij}(\text{ old }) + \Delta w_{ij}$

For bias: $\Delta w_{0j} = -\alpha. \, \delta w_j$

Hence, $w_{0j}(\text{new}) = w_{0j}(\text{old}) + \Delta w_{0j}$

Note:

Learning rate is a user parameter which increases or decreases the speed with which the interconnection weights of a neural network is to be adjusted. If the learning rate is too high, the adjustment done as a part of the gradient descent process may miss the minima. Then, the training may not converge, and it may even diverge. On the other hand, if the learning rate is too low, the optimization may consume more time because of the small steps towards the minima.

A balanced approach is to start the training with a relatively large learning rate (say 0.1), because in the beginning, random weights are far from optimal. Then, the learning rate should be decreased during training (say exponentially lower values, e.g. 0.01, 0.001, etc.) to allow more fine-grained weight updates.

For implementing neural network in Python, *neurolab* is a great option. It is a simple and powerful neural network library for Python. You can install *neurolab* by using the command below from the command prompt:

```
$ pip install neurolab
```

Please refer to the Figure B.9 for more details.

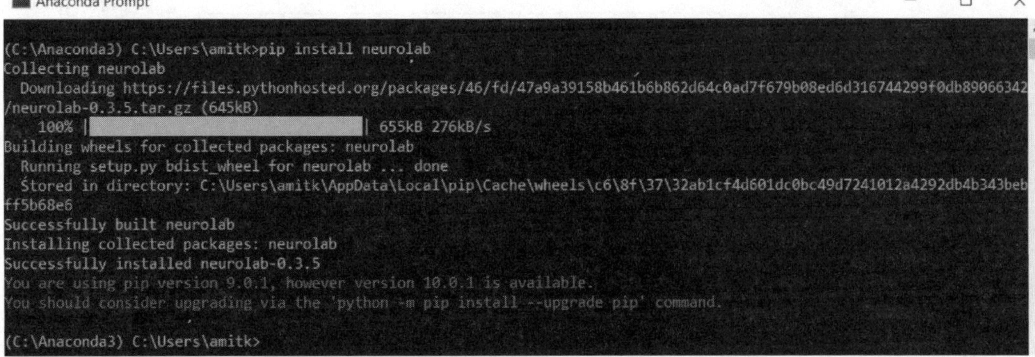

FIG. 11.23
Installing *neurolab* from command prompt

Let's first implement a single layer feed forward neural network. We can use the same set of data as provided as an example in Chapter 10, Section 10.6.2. The data is as below and output shown in Figure B.10.

- p1 = (5, 2) and p2 = (−1, 12) belonging to c1
- p3 = (3, −5) and p4 = (−2, −1) belonging to c2

This can summarized as

FEATURE 1	FEATURE 2	TARGET (OR CLASS)
5	2	1
−1	12	1
3	−5	2
−2	−1	2

So let's do the programming now.

```
>>> import neurolab as nl
>>> import matplotlib.pyplot as plt    # Plot results

>>> input = [[5, 2], [-1, 12], [3, -5], [-2, -1]]
>>> target = [[1], [1], [2], [2]]

# Create single layer neural net with 2 inputs and 1 neuron
>>> net = nl.net.newp([[-2, 12],[1, 2]], 1)  # Function newp is for
implementing single layer perceptron ...
>>> error = net.train(input, target, epochs=10, show=10, lr=0.1)

>>> plt.plot(error)
>>> plt.xlabel('Epoch number')
>>> plt.ylabel('Train error')
>>> plt.grid()
>>> plt.show()
```

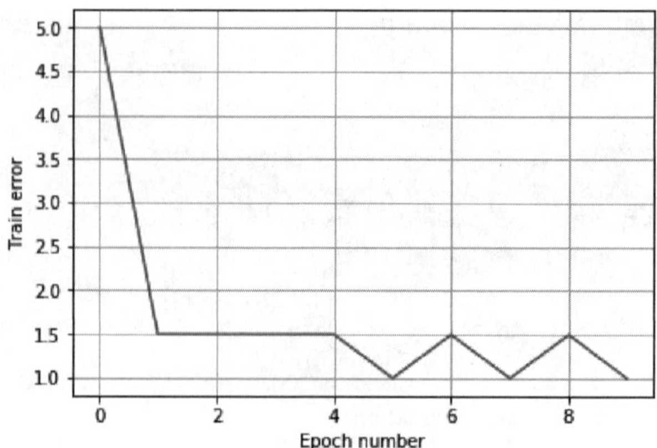

FIG. 11.24
Epoch number vs. error in a single-layer NN

Next let's implement a multi layer feed forward neural network. We can have multiple hidden layers in this case. In this case, we will use multi layer neural network as a regressor i.e. to predict a continuous variable. A set of 75 values of predictor variable is first generated within a specified range. The corresponding target values are generated using the equation $y = 4x^2 + 7.6$ and normalized. Using these set of points, a multi layer neural network is trained. Then using the trained model, predictions are generated and compared with the actual data points generated from the regression function.

```
>>> import neurolab as nl
>>> import matplotlib.pyplot as plt

# Create train samples assuming minimum value = -2, maximum value
= 2 and number of training points = 75
>>> minm_val = -2
>>> maxm_val = 2
>>> no_points = 75
>>> x = np.linspace(minm_val, maxm_val, no_points)
>>> y = 4*np.square(x) + 7.6
>>> y /= np.linalg.norm(y)

>>> input_data = x.reshape(no_points,1)
>>> target = y.reshape(no_points,1)

# Create network with 2 hidden layers - with 12 neurons in the
first layer and 8 neurons in the second layer.
# Task is to predict the value, so the output layer will contain
1 neuron ...
>>> net = nl.net.newff([[minm_val, maxm_val]],[12, 8, 1])
```

```
# Then the training algorithm is set to gradient descent ...
>>> net.trainf = nl.train.train_gd

# Now do the real training
>>> error = net.train(input_data, target, epochs=2000, show=100,
goal=0.01)

# Simulate network to generate prediction ...
>>> output_data = net.sim(input_data)
>>> pred_val = output_data.reshape(no_points)

# Plotting the results ...
>>> plt.figure()
>>> plt.plot(error)
>>> plt.xlabel('Epoch number')
>>> plt.ylabel('Train error')
>>> plt.grid()
>>> plt.show()

>>> x_dash = np.linspace(minm_val, maxm_val, no_points*2)
>>> y_dash = net.sim(x_dash.reshape(x_dash.size,1)).reshape(x_
dash.size)

>>> plt.figure()
>>> plt.plot(x_dash, y_dash, '.', x, y, '+', x, pred_val, 'p')
>>> plt.legend(['Actual', 'Predicted'])
>>> plt.title('Actual vs predicted')
>>> plt.show()
```

Output is presented in Figures B.11 and B.12.

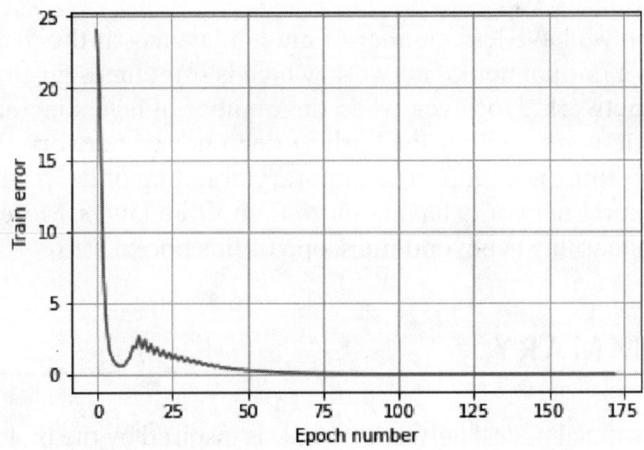

FIG. 11.25
Epoch number vs. error in a multi layer NN

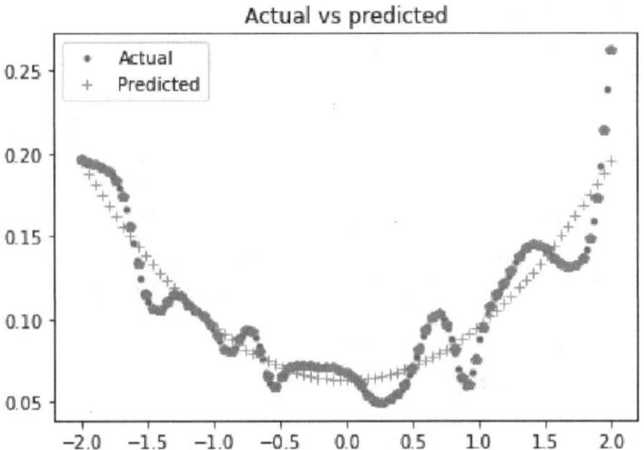

FIG. 11.26
Actual vs. predicted in a multi layer NN

11.9   DEEP LEARNING

Neural networks, as we have already seen in this chapter, are a class of machine learning algorithms. As we have also seen, there are multiple choices of architectures for neural networks, multi-layer neural network being one of the most adopted ones. However, in a multi-layer neural network, as we keep increasing the number of hidden layers, the computation becomes very expensive. Going beyond two to three layers becomes quite difficult computationally. The only way to handle such intense computation is by using graphics processing unit (GPU) computing.

When we have less number of hidden layers – at the maximum two to three layers, it is a normal neural network, which is sometimes given the fancy name 'shallow neural network'. However, when the number of layers increases, it is termed as deep neural network. One of the earliest deep neural networks had three hidden layers. Deep learning is a more contemporary branding of deep neural networks, i.e. multi-layer neural networks having more than three layers. More detailed understanding of deep learning is beyond the scope of this book.

11.10   SUMMARY

- Artificial neural network (ANN) is inspired by the biological neural network. In an ANN, the biological form of neuron is replicated in the electronic or digital form of neuron.
- Each neuron has three major components:
  - ❖ A set of synapses having weight

- ❖ A summation junction for the input signals weighted by the respective synaptic weight
- ❖ A threshold activation function results in an output signal only when an input signal exceeding a specific threshold value comes as an input
- Different types of activation functions include:
  - ❖ Threshold/Step function
  - ❖ Identity function
  - ❖ ReLU function
  - ❖ Sigmoid function
  - ❖ Hyperbolic tangent function
- Some of the earlier implementations of ANN include
  - ❖ McCulloch–Pitts Model of Neuron
  - ❖ Rosenblatt's Perceptron
  - ❖ ADALINE Network Model
- Some of the architectures of neural network include
  - ❖ Single-layer feed forward ANNs: simplest and most basic architecture consisting on an input and output layer.
  - ❖ Multi-layer feed forward ANNs – there are one or more hidden intermediate layers of neurons between the input and the output layers
  - ❖ Competitive network – similar to single-layer feed forward network. The only difference is that the output neurons are connected with each other (either partially or fully).
  - ❖ Recurrent networks – single or multi-layer, with a feedback loop from the neurons in the output layer to the input layer neurons. There may also be self-loops.
- There are four major aspects which need to be decided while learning using ANN
  - ❖ The number of layers in the network
  - ❖ The direction of signal flow
  - ❖ The number of nodes in each layer
  - ❖ The value of weights attached with each interconnection between neurons
- In the backpropagation algorithm, errors are propagated back from the output layer to the preceding layers. The backpropagation algorithm is applicable for multi-layer feed forward network.
- A technique termed as gradient descent is used to adjust the interconnection weights between neurons of different layers.
- When the number of hidden layers in multi-layer neural networks is higher than three, it is termed as deep neural network. Deep learning is a more contemporary branding of deep neural networks.

SAMPLE QUESTIONS

MULTIPLE-CHOICE QUESTIONS

1. ANN is made up of ___ neurons.
   (a) biological
   (b) digital
   (c) logical
   (d) none of the above

2. Biological neuron does not consist:
   (a) dendrite
   (b) synapse
   (c) soma
   (d) axon

3. A neuron is able to ___ information in the form of chemical and electrical signals.
   (a) receive
   (b) process
   (c) transmit
   (d) all of the above

4. A summation junction is a ____ for the input signals.
   (a) tokenizer
   (b) multiplier
   (c) linear combiner
   (d) None of the above

5. Step function gives __ as output if the input is either 0 or positive.
   (a) 0
   (b) -1
   (c) 1
   (d) None of the above

6. A binary sigmoid function has range of ___.
   (a) $(-1, +1)$
   (b) $(0, -1)$
   (c) $(0, 1)$
   (d) $(1, 0)$

7. A bipolar sigmoid function has range of ___.
   (a) $(-1, +1)$
   (b) $(0, -1)$
   (c) $(0, 1)$
   (d) $(1, 0)$

8. The inputs of the McCulloch–Pitts neuron could be ___.
   (a) either -1 or 1
   (b) either 0 or 1
   (c) either 0 or -1
   (d) none of the above

9. Single-layer perceptron is able to deal with
   (a) linearly separable data
   (b) non-linearly separable data
   (c) linearly inseparable data
   (d) none of the above

10. Single-layer feed forward network consists of ___ layers.
   (a) two
   (b) one
   (c) three
   (d) many

11. Multi-layer feed forward network consists of ___ layers.
   (a) two
   (b) one
   (c) three
   (d) many

12. In competitive networks, output neurons are connected with __.
   (a) each other
   (b) input neurons
   (c) synapse
   (d) none of the above

13. Recurrent networks
   (a) are similar to multi-layer feed forward networks
   (b) may have self-loops
   (c) have feedback loops
   (d) all of the above

14. Which of the following are critical aspects of learning in ANN?
(a) The number of layers in the network
(b) The number of nodes in each layer
(c) The interconnection weights
(d) all of the above

15. In the backpropagation algorithm, multiple iterations are known as
(a) degree
(b) epoch
(c) cardinality
(d) none of the above

16. Each epoch consists of phases –
(a) forward
(b) backward
(c) both a and b
(d) none of the above

17. Deep neural networks generally have more than ___ hidden layers.
(a) 1
(b) 2
(c) 3
(d) none of the above

18. To handle intense computation of deep learning, ___ is needed.
(a) parallel computing
(b) CPU-based traditional computing
(c) GPU computing
(d) none of the above

SHORT-ANSWER TYPE QUESTIONS (5 MARKS EACH)

1. What is the function of a summation junction of a neuron? What is threshold activation function?

2. What is a step function? What is the difference of step function with threshold function?

3. Explain the McCulloch–Pitts model of neuron.

4. Explain the ADALINE network model.

5. What is the constraint of a simple perceptron? Why it may fail with a real-world data set?

6. What is linearly inseparable problem? What is the role of the hidden layer?

7. Explain XOR problem in case of a simple perceptron.

8. Design a multi-layer perceptron to implement A XOR B.

9. Explain the single-layer feed forward architecture of ANN.

10. Explain the competitive network architecture of ANN.

11. Consider a multi-layer feed forward neural network. Enumerate and explain steps in the backpropagation algorithm used to train the network.

12. What are the advantages and disadvantages of neural networks?

13.   Write short notes on any two of the following:
      (a) Biological neuron
      (b) ReLU function
      (c) Single-layer feed forward ANN
      (d) Gradient descent
      (e) Recurrent networks

LONG-ANSWER TYPE QUESTIONS (10 MARKS EACH)

1.   Describe the structure of an artificial neuron. How is it similar to a biological neuron? What are its main components?

2.   What are the different types of activation functions popularly used? Explain each of them.

3.   (a) Explain, in details, Rosenblatt's perceptron model. How can a set of data be classified using a simple perceptron?
     (b) Use a simple perceptron with weights w_0, w_1, and w_2 as $-1, 2$, and 1, respectively, to classify data points $(3, 4)$; $(5, 2)$; $(1, -3)$; $(-8, -3)$; $(-3, 0)$.

4.   Explain the basic structure of a multi-layer perceptron. Explain how it can solve the XOR problem.

5.   What is artificial neural network (ANN)? Explain some of the salient highlights in the different architectural options for ANN.

6.   Explain the learning process of an ANN. Explain, with example, the challenge in assigning synaptic weights for the interconnection between neurons? How can this challenge be addressed?

7.   Explain, in details, the backpropagation algorithm. What are the limitations of this algorithm?

8.   Describe, in details, the process of adjusting the interconnection weights in a multi-layer neural network.

9.   What are the steps in the backpropagation algorithm? Why a multi-layer neural network is required?

10. (a) Write short notes on any two of the following:
         (i)   Artificial neuron
         (ii) Multi-layer perceptron
         (iii) Deep learning
         (iv) Learning rate

     (b) Write the difference between (any two)
         (i)   Activation function vs threshold function
         (ii) Step function vs sigmoid function
         (iii) Single layer vs multi-layer perceptron

Chapter 12
Other Types of Learning

OBJECTIVE OF THE CHAPTER:

In the previous chapters, you have got a good understanding of supervised learning algorithms and unsupervised learning algorithms. In this chapter, we will discuss learning types that were not covered in the earlier chapters such as representation learning, active learning, instance-based Learning, association rule, and ensemble learning. By the end of this chapter, you will gain sufficient knowledge in all aspects of learning and become ready to start solving problems independently..

12.1 INTRODUCTION

In this chapter, we will discuss learning types that were not covered in the earlier chapters such as representation learning, active learning, instance-based Learning, association rule, and ensemble learning.

12.2 REPRESENTATION LEARNING

Another name for representation learning is feature learning. While many enterprises nowadays retain substantial amounts of business-related data, most of those are often unstructured and unlabelled. Creating new labels is generally a time-consuming and expensive endeavor. As a result, machine learning algorithms that can straight away mine structures from unlabelled data to improve business performance are reasonably valued. Representation learning is one such type where the extraction from the overall unlabelled data happens using a 'neural network'. The main objective of representation learning (feature learning) is to find an appropriate representation of data based on features to perform a machine learning task. Representation learning has become a field in itself because of its popularity. Refer the Chapter 4 titled 'Basics of Feature Engineering' to understand more about the feature and feature selection process. An example of some of the characteristics of a triangle are its corners (or vertices), sides, and degree of angle. Every triangle has three corners and three angles. The sum of the three angles of a triangle is equal to 180°. The types of triangles with their characteristics are given below.

Consider you are tasked to classify/identify the types of triangles (Refer **to Table 12.1**). The way you do that is to find unique characteristics of the type of triangle given as input.

The system may work something like this

Input – Triangular image

Representation – Three angles, length of sides.

Model – It gets an input representation (angles, length of sides) and applies rules as per Table 12.1 to detect the type of triangle.

Great! Now, we have a primary representational working system to detect the type of triangle.

What happens when we begin to input shapes like squares, rectangles, circles, or all sorts of shapes instead of a triangle? What if the image contains both a triangle and a circle? Designing to adapt to this kind of feature requires deep domain expertise as we start working with real-world applications. Deep Learning goes one step further and learns/tries to learn features on its own. All we would do is feed in an image as input and let the system learn features like human beings do

Representation learning is most widely used in words, speech recognition, signal processing, music, and image identification. For example, a word can have meaning based on the context.

Table 12.1
Types of Triangles

S. No	Types of triangles	Characteristics
1	Acute triangle	A triangle in which all three angles are less than 90°
2	Obtuse triangle	An obtuse triangle is a triangle in which one of the angles is greater than 90°.
3	Right triangle	A right triangle is triangle with an angle of 90°.
4	Scalene triangle	A triangle with three unequal sides.
5	Isosceles triangle	An isosceles triangle is a triangle with (at least) two equal sides.
6	Equilateral triangle	An equilateral triangle is a triangle with all three sides of equal length.
7	Equiangular triangle	An equiangular triangle is a triangle, which has three equal angles.

Generation and Recognition in Representation Learning

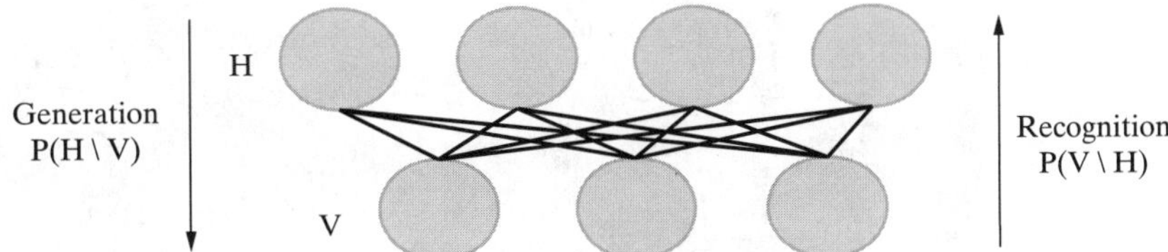

FIG. 12.1
Generation versus recognition

In Figure 12.1, V represents the input data, and H represents the causes. When the causes (H) explain the data (V) we observe, it is called Recognition. When unknown causes (H) are combined, it can also generate the data (V), it is called generative (or) Generation.

Representation learning is inspired by the fact that machine learning tasks such as classification regularly require numerical inputs that are mathematically and computationally easy to process. However, it is difficult to define the features algorithmically for real-world objects such as images and videos. An alternative is to discover such features or representations just through examination, without trusting on explicit algorithms. So, representation learning can be either supervised or unsupervised.

1. Supervised neural networks and multilayer perceptron

2. Independent component analysis (unsupervised)

3. Autoencoders (unsupervised) and

4. Various forms of clustering.

12.2.1 Supervised neural networks and multilayer perceptron

Refer the Chapter 10 titled 'Basics of Neural Network' to understand more on the topic of the neural network.

12.2.2 Independent Component Analysis (Unsupervised)

Independent component analysis, or ICA is similar to principal component analysis (PCA), with the exception that the components are independent and uncorrelated. ICA is used primarily for separating unknown source signals from their observed linear mixtures after the linear mixture with an unfamiliar matrix (A) . Nil information is known about the sources or the mixing process except that there are N different recorded mixtures. The job is to recuperate a version(U) of the sources (S) which are identical except for scaling and permutation, by finding a square matrix (W) specifying spatial filters that linearly invert the mixing process, i.e. $U = WX$. Maximizing the joint entropy, H(y), of the output of a neural processor minimizes the mutual information among the output components (Refer Fig. 12.2).

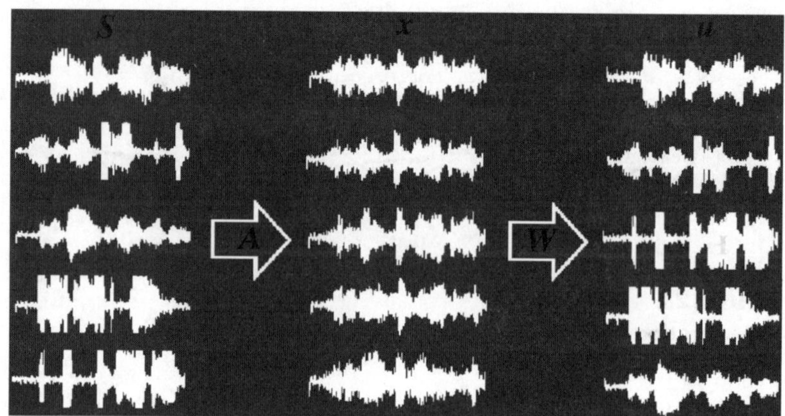

FIG. 12.2
Independent component analysis

12.2.3   Autoencoders

Autoencoders belong to the neural network family (Refer to Fig. 12.3) and are similar to Principal Component Analysis (PCA). They are more flexible than PCA. Autoencoders represent both linear and non-linear transformation, whereas PCA represents only linear transformation. The neural network's (autoencoder) target output is its input (x) in a different form (x'). In Autoencoders, the dimensionality of the input is equal to the dimensionality of the output, and essentially what we want is x' = x. x' = Decode (Encode(x))

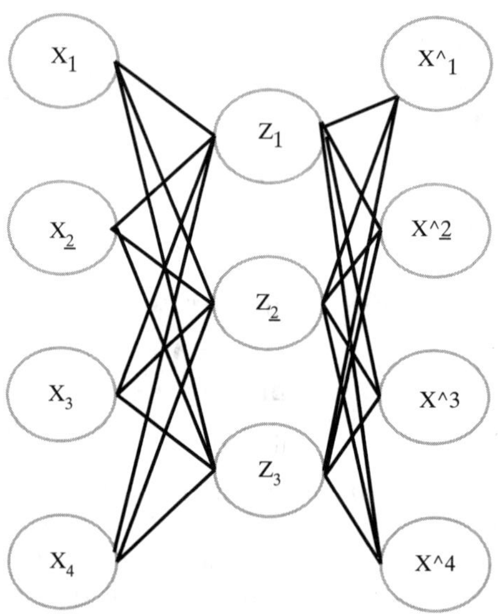

FIG. 12.3
Autoencoders

To get the value from the hidden layer, we multiply the (input to hidden) weights by the input. To get the value from the output, we multiply (hidden to output) weights by the hidden layer values.

$Z = f (Wx)$

$Y = g (Vz)$

$So\ Y = g(V f (Wx)) = VWx$

So Objective Function $J = \Sigma\ [Xn - VWx\ (n)]^2$

Heuristics for Autoencoders

The autoencoder training algorithm can be summarized as below:

For each input x

1. Do a feed-forward pass to compute activations at all hidden layers, then at the output layer to obtain an output X'
2. Measure the deviation X' from the input X
3. Backpropagate the error through the net and perform weight updates.

12.2.4 Various forms of clustering

Refer Chapter 9 titled 'Unsupervised Learning' to know more about various forms of Clustering.

12.3   ACTIVE LEARNING

Active learning is a type of semi-supervised learning in which a learning algorithm can interactively query (question) the user to obtain the desired outputs at new data points.

Let P be the population set of all data under consideration. For example, all male students studying in a college are known to have a particularly exciting study pattern.

During each iteration, I, P (total population) is broken up into three subsets.

1. P(K, i): Data points where the label is known (K).
2. P(U, i): Data points where the label is unknown (U)
3. P(C, i): A subset of P(U, i) that is chosen (C) to be labelled.

Current research in this type of active learning concentrates on identifying the best method P(C, i) to choose (C) the data points.

12.3.1 Heuristics for active learning

1. Start with a pool of unlabeled data P(U, i)
2. Pick a few points at random and get their labels P(C, i)
3. Repeat

Some active learning algorithms are built upon Support vector machines (SVMs) to determine the data points to label. Such methods usually calculate the margin (W) of each unlabeled datum in P(U, i) and assume W as an n-dimensional space distance commencing covering datum and the splitting hyperplane.

Minimum marginal hyperplane (MMH) techniques consent that the data records with the minimum margin (W) are those that the SVM is most uncertain about and therefore should be retained in P(C, i) to be labeled. Other comparable approaches, such as Maximum Marginal Hyperplane, select data with the significant W (*n-dimensional* space). Other approaches to select a combination of the smallest as well as largest Ws.

12.3.2 Active Learning Query Strategies

Few logics for determining which data points should be labeled are

1. Uncertainty sampling
2. Query by committee
3. Expected model change
4. Expected error reduction
5. Variance reduction

Uncertainty sampling: In this method, the active learning algorithm first tries to label the points for which the current model is least specific (as this means a lot of confusion) on the correct output.

Query by committee: A range of models are trained on the current labeled data, and vote on the output for unlabeled data; label those points for which the 'committee' disagrees the most.

Expected model change: In this method, the active learning algorithm first tries to label the points that would most change the existing model itself.

Expected error reduction: In this method, the active learning algorithm first tries to label the points that would mostly reduce the model's generalization error.

Variance reduction: In this method, the active learning algorithm first tries to label the points that would reduce output variance (which is also one of the components of error).

12.4   INSTANCE-BASED LEARNING (MEMORY-BASED LEARNING)

In instance-based learning (memory-based learning), the algorithm compares new problem instances with instances already seen in training, which have been stored in memory for reference rather than performing explicit generalization. It is called instance-based as it constructs hypotheses from the training instances (memories) themselves. Computational complexity O(n) of the hypothesis can grow when we have some data (n). It can quickly adapt its model to previously unseen data. New instances are either stored or thrown away based on the previously set criteria.

Examples of instance-based learning include the K-nearest neighbor algorithm (K-NN), kernel machines (support vector machine, PCA), and radial basis function (RBF) networks.

All these algorithms store already known instances and compute distances or similarities between this instance and the training instances to make the final decision.

The instance reduction algorithm can be used to overcome memory complexity problem and overfitting problem. Let us look into the radial basis function (RBF) in detail.

12.4.1 **Radial basis function**

Radial basis function (RBF) networks typically have three layers: one input layer, one hidden layer with a non-linear RBF activation function, and one linear output layer (Refer Fig. 12.4).

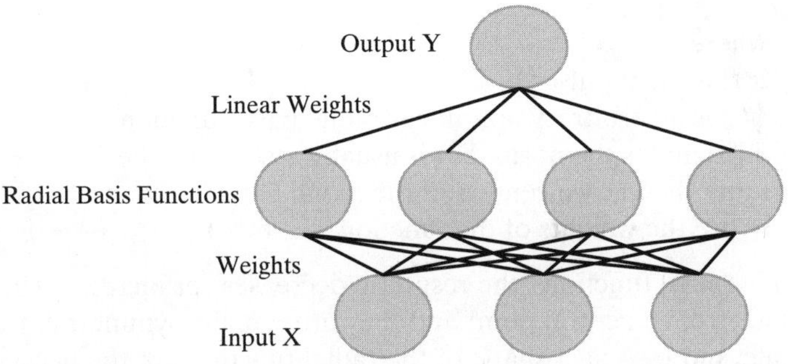

FIG. 12.4
Radial Basis Function

In the above diagram, an input vector(x) is used as input to all radial basis functions, each with different parameters. The input layer (X) is merely a fan-out layer, and no processing happens here. The second layer (hidden) performs radial basis functions, which are the non-linear mapping from the input space (Vector X) into a higher - order dimensional space. The output of the network (Y) is a linear combination of the outputs from radial basis functions. If pattern classification is required (in Y), then a hard-limiter or sigmoid function could be placed on the output neurons to give 0/1 output values.

The distinctive part of the radial basis function network (RFFN) is the procedure implemented in the hidden layer. The idea is that the patterns in the input space form clusters. Beyond this area (clustering area, RFB function area), the value drops dramatically. The Gaussian function is the most commonly used radial-basis function. In an RBF network, r is the distance from the cluster center.

Space (distance) computed from the cluster center. is usually the Euclidean distance. For each neuron that is part of the hidden layer, the weights represent the coordinates of the centre of the cluster. Therefore, when that neuron receives an input pattern, X, the distance is found using the following equation:

$$r_j = \sqrt{\sum_{i=1}^{n}\left(x_i - w_{ij}\right)^2}$$

The variable sigma, σ, denotes the width or radius of the bell shape and is to be determined by calculation. When the distance from the center of the Gaussian reaches σ, the output drops from 1 to 0.6.

$$(hidden_{unit})\phi_j = \exp\left(-\frac{\sum_{i=1}^{n}\left(x_i - w_{ij}\right)^2}{2\sigma^2} \right)$$

The output $y(t)$ is a weighted sum of the outputs of the hidden layer, given by

$$y(t) = \sum_{i=1}^{n} w_i \phi\left(\|u(t) - c_i\|\right),$$

where
$u(t)$ is the input
$\phi(.)$ is an arbitrary non-linear radial basis function
$\|.\|$ denotes the norm that is usually assumed to be Euclidean
c_i are the known centers of the radial basis functions
w_i are the weights of the function

In radial functions, the response decreases (or increases) monotonically with distance from a central point and they are radially symmetric. The center, the distance scale, and the exact shape of the radial function are the necessary considerations of the defined model. The most commonly used radial function is the Gaussian radial filter, which in the case of a scalar input is

$$h(x) = \exp\left(-\frac{(x-c)^2}{\beta^2} \right)$$

Its parameters are its centre c and its radius β (width), illustrates a Gaussian RBF with centre $c = 0$ and radius $\beta = 1$. A Gaussian RBF monotonically decreases with distance from the center.

12.4.2 Pros and cons of instance-based learning method

Advantage: Instance-based learning (IBL) methods are particularly well suited to problems where the target function is highly complex, but can also be defined by a group of not as much complex local approximations.

The disadvantage I: The cost of classification of new instances can be high (a majority of the calculation takes place at this stage).

Disadvantage II: Many IBL approaches usually study all characteristics of the instances leading to dimensionality-related problems.

12.5   ASSOCIATION RULE LEARNING ALGORITHM

Association rule learning is a method that extracts rules that best explain observed relationships between variables in data. These rules can discover important and commercially useful associations in large multidimensional data sets that can be exploited by an organization. The most popular association rule learning algorithms are the Apriori algorithm and the Eclat process.

12.5.1 Apriori algorithm

Apriori is designed to function on a large database containing various types of transactions (for example, collections of products bought by customers, or details of websites visited by customers frequently). Apriori algorithm uses a 'bottom-up' method, where repeated subsets are extended one item at a time (a step is known as candidate generation, and groups of candidates are tested against the data). The Apriori Algorithm is a powerful algorithm for frequent mining of item sets for boolean association rules. Refer to chapter 9 titled 'Unsupervised learning' to understand more on about this algorithm.

12.5.2 Eclat algorithm

ECLAT stands for 'Equivalence Class Clustering and bottom-up Lattice Traversal'. The Eclat algorithm is another set of frequent item set generation similar to the Apriori algorithm. Three traversal approaches such as 'Top-down', 'Bottom-up', and Hybrid approaches are supported. Transaction IDs (TID list) are stored here. It represents the data in vertical format.

Step 1: Get Transaciton IDs : tidlist for each item (DB scan).

Step 2. Transaciton IDs (tidlist) of {a} is exactly the list of transactions covering {a}.

Step 3. Intersect tidlist of {a} with the tidlists of all other items, resulting in tidlists of {a,b}, {a,c}, {a,d}, ... = {a}–conditional database (if {a} removed).

Step 4. Repeat from 1 on {a}–conditional database 5. Repeat for all other items.

12.6   ENSEMBLE LEARNING ALGORITHM

Ensemble means collaboration/joint/group. Ensemble methods are models that contain many weaker models that are autonomously trained and whose forecasts are combined approximately to create the overall prediction model. More efforts are required to study the types of weak learners and various ways to combine them.

The most popular ensemble learning algorithms are

Bootstrap Aggregation (bagging)

Boosting

AdaBoost

Stacked Generalization (blending)

Gradient Boosting Machines (GBM)

Gradient Boosted Regression Trees (GBRT)

Random Forest

12.6.1 Bootstrap aggregation (Bagging)

Bootstrap Aggregation (bagging) works using the principle of the Bootstrap sampling method. Given a training data set D containing m examples, the bootstrap drawing method draws a sample of training examples D_i, by selecting m examples in uniform random with replacement. It comprises two phases namely Training phase and Classification Phase.

Training Phase:

1. Initialize the parameters
2. $D = \{\Phi\}$
3. H = the number of classification
4. For $k = 1$ to h
5. Take a bootstrap sample S_k from training set S
6. Build the classifier D_k using S_k as a training set
7. $D = D \bigcup D_i$
8. Return D

Classification Phase:

1. Run $D_1, D_2, \ldots\ldots\ldots D_k$ on the input k
2. The class with a maximum number of the votes is chosen as the label for X.

Original Sample	1	2	3	4	5	6	7	8

Bootstrap Sample 1	1	1	2	8	3	4	5	3
Bootstrap Sample 2	1	4	5	7	4	5	1	2
Bootstrap Sample 3	5	2	1	2	1	8	4	2
Bootstrap Sample 4	7	4	2	8	5	6	6	6

In the above example, the original sample has eight data points. All the Bootstrap samples also have eight data points. Within the same bootstrap sample, data points are repeated due to selection with the replacement.

12.6.2   Boosting

Just like bagging, boosting is another key ensemble-based technique. Boosting is an iterative technique. It decreases the biasing error. If an observation was classified incorrectly, then it boosts the weight of that observation. In this type of ensemble, weaker learning models are trained on resampled data, and the outcomes are combined using a weighted voting approach based on the performance of different models. Adaptive boosting or AdaBoost is a special variant of a boosting algorithm. It is based on the idea of generating weak learners and learning slowly.

12.6.3 Gradient boosting machines (GBM)

As we know already, boosting is the machine learning algorithm, which boosts weak learners to strong learners . We may already know that a learner estimates a target function from training data. Gradient boosting is the boosting with Gradient.

Gradient: Consider L as a function of an ith variable, other $N - 1$ variables are fixed at the current point, by calculating the derivative of L at that point (L is differentiable), we have – if the derivative is positive/negative – a decrease/increase value of the ith variable to make the loss smaller (*). Applying the above calculation for all $i = 1 \ldots N$, we will get N derivative values forming a vector, the so-called gradient of an N-variable function at the current point.

12.7   REGULARIZATION ALGORITHM

This is an extension made to another method (typically regression method) that penalizes models based on their complexity, favoring simpler models that are also better at generalizing. Regularization algorithms have been listed separately here because they are famous, influential, and generally simple modifications made to other methods.

The most popular regularization algorithms are

> Ridge Regression
> Least Absolute Shrinkage and Selection Operator (LASSO)
> Elastic Net
> Least-Angle Regression (LARS)

Refer chapter 8 titled "Supervised Learning: Regression" for Ridge regression and the LASSO method.

Elastic Net

When we are working with high-dimensional data sets with a large number of independent variables, correlations (relationships) amid the variables can often result in multicollinearity. These correlated variables which are strictly related can sometimes form groups or clusters called an elastic net of correlated variables. We would want to include the complete group in the model selection even if just one variable has been selected.

12.8   EVOLUTIONARY ALGORITHMS

Optimization of machine learning algorithms has been a highly researched area that aims at improving a model's performance. We have discussed some of the optimization algorithms like Gradient Descent and Stochastic Gradient Descent in earlier chapters. We will discuss a set of optimization algorithms that uses the principles of Evolutionary Computation, called the Evolutionary Algorithm in this section.

Evolutionary Computation is a field that explores computational systems drawing insights from natural evolution. It adopts the principle of "survival of the fittest" from natural evolution. The process involves working with a population of data structures and introducing variations by randomly modifying these structures and combining different structures. This is achieved through two processes known as mutation and crossover, collectively referred to as variation operators. Techniques from Evolutionary Computation can be applied in optimization, learning, and design.

Evolutionary Algorithms (EA), a subset of evolutionary computation, primarily incorporate techniques that emulate biological evolution processes such as reproduction, mutation, recombination, natural selection, and survival of the fittest. In this context, potential solutions to an optimization problem are considered as individuals within a population, and their quality is assessed using a fitness function. The population evolves through repeated application of these processes like reproduction, mutation, etc.

Evolutionary Algorithms (EAs) are often effective in estimating solutions for a wide range of problems, mainly because they typically don't presuppose anything about the underlying fitness landscape. However, the computational complexity associated with EAs often poses a challenge in their real-world applications. We will discuss the two most popular EAs – Genetic Algorithm and Ant Colony Optimization in detail.

12.8.1 Genetic algorithm

A Genetic Algorithm (GA) is an optimization method that is a subset of the broader field of evolutionary algorithms. This draws inspiration from the process of natural selection and genetic principles. GA works on the evolutionary generational cycle to generate high-quality solutions algorithms that either enhance or replace the population to give an improved fit solution through the use of different variation operations. GA is employed to produce superior solutions for search and optimization challenges. Some key components of Genetic Algorithms are (see Figure 12.5):

o Population: A given problem can have a set of possible or probable solutions. A subset of these solutions is considered in the algorithm to find out the optimal solution. This subset is called the population.

o Chromosomes: To draw a similarity with the genetics, individual solutions within the population are termed chromosomes.

o Gene: A chromosome is divided into different genes. Genes define the characteristics of the chromosomes. In the context of computing, if we consider the value of each variable in 8-bit binary values, then each bit will represent a gene.

o Allele: each gene within a particular chromosome contains a value, which is called Allele.

o Fitness Function: The individual solutions within a set are compared to each other in terms of their fitness values. This normally denotes the quality of the solution and determines its ability to compete with other individuals in the population. A fitness function enables the evaluation of the fitness value.

o Genetic Operators: Two important genetic operators used in GA are Crossover and Mutation. The best two individuals mate and a crossover of the chromosomes happens to regenerate offspring better than parents. A chromosome can also mutate or change its genetic values to improve its fitness value. So, genetic operators play a role in changing the genetic composition of the next generation

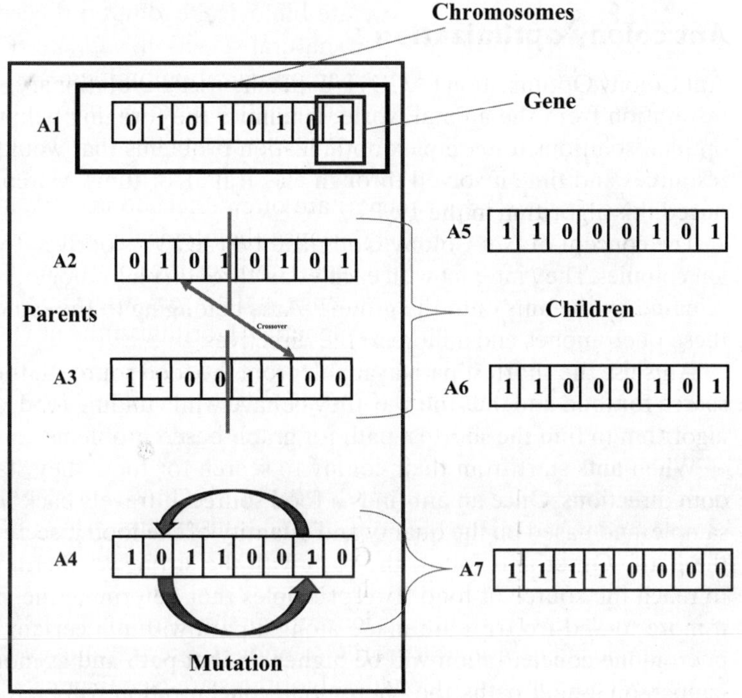

FIG. 12.5
Genetic Algorithm Concepts

GA involves five phases to solve complex optimization problems, which are given below:

1. Initialization: The GA procedure commences by creating a group of entities, referred to as a population. In this context, each entity represents a solution to the problem at hand.

2. Fitness Assignment: Post initialization, a fitness score is allocated to each entity, indicating its competitive ability.

3. Selection: Entities with superior fitness scores are chosen. These entities mate and yield improved offspring by merging the parents' chromosomes.

4. Reproduction: This stage involves the application of genetic operators to generate new offspring.

5. Termination: The algorithm ceases if the population has converged (i.e., there is minimal variation in fitness across generations) or if a maximum number of generations has been attained.

Genetic Algorithms are being widely used in different real-world applications, for example, designing electronic circuits, code-breaking, image processing, and artificial creativity

12.8.2 Ant colony optimization

Ant Colony Optimization (ACO) is a metaheuristic evolutionary algorithm that takes inspiration from the animal world. It mimics the foraging behavior of ants to find optimal solutions for complex optimization problems that would take much higher resources and time if solved through classical algorithms. Marco Dorigo first introduced this algorithm in the 1990s

The concept of Ant Colony Optimization (ACO) is derived from the behavior of ant colonies. They interact with each other through pheromones, which are chemicals released by the ants onto the ground. Ants belonging to the same colony can detect these pheromones and adhere to the directives.

Ants use the shortest path available from the food source to the colony when they search for food and thus the way they behave while finding food is used to design the algorithm to find the shortest path for graph-based problems.

When ants start from their colony to search for food, they start in multiple random directions. Once an ant finds a food source, it travels back to the colony with a sample, and based on the quality and quantity of the food it secretes pheromones on the path. Other ants follow the path with the strongest pheromone concentration to reach the source of food. Two principles that determine the shortest route are – if more to-and-fro trips are made along a path within a certain time interval, then pheromone concentration will be higher on that path and as more evaporation will happen on longer paths, the pheromone concentration will be reduced there. These are the two major factors to determine the shortest path from the food source to the colony. Refer to Figure 12.6.

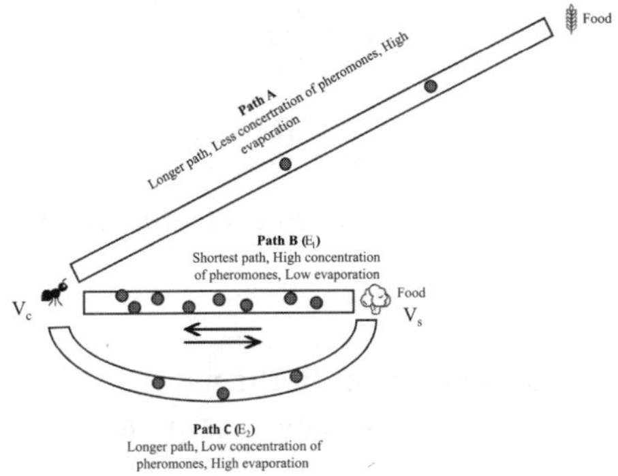

FIG. 12.6
Ant Colony Optimization Concept

The ant colony and the food sources can be considered as the nodes or vertices of the graph and the paths as the edges to these vertices. The pheromone concentration can be assumed as the weightage associated with each path.

The ACO algorithm involves the following stages:

1. **Stage 1**: There is no pheromone in the path, and there are empty paths from food to the ant colony.

2. **Stage 2:** Ants are divided into two groups following two different paths with a probability of 0.5.

3. **Stage 3:** The ants that follow the shorter path will reach the food first, and then the pheromone concentration will be higher on this path as more ants from the colony will follow the shorter path. More ants will return from the shortest path, and the concentration of pheromones will be higher.

4. **Stage 4:** Also, the rate of evaporation from the longer path will be higher as fewer ants are using that path. Now more ants from the colony will use the shortest path.

ACO has been used to solve computational problems which can be reduced to finding good paths through graphs. It is a population-based metaheuristic that can be used to find approximate solutions to difficult optimization problems. The algorithmic design of ACO can be understood based on Figure 12.6. Let's consider only one food source (Vs) and one colony (Vc) for simplicity. In a graphical representation, these are the two vertices of the graph. Let's also assume that there are only two possible paths between Vc and Vs which are edges of the graph E1 and E2 having lengths L1 and L2 respectively. The pheromone strengths corresponding to E1 and E2 are denoted as R1 and R2.

The probability of an ant to start on either of the paths E1 or E2 is dependent on the pheromone concentration on those paths:

$$P_i = \frac{R_1}{R_1 + R_2} \qquad \text{---- Equation (1)}$$

where Pi denotes the probability, Ri denotes the pheromone concentration and i $\in [1,2]$

Now, the pheromone concentration gets updated according to the path length and the evaporation rate:

$$R_i \leftarrow R_i + \frac{K}{L_i} \qquad \text{---- Equation (2)}$$

where i $\in [1,2]$, K is a parameter of the model

Based on equation (2), if the length of path increases, the pheromone deposit decreases.

The update due to evaporation can be expressed as

$$R_i \leftarrow (1 - v)^* R_i \qquad \text{---- Equation (3)}$$

where v controls the pheromone evaporation and $0 \leq v \leq 1$

in each iteration of the travel, Ri gets updated. From the above three equations, we can see that the probability of choosing path E1 over path E2 increases and the shortest path is identified in the process.

The Traveling Salesman Problem (TSP) is an example that can be solved using the ACO algorithm.

The TSP is a classic algorithmic problem in the field of computer science and operations research which focuses on optimization. In this problem, a salesman is given a list of cities and must determine the shortest route that allows him to visit each city once and return to his original location.

The steps involved in using ACO to solve the TSP:

1. **Initialization:** Ants are placed on the cities of the graph (which represents the map of the cities the salesman has to visit). Each city is visited by exactly one ant, which is equivalent to saying that each ant starts from a different city.

2. **Construct Ant Solutions:** Each ant constructs a solution to the problem. An ant chooses to move from city i to city j with a probability that is proportional to the amount of pheromone on the edge connecting i and j, and inversely proportional to the length of the edge. This means that the shorter the edge and the more the pheromone on the edge, the higher the probability that the ant will choose that edge.

3. **Update Pheromones:** After all ants have constructed their solutions, they update the pheromones on the edges. Each ant deposits an amount of pheromone on the edges it traversed that is inversely proportional to the length of its tour. That is, the shorter the tour, the more pheromone is deposited.

4. **Evaporation:** To simulate the natural evaporation of pheromones in nature, a certain percentage of the pheromones on all edges is evaporated.

5. **Best Solution:** The best solution is then chosen as the one that represents the shortest complete tour.

This process is repeated for a certain number of iterations, or until a satisfactory solution is found.

ACO has been successfully applied to several optimization problems, like vehicle routing, robot navigation, and many more with good results

12.9   SUMMARY

- Another name for Representation learning is feature learning.
- Representation learnings are most widely used in words, speech recognition, signal processing, music, and image identification. For example, a word can have meaning based on the context
- Independent component analysis, or ICA) is similar to principal components analysis (PCA), with the exception that the components are independent and uncorrelated.
- Autoencoders belong to the neural network family and are similar to PCA (Principal Component Analysis). They are more flexible than PCA.
- Active learning is a type of semi-supervised learning in which a learning algorithm can interactively query (question) the user to obtain the desired outputs at new data points.
- Uncertainty sampling: In this method, the active learning algorithm first tries to label the points for which the current model is least specific (that means much confusion) on the correct output.
- In instance-based learning (memory-based learning), the algorithm compares new problem instances with instances already seen in training, which have been stored in memory for reference rather than performing explicit generalization.
- Examples of instance-based learning include K-nearest neighbor algorithm (K-NN), Kernel machines (Support Vector Machine, PCA), and Radial Basis Function networks (RBF networks).
- Radial basis function (RBF) networks typically have three layers: one input layer, one hidden layer with a non-linear RBF activation function, and one linear output layer.
- Association rule learning is a method that extracts rules that best explain observed relationships between variables in data. These rules can discover important and commercially useful associations in large multidimensional datasets that can be exploited by an organization.
- Apriori is designed to function on a large database containing various types of transactions (for example, collections of products bought by customers, or details of websites visited by customers frequently).
- ECLAT stands for "Equivalence Class Clustering and bottom-up Lattice Traversal." The Eclat algorithm is another set of frequent item set generation similar to the Apriori algorithm. Three traversal approaches such as "Top-down," "Bottom-up" and Hybrid approaches are supported.
- Ensemble means collaboration/joint/Group. Ensemble methods are models that contain many weaker models that are autonomously trained and whose forecasts are joined approximately to create the overall prediction model.
- *Evolutionary Algorithms* (EA), a subset of evolutionary computation, primarily incorporate techniques that emulate biological evolution processes such as reproduction, mutation, recombination, natural selection, and survival of the fittest

SAMPLE QUESTIONS

MULTIPLE-CHOICE QUESTIONS (1 MARK QUESTIONS)

1. Another name for Representation learning is ___
   - (a) Feature learning
   - (b) Active learning
   - (c) Instance-based learning
   - (d) Ensemble learning

2. In representation learning, when unknown causes (H) are combined, it can also generate the data (V), Which is called ___
   - (a) Recognition
   - (b) Generation
   - (c) Representative
   - (d) Combinative

3. When the causes (H) explain the data (V) we observe, it is called ___
   - (a) Recognition
   - (b) Generation
   - (c) Representative
   - (d) Combinative

4. When unknown causes (H) are combined, it can also generate the data (V), it is called as ___
   - (a) Recognition
   - (b) Generation
   - (c) Representative
   - (d) Combinative

5. Independent component analysis is similar to
   - (a) Dependent analysis
   - (b) Sub Component analysis
   - (c) Data analysis
   - (d) Principal component analysis

6. In this method, the active learning algorithm first tries to label the points for which the current model is least specific (as this means a lot of confusion) on the correct output.
   - (a) Expected model change
   - (b) Query by committee
   - (c) Uncertainty sampling
   - (d) Expected error reduction

7. A range of models are trained on the current labeled data, and vote on the output for unlabeled data; label those points for which the 'Group of people' disagrees the most.
   - (a) Expected model change
   - (b) Query by committee
   - (c) Uncertainty sampling
   - (d) Expected error reduction

8. In this method, the active learning algorithm first tries to label the points that would most change the existing model itself
   - (a) Expected model change
   - (b) Query by committee
   - (c) Uncertainty sampling
   - (d) Expected error reduction

9. In this method, the active learning algorithm first tries to label the points that would mostly reduce the model's generalization problem.
   - (a) Expected model change
   - (b) Query by committee
   - (c) Uncertainty sampling
   - (d) Expected error reduction

10. Which of the following is not a type of Ensemble learning algorithm?
    - (a) Boosting
    - (b) AdaBoost
    - (c) GBM
    - (d) Elastic Net

SHORT-ANSWER TYPE QUESTIONS (5 MARKS QUESTIONS)

1. What is the main objective of Representation Learning?
2. What are the applications of Representational Learning?
3. Define Independent Component Analysis? What is the primary usage of it?
4. What is Uncertainty sampling in Active learning?
5. What is Query by committee in Active learning?
6. What are the Pros and Cons of Instance-Based Learning (IBL) Method?
7. Write notes on Elastic Net
8. List down various types of regularization algorithms
9. What is Gradient?
10. What is Bootstrap Aggregation (Bagging)?
11. List down various types of Ensemble learning algorithms

LONG-ANSWER TYPE QUESTIONS (10 MARKS QUESTIONS)

1. Derive a primary representational working system to detect the type of triangle.
2. Discuss Generation and Recognition in the Representation of Learning
3. Discuss Independent component analysis (unsupervised)
4. Discuss Autoencoders in detail with a diagram
5. What is active learning? Explain its heuristics
6. Discuss various Active learning Query Strategies
7. Discuss Instance-based Learning (Memory-based learning)
8. Discuss the Radial Basis Function in detail
9. Discuss various Association Rule Learning Algorithms in detail
10. What is Ensemble Learning Algorithm? Discuss various types.

Chapter 13

End-to-end ML implementations

OBJECTIVE OF THE CHAPTER:

Now that the fundamental concepts of machine learning have been covered along with detailed exposure to the programming practices in the two most popular programming languages – Python and R, it is good to look at a few reference implementations in machine learning. The implementations related to both supervised and unsupervised learning have been presented to give a complete perspective of the machine-learning domains.

The first implementation is a simple one. It is a supervised learning (classification) problem with a structured dataset – the very popular iris dataset. The solution is done using a popular machine-learning model, wrapped with a GUI. The next two implementations relate to two advanced implementations. The second implementation is related to the recognition of hand-written digits. It uses the MNIST dataset of handwritten digits. The solution is implemented using another machine learning model (a classification model). The third implementation is related to sentiment-based clustering of text data. For this, a popular unsupervised learning model has

13.1 IMPLEMENTATION 1 - DETECTION OF IRIS FLOWER SPECIES

This implementation is related to the identification of Iris flower species. The Iris flower dataset is a multivariate dataset prepared by the British statistician and biologist Ronald Fisher in 1936. The dataset consists of 50 samples each from the three species of Iris - setosa, virginica, and versicolor. Four features were measured, in centimeters, from each sample - the length and the width of the sepals and petals.

This problem, which relates to the identification of species of an Iris flower, is a classic classification problem. It's a multiclass classification problem, a popular kind of problem in supervised learning, where the goal is to categorize instances into one of three or more classes.

The implementation program has been developed in Python. In this case, a Decision Tree model is trained to classify whether an iris flower belongs to either of the species 'setosa', 'virginica', or 'versicolor'. The Decision Tree algorithm is a widely used model in machine learning for classification tasks. Because of its simplicity and interpretability, this model is very effective for solving the Iris classification problem. It constructs a tree-like model of decisions and their possible consequences. In applying a decision tree model to the Iris dataset:

- The algorithm begins by examining each feature (sepal length, sepal width, petal length, petal width) to determine which feature best separates the flowers into their respective species.

- The dataset is split at nodes based on these features. For instance, if petal length is the most significant feature in separating the species, the dataset will be split into groups based on petal length values.

- This process continues, with the algorithm making further splits to classify the flowers more accurately.

- The resulting tree is a model that, given a new flower's measurements, can predict with a certain degree of accuracy what species it belongs to.

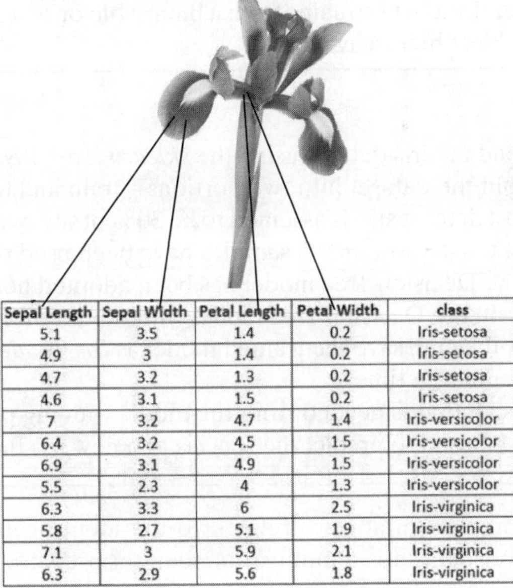

Sepal Length	Sepal Width	Petal Length	Petal Width	class
5.1	3.5	1.4	0.2	Iris-setosa
4.9	3	1.4	0.2	Iris-setosa
4.7	3.2	1.3	0.2	Iris-setosa
4.6	3.1	1.5	0.2	Iris-setosa
7	3.2	4.7	1.4	Iris-versicolor
6.4	3.2	4.5	1.5	Iris-versicolor
6.9	3.1	4.9	1.5	Iris-versicolor
5.5	2.3	4	1.3	Iris-versicolor
6.3	3.3	6	2.5	Iris-virginica
5.8	2.7	5.1	1.9	Iris-virginica
7.1	3	5.9	2.1	Iris-virginica
6.3	2.9	5.6	1.8	Iris-virginica

FIG. 13.1
Iris dataset

To start with, a new Python file was created. The implementation consists of two salient parts –

(i) A machine learning part for predicting the species of a new flower

(ii) A GUI application that allows users to input the features of an iris flower and receive a prediction result.

MODEL PREPARATION FOR SPECIES PREDICTION

First, let's import all necessary libraries. We will need the following libraries:

- sklearn library for the different machine learning related functionalities. The iris dataset can also be obtained from the sklearn library.
- Joblib library for saving the trained model as .pkl (also called 'pickle' file)

```
from sklearn.datasets import load_iris
from sklearn.tree import DecisionTreeClassifier
from sklearn.model_selection import train_test_split
from sklearn.metrics import accuracy_score
from sklearn.datasets import load_iris
import joblib
```

Then, define a function *build_model()* to do the following:

Did you know?

The pickle module in Python implements binary protocols for serializing and de-serializing a Python object structure. "Pickling" is the process whereby a Python object hierarchy is converted into a byte stream. "Unpickling" is the inverse operation, whereby a byte stream (from a binary file or bytes-like object) is converted back into an object hierarchy.

- load the iris dataset using the *sklearn load_iris()* function
- split the dataset into two portions – train and test
- test dataset size is assumed to be 30% of the overall dataset, which means 70% of the dataset or 105 samples have been used to train the model
- The Decision Tree model has been adopted here
- train the Decision Tree model with the training data samples
- at the end, save the trained model as *iris_model.pkl* file so that it can be used at a later point in time

This is all that is needed from the model training perspective. This trained model can now be used to predict the species of a new iris flower.

```python
def build_model():
    # Load dataset
    iris = load_iris()
    X, y = iris.data, iris.target

    # Split dataset into training set and test set
    X_train, X_test, y_train, y_test = train_test_split(X, y, test_
size=0.3, random_state=1)

    # Create Decision Tree classifer object
    clf = DecisionTreeClassifier()

    # Train Decision Tree Classifer
    clf = clf.fit(X_train, y_train)

    # Save the model to disk
    joblib.dump(clf, 'iris_model.pkl')
```

BUILDING GUI APPLICATION FOR USER INPUT & PREDICTION

Once the model is trained and the model file is saved for future use, then the next step
is to develop a simple GUI to take user inputs related to the feature values of a new
iris flower. As we know, the user inputs are needed for four features, namely sepal
length, sepal width, petal length, and petal width. Though there are multiple options
for building GUI in Python, we will use the *Tkinter* library for the GUI front end.
Note, that while *Tkinter* is more straightforward and comes with Python's standard
library, *PyQt* is more feature-rich and complex but requires additional installation.
Let's first import the Tkinter library.

```python
import tkinter as tk
from tkinter import messagebox
```

After that, define a function *show_dialogue()* to do the following:
- load the trained model from *iris_model*.pkl file
- create the dialogue box for taking user inputs using *Tkinter* library widgets
  e.g., Label, Entry box, Button
- define a sub-function *classify()* which picks the user inputs from the Entry
  boxes and use them to generate prediction from the trained model
- the function *classify()* is invoked when the Button is clicked

```python
def show_dialogue():
    # Load the trained model
    model = joblib.load('iris_model.pkl')
    # Load dataset
    iris = load_iris()

def classify():
  try:
    sepal_length = float(sepal_length_entry.get())
    sepal_width = float(sepal_width_entry.get())
    petal_length = float(petal_length_entry.get())
    petal_width = float(petal_width_entry.get())
    features = [sepal_length, sepal_width, petal_length,
petal_width]
    result = iris.target_names[model.predict([features])[0]]
    messagebox.showinfo("Result", f"The Iris flower is classified
as: {result}")
    except ValueError:
    messagebox.showerror("Error", "Please enter valid numbers")

    app = tk.Tk()
    app.title("Iris Flower Classification")

    tk.Label(app, text="Sepal Length (cm):").grid(row=0, column=0,
padx=10, pady=10)
    sepal_length_entry = tk.Entry(app)
    sepal_length_entry.grid(row=0, column=1, padx=10, pady=10)

tk.Label(app, text="Sepal Width (cm):").grid(row=1, column=0,
padx=10, pady=10)
sepal_width_entry = tk.Entry(app)
sepal_width_entry.grid(row=1, column=1, padx=10, pady=10)

    tk.Label(app, text="Petal Length (cm):").grid(row=2, column=0,
padx=10, pady=10)
    petal_length_entry = tk.Entry(app)
    petal_length_entry.grid(row=2, column=1, padx=10, pady=10)

    tk.Label(app, text="Petal Width (cm):").grid(row=3, column=0,
padx=10, pady=10)
    petal_width_entry = tk.Entry(app)
    petal_width_entry.grid(row=3, column=1, padx=10, pady=10)

    classify_btn = tk.Button(app, text="Classify", command=classify)
    classify_btn.grid(row=4, column=0, columnspan=2, pady=20)

    app.mainloop()
```

Finally, define the *main* function as an entry point to the Python file. From this function, the other two functions defined in the file, i.e., *build_model()* and *show_dialogue()* are being called.

```
# Defining main function
if __name__ == "__main__":
    build_model()
    show_dialogue()
```

Now that the program is written, let's see the execution of the program. When the program is run, the model is trained in the background. What you get to see is the dialog box 'Iris Flower Classification' with the user input boxes 'Sepal Length (cm)', 'Sepal Width (cm)', 'Petal Length (cm)' and 'Petal Width (cm)'. Also, there is a button 'Classify'.

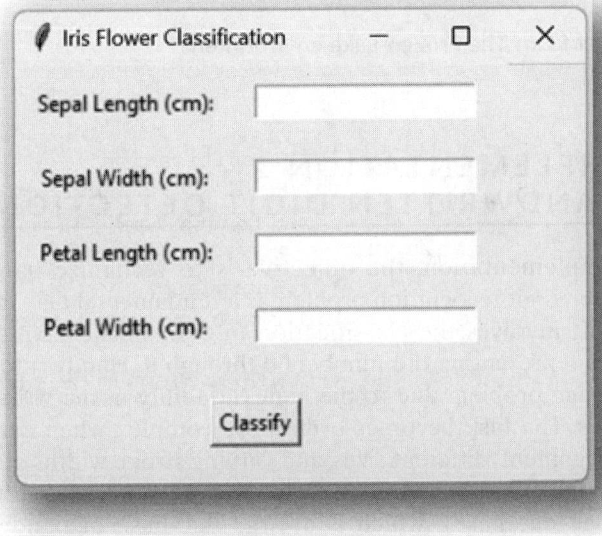

FIG. 13.2
Blank dialogue box

Now, user values need to be entered and 'Classify' button pressed. A MessageBox is thrown giving the species of the flower for which the feature values have been entered.

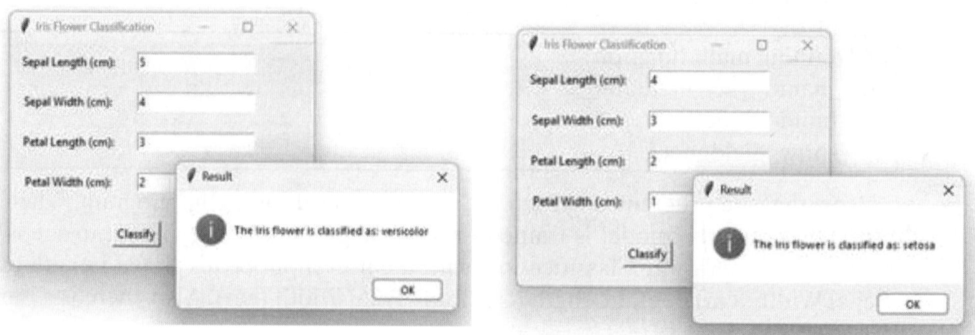

FIG. 13.3
Different elements of RL in The Frozen Lake environment

13.2:   IMPLEMENTATION 2 – HANDWRITTEN DIGIT DETECTION

In this implementation, the objective is to recognize handwritten digits. The handwritten digit recognition problem is a fundamental task in the field of machine learning. It involves the classification of digit images, typically into one of ten categories representing the numbers 0 through 9. Handwritten digit recognition is a challenging problem due to the high variability in the writing styles of different individuals. The task becomes even more complex when considering factors like skewed alignment, different sizes, and varying stroke widths of the digits.

The dataset used is MNIST (Modified National Institute of Standards and Technology database), which is a large database of handwritten digits that is commonly used for training various models. The dataset, created in 1994, contains images of handwritten numbers from 0 to 9. The size of all the small images is 28*28 pixels. Below are some sample images from the MNIST dataset. The MNIST database contains 60,000 training images and 10,000 testing images.

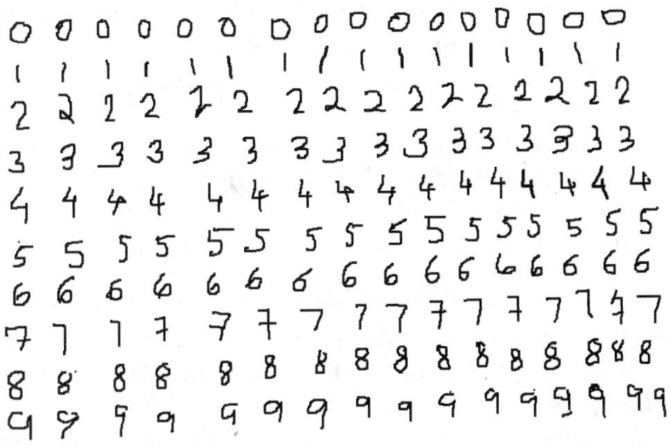

FIG. 13.4
Sample digit images as present in MNIST dataset

The implementation program has been developed in Python. The primary objective of this implementation is to develop a model that can correctly identify the digit presented in an image. This task is a multiclass classification problem, where the goal is to categorize an image into one of several classes (in this case, ten classes, one for each digit between 0 and 9). SVM is a powerful supervised machine learning algorithm used for classification and regression tasks. It is particularly well-suited for complex classification problems with medium-sized datasets, such as handwritten digit recognition. With its robustness and effectiveness, SVM offers a good approach to solving the handwritten digit recognition problem. When properly tuned, an SVM model can achieve high accuracy. While applying the SVM model in the context of handwritten digit recognition:

- Each image in the dataset is transformed into a feature vector, which represents various aspects of the image, such as the presence or absence of lines, edges, etc.

- SVM is trained on this feature set, learning to differentiate between digits based on these features. It tries to draw a hyperplane (or set of hyperplanes in higher-dimensional space) to segregate the digits into classes.

- The performance of the SVM model can be further enhanced by using appropriate kernel functions, which can handle the non-linear nature of the image data.

MODEL PREPARATION AND SPECIES PREDICTION

First, we need to import all libraries that are needed to invoke different functions which are:

- *sklearn* library for machine learning related functionalities that can be used to predict the handwritten digit.
- *Joblib* library for saving the trained model (Note that here the model is stored in .joblib format in place of .pkl format. .joblib (which has functions .dump for saving a model and .load for loading a saved model) is significantly faster on

large numpy arrays because it has a special handling mechanism for the array buffers of the numpy data structure.

```
from sklearn import datasets, svm
from sklearn.datasets import fetch_openml
from sklearn.model_selection import train_test_split
from sklearn.preprocessing import StandardScaler
from sklearn.metrics import classification_report
from joblib import dump, load
```

Then, the following activities are done to train the model:
- loaded the MNIST dataset from sklearn – datasets library using *fetch_openml()* function
- scaled the dataset using sklearn *StandardScaler()* function
- split the dataset into two portions – train and test
- adopted the Support Vector Machine (SVM) model
- trained the SVM model with the training data samples
- at the end, save the trained model as *svm_digits_model*.joblib file so that it can be used at a later point of time

This is all that is needed from the model training perspective. This trained model can now be used to predict the new handwritten digits.

```python
# Load the MNIST dataset
#digits = datasets.load_digits()
#X, y = digits.data, digits.target
X, y = fetch_openml('mnist_784', version=1, return_X_y=True)

# Scale data to normalize pixel intensity values
scaler = StandardScaler()
X_scaled = scaler.fit_transform(X)

# Split data into training and test sets
X_train, X_test, y_train, y_test = train_test_split(X_scaled, y,
test_size=0.3, random_state=0)

# Train an SVM model
model = svm.SVC(gamma=0.001)
model.fit(X_train, y_train)

# Evaluate the model
predicted = model.predict(X_test)
print(classification_report(y_test, predicted))

# Save the trained model and scaler
dump(model, 'svm_digits_model.joblib')
dump(scaler, 'svm_digits_scaler.joblib')
```

Output of trained model:

	precision	recall	f1-score	support
0	0.98	0.98	0.98	2077
1	0.98	0.99	0.98	2385
2	0.95	0.96	0.96	2115
3	0.96	0.94	0.95	2117
4	0.95	0.96	0.96	2004
5	0.96	0.95	0.95	1900
6	0.98	0.97	0.97	2045
7	0.93	0.97	0.95	2189
8	0.96	0.95	0.95	2042
9	0.96	0.93	0.94	2126
accuracy			0.96	21000
macro avg	0.96	0.96	0.96	21000
weighted avg	0.96	0.96	0.96	21000

BUILDING GUI APPLICATION FOR USER INPUT AND PREDICTION

Once the model is being trained and the model file is saved for future use, a simple GUI was developed to take user inputs related to the handwritten digits. A small canvas is positioned in the application where the digits can be written using the mouse. The *Tkinter* library was used for the GUI front end. Let's first import the *Tkinter* library along with the different widgets.

```
import tkinter as tk
from tkinter import Canvas, Button, Label
from PIL import Image, ImageDraw, ImageGrab
import numpy as np
from joblib import load
from tkinter import messagebox
```

After that, the GUI was developed with the following steps:
-   loaded the trained model from the *svm_digits_model*.joblib file and the Scaler using the *svm_digits_scaler.joblib* file.
-   defined the sub-functions *event_activation()* for activating the canvas, *draw_lines()* to enable writing the digit on the canvas and *clear_canvas()* to clear the written digit on the canvas
-   create the dialogue box for taking user inputs using *Tkinter* library widgets e.g., Label, Canvas, Button
-   defined the predict_digit() sub-function to grab the handwritten digit image from the canvas and predict the label i.e., the digit value, corresponding to the image

```python
window = tk.Tk()
window.title("Handwritten digit recognition")
window.geometry (300 * 250)
# To predict the digit written in canvas
def predict_digit():...
# Clears the canvas
def clear_canvas():...
# Activate canvas
def event_activation(event):...
# To draw on canvas
def draw_lines(event):...


L1 = Label(window, text='Write a digit:', font=('Helvetica', 14))
L1.place(x=20, y=20)


C1 = Canvas(window, width=200, height=200, bg='white')
C1.place(x=90, y=60)
C1.bind("<Button-1>", event_activation)


B1 = Button(window, text='Predict Digit', font=('Helvetica', 10),
command=self.predict_digit)
B1.place(x=150, y=170)


B2 = Button(window, text='Clear Canvas', font=('Helvetica', 10),
command=self.clear_canvas)
B2.place(x=30, y=170)


window.mainloop()

# To predict the digit written in canvas
def predict_digit():
    global l1

    # Load the model and scaler
    model = load('svm_digits_model.joblib')
    scaler = load('svm_digits_scaler.joblib')
    widget = cv

    # Setting co-ordinates of canvas
    x = window.winfo_rootx() + widget.winfo_x()
    y = window.winfo_rooty() + widget.winfo_y()
    x1 = x + widget.winfo_width()
    y1 = y + widget.winfo_height()
```

```python
    # Image is captured from canvas and is resized to (28 X 28) px
    img = ImageGrab.grab().crop((x, y, x1, y1)).resize((28, 28))

    # Converting RGB to a grayscale image
    img = img.convert('L')

    img_array = np.array(img).reshape(1, -1)

    # Preprocess the image for the model
    img_array = scaler.transform(img_array)

    # Make prediction
    prediction = model.predict(img_array)
    messagebox.showinfo("Result",   f"Predicted   Digit:
{prediction[0]}")

# Clears the canvas
def clear_canvas():
    global cv, l1
    cv.delete("all")
    l1.destroy()

# Activate canvas
def event_activation(event):
    global lastx, lasty
    cv.bind('<B1-Motion>', draw_lines)
    lastx, lasty = event.x, event.y

# To draw on canvas
def draw_lines(event):
    global lastx, lasty
    x, y = event.x, event.y
    cv.create_line((lastx, lasty, x, y), width=5, fill='white',
splinesteps=2)
    lastx, lasty = x, y
```

Now that the program is written, let's see the execution of the program. When the program is run, the model is trained in the background. What you get to see is the dialog box 'Handwritten digit recognition' with the user input Canvas and buttons 'Predict Digit' and 'Clear Canvas'.

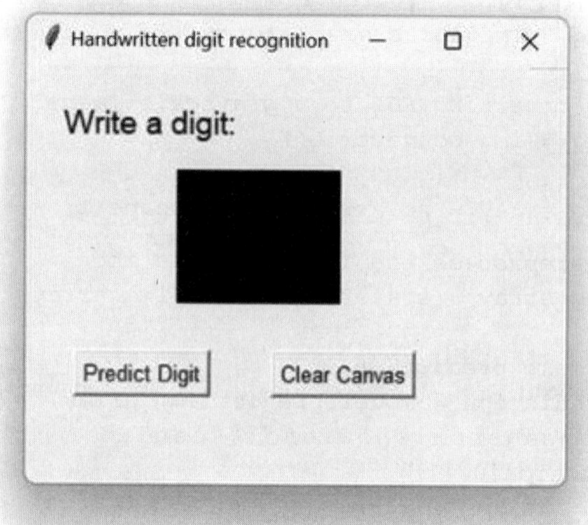

FIG. 13.5
Blank dialogue box (for Handwritten digit detection)

Using the mouse, write a digit on the canvas and press the 'Predict Digit' button. A MessageBox is thrown giving the digit which has been written on the canvas.

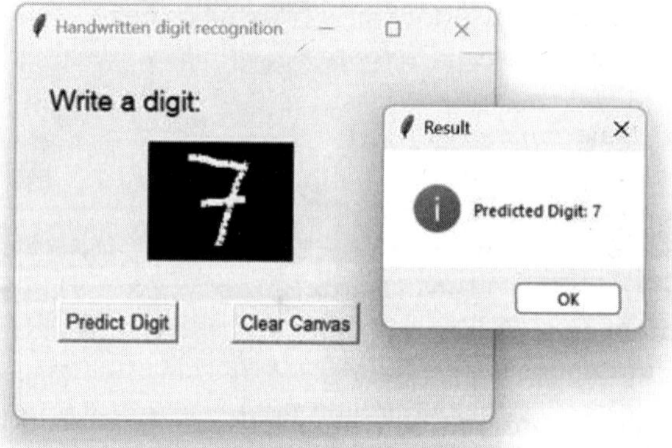

FIG. 13.6
Digit written on canvas for which prediction is given

13.3: IMPLEMENTATION 3 – SENTIMENT-BASED CLUSTERING OF TEXT DATA

The exponential increase in the volume of text data generated online, has made automated text analysis methods indispensable. Sentiment analysis, a subfield of Natural Language Processing (or NLP), involves determining whether a piece of writing is positive, negative, neutral, or irrelevant. Clustering, on the other hand, is a method of unsupervised machine learning used to group data points into clusters where items in the same cluster are more similar to each other than to those in other clusters.

The dataset used in this implementation, with a source in Kaggle (https://www.kaggle.com/datasets/thedevastator/movie-reviews-dataset-with-sentiment-labels), contains thousands of movie reviews from hundreds of movie-watchers across the globe. This dataset can be used for sentiment-based clustering of movie reviews. The data includes reviews from multiple sources, each with a label indicating whether the review is positive or negative, given by the viewer. This labeled dataset has been used intentionally in the clustering problem to do a reality check of the clustered reviews.

The implementation program has been developed in R. In this implementation, a clustering technique - k-Means, has been used. The main objective in sentiment-based clustering of text data is to automatically categorize a set of texts into groups based on the sentiment they express. This categorization should ideally reflect the underlying emotional tone or subjective opinion conveyed in the text. The k-means algorithm is one of the most popular clustering methods. It is a centroid-based algorithm, which partitions the data into 'k' distinct clusters based on distance metrics.

In applying k-Means to sentiment-based clustering of text data:

- The text data is first preprocessed (cleaned and normalized), and features are extracted.
- The k-Means algorithm is applied to these numerical representations, often using the sentiment scores as features, to group the text data into clusters.
- Each resulting cluster is analyzed to understand the common sentiment shared by the texts within it.

First, all necessary libraries will be installed and loaded. The libraries to be used are *tm* for text mining, *tidytext* and *syuzhet* for sentiment analysis, *textdata* for accessing lexicons, *dplyr* for data manipulation, and *factoextra* for better clustering visualization.

```
install.packages(c("tm", "tidytext", "textdata", "syuzhet", "dplyr", "factoextra", "data.table"))
library(tm)
library(tidytext)
library(syuzhet)
library(dplyr)
library(factoextra)
library(data.table)
```

Then the data is loaded and pre-processed. This involves reading the text data, cleaning it (like removing stop words, punctuation, and stemming), and converting it into a format suitable for analysis.

```
# Example: Reading text data from a CSV file
# Load the data from .csv file to the data object and select the
column with name 'text'
data <- read.csv("moviereviews.csv")
texts <- data$text


# Text preprocessing
clean_text <- function(text) {
  text <- tolower(text)
  text <- removePunctuation(text)
  text <- removeNumbers(text)
  text <- removeWords (text, stopwords("en"))
  text <- stripWhitespace(text)
  return(text)
}


texts_clean <- sapply (texts, clean_text)
corpus <- Corpus (VectorSource(texts_clean))
```

Then, calculate sentiment scores for each text. Since this can be computationally intensive, parallel processing for large datasets can be an option.

```
get_sentiment_scores <- function(text) {
  sentiment <- get_nrc_sentiment(text)
  scores <- colSums(sentiment[,1:8]) # Summing scores across dif-
ferent emotions

  return(scores)
}

sentiment_scores  <-  sapply(sapply(corpus,  as.character),
get_sentiment_scores)
```

Convert the sentiment scores into a matrix and possibly scale them. Then use a clustering technique like k-means clustering, which can provide more insight for certain types of data.

```
sentiment_matrix <- as.matrix(sentiment_scores)
set.seed(123)  # For reproducibility
num_clusters <- 2  # Adjust the number of clusters as needed
kmeans_result <- kmeans(sentiment_matrix, centers = num_clusters)


# Merging cluster results with original texts
clustered_texts  <-  data.frame(Text  =  texts, Cluster  =
kmeans_result$cluster)
```

Visualizing the clusters can provide insights into how they are grouped. To get more insight, the most common words or sentiments within each cluster may be examined.

```
# Visualize clusters
fviz_cluster(kmeans_result, data = sentiment_matrix)

# Example: Examining words or sentiments in each cluster
for (cluster in 1:num_clusters) {
  cat("Cluster", cluster, ":\n")
  print(head(clustered_texts[clustered_texts$Cluster == cluster,
]))
}
```

The outcome from the code:

	Cluster
1	1
2	2
3	1
4	1
5	2
6	1
7	1
8	2
9	1
10	2
...	.
...	.
1991	1
1992	2
1993	1
1994	2
1995	1
1996	1
1997	2
1998	1
1999	1
2000	2

This program provides a structured approach to perform sentiment-based clustering using k-means in R. The number of clusters (*num_clusters*) and other parameters can be adjusted based on your specific data and requirements. It is critical to ensure that the data preprocessing steps are appropriately followed for the dataset used.

It is highly recommended that you try out these implementations to understand how ML models are developed and implemented end-to-end in the real world. You may also change some of the parameters and see the effect on the model performance, as we discussed in the previous chapters of this book.

## Chapter 14

Generative AI & Large Language Models

OBJECTIVE OF THE CHAPTER:

This chapter immerses into the transformative domains of Generative Artificial Intelligence (GenAI) and Large Language Models (LLMs), providing a brief yet comprehensive exploration of their principles and applications. As we navigate the intricate landscape of generative AI, the chapter elucidates the foundational concepts that underpin the creation of machines capable of human-like creativity. Through tangible examples, we will be able to discriminate how algorithms, neural networks, and diverse training data converge to generate innovative outputs across textual and visual domains.

A focal point of the chapter revolves around Large Language Models, with an emphasis on understanding their architecture and training methodologies. Delving into models such as GPT, readers will grasp how pre-training on extensive datasets equips these models with linguistic prowess, enabling them to comprehend context and produce coherent and contextually relevant language. The chapter also delves into the ethical dimensions surrounding generative AI and LLMs, leading to consider the responsible use of creative machines. By scrutinizing issues related to bias, misinformation, and societal impact, a nuanced perspective on the ethical considerations inherent in the deployment of these technologies can be developed. To reinforce theoretical understanding, the chapter integrates hands-on examples with prompt engineering. This practical approach enhances the skill set, fostering a holistic comprehension of the dynamic interplay between technology and creativity. In conclusion, this chapter serves as a gateway to appreciate the multifaceted nature of generative AI and LLMs, equipping them to navigate the evolving landscape of artificial intelligence with insight and proficiency.

14.1   OVERVIEW

Our exploration into the realm of Artificial Intelligence (AI) begins with the fundamental concept of machine learning. This initial stage focused on algorithms that learn patterns from data, laying the groundwork for more sophisticated technologies to emerge. The shift from machine learning to generative AI marks a significant turning point, where machines move beyond mere pattern recognition and exhibit a form of creativity reminiscent of human ingenuity.

Gradually, the concept of deep learning emerged as a pivotal milestone. This area of machine learning utilizes multi-layered neural networks, also known as deep neural networks, to unlock the intricacies of data. These networks excel at understanding complex features, enabling them to handle intricate patterns with remarkable proficiency. Their ability to learn hierarchical relationships within data elevates their capabilities, making them exceptional tools for various tasks. However, at the same time, deep learning models are computationally more intensive. Additionally, it requires a lot of good-quality data. The year 2012 marked a watershed moment for deep learning with the ImageNet competition. Alex Net, a deep neural network architecture, showcased unprecedented performance in image classification, heralding the dawn of a new era in deep learning and influencing subsequent developments in the field.

The transition from machine learning to generative AI represents a paradigm shift. No longer limited to recognizing patterns, generative AI actively creates new, contextually relevant content. This pivotal shift marks a significant leap forward as machines exhibit a level of creative potential previously unseen in traditional machine-learning models. Natural Language Processing (NLP) emerged as a key domain in this transformation, allowing machines to understand, interpret, and generate human-like language. Two revolutionary models stand out in this domain: Variational Autoencoders (VAEs) and Transformers. VAEs excel at learning latent data representations, fostering creativity by enabling diverse output generation. Transformers, on the other hand, revolutionize the way machines process sequential data, paving the way for more advanced language models.

VAEs introduce an element of creativity by focusing on learning latent representations of data. This enables them to generate diverse outputs by comprehending the underlying structure of the data. Their ability to capture variability in the input data contributes to the richness and diversity of generative AI outputs. Transformers, on the other hand, represent a revolutionary breakthrough in sequential processing. By allowing for parallelization, they fundamentally alter how machines understand and generate sequences of data, significantly impacting the capabilities of language models.

As we reach the pinnacle of technological evolution, we encounter Large Language Models (LLMs). These models not only understand but actively generate human-like language, with BERT (Bidirectional Encoder Representations from Transformers) and GPT (Generative Pre-trained Transformer) standing out as leading examples. BERT has revolutionized natural language understanding through its bidirectional approach, which considers both the left and right context of a word. This allows it to capture a more comprehensive understanding of language nuances, resulting in enhanced performance on various NLP tasks. Generative Pre-trained Transformers (GPT) exemplify the peak of generative AI. Through extensive pre-training on vast datasets, GPT learns to predict the next word in a sequence based on context. This empowers it to generate coherent and contextually relevant human-like text, solidifying its position as a leading model in the LLM landscape.

The journey from machine learning to generative AI and LLMs reveals the intricate interplay between technology and creativity. This evolution from passive learning to active creative engagement with data marks a transformative shift, shaping the future of artificial intelligence. As we stand at the threshold of this future, we are invited to unravel the layers of innovation, fostering a deeper understanding of the multifaceted nature of AI and its potential impact on the creative landscape. In the subsequent sections, we will cover the foundational areas of generative AI along with a deep dive into applying generative AI in solving practical problems.

Did you know?

Generative Pre-trained Transformer 4 (GPT-4) is a large language model released by OpenAI in late 2022. It has trained on trillions of words of text and many thousands of powerful computer chips. The cost of training has been over 100 Million USD. It has successfully passed the Uniform Bar Examination with a score of 297 (76%).

14.2   A BRIEF CONTEXT OF NLP

Natural Language Processing (NLP) is a subfield of artificial intelligence (AI) that focuses on enabling machines to understand, interpret, and generate human language in a way that is both meaningful and contextually relevant. NLP seeks to bridge the gap between human communication and machine understanding, allowing computers to process, analyze, and respond to natural language input. It involves a diverse range of tasks, including but not limited to text preprocessing, part-of-speech tagging, sentiment analysis, named entity recognition, and machine translation. The ultimate goal of NLP is to empower machines with the ability to comprehend the intricacies of human language, facilitating applications such as chatbots, virtual assistants, language translation, and more. NLP techniques leverage computational linguistics, machine learning, and deep learning methodologies to extract meaning from unstructured text data, paving the way for advancements in human-computer interaction and natural language understanding. The basic tasks of NLP include the following:

- Tokenization, the process of breaking down text into smaller units, such as words or subwords, is a basic task of NLP. For instance, the phrase "Jack and Jill went up the hill" would be tokenized into individual words: "Jack", "and", "Jill", "went", "up", "the" and "hill".

- In Part-of-Speech Tagging (POS), the goal is to assign grammatical labels to each word in a sentence, distinguishing between nouns, verbs, adjectives, and more. For example, in the sentence "The horse is running," POS tagging would involve labeling "horse" as a noun and "running" as a verb.

- Named Entity Recognition (NER) focuses on identifying and classifying entities within text, such as names of people, organizations, or locations. In the sentence "Mr. Bacchan stays in Mumbai," NER would recognize "Mr. Bacchan" as a person and "Mumbai" as a location.

- Sentiment Analysis involves determining the emotional tone expressed in text, whether it is positive, negative, or neutral. This task is commonly used for analyzing customer reviews or social media sentiment towards a product or service.

- Machine Translation is the automated translation of text from one language to another, such as converting an English sentence like "Life is good." into Spanish as "La vida es buena."

- Text Summarization condenses large volumes of text into concise summaries, facilitating efficient information consumption. This is particularly useful for distilling the key points of news articles or research papers.

- Speech Recognition, in which spoken language is converted into written text, enabling applications like voice commands or transcription services.

- Text Generation involves creating coherent and contextually relevant text based on a given input. This is utilized in chatbots, language models, and creative writing applications.

- Coreference Resolution addresses the identification of when different words or expressions in a text refer to the same entity. For example, resolving that the pronoun "he" in a sentence refers to a previously mentioned person.

- Question-answering tasks involve comprehending a question and providing a relevant answer based on available information, often applied in information retrieval systems or virtual assistants responding to user queries. These NLP tasks collectively underscore the versatility and practical applications of language understanding in the realm of artificial intelligence.

14.3 GENERATIVE MODELS – FOUNDATIONAL ARCHITECTURES

The architectures that deal with sequential data, especially natural language, went through a good number of changes by the means of encoder-decoder, attention mechanism, and transformer architecture. Another set of models underlying generative AI that came into prominence is GAN or Generative Adversarial Network, which tries to learn the generation process underlying a supervised problem.

The *encoder-decoder* architecture is a foundational structure in machine translation. In this setup, the encoder processes the input sequence and transforms it into a fixed-size context vector, capturing essential information. This context vector becomes the foundation for the decoder, which generates the output sequence based on the provided context. The encoder's role is to distill the input's salient features, and the decoder utilizes this information to produce a meaningful output. The encoder-decoder architecture improves greatly the performance over a vanilla sequence-to-sequence model.

The *attention mechanism* enhances the models' ability to process sequential data. Unlike traditional models that treat all parts of a sequence equally, attention allows the model to focus on specific elements selectively. In this mechanism, the model assigns different weights to different parts of the input sequence, emphasizing more on relevant components during processing. This dynamic focus on specific elements facilitates better understanding and context capture, proving especially beneficial in tasks like machine translation and natural language processing.

In 2017, there was a state-of-the-art paper by a few Google researchers, where they introduced a new architecture called *'Transformer'.* Some of the highlights of Transformer architecture are –

- There are multiple encoder and decoder blocks, stacked on one another.
- The attention layer is more involved.
- From a performance perspective, these architectures could be trained in parallel doing away with complex recurrences, hence are more efficient.

Generative Adversarial Network (GAN) is a class of deep learning algorithms proposed by Goodfellow et. al. in their 2014 paper "Generative Adversarial Nets". GAN is intended to estimate generative models via an adversarial process, in which two models are trained simultaneously – a generative model G that captures the data distribution and a discriminative model D that estimates the probability that a sample came from the training data rather than G. The generator tries to generate real-like images and the discriminator tries to prove that the image is fake. This process keeps on going through multiple iterations in a game-theoretic way. In the end, the generator can generate a fake image, which is successfully able to fool the discriminator into thinking it is a real image.

Below are some popular generative AI models:

1. **Generative Pre-trained Transformer (GPT):**
   Generative Pre-trained Transformers (GPT) are a type of large language model (LLM) based on Transformer architecture. These models are pre-trained on a large volume of unlabelled texts and are able to generate novel text content. GPT-4 is the version released in March 2023 by OpenAI.

2. **Bidirectional Encoder Representations from Transformers (BERT):**
   While not primarily a generative model, BERT, developed by Google, has redefined natural language understanding. Its bidirectional context understanding has left an indelible impact on subsequent models. BERT's pre-training involves predicting missing words in a sentence, contributing to its nuanced comprehension of context and semantics.

3. **StyleGAN:**
   NVIDIA's StyleGAN specializes in generating high-quality images. Introducing a style-based generator architecture, StyleGAN enables the manipulation of specific visual features in generated images. Its applications extend to creating photorealistic faces and intricate artwork, showcasing the versatility of generative AI in the realm of visual content.

4. OpenAI's DALL-E:

DALL-E, an extension of GPT's capabilities for image generation, exemplifies the versatility of generative AI across modalities. By generating images based on textual descriptions, DALL-E showcases the model's ability to transcend traditional boundaries and engage in cross-modal creative synthesis.

14.4   LARGE LANGUAGE MODELS (LLMS)

Extensively trained on massive text data (including Github, Common Crawl dataset, BookCorpus dataset, StackExchange, and so on) Large Language Models (LLMs) are advanced AI models capable of interacting with and generating human language. These models, like OpenAI's GPT-4, are characterized by their immense size and parameter count, enabling them to understand and generate human-like text across a wide range of contexts. Through training on extensive and diverse datasets, LLMs acquire proficiency in understanding intricate linguistic patterns, contextual nuances, and semantic subtleties. These capabilities have led to their successful application in diverse domains, including natural language processing, machine translation, content generation, and even code completion. Another key feature of LLMs lies in their ability to leverage transfer learning. By initially undergoing pre-training on a comprehensive language understanding task, LLMs can then be fine-tuned for specialized applications. This significantly reduces the dependence on large, task-specific datasets, facilitating efficient adaptation to various domains and requirements.

14.4.1. Few Popular LLMs

There are many different LLMs available, but some of the most popular include:

- GPT-n, a series of Large Language Models (LLMs) developed by OpenAI, includes the well-known GPT-3, released in 2020 with a staggering 175 billion parameters. Renowned for its capacity to produce realistic and innovative text, GPT-n has been applied across diverse domains, generating poetry, code, scripts, music, emails, and letters. Built on the Transformer architecture, GPT-n employs "self-attention," a technique facilitating simultaneous focus on various parts of the input sequence, enhancing its ability to determine long-range dependencies in the data.

- BARD AI, a factual language model from Google AI, is trained on an extensive dataset of text and code. Similar to GPT-n, it can generate creative text formats such as poems, code, scripts, music, emails, and letters. Utilizing the Transformer architecture, BARD AI incorporates "factual attention," allowing the model to concentrate on the most pertinent aspects of the input data based on its trained factual knowledge, striving to meet user requirements effectively.

- Meta AI, previously Facebook AI, has introduced various LLMs, including BlenderBot3 (175 billion parameters, released in 2022) and Megatron-Turing NLG (530 billion parameters, released in 2022). BlenderBot3 is acclaimed for generating realistic and engaging dialogue, applicable in chatbots and virtual assistants. Megatron-Turing NLG, one of the largest LLMs globally, excels in producing high-quality text for tasks like translation and diverse creative content. Meta AI's LLM incorporates different architectures, including the Transformer, enabling the model to learn multiple representations of the data and enhancing its performance across various tasks.

14.4.2. Challenges / Risks with LLMs

Large Language Models (LLMs) have demonstrated remarkable capabilities in natural language processing, but they also come with a set of challenges that warrant attention and consideration:

- **Model Bias and Fairness**
  Fueled by massive datasets, LLMs are susceptible to replicating and amplifying biases present in the real world. This is because the training data reflects the world's imperfections, including societal prejudices, historical injustices, and discriminatory language. As a result, LLMs can generate outputs that are unfair, discriminatory, and perpetuate harmful stereotypes. Addressing bias in LLMs is a crucial ethical consideration to ensure fairness and equity in their applications.

- **Privacy**
  The vast datasets used to train LLMs often contain information about individuals, including their names, addresses, and even personal opinions. This raises concerns that such sensitive information could be inadvertently leaked or misused. Additionally, individuals may not be aware that their data is being used to train LLMs, raising ethical considerations about informed consent and data ownership. Striking a balance between model performance and protecting user privacy is a critical consideration in the development and deployment of LLMs.

- **Transparency and Accountability**
  Though LLMs have emerged as powerful tools, their opaque nature poses a significant challenge. Their internal workings, often compared to "black boxes," make it difficult to understand how they reach their outputs, particularly in critical domains like healthcare and finance. Transparency becomes paramount in these sensitive fields, where trust and accountability hinge on comprehending the reasoning behind LLM decisions. Techniques like Explainable AI allow us to look into the internal representations used by LLMs, offering insights into how they arrive at their decisions.

- **Resource Intensive Training**
  The remarkable capabilities of large language models (LLMs) come at a cost: the immense computational resources required for training and fine-tuning. This dependence on powerful hardware translates to substantial energy consumption, raising environmental concerns and accessibility challenges that hinder the widespread adoption of these models. Developing hardware specifically designed to be more energy-efficient during LLM training could significantly

reduce their environmental footprint. Optimizing the training algorithms themselves to require less computational power can minimize energy consumption and make LLMs more accessible.

- **Lack of real-world knowledge**

  While LLMs excel at generating fluent and even human-quality text, they often falter when it comes to grasping context and applying common-sense reasoning. This can lead to situations where LLMs produce seemingly plausible responses that are ultimately nonsensical or factually incorrect due to a lack of context awareness. Integrating human oversight and judgment into LLM systems can provide a safety net and ensure that outputs are accurate and contextually relevant.

- **Ethical Concerns**

  The impressive language generation capabilities of LLMs come with a double-edged sword. While they offer immense potential for progress and innovation, their powerful tools can also be exploited for malicious purposes. The potential for LLMs to be used to spread misinformation, create sophisticated propaganda, and generate convincing deepfakes raises serious ethical concerns and necessitates the development of robust safeguards. Establishing clear and comprehensive ethical guidelines and regulations for the development and deployment of LLMs can help ensure their responsible use and mitigate potential harm.

- **Potential ownership/copyright issues**

  LLMs, trained on vast datasets collected from diverse sources, pose intriguing legal questions. Determining ownership and copyright of this training data becomes complex due to the often fragmented nature of contributions from various authors and publishers. Further complicating matters is the open-source nature of some LLMs, components, and frameworks, each subject to specific licenses. Understanding and adhering to these licenses is crucial to avoid legal repercussions associated with model usage, modification, and distribution.

  Furthermore, LLMs have the potential to unintentionally reproduce copyrighted material in their generated outputs, raising concerns about copyright infringement. This necessitates a careful approach from developers and users to ensure their content does not infringe upon existing copyrights.

- **Potential Cultural and Linguistic issues**

  LLMs face challenges with cultural and linguistic nuances, including biases in training data, struggles with diverse dialects, cultural insensitivity, and difficulties in handling idiomatic expressions and contextual understanding. Translation issues, lack of inclusivity, and representation pose additional hurdles. Addressing these challenges requires efforts in diversifying training data, enhancing cultural sensitivity, and ensuring inclusivity in LLM development. Regular feedback and collaboration with users from various linguistic and cultural backgrounds are essential for continual improvement and mitigating biases in language generation.

14.4.3. Hallucination

Hallucination in Large Language Models (LLMs) refers to instances where they generate inaccurate or fictional content despite seemingly plausible and relevant outputs. This arises from their vast training data, which often encompasses a mix of factual information, fictional stories, and even speculative content. As LLMs lack a clear "ground truth" during training, they can learn patterns and associations that are not grounded in reality, leading to hallucinated outputs that mislead users.

The consequences of hallucination are particularly concerning in applications where accuracy and reliability are paramount, such as medical diagnoses, legal document analysis, and news reporting. To combat this issue, researchers and developers are exploring various approaches:

✓ **Data Refinement:** By carefully curating and refining training data to minimize fictional or misleading content, the risk of hallucination can be significantly reduced.

✓ **Validation and Fact-Checking:** Implementing robust validation and fact-checking mechanisms helps identify and filter out potentially false or inaccurate outputs generated by the LLM.

✓ **Prioritizing Factual Accuracy:** Fine-tuning the LLM with a focus on factual accuracy can help the model better distinguish between real and fictional information, leading to more reliable outputs.

These efforts highlight the importance of responsible AI development in ensuring the reliability and trustworthiness of LLM-generated content. By continuously refining training data, implementing safeguards, and prioritizing factual accuracy, we can mitigate the risks associated with hallucination and unlock the true potential of LLMs responsibly and ethically.

14.5 HOW IS CHATGPT TRAINED?

As we discussed above, GPT models are trained on massive datasets of text for processing and generating human-like language. ChatGPT is a variation of the GPT model that is specifically designed for chatbots and conversational AI applications. It employs a technique known as Reinforcement Learning from Human Feedback (RLHF) to fine-tune its language model and generate superior responses. Here's a detailed explanation of how it works (refer to Figure 14.1):

1. **Training on a large dataset:** ChatGPT is initially trained on a large dataset of text conversations. This allows the model to learn patterns and relationships in language.

2. **Fine-tuning with RLHF:** After the initial training, RLHF is used to fine-tune ChatGPT. Here humans/trainers play the role of assistant and user. The trainers check the model-written suggestions and help with composing the responses. This way human feedback is incorporated into the training loop to minimize harmful, untruthful, and/or biased outputs.

3. **Ranking Responses:** As part of RLHF, a reward model is developed. The responses generated in the previous step are ranked by human trainers based on their quality and human preferences. This helps the model provide better and more contextually appropriate answers.

4. **Adaptation:** a reinforcement learning task is created that uses this rewards model to fine-tune the language model over time. The reinforcement learning algorithm used in ChatGPT is Proximal Policy Optimization (PPO). In this way, ChatGPT adapts to different types of prompts, styles, and tones.

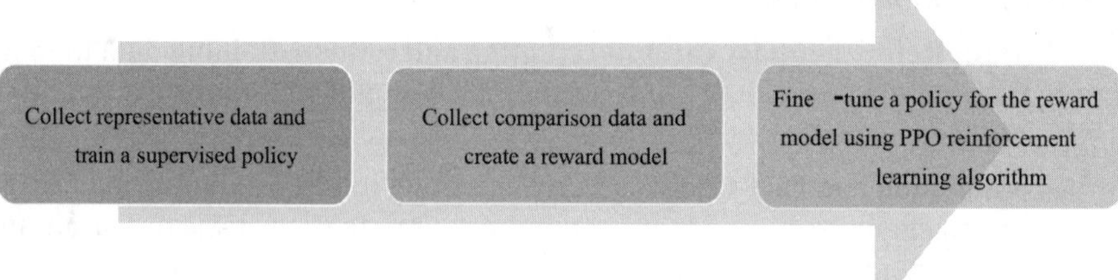

FIG. 14.1
Steps of training ChatGPT

The use of RLHF makes ChatGPT unique and allows it to generate responses that align more closely with human values and expectations.

14.6   APPLICATIONS OF GENERATIVE AI

Generative AI, which includes technologies like Generative Adversarial Networks (GANs) and other generative models, has a wide range of applications across various industries. Generative AI, which includes technologies like Generative Adversarial Networks (GANs) and other generative models, has a wide range of applications across various industries.

✓ **Text Generation:** News agencies, bloggers, and content creators use generative models to automatically generate articles, blog posts, and other written content. This can be particularly useful for generating news updates or creating content at scale. Conversational agents powered by generative models enhance user interactions by providing more natural and contextually relevant responses. Customer service, virtual assistants, and online support systems benefit from these advanced chatbot capabilities.

✓ **Code Generation:** Generative AI assists developers by automatically generating code snippets, completing code blocks, or suggesting relevant functions. This accelerates the software development process and improves coding efficiency.

✓ **Image Generation:** Generative models, particularly GANs, are employed to create unique and visually appealing artwork, digital paintings, and designs. Artists and designers can leverage these tools to explore new creative possibilities and styles. In the entertainment industry, generative AI is used to synthesize realistic human faces for video games, movies, and special effects.

✓ **Video Generation:** Generative models enable the creation of deepfake videos, where faces or content in existing videos are convincingly altered. This has applications in the film industry, as well as potential concerns related to misinformation and privacy. Generative AI is used in animation production to generate realistic movement sequences and enhance the efficiency of the animation process.

✓ **Gaming:** Procedural Content Generation: In the gaming industry, generative AI is employed to dynamically create game environments, characters, and levels. This enhances the gaming experience by providing diverse and unpredictable content.

✓ **3D modeling:** Generative AI has found compelling applications in the field of 3D modeling. Its application in 3D modeling spans terrain generation, facilitating realistic landscapes to 3D characters by generating variations in appearance, clothing, and accessories. It is also applied to create detailed and accurate 3D models of anatomical structures from medical imaging data.

✓ **Voice synthesis:** Generative AI revolutionizes voice synthesis by creating natural and expressive synthetic voices for text-to-speech applications, enabling personalized voice cloning, and supporting multilingual synthesis. It enhances entertainment with realistic character voices, facilitates voice conversion for audio post-production, and aids accessibility by providing customized voices for individuals with speech impairments. Generative AI also powers more natural conversational agents in voice assistants and chatbots contributing to podcasting and content creation with diverse voices.

These detailed applications showcase the breadth and depth of generative AI's impact on diverse industries, ranging from entertainment and art to healthcare, finance, and technology. As these technologies continue to advance, their potential applications are likely to expand even further, contributing to innovation and efficiency across various domains.

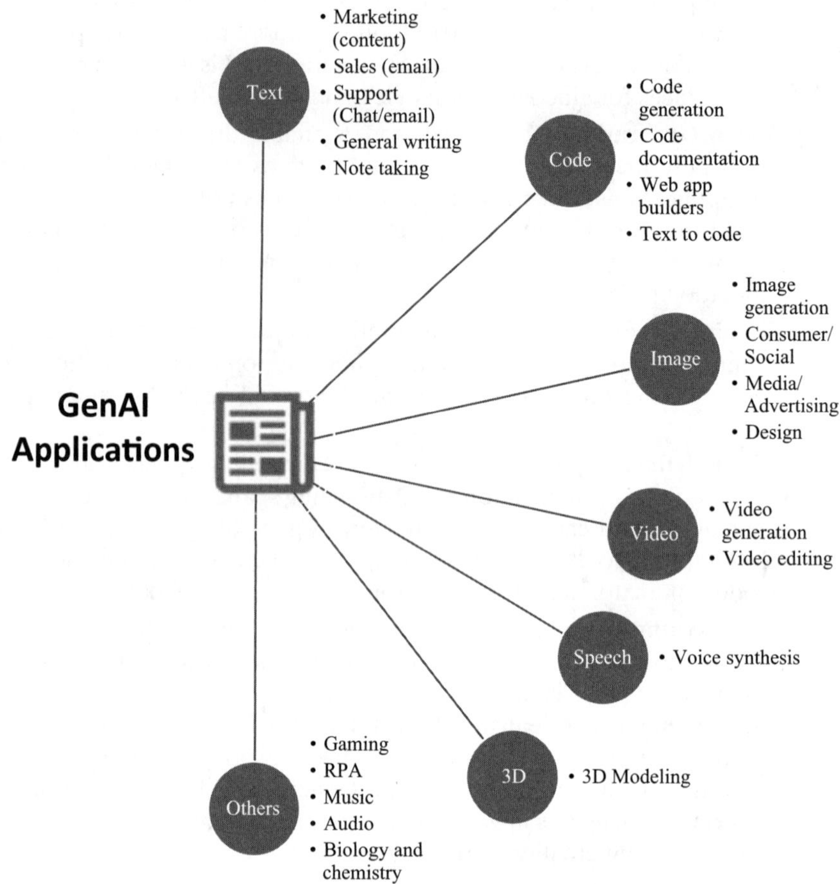

FIG. 14.2
Application Domains of Generative AI

14.7   PROMPT ENGINEERING

A prompt is an input given to an LLM to generate the desired output. Using prompts, one can get a response to a question, just in the same fashion as a normal human being would answer a question asked. A small example is given below:

> **Prompt:** What is the distance between the earth and the moon?
>
> **Response:** The average distance between Earth and the Moon is approximately 238,855 miles (384,400 kilometers).

Prompt engineering is a methodical approach to designing and refining the instructions or queries given to LLM-based applications like ChatGPT. The goal is to optimize the performance and output of these models by carefully crafting the prompts they receive. In other words, prompt engineering tools like "AI Whisperer" speaks the secret language of AI. The right words are crafted in the right way, and suddenly, machines understand humans like never before. In the age of intelligent machines, prompt engineering is the bridge between humans and machines (i.e., the AI-based LLMs in this case).

The first and obvious question that will come to everyone's mind is how can we make prompt engineering effective, i.e., in other words, how can we make good prompts to get the best responses? Following are some of the guardrails for writing good prompts.

1. **Clarity and Precision:**
   Use unambiguous language to convey the intent. Ambiguous prompts may lead to unpredictable or irrelevant outputs. Be precise in your instructions. Clearly define what you are asking for to guide the model accurately. In this context, one important point to note is instructions should be given on what is required rather than what is not required. LLMs often have difficulty understanding the negative tone of prompts.

2. **Use of persona:**
   Give the prompt with a clear indication of what role needs to be played while giving the response. Below is an example:

Prompt: What do you think why India got defeated to Australia in the 2023 Cricket World Cup? Think from the point of view of a sports critic.

Response:

Tactical missteps:
- Misreading the pitch: The Ahmedabad surface, expected to favor spin, surprised everyone by playing slower and drier. India's insistence on spinners early backfired, allowing Australia to build a substantial total.
- Middle-order conundrum: The much-vaunted middle order once again failed to click, with key batsmen falling cheaply after a promising start. This lack of solidity put immense pressure on the top order.
- Dew factor ignored: The dew played a significant role later in the game, negating India's spin advantage and making the ball skid off the pitch. Failing to adapt to these changing conditions proved costly.

Execution lapses:
- Fielding woes: Uncharacteristic dropped catches and sloppy ground fielding gifted Australia extra runs and momentum. This lack of sharpness in the field was a stark contrast to Australia's clinical performance.
- Risky shot selection: Several Indian batsmen played reckless shots early in their innings, throwing away their wickets cheaply. This lack of discipline and composure under pressure ultimately hurt their chances.

> • Captaincy under scrutiny: Rohit Sharma's decision-making, particularly bowling changes and field placements, came under fire for being inconsistent and failing to adapt to the situation.
>
> **Australian dominance:**
> • Ruthless batting: Australia's top order, led by Travis Head and Marnus Labuschagne, played with aggression and intent, building a formidable foundation for their score. Their ability to adapt to the changing conditions and capitalize on India's mistakes was remarkable.
> • Clinical bowling: The Australian bowlers, led by Pat Cummins and Mitchell Starc, were disciplined and accurate, restricting India's scoring and taking key wickets at crucial junctures. Their ability to exploit the dew factor further tilted the game in their favor.
> • Mental fortitude: Australia played with a calm and composed demeanor throughout the final, showcasing their experience and ability to handle pressure situations. This mental toughness proved crucial in the tense final overs.
>
> It's important to note that these are just potential factors, and cricket is a complex game where a multitude of elements can contribute to the outcome. However, as a sports critic, analyzing these aspects can help us understand the nuances of the match and appreciate the strengths and weaknesses of both teams.
>
> Remember, this is just one perspective. There are many other valid viewpoints on this topic, and I encourage you to explore them all to form your own informed opinion.

3. **Format-related Instructions:**

   Clearly outline the desired format of the response, such as a paragraph, list, or specific structure. This helps in obtaining responses that meet your expectations. In continuation of the previous prompt, the following example adds a sense of format to it.

> **Prompt:** Make it less than 100 words. Give in a paragraph format.
>
> **Response:** India's World Cup dreams were shattered by tactical blunders and execution lapses. A slow pitch misread, a shaky middle order, and dew-ignoring spin tactics gifted Australia a hefty total. Fielding errors and reckless batting compounded the woes. Meanwhile, Australia's ruthless batting, disciplined bowling, and mental fortitude proved too much. India's potential remains, but questions loom about their captaincy and ability to handle pressure on the big stage.

4. **Context Awareness:**

   Include relevant context to help the model understand the desired tone, style, or information. Context-rich prompts yield more coherent and contextually appropriate responses. If necessary, supply background information to give the model a foundation for generating content in a specific domain.

> **Prompt:** Be sensitive to readers who may be supporters of the Indian team.
>
> **Response:** In the crucible of the World Cup final, India's hopes flickered and faded. A misjudged pitch and uncharacteristic middle-order jitters left them chasing a formidable target. Though the spinners found early success, the dew's touch later nullified their magic. Australia, clinical and composed, capitalized on every opening, their batsmen ruthless, their bowlers disciplined. While questions linger about tactics and execution, India's spirit remains unbroken. They will rise again, their passion for the game undimmed. This is not an ending, but a chapter closed, awaiting a new, thrilling beginning.

5. **Additional information:**

   Emphasize any additional important element you want the model to focus on. Specify the information or aspects that should be included in the response.

> **Prompt:** Please add if there is any potential umpiring decision which is in debate.
>
> **Response:** The World Cup final's embers still glow, tinged with questions for India. Misread pitch, faltering middle-order, and dew's fickle touch all conspired against them. The spinners' early bite succumbed to the evening's dampness, while Australia's batsmen and bowlers wove a web of ruthless precision. Yet, a whisper of debate lingers. A contentious LBW call, shrouded in replays and pixelated angles, still sparks heated discussions. Was it a game-changer, a turning point in the tide of fortune? India's spirit, though bruised, remains undefeated. They will rise again, their quest for the crown reignited, fueled by lessons learned and debates unresolved. The future beckons, another chapter waiting to be written, its pages blank but brimming with possibilities.

6. **Gradual Complexity:**

   Start with a simple prompt. Begin with straightforward prompts to ensure basic understanding. Gradually introduce complexity to avoid overwhelming the model and to assess its capabilities incrementally. As the model adapts, introduces more complex queries, and layering instructions to achieve nuanced and sophisticated responses. This is exactly what is in the above examples of the prompts.

7. **Iterative Testing:**

   Conduct iterative testing with different prompts to understand how the model responds to variations. This allows you to refine and optimize your prompts for better results. Establish a feedback loop by analyzing model outputs and adjusting prompts accordingly. Continuous improvement is essential for achieving desired outcomes.

8. **Avoiding Bias and Sensitivity:**

   Be mindful of bias in prompts. Use neutral and inclusive language to prevent unintended biases in generated content. Consider the potential sensitivity of topics and frame prompts in a way that respects ethical guidelines and societal norms. This is exactly what was done when we mentioned *"Be sensitive to readers"* in one of the previous prompts.

9. **Limitations and Constraints:**
Clearly define any limitations or constraints within the prompt. This helps manage expectations and ensures that the model operates within specified boundaries. This was done when, in one of the above prompts, it was mentioned "Make it less than 100 words".

10. **Human-in-the-Loop:**
Incorporate human review to assess the quality of generated content. Human feedback is valuable for refining prompts and enhancing the overall performance of the model.

11. **Ethical Considerations:**
Frame prompts with ethical considerations in mind. Avoid requests for harmful or inappropriate content and ensure that the generated responses align with ethical standards.

12. **Real-world Evaluation:**
Evaluate prompts in real-world scenarios to gauge the practical applicability of model outputs. Consider the context in which the generated content will be used.
Crafting the right questions unlocks the hidden potential of LLMs. It's like whispering instructions to a magic genie, guiding its responses toward accuracy and relevance. By understanding language nuances and fine-tuning prompts, we bridge the gap between human intent and AI capabilities, opening doors to new possibilities in tasks like language understanding and problem-solving.

14.7.1. Types of Prompts

Prompt engineering diversifies LLM interaction with a spectrum of prompt types. From zero-shot evaluations, where models navigate without training data, to few-shot and N-shot prompting with varying examples, to cross-domain prompts bridging knowledge gaps and adversarial prompts testing robustness, the landscape is rich. Optimizing LLM outputs hinges on this evolving art of crafting effective prompts. Let's delve into the specific types.

0-shot prompts:
In 0-shot prompts, models generate responses without specific examples or additional context. These prompts demonstrate a model's ability to perform tasks without any training examples. Let's look at the following example. In this case, a basic sentiment analysis is done for a sentence with the intent to understand whether the sentiment reflected is "good" "bad" or "neutral". As you can see, the model responded correctly because it understood the instructions given to it.

> **Prompt:** Classify the following text as good, bad, or neutral.
>
> Text: The dress is super cool!
>
> Classification:
>
> **Response:**
>
> Classification: Good

Few-shot prompts:

Few-shot prompts involve providing the model with a limited number of examples to guide its behavior. The model generalizes from these examples to respond appropriately. Following is an example of few-shot learning. This demonstrates the model's ability to infer task requirements from examples. It adopts the unique response terms ("Fab" for positive, "Drab" for negative) provided within the examples, showcasing its capacity to adapt its output language. So, instead of hand-holding, these few-shot prompts thrive on example-driven learning.

> **Prompt:**
>
> Text: What a wonderful movie it was!
>
> Classification: Fab
>
> Text: It was a real stupid decision on my part.
>
> Classification: Drab
>
> Text: That code is taking ages to execute.
>
> Classification: Drab
>
> Text: Having cinnamon cake after such a long time was exciting.
>
> Classification: Fab
>
> Text: The train is running quite later.
>
> Classification:
>
> **Response:**
>
> Classification: Drab

Chain-of-Thought (COT) prompts:

Chain-of-thoughts prompts involve building a narrative or sequence of ideas by instructing the model to continue generating text based on a given context. This type of prompt encourages coherent and logical development of ideas over multiple responses. It is especially helpful for complex problems which would be difficult to solve in a single prompt. As shown in the example below, the prompt as a part of Option 1 is a bit complex. The response yielded is grossly incorrect. However, when the same prompt is broken into multiple simple and logical prompts, the response yielded by the LLM is accurate.

Option 1 (without COT)

> **Prompt:**
>
> I've 600 rupees. I spend half of it for lunch. From the remaining half, I give one-third to my daughters. I got 300 rupees more from a friend. How much money do I have now? Answer in one sentence.
>
> **Response:**
>
> After spending 300 rupees for lunch, giving one-third of the remaining 300 rupees to your daughters, and receiving 300 rupees from a friend, you now have 600 rupees.

Option 2 (with COT)

> **Prompt:** I've 600 rupees. I spend half of it for lunch. How much is left with me.
>
> **Response:** After spending half of the 600 rupees for lunch, you have 300 rupees left.
>
> **Prompt:** From the remaining half, I give one-third to my daughters. How much is left with me.
>
> **Response:** After giving one-third of the remaining 300 rupees to your daughters, you have 200 rupees left with you.
>
> **Prompt:** I got 300 rupees more from a friend. How much money do I have now?.
>
> **Response:** After receiving an additional 300 rupees from your friend, you now have a total of 500 rupees (200 rupees remaining from lunch and 300 rupees from your friend)..

14.7.2. Applications of Prompt Engineering

As language models like GPT-3.5 become ever more powerful, the ability to control and direct them becomes crucial. This is where prompt engineering steps in, a rapidly evolving field that equips us with the skills to craft the perfect prompts, guiding these AI marvels toward meaningful results. In a world increasingly reliant on AI, mastering this art is no longer a luxury, it's a necessity. As businesses and developers increasingly integrate language models into various applications, the importance of effective prompt engineering becomes paramount, influencing outcomes in content creation, customer support, data analysis, and beyond.

1. **Customized Content Creation:**

   Prompt engineering is instrumental in generating diverse and compelling marketing content. By crafting prompts that specify the tone, style, and key messaging elements, businesses can efficiently create ad copies, social media posts, and product descriptions. This ensures consistency in brand communication and enables the model to produce content aligned with the company's unique voice and marketing strategy.

2. Intelligent Virtual Assistants for Customer Support:

Businesses can leverage prompt engineering to enhance the capabilities of customer support chatbots. Well-crafted prompts guide the chatbot in understanding and addressing customer queries more effectively. From troubleshooting common issues to providing product information, prompt engineering optimizes the chatbot's responses, improving customer satisfaction and reducing response times.

3. Text extraction and text summarization:

Prompt engineering facilitates text summarization by instructing the underlying LLM model to condense information coherently. Crafting prompts with a strategic balance influences the AI's ability to distill essential content, empowering users in tasks such as document summarization and information extraction. This capability enhances efficiency in extracting valuable insights and generating concise summaries, offering a versatile approach to handling textual data. An example of text summarization is given below.

Prompt: Write a 100-word summary of the following text.

###

The Indian Premier League (IPL) (also known as the TATA IPL for sponsorship reasons) is a men's Twenty20 (T20) cricket league that is annually held in India and contested by ten city-based franchise teams.[3][4] The BCCI founded the league in 2007. The competition is usually held in summer between March and May every year. It has an exclusive window in the ICC Future Tours Programme due to fewer international cricket tours happening during IPL seasons worldwide.[5]

. . . .

. . . .

Teams must include 15 players in their squad, with a maximum of eight overseas players.[70]

From the 2024 season, bowlers will be allowed to deliver two bouncers an over. This change in playing conditions was trialled during the 2023-24 Syed Mushtaq Ali Trophy, India's domestic T20 tournament.[71]

(Source: https://en.wikipedia.org/wiki/Indian_Premier_League)

Response: The Indian Premier League (IPL), sponsored by TATA, is an annual men's Twenty20 cricket league in India. Established by the BCCI in 2007, it features ten city-based franchise teams, with matches held between March and May. The IPL is globally renowned, ranking sixth in average attendance among sports leagues in 2014. Its brand value reached ₹90,038 crore (US$11 billion) in 2022, and it became a $10.9 billion decacorn in 2022. Notably, the 2023 final was the most-streamed live event on the internet. The league, with a rich history and substantial economic impact, continues to be a major force in international cricket.

Similarly, an example of keyword extraction is given below.

> **Prompt:**
>
> List down the top 10 prominent keywords / themes in a semi-colon separated format of the following text. *(as a continuation of the last prompt)*
>
> **Response:**
>
> Indian Premier League (IPL); TATA IPL; Twenty20 (T20) cricket; BCCI (Board of Control for Cricket in India); Franchise teams; Brand value; 2023 final; Media rights; Chennai Super Kings; Gujarat Titans

4. Automated Code Generation and Testing:

In software development, prompt engineering can be applied to automate code generation, code conversion (i.e. converting code from one programming language to another), code refactoring, code documentation, and testing processes. Developers can use prompts to instruct models to generate code snippets based on specific requirements or to identify potential vulnerabilities in existing code. This accelerates the development lifecycle and enhances the efficiency of code review processes.

Code Generation using prompts:

Following is a sample code generated in Python programming language.

> **Prompt:**
>
> Generate a Python code to generate Fibonacci series with 12 terms.
>
> **Response:**
> ```python
> # Function to generate Fibonacci series with n terms
> def generate_fibonacci(n):
>     fibonacci_series = [0, 1]
>     while len(fibonacci_series) < n:
>         next_term = fibonacci_series[-1] + fibonacci_series[-2]
>         fibonacci_series.append(next_term)
>     return fibonacci_series
>
> # Number of terms in the Fibonacci series
> num_terms = 12
>
> # Generate and print the Fibonacci series
> fibonacci_series = generate_fibonacci(num_terms)
> print(f"Fibonacci Series with {num_terms} terms: {fibonacci_series}")
> ```

Output after running the response:
>> Fibonacci Series with 12 terms: [0, 1, 1, 2, 3, 5, 8, 13, 21, 34, 55, 89]

Prompt engineering can also be used to generate SQL queries. Following is a sample.

Prompt:

Table name "Students", column names ["Roll No", "Name", "Age", "Height", "Weight"]. Create a t-SQL query to get a list of all students whose age is greater than 18 and height more than 140.

Response:

```
SELECT *
FROM Students
WHERE Age > 18 AND Height > 140;
```

Code conversion using prompts:
Following is an example of converting the Python code to R code and also the output after running the code.

Prompt:

Convert the following code to R.

\###

Function to generate Fibonacci series with n terms

```python
def generate_fibonacci(n):
    fibonacci_series = [0, 1]
    while len(fibonacci_series) < n:
        next_term = fibonacci_series[-1] + fibonacci_series[-2]
        fibonacci_series.append(next_term)
    return fibonacci_series
# Number of terms in the Fibonacci series
num_terms = 12
# Generate and print the Fibonacci series
fibonacci_series = generate_fibonacci(num_terms)
print(f"Fibonacci Series with {num_terms} terms: {fibonacci_series}")
```

```
Response:
# Function to generate Fibonacci series with n terms
generate_fibonacci <- function(n) {
  fibonacci_series <- c(0, 1)
    while (length(fibonacci_series) < n) {
    next_term <- tail(fibonacci_series, 1) + tail(fibonacci_series, 2)[1]
    fibonacci_series <- c(fibonacci_series, next_term)
  }
    return(fibonacci_series)
}
# Number of terms in the Fibonacci series
num_terms <- 12
# Generate and print the Fibonacci series
fibonacci_series <- generate_fibonacci(num_terms)
print(fibonacci_series)
```

Output after running the response:
>> [1] 0 1 1 2 3 5 8 13 21 34 55 89

Refactor code using prompts:

Following is an example of refactoring a piece of monolithic code to a more structured version of the code using prompt engineering.

```
Prompt:
Refactor the following code.
###
num_terms = 12

fibonacci_series = [0, 1]
while len(fibonacci_series) < num_terms:
    next_term = fibonacci_series[-1] + fibonacci_series[-2]
    fibonacci_series.append(next_term)

print(f"Fibonacci Series with {num_terms} terms: {fibonacci_series}")
```

```
Response:
def generate_fibonacci_series(num_terms):
    fibonacci_series = [0, 1]
    while len(fibonacci_series) < num_terms:
        next_term = sum(fibonacci_series[-2:])
        fibonacci_series.append(next_term)
return fibonacci_series
num_terms = 12
fibonacci_series = generate_fibonacci_series(num_terms)
print(f"Fibonacci Series with {num_terms} terms: {fibonacci_series}")
```

Document code using prompts:
Following is an example of refactoring a piece of monolithic code to a more structured
version of the code using prompt engineering.

```
Prompt:
Add inline documentation to the code.
###
def generate_fibonacci_series(num_terms):
    fibonacci_series = [0, 1]

    while len(fibonacci_series) < num_terms:
        next_term = sum(fibonacci_series[-2:])
        fibonacci_series.append(next_term)

    return fibonacci_series


num_terms = 12
fibonacci_series = generate_fibonacci_series(num_terms)
print(f"Fibonacci Series with {num_terms} terms: {fibonacci_series}")
```

Response:

```
def generate_fibonacci_series(num_terms):
    """
    Generate Fibonacci series with a specified number of terms.

    Parameters:
    - num_terms (int): The number of terms in the Fibonacci series.

    Returns:
    - list: The generated Fibonacci series.
    """
    fibonacci_series = [0, 1]

    while len(fibonacci_series) < num_terms:
        next_term = sum(fibonacci_series[-2:])
        fibonacci_series.append(next_term)

    return fibonacci_series


# Number of terms in the Fibonacci series
num_terms = 12
# Generate Fibonacci series
fibonacci_series = generate_fibonacci_series(num_terms)

# Print the generated Fibonacci series
print(f"Fibonacci Series with {num_terms} terms: {fibonacci_series}")
```

Instead of inline documentation, if overall documentation is needed, that can also be done using prompt engineering. Let's look at an example.

Prompt:

Provide a brief documentation of the following code.

```
###
def generate_fibonacci_series(num_terms):
    fibonacci_series = [0, 1]

    while len(fibonacci_series) < num_terms:
        next_term = sum(fibonacci_series[-2:])
        fibonacci_series.append(next_term)
    return fibonacci_series
num_terms = 12
fibonacci_series = generate_fibonacci_series(num_terms)
print(f"Fibonacci Series with {num_terms} terms: {fibonacci_series}")
```

Response:

Function: generate_fibonacci_series

This Python function generates a Fibonacci series with a specified number of terms.

Parameters:

num_terms (int): The number of terms to be included in the Fibonacci series.

Returns:

list: The generated Fibonacci series as a list.

Function Logic:

1. Initialize the Fibonacci series with the first two terms $[0, 1]$.

2. Use a while loop to continue generating the series until it reaches the specified number of terms (num_terms).

3. In each iteration, calculate the next term by summing the last two terms of the existing series.

4. Append the calculated next term to the series.

5. Once the series has the desired number of terms, return the generated Fibonacci series.

Generate test cases using prompts:

Following is an example of generating test cases using prompt engineering.

Prompt:

Generate test cases for the following code.

###

```python
def generate_fibonacci_series(num_terms):
    fibonacci_series = [0, 1]
    while len(fibonacci_series) < num_terms:
        next_term = sum(fibonacci_series[-2:])
        fibonacci_series.append(next_term)
    return fibonacci_series

num_terms = 12

fibonacci_series = generate_fibonacci_series(num_terms)

print(f"Fibonacci Series with {num_terms} terms: {fibonacci_series}")
```

Response:

Test Case: Zero Terms
Input: num_terms = 0
Expected Output: [] (An empty list since no terms are generated.)
Test Case: One Term
Input: num_terms = 1
Expected Output: [0] (The first term of the Fibonacci series.)
Test Case: Two Terms
Input: num_terms = 2
Expected Output: [0, 1] (The first two terms of the Fibonacci series.)
Test Case: Three Terms
Input: num_terms = 3
Expected Output: [0, 1, 1] (The first three terms of the Fibonacci series.)
Test Case: Large Number of Terms
Input: num_terms = 20
Expected Output: [0, 1, 1, 2, 3, 5, 8, 13, 21, 34, 55, 89, 144, 233, 377, 610, 987, 1597, 2584, 4181] (The first 20 terms of the Fibonacci series.)
Test Case: Negative Number of Terms
Input: num_terms = -5
Expected Output: [] (An empty list since a negative number of terms is not meaningful.)
These test cases cover a range of scenarios, including edge cases and common scenarios, to ensure the generate_fibonacci_series function behaves as expected.

5. Data generation

In data generation, prompts guide the model to produce specific content. By formulating precise queries or instructions, users can shape the AI's responses to generate desired datasets. This capability enables synthetic data generation. However, prompt engineering requires a detailed understanding of the model's behavior and limitations, ensuring effective communication to achieve the desired outcomes in data generation applications.

Prompt:

1. Create a list of 10 Roll No.

2. Create a list of 10 Last Name.

3. Create a list of 10 First Name.

4. Combine them to a list of Full Name.

5. Create a list of 10 Age.

6. Create a list of 10 Height.

7. Create a list of 10 Weight.

8. Combine Roll No, Full Name, Age, Height, Weight randomly to create a table name Student.

Response:

```python
import random

# Lists of Roll No, Last Name, and First Name
roll_numbers = list(range(1, 11))
last_names = ["Smith", "Johnson", "Williams", "Jones", "Brown", "Davis", "Miller", "Wilson", "Moore", "Taylor"]
first_names = ["John", "Jane", "Robert", "Emily", "Michael", "Olivia", "William", "Sophia", "Daniel", "Emma"]

# Combine last names and first names to create a list of full names
full_names = [f"{random.choice(first_names)} {random.choice(last_names)}" for _ in range(10)]

# Lists of Age, Height, and Weight
ages = [random.randint(18, 25) for _ in range(10)]
heights = [random.randint(150, 180) for _ in range(10)]
weights = [random.randint(50, 80) for _ in range(10)]

# Combine Roll No, Full Name, Age, Height, Weight to create the "Student" table
students = list(zip(roll_numbers, full_names, ages, heights, weights))

# Print the "Student" table
for student in students:
    print(student)
```

Data generated as the output of the code:

(1, 'Daniel Davis', 21, 172, 53)
(2, 'Michael Davis', 22, 165, 76)
(3, 'Robert Taylor', 24, 173, 74)
(4, 'William Johnson', 21, 162, 55)
(5, 'John Wilson', 19, 178, 72)
(6, 'William Williams', 21, 174, 52)
(7, 'Sophia Williams', 24, 154, 59)
(8, 'Emily Miller', 25, 175, 72)
(9, 'Daniel Taylor', 21, 157, 71)
(10, 'John Davis', 19, 178, 55)

6. **Data Analysis and Reporting Automation**

   In the area of data analysis, prompt engineering plays a crucial role in automating the generation of insights and reports. By formulating prompts that articulate specific analysis requirements or reporting formats, businesses can instruct language models to sift through complex datasets and present key findings. This accelerates the decision-making process and facilitates more efficient communication of data-driven insights to stakeholders.

14.7.3. Integrating LLMs into Python using LangChain

LangChain is a Python and JavaScript framework designed to simplify the creation of applications powered by large language models (LLMs). It offers a powerful and flexible framework for developers to leverage the capabilities of LLMs and build sophisticated language-driven applications. LangChain consists of several components:

- **Libraries:** The Python and JavaScript libraries provide interfaces and integrations for various components, a runtime for combining them, and ready-made implementations for building chains and agents.
- **Templates:** A collection of reference architectures for common tasks like question answering, dialogue generation, and text summarization.
- **LangServe:** A library for deploying LangChain applications as REST APIs.
- **LangSmith:** A developer platform for debugging, testing, evaluating, and monitoring LangChain applications, integrating seamlessly with various LLM frameworks.

A simple code sample to leverage the LangChain library and use prompt engineering from within Python code is given below. To use LangChain, the LangChain library must be installed first from the Python package manager. Also, the OpenAI Python wrapper needs to be installed.

```
pip install langchain == <<current version>>
pip install openai == <<current version>>
from langchain.llms import OpenAI

LLM = OpenAI (openai_api_key="How many rows are there in the Iris
dataset?")
prompt = "What would be a good company name for a company that makes
colorful socks?"
response = LLM.invoke (prompt)
print (response)


>>> The Iris dataset typically contains 150 rows. Each row represents an
individual iris flower, and the dataset is commonly used in machine learning
and statistics for tasks such as classification.
```

14.7.4. Pair programming powered by Prompt Engineering

Pair programming facilitates collaborative software development by allowing developers to work together in real-time, with AI-powered code completion tools. GitHub Copilot (https://github.com/features/copilot) is one such cloud-based, AI-powered code completion tool developed by GitHub (owned by Microsoft) in collaboration with OpenAI (49% owned by Microsoft). It is designed to assist developers by suggesting whole lines or blocks of code as they type. GitHub Copilot is built on the Codex model, which is a variant of OpenAI's GPT technology. It works best for users coding in Python, JavaScript, TypeScript, Ruby, and Go. Copilot integrates with popular Integrated Development Environments (IDEs) such as Visual Studio Code, allowing developers to seamlessly incorporate it into their coding workflow. Key features of GitHub Copilot include:

- **Collaborative coding:** Copilot provides intelligent code autocompletion suggestions based on the context of the code being written. It can generate entire lines or chunks of code.
- **Code review:** Review new code, see visual code changes, and confidently merge code changes with automated status checks.
- **Code search & code view:** Code search and code view enable developers to rapidly search, navigate, and understand code right from GitHub.com.
- **Natural Language Understanding:** Developers can write code in natural language comments, and Copilot will attempt to generate code snippets based on the comments.
- **Learning from Context:** Copilot learns from the context of the code it is generating, providing more contextually relevant suggestions over time.
- **Multi-line comments:** Clarify code reviews by referencing or commenting on multiple lines at once in a pull request diff view.

- **Test case generation:** Developers can use Copilot to generate unit test cases from a piece of code, saving time during the development process.

Other such popular AI-powered productivity tools are increasingly growing in terms of adoption. Amazon CodeWhisperer is one such tool. It also generates code suggestions ranging from snippets to full functions in real-time in the IDE based on your comments and existing code.

14.7.5. Best Practices in Prompt Engineering

The response to the prompts depends a lot on the way the prompts are being constructed. Following are some of the guidelines that can yield effective responses.

- **Clarity:** Craft prompts with clear instructions and goals
- **Specificity:** Be precise about the desired format, length, or type of response
- **Version of LLM:** Use the latest version of LLM as it is trained with the latest data, hence can answer more recent questions
- **Type of prompt:** Start with a 0-shot prompt and slowly move to a few-shot prompt
- **Iterative Refinement:** Experiment with different prompts, refining based on model outputs
- **Delimiters:** Use delimiters to separate the instruction from the context
- **Avoid using fluffy/indirect instructions:** Keep the instructions simple and crisp. Also, provide instructions regarding what to do rather than what not to do.
- **Leading words:** For code generation, use leading words i.e., a smaller snippet of starter code. This leads the LLM to generate code in a desired pattern.

14.8 SUMMARY

- ✓ Natural Language Processing (NLP) is a subfield of artificial intelligence (AI) that focuses on enabling machines to understand, interpret, and generate human language in a way that is both meaningful and contextually relevant.
- ✓ NLP techniques leverage computational linguistics, machine learning, and deep learning methodologies to extract meaning from unstructured text data, paving the way for advancements in human-computer interaction and natural language understanding.
- ✓ The architectures that deal with sequential data, especially natural language, went through a good number of changes by the means of encoder-decoder, attention mechanism, and transformer architecture.
- ✓ GAN or Generative Adversarial Network is another set of models underlying generative AI which came into prominence.
- ✓ Generative Pre-trained Transformers (GPT) are a type of large language model (LLM) based on Transformer architecture. These models are pre-trained on a large volume of unlabelled texts and are able to generate novel text content.

- ✓ Extensively trained on massive text data (including Github, Common Crawl dataset, BookCorpus dataset, StackExchange, and so on) Large Language Models (LLMs) are advanced AI models capable of interacting with and generating human language.
- ✓ Some of the most popular include:
  - & GPT-n, a series of Large Language Models (LLMs) developed by OpenAI
  - & BARDAI, a factual language model from Google AI
  - & Meta AI, previously Facebook AI
- ✓ Challenges related to LLMs include:
  - & Model Bias and Fairness
  - & Privacy
  - & Transparency and Accountability
  - & Resource Intensive Training
  - & Lack of real-world knowledge
  - & Ethical Concerns
  - & Potential ownership/copyright issues
  - & Potential Cultural and Linguistic issues
- ✓ Hallucination in Large Language Models (LLMs) refers to instances where they generate inaccurate or fictional content despite seemingly plausible and relevant outputs.
- ✓ ChatGPT is a variation of the GPT model that is specifically designed for chatbots and conversational AI applications. It employs a technique known as Reinforcement Learning from Human Feedback (RLHF) to fine-tune its language model and generate superior responses.
- ✓ GenAI has a wide range of applications across various industries:
  - & Text Generation
  - & Code Generation
  - & Image Generation
  - & Video Generation
  - & Gaming
  - & 3D modelling
  - & Voice synthesis
- ✓ Prompt engineering is a methodical approach to designing and refining the instructions or queries given to LLM-based applications like ChatGPT. A prompt is an input given to an LLM to generate the desired output.
- ✓ Some of the guardrails for writing good prompts include:
  - & Clarity and Precision
  - & Use of persona
  - & Format-related Instructions
  - & Context Awareness

- & Additional information
- & Gradual Complexity
- & Iterative Testing
- & Avoiding Bias and Sensitivity
- & Limitations and Constraints
- & Human-in-the-Loop
- & Ethical Considerations
- & Real-world Evaluation

✓ Types of Prompts are -

- & 0-shot prompts
- & Few-shot prompts
- & Chain-of-Thought (COT) prompts

✓ As businesses and developers increasingly integrate language models into various applications, the importance of effective prompt engineering becomes paramount, influencing outcomes in content creation, customer support, data analysis, and beyond.

✓ Some of the applications of prompt engineering are:

- & Customized Content Creation
- & Intelligent Virtual Assistants for Customer Support
- & Text extraction and text summarization
- & Automated code generation and testing
  - ▪ Code Generation
  - ▪ Code conversion
  - ▪ Refactor code
  - ▪ Document code
- & Generate test cases
- & Data generation
- & Data Analysis and Reporting Automation

✓ LangChain is a Python and JavaScript framework designed to simplify the creation of applications powered by large language models (LLMs). It offers a powerful and flexible framework for developers to leverage the capabilities of LLMs and build sophisticated language-driven applications.

✓ Pair programming facilitates collaborative software development by allowing developers to work together in real-time, with AI-powered code completion tools. GitHub Copilot is one such cloud-based, AI-powered code completion tool developed by GitHub in collaboration with OpenAI.

SAMPLE QUESTIONS

MULTIPLE-CHOICE QUESTIONS (1 MARK QUESTIONS):

1.   Which event in 2012 is mentioned as a watershed moment for deep learning in the text?
     (a) Introduction of GANs
     (b) ImageNet competition
     (c) Development of Transformers
     (d) Release of GPT-4

2.   What is the primary focus of Variational Autoencoders (VAEs) in generative AI?
     (a) Image classification
     (b) Learning latent data representations
     (c) Sequential data processing
     (d) Text summarization

3.   How do Transformers differ from traditional models in processing sequential data?
     (a) They use recurrent layers.
     (b) They allow for parallelization.
     (c) They focus on generative tasks.
     (d) They have fewer encoder-decoder blocks.

4.   What distinguishes Large Language Models (LLMs) from traditional models?
     (a) They are trained on small datasets.
     (b) They focus only on image processing.
     (c) They understand and generate human-like language.
     (d) They use unsupervised learning exclusively.

5.   Which architecture is foundational in machine translation and involves an encoder-decoder structure?
     (a) Transformer
     (b) GAN
     (c) Attention mechanism
     (d) Encoder-decoder

6.   What is the primary goal of the attention mechanism in models processing sequential data?
     (a) Sequential data generation
     (b) Sequential data processing
     (c) Sequential data parallelization
     (d) Sequential data encryption

7.   What risk is associated with Large Language Models (LLMs) regarding user privacy?
     (a) Hallucination
     (b) Bias and fairness
     (c) Lack of real-world knowledge
     (d) Resource-intensive training

8. What is a potential challenge with LLMs mentioned in the text regarding ethical concerns?
(a) Speech recognition issues
(b) Model hallucination
(c) Cultural and linguistic insensitivity
(d) Lack of real-world knowledge

9. What is the primary purpose of prompt engineering in the context of language models like ChatGPT?
(a) Enhancing model aesthetics
(b) Optimizing model performance and output
(c) Improving model physical design
(d) Minimizing model training time

10. Why is clarity important in crafting prompts for language models?
(a) To confuse the model for better creativity
(b) To achieve ambiguity in generated content
(c) To optimize model understanding and response
(d) To challenge the model's comprehension limits

11. In prompt engineering, what is the role of the persona in generating responses?
(a) Enhancing the model's self-awareness
(b) Providing a clear indication of the role in the response
(c) Confusing the model with identity shifts
(d) Making the model more human-like

12. What is the significance of including format-related instructions in prompts?
(a) To limit the model's creativity
(b) To discourage the use of paragraphs in responses
(c) To guide the desired structure of the response
(d) To confuse the model with conflicting instructions

13. How can prompt engineering contribute to avoiding bias in generated content?
(a) By promoting biased language in prompts
(b) By using ambiguous and vague instructions
(c) By avoiding any context in prompts
(d) By using neutral and inclusive language

14. What does iterative testing involve in the context of prompt engineering?
(a) Training the model from scratch
(b) Continuous refinement of prompts based on testing variations
(c) Ignoring model outputs and sticking to initial prompts
(d) Using identical prompts for every test iteration

15. How can human-in-the-loop contribute to prompt engineering?
(a) By replacing the model's role in generating responses
(b) By incorporating human review to assess generated content
(c) By restricting the model's autonomy in generating responses
(d) By minimizing human involvement in the prompt design

SHORT-ANSWER TYPE QUESTIONS (5 MARKS QUESTIONS):

1. Explain the significance of the ImageNet competition in 2012 and its impact on the field of deep learning.

2. How do Variational Autoencoders (VAEs) contribute to the richness and diversity of generative AI outputs?

3. Compare the roles of Transformers and Variational Autoencoders (VAEs) in the realm of generative AI, highlighting their respective strengths.

4. Examine the key features of Large Language Models (LLMs), such as BERT and GPT, and how they represent a significant advancement in natural language understanding.

5. Explain the importance of clarity and precision in prompt engineering. Provide examples to illustrate how ambiguous prompts can lead to unpredictable or irrelevant outputs from language models.

6. Why is it important to outline the desired format of the response in prompt engineering? Provide an example of a prompt that includes a format-related instruction and explain how it contributes to obtaining responses that meet expectations.

7. Explain the significance of including relevant context in prompts for language models. Provide an example of a prompt that emphasizes sensitivity to readers and describe how context-rich prompts contribute to coherent and contextually appropriate responses.

8. Explain the importance of using the latest version of language models in prompt engineering. Provide examples of how the version of the language model can impact responses and why staying updated is crucial.

9. Compare the characteristics of GANs (Generative Adversarial Networks) with other generative AI models. How does the adversarial process contribute to GANs' ability to generate realistic content?

10. Briefly describe the Generative Pre-trained Transformer (GPT) and its role as a Large Language Model (LLM). How does GPT-4 exemplify the pinnacle of generative AI?

LONG-ANSWER TYPE QUESTIONS (10 MARKS QUESTIONS):

1. Discuss the evolution of artificial intelligence from machine learning to generative AI and Large Language Models (LLMs). Highlight key milestones and breakthroughs, emphasizing the transformative shifts in technology and creativity. Provide examples of influential models in each stage.

2. Explain the foundational architectures in generative AI, focusing on the encoder-decoder, attention mechanism, and Transformer architecture. Illustrate how these architectures contribute to sequential data processing, especially in the context of natural language. Provide examples of models that utilize these architectures.

3. Provide an overview of Natural Language Processing (NLP), highlighting its goals, tasks, and significance in bridging the gap between human communication and machine understanding. Discuss key tasks within NLP and how they contribute to applications such as chatbots, virtual assistants, and language translation.

4. Discuss the challenges and risks associated with Large Language Models (LLMs). Highlight specific concerns such as model bias, privacy, transparency, resource-intensive training, lack of real-world knowledge, ethical concerns, and potential ownership/copyright issues. Propose potential solutions or mitigations for these challenges.

5. Examine the concept of hallucination in Large Language Models (LLMs), outlining instances where LLMs may generate inaccurate or fictional content. Discuss the potential consequences of hallucination, particularly in critical domains like medical diagnoses and news reporting. Propose strategies such as data refinement, validation, and prioritizing factual accuracy to mitigate the risks associated with hallucination.

6. Explain the significance of clarity and precision in prompt engineering. Provide examples to illustrate how clear and unambiguous language can impact the output of language models like ChatGPT.

7. Explain the importance of incorporating personas in prompts for language models. Provide an example prompt and response that demonstrates the use of personas in obtaining nuanced and role-specific outputs.

8. Discuss the importance of format-related instructions in prompt engineering. Provide an example prompt and response that illustrates how specifying the desired format enhances the quality of the language model's output.

9. Explain the role of context awareness in prompt engineering. Provide an example prompt and response that showcases how incorporating relevant context improves the coherence and appropriateness of language model outputs.

10. Discuss the importance of gradual complexity and iterative testing in prompt engineering. Provide examples to illustrate how starting with simple prompts and refining through iterations contribute to the optimization of language model outputs.

Appendix A

Programming Machine Learning in R

A.1   PRE-REQUISITES

Before starting with machine learning programming in R, we need to fulfil certain pre-requisites. Quite understandably, the first and foremost activity is to install R and get started with the basic programming interface of R, i.e. R console. Then, we need to become familiar with the R commands and scripting in R. In this section, we will have a step-by-step guide of fulfilling these pre-requisites.

A.1.1   Install R in Your System

- R 4.3.2 or higher (https://cran.r-project.org/bin/windows/base/)
- RStudio 1.7.0 or higher (*Optional*, only if you want to leverage the advantage of using an integrated development environment (IDE). Otherwise, R console is sufficient.) (https://www.rstudio.com/products/rstudio/download/)

A.1.1.1   Note

- The Comprehensive R Archive Network (or CRAN) is a worldwide network of ftp and web servers that store identical and up-to-date versions of code and documentation for R.
- RStudio is a free and open-source IDE for R.

436

A.1.2   Know How to Manage R scripts

- Open new / pre-existing scripts in R console as shown in Figure A.1:

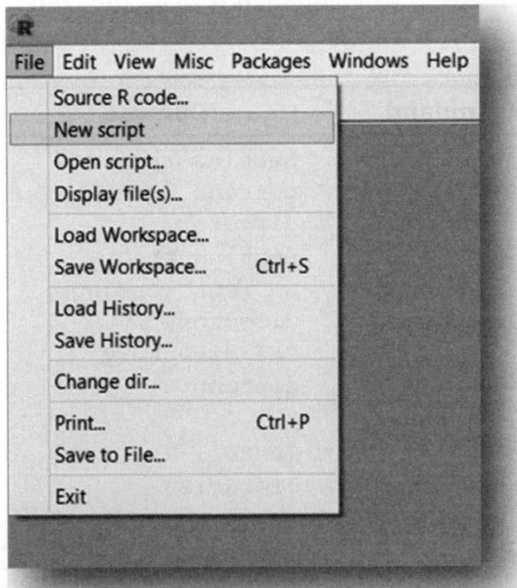

Copyright © The R Foundation

FIG. A.1
Opening a script in R console

- Scripts can be written / edited on the R editor window, and console commands can be directly executed on the R console window as shown in Figure A.2:

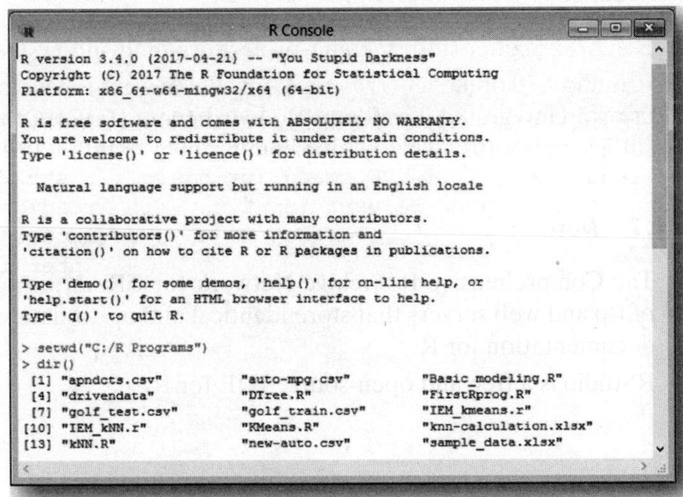

Copyright © The R Foundation

FIG. A.2
Writing code in R console

A.1.3   Know How to do Basic Programming Using R

A.1.3.1   Introduction to basic R commands

Try each of the following commands from the command prompt in R console (or from RStudio, if you want).

Sr #	Command	Purpose	Sample code with output
1	getwd ()	Getting the current working directory	> getwd() [1] "C:/"
2	setwd ()	Setting the current working directory	> setwd("C:/R Programs")
3	dir()	See directory content	> dir() [1] "Example.doc" "HelloWorld.R"
4	install. packages()	Install R libraries	> install. packages('caret') Installing package into 'F:/R/library' (as 'lib' is unspecified) --- Please select a CRAN mirror for use in this session ---
5	library(package)	Load a package which is installed.	> library (caret)
6	source ()	Enables R to accept inputs from a source file (i.e. a .R file)	> source("HelloWorld.R")
7	print()	Command for basic user output	> print("Hello") [1] Hello
8	readline ()	Command for basic user input	> str <- readline("Enter input:") Enter input: Hello

(Continued)

(*Continued*)

Sr #	Command	Purpose	Sample code with output
9	class()	Gives the type of an object	> num <- 10 > class(num) [1] "numeric"
10	help(<<keyword>>) / ? <<keyword>>	Access help related to some function. **Note**: To access help for a function in a package that is not currently loaded, specify name of the package as follows: *help(<<keyword>>, package= <<package>>)*	> ?setwd / > help(setwd) > help(train, package = caret)
11	rm ()	Remove objects from memory	> rm(list = ls()) > rm(list = c("g","x")) where g and x are variables created

Note:

"#" is used for inserting inline comments
<- and = are alternative / synonymous assignment operators

A.1.3.2 Basic data types in R

- **Vector:** This data structure contains similar types of data, i.e. integer, double, logical, complex, etc. The function c () is used to create vectors.

```
> num <- c(1,3.4,-2,-10.85) #numeric vector
> char <- c("a","hello","280") #character vector
> bool <- c(TRUE,FALSE,TRUE,FALSE,FALSE) #logical vector
> print(num)
[1] 1.0 3.4 -2.0 -10.85
```

- **Matrix:** Matrix is a 2-D data structure and can be created using the matrix () function. The values for rows and columns can be defined using 'nrow' and 'ncol' arguments. However, providing both is not required as the other dimension is automatically acquired with the help of the length parameter (first index : last index).

```
> mat<-matrix(1:12, nrow=3,ncol=4)
> print(mat)
     [,1] [,2] [,3] [,4]
[1,]   1    4    7   10
[2,]   2    5    8   11
[3,]   3    6    9   12
```

- **List:** This data structure is slightly different from vectors in the sense that it contains a mixture of different data types A list is created using the list () function.

```
> L <- list(num=10.5, str="Goodbye", matrix=mat)
> print(L)
$num
[1] 10.5
$str
[1] "Goodbye"
$matrix
     [,1] [,2] [,3] [,4]
[1,]   1    4    7   10
[2,]   2    5    8   11
[3,]   3    6    9   12
> print (L[1])#1st component of the list
$num
[1] 10.5 #to truncate '$num', use double indexing, i.e. '[[]]'
```

- **Factor:** The factor stores the nominal values as a vector of integers in the range $[1...k]$ (where k is the number of unique values in the nominal variable) and an internal vector of character strings (the original values) mapped to these items.

```
> data <- c('A','B','B','C','A','B','C','C','B')
> fact <- factor(data)
> fact
[1] A B B C A B C C B
Levels: A B C
> table(fact) #arranges argument item in a tabular format
fact
A B C #unique items mapped to frequencies
2 4 3
```

- **Data frame:** This data structure is a special case of list where each component is of the same length. Data frame is created using the frame () function.

```
> DF <- data.frame("Num" = 3:5, "Name" = c("Nolan","Kubrick",
"Tarantino"), "Color" = c("Blue",NA,"Red"))
> print(DF)
 Num       Name  Color
1 3        Nolan  Blue
2 4      Kubrick  <NA>
3 5    Tarantino   Red
```

A.1.3.3 Loops

For loop
Syntax:

```
for (variable in sequence)
{
  (loop_body)
}
```

Example: Printing squares of all integers from 1 to 3.

```
for (i in c(1:3))
{
  j = i*i
  print(j)
}
[1] 1
[1] 4
[1] 9
```

While loop
Syntax:

```
while (condition)
{
  (loop_body)
}
```

Example: Printing squares of all integers from 1 to 3.

```
i <- 1
while(i<=3)
{
  sqr <- i*i
  print(sqr)
  i <- i+1
}
[1] 1
[1] 4
[1] 9
```

If-else statement
Syntax:

```
if (condition 1)
{
  Statement 1
}
```

```
else if (condition 2)
{
Statement 2
}
else
{
Statement 4
}
```

Example:

```
x = 0
if (x > 0)
{
print ("positive")
} else if (x == 0)
{
print ("zero")
} else
{
print ("negative")
}
[1] "zero"
```

A.1.3.4 Writing functions

Writing a function (in a script):

Syntax:

```
function_name <- function(argument_list)
{
  (function_body)
}
```

Example: Function to calculate factorial of an input number n.

```
factorial <- function (n)
{
  fact<-1
for(i in 1:n)
{
  fact <-fact*i
}
return(fact)
}
```

Running the function (after compiling the script by using source ('script_name')):

```
> f <- factorial(6)
> print(f)
[1] 720
```

A.1.3.5 Mathematical operations on data types

- **Vectors:**

```
> n <- 10
> m <- 5
> n + m #addition
[1] 15
> n - m #subtraction
[1] 5
> n * m #multiplication
[1] 50
> n / m #division
[1] 2
```

- **Matrices:**

```
> mat1 <- matrix(1:6,2)
> mat1
     [,1] [,2] [,3]
[1,]   1    3    5
[2,]   2    4    6
> mat2 <- matrix(c(rep(1, 3), rep(2, 3)), 2, byrow=T)
> mat2
     [,1] [,2] [,3]
[1,]   1    1    1
[2,]   2    2    2
> t(mat2) #transpose
[,1] [,2]
[1,] 1 2
[2,] 1 2
[3,] 1 2
> mat1 + mat2 #element-wise addition
[,1] [,2] [,3]
[1,]     246
[2,]     468
> mat1 - mat2 #element-wise subtraction
[,1] [,2] [,3]
[1,]     024
[2,]     024
> mat1 * mat2 #element-wise multiplication
[,1] [,2] [,3]
[1,]     135
[2,]     4812
> mat1 %*% t(mat2) #conventional matrix multiplication
[,1] [,2]
[1,] 9 18
[2,] 12 24
```

```
> mat1 / mat2 #element-wise division
[,1]  [,2] [,3]
[1,]      135
[2,]      123
```

A.1.3.6 Basic data handling commands

```
> data <- read.csv("auto-mpg.csv") # Uploads data from a .csv file


> class(data) # To find the type of the data set object loaded
[1] "data.frame"
> dim(data) # To find the dimensions, i.e. the number of rows and
columns of the data set loaded
[1] 398 9


> nrow(data) # To find only the number of rows
[1] 398


> ncol(data) # To find only the number of columns
[1] 9


> names (data) #
[1] "mpg" "cylinders" "displacement" "horsepower" "weight"
[6] "acceleration" "model.year" "origin" "car.name"


> head (data, 3) # To display the top 3 rows


> tail(data, 3) # To display the bottom 3 rows


> View(data) # To view the data frame contents in a separate UI
> data[1,9] # Will return cell value of the 1st row, 9th column
of a data frame
[1] chevrolet chevelle malibu


> write.csv(data, "new-auto.csv") # To write the contents of a data
frame object to a .csv file


> rbind(data[1:15,], data[25:35,]) # Bind sets of rows


> cbind(data[,3], data[,5]) # Bind sets of columns, with the same
number of rows


> data <- data[!data$model.year > 74,] #Remove all rows
with model year greater than 74
```

Note:

For advanced data manipulation, the **dplyr** library of R (developed by Hadley Wickham et al) can be leveraged. It is the next version of the **plyr** package focused on working with data frames (hence the name "d"plyr).

A.1.3.7 Advanced data manipulation commands

```
> library("dplyr")
# Functions to project specific columns
> select (data, cylinders) #Selects a specific feature
> select(data, -cylinders) # De-selects a specific feature
> select(data,2) #selects columns by column index
> select(data,2:3) #selects columns by column index range
> select(data,starts_with("Cyl"))#Selects features by pattern
match
```

Some additional options to project data elements on the basis of conditions are as follows:

- **ends_with ()** = Select columns that end with a character string
- **contains ()** = Select columns that contain a character string
- **matches ()** = Select columns that match a regular expression
- **one_of ()** = Select column names that are from a group of names

```
# Functions to select specific rows
> filter(data, cylinders == 8) #selects rows based on conditions
> filter(data, cylinders == 8, model.year > 75)
```

In R, the **pipe** (%>%) operator allows to pipe the output from one function to the input of another function. Instead of nesting functions (reading from inside to outside), the idea of piping is to read the functions from left to right.

```
> data %>% select(2:7) %>% filter(cylinders == 8, model.year > 75)
%>% head(3)
```

	cylinders	displacement	horsepower	weight	acceleration	model.year
1	8	304	150	3433	12	87
2	8	307	200	4376	15	85
3	8	305	140	4215	13	76

```
> arrange(data,model.year) #Sorts ascending rows by a feature
> arrange(data,- model.year) #Sorts descending rows by a feature
> mutate(data,Total = mpg*2) #Adds new columns
```

	mpg	cylinders	displacement	horsepower	weight	acceleration	model. year	origin
1	18	8	307	130	3504	12.0	70	1
2	15	8	350	165	3693	11.5	70	1
3	18	8	318	150	3436	11.0	70	1

	car.name	total
1	chevrolet chevelle malibu	36
2	buick skylark 320	30
3	Plymouth satellite	36

```
> mutate(data, mpg = mpg*2) #Also, transforms existing columns
```

	mpg	cylinders	displacement	horsepower	weight	acceleration	model. year	origin
1	36	8	307	130	3504	12.0	70	1
2	30	8	350	165	3693	11.5	70	1
3	36	8	318	150	3436	11.0	70	1

	car name
1	chevrolet chevelle malibu
2	buick skylark 320
3	plymouth satellite

```
> data %>% select(2:7) %>% filter(cylinders == 8, acceleration >
15.3) %>% group_by(model.year) #Groups rows together according to
attribute values

Source : local data frame [10 x 6]
Groups : model. year [7]
```

	cylinders	displacement	horsepower	weight	acceleration	model. year
	<int>	<dbl>	<fctr>	<int>	<dbl>	<int>
1	8	304	193	4732	18.5	70
2	8	302	140	4294	16.0	72
3	8	302	140	4638	16.0	74
4	8	304	150	4257	15.5	74
5	8	260	110	4060	19.0	77
6	8	260	110	3365	15.5	78
7	8	305	130	3840	15.4	79
8	8	350	125	3900	17.4	79
9	8	260	90	3420	2 2.2	79
10	8	350	105	3725	19.0	81

A.2   PREPARING TO MODEL

Now that we are reasonably familiar with the basic R commands, we have acquired the ability to start machine learning programming in R. But before starting the actual modelling work, we have to first understand the data using the concepts highlighted in Chapter 2. Also, there might be some issues in the data, which we will reveal during data exploration. We have to remediate that too.

So first, let us find out how to do data exploration in R. There are two ways to explore and understand data:

1. By using certain statistical functions to understand the central tendency and spread of the data
2. By visually observing the data in the form of plots or graphs

A.2.1   Basic Statistical Functions for Data Exploration

Let us start with the first approach of understanding the data through statistical techniques. As we have seen in Chapter 2, for any data set, it is critical to understand the central tendency and spread of the data. We have also seen that the standard statistical measures used are as follows:

1. Measures of central tendency – mean, median, mode
2. Measures of data spread
   (a) Dispersion of data – variance, standard deviation
   (b) Position of the different data values – quartiles, interquartile range (IQR)

In R, there is a function ***summary***, which generates the summary statistics of the attributes of a data set. It gives the first basic understanding of the data set, which can trigger thoughts about the data set and the anomalies that may be present. We will use another diagnostic function, str, which compactly provides the structure of a data frame along with the data types of the different attributes. So, let us start exploring a data set **Auto MPG data set** from the University of California, Irvine (UCI) machine learning repository. We will run the *str* and *summary* commands for the Auto MPG data set.

```
> str(data)
'data. frame' :  398 obs. of 9 variables:
 $ mpg         : num 18 15 18 16 17 15 14 14 14 15 ...
 $ cylinders   : int 8888888888 ...
 $ displacement: num 307 350 318 304 302 429 454 440 455 3000 ...
 $ horsepower  : int 130 165 150 150 140 198 220 215 225 190 ...
 $ weight      : int 3504 3693 3436 3433 3449 4341 4354 4312 4425
                     3850 ...
 $ acceleration: num 12 11.5 11 12 10.5 10 9 8.5 10 8.5 ...
 $ model.year  : int 70 70 70 87 70 70 70 70 70 70 ...
 $ origin      : int 1111111111 ...
 $ car.name    : Factor w/ 305 levels "amc ambassador
                     brougham",..: 50 37 232 1$
```

```
> summary(data)
```

mpg	cylinders	displacement	horsepower	weight
Min. :9.00	Min. :3.000	Min. : 68.0	Min. :46.0	Min. :1613
1st Qu.:17.50	1st Qu.:4.000	1st Qu.: 104.2	1st Qu.:75.0	1st Qu.:2224
Median :23.00	Median :4.000	Median : 148.5	Median :93.5	Median :2804
Mean :23.51	Mean :5.455	Mean : 200.0	Mean :104.5	Mean :2970
3rd Qu.:29.00	3rd Qu.:8.000	3rd Qu.: 262.0	3rd Qu.:126.0	3rd Qu.:3608
Max :46.60	Max. :8.000	Max. :3000.0	Max. :230.0	Max. :5140
			NA's :6	

acceleration	model.year	origin	car.name	
Min. :8.00	Min. :60.00	Min. :1.000	ford pinto	: 6
1st Qu.:13.82	1st Qu.:73.00	1st Qu.:1.000	amc matador	: 5
Median :15.50	Median :76.00	Median :1.000	ford maverick	: 5
Mean :15.57	Mean :76.07	Mean :1.573	toyota corolla	: 5
3rd Qu.:17.18	3rd Qu.:79.00	3rd Qu :2.000	amc gremlin	: 4
Max. :24.80	Max. :90.00	Max. :3.000	amc hornet	: 4
			(other)	:369

Looking closely at the output of the *summary* command, there are six measures listed for the attributes (well, most of them). These are

1. Min. – minimum value of the attribute

2. 1st Qu. – first quartile (for details, refer to Chapter 2)

3. Median

4. Mean

5. 3rd Qu. – third quartile (for details, refer to Chapter 2)

6. Max. – maximum value of the attribute

These measures give quite good understanding of the data set attributes. Now, note that the attribute car.name is not showing these values and showing something else. Why is that so and what are the values that it is showing? Let us try to understand the reason for this difference.

The attribute car.name is a nominal, i.e. categorical attribute. As we have already seen in Chapter 2, mathematical or statistical operations are not possible for a nominal variable. Hence, only the unique values for the attribute along with the number of occurrences or frequency are given. We can obtain an exhaustive list of nominal attributes using the following R command.

```
> summary(data$car.name)
        ford pinto            amc matador
                 3                      5
     ford maverick         toyota corolla
                 5                      5
       amc gremlin             amc hornet
                 4                      4
```

Chevrolet chevette		Chevrolet impala	
4		4	
Peugeot 504		toyota corona	
4		4	
Chevrolet caprice		Chevrolet citation	
classic			
3		3	
Chevrolet nova		Chevrolet vega	
3		3	
dodge colt		ford galaxie 500	
3		3	
ford gran torino		honda civic	
3		3	

Next, let us try to explore whether any variable has any issue with the data values where a cleaning may be required. As discussed in Chapter 2, there may be two primary data issues: missing values and outliers.

Let us first try to determine whether there is any missing value for any of the attributes. Let us use a small piece of R code to find out whether there is any missing/unwanted value for an attribute in the data. If there is such issue, return the rows in which the attribute has missing/unwanted values. By checking all the attributes, we find that the attribute 'horsepower' has missing values.

```
> data[is.na(data$horsepower),]
```

	mpg	cylinders	displacement	horsepower	weight	acceleration	model.year	origin
33	25.0	4	98	NA	2046	19.0	71	1
127	21.0	6	200	NA	2875	17.0	74	1
331	40.9	4	85	NA	1835	17.3	80	2
337	23.6	4	140	NA	2905	14.3	80	1
335	34.5	4	100	NA	2320	15.8	81	2
375	23.0	4	151	NA	3035	20.5	82	1

	car.name
33	ford pinto
127	ford maverick
331	renault lecar deluxe
337	ford mustang cobra
355	renault 18i
375	amc concord dl

There are six rows in the data set, which have missing values for the attribute 'horsepower'. We will have to remediate these rows before we proceed with the modelling activities. We will do that shortly.

The easiest and most effective method to detect outliers is from the box plot of the attributes. In the box plot, outliers are very clearly highlighted. When we explore the attributes using box plots in a short while, we will have a clear view of this aspect.

Let us quickly see the other R commands for obtaining statistical measures of the numeric attributes.

```
> range(data$mpg) #Gives minimum and maximum values
[1] 9.0 46.6
> diff(range(data$mpg))
[1] 37.6
> quantile(data$mpg)
0% 25% 50% 75% 100%
9.0 17.5 23.0 29.0 46.6
> IQR(data$mpg)
[1] 11.5
> mean(data$mpg)
[1] 23.51457
> median(data$mpg)
[1] 23
> var(data$mpg)
[1] 61.08961
> sd(data$mpg)
[1] 7.815984
```

Note:

To perform data exploration (as well as data visualization), the **ggplot2** library of R can be leveraged. Created by Hadley Wickham, the ggplot2 library offers a comprehensive graphics module for creating elaborate and complex plots.

A.2.2   Basic Plots for Data Exploration

To start using the library functions of *ggplot2*, we need to load the library as follows:

```
> library(ggplot2)
```

Let us now understand the different graphs that are used for data exploration and how to generate them using R code.

A.2.2.1 Box plot

Syntax: boxplot (x, data, notch, varwidth, names, main)
  Usage:

```
> boxplot(iris) # Iris is a popular data set used in machine learn-
ing, which comes bundled in R installation
```

A separate window opens in R console with the box plot generated as shown in Figure A.3.

As we can see, Figure A.3 shows the box plot of the entire iris data set, i.e. for all the features in the iris data set, there is a component or box plot in the overall plot. However, if we want to review individual features separately, we can do that too using the following R command.

```
> boxplot(iris$Sepal.Width, main="Boxplot", ylab = "Sepal.Width")
```

The output of the command, i.e. the box plot of an individual feature, sepal width, of the iris data set is shown in Figure A.4.

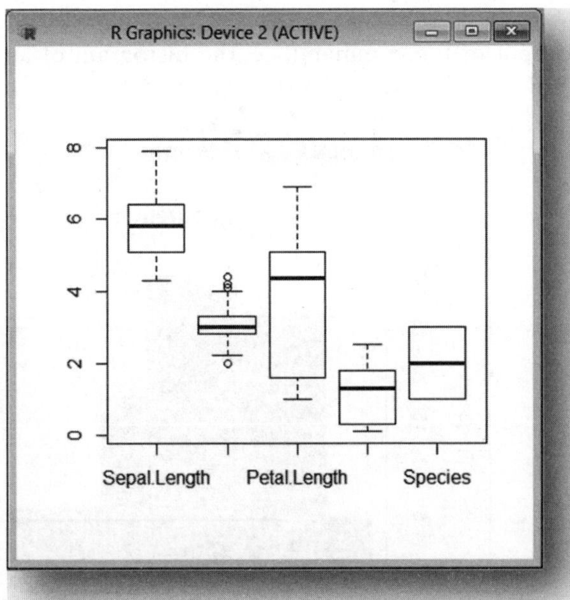

FIG. A.3
Box plot of an entire data set

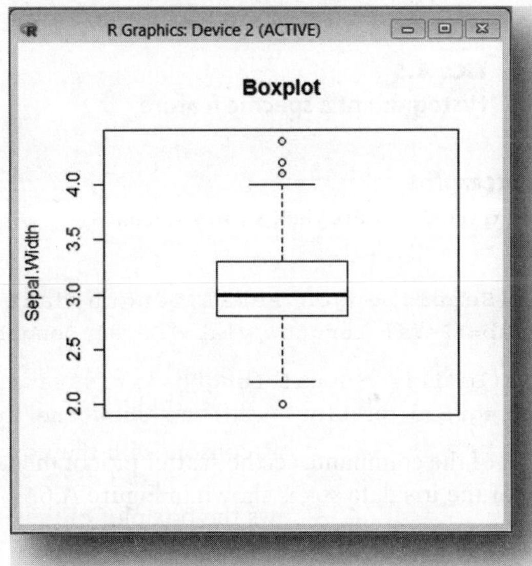

FIG. A.4
Box plot of a specific feature

A.2.2.2 *Histogram*

Syntax: hist (v, main, xlab, xlim, ylim, breaks, col, border)
   Usage:

```
> hist(iris$Sepal.Length, main = "Histogram", xlab = "Sepal
Length", col = "blue", border = "green")
```

The output of the command, i.e. the histogram of an individual feature, petal length, of the iris data set is shown in Figure A.5.

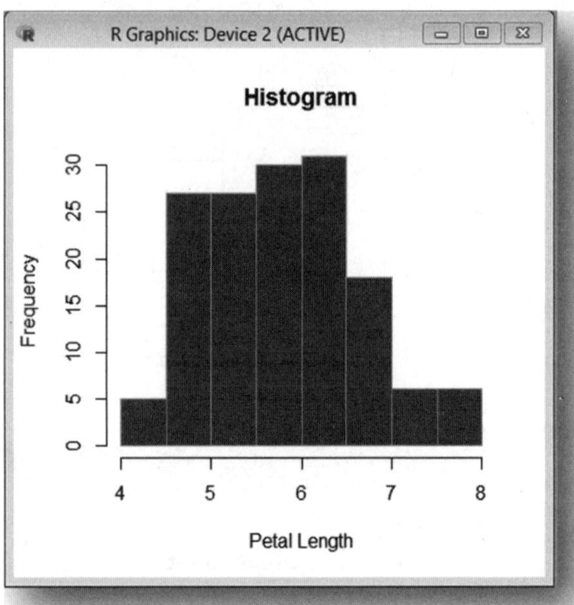

FIG. A.5
Histogram of a specific feature

A.2.2.3 *Scatterplot*

Syntax: plot (x, y, main, xlab, ylab, xlim, ylim, axes)
   Usage:

```
>  plot(Sepal.Length~Petal.Length,data=iris,main="Scatter
Plot",xlab="Petal Length",ylab="Sepal Length")

> abline(lm(iris $Sepal.Length~ iris$Petal.Length), col="red")
# Fit a regression line (red) to show the trend
```

The output of the command, i.e. the scatter plot of the feature pair petal length and sepal length of the iris data set, is shown in Figure A.6.

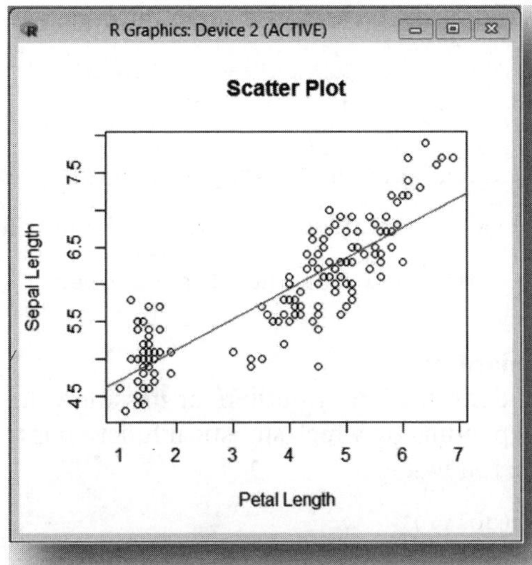

FIG. A.6
Scatter plot of petal length vs sepal length

A.2.3   Data Pre-Processing

The primary data pre-processing activities are remediating data issues related to outliers and missing values. Also, feature subset selection is quite a critical area of data pre-processing. Let us understand how to write programmes for achieving these purposes.

A.2.3.1 Handling outliers and missing values

As we saw in Chapter 2, the primary measures for remediating outliers and missing values are as follows:

- Removing specific rows containing outliers/missing values
- Imputing the value (i.e. outlier/missing value) with a standard statistical measure, e.g. mean or median or mode for that attribute
- Estimate the value (i.e. outlier/missing value) on the basis of value of the attribute in similar records and replace with the estimated value.
- Cap the values within 1.5 times IQR limits

Removing outliers/missing values

We have to first identify the outliers. We have already seen in boxplots that outliers are clearly visible when we draw the box plot of a specific attribute. Hence, we can use the same concept as shown in the following code:

```
> outliers <- boxplot.stats(data$mpg)$out
```

Then, those rows can be removed using the code:

```
> data <- data[!(data$mpg == outliers),]
```

OR,

```
> data <- data[-which(data$mpg == outliers),]
```

For missing value identification and removal, the below code is used:

```
> data1 <- data[!(is.na(data$horsepower)),]
```

Imputing standard values

The code for identification of outliers or missing values will remain the same. For imputation, depending on which statistical function is to be used for imputation, the code will be as follows:

```
> library(dplyr)

# Only the affected rows are identified and the value of the
attribute is transformed to the mean value of the attribute

> imputedrows <- data[which(data$mpg == outliers),] %>% mutate(mpg =
mean(data$mpg))

# Affected rows are removed from the data set

> outlier_removed_rows <- data[-which(data$mpg == outliers),]

# Recombine the imputed row and the remaining part of the data set

> data <- rbind(outlier_removed_rows, imputedrows)
```

Almost the same code can be used for imputing missing values with the only difference being in the identification of the relevant rows.

```
>  imputedrows  <-  data[(is.na(data$horsepower)),]%>%  mutate
(horsepower = mean(data$horsepower))
> missval_removed_rows <- data[!(is.na(data$horsepower)),]
> data <- rbind(outlier_removed_rows, imputedrows)
```

Capping of values

The code for identification of outlier values will remain the same. For capping, generally a value of 1.5 times the IQR is used for imputation, and the code will be as follows:

```
> library(dplyr)


> outliers <- boxplot.stats(data$mpg)$out
```

```
> imputedrows <- data[which(data$mpg == outliers),] %>% mutate(mpg =
1.5*IQR(data$mpg))
> outlier_removed_rows <- data[-which(data$mpg == outliers),]
> data <- rbind(outlier_removed_rows, imputedrows)
```

A.3   MODELLING AND EVALUATION

Note:

The **caret** package (short for Classification And REgression Training) contains functions to streamline the model training process for complex regression and classification problems. The package contains tools for
- data splitting
- different pre-processing functionalities
- feature selection
- model tuning using resampling
- model performance evaluation

as well as other functionalities.

A.4   MODEL TRAINING

To start using the functions of the *caret* package, we need to include the *caret* as follows:

```
> library(caret)
```

A.4.1   Holdout

The first step before the start of modelling, in the case of supervised learning, is to load the input data, holdout a portion of the input data as test data, and use the remaining portion as training data for building the model. Below is the standard procedure to do it.

```
> inputdata <- read.csv("btissue.csv")
> split = 0.7 #Ratio in which the input data is to be split to
training and test data. A split value = 0.7 indicates 70% of the
data will be training data, i.e. 30% of the input data is retained
as test data
> set.seed(123) # This step is optional, needed for result
reproducibility
> trainIndex <- createDataPartition (y = inputdata$class, p = split,
list = FALSE) # Does a stratified random split
of data into training and test sets
> train_ds <- inputdata [trainIndex,]
> test_ds <- inputdata [-trainIndex,]
```

A.4.2   K-Fold Cross-Validation

Let us do a 10-fold cross-validation. For creating the cross-validation, functions `from` the *caret* package can be used as follows:

```
> ten_folds <- createFolds(data$weight, k = 10)> head(ten_folds,3)
$Fold01
 [1]    7   14   29   38   41   75   82   85   91  106 108 111 112 118 119 131 145 151 156 168 169
[22]  204 205 208 216 226 232 233 234 243 264 272 287 298 311 317 368 390 394

$Fold02
 [1]    9   11   40   44   55   62   67   72   79   89   92 115 133 138 149 153 154 176 182 190 192
[22]  206 215 227 236 245 246 250 278 291 300 302 304 327 332 333 340 342 372 393

$Fold03
 [1]   34   45   51   52   81   90  101 107 110 116 123 124 136 141 159 167 179 181 189 195 197
[22]  199 237 239 251 254 262 265 271 280 290 301 308 316 331 344 358 377 384
```

Next, we perform the data holdout.

```
train_ds <- inputdata [-ten_folds$Fold01,]

test_ds <- inputdata [ten_folds$Fold01,]
```

Note:

When we perform data holdout, i.e. splitting of the input data into training and test data sets, the records selected for each set are picked randomly. So, it is obvious that executing the same code or R function may result in different training data sets. The model trained will also be somewhat different.

In R, there is a **set.seed** function which sets the starting point of the random number generator used internally to pick the records. This ensures that random numbers of a specific sequence are used every time, and hence, the same records (i.e. records having the same sequence number) are picked every time and the model is trained in the same way. This is extremely critical for the reproducibility of results, i.e. every time, the same machine learning program generates the same set of results. The code is as follows:

```
> set.seed (5)
```

A.4.3   Bootstrap Sampling

To generate a bootstrap sample for any statistics, R package **boot** can be used. A sample code is given below.

```
> install.packages ("boot")
> library (boot)

myfunc <- function (){
# body of the function ...
return (someval)
}

> bootcorr <- boot(data = mydata, statistic = myfunc, R = 500) #
R is the number of bootstrap samples
```

A.4.4   Training the Model

Once the model preparatory steps such as data holdout, etc. are completed, the actual training starts using the following code or similar codes.

```
> model <- train(class ~ ., method = "rpart", data = train_ds) #
Code for the decision tree model
```

A.4.5   Evaluating Model Performance

There are different ways to evaluate the different models in supervised and unsupervised learning. Some of them, as we have seen, have been discussed in Chapter 3. Now, it is time to see how we can implement them through R code.

A.4.5.1 Supervised learning - classification

In supervised learning, model accuracy is the most critical measure for evaluating a model's performance. There are also other measures such as sensitivity, specificity, precision, recall, etc., each of which we have studied in Chapter 3. R library *caret* gives a function *confusionMatrix* to reveal the confusion matrix of a model, and on the basis of the confusion matrix, values of the different measures, namely accuracy, sensitivity, specificity, precision, recall, etc., are obtained. Figure A.7 presents a snapshot of the *confusionMatrix* output for a specific data set.

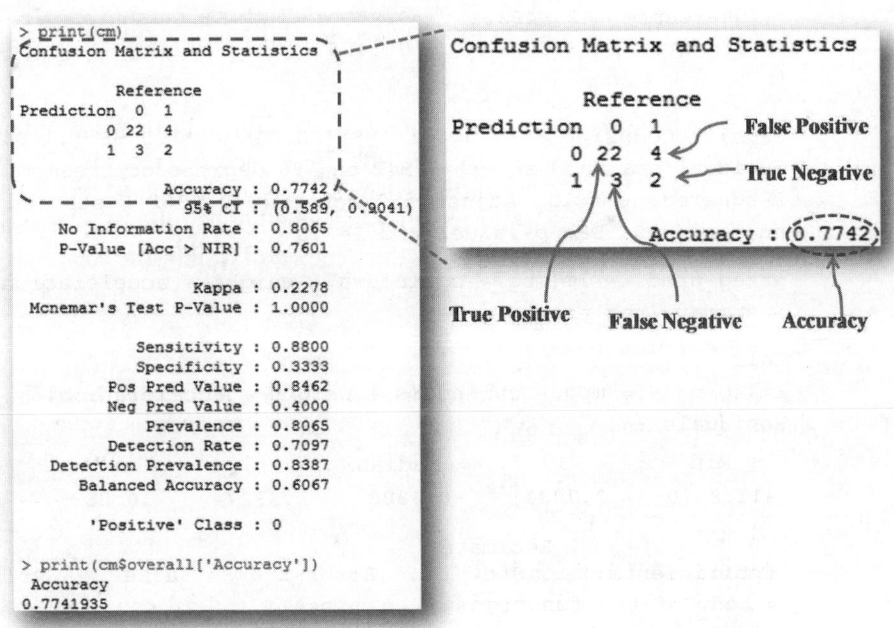


```
> print(cm)
Confusion Matrix and Statistics

          Reference
Prediction  0  1
         0 22  4
         1  3  2

               Accuracy : 0.7742
                 95% CI : (0.589, 0.9041)
    No Information Rate : 0.8065
    P-Value [Acc > NIR] : 0.7601

                  Kappa : 0.2278
 Mcnemar's Test P-Value : 1.0000

            Sensitivity : 0.8800
            Specificity : 0.3333
         Pos Pred Value : 0.8462
         Neg Pred Value : 0.4000
             Prevalence : 0.8065
         Detection Rate : 0.7097
   Detection Prevalence : 0.8387
      Balanced Accuracy : 0.6067

       'Positive' Class : 0

> print(cm$overall['Accuracy'])
 Accuracy
0.7741935
```

FIG. A.7

Performance evaluation of a classification model (Decision Tree)

```
> predictions <- predict(model, test_ds, na.action = na.pass)
> cm <- confusionMatrix(predictions, test_ds$class)
> print(cm)
> print(cm$overall['Accuracy'])
```

A.4.5.2 *Supervised learning - regression*

The *summary* function, when applied to a regression model, displays the different performance measures such as residual standard error, multiple R-squared, etc., both for simple and multiple linear regression.

```
> data <- read.csv("auto-mpg.csv")
> attach(data)
> reg_pred <- lm(mpg ~ cylinders)
> summary(reg_pred)

Call:
lm(formula = mpg ~ cylinders)
Residuals :
```

Min	1Q	Median	3Q	Max
-14.2607	-3.3841	-0.6478	2.5538	17.9022

```
Coefficients:
```

	Estimate Std.	Error t	Value	Pr(>| t |)
(Intercept)	42.9493	0.8330	51.56	<2e-16***
cylinders	-3.5629	0.1458	-24.43	<2e-16***

```
- - -

Signif. Codes: 0'***' 0.001 '***' 0.01 '***' 0.05 '.' 0.1 ' ' 1
Residual standard error: 4.942 on 396 degrees of freedom. Multiple
R-squared: 0.6012, Adjusted R-squared: 0.6002 F-statistic: 597.1
on 1 and 396 DF, p-value: < 2.2e-16

> reg_pred <- lm(mpg ~ cylinders + weight + acceleration)
> summary(reg_pred)

Call
lm(formula = mpg ~ cylinders + weight + acceleration)
Residuals :
```

Min	1Q	Median	3Q	Max
-11.8070	-2.7084	-0.3802	2.3327	16.2891

	Estimate Std.	Error t	Value	Pr(>| t |)
Coefficients:	42.3810831	1.9596811	21.627	<2e-16***
	-0.4827342	0.3019075	-1.599	0.1106
	-0.0065312	0.0005758	-11.342	<2e-16***
	0.2034431	0.0909951	2.236	0.0259

```
Signif. Codes: 0'***' 0.001 '***' 0.01 '***' 0.05 '.' 0.1 ' ' 1
Residual standard error: 4.296 on 394 degrees of freedom. Multiple
R-squared: 0.7002, Adjusted R-squared: 0.6979 F-statistic: 306.7
on 1 and 396 DF, p-value: < 2.2e-16
```

A.4.5.3 *Unsupervised learning - clustering*

As we have seen in Chapter 3, there are two popular measures of cluster quality: purity and silhouette width. Purity can be calculated only when class label is known for the data set subjected to clustering. On the other hand, silhouette width can be calculated for any data set.

Purity

We will use a Lower Back Pain Symptoms data set released by Kaggle (https://www. kaggle.com/sammy123/lower-back-pain-symptoms-dataset). The data set *spine.csv* consists of 310 observations and 13 attributes (12 numeric predictors, 1 binary class attribute).

```
> library(fpc)


> data <- read.csv("spine.csv") #Loading the Kaggle data set
> data_wo_class <- data[,-length(data)] #Stripping off the class
attribute from the data set before clustering
> class <- data[,length(data)] #Storing the class attribute in a
separate variable for later use
> dis = dist(data_wo_class)^2
> res = kmeans(data_wo_class,2) #Can use other clustering
algorithms too
#Let us define a custom function to compare cluster value with the
original class value and calculate the percentage match

ClusterPurity <- function(clusters, classes) {
sum(apply(table(classes, clusters), 2, max)) / length(clusters)
}
> ClusterPurity(res$cluster, class)
```

Output

```
[1] 0.6774194
```

Silhouette width

Use the R library *cluster* to find out/plot the silhouette width of the clusters formed. The piece of code below clusters the records in the data set *spinem.csv* (the same data set as spine.csv with the target variable removed) using the *k-means* algorithm and then calculates the silhouette width of the clusters formed.

```
> library (cluster)


> data <- read.csv("spinem.csv")
> dis = dist(data)^2
```

```
> res = kmeans(data,2) #Can use other clustering algorithms too
> sil_width <- silhouette (res$cluster, dis)
> sil_summ <- summary(sil_width)
> sil_summ$clus.avg.widths # Returns silhouette width of
each cluster

> sil_summ$avg.width # Returns silhouette width of the
overall data set
```

Output

Silhouette width of each cluster:

```
1            2

0.7473583 0.1921082
```

Silhouette width of the overall data set:

```
[1] 0.5413785
```

A.5   FEATURE ENGINEERING

A.5.1   Feature Construction

For performing feature construction, we can use *mutate* function of the **dplyr** package.
Following is a small code for feature construction using the iris data set.

```
> data <- iris
> data <- mutate(data, Sepal.Area = Sepal.Length*Sepal.Width,
Petal.Area = Petal.Length*Petal.Width)
> head(data)
```

	Sepal. Length	Sepal. Width	Petal. Length	Petal. Width	Species	Sepal. Area	Fetal. Area
1	5.1	3.5	1.4	0.2	setosa	17.85	0.28
2	4.9	3.0	1.4	0.2	setosa	14.70	0.28
3	4.7	3.2	1.3	0.2	setosa	15.04	0.26

A.5.1.1 Dummy coding categorical (nominal) variables

As in the above case, we can use the *dummy.code* function of the **psych** package to
encode categorical variables. Following is a small code for the same.

```
> library(psych)

> age <- c(18,20,23,19,18,22)
> city <- c('City A','City B','City A','City C','City B')
> data <- data.frame(age, city)
> data
```

```
          age      city
    1     18     City A
    2     20     City B
    3     23     City B
    4     19     City A
    5     18     City C
    6     22     City B

> data1 <- dummy.code(data$city)
> data <- cbind(data[,1],data1)
> data

                 City A   City B   City C
    [1,]     18      1        0        0
    [2,]     20      0        1        0
    [3,]     23      0        1        0
    [4,]     19      1        0        0
    [5, ]    18      0        0        1
    [6, ]    22      0        1        0
```

A.5.1.2 Encoding categorical (ordinal) variables

```
> marks_science <- c(78,56,87,91,45,62)
> marks_maths <- c(75,62,90,95,42,57)
> grade <- c('B','C','A','A','D','B')
> data <- data.frame(marks_science, marks_maths, grade)
> data

        marks_science    marks_maths      grade
    1        73              75              B
    2        56              62              C
    3        87              90              A
    4        91              95              A
    5        45              42              D
    6        62              57              B

> data[,3] <- ifelse(data[,3] == "A", 1, ifelse(data[,3] == "B",
2, ifelse(data[,3] == "C", 3, ifelse(data[,3] == "D", 4, 99))))

> data

        marks_science    marks_maths      grade
    1        78              75              2
    2        56              62              3
    3        87              90              1
    4        91              95              1
    5        45              42              4
    6        62              57              2
```

A.5.1.3 Transforming numeric (continuous) features to categorical features

```
> apartment_area <- c(4720,2430,4368,3969,6142,7912)
> apartment_price <- c(2360000,1215000,2184000,1984500,3071000,
3956000)
> data <- data.frame(apartment_area, apartment_price)
> data
```

	apartment_area	apartment_price
1	4720	2360000
2	2430	1215000
3	4368	2184000
4	3969	1984500
5	6142	3071000
6	7912	3956000

```
> data[,2] <- ifelse(data[,2] > 3000000, 'High', ifelse(data[,2]
< 2000000, 'Low', 'Medium'))
> data
```

	apartment_area	apartment_price
1	4720	Medium
2	2430	Low
3	4368	Medium
4	3969	Low
5	6142	High
6	7912	High

```
> data[,2] <- ifelse(data[,2] == 'High', 3, ifelse(data[,2] ==
'Low', 1, 2))
> data
```

	apartment_area	apartment_price
1	4720	2
2	2430	1
3	4368	2
4	3969	1
5	6142	3
6	7912	3

A.5.2   Feature Extraction

A.5.2.1 Principal Component Analysis (PCA)

For performing principal component analysis (PCA), we can use the *prcomp* function of the **stats** package. Following is the code using the iris data set. PCA should be applied to the predictors. The class variable can be used to visualize the principal components.

```
> library(stats)


> data <- iris
> principal_comp <- prcomp(data[,1:4], center = TRUE, scale = TRUE)
> print(principal_comp)

Standard deviations (1,.., P=4):
[1] 1.7083611 0. 9560494 0.3830886 0.1439265
Rotation (n x k) = (4 x 4) :
                   PC1           PC2           PC3           PC4
Sepal.Length    0.5210659   -0.37741762    0.7195664    0.2612863
Sepal.Width -   -0.2693474   -0.92329566   -0.2443818   -0.1235096
Petal.Length    0.5804131   -0.02449161   -0.1421264   -0.8014492
 Petal.WIdth    0.5648565   -0.06694199   -0.6342727    0.5235971

> biplot(principal_comp, scale = 0)
```

The output of the *biplot* function is given in Figure A.8

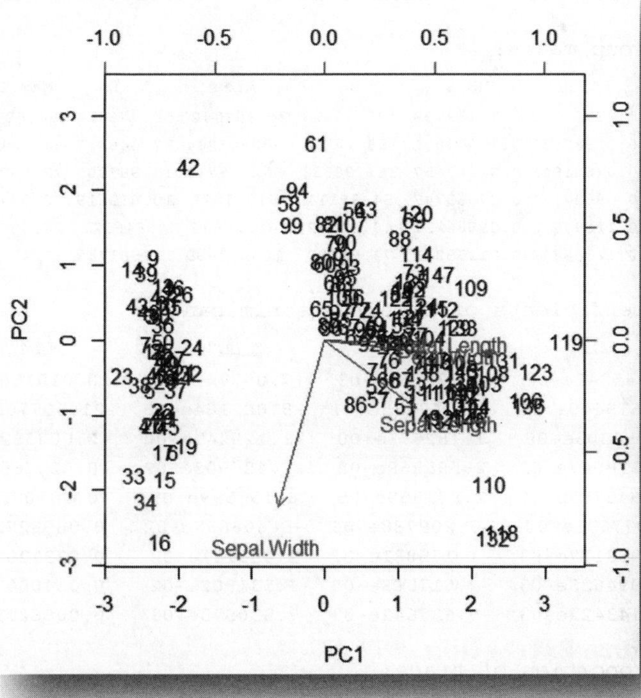

FIG. A.8
Principal components of the iris data set

A.5.2.2 *Singular Value Decomposition (SVD)*

For performing singular value decomposition, we can use the *svd* function of the **stats** package. Following is the code using the iris data set.

```
> sing_val_decomp <- svd(iris[,1:4])
> print(sing_val_decomp$d)
```

Output:

```
[1]  95.959914 17.761034 3.460931 1.884826
```

A.5.2.3 *Linear Discriminant Analysis (LDA)*

For performing linear discriminant analysis, we can use the *lda* function of the **MASS** package. Following is the code using the UCI data set *btissue*.

```
> library(MASS)


> df <- read.csv("btissue.csv")
> lda.fit <- lda(class ~ ., data = df)
> lda.fit
```

```
Prior probabilities of groups:
      adì        car        con        fad        gla        mas
0.2075472  0.1981132  0.1320755  0.1415094  0.1509434  0.1698113
```

```
Group means:
        IO       PA500        HE'S        DA       Area        A. DA     Max.IP        DR          P
adì 2052.0503 0.07355193 0.13437299 396.99723 24389.7428 50.775814 194.59726 324.71471 2138.7537
car  394.2320 0.21985331 0.18434001 168.27116  5723.1214 32.046327  64.53152 153.00799  479.9726
con 1212.8643 0.07021849 0.05223457 367.98583  5324.5712 13.997809  72.95797 357.98242 1064.9929
fad  245.8626 0.09527171 0.07069747  54.39114   610.1829 10.013219  22.97410  47.84468  268.8740
gla  233.3162 0.11694797 0.09586221  40.35142   411.6635  7.846327  26.35023  27.50161  261.5028
mas  290.3108 0.12309419 0.11135201  73.29728  1082.3999 12.581749  31.47139  63.60999  314.9211
```

```
Coefficients of linear discriminants:
              LD1            LD2            LD3            LD4            LD5
10      1.345342e-02   8.673261e-03  -7.057711e-03  -0.010160021  -2.1366Q6e-02
PAS 00 -4.519440e+00  -1,748635e+01  -5.002164e+00  -21.807706742   1.107125e+Q1
HFS     3.853303e+00   1.182€71e+00  -1.129247e+00  -2.002382722   -1.395844e+01
DA     -3.278047e-03   2.595269e-02  -2.486903e-02  -0.025760913    2.280775e-02
Area   -2.946759e-06   2.871859e-05   8.19€599e-05  -0.000089572    4.214914e-05
A. DA   4.077671e-02  -3.209788e-03  -5.608637e-02   0.065927280   -1.278080e-01
Max.IP -6.958177e-03  -1.185881e-02   1.455111e-02   0.023725953   -4.711875e-03
DR     -4.99462Se-03  -2.5175€3e-02   1.531902e-02   0.034000735   -8.722856e-03
P      -7.143422e-03  -9.637642e-03   7.330575e-03   0.006626973    2.097651e-02
```

```
Proportion of trace:
   LD1       LD2       LD3       LD4       LD5
0.8479    0.0946    0.0535    0.0034    0.0006
```

```
> plot(lda.fit)
```

The output of the above function is given in Figure A.9

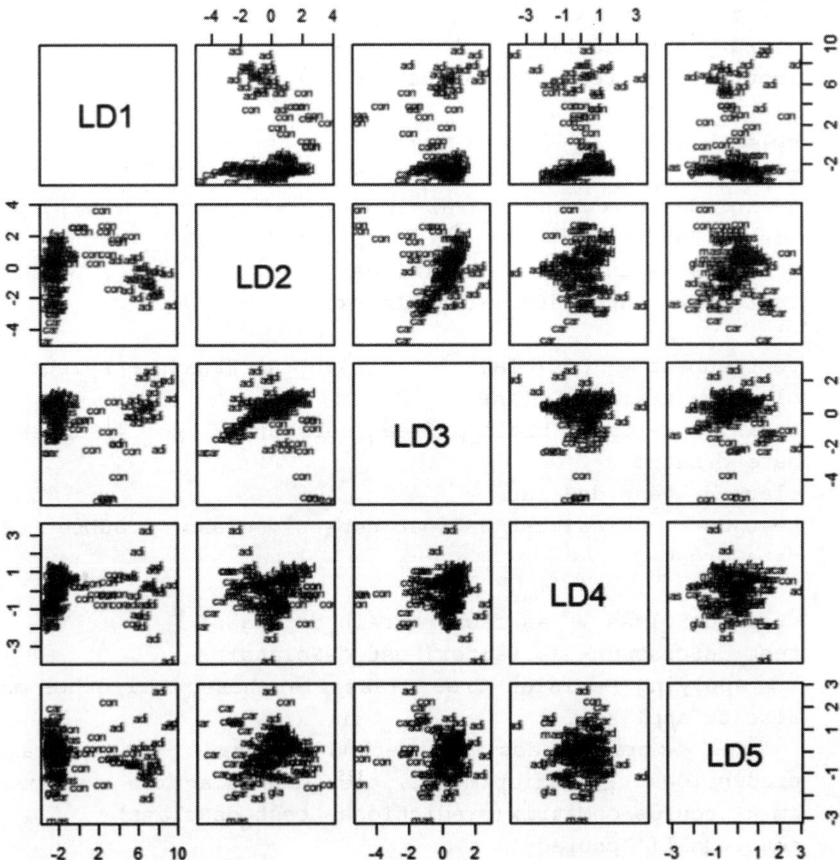

FIG. A.9
LDA of the btissue data set

A.5.3   Feature Subset Selection

Feature subset selection is a topic of intense research. There are many approaches to select a subset of features which can improve model performance. It is not possible to cover all such approaches as a part of this text. However, only for basic feature selection functionalities, the ***FSelector*** package of R can be used.

```
library(FSelector)
```

```
data <- iris
feat_subset <- cfs(Species ~ ., data) # Selects feature subset
using correlation and entropy measures for continuous and discrete
data
```

Below is a programme to perform feature subset selection before applying the same for training a model.

```
library(caret)
library(FSelector)
inputdata <- read.csv("apndcts.csv")

split = 0.7
set.seed(123)
trainIndex <- createDataPartition (y = inputdata$class, p = split,
list = FALSE)
train_ds <- inputdata [trainIndex,]
test_ds <- inputdata [-trainIndex,]

feat_subset <- cfs(class ~ ., train_ds) #Feature selection done
class <- train_ds$class
train_ds <- cbind(train_ds[feat_subset], class) # Subset training
data created
class <- test_ds$class
test_ds <- cbind(test_ds[feat_subset], class) # Subset test
data created

train_ds$class <- as.factor(train_ds$class)
test_ds$class <- as.factor(test_ds$class)
  # Applying Decision Tree classifier here. Any other model can
also be applied …
  model <- train(class ~ ., method = "rpart", data = train_ds)
predictions <- predict(model, test_ds, na.action = na.pass)
cm <- confusionMatrix(predictions, test_ds$class)
cm$overall['Accuracy']
```

Note:

The **e1071** package is an important R package which contains many statistical functions along with some critical classification algorithms such as Naïve Bayes and support vector machine (SVM). It is created by David Meyer and team and maintained by David Meyer.

A.6   MACHINE LEARNING MODELS

A.6.1   Supervised Learning – Classification

In Chapters 6, 7, and 8, conceptual overview of different supervised learning algorithms has been presented. Now, you will understand how to implement them using R. For the sake of simplicity, the code for implementing each of the algorithms is kept as consistent as possible. Also, we have used benchmark data sets from UCI repository (these data sets will also be available online, refer to the URL https://archive.ics.uci.edu/ml).

A.6.1.1 *Naïve Bayes classifier*

To implement this classifier, the *naiveBayes* function of the *e1071* package has been used. The full code for the implementation is given below.

```
> library(caret)
> library (e1071)

> inputdata <- read.csv("apndcts.csv")
> split = 0.7
> set.seed(123)
> trainIndex <- createDataPartition (y = inputdata$class, p =
split, list = FALSE)
> train_ds <- inputdata [trainIndex,]
> test_ds <- inputdata [-trainIndex,]
> train_ds$class <- as.factor(train_ds$class) #Pre-processing step
> test_ds$class <- as.factor(test_ds$class) #Pre-processing step

> model <- naiveBayes (class ~ ., data = train_ds)
> predictions <- predict(model, test_ds, na.action = na.pass)
> cm <- confusionMatrix(predictions, test_ds $class)
> cm$overall['Accuracy']
```

Output Accuracy:

```
0.8387097
```

A.6.1.2 *kNN classifier*

To implement this classifier, the *knn* function of the ***class*** package has been used. The full code for the implementation is given below.

```
> library(caret)
> library (class)

> inputdata <- read.csv("apndcts.csv")
> split = 0.7
> set.seed(123)
> trainIndex <- createDataPartition (y = inputdata$class, p =
split, list = FALSE)
> train_ds <- inputdata [trainIndex,]
> test_ds <- inputdata [-trainIndex,]
> train_ds$class <- as.factor(train_ds$class) #Pre-processing step
> test_ds$class <- as.factor(test_ds$class) #Pre-processing step
> model <- knn(train_ds, test_ds, train_ds$class, k = 3)
> cm <- confusionMatrix(model, test_ds$class)
> cm$overall['Accuracy']
```

Output Accuracy:

```
1
```

A.6.1.3 Decision tree classifier

To implement this classifier implementation, the *train* function of the **caret** package can be used with a parameter *method* = *"rpart"* to indicate that the train function will use the decision tree classifier. Optionally, the *rpart* function of the **rpart** package can also be used. The full code for the implementation is given below.

```
> library(caret)
> library(rpart) # Optional
> inputdata <- read.csv("apndcts.csv")

> split = 0.7
> set.seed(123)
> trainIndex <- createDataPartition (y = inputdata$class, p =
split, list = FALSE)
> train_ds <- inputdata [trainIndex,]
> test_ds <- inputdata [-trainIndex,]
> train_ds$class <- as.factor(train_ds$class) #Pre-processing step
> test_ds$class <- as.factor(test_ds$class) #Pre-processing step

> model <- train(class ~ ., method = "rpart", data = train_ds,
prox = TRUE)
# May also use the rpart function as shown below …
#> model <- rpart(formula = class ~ ., data = train_ds) # Optional

> predictions <- predict(model, test_ds, na.action = na.pass)
> cm <- confusionMatrix(predictions, test_ds $class)


> cm$overall['Accuracy']
```

Output Accuracy:

```
0.8387097
```

A.6.1.4 Random forest classifier

To implement this classifier, the *train* function of the **caret** package can be used with the parameter *method* = *"rf"* to indicate that the train function will use the decision tree classifier. Optionally, the *randomForest* function of the **randomForest** package can also be used. The full code for the implementation is given below.

```
> library(caret)
> library(randomForest) # Optional

> inputdata <- read.csv("apndcts.csv")

> split = 0.7
> set.seed(123)
```

```
> trainIndex <- createDataPartition (y = inputdata$class, p =
split, list = FALSE)
> train_ds <- inputdata [trainIndex,]
> test_ds <- inputdata [-trainIndex,]
> train_ds$class <- as.factor(train_ds$class) #Pre-processing step
> test_ds$class <- as.factor(test_ds$class) #Pre-processing step

> model <- train(class ~ ., method = "rf", data = train_ds, prox
= TRUE)
# May also use the randomForest function as shown below …
#> model <- randomForest(class ~ . , data = train_ds, ntree=400)

> predictions <- predict(model, test_ds, na.action = na.pass)
> cm <- confusionMatrix(predictions, test_ds $class)


> cm$overall['Accuracy']
```

Output Accuracy:

```
0.8387097
```

A.6.1.5 SVM classifier

To implement this classifier, the *svm* function of the *e1071* package has been used.
The full code for the implementation is given below.

```
> library(caret)
> library (e1071)

> inputdata <- read.csv("apndcts.csv")

> split = 0.7
> set.seed(123)
> trainIndex <- createDataPartition (y = inputdata$class, p =
split, list = FALSE)
> train_ds <- inputdata [trainIndex,]
> test_ds <- inputdata [-trainIndex,]
> train_ds$class <- as.factor(train_ds$class) #Pre-processing step
> test_ds$class <- as.factor(test_ds$class) #Pre-processing step

> model <- svm(class ~ ., data = train_ds)
> predictions <- predict(model, test_ds, na.action = na.pass)
> cm <- confusionMatrix(predictions, test_ds $class)


> cm$overall['Accuracy']
```

Output Accuracy:

```
0.8709677
```

A.6.2   Supervised Learning – Regression

As discussed in Chapter 9, two main algorithms used for regression are simple linear regression and multiple linear regression. Implementation of both the algorithms in R code is shown below.

```
> data <- read.csv("auto-mpg.csv")
> attach(data) # Data set is attached to the R search path, which
means that while evaluating a variable, objects in the data set
can be accessed by simply giving their names. So, instead of
"data$mpg", simply giving "mpg" will suffice.

> data <- data[!is.na(as.numeric(as.character(horsepower))),]
> data <- mutate(data, horsepower = as.numeric(horsepower))

> outliers_mpg <- boxplot.stats(mpg)$out
> data <- data[-which(mpg == outliers_mpg),]
> outliers_cylinders <- boxplot.stats(cylinders)$out
> data <- data[-which(cylinders == outliers_cylinders),]
> outliers_displacement <- boxplot.stats(displacement)$out
> data <- data[-which(displacement == outliers_displacement),]
> outliers_weight <- boxplot.stats(weight)$out
> data <- data[-which(weight == outliers_weight),]
> outliers_acceleration <- boxplot.stats(acceleration)$out
> data <- data[-which(acceleration == outliers_acceleration),]
```

A.6.2.1 Simple linear regression

```
> reg_pred <- lm(mpg ~ cylinders)
> summary(reg_pred)
```

A.6.2.2 Multiple linear regression

```
> reg_pred <- lm(mpg ~ cylinders + displacement)
> reg_pred <- lm(mpg ~ cylinders + weight + acceleration)
> reg_pred <- lm(mpg ~ cylinders + displacement + horsepower +
 weight + acceleration)
```

A.6.3   Unsupervised Learning

To implement the *k-means* algorithm, the *k-means* function of the **cluster** package has been used. Also, because silhouette width is a more generic performance measure, it has been used here. The complete R code for the implementation is given below.

```
> library (cluster)

> data <- read.csv("spinem.csv")
> dis = dist(data)^2
> res = kmeans(data,2)
```

```
> sil_width <- silhouette (res$cluster, dis)
> sil_summ <- summary(sil_width)
> sil_summ$avg.width # Returns silhouette width of the
overall data set
```

Output Accuracy:

```
[1] 0.5508955
```

A.6.4   Neural Network

To implement this classifier, the *neuralnet* function of the ***neuralnet*** package has been used. The full code for the implementation is given below.

A.6.4.1 Single-layer feedforward neural network

```
> library(caret)
> library(neuralnet)


> inputdata <- read.csv("apndcts.csv")
> split = 0.7
> set.seed(123)
> trainIndex <- createDataPartition (y = inputdata$class, p =
split, list = FALSE)
> train_ds <- inputdata [trainIndex,]
> test_ds <- inputdata [-trainIndex,]


> model <- neuralnet(class ~ At1 + At2 + At3 + At4 + At5 + At6 +
At7, train_ds)
> plot(model)
```

Output is presented in Figure A.10.

A.6.4.2 Multi-layer feedforward neural network

```
> library(caret)
> library(neuralnet)


> inputdata <- read.csv("apndcts.csv")
> split = 0.7
> set.seed(123)
> trainIndex <- createDataPartition (y = inputdata$class, p =
split, list = FALSE)
> train_ds <- inputdata [trainIndex,]
> test_ds <- inputdata [-trainIndex,]
```

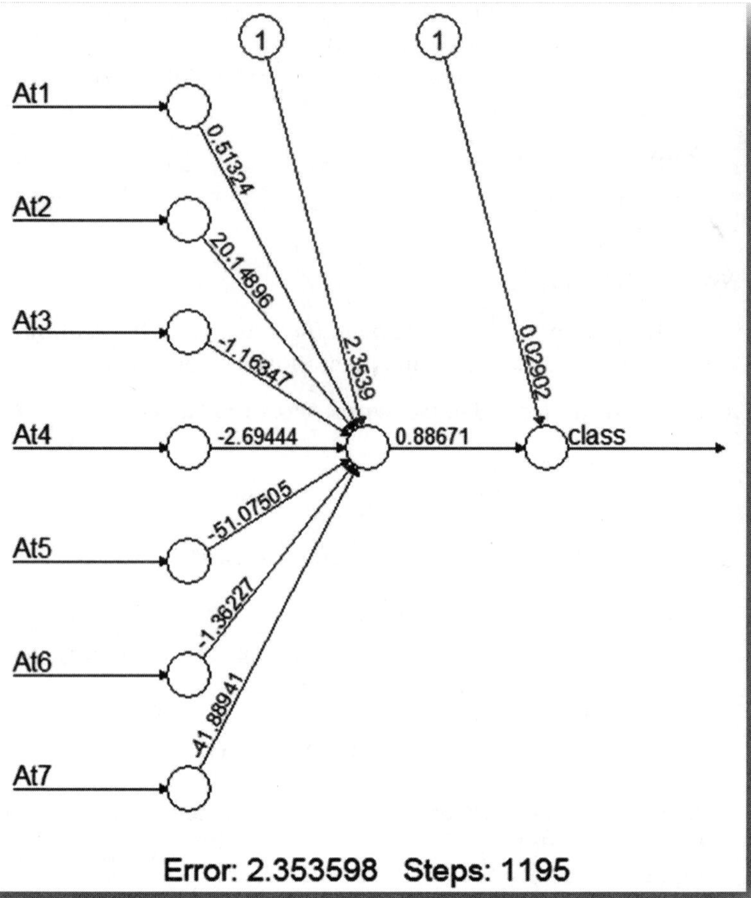

FIG. A.10
Single-layer NN

```
> model <- neuralnet(class ~ At1 + At2 + At3 + At4 + At5 + At6 +
At7, train_ds, hidden = 3) # Multi-layer NN
> plot(model)
```

Output is presented in Figure A.11.

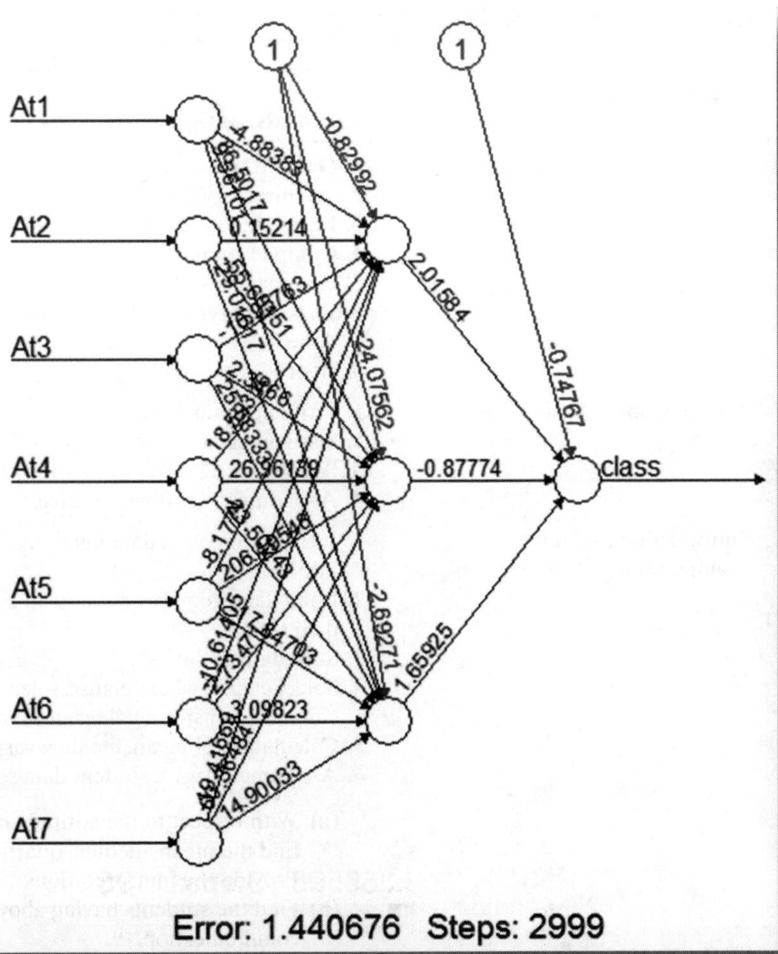

FIG. A.11
Multi-layer NN

A.7   MACHINE LEARNING LAB SCHEDULE

Day #	Topic/assignment of the day	Commands/assignment covered
1	Introduction to basic commands	**1.** Get and set working directory **2.** See directory content **3.** Install and load libraries/packages **4.** Compile source file for execution **5.** Commands for basic user input/output **6.** Basic data types and manipulations that can be done **7.** Loops
2	Introduction to basic commands (contd.)	**1.** Write new functions **2.** Assignment 1 – Implementing Fibonacci series **3.** Assignment 2 – Depth first search **4.** Assignment 3 – Binary search

3	Introduction to data manipulation	**1.** Introducing basic data manipulation library - dplyr
		2. Load data from .csv file as well as other types of data set
		3. Save data to data set
		4. Select clause, where clause, select specific columns, transform values in a column, etc.
		5. Calculation of mean, median, variance, quartiles
		6. Assignment (w.r.t. student data set) –
		
		   (a) With respect to the aptitude of the students, find the mean, median, quartiles, and variance. Provide the interpretations.
		   (b) Find the students having above average communication.
		   (c) Find the students having both above average aptitude and communication.
		   (d) Add a column to the data set having a weighted score on the basis of aptitude and communication (2:1).
		   (e) Print the name of the students having highest and lowest score as calculated in point d.
		   (f) Print name of all students whose name start with letter 'J'.
		   (g) Print name of all students whose name has letter 'J'.

4	Introduction to other standard library functions	• For R, ggplot2, caret, etc. • Plotting data – box plots • Plotting data – scatter diagram • Plotting data – histogram • Two-way cross-tabulations

(Continued)

(Continued)

Day #	Topic/assignment of the day	Commands/assignment covered
5	Basic data exploration	• Assignment to be done using auto-mpg data set • Following are the basic points of exploration – ✓ Is there any correlation between mpg and acceleration? ✓ Is there any correlation between horsepower and cylinder? ✓ How many Ford cars of 8 cylinders were manufactured in 1970s? ✓ Draw a histogram of 4-, 6-, and 8-cylinder cars manufactured in 1980s. ✓ Which are related attributes in the data set? ✓ Are there any missing values in the data set? Impute the missing values using the strategy of taking average value of the attribute value for the respective number of cylinders.
6	Starting to model	1. Data holdout 2. K-fold cross-validation 3. Use a simple supervised learning model, for example kNN 4. Derive confusion matrix and observe different elements of the confusion matrix 5. Assess model accuracy, sensitivity, specificity, etc. 6. Use a simple unsupervised learning model, for example k-means 7. Assess cluster quality measures such as silhouette width and purity
7	Start with learning algorithms – k-Nearest Neighbour (kNN) Linear Regression	
8	Unsupervised algorithm – k-means	
9	Supervised algorithm – Naïve Bayes	
10	1. Implement supervised algorithm - Decision Tree 2. Implement supervised algorithm – support vector machine (SVM)	Implement the algorithm using library functions
11	Basic programming using Neural Network	Implement the algorithm using library functions
12	Assignment – Text mining	

Appendix B

Python Basics and Setup for Machine Learning Programming

B.1   PRE-REQUISITES

B.1.1   Install anaconda in your system

Before starting to do machine learning programming in Python, please install **Python Anaconda** distribution from https://anaconda.org/anaconda/python. To write any python script, open any text editor and write your python script and save with the extension *.py.* You may also use the **Spyder** (Scientific PYthon Development EnviRonment), which is a powerful and interactive development environment for the Python language with advanced editing, interactive testing, debugging, and introspection features. In this chapter, all the examples have been created working in Spyder.

B.1.2   Know how to manage Python scripts

- Open new/pre-existing .py script in Spyder as shown in Figure B.1:

B.1.3   Know how to do basic programming using Python

B.1.3.1   Introduction to basic Python commands

First install a couple of basic libraries of Python namely

- 'os' for using operating system dependent functions
- 'pandas' for extensive data manipulation functionalities

In general, Annaconda Python by default contains all the basic required packages for starting programming in machine learning. But in case, any extra package is needed, 'pip' is the recommended installer.

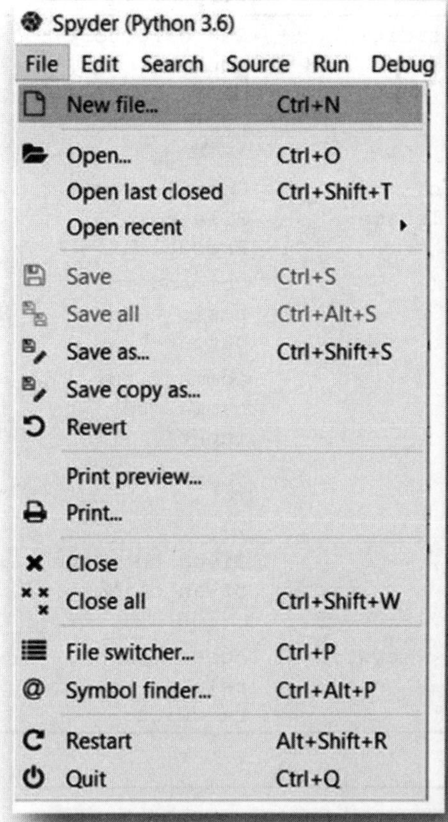

Copyright © 2018. Python Software Foundation

FIG. B.1
Opening a script in Spyder

Command: pip install
Syntax: pip install 'SomePackage'

After installing, libraries need to be loaded by invoking the command:

Command: import <<library-name>>
Syntax: import os

Try out each of the following commands.

Sr #	Command	Purpose	Sample code with output
1	os.getcwd()	Getting the current working directory	>>> os.getcwd() C:\Users\amitk
2	os.chdir()	Setting the current working directory	>>> os.chdir('C:\\ Python programs')

Sr #	Command	Purpose	Sample code with output
3	os.listdir()	See directory content	>>> os.listdir('C:\\ Python programs') Out[16]: ['Machine_Learning_ Python.py']
4	python '<<filename>>'	Compile Source File for Execution	>>> python new1.py
5	print()	Command for basic user output	>>> print("Hello") Hello

6	input ()	Command for basic user input	>>> a = input("Give input: ")
			Give input: 12
			>>> print("Your input: ", a)
			Your input: 12

7	type()	Gives the type of an object	>>> x = 5
			>>> type(x)
			Out[28]: int

8	help(<<keyword>>)	Access help related to some function.	>>> help(print) >>> help(os.listdir)

Note:

'#' is used for inserting inline comments
'+' is the assignment operator

B.1.3.2   Basic data types in Python

Python has five standard data types –

1. Number
2. String
3. List
4. Tuple
5. Dictionary

Though Python has all the basic data types, Python variables do not need explicit declaration to reserve memory space. The declaration happens automatically when you assign a value to a variable. The equal sign (=) is used to assign values to variables.

The operand to the left of the = operator is the name of the variable and the operand to the right of the = operator is the value stored in the variable. For example –

```
>>> var1 = 4
>>> var2 = 8.83
>>> var3 = "Machine Learning"

>>> type(var1)
Out[38]: int
>>> print(var1)
4

>>> type(var2)
Out[39]: float
>>> print(var2)
8.83

>>> type(var3)
Out[40]: str
>>> print(var3)
Machine Learning
```

Python variables can be easily typecasted from one data type to another by using its datatype name as a function (actually a wrapper class) and passing the variable to be typecasted as a parameter. But not all data types can be transformed into another like String to integer/number is impossible (that's obvious!).

```
>>> var2 = int(var2)
>>> print (var2)
8
>>> type (var2)
Out[42]: int
```

B.1.3.3   *for–while Loops & if–else Statement*

For loop
Syntax:

```
for i in range(<lowerbound>,<upperbound>,<interval>):
    print(i*i)
```

Example: Printing squares of all integers from 1 to 3.

```
for i in range(1,4):
    print(i*i)
1
4
9

for i in range(0,4,2):
    print(i)
```

```
0
2
```

While loop
Syntax:
```
while < condition>:
    <do something>
```

Example: Printing squares of all integers from 1 to 3.
```
i = 1
while i < 4:
    print(i*i)
    i = i + 1

1
4
9
```

if-else statement
Syntax:
```
if < condition>:
    <do something>
else:
    <do something else>
```

Example:
```
i = -5
if i < 0:
    print(i*i)
else:
    print(i)

25
```

B.1.3.4   *Writing functions*

Writing a function (in a script):
Syntax:

```
def functionname(parametername,…):
(function_body)
```

Example: Function to calculate factorial of an input number n.

```
def factorial(n):
    fact = 1
    for i in range(1,n+1):
        fact = fact*i
    return(fact);
```

Running the function (after compiling the script using source ("script_name"):

```
>>> factorial(6)
720
```

B.1.3.5 *Mathematical operations on data types*

Vectors:

```
>>> n = 10
>>> m = 5
>>> n + m     #addition
Out[53]: 15

>>> n - m  #subtraction
Out[55]: 5

>>> n * m     #multiplication
Out[56]: 50

>>> n / m     #division
Out[57]: 2.0
```

Matrices:

```
>>> mat1 = range(0,16)
>>> mat1 = reshape(mat1,(4,4))
>>> print(mat1)
[[ 0  1  2  3]
 [ 4  5  6  7]
 [ 8  9 10 11]
 [12 13 14 15]]
>>> type(mat1)
numpy.ndarray

>>> mat2 = range(17,33)
>>> mat2 = reshape(mat2,(4,4))
>>> print(mat2)
[[17 18 19 20]
 [21 22 23 24]
 [25 26 27 28]
 [29 30 31 32]]
>>> type(mat2)
numpy.ndarray

>>> mat3 = mat1 + mat2    # Adds element in one matrix to the cor-
responding element in the other matrix
>>> print(mat3)
[[17 19 21 23]
 [25 27 29 31]
 [33 35 37 39]
 [41 43 45 47]]
```

```
>>> mat4 = mat2 - mat1       # Subtracts element in one matrix from
the corresponding element in the other matrix
>>> print(mat4)
[[17 17 17 17]
 [17 17 17 17]
 [17 17 17 17]
 [17 17 17 17]]
```

Note:

pandas is a Python package providing fast and flexible functionalities designed to work with "relational" or "labelled" data.

B.1.3.6   Basic data handling commands

```
>>> import pandas as pd   # "pd" is just an alias for pandas

>>> data = pd.read_csv("auto-mpg.csv") # Uploads data from a .csv file
>>> type(data)   # To find the type of the data set object loaded
pandas.core.frame.DataFrame

>>> data.shape   # To find the dimensions i.e. number of rows and
columns of the data set loaded
(398, 9)

>>> nrow_count = data.shape[0]   # To find just the number of rows
>>> print(nrow_count)
398

>>> ncol_count = data.shape[1]   # To find just the number of columns
>>> print(ncol_count)
9

>>> data.columns   # To get the columns of a dataframe

Index(['mpg', 'cylinders', 'displacement', 'horsepower', 'weight',
       'acceleration', 'model year', 'origin', 'car name'],
      dtype='object')

>>> list(data.columns.values)# To list the column names of a
dataframe
```

We can also use:

```
>>> list(data)

['mpg',
 'cylinders',
 'displacement',
 'horsepower',
```

```
'weight',
'acceleration',
'model year',
'origin',
'car name']

# To change the columns of a dataframe ...

>>> data.columns = ['miles_per_gallon', 'cylinders', 'displacement',
'horsepower', 'weight', 'acceleration', 'model year', 'origin',
'car name']
```

Alternatively, we can use the following code:

```
>>> data.rename(columns={'displacement': 'disp'}, inplace=True)
>>> data.head()   # By default displays top 5 rows
>>> data.head(3)   # To display the top 3 rows

>>> data. tail ()  # By default displays bottom 5 rows
>>> data. tail (3)  # To display the bottom 3 rows

>>> data.at[200,'cylinders']   # Will return  cell value of  the
200th row and column 'cylinders' of the data frame
6
```

Alternatively, we can use the following code:

```
>>> data.get_value(200,'cylinders')
```

To select a specific column of a dataframe:

```
>>> data_cyl = data.loc[: , "car name"]
>>> data_cyl.head()

0     chevrolet chevelle malibu
1             buick skylark 320
2           plymouth satellite
3                  amc rebel sst
4                    ford torino
Name: car name, dtype: object
```

To select multiple columns of a dataframe:

```
>>> data_cyl = data[["miles_per_gallon", "origin", "car name"]]
>>> data_cyl.head()

   miles_per_gallon   origin                        car name
0             18.0        1    chevrolet chevelle malibu
1             15.0        1            buick skylark 320
2             18.0        1           plymouth satellite
3             16.0        1                  amc rebel sst
4             17.0        1                    ford torino
```

To extract specific rows:

```
>>> data[1:3]

  miles_per_gallon cylinders  disp horsepower weight acceleration \
1             15.0         8 350.0        165   3693         11.5
2             18.0         8 318.0        150   3436         11.0

    model year  origin                 car name
1          70       1    buick skylark 320
2          70       1    plymouth satellite

>>> data.loc[1, : ]
miles_per_gallon                      15
cylinders                              8
disp                                 350
horsepower                           165
weight                              3693
acceleration                        11.5
model year                            70
origin                                 1
car name              buick skylark 320
Name: 1, dtype: object
```

Bind sets of rows of dataframes:

```
>>> data1 = data[0:2]
>>> data1.head()
  miles_per_gallon cylinders  disp horsepower  weight  acceleration \
0             18.0         8 307.0        130    3504          12.0
1             15.0         8 350.0        165    3693          11.5

    model year  origin                        car name
0          70       1  chevrolet chevelle malibu
1          70       1          buick skylark 320

>>> data2 = data[3:5]
>>> data2.head()

  miles_per_gallon cylinders  disp horsepower  weight  acceleration \
3             16.0         8 304.0        150    3433          12.0
4             17.0         8 302.0        140    3449          10.5

    model year  origin        car name
3          87       1  amc rebel sst
4          70       1     ford torino
```

```
>>> data3 = data1.append(data2, ignore_index=True)
>>> data3.head()
 miles_per_gallon cylinders disp horsepower  weight  acceleration \
0               18.0         8 307.0        130    3504          12.0
1               15.0         8 350.0        165    3693          11.5
2               16.0         8 304.0        150    3433          12.0
3               17.0         8 302.0        140    3449          10.5

    model year   origin                   car name
0           70        1 chevrolet chevelle malibu
1           70        1         buick skylark 320
2           87        1             amc rebel sst
3           70        1                ford torino

>>> data3.shape
(4, 9)
```

Bind sets of columns of dataframes:

```
>>> data1 = data[["miles_per_gallon"]]
>>> data1.head()

    miles_per_gallon
0               18.0
1               15.0
2               18.0
3               16.0
4               17.0

>>> data2 = data[["car name"]]
>>> data2.head()
                  car name
0  chevrolet chevelle malibu
1          buick skylark 320
2         plymouth satellite
3              amc rebel sst
4                ford torino

>>> data3 = pd.concat([data1.reset_index(drop=True), data2], axis=1)
>>> data3.head()

    miles_per_gallon                  car name
0               18.0 chevrolet chevelle malibu
1               15.0         buick skylark 320
2               18.0        plymouth satellite
3               16.0             amc rebel sst
4               17.0               ford torino
```

To save dataframes as .csv files:

```
>>> data3.to_csv('data3.csv')   #Save dataframe with index column
>>> data3.to_csv('data3.csv', index=False) #Save dataframe without
index column
```

Often, we get data sets with duplicate rows, which is nothing but noise. Therefore, before training the model, we need to make sure we get rid of such inconsistencies in the data set. We can remove duplicate rows using code:

```
>>> data = data.drop_duplicates()
```

We frequently find missing values in our data set. We can drop the rows/columns with missing values using the code below.

```
>>> data.dropna(axis=0, how='all') #Remove all rows where values
of all columns are 'NaN'

>>> data.dropna(axis=1, how='all') ) #Remove all columns where
values of all rows are 'NaN'

>>> data.dropna(axis=0, how='any') #Remove all rows where value
of any column is 'NaN'

>>> data.dropna(axis=1, how='any') ) #Remove all columns where
value of any row is 'NaN'
```

B.2   PREPARING TO MODEL

Now that we are kind of familiar with the basic Python commands, we have the ability to start machine learning programming in Python. But before starting to do actual modelling work, we have to first understand the data using the concepts highlighted in Chapter 2. Also, there might be some issues in the data which you will unveil during data exploration. You have to remediate that too.

So first, let's find out how to do data exploration in Python. There are two ways to explore and understand data:

1. By using certain statistical functions to understand the central tendency and spread of the data
2. By visually observing the data in the form of plots or graphs

B.2.1   Basic statistical functions for data exploration

Let's start with the first approach of understanding the data through the statistical techniques. As we have seen in Chapter 2, for any data set, it is critical to understand the central tendency and spread of the data. We have also seen the standard statistical measures are as follows:

(a) Measures of central tendency – Mean, median, mode

(b) Measures of data spread

    (i) Dispersion of data – variance, standard deviation

    (ii) Position of the different data values – quartiles, inter-quartile range (IQR)

In Python, *info* function provides the structure of the data frame along with the data types of the different attributes. Also, there is a function *describe* which generates the summary statistics of a data set. It gives the first basic understanding of the data set which can trigger thought about the data set and the anomalies that may be present. So, let's start off exploring a data set **Auto MPG data set** from the University of California, Irvine (UCI) machine learning repository. We will run the *info* and *describe* commands for the Auto MPG data set.

```
>>> data = pd.read_csv("auto-mpg.csv")
>>> data.info()
<class 'pandas.core.frame.DataFrame'>
RangeIndex: 398 entries, 0 to 397
Data columns (total 9 columns):
mpg             398 non-null float64
cylinders       398 non-null int64
displacement    398 non-null float64
horsepower      398 non-null object
weight          398 non-null int64
acceleration    398 non-null float64
model year      398 non-null int64
origin          398 non-null int64
car name        398 non-null object
dtypes: float64(3), int64(4), object(2)
memory usage: 28.1+ KB

>>> data.describe()   # To get a quick analysis of data set
              mpg   cylinders  displacement      weight  acceleration \
count  398.000000  398.000000    398.000000  398.000000    398.000000
mean    23.514573    5.454774    199.983668  2970.424623     15.568090
std      7.815984    1.701004    174.850524   846.841774      2.757689
min      9.000000    3.000000     68.000000  1613.000000      8.000000
25%     17.500000    4.000000    104.250000  2223.750000     13.825000
50%     23.000000    4.000000    148.500000  2803.500000     15.500000
75%     29.000000    8.000000    262.000000  3608.000000     17.175000
max     46.600000    8.000000   3000.000000  5140.000000     24.800000

       model year      origin
count  398.000000  398.000000
mean    76.067839    1.572864
```

```
std         4.113983      0.802055
min        60.000000      1.000000
25%        73.000000      1.000000
50%        76.000000      1.000000
75%        79.000000      2.000000
max        90.000000      3.000000
```

Looking closely at the output of the *describe* command, there are seven measures listed for the attributes (well, most of them). These are

1. mean – mean of the specific attribute
2. std – Standard deviation of the specific attribute
3. min – minimum value of the attribute
4. 25% – First quartile (for details, refer to Chapter 2)
5. 50% – Median of the attribute
6. 75% – Third quartile (for details, refer to Chapter 2)
7. max – maximum value of the attribute

These gives a pretty good understanding of the data set attributes. Now, note that one attribute – car.name, has a data type object whereas the remaining attributes have either integer or float data type. Why is that so? This is because this attribute is a categorical attribute while the other ones are numeric.

Note:

Numpy is a Python library which is used for scientific computing. It contains among other things – a powerful array object, mathematical and statistical functions, and tools for integrating with C/C++ and Fortran code.

Let's try to explore if any variable has any problem with the data values where a cleaning may be required. As discussed in Chapter 2, there may be two primary data issues – missing values and outliers.

Let's first try to figure out if there is any missing value for any of the attributes. Let's use a small piece of Python code find out if there is any missing/unwanted value for an attribute in the data. If there is, return the rows in which the attribute has missing/unwanted values. Checking for all the attributes, we find that the attribute 'horsepower' has missing values.

```
>>> data[data['horsepower'].isnull()]
     mpg  cylinders  displacement  horsepower  weight  acceleration  \
32   25.0          4          98.0         NaN    2046          19.0
126  21.0          6         200.0         NaN    2875          17.0
330  40.9          4          85.0         NaN    1835          17.3
336  23.6          4         140.0         NaN    2905          14.3
354  34.5          4         100.0         NaN    2320          15.8
374  23.0          4         151.0         NaN    3035          20.5
```

```
        model year   origin                       car name
32             71        1                       ford pinto
126            74        1                    ford maverick
330            80        2            renault lecar deluxe
336            80        1             ford mustang cobra
354            81        2                      renault 18i
374            82        1                  amc concord dl
```

There are six rows in the data set which have missing values for the attribute 'horsepower'. We will have to remediate these rows before we proceed with the modelling activities. We will do that shortly.

The easiest and most effective way to detect outliers is from the box plot of the attributes. In the box plot, outliers are very clearly highlighted. When we explore the attributes using box plots in a short while, we will have a clear view of this.

We can get the other statistical measure of the attributes using the following Python commands from the *Numpy* library:

```
>>> np.mean(data[["mpg"]])
23.514573
>>> np.median(data[["mpg"]])
23.0
>>> np.var(data[["mpg"]])
60.936119
>>> np.std(data[["mpg"]])
7.806159
```

Note:

Matplotlib is a plotting library for the Python programming language which produces 2D plots to render visualization and helps in exploring the data sets. matplotlib.pyplot is a collection of command style functions that make matplotlib work like MATLAB

B.2.2   Basic plots for data exploration

In order to start using the library functions of *matplotlib*, we need to include the library as follows:

```
>>> import matplotlib.pyplot as plt
```

Let's now understand the different graphs that are used for data exploration and how to generate them using Python code.

We will use the "iris" data set, a very popular data set in the machine learning world. This data set consists of three different types of iris flower: Setosa, Versicolour, and Virginica, the columns of the data set being - Sepal Length, Sepal Width, Petal Length, and Petal Width. For using this data set, we will first have to import the Python library *datasets* using the code below.

```
>>> from sklearn import datasets
# import some data to play with
>>> iris = datasets.load_iris()
```

B.2.2.1   Box plot

```
>>> import matplotlib.pyplot as plt
>>> X = iris.data[:, :4]
>>> plt.boxplot(X)
>>> plt.show()
```

A box plot for each of the four predictors is generated as shown in Figure B.2.

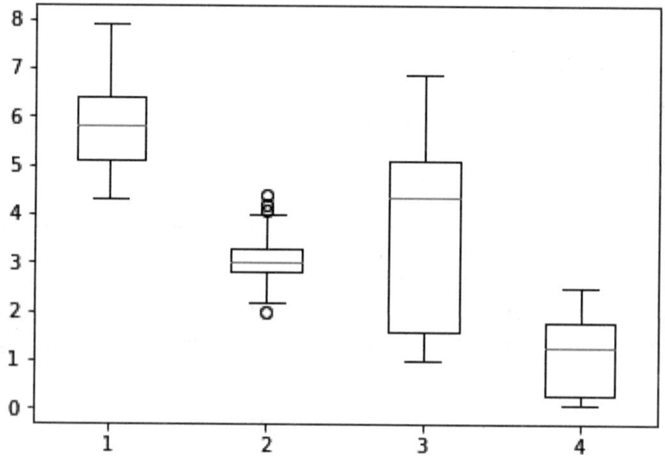

FIG. B.2

Box plot for an entire data set

As we can see, Figure B.2 gives the box plot for the entire iris data set i.e. for all the features in the iris data set, there is a component or box plot in the overall plot. However, if we want to review individual features separately, we can do that too using the following Python command.

```
>>> plt.boxplot(X[:, 1])
>>> plt.show()
```

The output of the command i.e. the box plot of an individual feature, sepal width, of the iris data set is shown in Figure B.3.

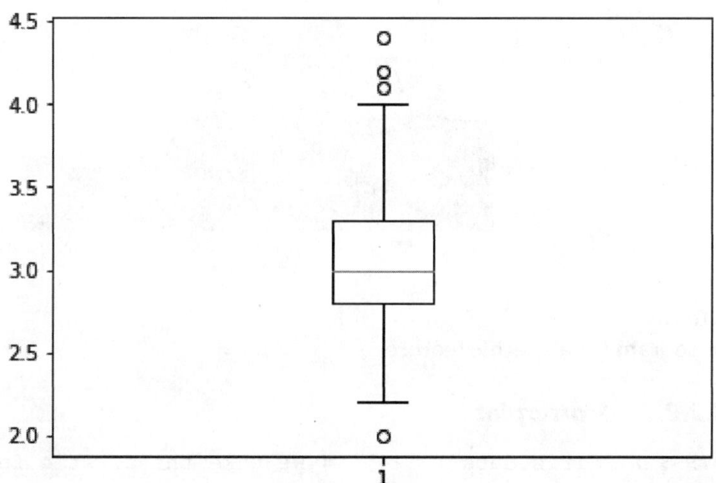

FIG. B.3
Box plot for a specific feature

To find out the outliers of an attribute, we can use the code below:

```
>>> outliers = plt.boxplot(X[:, 1])["fliers"][0].get_data()[1]
>>> print(outliers[1])    # All outliers for the attribute
[ 2.   4.4  4.1  4.2]

>>> print(outliers[1])    # Examine each outlier separately
4.4
```

B.2.2.2   Histogram

```
>>> import matplotlib.pyplot as plt

>>> X = iris.data[:, :1]
>>> plt.hist(X)
>>> plt.xlabel('Sepal length')
>>> plt.show()
```

The output of the command, i.e. the histogram of an individual feature, Sepal Length, of the iris data set is shown in Figure B.4.

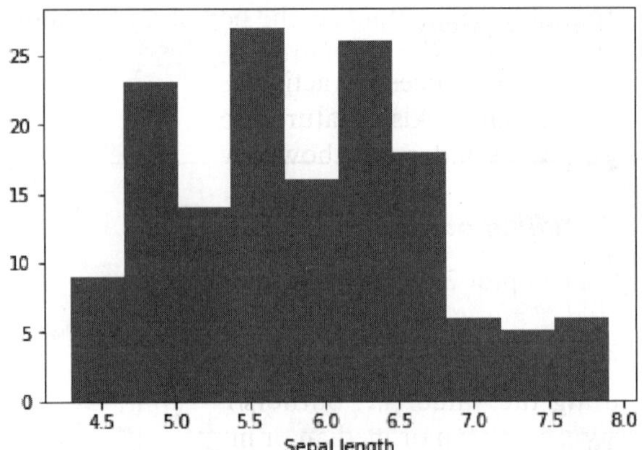

FIG. B.4
Histogram for a specific feature

B.2.2.3   Scatterplot

```
>>> X = iris.data[:, :4]  # We take the first 4 features
>>> y = iris.target

>>> plt.scatter(X[:, 2], X[:, 0], c=y, cmap=plt.cm.Set1,
edgecolor='k')
>>> plt.xlabel('Petal length')
>>> plt.ylabel('Sepal length')
>>> plt.show()
```

The output of the command, i.e. the scatter plot for the feature pair petal length and sepal length of the iris data set is shown in Figure B.5.

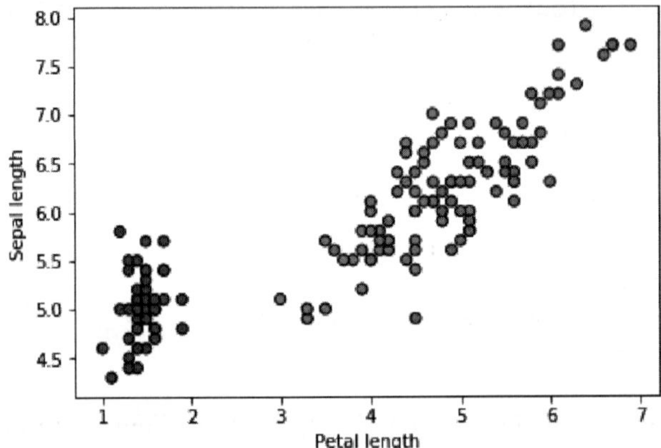

FIG. B.5
Scatter plot of Petal Length vs. Sepal Length

B.2.3   Data pre-processing

The primary data pre-processing activities are remediating data issues related to outliers and missing values. Also, feature subset selection is quite a critical area of data pre-processing. Let's understand how to write programs for achieving these purposes.

B.2.3.1   Handling outliers and missing values

As we saw in Chapter 2, the primary measures for remediating outliers and missing values are

- Removing specific rows containing outliers/missing values
- Imputing the value (i.e. outliers/missing value) with a standard statistical measure, e.g. mean or median or mode for that attribute
- Estimate the value (i.e. outlier / missing value) based on value of the attribute in similar records and replace with the estimated value.
- Cap the values within 1.5 X IQR limits

B.2.3.1.1 Removing outliers / missing values

We have to first identify the outliers. We have already seen in boxplots that outliers are clearly found out when we draw the box plot of a specific attribute. Hence, we can use the same concept as shown in the following code:

```
>>> outliers = plt.boxplot(X[:, 1])["fliers"][0].get_data()[1]
```

There is an alternate option too. As we know, outliers have abnormally high or low value from other elements. So the other option is to use threshold values to detect outliers so that they can be removed. A sample code is given below.

```
def find_outlier(ds, col):
    quart1 = ds[col].quantile(0.25)
    quart3 = ds[col].quantile(0.75)
    IQR = quart3 - quart1 #Inter-quartile range
    low_val  = quart1 - 1.5*IQR
    high_val = quart3 + 1.5*IQR
    ds = ds.loc[(ds[col] < low_val) | (ds[col] > high_val)]
    return ds

>>> outliers = find_outlier(data, "mpg")
```

Then those rows can be removed using the code:

```
def remove_outlier(ds, col):
    quart1 = ds[col].quantile(0.25)
    quart3 = ds[col].quantile(0.75)
    IQR = quart3 - quart1 #Interquartile range
    low_val  = quart1 - 1.5*IQR
    high_val = quart3 + 1.5*IQR
    df_out = ds.loc[(ds[col] > low_val) & (ds[col] <
high_val)]
    return df_out
```

```
>>> data = remove_outlier(data, "mpg")
```

Rows having missing values can be removed using the code:

```
>>> data.dropna(axis=0, how='any') #Remove all rows where value
of any column is 'NaN'
```

B.2.3.1.2 Imputing standard values

The code for identification of outliers or missing values will remain the same. For imputation, depending on which statistical function is to be used for imputation, code will be as follows:

Only the affected rows are identified and the value of the attribute is transformed to the mean value of the attribute.

```
>>> hp_mean = np.mean(data['horsepower'])
>>> imputedrows = data[data['horsepower'].isnull()]
>>> imputedrows = imputedrows.replace(np.nan, hp_mean)
```

Then the portion of the data set not having any missing row is kept apart.

```
>>> missval_removed_rows  =  data.dropna(subset=['horsepower'])
```

Then join back the imputed rows and the remaining part of the data set.

```
>>> data_mod  =  missval_removed_rows.append(imputedrows,
ignore_index=True)
```

In a similar way, outlier values can be imputed. Only difference will be in identification of the relevant rows.

B.2.3.1.3 Capping of values

The code for identification of outliers values will remain the same. For capping, generally a value 1.5 times the (inter-quartile range) IQR is to be used for imputation, code will be as follows:

```
>>> outliers = find_outlier(data, "mpg")
>>> quart1 = data["mpg"].quantile(0.25)
>>> quart3 = data["mpg"].quantile(0.75)
>>> IQR = quart3 - quart1    #Getting the value of IQR

>>> outliers.loc[:, "mpg"] = 1.5*IQR  #Capping the outlier values
                                  with 1.5 times IQR value …
>>> outlier_removed_rows = remove_outlier(data, "mpg")
>>> data_mod  =  outlier_removed_rows.append(outliers,
ignore_index=True)
```

Note:

Scikit-learn ("SciKit" = SciPy Toolkit) is a machine learning library for the Python programming language. It contains various classification, regression and clustering algorithms including support vector machines, random forests, gradient boosting, k-means, etc. Built on NumPy, SciPy, and matplotlib, it is designed to interoperate smoothly between the libraries.

B.3   MODEL TRAINING

B.3.1   Bootstrap sampling

As discussed in Capter 3

```
          I0      PA500      HFS            DA          Area        A/DA  \
0   524.794072  0.187448  0.032114  228.800228   6843.598481  29.910803
1   330.000000  0.226893  0.265290  121.154201   3163.239472  26.109202
2   551.879287  0.232478  0.063530  264.804935  11888.391830  44.894903
3   380.000000  0.240855  0.286234  137.640111   5402.171180  39.248524
4   362.831266  0.200713  0.244346  124.912559   3290.462446  26.342127
5   389.872978  0.150098  0.097738  118.625814   2475.557078  20.868620
6   290.455141  0.144164  0.053058   74.635067   1189.545213  15.938154

         Max IP          DR           P
0     60.204880  220.737212  556.828334
1     69.717361   99.084964  400.225776
2     77.793297  253.785300  656.769449
3     88.758446  105.198568  493.701813
4     69.389389  103.866552  424.796503
5     49.757149  107.686164  429.385788
6     35.703331   65.541324  330.267293

           I0      PA500      HFS            DA          Area        A/DA  \
44   172.515797  0.127235  0.038397   37.543673    192.218148   5.119855
47   370.395725  0.104720  0.000000  115.923253   1308.120430  11.284366
64   391.000000  0.058119  0.011170   35.780061    265.149790   7.410546
67   145.000000  0.117635  0.110305   21.218942     82.455562   3.885941
67   145.000000  0.117635  0.110305   21.218942     82.455562   3.885941
103 1600.000000  0.071908 -0.066323  436.943603  12655.342130  28.963331

          Max IP          DR            P
44    19.322081   32.189821   174.933770
47    31.367031  112.715102   365.977651
64    22.131472   28.114244   400.994818
67    20.303082    6.166715   162.510927
67    20.303082    6.166715   162.510927
103  103.732704  432.129749  1475.371534
```

Once you complete the suggested Python setup you are ready to run
the codes shown in the previous chapters.

B.4   MACHINE LEARNING LAB USING PYTHON – PROPOSED DAY-WISE SCHEDULE

Below is the proposed structure for a machine learning lab using Python.

Day #	Topic / Assignment of the day	Commands / assignment covered
1	Introduction to basic commands	**1.** Get and set working directory **2.** See directory content **3.** Install from command prompt using "pip" **4.** Commands for basic user input output **5.** Basic data types in Python and related operations **6.** Loops – For and While **7.** If…Else statement
2	Introduction to basic commands (contd.)	**1.** Write new functions **2.** Assignment 1 – Implementing recurrent functions **3.** Assignment 2 – Breadth first search **4.** Assignment 3 – Bubble sort

3	Introduction to data manipulation	**1.** Introduction to data manipulation using *pandas*
		2. Load data from .csv file
		3. Save data to .csv file
		4. Calculation of mean, median, variance, quartiles, inter-quartile range
		5. Introduction to *numpy* library
		6. Assignment (w.r.t. student data set)
		  (a) With respect to the aptitude of the students, find the mean, median, quartiles, and variance. Provide the interpretations.
		  (b) Find the students having above average communication
		  (c) Find the students having both above average aptitude and communication
		  (d) Add a column to the data set having a weighted score based on aptitude and communication (2:1)
		  (e) Print the name of the students having highest and lowest score as calculated in point d.
		  (f) Print name of all students whose name start with the word "J".
		  (g) Print name of all students whose name has the word "J".

4	Introduction to other standard library functions	• Understanding *matplotlib* library
		• Hands-on with basic plots -
		  ✓ Box plots
		  ✓ Scatter diagram
		  ✓ Histogram

(Continued)

Day #	Topic / Assignment of the day	Commands / assignment covered

5	Basic data exploration	• Assignment to be done using auto-mpg data set
		• Following are the basic points of exploration –
		  ✓ Is there any correlation between mpg and acceleration?
		  ✓ Is there any correlation between horsepower and cylinder?
		  ✓ How many Ford cars of 8 cylinders were manufactured in 1970s?
		  ✓ Draw a histogram of 4, 6, and 8 cylinder cars manufactured 1980s.
		  ✓ Which are related attributes in the data set?
		  ✓ Are there any missing values in the data set? Impute the missing values using the strategy of taking average value of attribute value for the respective number of cylinders.

6	Preparing to model	**1.** Introduction to *Scikit-learn* library **2.** Data holdout **3.** How to ensure result reproducibility **4.** K-fold cross validation **5.** Finding data issues and remediating them **6.** Basic feature selection

7	Starting with learning algorithms –
	• k- Nearest Neighbour (kNN)
	• Linear Regression
		1. Basic classification modelling with kNN
		  (i) Derive confusion matrix and observe different elements of confusion matrix
		  (ii) Inspect model accuracy, sensitivity, specificity, etc.
		2. Basic regression modelling and review error in prediction

8	Unsupervised algorithm – K-Means	**1.** Basic modelling using K-Means **2.** Inspect cluster quality measures like Silhouette Width and Purity **3.** Test the result if value of k is increased
9	Implement supervised algorithm – • Naive Bayes • Decision Tree • SVM	
10	Implement single layer FF Neural Network	
11	Implement multi layer FF Neural Network	
12	Assignment – Text mining	

A Case Study on Machine Learning Application: Grouping Similar Service Requests and Classifying a New One

In the previous two appendices, we have discussed how R and Python can be used to create the machine learning algorithms. We also talked about different sets of libraries available for easy deployment of machine learning. With that perspective, let's now see how machine learning is used in real life to solve a business problem, which otherwise would have taken significant manual effort.

C.1   BUSINESS CASE

In a telecom service center, the operators are responsible for providing the technical resolution to the problems that the customers face. Recently, due to huge surge in telecom user base, the service center of Newtel Infocomm is facing a huge challenge in dealing with the increase in service request volume. Newtel has two options – either it can increase the number of operators, thus increasing the operating cost substantially. Alternatively, it can explore if technology can help to solve the problem, without much additional cost, and thus help it remain profitable. The service center of Newtel engaged Global Tech (GT), a company known for providing state-of-the-art machine learning solutions to solve customer problems. After careful review of the problem and the underlying root cause, GT come up with a Machine Learning solution, briefly highlighted below.

C.2   SOLUTION APPROACH

GT observed that there are many service requests coming to Newtel service centers, which are repetitive in nature in terms of the type of problem. This was evident from the text of the service requests. Also, in most of the cases, there are some standard steps that the customer needs to follow to get the issue resolved. So, GT experts inferred, that buckets of service requests can be created through machine learning algorithm based on the past service requests. For each bucket, a set of corresponding standard resolutions can be associated. Whenever a new service request comes to Newtel service center, another machine learning algorithm should identify the bucket to which the new request should be tagged to, pull out the corresponding standard resolution, and send it to the customer. All these will happen without any human intervention. So, additional call volumes can be handled without any additional personnel in place. This will significantly reduce the additional manpower requirement leading to an impact on operating cost and profitability.

In the solution provided by GT, service requests in the repository were clustered using a combination of text analytics of select descriptive fields, time taken to resolve each request, and a user-selected categorical variable. The specific text analytics technique chosen was Word2Vector and the clustering technique was DBSCAN. For text classification to classify the new service request to one of the buckets created, Cosine Similarity algorithm was used. Let's review the technical solution in some more details.

(I) Getting Python ready

Algorithm:

1. Load required libraries of Python. These sets of libraries are needed to load data, perform computations and display output. Some of the important libraries are

   (a) Pandas—Data analysis library

   (b) numpy—array processing library in Python

   (c) nltk.data and nltk.corpus—Natural language processing library

   (d) import genism—for text analytics and clustering we will be converting word to vector. Word2vec function implemented by genism is useful here

   (e) from gensim.models import word2vec

   (f) from gensim.models.keyedvectors import KeyedVectors

   (g) matplotlib.pyplot—To visualize the clusters

   (h) from sklearn.cluster import DBSCAN—For clustering

   (i) from sklearn.metrics.pairwise import cosine_similarity—To compute service request description similarity

Sample code snippet

```
import os
import pandas as pd
import numpy as np
from numpy import array
from IPython.display import display

#Python's powerful natural language processing library
import nltk.data
from nltk.corpus import stopwords

#word2vec is implemented through the gensim libraries
import gensim
from gensim.models import word2vec
from gensim.models.keyedvectors import KeyedVectors

import matplotlib.pyplot as plt          #to visualize the clusters
import matplotlib.cm as cm
from sklearn.cluster import DBSCAN          #for clustering
import sklearn.metrics as metrics

from sklearn.metrics.pairwise import cosine_similarity #to compute service request
(SR) description similarity
```

(II) Data load

Algorithm:

Based on the source of data, like spreadsheet or csv dump of service requests or a direct access to service request database, load the data into the program in form of array of strings. The csv file containing the data set is available as online material for this book. The structure of the file is given below:

SR number	Short_description	Assignment_group
SRN49099	Caused by:com.XCException	Store Transaction Hub
SRN50248	Order missing	Store Mobility Support
SRN53087	Receiving – Count is not increasing	Store Mobility Support
SRN49497	Not giving notification for bogus orders	Store Mobility Support
SRN49802	Store is getting notifications to assign a request	Store Mobility Support
SRN49164	Event description: illegal transactions filtered out	Payment and Tax Systems

Code snippet

```
f = 'old_service_request.csv' # this file contains the details of the old service requests
data_1 = pd.read_excel(f, sheet_name='SRN', converters={'short_description':str})
```

(III) Filtering for the assignment groups listed by the business users. This will ensure that the clusters are created as per business units.

Algorithm:

Identify the information from the data set that can help in making the data categorization or the clustering easy. In our example, we will use the service center's assignment group or department as the driver for clustering. Below is some example of the assignment groups that can categorize the service requests.

```
[ 'Store Transaction Hub',
'Store Sales Reporting',
'Store Sales Floor Sign',
'Store Pricing',
'Store Mobility Support',
'Store Web Services',
'Store Alternative Systems Support',
'Return Web Services',
'Payment and Tax Systems – Online',
'Payment and Tax Systems – Offline',
'Managed Services – In Store Applications',
'Intranet',
'In-store applications',
'Accounts Payable']
```

Code snippet

```
assignment_group_subset = [
    'Store Transaction Hub',
    'Store Sales Reporting',
    'Store Sales Floor Sign',
    'Store Pricing',
    'Store Mobility Support',
    'Store Web Services',
    'Store Alternative Systems Support',
    'Return Web Services',
```

```
    'Payment and Tax Systems – Online',
    'Payment and Tax Systems – Offline',
    'Managed Services – In-Store Applications',
    'Intranet',
    'In-store applications',
    'Accounts Payable'
]
```

```
data_1 = data_1 [data_1.assignment_group.isin(assignment_group_subset)]
```

(IV) Text analytics to create the training data for machine learning algorithm.

Algorithm:

1. Create training data by averaging vectors for the words in the SR.
2. Calculate the average feature vector for each one and return a 2D numpy array.
3. This array set is now your training data for running the clustering.

Code snippet

```
# Load Google's pre-trained Word2Vec model trained on part of Google News data
set (about 100 #billion words). The model contains 300-dimensional vectors for 3
million words and phrases

model_google3M  =  gensim.models.KeyedVectors.load_word2vec_format('./
GoogleNews-vectors-negative300.bin', binary=True)

#Creating training data by averaging vectors for the words in the " vShortDescrip-
tion" column, by SR

def createFeatureVec (words, model, num_features):
    # Function to average all of the word vectors in a given paragraph
    # Index2word is a list that contains the names of the words in
    # the model's vocabulary. Convert it to a set, for speed
    index2word_set = set(model.wv.index2word)
    #
    # Loop over each word in the vShortDescription and, if it is in the model's
    # vocabulary, add its feature vector to the total
    for word in words:
        if word in index2word_set:
            nwords = nwords + 1.
            featureVec = np.add(featureVec,model[word])
    #
    # Divide the result by the number of words to get the average
```

```python
featureVec = np.divide(featureVec,nwords)
return featureVec

def getAvgFeatureVecs(vShortDescription_s, model, num_features):
    # Given a set of vShortDescription (each one a list of words), calculate
    # the average feature vector for each one and return a 2D numpy array
    #
    # Initialize a counter
    counter = 0.
    #
    # Preallocate a 2D numpy array, for speed
vShortDescriptionVecs  =  np.zeros((len(vShortDescription_s),num_
features),dtype="float32")
    #
    # Loop through the vShortDescription_s
    for vShortDescriptionin vShortDescription_s:
    # Call the function (defined above) that makes average feature vectors
vShortDescriptionVecs[int(counter)]  =  createFeatureVec(vShortDescription,
model, \
        num_features)
        #
        # Increment the counter
        counter = counter + 1.
    return vShortDescriptionVecs

clustering_vec = getAvgFeatureVecs(data_1['short_description'], model_google3M, 300)
```

(IV) Running the clustering

Algorithm:

DBSCAN algorithm is used for this clustering which will take the density-based clustering approach. The position of vectors created above are checked and the high-density areas are taken as a new cluster whereas clusters are separated by low-density areas.

Code snippet

```python
#clustering using DBSCAN
db = DBSCAN(eps=0.3, min_samples=10).fit(clustering_vec)
core_samples_mask = np.zeros_like(db.labels_, dtype=bool)
core_samples_mask[db.core_sample_indices_] = True
labels = db.labels_
```

The cluster that is generated as the result of DBSCAN is shown in Figure C.1. The estimated number of clusters: 14 and Silhouette Coefficient: 0.367

```python
# Plot result
import matplotlib.pyplot as plt

# Black removed and is used for noise instead.
unique_labels = set(labels)
colors = [plt.cm.Spectral(each)
          for each in np.linspace(0, 1, len(unique_labels))]
for k, col in zip(unique_labels, colors):
    if k == -1:
        # Black used for noise.
        col = [0, 0, 0, 1]

    class_member_mask = (labels == k)

    xy = clustering_vec[class_member_mask & core_samples_mask]
    plt.plot(xy.iloc[:, 0], xy.iloc[:, 1], 'o', markerfacecolor=tuple(col),
        markeredgecolor='k', markersize=14)

    xy = clustering_vec[class_member_mask & ~core_samples_mask]
    plt.plot(xy.iloc[:, 0], xy.iloc[:, 1], 'o', markerfacecolor=tuple(col),
        markeredgecolor='k', markersize=1)

plt.title('Estimated number of clusters: %d' % n_clusters_)
plt.show()
```

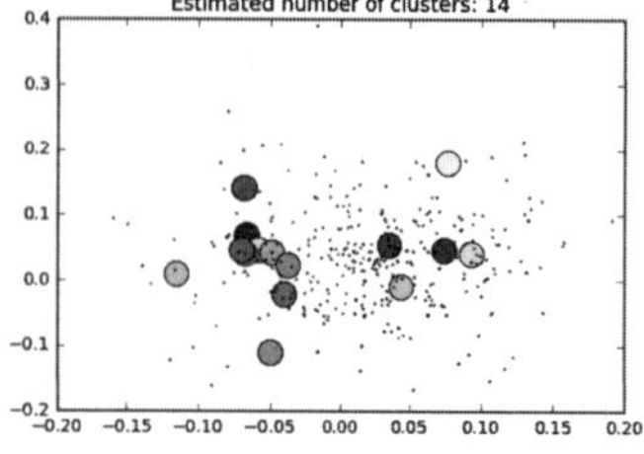

FIG. C.1
Clustering output

(V) New SR assigned to correct bucket – Cosine similarity function

Algorithm:

1. Create the vector from the description text of the SR using word2vec function
2. Calculate the similarity score for the vector using the cosine_similarity function
3. Find the cluster the service request is assigned to, based on the max similarity score, averaged across all service requests in the cluster
4. If no cluster is found matching this SR vector, then this SR is unlike any in the training repository and is not assigned to any cluster

Code snippet

```python
def newSRClusterer(newSRText):# Function to assign a new SR to one of the previously grouped service request clusters
    #vectorize SR text
    newSRVector = getAvgFeatureVecs(newSRText, model_google3M, 300)

    #building the dataframe with SR meta data + similarity scores
    data_8 = pd.concat([pd.DataFrame(labels),data_6_1[['number','short_description','assignment_group']]], axis=1)
    data_8.rename(columns = {0:'Cluster'}, inplace = True)
    data_8['similarityScore'] = cosine_similarity(data_6_1.iloc[:,26:326], newSRVector)
    #find the cluster the service request is assigned to based on max similarity score, averaged across all service requests in the cluster
    similarityScoreMean = data_8.groupby('Cluster')['similarityScore'].mean().max()
    newSRCluster = data_8.groupby('Cluster')['similarityScore'].mean().idxmax()

    return similarityScoreMean, newSRCluster

#sample service request texts
newSRText = 'Receiving - Percentage of cartons scanned is 0'

#produces output of new service request clustering
similarityScoreMean, newSRCluster = newSRClusterer(newSRText)
if similarityScoreMean >= 0.7: #this threshold needs to be tuned to ensure noise is not incorrectly assigned
    newSRCluster = newSRCluster
    print('This SR is assigned to the cluster', newSRCluster)
    print('This SR similarity to the assigned cluster is',round(similarityScoreMean,2))
else:
    newSRCluster = -1
    print('This SR is unlike any in the training repository and is not assigned to any cluster')
```

C.3   OUTCOME

The service request processing of Newtel Infocomm has been automated now. GT has used machine learning technique to achieve the automation. As a part of the solution, the unlabeled service requests have been grouped into logical clusters using the DBSCAN algorithm. Also, whenever any new service request arrives, the cosine similarity algorithm finds out the relevant bucket for it so that some predefined, standard resolution can be sent automatically to the customer. There can be more such ways to solve this same business problem, as well as many scenarios which can be addressed through this same approach. So, look out for real-life business problems and think about automating the resolutions thorough intelligent use of machine learning.

Model Question Paper-1

<< NAME OF THE INSTITUTE >>

DEPARTMENT OF << XXX >>

Final Semester Examination

SUBJECT NAME: Basics of Machine Learning

SUBJECT CODE: <XXX>

TIME: 3 HOUR   **FULL MARKS: 80**

PART A (Multiple Choice Type Questions)

1. Answer any ten questions.   **10 X 1 = 10**

i. A computer program is said to learn from __________ with respect to some class of tasks T and performance measure P, if its performance at tasks in T, as measured by P, improves with it.

   A. Training
   B. Experience
   C. Database
   D. Algorithm

ii. This type of learning to be used when there is no idea about the class or label of a particular data

   A. Supervised learning algorithm
   B. Unsupervised learning algorithm
   C. Semi-supervised learning algorithm
   D. Reinforcement learning algorithm

iii. Temperature is an example of

   A. Interval data
   B. Ratio data
   C. Discrete data
   D. None of the above

iv. For understanding relationship between two variables, _____ can be used.

   A. Box plot
   B. Scatter plot
   C. Histogram
   D. None of the above

v. Which of the following is a performance measure for regression?

    A. Accuracy
    B. Recall
    C. RMSE
    D. Error rate

vi. Hamming distance between binary vectors 1001 and 0101 is

    A. 1
    B. 2
    C. 3
    D. 4

vii. In a certain basketball club, there are 4% of male players who are over 6 feet tall and 1% of female players who are over 6 feet tall. The ratio of male to female players in the total player population is male:female = 2:3. A player is selected at random from among all those over 6 feet tall. What is the probability that the player is a female?

    A. 3/11
    B. 2/5
    C. 2/11
    D. 1/11

viii. The probability that a particular hypothesis holds for a data set based on the Prior is called

    A. Independent probabilities
    B. Posterior probabilities
    C. Interior probabilities
    D. Dependent probabilities

ix. Predicting whether a tumour is malignant or benign is an example of

    A. Unsupervised learning
    B. Supervised regression problem
    C. Supervised classification problem
    D. Categorical attribute.

x. _____ are the data points (representing classes), the important component in a data set, which are near the identified set of lines (hyper plane).

    A. Hard Margin
    B. Soft Margin
    C. Linear Margin
    D. Support Vectors

xi. A binary sigmoid function has range of ___.

    A. $(-1, +1)$
    B. $(0, -1)$
    C. $(0, 1)$
    D. $(1, 0)$

xii.   Which of the following is not an inductive bias in a decision tree?

    A.   It prefers longer tree over shorter tree
    B.   Trees that place nodes near the root with high information gain are preferred
    C.   Overfitting is a natural phenomenon in a decision tree
    D.   Prefer the shortest hypothesis that fits the data

xiii.   When you find many noises in data, which of the following options would you consider in k-NN?

    A.   Increase the value of k
    B.   Decrease the value of k
    C.   Noise does not depend on k
    D. $K = 0$

Part B (Short Answer Type Questions)

Answer any five questions   **5 X 5 = 25**

2.   **a)**   Define the concept of consistent learners.

    b)   Explain how Naïve Bayes classifier is used for Online Sentiment Analysis.?

3.   What is supervised learning? Give any two examples.

4.   Write the difference between

    a.   Activation function and threshold function

    b.   Filter and wrapper method of feature selection

5.   Write short notes on

    a.   Feature construction

    b.   Deep neural network

6.   Why is cosine similarity a suitable measure in context of text categorization? Two rows in a document-term matrix have values – $(2, 3, 2, 0, 2, 3, 3, 0, 1)$ and $(2, 1, 0, 0, 3, 2, 1, 3, 1)$. Find the cosine similarity.

7.   Explain the competitive network architecture of ANN.

Part C (Long Answer Type Questions)

Answer any three questions   **3 X 15 = 45**

8.   **a)**   Compare supervised, unsupervised, and reinforcement learning.   **7**

    b)   An antibiotic resistance test (random variable T) has 1% false positives (i.e. 1% of those not resistance to an antibiotic show positive in the test), and 5% false negatives (i.e. 5% of those actually resistant to an antibiotic test negative). Let's assume that 2% of those tested are resistant to antibiotics. Determine the probability that somebody who tests positive is actually resistant (random variable D).   **8**

9. **a)** What are the different techniques for data pre-processing? Explain the filter approach of feature selection. How is it different from the wrapper approach?   **8**

b) Use a simple perceptron with weights w0, w1, and w2 as $-1, 2$, and 1, respectively, to classify data points $(3, 4); (5, 2); (1, -3); (-8, -3); (-3, 0)$.   **7**

10. **a)** Explain, in details, the different components of a box plot? When will the lower whisker be longer than the upper whisker? How can outliers be detected using box plot?   **7**

b) During a research work, you found seven observations as described with the data points below. You want to create three clusters from these observations using K-means algorithm.

After first iteration, the clusters C1, C2, C3 has following observations:

  C1: $\{(2,2), (4,4), (6,6)\}$

  C2: $\{(0,4), (4,0)\}$

  C3: $\{(5,5), (9,9)\}$

If you want to run a second iteration then what will be the cluster centroids?   **8**

11. **a)** What is over-fitting? When does it happen? How can we avoid over-fitting?   **5**

b) In an exam, there were 20 multiple-choice questions. Each question had 44 possible options. A student knew the answer to 10 questions, but the other 10 questions were unknown for him and he chose answers randomly. If the score of the student X is equal to the total number of correct answers, then find out the PMF of X. What is $P(X > 15)$?   **5**

c) There are 100 men on a ship. If X_i is the weight of the ith man on the ship and X_i's are independent and identically distributed and also $E(X_i) = \mu = 170$ and $\sigma X_i = \sigma = 30$. Find the probability that the total weight of the men on the ship exceeds 18,000.   **5**

Model Question Paper-2

<< NAME OF THE INSTITUTE >>

DEPARTMENT OF << XXX >>

Final Semester Examination

SUBJECT NAME: Basics of Machine Learning

SUBJECT CODE: <XXX>

TIME: 3 HOUR   **FULL MARKS: 80**

PART A (Multiple Choice Type Questions)

1. **Answer any ten questions.**   **10 X 1 = 10**

   i.   Which of the following is not a type of Ensemble learning algorithms?

       A. Boosting
       B. AdaBoost
       C. GBM
       D. Elastic Net

   ii. A neuron is able to ___ information in the form of chemical and electrical signals.

       A. Receive
       B. Process
       C. Transmit
       D. All of the above

   iii. In SVM, ___ functions take low-dimensional input space and transform it to a higher dimensional space.

       A. Kernel
       B. Vector
       C. Support vector
       D. Hyper plane

   iv. Feature ___ involves transforming a given set of input features to generate a new set of more powerful features.

       A. Selection
       B. Engineering
       C. Transformation
       D. Re-engineering

v.   Principal component is a technique for

   A.   Feature selection
   B.   Dimensionality reduction
   C.   Exploration
   D.   None of the above

vi.   Which of the following is the measure of cluster quality?

   A.   Purity
   B.   Distance
   C.   Accuracy
   D.   All of the above

vii.   Out of 200 emails, a classification model correctly predicted 150 spam emails and 30 ham emails. What is the accuracy of the model?

   A.   10%
   B.   90%
   C.   80%
   D.   60%

viii.   Conversion of a text corpus to a numerical representation is done using ___ process.

   A.   Tokenization
   B.   Normalization
   C.   Vectorization
   D.   None of the above

ix.   Intelligent robots are best example of

   A.   Supervised learning algorithm
   B.   Unsupervised learning algorithm
   C.   Semi-supervised learning algorithm
   D.   Reinforcement learning algorithm

x.   Single-layer feed forward network consists of ___ layers.

   A.   Two
   B.   One
   C.   Three
   D.   Many

xi.   ____ refers to the transformations applied to the identified data before feeding the same into the algorithm.

   A.   Problem identification
   B.   Identification of required data
   C.   Data pre-processing
   D.   Definition of training data set

xii. Which of the following will be Euclidean distance between the two data points A $(4, 3)$ and B $(2, 3)$?

    A. 5
    B. 4
    C. 2
    D. 7

xiii. For nominal data, only _____ can be measured.

    A. Mean
    B. Mode
    C. Median
    D. Quartile

Part B (Short Answer Type Questions)

Answer any five questions　　　　　　　　　　　**5 X 5 = 25**

2. Explain, in brief, how the Market Basket Analysis uses the concepts of association analysis.

3. What is feature transformation? Explain the process of transforming numeric features to categorical features.

4. Write the difference between
    a) Model accuracy and error rate
    b) Overfitting and underfitting

5. Write short notes on
    a) 'No Free Lunch' theorem
    b) ReLU function

6. If X is a continuous random variable with pdf

$$f_x(x) = \begin{cases} 4x^3 & 0 < x \leq 1 \\ 0 & otherwise \end{cases}$$

Find $P(X \leq 2/3 \mid X > 1/3)$

7. Explain the recurrent network architecture of ANN.

Part C (Long Answer Type Questions)

Answer any three questions　　　　　　　　　　**3 X 15 = 45**

8. **a)** Explain the process of feature engineering in context of text categorization problem.　　　　　　　　　　　　　　　　　　　　　　　7

    b) For preparation of the exam, a student knows that one question is to be solved in the exam, which is either of the types A, B, or C. The probabilities of A, B, or C appearing in the exam are 30%, 20%, and 50%, respectively. During the preparation, the student solved 9 of 10 problems of type A, 2 of 10 problems of type B, and 6 of 10 problems of type C. Given that the student solved the problem, what is the probability that it was of type A?   **8**

9. **a)** What are the two major data issues in machine learning? How can these issues be remediated?   **8**

   b) Following is the training data for a group of athletes. Based on this data, use k-NN algorithm and classify Sayan (Weight = 56 kg., Speed = 10 kmph) as a Good, Average, or Poor sprinter.   **7**

Name	Weight (kg.)	Speed (kmph)	Class
Nitesh	55	9	Average
Gurpreet	58	8	Poor
Goutam	60	7.5	Poor
Gulshan	59	8.5	Average
Mohit	57	10	Good
Sahil	53	10.5	Good
Samyak	53	10	Good

10. **a)** What are different shapes of histogram? What are 'bins'?   **7**

   b) You are given a set of one-dimensional data points: $\{5, 10, 15, 20, 25, 30, 35\}$. Assume that $k= 2$ and first set of random centroid is selected as $\{15, 32\}$ and then it is refined with $\{12, 30\}$.

   i. Create two clusters with each set of centroid mentioned above following the K-means approach

   ii. Calculate the SSE for each set of centroid   **8**

11. **a)** Why a multilayer neural network is required? What are the steps in backpropagation algorithm?   **10**

   b) Compare the Jaccard index and similarity matching coefficient of two features having values $(1, 1, 1, 1, 0, 0, 1, 1)$ and $(1, 0, 1, 1, 0, 1, 0, 1)$.   **5**

Model Question Paper-3

<< NAME OF THE INSTITUTE >>

DEPARTMENT OF << XXX >>

Final Semester Examination

SUBJECT NAME: Basics of Machine Learning

SUBJECT CODE: <XXX>

TIME: 3 HOUR   **FULL MARKS: 80**

PART A (Multiple Choice Type Questions)

1. **Answer any ten questions.**   **10 X 1 = 10**

 i.   Ordinal data can be naturally ____.

    A.   Measured
    B.   Ordered
    C.   Divided
    D.   None of the above

 ii. For box plot, the upper and lower whisker length depends on:

    A.   Median
    B.   Mean
    C.   IQR
    D.   All of the above

 iii. LOOCV in machine learning stands for:

    A.   Leave-one-out cross-validation
    B.   Leave-Object Oriented cross-validation
    C.   Leave-one-out class-validation
    D.   None of the above

 iv. Which of the following will be Manhattan Distance between the two data point A (8,3) and B (4,3)?

    A.   1
    B.   2
    C.   4
    D.   8

v.   Cosine similarity is most popularly used in:

   A.   Text classification
   B.   Image classification
   C.   Feature selection
   D.   None of the above

vi.   In this method, the active learning algorithm first tries to label the points that would mostly reduce the model's generalization problem

   A.   Expected Model Change
   B.   Query by committee
   C.   Uncertainty sampling
   D.   Expected Error Reduction

vii.   Two boxes containing chocolates are placed on a table. The boxes are labelled B1 and B2. Box B1 contains 6 Cadbury chocolates and 5 Amul chocolates. Box B2 contains 3 Cadbury chocolates and 8 Nestle chocolates. The boxes are arranged so that the probability of selecting box B1 is 1/3 and the probability of selecting box B2 is 2/3. Sneha is blindfolded and asked to select a chocolate. She will win Rs. 10,000 if she selects a Cadbury chocolate. If she wins Rs 10,000, what is the probability that she selected Cadbury from the first box?

   A.   7/12
   B.   6/12
   C.   11/12
   D.   10/33

viii.   Single-layer perceptron is able to deal with

   A.   linearly separable data
   B.   non-linearly separable data
   C.   linearly inseparable data
   D.   none of the above

ix.   What sizes of training data sets are not best suited for SVM?

   A.   Large data sets
   B.   Very small training data sets
   C.   Medium size training data sets
   D.   Training data set size does not matter.

x.   In ___ approach, identification of best feature subset is done using the induction algorithm as a black box.

   A.   Embedded
   B.   Hybrid
   C.   Wrapper
   D.   Filter

xi.   Which of the following is not a data issue?

    A.   Boundary value
    B.   Missing value
    C.   Threshold value
    D.   Outlier

xii.   Which of the following clustering algorithm is most sensitive to outliers?

    A.   K-means clustering algorithm
    B.   K-medians clustering algorithm
    C.   K-medoids clustering algorithm
    D.   K-modes clustering algorithm

xiii.   The Q-learning algorithm is a

    A.   Supervised learning algorithm
    B.   Unsupervised learning algorithm
    C.   Semi-supervised learning algorithm
    D.   Reinforcement learning algorithm

Part B (Short Answer Type Questions)

Answer any five questions   **5 X 5 = 25**

2.   **a)**   What is Query by committee in Active learning?

    b)   Mention about some of the applications of Representational learning.

3.   What is reinforcement learning? Give any 2 examples.

4.   Write the difference between:
    a)   Cross-validation vs. Bootstrapping

    b)   Lazy vs. eager learning

5.   Write short notes on:
    a)   Silhouette width

    b)   Logistic regression

6.   While predicting win-loss of teams in World Cup Football using a classification model, following are the data recorded:
    a)   Correct predictions – 73 wins, 13 losses

    b)   Incorrect predictions – 9 wins, 5 losses

Calculate the accuracy, sensitivity, precision and F-measure of the model.

7.   Explain the single-layer feed forward architecture of ANN.

Part C (Long Answer Type Questions)

Answer any three questions   **3 X 15 = 45**

8.   **a)**   What is a target function? Express target function in context of a real-life example. Explain bias-variance trade-off in context of model fitting.

b) In an airport security checking system the passengers are checked to find out any intruder. Let I with i $\in$ {0, 1} be the random variable which indicates whether somebody is an intruder (i = 1) or not (i = 0) and A with a $\in$ {0, 1} be the variable indicating alarm. An alarm will be raised if an intruder is identified with probability P (A = 1| I = 1) = 0.98, a non-intruder with probability P (A = 1| I = 0) = 0.001 which implies the error factor. In the population of passengers, the probability of someone is intruder is, P (I = 1) = 0.00001. What is the probability that an alarm is raised when a person actually is an intruder?   **8**

9. **a)** Explain the learning process of an ANN. What are the limitations of backpropagation algorithm?   **8**

b) A CCTV is installed in a bank to monitor the incoming customers and take a photograph. Though there is continuous flow of customers we create bins of timeframe of 5 minutes each. In each time frame of 5 min there may be a customer moving into the bank with probability 5%, or there is no customer (again, for simplicity we assume that either there is 1 customer or none, not the case of multiple customers). If there is a customer, it will be detected by the CCTV with a probability of 99%. If there is no customer, the camera will take false photograph by detecting other thing's movement with a probability of 10%. How many customers enter the bank on average per day (10 hours)? How many false photographs (there is a photograph taken even though there is no customer) and how many missed photographs (there is no photograph even though there is a customer) are there on average per day.   **10**

10. **a)** Can the performance of a learning model be improved? Elaborate your answer. **6**

b) Present the Decision Tree classifier algorithm. Using the algorithm and the following training data, find the class label for a test record {"Sohrab", CGPA = High, Communication = Bad, Programming skills = Bad}   **9**

CGPA	Communication	Programming Skill	Employable
High	Good	Good	Yes
Medium	Good	Good	Yes
High	Good	Bad	Yes
High	Good	Good	Yes
High	Bad	Good	Yes
Medium	Good	Good	Yes
Low	Bad	Bad	No
Low	Bad	Bad	No
Medium	Good	Bad	Yes
Medium	Bad	Good	No
Medium	Good	Bad	Yes

11. **a)** Explain the process how a Random Forest classifier works.   **5**

b) Explain some strengths and weaknesses of Decision Tree classifier.   **5**

c) What are the broad three categories of clustering techniques? Explain the characteristics of each briefly.   **5**

Index

Credits

FIG. 10.1: The Frozen Lake Screenshot, © The Farama Foundation, used with permission.
FIG. 10.2: The Frozen Lake Screenshot, © The Farama Foundation, used with permission
FIG. 10.3: The Frozen Lake Screenshot, © The Farama Foundation, used with permission
FIG. 10.4: The Frozen Lake Screenshot, © The Farama Foundation, used with permission
Page 306: Turing [1948] 2004, 425
FIG. 11.23: Copyright ©2001-2023. Python Software Foundation
FIG. 13.1: Petr Malyshev / Shutterstock
FIG. 13.2: © R Foundation, from http://www.r-project.org
FIG. 13.3: © R Foundation, from http://www.r-project.org
FIG. 13.5: © R Foundation, from http://www.r-project.org
FIG. 13.6: © R Foundation, from http://www.r-project.org
FIG. A.1: © R Foundation, from http://www.r-project.org
FIG. A.2: © R Foundation, from http://www.r-project.org
FIG. A.3: © R Foundation, from http://www.r-project.org
FIG. A.4: © R Foundation, from http://www.r-project.org
FIG. A.5: © R Foundation, from http://www.r-project.org
FIG. A.6: © R Foundation, from http://www.r-project.org
FIG. B.1: Copyright © 2018. Python Software Foundation